AN APPETITE FOR POWER

AN APPETITE FOR POWER

A HISTORY OF
THE CONSERVATIVE PARTY
SINCE 1830

John Ramsden

HarperCollins*Publishers*

HarperCollins*Publishers*
77–85 Fulham Palace Road,
Hammersmith, London W6 8JB

Published by HarperCollins 1998
1 3 5 7 9 8 6 4 2

Copyright © John Ramsden 1998

John Ramsden asserts the moral right to
be identified as the author of this work

ISBN 0 00 255686 3

Set in PostScript Linotype Minion with Castellar by
Rowland Phototypesetting Ltd, Bury St Edmunds, Suffolk

Printed and bound in Great Britain by
Clays Ltd, St Ives plc

All rights reserved. No part of this publication may be reproduced, stored in a retrieval system, or transmitted, in any form or by any means, electronic, mechanical, photocopying, recording or otherwise, without the prior permission of the publishers.

This book is sold subject to the condition that it shall not, by way of trade or otherwise, be lent, re-sold, hired out or otherwise circulated without the publisher's prior consent in any form of binding or cover other than that in which it is published and without a similar condition including this condition being imposed on the subsequent purchaser.

CONTENTS

LIST OF ILLUSTRATIONS   vii
LIST OF CARTOONS   ix
ACKNOWLEDGEMENTS   xiii

1. Introduction: The Conservative Party and
    Conservative History   1
2. Origins: Tories into Conservatives   13
3. Peel's Conservative Party, 1832–46   50
4. Wilderness Years, 1846–68   77
5. Disraeli's Indian Summer, 1868–76   101
6. Salisbury and Unionism: 1876–86   130
7. The First Summit: The Hotel Cecil, 1886–1900   162
8. Drifting, 1900–1914   190
9. Clambering Back, 1914–22   222
10. The Second Summit: Baldwin's Party, 1922–29   247
11. The Centre Holds, 1929–39   271
12. War and Aftermath, 1939–47   292
13. 'Post-War', 1947–57   325
14. The Third Summit: Macmillan's Party, 1957–65   353
15. Conservatives for a Change, 1965–74   385
16. Thatcherism: The Way Up, 1974–87   417
17. Thatcherism: The Way Down, 1987–97   449
18. Ghosts and Portents   486

APPENDICES: 1. Sources   501
             2. Officeholders in the party since 1830   511
             3. Conservative and Coalition
                Governments since 1834   518

4. Conferences of the National Union of Conservative and Unionist Associations   521
5. Glossary of Organizations and Principal Personalities   525
6. The Conservative Party's Electoral Performance   540

INDEX   543

LIST OF ILLUSTRATIONS

Between pages 178 and 179

Arthur Wellesley, 1st Duke of Wellington (1796–1852) with Sir Robert Peel (1788–1850) by Franz Xaiver Winterhalter (1805–1873). © Her Majesty Queen Elizabeth II.

Lord George Cavendish Bentinck (1802–1848) by Samuel Lane, c. 1836. Reproduced courtesy of the National Portrait Gallery, London.

Edward Stanley, 14th Earl of Derby (1799–1869) by Frederick Richard Say, 1844. Reproduced courtesy of the National Portrait Gallery, London.

Benjamin Disraeli, the most popular engraving, based on a photograph by Mayall. Photograph © Hulton/Getty Images.

Members of Disraeli's 1874 Cabinet photographed c. 1876. Photograph © Hulton/Getty Images.

Lord Randolph Churchill, photographed in 1874. Photograph © Hulton/Getty Images.

Arthur James Balfour and Joseph Chamberlain on the Front Bench by Sydney Prior Hall, 1902. Reproduced courtesy of the National Portrait Gallery, London.

Andrew Bonar Law addressing a Rally of Unionists at Blenheim Palace on 29 July 1912. Photograph © PA News.

Andrew Bonar Law and J. C. C. Davidson leaving the Carlton Club after the meeting that overthrew Austen Chamberlain as Conservative leader, 19 October 1922. Photograph © Hulton/Getty Images.

Stanley Baldwin greeting photographers outside the Caxton Hall, before a meeting with his Party critics, 1930. Photograph © Hulton/Getty Images.

Stanley Baldwin recording a newsreel film in the gardens of No. 10. Photograph © Hulton/Getty Images.

Stanley Baldwin is given a presentation book by Neville Chamberlain on his retirement in May 1937. Photograph © Topham Picturepoint.

Winston Churchill speaking at Walthamstow on 4 July 1945, during the General Election campaign. Photograph © Hulton/Getty Images.

Harold Macmillan helping to launch *The Right Road for Britain* at the 1949 Conservative Party Conference. Photograph © Hulton/Getty Images.

Members of Churchill's shadow cabinet shortly before the 1950 General Election. Photograph © Hulton/Getty Images.

Between pages 370 and 371

Anthony Eden with Conservative candidates for Kent constituencies at a Rally in the Dartford football stadium, 1951. Photograph © Kent Messenger.

Sir David and Lady Maxwell Fyfe campaigning in Derbyshire, 1950. Photograph © Hulton/Getty Images.

Peter Rawlinson in a characteristic 1950s Conservative campaign. Photograph © Hulton/Getty Images.

Lord Hailsham ringing the Conference chairman's bell at the 1957 Party Conference in Brighton. Photograph © PA News.

Harold Macmillan entertains President Eisenhower. Photograph © Associated Press Photo.

Harold Macmillan at Birch Grove House, 1960. Photograph © Hulton/Getty Images.

R. A. Butler is applauded after his speech at the 1963 Conservative Conference. Photograph © Topham Picturepoint.

Sir Alec Douglas-Home, apparently unimpressed with his own television image, 1964. Photograph © Hulton/Getty Images.

Edward Heath is applauded after his first Conference speech as Leader of the Party. Photograph © Hulton/Getty Images.

Edward Heath's Cabinet in the garden at Number 10. Photograph © Hulton/Getty Images.

Edward Heath and Sir Keith Joseph, autumn 1974. Photograph © Camera Press.

Kenneth Clarke's wedding in 1964. Photograph from *Kenneth Clarke* by Michael Balen.

John Major campaigning in March 1992. Photograph © PA News.

Labour poster – Major and Clarke as Laurel and Hardy, May 1996. BMP DDB. Art Director: Richard Flintham, Copywriters: Tony Cox and Andy McLeod.

LIST OF CARTOONS

1. Gillray's satire on the anti-Jacobin rhetoric of the 1790s. (Photograph © The British Museum.) — 30
2. Peel as depicted in *Punch*, 29 November 1845. (© *Punch*.) — 71
3. Peel's statue being unveiled at Bury and attracting an appreciative crowd, 18 September 1852. © The *Illustrated London News* Picture Library. — 81
4. Disraeli nimbly avoiding the breaking of Reform eggs in a *Punch* cartoon of 1867. (© *Punch*.) — 96
5. *Punch* on Disraeli's speech at the Crystal Palace, 6 July 1872. (© *Punch*.) — 118
6. *Punch* on Disraeli's eventual return as majority Prime Minister, 28 February 1874. (© *Punch*). — 123
7. Disraeli as a hero for the young, *Punch* 1910. (© *Punch*.) — 141
8. Salisbury at the dispatch box, 1891, drawn by Harry Furniss (1854–1925). (Reproduced courtesy of the National Portrait Gallery, London.) — 146
9. The Home Rule Card Game in a cartoon of 1885, showing Parnell awaiting the end of the four-handed game between Churchill, Salisbury, Gladstone and Chamberlain. — 154
10. Drawing of Churchill addressing an Orange meeting in Belfast, February 1886. Photograph © Hulton/Getty Images. — 157
11. The Marquess of Hartington, later eighth Duke of Devonshire, drawn by Sir Francis Carruthers Gould (1844–1925). (Reproduced courtesy of the National Portrait Gallery, London.) — 159
12. Arthur Balfour drawn by Harry Furniss. (Reproduced courtesy of the National Portrait Gallery, London.) — 165
13. An Irish nationalist view of Balfour's Irish policy, 17 September 1887. — 169

14. *Punch* on Salisbury's equivocal response to the agricultural depression, 30 November 1895. (© *Punch*.) 175
15. Balfour adrift between Hartington and Chamberlain in the *Westminster Gazette*, 20 January 1904. Cartoon by Sir Francis Carruthers Gould. (Courtesy of the Centre for the Study of Cartoons and Caricature, University of Kent, Canterbury.) 204
16. *Punch* on the peers' attempt to stave off the 1911 Parliament Act, 19 April 1911. (© *Punch*.) 211
17. Punch on the advantage to the Unionists of three-party contests, 10 July 1912. (© *Punch*.) 220
18. Baldwin's homely features, as drawn by David Low, *New Statesman*, 4 November 1933. Cartoon by David Low. (Courtesy of Solo Syndication/Centre for the Study of Cartoons and Caricature, University of Kent, Canterbury.) 252
19. The Conservatives' 'anti-sosh'[ialist] campaign, with Beaverbrook and Rothermere looking after the banner, wins over Churchill, from the *Star*, 7 October 1924. Cartoon by David Low. (Courtesy of Solo Syndication/Centre for the Study of Cartoons and Caricature, University of Kent, Canterbury.) 263
20. *Punch* on Baldwin the peacemaker, 28 March 1925. (© *Punch*.) 266
21. No new Zinoviev Letter appears in time to save the Conservatives' 1929 campaign, *Evening Standard*, May 1929. Cartoon by David Low. (Courtesy of Solo Syndication/Centre for the Study of Cartoons and Caricature, University of Kent, Canterbury.) 269
22. Rothermere and Beaverbrook against Baldwin, *Star*, 11 August 1925. Cartoon by David Low. (Courtesy of Solo Syndication/Centre for the Study of Cartoons and Caricature, University of Kent, Canterbury.) 275
23. The impact of Churchill's Indian campaigning on his reputation, *Daily Herald*, 30 March 1933. 286
24. A view of Churchill from the left before 1940, *Sunday Worker*, 8 August 1926. 300
25. *Punch* gives Butler due credit for the Education Bill, December 1943. (© *Punch*.) 307
26. Labour leaflet in the 1945 campaign, attacking Churchill's 'National' credentials and bringing up his past to embarrass him. 314
27. Low on Conservative efforts to woo the Liberals, *Daily Herald*, 10 February 1950. 319

LIST OF CARTOONS xi

28. Anti-nationalization campaigning on every sugar packet, c. 1949 Reproduced courtesy of Tate & Lyle. 337
29. Vicky on Macmillan's need to succeed as Housing Minister, *Daily Mirror*. (Courtesy of Centre for the Study of Cartoons and Caricature, University of Kent, Canterbury.) 350
30. Vicky on the appeal of 'Supermac' in 1959, Hailsham is the doorman saying, 'I told you this sort of stuff will fetch 'em back into the old cinema...', *Evening Standard*, 17 November 1958. 363
31. Trog on Macmillan and affluence, *Spectator*, 16 October 1959. (Courtesy of Centre for the Study of Cartoons and Caricature, University of Kent, Canterbury.) 368
32. *Evening Standard*, 13 July 1962. Cartoon by Vicky. (Courtesy of Solo Syndication/Centre for the Study of Cartoons and Caricature, University of Kent, Canterbury.) 371
33. *Daily Express*, 20 February 1963. Cartoon by Cummings. (Reproduced courtesy of Express Syndication.) 377
34. Cummings of the *Daily Express* on the leadership contest of 1963. (Reproduced courtesy of Express Syndication.)
35. Powell and Macleod regret the choice of Douglas-Home, *Guardian*, October 1963. 381
36. *Daily Telegraph*, 17 October 1967. Cartoon by Nicholas Garland. (Courtesy of MacNaughton Associates/Centre for the Study of Cartoons and Caricature, University of Kent, Canterbury.) 386
37. Powell kept out of the Conservative campaign, *Daily Telegraph*, 1 June 1970. Cartoon by Nicholas Garland. (Courtesy of MacNaughton Associates/Centre for the Study of Cartoons and Caricature, University of Kent, Canterbury.) 404
38. Powell and the Tory vote, *Sun*, 18 June 1970.
39. *Guardian*, 7 February 1974. Cartoon by Les Gibbard. (Courtesy of Centre for the Study of Cartoons and Caricature, University of Kent, Canterbury.) 412
40. *Daily Telegraph*, 18 January 1974. Cartoon by Nicholas Garland. (Courtesy of MacNaughton Associates/Centre for the Study of Cartoons and Caricature, University of Kent, Canterbury.) 413
41. *Morning Star*, 1 October 1974.
42. *New Statesman*, 31 January 1975. Cartoon by Nicholas Garland. (Courtesy of Centre for the Study of Cartoons and Caricature, University of Kent, Canterbury.) 422

43. *Sunday Express*, 6 May 1975. (Reproduced courtesy of Express Syndication.) 424
44. *Daily Telegraph*, 26 April 1979. Cartoon by Nicholas Garland. (Courtesy of MacNaughton Associates/Centre for the Study of Cartoons and Caricature, University of Kent, Canterbury.) 429
45. *Sun*, 11 February 1980. 438
46. Housewife Thatcher hangs out Jim Prior to dry, c. 1981. 440
47. *Daily Telegraph*, 30 April 1980. Cartoon by Nicholas Garland. (Courtesy of MacNaughton Associates/Centre for the Study of Cartoons and Caricature, University of Kent, Canterbury.) 444
48. *The Times*, 10 May 1987. Cartoon by Peter Brookes. (© Brookes/Times Newspapers Limited, 1987.) 450
49. Political postcard, c. 1989. 453
50. *The Times*, 13 May 1987. 'Cry God for Maggie . . .' Cartoon by Wilson. (© Wilson/Times Newspapers Limited, 1987.) 454
51. *Guardian*, 11 April 1992. 456
52. *The Times*, 11 December 1996. Cartoon by Peter Brookes. (© Brookes/Times Newspapers Limited, 1996.) 478

ACKNOWLEDGEMENTS

This book is in a real sense the fruit of nearly thirty years of work on the Conservative Party, which I began as a research student under Robert Blake's supervision in 1969. I owe to Lord Blake, therefore, a longstanding debt of gratitude for early encouragement and for commissioning me, together with the Advisory Board that he chaired and with Longman's Andrew Maclennan, to write all three of the twentieth-century volumes in the Longman History of the Conservative Party. I was also extremely fortunate to have the supervision at Nuffield College of David Butler, who has remained an encouraging friend and helpful colleague ever since.

I have learned a great deal over the years from the many practising and retired politicians who have generally given of their time generously, but I would wish to acknowledge in particular the assistance of Rab Butler, Ian Gilmour, Patrick Jenkin and Keith Joseph. Like all historians of post-war British Conservatism, I shall truly miss the late Michael Fraser, Lord Fraser of Kilmorack, who, while sometimes seeming to be (in David Butler's words) 'the Conservative Party's family solicitor' when dealing with outsiders, was nevertheless always ready to make time to help those young people writing on the party's history.

My colleagues at Queen Mary and Westfield College have been understanding, and in particular I am grateful to Peter Hennessy, John Miller, Sarah Palmer and Glyn Williams, who have all read parts of this text at various stages. Any errors and omissions that remain are entirely my own. Arabella Pike at HarperCollins has been a constructively helpful publisher, and I cannot thank Giles Gordon enough for placing me within her capable hands.

JOHN RAMSDEN,
January 1998

1

Introduction: The Conservative Party and Conservative History

THE NOTION OF PARTY has for over a century been seen as one of the key components of 'the Westminster model' of democratic politics, for since at least the last third of the nineteenth century it has been commonplace to assert that Britain's two-party system is the vital channel that links electors' preferences out there in the constituencies with the selection of the government and the passing of its legislation. As Sir Robert Peel observed when resigning office in 1845 in order to avoid the accusations of betrayal that would follow his reversal of course on the Corn Laws, 'a Government ought to have a natural support. A Conservative Government should be supported by a Conservative Party.' That crisis of 1845–46 was to prove one of the defining points of the history of party in Britain, and when Peel failed to escape office and then pursued his changed policy without the 'natural' support that Conservatives might otherwise have offered him, he was widely condemned. One of those who did resign in 1845, became Peel's effective successor as Party Leader and was three times Conservative Prime Minister, the 14th Earl of Derby, thought that

> the Conservative Party had been led to believe in Sir R. Peel's maintenance of the principle of effective protection [for agriculture]; and they had a right to complain of, and to resent, the ... total abandonment of a principle which he had led them to believe he would maintain, and in which belief he had accepted, and availed himself of, their Parliamentary support.

Party was thus a two-way street, down which loyal support from the party members flowed in one direction, but on the implied condition that fidelity to party principle flowed back to them from the leadership. In

1872 Derby's own successor as Party Leader, Benjamin Disraeli, told his supporters that 'without party Parliamentary Government is impossible'.

Sometimes Conservatives entered into this world of team-game loyalty without much forethought – Nigel Nicholson once pointed out that many – even Conservative MPs – had joined a party before they knew what the choice really meant, and then spent the rest of their lives trying to justify their decision to themselves and to others. But however unconsidered the original decision might have been, the significance of the later sense of belonging should not be underestimated, nor should the constant reinforcement of the group identity that is engendered simply by the regular acting together that partisanship involves. As Mark Twain somewhat cynically put it,

> Men think they think upon great political questions, and they do; but they think with their party, not independently; they read its literature, but not that of the other side; they arrive at convictions, but they are drawn from a partial view of the matter in hand, and are of no particular value. They swarm with their party, they feel with their party, they are happy in their party's approval, and where the party leads they will follow, whether for right and honour, or through blood and dirt and a mush of mutilated morals.

For every prominent Conservative – Robert Peel, say, or Winston Churchill – who seems to prove that 'it ain't necessarily so', there are dozens who may be cited in support of the herd instinct as one of the most significant motives in political activity. This is perhaps especially true for a conserving party, a party that is broadly resistant to change, for while radicals and reformers have generally not yet actually experienced the Utopias they dream of, and can therefore contemplate their postponement with some equanimity, in the meantime arguing among themselves about the exact topography of the Promised Land but confident in the optimistic view that time is on their side, the Conservative pessimist knows exactly what any undesirable change will cost him and his kind (since that which is at stake already exists and has perhaps been enjoyed for centuries). The tendency to herd together for self-preservation, and to place great emphasis on unity, on not rocking the boat, and on never, ever turning one's guns on one's allies, does not on this reading require any special explanation.

Such a strong sense of loyalty to the group could, of course, lead to high-flown expressions of distress when actual performance did not live up to expectations, as in the 'desertions' of the party by Winston Churchill in 1904, or by Enoch Powell in 1974. That 'unflinching Conservative', Mr Thorne in Anthony Trollope's *Barchester Towers* (1857), found that when repeal of the Corn Laws was carried out in 1846 'by the very men whom [he] had hitherto regarded as the only possible saviours of his country, he was for a time paralysed ... Not only must ruin come, but it must come through the apostasy of those who had been regarded as the truest of true believers. Politics in England, at least as a pursuit for gentlemen, must be at an end.' Occasionally, the party's top-brass have acted in a similarly uncompromising manner: when the Tory leaders prolonged coalition with Lloyd George in 1922, for rather longer than the party faithful thought desirable in the interests of Conservatism, the National Union Executive sternly warned Austen Chamberlain that his attitude as Leader constituted 'a breach of the understanding upon which the allegiance of the ... Party to its leaders depends'. R. A. Butler had the temerity to offer similar advice to Winston Churchill when he sought (unavailingly, as it turned out) to prolong his own Second World War coalition into peacetime in 1945, and there were similarly mutinous rumblings against Edward Heath in his pursuit of a centrist Government of National Unity in 1974: with respect to this latter period, Ian Gilmour has written of 'Ted Heath's fatal tendency – fatal for him – to act as a national statesman, subordinating the interests of his party to those of the country'. The ultimate sin in this partisan thought-world, even worse than combining unnecessarily with the enemy in office, was summarized in Disraeli's contemptuous dismissal of Peel as a leader who had appointed Tory men but then pursued Whig measures.

After 1846, though, such occasions were few and far between and Conservative leaders were more likely to be heard repeating Disraeli's dictum that 'England does not love coalitions' than asserting the need for national unity. They were also fond of recycling Disraeli's brutal advice to a follower: 'Damn your principles. Stick to your Party!' This assumption of an overriding partisan identity did not make it easy to mediate between the tribal prejudices of the party men, the quest for the votes of moderate electors, and the hard policy choices involved in being a national government. For Disraeli, the circle was to an extent squared by the claim that the Conservative Party was 'a national party or nothing' or, as he put it more quaintly to an audience of Tory Scotsmen in Edinburgh in 1868, 'the Conservative Party is the national party of England' (which became true only in 1997, when it failed to elect any MPs in Scotland, Wales or

Ireland). That reiterated claim that 'the great Conservative Party', even when being partisan in pursuing its own self-interest, was somehow also pursuing a national interest that was above and beyond the party contest, was a convenient rhetorical flourish that deceived few neutrals or rivals, but it was of recurrent value to Conservatives themselves in settling queasy stomachs among the crew. However, as Disraeli's and then Salisbury's party went on to develop and play the patriotic card more openly, through the exploitation of jingoism, imperialism and then Irish Unionism, such rhetoric did undoubtedly evoke a response in the electorate that went beyond mere partisan loyalty. Even when much later exponents of uninhibited, Union Jack-draped electioneering, such as Winston Churchill and Margaret Thatcher, pursued the same tactic after 1945, their opponents were always uneasily aware of its appeal to voters who could not be reached by the more prosaic programmes of domestic policy.

More often the practitioners of Conservative partisanship practised their arts more subtly, through cynicism and semantic obfuscation. For Arthur Balfour, the British political system actually depended on the determination to make it work, when all the partisan appearances suggested otherwise; indeed, late in his career he thought that the Westminster model worked *only* because the parties actually agreed on all matters of essential importance, which left them free to bicker with as much noise as they wished about 'inessentials'; the failure to maintain 'the Westminster model' of democracy in some former British colonies – regimes that Patrick Wall, MP, once memorably characterized as practising 'one man, one vote, once' – suggests that that truth has not been sufficiently understood.

In his own time, Balfour's stance of philosophic detachment allowed him both to be the partisan leader who unleashed the constitutional crisis of 1911 by employing the House of Lords to block the proposals of a large Commons majority, and also, in 1910, to consider on its merits a possible cross-party deal with the Liberals to settle all outstanding issues of difference between them, and then, from 1915, to become one of the most convinced of Tory coalitionists. There were pre-echoes here of the din of party battle in the 1950s, a period that most subsequent historians have seen as demonstrating at least some degree of consensus on central issues of policy, and of the bitterly rude Heath-against-Wilson duels which nevertheless prompted Samuel Brittan to entitle one of his books *Left versus Right, the Bogus Dilemma*. In the aftermath of the 1997 election, in which it was scarcely possible to detect a gap as thick as a piece of tissue paper between the parties (constitutional reform apart), despite a sustained barrage of unenlightening partisanship during the actual campaign, those echoes were positively deafening.

For Stanley Baldwin, the semantics were rather different, for here was a party man to the core, who had risen to prominence in 1922 precisely by detaching the Conservatives from a coalition with Lloyd George; he solved his dilemma by asserting that his 'New Conservatism' of 1924 was merely the Disraelian approach, brought up to date for a full-scale democracy. He then chose to emphasize the 'national' aspect of the Disraelian inheritance, which was especially useful in dealing with a Labour Party which could be defined in those terms as a sectarian threat to national unity, by reference to such events as the General Strike of 1926. It was, however, even more important when applied as a label to the anti-Labour 'National Government' of 1931, which dominated Britain in the Conservative interest for a decade but then demonstrated the hollowness of its claim when it had to give way to a genuinely National Government in 1940, incorporating Labour as well as anti-Labour parties so as to broaden its wartime base, and led by Churchill in a way that effectively denied party rather than simply acting as a vehicle for it. For the war period the Conservatives happily (or rather, unhappily) accepted all of this, but with the return of peace they insisted also on a return to party politics, even managing to impose that partisanship on Winston Churchill at the very height of his fame.

W. S. Gilbert famously observed in *Iolanthe* in 1882 that 'every boy and every gal,/that's born into the world alive,/Is either a little Liberal,/ Or else a little Conservative', voicing what was already such a common assumption in a world of polarized party politics that merely to exaggerate it produced a good joke. In the second verse, Gilbert's sentry outside the Houses of Parliament goes on to note that 'when in that House [of Commons], MPs divide', they 'have to leave their brains outside, and vote just as their leaders tell 'em to', a very topical reference to whipping practices that had only recently developed in the aftermath of the 1867 Reform Act. For it was after all in opposition to something as well as in favour of something that party derived its force. The future Prime Minister Lord Salisbury, for example, thought even as early as 1859, when the mood of British politics was scarcely partisan at all, that 'hostility to Radicalism, incessant, implacable hostility, is the essence of Conservatism. The fear that the radicals may triumph is the only final cause that the Conservative Party can plead for its own existence.' It is thus no accident that the great eras of Conservative success have all followed times of political, social and economic change, for all too many of the conservative British seem to agree with Queen Victoria's solemn advice to Gladstone, that 'change is so bad for the country'.

One of the most dominant myths in writing about British political history is that of 'the swing of the pendulum', the assumption that two parties have naturally alternated in office; this assumption produced in the early televising of election results Robert McKenzie's inimitable 'swingometer' and can still be seen in Peter Snow's more technological version today. The entire concept of 'swing' is difficult to apply to a political world of three or more strong parties, but what such visual devices do usefully demonstrate is the extent to which the electoral system itself has shaped the British parties, both positively – by such means as the single-member constituencies which then became the building blocks on which the Conservative Party structure and organization has always rested – and, above all, negatively, through the absence of any form of proportional representation.

The British first-past-the-post system of elections, unchanged in its essentials even when the franchise and other electoral rules were revolutionized after 1832, has had a profound influence both on the Conservative Party as an organism and on its long-term success. The lack of proportional representation has not of course been the only influence in determining which parties actually won elections, but it has constantly reinforced the parliamentary position of strong parties at the expense of the weak, and provided a steep gradient that third parties found almost impossible to climb in their quest for major party status. As one of the two strong parties in the state ever since modern politics began in Britain, and as a party that has had a remarkably tenacious hold over the loyalty of much of its vote, the Conservatives have thus benefited enormously and throughout their history from the electoral system. This has enabled them to profit disproportionately during their periods of success and to ride out their periods of unpopularity without ever quite facing a dangerous challenge for second place. If the gold medal was for the time being unattainable, then the silver was always the worst that the party could achieve, and this – to say the least – ensured that it invariably had a favourable draw in the next race.

It is not at all surprising, then, that with the exception only of a couple of periods in 1917–18 and in the later 1970s, when its usual self-confidence faltered, the Conservative Party has always been collectively unconvinced of the need for a change of electoral system. Its refusal to contemplate either conversion to PR or a change of name and a new start as a party, even when Winston Churchill, riding high after his wartime triumphs, proposed it to a shattered party after its defeat in 1945, is powerful evidence of the place that the electoral system has had in Tory confidence and self-identity. Quite how that tradition will play in a twenty-first century in which electoral reform is likely to be more insistently proposed than in the past is a moot point.

There is, though, something dangerously circular about the linkage just described between the electoral system and the party's success, for no party that loses too many votes can be saved by an electoral system. After all, the British Liberal Party spectacularly demonstrated the possibility of falling unexpectedly through the electoral system's trapdoor between 1918 (when it entered a general election with some 250 MPs) and the election of 1924 (from which it emerged with just forty), and how far such a fall, when once begun, could rapidly become self-generating. The Liberals have more recently enjoyed a forty-year recovery that has, even with their many gains in 1997, restored them only to the position that they had *after* their great 1920s collapse, a trend which demonstrates just how hard it is to work the trick in reverse. For the negotiation of such dangerous trapdoors – which the Conservatives themselves had to step carefully around in 1866–7, in 1885, in 1906–10, and in the 1920s, for example – we need to seek explanations in the more conventional areas of strategy, tactics and leadership, while remaining aware of the fact that the more solid ground in between the elephant traps was far from being a level playing field in itself.

Something like the regular alternation of two parties in office has been seen only rarely over the past two centuries; the two periods between 1865 and 1885, and during the 1960s and 1970s offer the best examples, apparent continuity being reinforced in each case by the fact that successive electoral contests were between the same potential prime ministers, Gladstone and Disraeli in the first case, Wilson and Heath in the second. More normally, though, British politics has produced longish periods in which one party has been dominant, with only the shortest periods of interruption of its hegemony, and ever since political and social forces were realigned to the advantage of the Conservatives in the 1880s (for which see Chapter Six below), it has usually been the Conservatives who dominated. This was the political pattern from 1886 to 1906, from 1918 to 1945, from 1951 to 1964, and from 1979 to 1997, each of them periods in which no other party ever won a Commons majority. For over a century, then, the Conservatives have controlled the Commons for two-thirds of the time (and the Lords for all the time, come to that), and have occupied governmental office either alone or with allies for even longer periods; in the 111 years between 1886 and 1997 there have been single-party majority governments formed by a party other than the Conservatives for less than twenty years. By any reckoning this is a quite extraordinary record of sustained success in the only contest that really matters to a political party – the winning of power and its denial to others. Since the Conservatives can also demonstrate a continuity of tradition, personnel and (to an extent) institutions that goes back to the period before democratic politics – even to before Britain became an industrialized nation, an era from which no other political party in the western world has survived *and* prospered – they may fairly be considered to be the most successful political party in the history of the world to date.

To *The Economist*'s editor Walter Bagehot in 1874 (when the long period of Conservative dominance had scarcely even started), all of this was quite right and proper, for

> in happy states, the Conservative party must rule upon the whole a much longer time than their adversaries. In well-framed politics, innovation – great innovation that is – can only be occasional. If you are always altering your house, it is a sign either that you have a bad house, or that you have an excessively restless disposition – there is something wrong somewhere.

Bagehot himself was a Liberal, but he was also a strong believer in the idea that there was much that was right about the British polity of his time (classically and admiringly described in his *The English Constitution*), and that it did not therefore need too much even of his own Liberal reformism, especially in relation to constitutional matters. For, both to Bagehot and to many political writers who followed in his footsteps, British restraint and British political moderation were both inborn and the product of long maturation within a system where evolution rather than revolution had always been the basis of the political process. Conservative political instincts were therefore entirely understandable in such a nation, at ease with itself politically and with the rules of the political game generally respected by all sides – much as in the domestic sphere Ralph Waldo Emerson had argued that 'men are Conservatives when they are least vigorous, or when they are most luxurious. They are Conservatives after dinner.'

In this light, it is surprising to note how little of the Conservative Party's history had been investigated and written about until relatively recently. In his novel *Contarini Fleming*, Disraeli advised people to 'read no history, nothing but biography, for that is life without theory', but those who followed after him actually had little choice in the matter. There were substantial 'tombstone' biographies of the Victorian and Edwardian Tory heroes from the earliest days, but these were often written for the edification of their successors and with the warts of their subjects quite ruthlessly excised, as, for instance, in W. R. Monypenny and G. E. Buckle's six-volume *Life of Benjamin Disraeli* (1910–20), though in this case the irrepressible personality of the subject kept breaking through whenever his own words were quoted by his biographers. Autobiographies were usually even more self-serving, and sometimes biographies too, like the young Winston Churchill's two volumes on his father, *Lord Randolph Churchill* (1906), which contrived to justify his own desertion of the Conservatives rather well but never quite got round to emphasizing Lord Randolph's steady sympathy for tariffs (which Winston shared neither then nor later). In the first half of the twentieth century the 'life and letters' school of biography produced several rather more valuable works, notably Lady Cecil's *Life of Robert, Marquess of Salisbury* (1921–32), Blanche Dugdale's *Arthur James Balfour* (1936), and lives of both Austen Chamberlain and Walter Long by Sir Charles Petrie (1936–40), but an entirely new standard was set in the writing of biographies with access to the archives by Robert Blake's life of Andrew Bonar Law, *The Unknown Prime Minister* (1955) – even if its title did more to bury Law than to praise him.

By comparison with this continuous flow of literature organized biographically, there was little in the way of formal history of the party as an organization or of institutions within it, an honourable exception being Charles Petrie's *The Carlton Club* (1955). The more interpretative general histories were partisan *within* the Tory world: R. L. Hill's *Toryism and the People* (1924) and Maurice Woods's *History of the Tory Party* (1929) both sought to show that Conservatives had an honourable history of humanitarian social reform, a claim that made a pro-Baldwin contribution to the party debate in their own times. Sir Keith Feiling's two volumes on the Tories of the seventeenth and eighteenth centuries, *The History of the Tory Party* (1924) and *The Second Tory Party* (1938), while more scholarly than most contributions in that period, fell into the same trap in emphasizing traits in the Tory tradition that fitted well with his own contributions to the contemporary debate.

Ironically, serious and systematic investigation of the Conservative Party's history as a whole began not with a British historian but with a Canadian political scientist, Robert McKenzie, who demonstrated in *British Political Parties* (1955) just how much could be synthesized by trawling through the biographical material which was by then in print and by putting it together with the first studies by political scientists into local organizations and voting behaviour, though it seems clear that McKenzie was influenced in his main findings as much by his observations of contemporary Conservatives as by systematic use of the available literature. Until then, Conservatives' public protestations of their deep loyalty to their leaders had often been taken at face value, at least as far as textbooks on British politics were concerned, and it had been traditional to portray the Conservatives as a 'top-down', hierarchical and leader-orientated party, especially when compared with Labour's more democratic, 'bottom-up' systems of delegation and consultation. McKenzie demonstrated, though, with an empiricism that political scientists were able to get away with in those days (if with a wealth of biographical evidence in support of his conclusions), that in practice the Conservative leaders of the previous fifty years had only survived in office when enjoying the consent of their followers, and that the traditional hierarchical assumptions were highly misleading; indeed McKenzie showed that it was possible to argue that hardly any Conservative leader had actually retired at a time of his own choosing, so mutinous had the party been over the years. His challenge to the previous orthodoxy, together with the overall explosion of academic research by both political scientists and historians as the 1950s and 1960s went on, opened the way for the serious study of the party's history. It was nevertheless still far more fashionable for much of the 1960s to study the parties of the left and centre than the Conservative Party, and few major historians active in that generation except Norman Gash and Robert Blake could be considered 'Conservative Party historians' as such.

Gash did more than any man to clarify the relationship between party and the politicians in the key period in which the party evolved, through *Politics in the Age of Peel* (1953), through biographical studies of Peel (1961, 1972 and 1976), and through the essays in *Reaction and Reconstruction in English Politics in the 1830s and 1840s* (1965), as well as through a veritable forest of articles on the organizational side of the party, its funding, whipping and structural development. Blake ranged more widely, producing in 1966 the biography *Disraeli*, which remains both a model of economy and lucidity in evoking the world of mid-Victorian politics and the essential guide to the man and his career. More importantly for our purposes here, perhaps, he offered in his Ford Lectures of 1968 (published in 1970 as *The Conservative Party from Peel to Churchill*, and subsequently extended to include the period up to Thatcher and then Major) the first overview of party history to appear from a serious pen – and still the only one to have commanded general respect, so that it has deservedly remained in print for more than a quarter of a century. Not the least of its effects was to prompt Longman to commission (and the party itself to agree to facilitate) a multi-volume series based on original research, the first parts of which appeared in 1978 and the last in 1996, bringing to a close what was by then a six-volume series on the party's history between 1830 and 1975.

By 1996, though, the world of research into Conservative history had been transformed, partly by established scholars contributing to our understanding of vital aspects of the party's history that had previously been neglected – Stuart Ball on *Baldwin and the Conservative Party* (1988), Martin Pugh on the Primrose League, *The Tories and the People* (1985), and Ewen Green's masterly *The Crisis of Conservatism, 1880–1914* (1995) being particularly influential examples. Beyond these, there has been a continuing outpouring of literature in academic journals, new biographies of old subjects – R. J. Q. Adams's forthcoming life of Bonar Law will be especially important here – and the published research of the youngest in the profession, now carried out with access to the party's own archives deposited in the Bodleian Library, of whom Nicholas Crowson, Martin Francis, Michael Kandiah and Ina Zweiniger-Bargielowska spring to mind.

Much of the recent literature is in fairly remote academic corners which only university libraries can be expected to shelve, while popularizing attempts to make the long-term history of the party available for readers more generally interested in British political history have all been disfigured by too many opinions and too little evidence. It seems more than time that an academic historian steeped in the work of the past generation had a go at synthesizing recent work and making it available to a wider audience. The timing could hardly be more appropriate, for in May 1997 the Conservative party was once again shattered by heavy electoral defeat after a period of dominance, and it now has to come to terms with its past, to re-examine its identity between the legacy of its history and the prospects for its future, as it approaches its third century of existence. This study may perhaps contribute a little to that process, both within the Conservative Party and for those outside who maintain an interest in its activities, for as Churchill wrote in 1948, 'pondering upon the past may give guidance in days to come [and] enable a new generation to repair some of the errors of former years'.

Such aspirations ought not perhaps to be pitched too high, for though de Tocqueville reminded us that history is a portrait gallery that more often contains copies than originals, it is often precisely in the detailed brushwork that distinguishes one copy from another that historical events are decided. Or, as A. J. P. Taylor more cynically put it when describing the Emperor Napoleon III's fascination with reading history, it is quite possible to learn to avoid repeating the mistakes of the past and thus to make only entirely new ones in the future. And yet, as Churchill also said, it is obviously better to learn from hindsight than to refuse to profit from experience. With the profusion of material now available to the historian of the Conservative Party, at least the next generation will no longer be able to say like Ezra Pound – except, that is, in the mood of deep nostalgia that conservatives find so appealing in itself – 'I can remember a day when historians left blanks in their writings, I mean for the things they didn't know.'

2

Origins:
Tories into Conservatives

SINCE THE BRITISH CONSERVATIVE PARTY, like the country itself, has to date had no written constitution, the question of how it first came into being is not easily answered. For the Labour Party a founding conference in 1900 set up a specific organization with rules, while the adoption of the name 'the Labour Party' in 1906 and the reformed constitution of 1918 provide easy answers to the equivalent question about starting points. For the Liberals, a meeting held in Willis's Rooms prior to the formation of the Palmerston government of 1859 has traditionally been accepted as the date at which the recognizable Victorian Liberal Party coalesced; if historians now question the importance of that 1859 meeting, and highlight earlier developments and the widespread use of the name 'Liberal' long before the 1850s, it nevertheless provides both an agreeable fiction on which most Liberal Party history could be based and an event which is still acknowledged to have been at the least a key moment in the evolution of the party.

For Conservatives and their historians, there have been no such certainties: it is not clear how far Tories of earlier centuries were true ancestors of Victorian Conservatives, as Sir Keith Feiling assumed in his studies of the earliest Tories, *The History of the Tory Party 1640–1714* (1924) and *The Second Tory Party, 1714–1832* (1938); it remains even more unclear how far Toryism as a concept was the basis on which the later official Conservatism rested, and whether even the party that Peel led under the name 'Conservative' between 1834 and 1846 deserved to be called a 'party' anyway. The issue has been further complicated by the fact that even when most politicians on the political right called themselves 'Conservatives' after 1830, they were nevertheless still labelled 'Tory' by their opponents, and sometimes themselves accepted that label as a badge both of honour and tradition. The assumption that 'Tory' and 'Conservative' were synonymous was frequently an unthinking and untested one, but for some politicians – Lord Randolph Churchill in the 1880s or Iain Macleod and Enoch Powell in the 1950s and 1960s, for example – 'Tory' has continued to mean something different from their 'Conservative' Party's official name.

To an extent this confusion arises from the fact that the lack of a constitution has allowed people to argue from different premisses and therefore to arrive quite naturally at different conclusions. If by 'party' is meant something like the organized, integrated, electioneering machinery of the twentieth century, then no such party existed anywhere at all on the political spectrum before the Second Reform Act of 1867. But is it sensible to ignore the fact that in the first half of the nineteenth century contemporaries almost universally spoke of 'party' as an essential ingredient in the political worlds of Westminster and the constituencies, or that they recognized that for most of the time a body of politicians on the political right had enough in common to work together for broadly agreed ends? For that earlier period, 'party' can usefully be approached from the definition given by Edmund Burke in 1770; 'a body of men united, for promoting by their joint endeavours the national interest, upon some particular principle on which they are all agreed'. In view of Burke's own considerable influence on British Conservatism, it makes sense to view it in just such terms, and by that kind of test it is clear that in the 1830s a 'party' existed and called itself 'Conservative'.

It did not of course emerge from the thin air, or from one single political crisis, though the constitutional revolutions of the period between 1827 and 1832 did play an important part in the process, rather as the kiln fires the pot and thereby fixes its shape, but only after the potter's prior and more creative efforts. The Conservative Party of the 1830s, which we shall take as our point of departure, needs to be explained as the convergence of three quite different streams of development. First, there was a philosophical tradition of conservatism as justification for those opposed to change. This owed something to earlier Toryism and to the theorists who wrote about the monarchy and the Anglican Church, but appeared in far sharper form in and after the 1790s as the dual consequence of the French Revolution and of the first stirrings of Britain's own urban, industrial class system. Second, there was the tradition of working together in office that began with the return to government of Tory politicians when their fifty years of political exile ended in the 1760s, a tradition shaped by the leadership of William Pitt after 1783 and through 'Pittite' alliances made with independents and former Whigs from the 1790s onwards. Gradually 'Pittites' were transmitted back into 'Tories' during the wars against Napoleon, and in collective resistance to radical reformers at home when they resurfaced after peace came in 1815. Lord Liverpool's long tenure of office as Prime Minister between 1812 and 1827 (and continuity established by many of his senior ministers too) was a key factor here, establishing trust and the habit of cooperation, as well as evolving a programme of actual policy over years in shared administration.

The limitation to all this lay in the fact that even a forty-seven-year dominance of ministerial office after 1783 did not quite make such men a party (in at least *some* of the modern senses), for holding office was still seen – at least partly – as a duty to the king rather than as loyalty to ministerial colleagues – especially by Tories, who had an elevated view of the monarchy – and the very fact that they were running the national political institutions removed any temptation to create their own. This was where the third factor, the crises of 1827 to 1832, was vital, for in detaching the Tories both from office and from the overriding idea of duty to the throne these events forced on them a collective redefinition of what they were about, what they had in common, and how they were to react effectively to a world which, after the 1832 Reform Act, would be much less comfortable for them. Under these final stimuli from events, steps were deliberately taken to create what all acknowledged at the time to be a party, and which almost everyone called by the new name of Conservative. In the 1840s the survival into high office of politicians who had formed most of their attitudes in a pre-Reform world ensured that this would not be an easy birth, and indeed in 1846–7 the sickly child seemed doomed to an early death. The Conservative Party of Peel appeared to have been a false start, but was not to prove so, for enough of the lessons of the 1830s lingered on even when Peel the teacher had been forced into early retirement by his unruly pupils. Since the 1830s, then, the Conservative Party has had a recognizably continuous history.

In summary, Peel's Conservatives in the 1830s were the product of three separate – and to some extent sequential – waves, by which the conservative forces in British politics acquired in stages their principles, their programme and, finally, their party. James Sack has identified the tradition as consisting in 'disposition; a peculiar form of rhetoric; a common historical vision; collective likes and, especially, dislikes; and, most important, a marked insistence, increasing in the early nineteenth century, on the spiritual, Christian, Anglican basis of English political life'. Noting that all of this convergence took place during a period in which actual party labels continued to be used capriciously and even contradictorily, he cites J. M. Roberts on the similar problem of identifying the French right in its formative years: 'There is a moment when a historical reality is coming to birth, is perhaps born, when it is not yet named, but when the awareness that there is something that needs to be named is spreading.' That view is given powerful reinforcement by the speed with which the word 'Conservative' was generally adopted in Britain in 1830–32.

We need to examine these three processes in turn, and to ask of each one how it contributed to what Harold Macmillan would in 1957 call 'the broad stream of our philosophy ... which makes us not only a national Party but a Party at the roots of whose philosophy lies the conviction that we are all in the same boat, with common problems to solve and a common destiny before us.' The image that Macmillan chose to illustrate the nature of the Party which he had just been elected to lead was characteristically derived mainly from the writings of Edmund Burke, and especially from Burke's emphasis on commonality and on the present's debts to the past and its duty to the future. Burke emerges as the key shaper of the process by which a distinctively conservative approach to British politics evolved, even though Burke considered himself a Whig and did not in any case separate himself off from earlier traditions of writing on his subject.

The first Tories, given by their opponents that offensive nickname which had originally described Irish cattle thieves, were politicians who operated in Britain at the end of the reign of Charles II. Even then, they traced their own roots back to the Royalists who had fought for Charles I a quarter of a century earlier. In later years too, the efforts and ideas of the moderate Royalists who sought unavailingly to prevent the English Civil War from breaking out in 1642 – such men as Edward Hyde and Viscount Falkland, MPs who did not blindly follow the king but rather sought a middle way between absolutism and radicalism – have been a continuing source of inspiration to later Conservatives. Falkland's dictum on the dangers of reform – that if it is not necessary to make a change in the state, then it is necessary *not* to change it – leads straight on to Burke and has been recited by Conservatives over the past three and a half centuries; in the heyday of Margaret Thatcher, Falkland was rendered into the twentieth-century vernacular by Dr Rhodes Boyson as 'if it ain't broke, don't fix it'. Others, generally the natural Cavaliers of the political world like Disraeli and Lord Randolph Churchill, have welcomed a more generalized association with the Royalists of the 1640s. Disraeli dubbed his fellow Leader, Stanley in the 1840s 'the Prince Rupert of parliamentary discussion', while Lord Randolph's son Winston was always both inordinately proud of the earlier Winston Churchill who had fought for King Charles and especially sensitive to charges that his greatest ancestor, the first Duke of Marlborough, had himself abandoned his king in 1688.

Falkland was killed in the Civil War, apparently seeking death willingly rather than live on in a land whose organic unity was riven by civil strife; Hyde, although he became Charles II's chief minister when the monarchy was restored in 1660, was no more successful in mediating between crown and parliament in the 1660s than he had been in 1642. It was, therefore, during the threatened breakdown of monarchical government in the Exclusion Crisis of 1679–81, rather than in earlier Stuart politics, that a distinct Tory Party emerged, and – fairly characteristically, as we shall see – it was only in reaction to a radical threat that this development took place. The Whig faction in the political nation reacted to the increasing age of a childless king by highlighting its fear of the consequences of his being succeeded by his only brother, James, Duke of York, a known and practising Catholic. They attempted to secure a parliamentary statute which would bar James from the throne and replace him with a Protestant, and although those who became Tories were almost to a man Anglicans who shared the Whigs' dislike and fear of Catholicism, they rallied to the House of Stuart as the cause of legitimacy and of the 'natural' rights of succession. Indeed, Tories tended to see this 'Exclusion Crisis' as merely a Whig pretext to bring back all the horrors of the 1640s: civil war, regicide republicanism, and the confiscation of property. That broad divide remained central to British political life: two centuries later the historian W. E. Lecky thought that before Victorians were Whigs or Tories, they were at heart Roundheads and Cavaliers.

In the short term, despite the hysteria whipped up by the Whigs during the 'Popish Plot' of 1679, the Tories rallied sufficiently well to allow Charles II to outwit the Whigs and then mount a counter-attack in which a number of them went to the scaffold, and rather more lost their places and preferment both nationally and in town corporations. When Charles II died, his brother duly became king, as James II, but this proved not so much a triumph as a disaster for the Tories: James rapidly moved to promote Catholics rather than Anglicans both in his household and in the army, and he sought a cynical alliance with the nonconformists (who had been more Whig than Tory in their own political allegiance, and were disliked by the Anglican Tories almost as much as Catholics). Most English politicians interpreted all of this as moving towards an absolutist monarchy on the French model, a development which threatened those very rights of property that Tories thought they had been fighting for at the king's side only five years earlier.

By the end of James's short reign in 1688 his Tory subjects had to make an unpalatable choice between loyalty to their king by due succession and allegiance to the Church, and Tories as well as Whigs were to be found signing the secret invitation to William of Orange to invade England and save its Protestant constitution. Fortunately for most Tories, the relatively bloodless revolution of 1688, and the flight of King James without calling them to his military defence, allowed them to avoid that truly horrendous choice. It could thereafter be maintained that James had by his flight simply vacated the crown (which had not therefore been taken from him either by force or by statute), while the fact that James's eldest daughter Mary now became queen regnant (and a good Anglican one at that) when her husband William III became king meant that for a few more years the Tories could convince themselves that they were remaining loyal both to legitimacy and to their Church. In any case, the transmission of the crown, once the settlement of 1688 had excluded James and his son, had to follow strict lines of inheritance, and it was only the failure of both of James II's Protestant daughters to produce a living heir that kept the issue open. The inconvenient fact that James also had a son was initially explained away for such tender Tory consciences by recourse to the rumour that he was not legitimate, though few serious politicians can have really believed this to be true. After 1688 they scarcely needed to believe such an improbable story anyway, for by voting with the Whigs in both Lords and Commons for the proposition that a Catholic king was incompatible with a Protestant kingdom, Tories had belatedly accepted the exclusion principle that they had so vigorously opposed in 1679.

Over the next quarter century, until James's Protestant issue failed on the death of the childless Queen Anne in 1714, Tories could for the most part remain loyal to the throne, and play an active part in the near-continuous wars between Britain and her allies on the one side and a France backing the return of James and his heirs on the other. They could also derive considerable political capital from their claim that they alone were to be trusted to govern in a way that would keep the Church safe. The 'rage of party' during the reign of Queen Anne, a false dawn for the

British two-party system in which the country was deeply polarized into competing factions in parliament, in the constituencies and in the press, derived largely from the Tories' hyping up of the threat to the Church, a convenient distraction from their own uncertainty about the monarchy. Tories shared in several ministries after 1688, and with the growing support for Queen Anne (whom the Vicar of Bray thought to be 'the Church of England's glory', sufficiently so to make him too a Tory – until 1714) they had the better of the Whigs in elections during her reign and were from 1710 the dominant party in both Houses of parliament and in the ministry.

Nevertheless, the compromise of 1688 in which most Tories had chosen to prioritize their religion over their king but claimed to have kept both loyalties intact, gradually ate away at their credibility and their confidence, which came to depend entirely on the Protestant daughters of King James. When Mary died in 1694, their acceptance of William III when he continued to govern alone had already shown the illogicality of their position, and its recovery when Anne succeeded in 1702 was limited by her frail health, by her inability to produce an heir, and by the fact that parliament (even with a Tory majority in the Commons) had already in 1701 entailed the crown to the Elector of Hanover, a distant Lutheran descendant of Anne's great-grandfather, on the sole ground that he was Protestant and should therefore have precedence over James II's Catholic offspring. In effect, the throne of England could be said to have become elective in 1701; this was confirmed when, on the death of Anne in 1714, the elector duly succeeded as George I, just as parliament had prescribed.

Many Tories were simply unable to accept this development, while the manoeuvrings of the final Tory government of Anne's reign for an alternative to the succession of a German-speaking alien only made their support for the Protestant succession look unreliable. In 1715 many Scottish Tories, dubbed 'Jacobites' after the Latin name for James, rose in rebellion against the newly arrived George I, and, although the majority of English Tories did not join them in arms, their lack of enthusiasm for Hanover damned them with the new king and allowed the Whigs to enjoy a monopoly of power for the next forty years. A second Jacobite rising in 1745 attracted rather more Scottish support and even less in England, and although the bloody defeat of James II's grandson Charles Edward actually removed the Jacobite threat to the house of Hanover for ever, it once again gave the Whigs a pretext for their continuing claim to be the only reliable supporters of the Protestant succession. No Tories served in ministries under either George I (1714–27) or George II (1727–60) and, with the

Whigs enjoying all of the fruits of office in those years, their ruthless control of patronage made it difficult for Tories to rise in the court, the army, the Church or in civil politics.

Nevertheless, it is clear that English and Welsh Toryism did not entirely wither during these long years of Whig dominance after 1714, for in many a village the alliance of squire and parson rested on just such a 'Church and King' political outlook as had launched the original Tories in the previous century. In that period when all constituencies had two MPs, many shires liked to divide their representation between a Whig and a Tory and so preserve 'the peace of the county', so that there were still over a hundred Tory MPs in 1760, while in towns there were frequently Tory as well as Whig factions keeping up the contest for local pre-eminence through elections, pamphleteering and the press. The continuing strength of the Church of England in the universities (which educated most clergymen, who went on to shape the views of future generations of squires) and the continuance of the Test and Corporation Acts, which denied attendance in those universities and office-holding in many other closed corporations across the land to all but Anglicans (unless, that is, they denied their nonconformity by occasional appearances in church), ensured that Anglican Tories remained at least a significant minority. Their political minority status was reconciled with their aspirations by their espousal of a 'country party' ideology, the traditional response to exclusion from the party of the 'court', from royal patronage and from power. In their case, though, 'country' often truly meant a preference for rural England, as well as the antithesis of 'court'. Tories could reassure themselves that by staying out of office they had at least avoided the cynical abandonment of principle which they professed to detect in the Whigs of the day. Some went so far as to assume that all who served in national government must become corrupt, so deep were their suspicions – though they retained a healthy interest as magistrates in the government and the parliamentary representation of their own spheres. Squire Western in Henry Fielding's novel *Tom Jones* (1749) was the epitome of this consolingly 'country' identity, a man who is scabrously contemptuous of London, lords, tradesmen, poachers and government alike, and who lives a cheerfully irreligious lifestyle while maintaining an Anglican clergyman in the house.

The situation nationally changed only with the accession of George III in 1760. This was partly because, as the first Hanoverian king who was thoroughly English in speech and in outlook, he did not suffer the resentment which had fuelled Tory Jacobitism under George I and George II, partly because the passage of time had made Jacobitism seem more and more of a lost cause anyway for politicians hungry for a share of the political spoils, partly because the break-up of Whig unity and the new king's coincident wish to have more freedom of manoeuvre in choosing his ministers opened the way for new types of ministerial appointment. In the 1760s, then, and especially in the 1770s and afterwards, Tories returned to the centre of the political world after half a century on the periphery, though in order to ease their passage in that direction they frequently gave up the label 'Tory' in favour of a more anodyne 'King's Friend' or 'independent' – or indeed no label at all except a protestation of loyalty and service to the king. From thence came the gradual construction of a prolonged 'Tory' dominance that dare not speak its name over the sixty years between 1770 and 1830.

What, though, was Toryism thought to stand for in its first century – for clearly something very positive was involved if it was able to keep the flame alive over fifty continuous years of minority status in the political nation? One rallying point was clearly support for a strict line of succession by primogeniture, which no doubt appealed to the squirearchy because the same principle legitimated their own position in society and their landed property. For – to reverse the argument put to the king by the Duke of York in Shakespeare's *Richard II* – the king's right to succeed was the mirror-image of a subject-heir's title to his own acres:

> Take Hereford's rights away, and take from Time
> His charters and his customary rights;
> Let not tomorrow then ensure today;
> Be not thyself – for how art thou a king
> But by fair sequence and succession?

There was also clearly a deep commitment to the Church of England and to the idea that the possession of land was in itself a public good, an essential qualification for the responsibility of government, both local and national, and a paternal duty that should not be shirked. It was after all a Tory-dominated parliament which had introduced a high property qualification for MPs in 1710: the possession of property worth £300 for a borough member; £600 for a knight of the shire (who would represent the landholders themselves).

The high value that Tories placed on the monarchy made it hard for them to rally to the first two Georges, who had both (as Tories saw it) had a weak hereditary claim and placed their sacred powers in the hands of cynical Whig manipulators, a group that certainly contained more than its share of the aristocracy but was also too closely tied for Tory taste to the commercial interests of the City of London and the political interests of nonconformity. For Dr Johnson, himself a staunch Tory of the mid-eighteenth century, a Tory's political make-up included an instinctive reverence for all that previous generations had handed down (a concept that the equally Tory Alexander Pope summarized brutally as 'Whatever is, is right'), a respect for the crown and its governance of the country, a fixed loyalty to the Church of England and a prejudice in favour of the landed interest.

The real difference between Tory and Whig by this time had more to do with attitude than with actual policy: Johnson thought that 'a wise Tory and a wise Whig . . . will agree'; for example, 'a Tory does not wish to give more power to Government; but that Government should have more reverence'. In saying that the Tory was essentially prejudiced in favour of 'establishment' and the Whig of 'innovation', Johnson was typically putting a civil debate into ecclesiastical language, but he was not defining things very differently from the Whig Macaulay when he attempted the same task in 1830. Macaulay thought that the Whig and the Tory were 'each of them representative of a great principle, essential to the welfare of nations': 'One is, in an especial manner, the guardian of liberty, and the other of order. One is the moving power, and the other the steadying power of the State. One is the sail, without which society would make no progress; the other, the ballast, without which there would be no safety in a tempest.' The merging of both Whig and Tory traditions into Conservative Unionism in 1886 led on to Stanley Baldwin's declaration in 1936 that for him Conservatism stood for 'ordered liberty', and to the sometimes schizophrenic appearance of the twentieth-century Party when trying to decide between progress and resistance. Or, as a backbencher put it in 1819, the Whigs anticipated danger to the political nation from the encroachments of the king, Tories from too great concessions to the mob, 'the encroaching and overbearing licence of the people'. Put in this way, a distinction between the parties that was on both sides not far from the debates of 1642 and 1679, it is not hard to demonstrate a broad continuity of attitude from Tories across to the Conservatives of later generations.

In a broader sense, too, writers about British politics before Edmund Burke had already articulated a distinctively conservative viewpoint, more moderate than theorists of royal absolutism like Robert Filmer or Thomas Hobbes, less oligarchic than Whig theorists like John Locke, less democratic than Tom Paine or Jean-Jacques Rousseau. That tradition's association with the compromise status which the Church of England claimed (perhaps spuriously, when the draconian legislation of the 1660s is considered) should not be overlooked, for both in theory and in practice the Church of England often saw itself (as a Chartist would famously quip in the 1830s) as 'the Conservative Party at prayer'. In establishing the Church of England during her long reign, Queen Elizabeth I had spoken of the golden mean, the 'via media', as her real objective, a concept that had as much to do with the mid-point between authoritarian and democratic forms of Church government as it had to do with theological dogma. As the preface to the 1662 Prayer Book put it, 'It hath been the wisdom of the Church of *England*, ever since the first compiling of her Publick Liturgy, to keep the mean between the two extremes, of too much stiffness in refusing, and of too much easiness in admitting any variation from it.' On this view, it is not surprising that it was an Anglican theologian, Richard Hooker, Queen Elizabeth's Bishop of Exeter, who was generally identified as the first writer in this English conservative tradition (though, once again, more for what he stood for personally than for the typicality of his beliefs among Anglicans of his time). Hooker's *Laws of Ecclesiastical Polity* (1594) set out to provide a theological and philosophical underpinning of the case for Anglicanism's 'mean between the two extremes', but in the context of a pamphleteering debate during the Counter-Reformation he again had to set his argument as much in the world of politics as in theology. Hooker was widely read and much cited by political philosophers of the seventeenth and eighteenth centuries, contributing to the thought of John Locke and admiringly cited as a source by both Viscount Bolingbroke, the most widely read Tory writer of the first half of the eighteenth century, and Edmund Burke in the 1790s.

Before Burke's contribution to the debate, and before Tories came almost to dominate the political scene again in the second half of the reign of George III, there was thus a pre-existent body of writing which asserted a middle way, but did so mainly on the basis of tradition, empiricism and the assumption of English and Anglican exceptionalism, rather than from the more theoretical, logical and rationalist premises from which Whigs like Locke tended to work. As Bolingbroke put it in 1735, 'our constitution is a system of government suited to the genius of our nation', based on 'the experience of many hundred years'. It was the fact of the French Revolution and Burke's reaction to it that gave these vague concepts a shape and form from which the later Conservative Party could draw two centuries of sustenance.

The French Revolution of 1789 was welcomed at first by most Britons, partly no doubt because it embarrassed and weakened an old enemy, partly because British politicians of every political stripe shared in the common assumption that the Catholic French monarchy was the polar, inferior opposite of English Protestant 'liberty'. It was not long, though, before opinion was transformed by the violence in Paris, the trial and execution of the king and queen (especially uncomfortable for Tories when French propagandists compared it with the fate of Charles I), the republican Terror that followed, and the ultimate recourse to a threatening military dictatorship under Napoleon Bonaparte. The French Revolution thus ushered in a wholly new era in European political life, symbolized neatly in the concepts of 'right' and 'left' that have been used ever since they first arose from the accidental seating plan of factions in the French Assembly of 1789. By 1795, as the conservative propagandist John Reeves put it in his *Thoughts on the English Government*, 'there are now no divisions in the Nation, but that of the friends of the Constitution as established by Law, and that of the Republicans, who are laying by for an opportunity to level everything to the Equality of a French Democracy.'

Burke, almost alone among British politicians and writers, took this view even in 1789, but he was absolutely alone in justifying his conservative position from a carefully thought-out analysis of the British tradition. Although he is often seen as an epitome of eighteenth-century rationalism, his political philosophy makes more sense as an early expression of the romantic movement that was to follow the Enlightenment, and many of Britain's greatest Romantics were themselves to be Burkeian in their politics. As a Romantic, he placed unusual emphasis on the irrational, the spiritual and the 'natural' within man. There was nothing wrong with inborn prejudice, for 'prejudice renders a man's virtue his habit; and not a series of unconnected acts. Through just prejudice, his duty becomes part of his nature.' For, as Norman Gash has put it, Burke reintroduced human nature into political theory, and when he applied his empiricism to the loosening of civil bonds brought about by the 1789 revolution, he was profoundly frightened by the consequences that he foresaw – and which then duly came to pass. Since Burke, it has been commonplace for

British Conservatives to argue against any utopian scheme on the reiterated assumption that weak, fallible man would never in practice be able to make such fine theories work; as Burke himself put it, 'the true touchstone of all theories which regard man and the affairs of man [is] does it suit his nature as modified by his habits?' The fundamental pessimism that characterized the Victorian Conservative Leader Lord Salisbury owed much to this concept.

In reaction to the democratic ideas unleashed in 1789 Burke stressed the organic nature of society, the relationship of the present to the past and future by a process of evolution, and the need to control the excesses of man's appetites through properly constituted authority:

> Society requires not only that the passions of individuals should be subjected, but that even in the mass and body, as well as in the individuals, the inclinations of men should frequently be thwarted, their will controlled, and their passions brought into subjection. This can only be done *by a power out of themselves*; and not, in the exercise of its function, subject to that will and to the passions which it is its office to bridle and subdue. In this sense the restraints on men, as well as their liberties, are to be reckoned among their rights.

That final sentence, with external restraint presented as a personal right rather than an encumbrance, echoed *The Book of Common Prayer*'s assertion that it is 'service' that is the 'perfect freedom'.

The overriding need, then, was to respect inherited authority, which had been constituted by the wisdom of the ages, for such respect removed the need to dispute about who should be given the necessary power to subdue men's lower natures. This led Burke into the classic defence of the conservative viewpoint: over time changes were both inevitable and desirable, since 'a state without the means of some change is without the means of its conservation', but those changes must be cautious and slow. 'A disposition to preserve, and an ability to improve, taken together, would be my standard of a statesman.'

Burke was a moderate in politics who spent almost all of his own career in opposition to the king's ministers, in seeking to limit the power of government, in impeaching Warren Hastings for abuses of colonial power in India, and in supporting the (socially conservative) American Revolution even though it was even more damaging to British interests than 1789 was to be in France. He was no blind reactionary then, as were most of the anti-Jacobin polemicists of the 1790s, but a constructive thinker. He was therefore able to mobilize his formidable powers as a writer of prose to give shape and substance to the emerging British conservative tradition of thought. Less vitriolically than Reeves, he too argued in 1796 that Britain was now divided between constructives and destructives, between those who stood for the 'conservation in England of the Ancient order of things' even while improving it with due care, and the other side 'which demands great changes here, and is so pleased to see them everywhere else'. Just as the mass sales of Tom Paine's *The Rights of Man* galvanized British radicals, Burke's impact on the more conservative reading public was huge: his *Reflections on the Revolution in France*, published in 1790, had by 1797 already sold over 300,000 copies – a quite colossal sale for a work of political theory, and when the total British population was still less than 10 million – and then not only went on selling in its own right but had its ideas propagated by a plethora of lesser writers like John Bowles well into the next century. In the short term, the reputation of Pitt (when carefully sanitized by his biographers) counted for more than the writings of Burke, but in the longer history of British Conservatism Burke's was the greater influence.

Disraeli later asserted that Burke 'effected for the Whigs what Bolingbroke in a preceding age had done for the Tories: he restored the moral existence of their party'. There is then much to be said for William Wordsworth's much later summary of the 'genius of Burke' who

> ... forewarns, denounces, launches forth,
> Against all systems built on abstract rights,
> Keen ridicule; the majesty proclaims
> Of Institutes and Laws, hallowed by time;
> Declares the vital power of social ties
> Endeared by Custom; and with high disdain,
> Exploding upstart theory, insists
> Upon the allegiance to which men are born ...

That summary, published only in 1850, gives a good indication of the authority with which Burke's contribution was by then viewed by the generation of orthodox, literary Conservatives who followed in his footsteps. For although Conservatives were (following John Stuart Mill) frequently to be derided as 'the stupidest party' by their Liberal opposites in the nineteenth century, Conservatism in its formative years had a high intellectual pedigree: following Burke in the full flowering of the Age of

Romanticism, Conservatives could claim the active literary support of the poets Wordsworth, Robert Southey and Samuel Taylor Coleridge, the novelists Thomas Love Peacock and Sir Walter Scott, and the essayists and journalists Thomas De Quincey, William Hazlitt, J. G. Lockhart and John Wilson Croker. In 1836, then, a Conservative journalist was able to cite a long list of 'great literary stars' who actively took the Conservative side in politics, listing many of those mentioned above as well as such scientists as Michael Faraday. The Whigs' *Edinburgh Review* was the first of a new genre of intellectual magazines, but by 1830 it was matched on the Tory side by the *Quarterly Review* (from whence Croker dabbled actively in the politics of the day), *Blackwood's Magazine* and *Fraser's*. In the founding generation, British Conservatives had not only acquired an agreed body of principle, they had also found outlets and persuasive voices for its propagation.

Fraser's told its readers that the party needed Conservatives 'who can render a reason for the faith that is in them, not men that only know that they abominate the radicals . . .', but it would be foolish to ignore the fact that all too many of the literary stars of Toryism were as anti-radical after witnessing the excesses of the Paris Jacobins as they were attracted to anything positive on their own side, and therefore all the more grateful to Burke for his work in giving them and their successors a respectable basis for their 'faith'. Nor was this Burkeian influence limited to the party's periodical press and its literary stars, for between the arrival of Liverpool as Prime Minister in 1812 and the fall of Peel in 1847 it was easy enough to spot in active politicians too. George Canning, for example, made his 1822 defence of the unreformed electoral system almost entirely on grounds drawn from Burke – its origins lost in the mists of time, respect for it built up over generations past, and the danger of making changes for the worse on the basis of untested theory. When Peel had to attempt the same task in 1830 he referred back to both Burke and Canning, and then argued in very similar terms. Disraeli, in one of his first commentaries on the British political system in 1835, argued that 'with us it is the growth of ages, and brooding centuries have watched over and tended its perilous birth and feeble infancy'. Such an inheritance from time itself defied theory, for 'it cannot be scribbled down . . . in a morning on the envelope of a letter . . . or sketched with ludicrous facility in the conceited commonplace book of an Utilitarian sage'. To Disraeli, 'respect for precedent . . . prescription . . . antiquity . . . have their origin in a profound knowledge of human nature . . .', a truly Burkeian approach.

Peel offers a more complex case, for he was too much the pragmatist to tie himself too closely to any body of theory, even as empirically based a theory as Burke's; however, he was not averse to proclaiming in 1838 that 'by conservative principles I mean a maintenance of the settled institutions of church and state ... and continuation of those laws, those institutions, that society, and those habits and manners which have contributed to mould and form the character of Englishmen ...' On another view, Peel was the only major Tory statesman of that age who took sufficiently seriously Burke's parallel view that a nation must reform *in order to* conserve, but this was a strategy that he was in the end unable to impose on his party. There has always remained a tendency, though, for Conservatives to see Burke as the rhetorician of resistance and to forget his equal insistence that government also be responsive to the needs of the people. Perhaps only Stanley Baldwin among twentieth-century leaders of the Conservative Party was truly following Burke, both in basing his politics on tradition and 'Englishness', and in insisting on the need for regular but moderate reform.

By Peel's time, what Conservatism meant had anyway as much to do with what men who by then called themselves Conservatives had actually done in office together as Tories earlier in their careers. In the first two decades of George III's reign Tories became once again reliable voting supporters for his ministers and helped to sustain Lord North in his vain efforts to retain the American colonies, but, having lost their 'country' mentality with their return to 'court', they tended also to drop their old 'Tory' label in the process. This habit became far more marked when giving continuing support to Pitt the Younger as Prime Minister from 1783 to 1801. Pitt had been very much the king's personal choice, against the predilections of most of the leading politicians of 1783, and that in itself rallied Tories to support him, but Pitt invariably called himself a Whig and rested his authority more on the premises of efficiency in administration, on managing parliamentary majorities through Treasury patronage, and on the duty of loyal men to support the king's ministers, than on the principles associated with any one historic party. To that extent, the tendency of Pitt's ministry was more to terminate Toryism than to promote it – or so it seemed until 1788–9.

In fact, despite his original dependence on the king's personal backing, Pitt's long ministry resumed the earlier process (to an extent halted in 1760) whereby practical power drifted from the palace to the Cabinet, especially when the king's first attack of mental illness in 1788 initiated a long period in which the actual monarch was enfeebled, or otherwise ineffective as a politician in his own right; as Frank O'Gorman puts it, 'when the King was no longer the first of party leaders, a Tory rather than a King's government could be said to exist'. The Tory tradition of loyalty to the king shifted, within the same period and for the same reason, to a practical loyalty to his ministers (especially since in almost every year between 1783 and 1827 these were men of whom they approved anyway – which is more than can be said of Tory views of George IV himself, either as prince regent or king). By 1822 Liverpool was prepared to face down George IV over Cabinet appointments, assuring him that if the Prime Minister was forced out then the rest of the Cabinet would go too, a milestone on the road to Cabinet government. By 1827, when Liverpool died, the king was even asking the Cabinet to choose its own Prime Minister, only to be told by the Duke of Wellington that this was a prerogative duty which the monarch could *not* shirk. The detachment of the Cabinet from the king and the emergence of a concept of 'His Majesty's Loyal Opposition', a phrase first used in about 1826, opened the way for Tory reverence for personal monarchy to be transmuted into Conservatism's more pragmatic relationship with the 'crown'.

In any case, the delayed reaction to the French Revolution, especially when Britain went to war against Revolutionary France in 1793 and then faced radical reformers at home who were perceived as black sheep within the national fold, ensured that Tory traditions suddenly became fashionable again – and overtly patriotic too. Having witnessed the fall of landed property in France alongside the abolition of the French monarchy, British property-owners were all too ready to display a self-interested resistance to anything that smacked of republicanism. George III was thus promoted into an avuncular national symbol of resistance to invasion by Napoleon, and almost all the 'haves' in society came naturally together for self-protection and to conserve the hierarchical status quo that the king symbolized; in 1827 Wellington was to argue that 'our Party consists of the Bishops & clergy, the great Aristocracy, the landed Interest, the Magistracy of the Country, the great Merchants and Bankers, in short the *parti conservateur* of the Country.' The splitting of the Whigs and the joining of Pitt's government by the more conservative Rockingham Whigs in 1794 (together with their chief theorist Edmund Burke), leaving only a rump of more ideological radicals in opposition to Pitt, was in effect a realignment of aristocracy and property in defence of the status quo. The effect was actually to make Pitt's government more hard-line in its treatment

Gillray's satire on the anti-Jacobin rhetoric of the 1790s. 'Promised Horrors of the French Invasion ... Vide the Authority of Edmund Burke', October 1796. Burke, with spectacles, is being tossed by the Bull, while Canning's head is hanging from a post, and the mob are storming the Tory White's Club.

of political dissent than it already was – the radical Whig leader Charles James Fox remarked sourly that 'our old friends are worse Tories than those whom they have joined'. Alliance with a later generation of Whigs between 1886 and 1895 would stiffen Salisbury's Conservatives in much the same way.

The political circumstances created by the long French wars also allowed a genuinely popular upsurge of Tory principles in the localities, too, though we have no effective way of knowing where sympathies had always existed but lain submerged throughout the previous century and where they were now created anew in these favourable conditions – and with the active encouragement, of course, of local propertied elites. In the regions, the rallying of opinion against both France and the British radicals led to the proliferation of Pitt clubs, King and Constitution clubs, and Constitutional Associations, and to popular participation in the military volunteers (which were then used for domestic repression as well as for defence against invasion). Such local bodies as Nottingham's patriotic White Lion Club, which was reorganized in 1797 as the 'True Blue Club', were the tributaries from which Conservative organization in the cities would later spring.

On the religious side, the French Revolution's process of secularization was denounced as atheism by British churchmen, who were already worried about their future in a world upset (from their viewpoint) by the recent rise of Methodism. Both sides of the political alliance of 'Church and King' were therefore from the mid-1790s once again highly topical for much of the political nation, and the fact that for over twenty years it was Britain that was the bedrock on which European resistance to dominance by Revolutionary and Napoleonic France depended meant that the Tory political identity became closely associated with the patriotic perspective too. Anglican clergymen came to the fore in offering, through sermons and tracts, Tory lessons in obedience to authority, and in general the tone of conservative politics became markedly more religious – so much so that after his death in 1806 the freethinking Pitt had to be redefined as a good Christian in order that his shrine would be a fit place at which Tories could worship. Disraeli in 1845 wrote that 'the name of Pitt remains fresh after forty years, a parliamentary beacon', while a young Conservative MP of 1914, a century after Pitt's death, could be described by a constituency newspaper as unusually principled, and therefore travelling down 'the great trunk road of which Pitt was the engineer in days of long ago'. Even as late as 1940, Rab Butler's reaction to the arrival of Winston Churchill as Prime Minister was that 'the good, clean tradition of English politics, that of Pitt as opposed to Fox, has been sold to the greatest adventurer of modern political history'.

It was in this sense that the founders of Methodism, John and Charles Wesley, called themselves Tories, even as early as 1785, since they put their trust in God rather than rational (and therefore Whiggish) man. As Conservatism evolved in the early nineteenth century its insistence on the link between Protestant Church and state (which even the Wesleys had not wished to break, though their followers subsequently did so) became steadily stronger.

There was, then, from the beginning of the nineteenth century an unusually deep cleavage between the groups that backed the government and those who opposed it, a bipolar divide that was in turn reinforced by the repressive actions that Tories in office continued to take against peacetime radicals after 1815, while Whigs denounced the repression as illiberal and unconstitutional. The habit of operating as two permanent groups of rivals became well-entrenched, lasting in effect right through to

1827; the introduction into Liverpool's government of the Grenvillites in 1822 brought to an end the last true family connection to operate independent of party, and though parties fragmented again for a time after 1827, it was henceforth to be more on the basis of policy than of family.

By 1807 a general election in which the war against France was the chief topic of contention offered an occasion in which the Whigs generally took to calling government supporters 'Tories' again, and though few government candidates yet used that label to describe themselves – George Canning was the first major politician to do so – the shape of things to come was becoming clearer. With the more ideological slant given to politics by the French Revolution, war and domestic economic distress, the Tory programme of 'Church and King' resistance could be readily contrasted with the reforming ideas of the remaining Whigs. That contrast owed a great deal to the uninterrupted tenure of office by Tories from 1807, first under the Duke of Portland, then from 1809 under Spencer Perceval, finally for fifteen years after 1812 under Lord Liverpool, a period which allowed for long continuities in office by individual ministers, for the habit to be finally established of working together (and in some cases getting on one another's nerves too, as in all good political parties), and for the unashamed readoption of the old label 'Tory'.

By 1830 Croker was writing in the *Quarterly* that 'party attachments and consistency are in the *first* class of a statesman's duties', and even going so far as to claim that party government was 'part of our well-understood, though unwritten, constitution'. This was an exaggeration, and would certainly not have represented the views of the more old-fashioned MPs of that time, but by then the management of Commons business had passed from the Speaker to the Whips, letters were sent out giving advice on forthcoming votes, Brooks's and White's clubs provided social networks for the rival parliamentary teams, and party meetings were held once or twice a session to coordinate backbench activities. The number of independent MPs was generally thought to have fallen to a handful, attendance in debate became somewhat more regular, and the tendency of the House of Lords to follow what were thought to be the king's personal wishes was also fast disappearing. This trend towards party must not of course be exaggerated: the country gentlemen on the Tory benches – of whom Lord Byron scoffed, 'For what were all the country patriots born? To hunt, and vote, and raise the price of corn' – were still all too apt to be there for the votes on corn but otherwise to give hunting a higher priority than politics.

Liverpool is no longer so easily dismissed as 'the Arch-mediocrity' that Disraeli thought him to be, and he has some claim to be the first in the line of sober, quiet team-players who would unexcitingly lead Conservative cabinets in the manner of Baldwin or John Major in the next century. Because he was surrounded by flashier and more brilliant men, his essential contribution in holding the team together was easy to underestimate, but the completeness of the disintegration that followed his death in 1827 was evidence enough of his importance. His first decade as Prime Minister was a period of continuous battle with outside forces – bringing the Napoleonic Wars to a triumphant conclusion in 1814–15 while coping with the severe industrial distress at home that produced Luddism, battling with parliament for sufficient resources to pay for the inflated National Debt and run other government services when peace came, moving into a second period of repression that culminated in 1819–20 with the 'Peterloo massacre' and the Cato Street conspiracy to assassinate the entire Cabinet, and finally battling with George IV over his unpopular wish to divorce Queen Caroline in 1820–21. Merely to hold the team together, to keep each problem at bay, and to play for time until the economy eventually restored prosperity, was a considerable achievement, and at times this seems to have been the limit of his policy. He was, though, quite conscious of his own position as the heir of the traditions described above, paying tribute to Burke as 'perhaps the greatest philosopher', and to Pitt in the Commons as 'certainly the greatest practical statesman, that ever existed'. For a party which would shortly be advised by Disraeli to 'read no history, only biography', an appeal to the legacy of Mr Pitt would long be a tactic used by leaders to secure approving nods from their followers.

It was when the government was at its most vulnerable in 1815 that it was in effect ambushed in the Commons (largely by its usual supporters) and forced to abolish the wartime income tax (which effectively ensured that more of the cost of government would have to be paid for through more regressive consumption taxes) and to pass the Corn Law, whose aim was to prevent the price of wheat from falling from its inflated wartime levels when normal trade resumed. Since income tax also fell most heavily on the landed property which was the interest still most substantially represented in both Houses of parliament (even though agriculture by now employed less than half the national workforce), both of these defeats for the government left it exposed to the charge that it had bowed to its own supporters' self-interest, and sacrificed the consumer's greater needs by doing so; later campaigns to cut government expenditure even further kept Liverpool and his ministers constantly under the threat of similar ambushes to come. The bitter politics of 1815–19, carrying over the heightened passions of the war through the transition to peace, owed much to that perception of governmental self-interest. In these circumstances the concept of 'Tory' as the defender of the constitutional and social status quo carried over into peacetime fairly naturally.

It was traditional to describe a change in the character of Liverpool's government, from a period of 'High Toryism', repression and confrontation, to a 'Liberal Tory' period of humanitarian reform, political flexibility and sensible economic management between 1822 and 1827. Such a stark comparison can now be seen to have been much exaggerated, for the chief difference between the two periods may have as much to do with the fact that returning prosperity improved the government's confidence and increased its room for manoeuvre as with any difference of actual approach. Nevertheless, the ministers who joined Liverpool (or in some cases rejoined after an interval) for his last five years – Peel at the Home Office, Canning at the Foreign Office, William Huskisson at the Board of Trade and F. J. Robinson at the Exchequer – were markedly different from predecessors like Lords Sidmouth and Castlereagh. A different impression also arose from the fact that these more articulate ministers were able to explain constructively the purpose of their policies, while Canning's 'liberal' foreign policy was pursued with enthusiasm where Castlereagh had proceeded along similar lines but with obvious reluctance. Some of those who served at the time were not at all happy with the inconsistency that all this seemed to denote, Wellington exploding in 1824 that 'Ld Liverpool had *changed his politics* . . . but it was not Lord Liverpool's line until he became the slave of Mr Canning, & it was at direct variance with the principles on which his Government was originally formed'.

There was, then, a change of mood as well as some change of policy. As Peel asked Croker, scenting the new wind even in 1820, 'do you think that the tone of England . . . is more liberal . . . than the policy of the Government? Do you not think that there is a feeling, becoming daily more general and more confirmed . . . in favour of some undefined change in the mode of governing the country?' Peel's own contribution was to set in motion a process of liberalizing penal reform of which many Tories were suspicious, but the area in which change was most contentious was in the move towards free trade orchestrated by Huskisson and Robinson, with the first real free trade budget coming in 1824 and with changes even to the operation of the Corn Law being introduced in 1826 (though passed only with the support of those who more often opposed the government than supported it).

With the return of prosperity in the 1820s it was increasingly difficult for ministers to ignore the growing needs of industry and of trade in industrial goods as the Industrial Revolution gathered pace, or to place those needs always as a lower priority to the agricultural interest that so many of their supporters held to be central to what Toryism was about. In 1820 Liverpool, a disciple of Adam Smith in political economy, had told the House of Lords that British prosperity had come in spite of rather than because of trade protection, and he went on to shock his party further by later telling the Lords that agriculture 'is not the only interest in Great Britain. It is not even the most numerous.' For his part, Robinson announced that Britain's protectionist trading policy was 'founded in error and calculated to defeat the object for which it was adopted'. Since the growth of industry had been largely unaccompanied by political reform, there were now significant social forces entirely outside the political (and especially the electoral) system, and although, as Canning put it in 1824, the battle against the revolutionaries 'is now fought. I think we have gained the victory', the mismatch between economic and political power was a growing source of instability, a divide in which some radical reformers were now to be found among the wealthy.

Though a colleague could assure Liverpool in 1825 that he was 'at the height of your power, at the head of the most popular administration which the country has for some time had', the internal divisions produced by the last five years of his premiership clearly prefigured the disintegration that was to follow. As more flexible policies were implemented by Liverpool's younger colleagues, and with his full support, it was more and more frequently said by his Tory critics that he had fallen unhealthily under the spell of Canning, a man they had long hated on personal grounds. The less flexible Tories in the government and in parliament began increasingly to regard themselves as the only reliable guardians of the true spirit of Toryism, which less-principled men were beginning to betray. For the time being, although the government's majority sometimes fell alarmingly on specific issues, it was generally over a hundred in the Commons on votes of confidence, but this depended on two things: the continuing vitality of Liverpool himself at the head of a team of increasingly discordant colleagues, and the postponement of the two great issues of the day – Catholic emancipation and electoral reform.

Ironically for a group that professed to venerate Pitt, both of these were issues on which most Tories now differed entirely from his views. Pitt had sought when first Prime Minister to modernize the electoral system with a moderate Reform Bill, but when it failed to pass the Commons he had remained in office in deference to the king's wishes and had not subsequently reopened the issue. As long as all reform was off the practicable political agenda in the 1790s as a result of war and the anti-radical hysteria that war unleashed, this caused no problem, but when the reasoned case for the abolition of 'Rotten Boroughs' and the reallocation of their MPs to new industrial towns resurfaced in the 1820s it was far more difficult to deal with. The Tory identity depended on veneration for the inherited constitution, and many Tories would never forgive a minister for destroying the unreformed electoral system whose beauties they regularly hymned, so although tiny changes were made from time to time through the disfranchisement of individual (mainly non-existent) boroughs, even that process had effectively ground to a halt by 1827–8.

The Catholic issue was if anything even more difficult. Pitt had negotiated the Act of Union with Ireland in 1801, to a large extent to offset the danger of French invasion through Ireland, and had promised that Catholics' civil disabilities would be ended in return for the Irish parliament also passing the Act. He had, though, been unable to persuade the king to back him, and had as a result left office. Pitt's legacy therefore pointed both ways on a crucial issue for 'Church and King' Tories, and it did so in terms of conservative ideology too; the Burkeian 'disposition to preserve' argued against reform, but the impossibility of governing Catholic Ireland for ever through a narrow, exclusively Protestant elite suggested that the best means of conserving the Union would be the acceptance of the equal civil rights of Catholics. For George IV, the Protestant supremacy was central to his coronation oath, while for the Church of England the privileged position of the Anglican Church of Ireland was seen as the first line of defence for its own established status in England and Wales. It was thus a question of increasing insistence – even the hawkish, Anglo-Irish Duke of Wellington, who detested the idea, could see by 1825 that Catholic emancipation must come soon – and at the same time an issue that no Tory government of the period could possibly tackle without falling apart very messily indeed. Liverpool's government was therefore explicitly formed and continued to exist throughout its life on the basis that Catholic rights would be an 'open question', on which individual ministers must make up their own minds and the government as such would have no policy. But since regular votes in both Houses obliged individual ministers to show their hands, each one was also well-known to be a 'Catholic' (in favour of emancipation) or a 'Protestant' (opposed to it). This was an explosion just waiting to be ignited when a stroke incapacitated Liverpool in February 1827.

In this sense, despite the polarization towards a party division of the political world that had taken place over the past decades, a trend that led many to view the mixed Tory–Whig ministry that succeeded Liverpool's as unnatural and even unconstitutional, the Tories were in fact deeply split among themselves. The king, after a period of paralysing indecision and consultation, made Canning his new Prime Minister, and this shattered Tory unity anyway, producing the resignations of Wellington, Peel, four other Cabinet ministers and forty junior members of the administration (which was in itself a sign of how far the Tories had by now diverged from the concept of backing the preferences of the monarch).

There seems little doubt that personal dislike and suspicion of Canning himself played a great part in this, for the more austere High Tories saw his regular bids for popularity outside Westminster as a low, dishonourable way for a minister to behave (Liverpool, by contrast, never made a public speech outside parliament at all), while his sheer enjoyment of the political game provoked others to declarations that they would never trust him as Prime Minister. Croker spoke for many Tories in saying that Canning could not even take a cup of tea without its being part of a stratagem, while Wellington amazedly asked the king himself how he could be surprised to learn that 'the Tory Party detest Mr. Canning'.

Personality thus counted greatly in the Tories' reaction to Canning succeeding Liverpool, but there were real policy issues at stake as well. The official reason given by Peel and Wellington for their resignations was that Catholic emancipation, which had already passed the Commons on more than one occasion but failed in the Lords, would be given a great boost by the appointment of a 'Catholic' Prime Minister, even though Canning was determined to keep it the open question that it had been for years past, and had no intention of making it a government measure. The fact was that High Tories – increasingly attracting the nickname 'Ultras' after the equivalent party of the extreme right in France – knew that concessions would soon have to be made on what Norman Gash has called 'the revolutionary trilogy of great constitutional reforms' (repeal of the Test Acts, Catholic emancipation and the reform of electoral system), suspected Canning of being too flexible to be an effective leader of resistance, and in any case would not taint their own consistency and honour by now carrying out policies they had rejected throughout their political lives. This promotion of honour and consistency into the ultimate political virtue is a good example of a principle largely derived by the Tories of the 1820s from their junction with the extremely conservative Rockingham Whigs in 1794. It was not a helpful inheritance in a rapidly changing world.

Such reasoning was self-fulfilling, for since Canning was unable to found his new government on Tory solidarity, he had little option but to form a coalition with some of the Whigs, a development which allowed the Ultras then to conclude that they had been right about his unsoundness all along. In principle this split both parties, since there were also orthodox Whigs of high principle who refused to back Canning, but in practice its main effect was to undermine Toryism at precisely the moment when the party desperately needed to act together to deal with the urgent issues of the day. In effect, by dividing the party of resistance, it brought reform (of the electoral system) closer and at the same time denied the Tories the chance to defuse the crisis by carrying reform on terms of their own. Canning insisted that since the Catholic issue was to remain an open one, then his Cabinet must be unitedly hostile to changes on the other major fronts, but this was more a case of protecting his flank than good strategy.

In any case, things rapidly became far worse as 1827 went on, for Canning's promotion had come too late to be of much use anyway. His death in the summer left his coalition broken, and the passing of the baton to the nerveless hands of Robinson (promoted to the Lords as Viscount Goderich) was a sign of the king's desperation; Goderich did not even remain in office long enough to meet parliament, resigning at the start of 1828. The thirty or so 'Canningites' were now entirely leaderless, but also bitter about the way in which their eponymous hero had been treated. Although Disraeli was to accuse Peel of killing Canning in 1827, it was rather the old Liverpool Tory Party that was assassinated by Peel and Wellington in 1827. Since George IV still had a deep loathing of the Whig Leader, Earl Grey, once he had tried and failed to run the government through moderate Tories, he now had no option but to return to the Ultras.

Wellington thus became Prime Minister, with Peel as Leader of the Commons, but hardly surprisingly it was now some of the Canningites (or Huskissonites, as they now had to be called – at least until 1830, when

Huskisson became the country's first distinguished casualty from a railway accident) who stayed ostentatiously in their tents. Wellington himself had a thoroughly idiosyncratic view of the life political, writing after his first Cabinet that it had been 'an extraordinary affair. I gave them their orders and they wanted to stay and discuss them.' He prided himself on his consistency and high principle, but also on his loyalty to king and country; in practice, therefore, his reiterated view that 'the King's Government must be carried on' made him something of a pragmatist in office – and a huge disappointment to his Ultra supporters. In 1846 he was to remark bluntly that 'good government is more important than Corn Laws', a pragmatic view which, though extremely unpopular at the time, he did much to transmit from Pitt into the later Conservative approach to politics.

Wellington's 1828 government had a substantial theoretical majority in the Commons, perhaps as much as 400 to 200 over the Whigs, but a narrow political base none the less. Within a few weeks, a misunderstanding led to Huskisson's departure, and in order to end in-fighting in his own administration Wellington seized on this as an excuse to get rid of the other surviving Canningites too. Peel asked how government could even be carried on 'by the mere Tory party', without the votes and more importantly the speaking powers of the departed Canningites. They would be 'supported by very warm friends, no doubt, but those warm friends being prosperous country gentlemen, foxhunters etc. etc., most excellent men, who will attend one night, but who will not leave their favourite pursuits to sit up till two or three o'clock fighting questions of detail ...' In these circumstances, with the government's patronage influence in the Commons now reduced to at most some fifty votes, they could not expect to survive long.

Almost as soon as he took office, and without having the usual time to prepare for the meeting of parliament, Wellington suffered the embarrassment of defeat on the repeal of the Test and Corporation Acts, which duly went through. This was the least contentious of the three major constitutional questions facing him, for even Ultras could see that the respectable nonconformists of 1828 were not much like those religious radicals at whom the original acts had been aimed in the reign of Charles II: the allowance of their civil rights would hardly be the start of a revolutionary terror. But as a signal to suspicious men on his own benches, it was for Wellington an inauspicious start.

Much worse, the arrival of Ultra government coincided fatally with events in Ireland that made it impossible to avoid Catholic emancipation either. The appointment of Vesey Fitzgerald as Wellington's President of the Board of Trade required him to seek re-election in his constituency, County Clare, and this gave the Catholic League in Ireland, and its fiery leader Daniel O'Connell, exactly the chance that they had been awaiting: Fitzgerald duly lost his seat to O'Connell when Catholic farmers would not vote for him. No government would ever again be able to appoint to office an MP for a Catholic Irish constituency without an immediate collision with the electors, but O'Connell was unable to become an MP either, because of the statutory ban on Catholics (who were now allowed to stand for parliament but not actually to take their seats). Feelings ran high on both sides of the Irish Sea but it was clear that, without a rapid concession to allow the voters' choice to enter the Commons, Ireland could soon become ungovernable. The Commons had already approved the principle of changing the law on a free vote in May 1829, and Wellington had told the Lords in June, even before County Clare voted, that he had decided that the issue was one of expediency rather than principle. Now pessimistically fearing (as he was wont to do) the entire breakdown of good government, Wellington sounded the retreat, and carried a bill to restore civil rights to Catholics, much as they had just been given to Protestant Nonconformists.

As might have been expected, the Ultras were apoplectic with rage, scarcely even acknowledging Peel's reasonable defence that repeal was in itself the conservative act best calculated to save the Irish Union: 'I yield therefore to a moral necessity which I cannot control, unwilling to push resistance to a point which might endanger the Establishments that I wish to defend.' The bill passed, even though half the government's Tory supporters in the Commons had voted with the noes. It seemed that the Canningites had been lost to the party for no good reason and that honour and consistency had been fatally undermined; a Whig insultingly told the Tories that this act of their own government 'explode[d] the real Tory doctrine that Church and State are indivisible'. Wellington had to fight a duel with an angry Ultra, and Peel was defeated in a by-election for the staunchly Anglican Oxford University constituency. About forty Ultra MPs formed a ginger group to oppose Wellington and, if possible, drive him from office, while Brunswick clubs and Orange lodges out in the country began to whip up local Protestant feeling too. For the rest of the session, it was from time to time necessary for Whig votes to keep Wellington in power. The Ultra Duke of Newcastle now thought Wellington to be 'the most unprincipled, most artful, most heartless, most ambitious and most dangerous man, not excepting Cromwell, that this country has seen for many a long year'. For a Tory, comparison with the regicide Oliver Cromwell was just about as low as you could go, but factional feelings were then raised even further by the prosecution of the Ultra *Morning Journal* for seditious libel of the government.

On the lesson that the crisis of 1829 offered for the future, however, the Ultra response was ambiguous. There were certainly some who decided that no electoral system could be worth defending if it allowed a government to knuckle under to Catholic pressure when the mass of British opinion opposed emancipation (as it almost certainly did); some Ultras thus became supporters of parliamentary reform, and the Ultra Duke of Richmond even went so far as to join the Whig government that was formed in 1830 with the specific intention of bringing it about. Others argued more mournfully that the Tories had simply given lessons to the Whigs in how to do it, by themselves removing obstacles to revolution; Lord Falmouth asked, 'Upon what principle will you talk of preserving the tree of the constitution, when you have laid your axe to the root?'

The Wellington government's final stroke of bad luck was the death of the king in June 1830, for although George IV had been a difficult and capricious man to deal with, he had refused ever since 1812 to have dealings with the Whig Leader Grey, and this had contributed significantly to the Tory monopoly of office. William IV was an unknown quantity who turned out to be more open-minded both on Whiggism and on reform than his brother had been. Most crucially, the death of the king involved the immediate dissolution of parliament and new elections (still then a legal requirement since parliament's authority flowed personally from the crown). These would take place before the government had had any chance to recover from the batterings of 1828–9 and during a period of deep economic distress; even agricultural depression was linked to the debate on reform, with reformers claiming that a system that produced such thoroughly bad results was in need of change, while defenders of the unreformed system were inhibited from their usual argument that if the system might not be theoretically perfect then it did at least produce good government.

No British government until the last third of the century was overthrown as the direct result of a general election, but it was usual for the results in the more 'open' constituencies (counties and larger towns with significant numbers of electors) to be scrutinized for evidence of the political nation's wishes, and for at least some of the MPs from narrower electorates then to realign themselves in the direction of any perceived change of public opinion. By that test, there was little doubt that Wellington 'lost' the 1830 general election, even though he retained a substantial nominal majority when it was over. The government continued to do well in Scotland, whose tiny electorate was managed as venally as ever, and held its ground in the restricted boroughs further south, but the *Annual Register* concluded that it had held only a third of the seats where there were 'open' contests, for 'no candidate found himself a gainer by announcing that he had been, or intended to be, an adherent of the existing government'. Indeed, even Tories who won in county contests often did so only by pledging themselves to vote for reform.

Wellington was now thoroughly rattled, noting the (apparent) similarities with recent events which had overthrown the Bourbon monarchy in France. He read Clarendon's *History of the Great Rebellion* and decided that Britain in the early 1830s was much as it had been in the 1640s – on the eve of civil war. He compounded the issue, perhaps in an effort to mend his fences with the Ultras and so consolidate the forces of resistance, by greeting the new parliament in November 1830 with the statement that he had no intention whatsoever of introducing a Reform Bill, since he believed that the existing electoral system had 'the full and entire confidence of the country'. This only ensured that the Whigs would now withdraw their tacit support before the Ultras had forgiven him for the betrayal of 1829. Two weeks later his government was duly beaten in the Commons on a procedural motion, with only nine of the sixty staunchest Ultras coming to his aid; only fifteen of the eighty-two English county MPs, the backbone of the Tories in the Commons then and later, supported Wellington, a direct consequence of the uncomfortable time they had recently endured at the hustings.

The king summoned Grey to office and a mainly Whig ministry was formed for the first time in decades, though in order to hold his own in parliament Grey too looked for support outside; in addition to the Ultra Richmond, his government included the Canningites Melbourne and Palmerston (neither of whom would ever be on the Tory side again) and others like Goderich and Lord Stanley, who would drift back to the right once the reform issue was settled. For since Wellington had really fallen because of his speech on reform, the principle on which Grey's government was formed was bound to be the promise of an immediate settlement of the issue; as Robert Stewart has argued, all the various differences between the parties became subsumed in that one great debate. This was in itself exceptionally bad news for the Tories, for they had a high degree of dependence on the unreformed electoral system, which had itself contributed quite a bit to their long tenure of power since the 1770s. Tory strength in Scotland depended entirely on manipulation of the old system, and after 1832 the party never again won even half the Scottish seats until 1900 – and usually had only a small minority. In 1827 Croker's calculation was that the Tory peers alone controlled between them 200 borough seats, and, although the 1832 Act did not completely terminate that system of influence-politics, it did severely curtail it. In the 1831 election – still under the old electoral rules – Tories won eighty-two of the 111 borough seats that the Whigs had by then determined to abolish. The Tory resistance to the Whigs in the reform crisis of 1830–32 was thus fatally weakened by their obvious self-interest in preserving the unreformed system, and when they eventually lost the battle they also lost much of their parliamentary strength.

Given their recent fissiparous performance in office, it is not surprising that the Tories did not do well in opposition to a Grey government that had the country behind it in carrying a policy the Tories hated. Wellington veered back and forth between a desire to be consistent in opposing reform and his core belief of service to the crown and state, though he thought despondently that 'when the crown joins the mob all balance is lost'. In 1832 he briefly tried to form a Cabinet to carry reform himself, only to face the 'May days' of mob violence, a run on the banks and massive Tory relief when he failed; after his experiences in 1829, even the idea of settling the issue on his own terms could not persuade Peel to accept office. In the end, Wellington organized the final retreat himself when he persuaded the Lords to pass reform without pushing the king into creating sufficient Whig peers to outvote the Tory majority, a tactic that preserved that Tory majority in the Upper House to fight another day, but earned him little respect from those who wanted to go down fighting for honour and principle. Strength in the Lords was to prove of great value, though, after 1832, for with the drift of the bench of bishops over to the Conservative side in response to what they saw as a threat to their Church from radicals and Liberals, and the final disappearance of the king's personal party in the Upper House, the Conservatives were able to consolidate a strong *party* majority. And since neither the Whigs nor their Liberal successors were actually the radical revolutionaries that Conservatives thought them to be, but rather had great respect for the

Lords as a bulwark against democracy, there would be no serious attempt to reduce the Upper House's powers until 1911. The Conservative peerage thus gave their party a good deal of leverage for the rest of the nineteenth century, even when the Conservatives were out of office and in a minority in the Commons.

Once the act was on the statute book, Wellington characteristically set out to make the best of it. Although he had himself once declared in the heat of battle that after reform he would never again set foot in the Lords, when Croker told him that he must give up his Commons seat because the post-1832 parliament would be a 'usurpation', a new Long Parliament aimed at wrecking 'the Church, the Peerage and the throne', the duke despairingly responded, 'I am very sorry that you do not intend to serve in Parlt. I cannot comprehend for what reason.' The duke's determination that the show must go on, however bad the barracking was getting, was in its way as important a contribution to Conservatism as any of Peel's activities in the age of reform. Almost a century later Balfour referred back to Wellington in defining his own ideas on 'representative government' and Britain's contribution to the world's stock of democratic ideas:

> I doubt if you would find it written in any book on the British Constitution that the whole essence of British Parliamentary government lies in the *intention to make the thing work*. We take that for granted . . . But it isn't so obvious to others. These peoples – Indians, Egyptians and so on . . . learn about our Parliamentary methods of obstruction, but nobody explains to them that when it comes to the point all our Parliamentary parties are determined that the machinery shan't stop. 'The King's government must go on', as the Duke of Wellington said. But their idea is that the function of opposition is to stop the machine. Nothing easier of course, but hopeless.

Even before Balfour's niece and biographer had put this private conversation into print in 1936, the concept was widely known: according to a routine Conservative research pamphlet three years earlier there had been an approving reference to the 'tradition that the King's Government must be carried on'.

The learning by the Conservatives of this hard lesson about what it meant to be a loyal opposition was a key factor in saving them from the reactionary path taken by most parties of the aristocratic, confessional right in other European countries in the 1830s, and from the oblivion to which it led. For British Conservatives, there would be instead a process of constant adaptation, making the best even of times when 'change and decay in all around I see', and therein lay one of the most basic causes of the party's subsequent longevity. Indeed, the party was frequently to prosper most in precisely those periods just after radical changes had been carried out against Tory wishes, but when the party had resisted the temptation to promise to reverse those changes when back in office.

Peel made the most effective speeches against reform in the Commons, but refused formally to take the lead there, mainly because he did not want to tie his future too closely to the Ultras, who necessarily made up most of the anti-reform vote; for his part the duke mused that 'I did pretty well with him [Peel] while we were in office, but I cannot manage him at all now.' Peel was saving himself for the next contest and determined that next time he would take the top job himself, while Wellington apparently had forgotten his own remark about Peel made in 1828, that 'whenever the R[oman] C[atholic] question is out of the way he will be most troublesome and out-libertize the most Liberal'.

The reform crisis marked the final separation of the Tories from residual loyalty to the king, in part simply because they were no longer actually the king's ministers, but also because they were desperately mobilizing to oppose polices that the king was actively supporting, and this freed them to take important steps both in accepting at last their identity as a 'party', and in creating a rudimentary organization with which to run one. In debate, the Tories generally made points that were validated by time, notably in their assertion that this first Reform Bill would not be the last (as 'Finality Jack', Lord John Russell, asserted for the Whigs), and they also predicted correctly some of the actual consequences of reform in terms of legislation that a reformed parliament would go on to pass – though this probably owed more to inborn pessimism than to foresight. They also managed to insert two significant amendments into the bill during debate: first General Gascoigne's proposal that the bill should not reduce the number of English MPs (vital for the long-term future of a party that would always do better in England than in any other part of the United Kingdom), and second the proposal of Viscount Chandos actually to enlarge further the new county electorate by adding to it the 'fifty pound tenants at will' – tenant farmers who occupied but did not own land to that rental value; since the words 'at will' accurately represented such farmers' dependence on their landlords, this 'Chandos clause' was a substantial reinforcement of the influence of landowners in county seats (the number of which would anyway be increased by the bill), and this could to some extent offset the loss of the nomination boroughs where the Conservative peers had previously selected MPs 'at will'.

The party could, though, do nothing effective to stop the headlong impetus of reform itself, nor prevent the damage to Tory interests caused by the Act when it was passed. When the Whigs went for another election in 1831 in order to seek the electorate's endorsement of their bill, the results were worse for Tories even than in 1830, with virtually no Tories at all returned in open contests; Croker reported Wellington saying that 'he looks upon the result of the general election as decisive in favour of the Ministers' Reform Bill, and in that Bill he sees . . . nothing but revolution'. And when in 1832 yet another election was held, this time under the new franchise and boundaries, the results were still worse, with a mere 179 Conservatives returned to face almost 500 on the government side. The only bright spot in this tally of disaster was the first signs of the party's recovery in the English counties, where the mere six seats held in 1831 rose to forty-three a year later (though the increased number of actual county members meant that these forty-three were still less than a third of the available seats). In the years ahead, the fact that English and Welsh counties were now a major component of the Commons would be a factor of great value in building Conservative majorities – or at least in ensuring that their minority remained a large one. In the towns the story was far more bleak, for though new borough constituencies returned sixty-four MPs in 1832, only two of them were Conservatives.

More generally, the representation of the great industrial towns proved to be a long-term factor of Conservative weakness, for over the entire period between the first and second stages of parliamentary reform, 1832–67, the Conservatives won less than a quarter of the seats in the most industrial towns, failing, for example, to elect a single MP in over thirty years in Manchester, Birmingham or Sheffield. Liverpool was the only major manufacturing town that remained a Tory stronghold over the next generation, but that owed more to its imperial trade (which also tilted Bristol to the right) and to its peculiar propensity for religious politics than to its manufacturing population. All too many Conservatives agreed with Wellington's conclusion in 1833 that 'the revolution is made, that is to say that power is transferred from one class of society, the gentlemen of England professing the faith of the Church of England, to another class of society, the shopkeepers, being dissenters from the Church, many of them being Socinians, others atheists'.

However, Toryism had emerged from the reform crisis with the first elements of an organization and with a new name. Although the party's recovery from its nadir is usually associated with Peel and his work from 1834 onwards, the first steps took place without any input from Peel and during the earlier crisis. In June 1831, still intent on fighting reform rather than recovering from it, a group of fifteen party men, including Wellington, met at the Charles Street house of Joseph Planta, already an active political organizer. Those present set up a party fund and agreed to subscribe to it (though initially only £5 each) and used the income generated to pay for an organizer's salary, the cost of premises, and to set up a fund for managing the press and fighting elections. The novelty of such an oppositional organization, for Tories more used to backing the king's ministers, led to its being dubbed the 'Charles Street gang', but it was nevertheless the tentative beginnings of an approach which would lead on to great things under Captain Middleton in the 1890s and Lord Woolton in the 1940s.

The actual work done from Charles Street was not very effective – in press management these infant organizers soon found themselves entirely out of their depth – and by 1832 they had little money left in any case to influence the elections of that year. Other initiatives were of more immediate importance. The Carlton Club, founded with Wellington's approval in March 1832 to mobilize the social forces that lay behind the party and counterbalance the Whigs' Reform Club, had by the end of the year about 200 MPs in membership and almost as many peers; in 1833 the membership reached 800. In 1835 the club moved from rented lodgings into purpose-built premises in Pall Mall, where it remained until bombed out in 1940, which prompted the post-war move to St James's Street. Membership of the Carlton became the public definition of association with the party, and when Disraeli became a Conservative in 1835, his first move up the greasy pole was getting himself elected to the Carlton.

But the Carlton was not only the social headquarters of the party; it was also, until Central Office opened in 1870, the nearest thing to a party office, replacing the more cramped and less convenient rooms in Charles Street. In the constituencies, too, the fact of constitutional crisis and three elections in three years had stimulated organization: in Gloucester there had been a Conservative Association as early as 1818, while Banbury acquired one in the early 1830s, and Nottingham turned its Constitutional

Club into a more partisan Conservative Club in 1832. Some of these local initiatives died soon after birth, but under the impetus of religious and protectionist activities during the later 1830s a network of such local *party* structures did gradually come into existence.

These new bodies were for the most part called 'Conservative', for in the course of the reform struggle a change of nomenclature had become fairly general. The first decisive entry of the concept into the national political debate came when in January 1830 the lawyer John Miller wrote in the *Quarterly Review* (in an article long misattributed to the better-known Croker) that 'we are now, as we have always been, decidedly and conscientiously attached to what is called the Tory, and might with more propriety be called the Conservative Party', a form of words which suggests continuity and change at the same time. The word Conservative had been on the edge of the national debate for some time; its association with the concept of 'conservation' by Burke has been quoted, and in 1819 a contributor to the *Anti-Jacobin Review* had argued, in that Burkeian sense, that the Pitt clubs embodied 'those conservative principles which all good men ought not passively to foster and cherish, but actually to promote, and sedulously, by combining, to perpetuate'. Such principles therefore enjoined collective action as well as ideological acceptance, and eight years later Wellington did indeed think of himself as being a leader of the *parti des conservateurs*; his use of the French term denoted its still relatively novel application in Britain, much as '*clôture*' was used in Commons procedure for some years before the more homely 'closure' was ever applied to the rules of debate.

Disraeli once remarked that 'in times of great political change and rapid political transition, it will generally be observed that political parties find it convenient to re-baptise themselves', and both New Liberalism in the 1900s and New Labour in the 1990s are good examples of that process. In the storm and stress of the reform crisis, the Burkeian concepts associated with 'conserving' came very much into their own, and it was hardly surprising that the party's leaders drew on such inherited language to signify their relative moderation when compared to the allegedly revolutionary Whigs. That Conservative identification of themselves owed something, then, to their appreciation of the renewed role of the Whigs as the reforming party in the state. For as Croker put it, 'two parties are now generated which will never die'.

The trend to the general adoption of 'Conservative' as a self-description denoted the end of the limited, 'mere Tory' (as Peel had put it) phase of party history, but it also represented the desire to stand for something wider than the Ultras, and for something less associated with the *ancien régime* just then passing away than 'Tory'. In November 1831 a party rally in Edinburgh produced several routine references to the party as 'Conservative' and one speaker there seems to have coined the phrase 'the great Conservative Party' when he dwelt on its patriotic inheritance from Pitt, a form that would be much used in the years to come. In April 1832 Croker routinely noted in his diary that he had dined 'with a large Conservative party', and by the end of 1831 the supportive *Evening Standard* was already referring to the party as 'Conservative' as a matter of course. The new label, and the less backward-looking approach that it suggested had to await *The Tamworth Manifesto* of 1835 for any effective presentation of its meaning, but it did nevertheless open up great strategic opportunities: for alliances with northern working-class radicals like Michael Sadler and Richard Oastler, and even with Chartists who were equally upset by Whiggism; for a later appeal to urban, middle-class voters who naturally associated 'Toryism' with a vanishing agrarian past; and for a modernization of policy of the sort that Liverpool's ministers had striven to initiate as 'Liberal Tories' in the 1820s. The great problem in all of this was that the Conservative Party, despite its new name and its widened identity, still contained nearly all the same old Tories who had just made life so difficult for Liverpool, Canning and Wellington.

3

Peel's Conservative Party, 1832–46

IN THE FLUX OF PARTIES and the constitutional revolution of 1827–32, the Tory grip on office had been relaxed and the policy that Tories most feared had been enacted. It seemed all too likely that in a reformed Commons the Whigs would sooner or later introduce other reforms which would help to push Tories further down into the abyss – for example, by crushing the political influence of the landed interest with an attack on the Corn Laws and on protectionism in general. It was entirely plausible that from this point Toryism might have dwindled to impotence and oblivion, as did many of the equivalent groupings representing land, aristocracy and established religion throughout Europe when confronted by the convulsive forces of Napoleonic nationalism, middle-class liberalism and industrial urbanization. That British – and especially English – Toryism did not enter on a period of further decline, but survived, and even governed again with the support of queen, Lords and Commons less than ten years after the Reform Act, says something about the underlying vitality of the tradition. It also demonstrates the importance of Sir Robert Peel, who was Party Leader from 1834 to 1847.

All the same, the disappointing end to Peel's government of 1841–6, prelude to twenty-seven years in which the party never again enjoyed a Commons majority, suggested that the difficulties of 1832 had not yet been properly surmounted, and ensured that despite Peel's enormous services to his party he would go down in Conservative Party history as the yardstick of how *not* to act as Leader. The Marquess of Salisbury thought in 1872 that to act like Peel was to inflict 'the heaviest disaster their party could undergo', while, confronted by a disintegrating party in 1903, Arthur Balfour was declaring, 'I will not be another Sir Robert Peel.'

Sixty years later Rab Butler thought that Peel's splitting of his party had been 'the supremely unforgettable lesson of history' for Conservatives and resolved not to do likewise when his leadership aspirations were thwarted by Harold Macmillan, and even in the 1990s John Major and Douglas Hurd were reminding Conservatives of the lesson of 1846 – though with no apparent effect. Since they so often followed Disraeli's flippant advice to read biography rather than history, and not least Monypenny and Buckle's standard life of the hero Disraeli himself, this moral echoed down the ages of Conservatism and goes far towards explaining what Lord Kilmuir was to call in the 1960s the party's 'secret weapon' of loyalty and discipline.

The Conservative party that emerged apparently wrecked by the reform crisis had retained considerable elements of strength on which a recovery could be based, so that things did not – at least at first – turn out as badly as they had feared: *Blackwood's* conceded in 1834 that 'the great process of dissolution has been much slower than was anticipated ... The great institutions of society, the church, the funds, the corn laws, primogeniture, the house of peers, though threatened, are not overthrown.' Wellington had saved the Tory majority in the Lords and kept within reasonable bounds the gulf between the party and the monarchy. The small print of the Reform Act, which created an additional sixty-five county seats (from which radical suburban voters had been excluded by widening borough boundaries), together with the Chandos clause, had provided the means by which the landed interest could actually increase its influence in parliamentary elections, so allowing Conservatives to win back in the 1830s and to hold almost invariably at subsequent elections the representation of the agricultural areas.

Other traditional economic interests were also suspicious of Whig reformers and their links with new industrial capital, as were, for example, the old colonial trades like sugar (which depended on the maintenance of protection just as much as did domestic agriculture), and these would provide the means by which Conservatives could maintain a strong position in commercial centres such as Bristol. The Church of England was beginning a period of revitalizing growth, and fears that it was in danger from both nonconformity and Rome would provide opportunities for Tories to exploit the country's Protestant tradition (so closely linked with the very idea of British nationality since the century and more of wars against France), especially in relation to Britain's Irish policy. And industrialization in the North of England had created a backwash of working-class resistance, some of which was distinctly subversive and opposed to everything which an aristocratic and gentry party could stand for, but a part of which looked to the traditions of Tory paternalism and humanitarianism. Yorkshire radicals led by Richard Oastler urged Conservatives to use the machinery of the state to regulate and order the economy for the public good, to protect industrial workers from the excesses of unbridled capitalism along the lines that Peel's own father had proposed in one of the first Factory Acts. With such men as the humanitarian reformer Lord Ashley (better known by his post-1851 title as the Earl of Shaftesbury) sitting in the Commons as a Conservative, the party could build on such links against a common enemy. These were all to be valuable assets in restoring the party, though it would take political skills of the highest order to maintain such a widely disparate bundle of interests in harmonious partnership. That task would eventually prove impossible in 1846, but the survival of the Conservatives as a serious force even in the wilderness years of 1846–65 would be further testament to the residual strength of these supportive interests.

Peel started as Party Leader with a mixed inheritance from his earlier career. On the positive side, he embodied as much as any man in his generation the idea of the scrupulous, assiduous 'man of government', deriving his claim on office as much from his reputation for administrative competence as from any particular policy that he might pursue. His pragmatic, reforming record at the Home Office (where he had, for example, created the Metropolitan Police) provided the best evidence of the governing tradition that he had inherited from Pitt via Liverpool and would pass on to the next generation, but especially to Gladstone and those who later called themselves not Conservatives but Peelites. Nevertheless, this was to be a continuing strain of Conservatism long after Peel and Gladstone had left the party: soon after the triumph of reform in 1832, Peel earnestly counselled the new MPs to think practically rather than wasting their energies in discussing abstract resolutions, using in the process arguments largely replicated later by Stafford Northcote, by Neville Chamberlain, by R. A. Butler and by John Major – none of them, incidentally, men who made many party friends by advocating the avoidance of theory.

Peel had been rising through the Tory ranks for years, and as the Leader in the Commons under Wellington had clearly become the party's second man and a potential prime minister. On the other hand, his apostasy over Catholic emancipation, when 'Orange' Peel (a soubriquet that referred both to his hair colour and to his religion) had reversed course so smartly, and his tactical ambivalence over reform in the years since, had made him a man whom some Tory MPs never quite trusted. The Whig statesman and poet Lord Macaulay wrote of Conservatives following 'reluctantly, and mutinously, a leader whose experience and eloquence are indispensable to them, but whose cautious and moderate opinions they abhor'. Whereas Wellington, whose military reputation left no room for charges of cowardice and who did not show many signs of personal ambition, had survived reversals of course with his reputation merely battle-scarred, the more obviously ambitious Peel was henceforth watched carefully for signs of another betrayal. This legacy from before 1834 was to make his position more vulnerable in the 1840s than it might otherwise have been, and could even be put in the form of Disraeli's outrageous allegation that it was Peel's desertion in 1827 that had caused the early death of the Tory romantics' lost leader, Canning.

The party needed Peel, however, as much as he aspired to lead it. When, in 1834, the Whig government was racked by an internal dispute which produced ministerial resignations and lost it the backing of the king, it was dismissed from office, and it was Peel who became Prime Minister on the duke's personal recommendation. Wellington even undertook to run the country on his behalf for three weeks until he could get back from Italy. The duke recognized that a leader in the Commons and one less directly associated with resistance to reform in 1832 was needed if a Conservative ministry was to have a chance, and Peel was so obviously the man that even reservations about his past did not prevent a reunion of almost all the Tory forces behind the new ministry. Some former Canningites like Palmerston did still remain aloof, but this was as much a matter of their calculating that the Whigs would be back in office fairly soon as of any disagreement with Peel on principles. The opportunity to show that Toryism could still govern in the post-reform parliamentary situation was too good to miss, but it would be a difficult one to bring off successfully: Peel would have the backing of the king and the Lords, but would have to face a hostile Commons with a continuing Whig majority, unless new elections could restore Tory fortunes there. It was in effect a caretaker government which would last for barely three months – 'Peel's Hundred Days' were compared with Napoleon's in 1815, Peel meeting his own Waterloo at the hands of the electorate. When the Tories failed to win a parliamentary majority at the 1835 election he recognized the inevitable and, when defeated in the Commons, resigned, thus obliging the king to take back the Whig ministers that he had just sacked.

Peel had, however, used his hundred days to show that his party really had accepted that the reform of 1832 was final, since Conservatives would make no attempt to turn the clock back. He could show in a limited way his willingness to engage in further reforms of a pragmatic type (as he did by setting up through an Ecclesiastical Causes Act a commission to transfer endowments from the wealthiest to the least wealthy Anglican dioceses); and by the nature of his appeal to the new electorate in 1835 he could extend this approach to other policy areas too. Since prime ministers did not campaign as such in elections for two more generations, it was the document that he issued in his own constituency of Tamworth which summed up this new approach, and his *Tamworth Manifesto* thus became a founding document of Conservatism. The *Manifesto* was discussed and approved by the Cabinet, and was widely used by candidates across the country in their own campaigns, so it may fairly be said to represent the face that the newly converging party collectively wished to show to the world.

First, after defending himself against charges of inconsistency in his earlier career, Peel reiterated the view that he had already offered in the Commons, that the Reform Bill 'constitute[d] a new era', as it had been 'a final and irrevocable settlement of a great Constitutional question – a settlement which no friend to the peace and welfare of this country would attempt to disturb'. That appeal to order – to the Tory Alexander Pope, order was 'heaven's first law' – was the first that many Conservative leaders would make in persuading their followers to swallow distasteful medicine from the other side rather than themselves initiating disorder by spitting it out. Peel then outlined two alternative ways of operating politically within 'the spirit of the Reform Bill', the first of which clearly represented his version of Whiggism:

> If ... it be meant that we are to live in a perpetual vortex of agitation; that public men can only support themselves in public estimation by adopting every popular impression of the day – by promising the instant redress of anything which anyone may call an abuse, by abandoning altogether that great aid of government – more powerful than either law or reason – the respect for ancient rights, and the defence to prescriptive authority; if this be the spirit of the Reform Bill, I will not undertake to adopt it.

In claiming to respect 'Victorian values', the Conservative Party of the 1980s (if indeed it ever deserved to be called conservative at all by Peel's standard) rather forgot this classic Victorian definition of what Conservatism was *not* about. On the other hand Peel would happily undertake, 'for myself and my colleagues', to carry out 'a careful review of institutions, civil and ecclesiastical, undertaken in a friendly temper, combining, with the firm maintenance of established rights the correction of proved abuses and the redress of real grievances.' There followed more detailed instances of how that 'necessarily vague' distinction would apply to specific cases of current political controversy, notably on reform of municipal corporations, of the Church and of the universities, and a conclusion which reiterated his party's commitment to maintaining peace, 'the support of public credit, the enforcement of strict economy, and the just and impartial consideration of what is due to all interests – agricultural, manufacturing and commercial . . .'

There was little here that conflicted with the approach to government that Liverpool had practised in the 1820s, or indeed Pitt in the 1780s; but in his refusal to commit himself always to support agriculture against other economic interests there lay the seeds of future problems. The repudiation of direct accountability to the reformed electorate (albeit dressed up in anti-Whig language as necessary for good government) would also be at the heart of Peel's battles in the 1840s. This was, then, a facing-both-ways document from a politician whose own learning of the trade had come entirely before the 1832 watershed, and who was unlikely now to change his approach. As the member for the quiet borough of Tamworth, Peel had only ever needed to fight one contest – and even that had been in 1829, before reform widened the electorate – and he did not therefore easily grasp the changes that a turbulent, post-reform electorate demanded of candidates fighting the larger constituencies. Even after the 1832 changes, Tamworth had only 586 electors (a number that anyway then fell when electors qualifying under old franchises gradually died off), while the North Lancashire county seat held by Lord Stanley had 6,593 electors in 1832, a figure that then rose to over 12,000 by the time he left the Commons in 1851 – thirty times the size of Peel's Tamworth electorate by that time.

Nevertheless, *The Tamworth Manifesto*, and the approach to political life that it represented in summing up Peel's 1834–5 government, was also a step forward, for it clearly articulated three possibilities, even if the pure High Tory/Ultra approach was dismissed right from the start. On Peel's view of things, his party now represented the moderate, middle way between a reactionary Toryism pledged actually to reverse changes already made, and a radicalism that would tear things up by the roots without concern for orderly progression or for the Burkeian inherited wisdom of earlier generations, for both of those extreme approaches would create a threat to the country's peace and welfare. The middle position which he claimed for his party would alone offer peaceful progress without the risk of either revolutionary or counter-revolutionary violence. This was the essence of what Peel's Conservatism meant to him, for his objective was, as he put it in 1833, 'to conciliate the goodwill of the sober-minded and well-disposed portion of the Community, and thus lay the foundation of our future strength'.

To 'conserve' would, on this reading of *The Tamworth Manifesto*, not imply any going back, but nor would it rule out the sensible reform of 'abuses', a strategy aimed at broadening support for the regime by reducing its top-hamper of unpopularity with those who felt themselves to be abused. Peel himself was happy to adopt the newly fashionable party label as an accurate description of his own strategy, though the word 'Conservative' did not appear in the *Manifesto* as such. There was thus more than a little justice in the claim of the *Quarterly Review*'s John Hookham Frere that 'a Conservative is only a Tory who is ashamed of himself'. From this time forth, while 'Tory' was to remain a shorthand title used both by friends and enemies alike, and be claimed by partisans to represent something purer and less sullied by compromise than 'Conservative', the new umbrella title generally took the place of 'Tory' as the party name. Disraeli would in 1844 denounce the very idea of a Conservative government as 'Tory men and Whig measures' and as 'an organized hypocrisy', but Conservatism was a label that he was happy enough to accept only a few years later when himself pursuing a Peelite, middle-of-the-road strategy.

In the short term, neither the *Manifesto* nor the official adoption of the new name seemed to have helped very much, for the 1835 election produced a Whig majority of around a hundred in the Commons, and Peel returned to opposition for a further six years. But there were ninety-four more Conservative MPs than in 1832, seventy-eight of these gains coming in England, and the party was once again a serious parliamentary force rather than a rump which might shortly disintegrate altogether. Some of that recovery was no doubt owed to a natural fall-back of the Whigs from the runaway victory they had won in the high days of reform in 1832, but even that fall-back would not have occurred unless the Conservatives had shown by 1835 that they remained relevant in post-reform

Britain. The first stage of the recovery was therefore quickly achieved, and at least the party's survival assured. It would take much more effort and patience to climb back into office as the majority party, and this second phase of recovery had to be conducted on three overlapping but distinct levels. First, there was the attraction to Conservatism of moderate Whigs who were worried about the pace of radical reform after 1832; second, the consolidation of the party into a more cohesive parliamentary force; and third, the development of organizational machinery in the country.

The capture of former Whigs (or more often the recapture of former Tories and Canningites who had allied with the Whigs only since 1827) was already under way in 1834-5, for it was Lord Stanley's resignation from the Whig government that prompted the crisis that brought Peel briefly into office. Stanley and his supporters, though refusing office under Peel, did support the Conservative government in debate. The Stanley group of four ex-Cabinet ministers and about forty MPs were dubbed the 'Derby Dilly' ('Dilly' being short for diligence, a type of coach which in this case conveyed Stanley and his followers from one political side to the other; Derby denoting Stanley's future title), and for a time he envisaged its becoming a new centre party, but in the election of 1835 and the return of a Whig ministry such hopes evaporated. From 1837, the Stanley group (now more like twenty MPs than forty) were treated as Conservatives, and when Peel returned to office in 1841 three of the four ex-Whig ministers joined his Cabinet: Stanley at the War Office, Sir James Graham at the Home Office, and Lord Ripon (formerly Prime Minister Goderich) at the Board of Trade. Graham and Stanley became Peel's closest confidants in the Commons and Stanley – Disraeli's [Prince] 'Rupert of discussion' – was a valued reinforcement to the firepower of the front bench too.

The Derby Dilly thus became the first of a number of bridges over which Whig and Liberal politicians passed in their journey to the right, an example followed by Liberal Unionists after 1886, Coalition Liberals from 1916 and National Liberals after 1931. Unfortunately for the Conservative Party, the 'Peelites' were to provide a much earlier example of the same journey in the opposite direction, as former Conservatives like Gladstone crossed to Liberalism between 1846 and 1859.

Something similar was also going on at a lower level and in less organized form, as individual Whigs became disenchanted by the legislation demanded in a reformed parliament; there were foreshadowings of this even in the disastrous 1832 election, when ten former Whigs (nine of whom had voted *for* the Reform Bill) were returned as Tories, though it was again notable that six of these had been considered to be Tories in the mid-1820s. Peel's task after 1835 was thus to a large extent to put back together the coalition of forces that Liverpool had operated before 1827. Apart from the Stanley group, forty more Whig MPs defected to the Conservatives between 1835 and 1841, a vital factor in constructing a parliamentary majority in an age in which elections were still remote from the practice of democracy. Edward Stanley's own case provides a good example of this process, for the family's regional influence was so strong that he could easily get himself elected for North Lancashire with any label that he chose to adopt, and the Stanleys also had the nomination of a number of other Lancashire representatives, so that the only way for Conservatives to 'gain' North Lancashire was to win over its sitting MP, who would then bring others with him. Not all MPs had such independence from the voters – Graham lost his Cumberland seat as a consequence of defecting to the Conservatives, and thereafter he carpet-bagged around four different constituencies across the length of England and Wales to keep his career going over the next quarter century, relying on the support of successive Conservative and Peelite patrons to gain election – but it was possible in enough places to make the conversion of a fifth of the Whigs in the Commons a highly significant advance for the Conservatives. Equally valuable, the more that moderate Whigs defected, the more the Whig government had to rely on radical and Irish MPs whose policy preferences would reinforce the reasons for the original defections, and probably stir up the hostility of moderate voters in the more open constituencies too.

The opposite was true on the other side, where the accession of former Whigs strengthened Peel's hand as a moderate Conservative leader in his own party; hence the value he placed on Stanley and Graham. Peel's reputation had risen enormously as a result of his 1834 ministry, and this in turn increased his own confidence. The diarist Charles Greville, clerk to the Privy Council, thought that Peel 'stands so proudly eminent, and there is such a general lack of talent, that he must be recalled by the voice of the nation and by the universal admission that he is indispensable to the country'. And the young William Gladstone, who held his first junior office under Peel in 1834, even though at that stage 'the rising hope of the stern, unbending Tories', paid the pragmatic Peel an even greater compliment at the end of his first premiership: 'The rare self-command, the quick and far-sighted tact, the delicacy and purity of principle and temper by which the speeches of this great man have been distinguished in a period of extraordinary stress and trial, bear the marks, it may fairly be said, of a Providential governance.'

Using this new authority, and with Wellington's reliable support in the Lords, Peel in opposition held his party in both Houses in check, mobilizing Conservative votes against the restored Whig government only when it pursued advanced radical measures, but offering constructive support at other times in order to avoid the charge of factiousness in an age in which Tory gentlemen still did not quite think it 'loyal' to oppose the king's government. In getting the Ultras firmly under control he was partly fortunate, for their most unmanageable figure, the (Royal) Duke of Cumberland, was exported from British politics to become King of Hanover when Victoria became Britain's queen in 1837. Others gradually came to the conclusion that Lord Londonderry voiced in 1837, that in the absence of unity on the Conservative side the radicals would carry a programme that Ultras loathed: 'there is but one man and one party for us now, and that is Peel; and bad as the Conservative chance may be, rely upon it that if that party is split into any section, the Whigs are in for ever.' The lessons of 1827–32 had been well-learned.

In the Commons Peel played the role of an active party manager as he had not done before (and would not do as Prime Minister after 1841, to his cost), with the innovative Sir Thomas Fremantle as his Chief Whip from 1837, and they achieved an unprecedented degree of cohesion. Party meetings with backbenchers were regularly held, so that Peel could personally explain his advice on voting and the reasoning behind it, while the introduction of a weekly whip's letter ensured that the advice would not be forgotten. The weekly whip was at first available only in return for a subscription (since the party had no permanent fund to pay for such continuous services), but by the 1838 session some ninety-four peers and 238 MPs were already paying for the service and increased cohesion in the lobbies demonstrated its effect, while the central organization of pairing by the whips (previously a matter of backbenchers' private whim) ensured that for the first time the Chief Whip knew just how many votes he could rely on each evening; as a country gentleman himself, Fremantle was effective in persuading his fellow-squires to remain in London until the end of the session. When he analysed fourteen key divisions between 1838 and 1840, he noted that in eleven cases his records showed no doubtfuls at all (since every MP was committed in advance of the debate), while the total number of Conservatives voting was never below 311 and never above 324, a quite remarkable (and again unprecedented) degree of continuity, and a landmark in the history of party in the voting lobbies.

Unity was placed at a premium: Graham wrote that 'the one thing on which the Salvation of the State depends [is] to keep *the Party together*', while Croker noticed from the outside that the 1837 parliament showed the polarization created by the 1832 Reform Act.

> The essential difference from the old Parliaments [is] that there were no neutral or individual men – no floating party to be swayed by future considerations ... We had all foreseen that the Reform Bill must tend to a system of delegation and dependence [on the electorate], but no one had ever expected to see it so soon, and so marked, and that there should not be one unpledged member in the new House.

The next quarter century would show just how premature this analysis was, for the fall of Peel in 1846 was followed by a long period of unstable parliamentary majorities sometimes known as 'the golden age of the independent Member', but that only underlines the achievement of Peel and Fremantle in the late-1830s. Cohesion was also helped by social forces, for almost every Tory MP and peer was now a member of the Carlton Club, and during sessions it was the daily battle-headquarters of the party, combining in one suite of rooms the functions of commissariat, general staff and officers' mess.

The Carlton was the place to which the whips and the party organizer F. R. Bonham repaired when they needed to raise funds for organization and campaigning, and it was also the party crossroads to which aspirant candidates would go in search of intelligence about vacancies in winnable constituencies. For this was also the period in which the first halting steps in recognizably modern party organization took place. In part this simply reflected the creation in 1832 of new, complex and fairly expensive methods of electoral registration, so that in many areas the local Tories set up standing organizations to ensure that the party's interests were protected in the annual process of revising the electoral registers; by 1837 there was some rudimentary form of party structure for this purpose in most constituencies. Peel, who had taken no part in the first phase of formal party organization in 1830–32, now espoused the process with a vengeance, as in an 1837 speech to his organizers:

> It may be disagreeable, and, indeed, inconvenient, to attend to the registration of voters which annually takes place throughout the country. All this may be revolting; but you may depend upon it that it is better that you should take the trouble than you should allow the Constitution to become the victim of false friends, or that you should be trampled under the hoofs of a ruthless democracy ... The advice that I give you is this – 'Register, register, register!'

Many of the new local organizations were extensions of local dining clubs, as at Banbury, or were so completely under the influence of a local patron as to be virtually private organizations, and there was no pretence whatsoever of either democracy or the representation of voter-supporters, but Bonham headed on Peel's behalf a confidential committee that sought to coordinate and encourage such activities, even if by later standards its work was primitive in the extreme.

Perhaps the most vital organizational process was the matching of candidates who could afford to stand with constituencies willing to have a contest, and it may well be that just contesting seats at all was the most important organizational achievement of the 1830s. There was, after all, a longstanding convention, in counties in particular, that contests should be avoided, for a fight was ruinously expensive and could anyway divide the gentry community for years. In 1830–32, with Toryism at a low ebb, many counties had elected two Whigs, and it was now up to Conservatives to make a challenge if they were to win seats back. So, for example, in the East Anglian counties, there were only sixteen Conservative candidates in 1835 (of whom fourteen were elected), but by 1841 there were twenty-five candidates and the party won twenty-four seats – ten of them in constituencies that it had previously surrendered without a fight. But organization should not be exaggerated as a factor in the advance, for even such gains in the counties owed as much to the growing local fervour of agricultural opinion in defence of protection as they did to organizational effort. By 1841 the farmers and the many county protection societies were positively demanding protectionist Conservatives as their MPs, and doing much of the necessary organization themselves. The party was largely reacting to this feeling as much as promoting it as a party cause.

The actual recovery was none the less steady and impressive. In 1835 the Conservatives again had a majority of English county members; in the 1837 election, caused by the death of William IV, the party gained thirty-four more seats and now had a majority in England as a whole; in 1841 a further fifty-nine gains produced an overall parliamentary majority of seventy-eight, and Peel again became Prime Minister. This was the first Conservative majority under the reformed franchise of 1832 – and, as it would turn out, also the last, for no Conservative majority would appear again until after the next franchise reform was carried by the Conservatives themselves in 1867.

In view of what followed, and the appeal back to 1841 as their justification by both sides in the party split of 1846, it is important to be aware of just what did happen in that 1841 election which returned Peel and his party to power. For those who became Peelites in 1846, the election had turned on Peel himself, and Conservative candidates had been proud to declare themselves his willing followers, so that he was personally chosen and with few policy commitments; for Peel's 1846 critics, candidates had given firm pledges to the electors, especially on protection and on Protestantism, and they could not later abandon those pledges without dishonour.

First, it can be established that although some part of the final Conservative advance was owed to the defections of landlords and borough patrons (who in effect brought parliamentary representation with them) there was also a distinct move of 'opinion' in the Conservative direction in the more open constituencies. So, for example, the poll books for Buckinghamshire show that a number of those who voted Whig in 1835 then switched to Conservative by 1837 and stayed with the party in 1841. The same pattern appears in the way in which electors disposed of their two votes in double-member boroughs: in 1835 about 18 per cent of these voters backed both a Whig and a Conservative candidate, but in 1837 polarization had reduced this to 15 per cent and in 1841 it fell to under 9 per cent, as more electors shifted their second vote as well as their first to the Conservatives; the end of that polarity, when the Corn Law crisis introduced a new period of political uncertainty, was reflected by the fact that in 1847 over a quarter of borough voters again split their ticket.

There is no doubt either that the growing Conservative support owed a good deal to Peel himself; Conservative candidates did indeed lose few opportunities at the hustings to declare their support for him, and Croker thought that in the first parliamentary session after the 1841 election 'all turns on the name of Sir Robert Peel', for almost every Conservative MP considered himself to be 'Peel's man'. What, though, did support for Peel entail in terms of policy? Peel himself explained that he now stood 'in the first place for strong executive government as the rock on which all else must stand', in other words for administration rather than legislation – and with no very definite policy pledges acknowledged in the process – for men rather than measures. Peel was claiming what would in 1931 be called 'a doctor's mandate' – to do whatever the nation as patient needed to return it to health.

On the other hand, the Conservatives as a whole were not in 1841 really the party of governing administrators that Peel proclaimed, and though his determination as Prime Minister to promote the country's commercial and industrial interests and to show that Conservatives could appreciate the value of these new factors was an important and positive move towards what has been called 'the great Victorian compromise' between capital and land, it was not what his party supporters believed that they stood for at the time, and nor did it follow logically from the way in which votes had recently been gained. The Conservatives had increased their support in the most urbanized constituencies, but in 1841 they still held only thirteen of those cities' forty-five seats (no larger a number in fact than they had already had in 1835, and the thirteen MPs they did have still mainly represented commercial rather than manufacturing constituencies).

The real bedrock of Conservatism in 1841 was still in the politics of the constitution, religion and land. The majority of Conservative candidates had made it clear that they would resist any diminution of the powers of the Church, whether to favour nonconformists or Catholics, and the cry of 'the Church in danger' had helped to pull in the vote; Lord Ashley, although himself a great humanitarian social reformer, argued that 'our great force has been Protestantism. We began the reaction [against the Whigs] with it; every step of our success has been founded upon it.' Politics in the 1830s was to a large extent determined by religious affiliation, and Conservatives were about twice as likely to win predominantly Anglican seats as those containing concentrations of Catholics and nonconformists (except only for the continuing tendency of Wesleyan Methodists to be Tory as their founder had been). In Christchurch in Hampshire in 1837, for example, the Conservative candidate had 108 Anglican votes, but only eight from nonconformists; while a broader analysis of the contemporary poll books published by John Vincent suggests that something like five out of every six Anglicans generally voted Conservative, while over 90 per cent of nonconformists voted Whig or radical, a degree of polarization sharper even than class-based Tory and Labour voting was to be in post-1945 Britain.

As a Dorset county member, Ashley would have known well that, alongside the Church militant, the party had also been solidly backed by farmers and by others whose economic dependence was on agriculture. Such people had become increasingly concerned by the propaganda waged since 1838 by Richard Cobden's Manchester-based Anti-Corn Law League. The *Buckinghamshire Herald* foresaw that 'the great struggle of the general election will arise from the question of whether the Agriculturalists of the Empire shall or shall not retain that protection which is virtually necessary to their existence as landowners, farmers and labourers.' With such an issue at their command, it was the 156 English, Welsh and Scottish county seats (the Whigs now had a mere thirty-three of the 137 they had held in 1832) that represented the Conservatives' heartland support, and even this understated the case, for there were also many Conservative MPs sitting for small market towns entirely dependent on farming too – as, for example, in Horsham and Aylesbury, where free trade Whigs did not even dare to stand for re-election in 1841, so strong was the demand for protection. In so far as 1841 was about issues in the seats that the Conservatives won, then the key issue was protection, and in order to win many of their candidates had to give to their local county protection societies binding pledges which would deeply embarrass them if the party's policy were to change.

Peel, therefore, had come to believe that he had been returned to power without binding pledges, while most Conservative MPs on whom his ministry would depend took a very different view. This was a recipe for disaster, though the fine start that Peel had in office masked the problem. His ministry was widely praised as an assemblage of talent: it contained five past and future prime ministers in addition to himself (Ripon, Wellington, Stanley, Aberdeen and Gladstone), and he saw no need to utilize the available talents of the young Disraeli, for which he paid a terrible price later on. The Peel government has generally been seen by historians as a key period in the process by which the country's commercial and legal institutions adapted themselves to the fact that Britain now had an industrial economy, and such reforms as the Bank Charter Act of 1844 stand as lasting memorials to Peel's formidable capacity for work and to his grasp of current political economy. Many such reforms received the full backing of his party, though they were scarcely opposed by the Whigs in any case, and fell mainly outside the party debate.

Far more seriously, Peel's economic policy had to respond to the fact that he entered office during a deep recession, which was also generating the major outburst of social and political disorder in the working class known as Chartism. He understood well enough that an industrial economy was less able than traditional society to ride out the alternation of boom and slump, for most industrial workers had no smallholdings to which they could turn to avoid starvation, while the cash economies which developed in industrialized areas had been slow to generate enough charitable provision for their huge concentrations of the poor and starving.

From his own side of the House, the 'Young England' group within which Disraeli cut his political teeth, but which mainly consisted of aristocratic sprigs like Lord John Manners, proclaimed the need to restore the social interdependence of the feudal, hierarchical past, when

> The Greatest owed connection with the least,
> From rank to rank the generous feeling ran
> And linked society as man to man...
> Oh would some noble choose again to raise
> The feudal banner of forgotten days
> And live, despising slander's harmless hate,
> The potent ruler of his petty state.
> Then would the different classes once again
> Feel the kind pressure of the social chain.

This policy was not easy to implement in practice during a trade depression – one of the characters in Disraeli's own novel *Coningsby* remarks of another that 'Henry thinks ... that the people are to be fed by dancing round a Maypole'. It was none the less a prescription that had a strong romantic appeal to the conservative mind, which still deplored such monstrosities as industrial Manchester in the first place, a phenomenon memorably described with a mixture of fascination and repulsion in Disraeli's novel *Sybil* (a book significantly subtitled *The Two Nations*). It was a similar mentality that produced the sham medievalism which made Sir Walter Scott's novels so popular, which generated the Victorian age's rediscovery of Arthurian (or at least Tennysonian) concepts of chivalry, and which left thousands of ladies and gentlemen standing in a downpour to watch the jousting of aristocratic knights in armour at 'the Eglinton tournament'. For a conservative party, these were dangerously backward-looking responses to the rise of an industrial society.

To the more prosaic Peel, industrial recession foreshadowed social revolution if it were not ameliorated by practical action from the government, though for a laisser-faire economist like Peel action would have to be at best indirect. He told Croker that: 'Something effectual must be done to revive the languishing commerce and manufacturing industry of this country. Look at the congregations of manufacturing masses, the amount of our debt, the rapid increase of poor rates ... and then judge whether we can with safety retrograde our manufactures.' Humanitarian reformers like Ashley were equally concerned about industrial problems, but their preferred solutions (such as tighter factory inspection, shorter hours, fewer children in employment and so on) were unwelcome to Peel as both likely to increase industrial costs (and so actually reduce output and employment) and involving an inappropriate role for government in any case.

His own response came with the budget of 1842, for Peel had become Chancellor of the Exchequer as well as Prime Minister. Income tax was reintroduced as a temporary measure to cut the rising public deficit (though for a temporary measure it was to prove remarkably permanent), the actual working of the Corn Laws was rationalized, and a mass of small tariffs were abolished in order to encourage trade – very much along the lines of policies begun in the Liberal Tory era before 1827. The budget of 1842 laid the foundations for much of Victorian public finance, and would be harked back to by Gladstone in particular as the basis of his own later work at the Exchequer, but it was also effective in the short term; by 1844 the public deficit was at an end and the economy had moved out of recession.

Conservatives in parliament were, however, mainly either indifferent to all of this or openly hostile. Income tax would be paid only by those with incomes over £150, and would be used in part to finance the abolition of tariffs, so that those who most wanted protection were in effect mainly the ones paying for its abolition, and in the process of removing these outworks their citadel of the Corn Laws was being made less defensible. It was only the low state of the economy and the real fear of social disorder – and, we might add, in modern parlance, the honeymoon effect of Peel's 1841 victory – that enabled him to carry his early economic reforms without any substantial opposition from his party. As the *Maidstone Advertiser* put the case of the new corn duty, 'injurious as we fear it is likely to prove ... it is far better for the agriculturalists to accept, with the best grace they can, a measure prepared by a friendly government ... rather than to trust to the tender mercies of those who repudiate the very principle of protection'. On this argument, much would depend on how long Conservatives continued to see Peel's as a 'friendly government', though over the next few years the general recovery of trade and the rise in prices took the heat out of most economic issues anyway. When they reappeared at the top of the agenda in 1845 the idea of Peel's being a 'friendly government' would already have been repudiated by many Conservative MPs for non-economic reasons.

This stemmed in part from the simple fact that, as Prime Minister, Peel did not make time for party business as he had done in opposition. An Ultra MP now thought him 'cold and uncourteous ... at times in manner almost insolent', and considered that 'no Minister ever possessed fewer friends, or would be personally less lamented' if he were to die. The more friendly Lord Ashley, offended by Peel's opposition to factory reform, noted that he had 'committed great and grievous mistakes' by not continuing with the practice of party meetings: 'a few minutes and a few words would have sufficed ... Men would have felt they were companions in arms; they now have the sentiment of being followers in a drill.' In personal opposition to Peel, Disraeli would take this lesson to heart and would not generally make the same mistakes when he became Leader, but in later generations the transition from opposition to power would all too often produce the same distancing between the grandees and the parliamentary lobby fodder, Arthur Balfour and Edward Heath being two good examples of this.

Unfortunately Peel's errors were not solely sins of omission, for in 1843, both over Canadian cattle and over Ireland, he was doing things that his supporters positively disliked (and which in the Canadian case provoked a revolt, albeit temporary, by seventy backbenchers). This alone explains the impact made by the four assorted eccentrics who made up the backbench ginger group 'Young England' – men whose collective grasp of political reality was practically non-existent and whose political importance was minimal, but whose witty attacks on Peel were vastly cheered by MPs on the Conservative side none the less.

In 1844–5 the earlier malaise moved on to sustained revolt, over sugar and then factory reform in 1844, and over Ireland again in 1845. In each of the 1844 disputes a Conservative revolt (by ninety-five and sixty-two MPs respectively) ensured that the House of Commons defeated the government, and in each case a stern threat to resign by the Prime Minister secured a reversal of the earlier vote. The unifying core of all these rebellions was a growing suspicion that their government was covertly moving the country towards a liberal economic policy, preparing the way for a great betrayal over the Corn Laws. In each case the government won the day and implemented its policy – mainly by calling up absentees and persuading abstainers, for in neither case did many rebels actually reverse their votes – but at the cost of using up reserves of party loyalty that could not be replenished. Peel's angry speech on factory reform, in which he described his determination to avoid 'the temptation of obtaining party support' by sacrificing his own view of what should be done, was hardly conciliatory. When party meetings were held in 1844, it was not for two-way exchanges of opinions but simply so that Peel could give his supporters their marching orders.

It is hardly surprising, then, that the even more emotive issue of Irish Catholicism really set the party alight in 1845. When in opposition, Conservatives had constantly sniped at the Whigs for their supposed dependence on Irish MPs' votes, but, once faced with the responsibility of governing Ireland, Peel strove to find a moderate policy that would strengthen Irish support for the Union and for the Irish administration, a path that led him into serious and continuous conflict with such supporters as the rabidly Protestant William Beresford (one of those who had still not forgiven Peel for 1829). The attempt to show that his Irish administration was sensitive to the genuine wishes of the Irish people led to the admission of Catholics to a new board to oversee charities, and to Peel's refusal to provide state funding for the building of Anglican churches which the majority of Irishmen would never enter. It was, however, difficult to influence Irish Catholic opinion in a positive direction when it was (as Peel thought) so much under the guidance of an ignorant, under-educated and superstitious Catholic priesthood, so in 1845 he proposed a building grant and a tripling of the annual budget of the seminary at Maynooth in which many priests were trained. Many Conservative MPs reacted in outrage to this plan, which they saw as promoting Catholicism with their taxes (when Peel had just refused to promote Anglicanism in the same way) and as weakening the beleaguered Irish Church, which was in their view the first line of defence for the Union. Peel grimly told Gladstone, himself so staunch a supporter of established Anglicanism that he felt obliged to resign office over Maynooth, that he would press on even though his plans would 'very probably be fatal to the Government'. Peel was already fatalistically expecting, and doing nothing much to prevent, 'a great smash'.

One hundred and forty-seven Conservatives, almost half of all the party's backbenchers, voted against the Second Reading of the Maynooth Bill, and on the Third Reading more Conservatives voted against than in favour. Whig support ensured a comfortable government majority each time, but Conservative rebels were still not willing to accept defeat. An Anti-Maynooth Committee was formed, with eighteen MPs among its organizers, funds were raised for a campaign in the country, and anti-government literature was sent to every Anglican clergyman. By-elections in 1845 had already shown an electorate demanding a strong line on Protestantism from their candidates, and there was now every sign that there would be at the next general election a full-scale Protestant appeal to the British electorate to throw Peel out of office.

Criticism now therefore exceeded the boundaries of the politically containable, even before the Corn Laws came back onto the agenda, and much of the attack on Peel was the result of the disillusion of former supporters. The Tory radical Richard Oastler, a ruined man after imprisonment for debt, produced a ceaseless flow of pamphlets, broadsheets and lampoons directed at Peel's betrayal of the Tory humanitarians, as evidenced by his resisting factory legislation; Disraeli, now emerging from the salons of Young England as a formidable politician in his own right, and one who had not forgiven Peel for not offering him a job, used his brilliance as a writer to make *Coningsby* both a polemic against Peel (who was portrayed as a hypocrite who would do anything to stay in power) and the hit novel among reading Conservatives in 1844–5; and Beresford lost no chance to denounce Peel as the appeaser of Catholics and Irish radicals. If for such people a Peel government really was no more than 'Tory men and Whig measures', then many of them would soon come to prefer the Whigs themselves – against whom they could at least mount an uninhibited Conservative opposition, while the effect of constant attacks was to undermine Peel's support among the more inarticulate country squires who made up the bulk of the party in the Commons.

For a long time after C. R. Fay published *The Corn Laws and Social England* in 1932, it was believed that the Corn Laws had been ineffective in giving real help to British agriculture, and that repeal in 1846 actually helped the farmers by forcing them to modernize their methods and so enter into the mechanized and prosperous era of 'high farming' that came in the middle years of the century. This followed substantially the argument of the Anti-Corn Law League at the time, and the effect was to make Peel's opponents seem ignorant even of their own best interests, and to make the battle of 1846 seem more politically symbolic than economically significant. More recent investigations have, however, shown that the Corn Laws did sustain rural prosperity in bad years and that their repeal caused real distress in the later 1840s; the 'high farming' boom of the 1850s owed as much to the building of railways as to the policy of free trade, and when world food prices then dropped in the 1870s the non-availability of tariff protection proved to be an unmitigated disaster for British agriculture in the twenty-year rural misery of the 'Great Depression'. In the debates of the 1840s the protectionists had therefore a better case than has often been acknowledged.

They also had a better case than they knew at the time when they claimed that Peel had been planning a final betrayal for years, and that his ostensible reason for repealing the Corn Laws – a famine in Ireland following the failure of 1845's potato harvest – was no more than an excuse. Peel and Graham certainly came into office to carry out a general policy of liberalizing the economy, reducing tariff restrictions, and raising government income from direct taxes rather than from duties, but it is equally clear that they did not at first envisage actually abolishing the Corn Laws. Once in office, though, their opinions began to drift more in the direction of Cobden's free trading views, and this was at least in part due to the winning of the argument (in their view) by his Anti-Corn Law League after 1841. They came to share Cobden's opinion that the feeding of Britain's rocketing population, at prices which did not themselves require wages which would price British manufactured goods out of export markets, could only be done with the free importation of food; any recessionary effect on British agriculture (which they did not concede anyway) would be offset by the positive value of growth in industrial trade (which would in turn more than pay for the necessary food imports). They were therefore placing industry and commerce ahead of agriculture in their assessment of the overall needs of the British economy and workforce, or at least refusing to give automatic pre-eminence to agriculture in that calculation. Farmers and the Conservative MPs who represented them were unlikely to take so balanced a view. As early as 1842 Peel had privately agreed with Graham that 'we must advance our present policy of relaxation' of tariffs, while Graham had stated even in the Commons in 1843 that 'free trade principles . . . are the principles of common sense'.

By 1845, then, Peel, Graham, Stanley and Gladstone (who at the Board of Trade was directly responsible for the policy) had all reached the conclusion that the repeal of the Corn Laws would have to be tackled if their overall policy was to be carried forward. Peel had no illusions about the difficulty of the task, and he seems to have planned to allow the passions of Maynooth to calm down over the rest of the 1845 session before announcing his new policy the following winter, prior to a general election in which this most unmandated Prime Minister would seek the electorate's leave to end the Corn Laws (a tactic which would also allow his backbench supporters to review any pledges they had themselves given in 1841).

It was only in that sense that the Irish potato blight of August 1845

THE KNAVE OF SPADES.

Peel as depicted in *Punch*, 29 November 1845.

determined events, for it altered the timing and removed the opportunity for Peel to prepare the ground for his public conversion, and this was why later Conservatives like Balfour could convict Peel of 'the unforgivable sin. He gave away a principle on which he had come into power – and, mind you, neither . . . had an unforeseen factor come into the case.' Faced with the threat of mass starvation in Ireland, Peel abandoned at once his careful strategy and seized instead the chance to make a bold move in his chosen direction. The level of import duties would be reduced at once by Orders in Council (the best emergency powers available) and a bill would be offered in the next session to suspend the Corn Laws altogether. But since it was agreed by all participants in the subsequent debate that, once suspended, the Corn Laws could never be reintroduced on anything like the old basis, the real argument at once turned on repeal rather than suspension or amendment. In November four Cabinet meetings and a week of debate demonstrated the depth of the division even within the ministry, for only three of the Cabinet fully backed Peel, while the majority gathered around Stanley in opposition to the Prime Minister.

Stanley's decision to oppose Peel was one of the key decisions in the Conservative Party's history, for it gave the critics an available, moderate leader if Peel were to fall, it guaranteed an effective and respected debater on the side of protection, and it represented a different view of the place of party in the post-1832 world from that articulated by the Leader. For although Stanley was quite capable of refuting in detail the economic case for repeal, in particular by exposing the fallacy that Irish peasants would ever be able to afford imported grain anyway, the crux of the case in his Cabinet paper was political, and deserves to be quoted at length:

> I fling aside at once in such a case all mere party considerations; I endeavour to put by all considerations of our character for capacity, foresight, and public consistency; but I must bear in mind that our support of the Corn Laws has been our main inducement to others to give us the support which placed us, and has kept us, in office; and it must not be forgotten that, come what may, if general distress prevails, we shall have to depend in great measure on the cooperation of the Landed proprietors in England and Ireland. Will not the abolition of the Corn Laws, at our suggestion, deprive (not *us*, but) the Government of that cooperation? . . . The effect of the abandonment of the Corn Laws at this time will not be that of deliberate conviction, but of hasty

flight from our position, in consequence of clamour, aided by most unfortunate, but temporary, circumstances.

This was masterly as a political statement, disclaiming party motivations but reeking of party, holding up the spectre of a withdrawal of labour by the magistracy on whom all local government in rural areas depended, accusing Peel (in effect) of both lack of foresight and inconsistency, and finally suggesting that repeal was just what *The Tamworth Manifesto* had said that Whiggism (but not Conservatism) was about – responding without due consideration to 'clamour'.

In all of this it was easy to miss the point that the grandee Stanley was also articulating a quasi-democratic attitude to electoral mandates which the manufacturer's son Peel found repugnant, or at least that he had a conception of the duties as well as the rights of party leadership which was far more forward-looking than Peel's own. For even the great landowners of England like the Stanleys owed their continuing influence not just to ownership as such, but also to their role as the articulators of their region's prevailing attitudes, and Stanley, as a keen huntsman and sportsman in his own locality as well as the member for a populous rural constituency, could have been in no doubt at all what Lancashire opinion wanted him to say on its behalf. And Lancashire's agriculturalists no doubt also thoroughly endorsed Stanley's stark claim that what was at stake was 'whether the legislative power is to rest with the land and those connected with it, or with the manufacturing interests of the country'. That conviction that the Corn Laws symbolized a once-for-all struggle for supremacy also turned the formidable pen of Peel's former friend and ally Croker against his chief, for Croker could never forgive a man who had betrayed the landed interest, a force which he thought to be to politics what gravity was to the physical world, the essential contribution towards balance, order and keeping things (and people) in their proper place.

Faced with a Cabinet which would not follow him, Peel tried to resign office in December 1845, but the Whigs were not about to take up the baton in the midst of an economic crisis and with a House of Commons still packed with Conservatives. By the end of the year Peel was back in office. All his late colleagues except Stanley now agreed to serve again – somewhat surprisingly in view of the fact that most of them had disagreed with the policy that Peel now had to pursue; for them it came down to the fact that (in Wellington's phrase) 'the Queen's Government must be carried on', but to backbenchers it constituted the final betrayal; the fact that Stanley now explicitly put party and consistency before country and 'necessity' by refusing to rejoin the Cabinet highlighted the compromise that his colleagues had had to make. Though even Stanley intended actually to vote for repeal, he just would not accept the need for Conservatives who were pledged not to do it at all to become the ones who proposed its adoption.

Rudimentary organizations already existed for the defence of the Corn Laws, created when the Cobdenites carried their own campaigning into the farming areas in 1843–4, and the Central Agricultural Protection Society also existed (with eighteen Conservative MPs on its committee) to coordinate the work of these county societies. In December 1845 the CAPS rescinded the rule that had previously debarred any intervention in party politics, and shortly afterwards it set up an election committee to ensure that only suitable candidates were supported when the time came. It was extremely successful in the winter of 1845–6 in extracting from Conservative MPs pledges that they would not vote for repeal, and publishing lists of those who had become so pledged. Where free trade candidates came forward at by-elections in county constituencies they found their position very uncomfortable indeed; Lord Lincoln, forced to seek re-election on his reappointment to office, lost his seat in Nottinghamshire (where his family influence had prevailed for generations) to an almost unknown protectionist, and when the two sitting MPs for Dorsetshire resigned their seats to fight for re-election as repealers (so conscientiously facing up to the pledges they had given in 1841), they found so little support in the county that they did not in the end dare to contest the by-election that they had deliberately created. The understandable refusal of other repealers to go through the fire of re-election only increased the protectionists' sense of betrayal.

The parliamentary contest against Peel could not, however, have been effective without the surprising emergence of a new leader from the backbenches. Stanley would not actually lead the fight against his old colleagues, men like Beresford were too extreme to be effective, and, though Disraeli certainly entertained Peel's enemies with his ever more polemical speeches, he could hardly – as an urban, literary Jew who never in his life learned to ride a horse – be the spokesman for rural England in its hour of need. Lord George Bentinck, on the other hand, fitted the situation perfectly: as a younger son of the Duke of Portland he had status; as a prominent racehorse-owner he had the perfect lifestyle; as a lifelong backbencher he had no previous record to live down; and as a declared man of principle who refused to be 'sold' by Peel he had the perfect stance with which to rally the squirearchy against their Leader. He was never much of a speaker, but then amateurism was of the essence among those that he came to lead, and the passion that he put into his denunciations of Peel made up for their lack of finesse. To Bentinck, ministers were 'no better than common cheats' and their actions were 'wholesale examples of political lying and pledge-breaking'. He would take up the cudgels from a sense of duty, because, 'for the sake of Political Morals and the character of public men ... a salutary lesson should in all cases be taught to delinquent politicians'. Such rudeness was just what protectionists wanted to hear, and if the political world was astounded by the effort that Bentinck put into the learning up of his case from parliamentary papers and the statistics of trade returns, this was after all perfect proof of the righteous indignation of a man previously more at home at Newmarket than in Whitehall.

Within a fortnight of Bentinck's sounding the trumpet he had enlisted 180 Conservative MPs behind him, and by the time parliamentary debates on repeal began in February 1846 the government whips were astonished to find an organized, well-prepared contingent of 220 MPs utterly opposed to their own Leader. Since the Whigs would vote for repeal (and were delighted to see Conservatives propose it and so wreck their party), there was never a doubt that Peel's bill would pass, but the delays that the protectionists created nevertheless deepened the Conservative split and eventually persuaded Stanley that he must accept their insistent demands that he take over the party, though because he had since 1844 been in the Lords he could still not head the campaign where it mattered.

The temperature of the debates now reached boiling point: on 15 May, for example, a speech by Disraeli which the parliamentary reports described as being punctuated by 'shouts of laughter and cheers' referred to Peel as a man who 'for between thirty and forty years ... has traded on the intelligence of others ... He is a burglar of others' intellect ...' Not since 1066 had there been any 'statesman who has committed political petty larceny on so great a scale'. But if Disraeli and Bentinck won the Tories' cheers, Peelites and Whigs had the votes, and in June repeal eventually passed, though with few Conservatives other than ministers voting for it. Peel now retained the support of only a third of Conservative MPs. There was some tendency for his supporters to be concentrated among the commercial and industrial representatives of the party (and thus to be pursuing the logic of Peel's own strategy), while almost every agricultural member was now ranged against him: repeal was opposed by 86 per cent of county members, and by 63 per cent of those from small towns, but by only half of the MPs from larger urban areas. The party, like the country, was split on broad lines of social and economic interest.

It was hardly to be expected that Peel's opponents would be content to see him remain Prime Minister after this self-inflicted party disaster, or indeed that he would want to, when the 'smash' towards which he had steered blindly over the past year finally came about. There was, however, some real vindictiveness in the fact that the issue chosen for his overthrow was one on which most Conservatives actually agreed with his policy – a Bill to authorize coercion in Ireland – but on which the rebels voted with the Whigs to force him out of office. Peel announced that he would never again be 'the leader of a party' or head a party government – not that he was ever likely to be offered the chance. Graham contemptuously resigned from the Carlton Club and Gladstone was made to feel most unwelcome there too. The party had been riven in the 1840s as it had been in 1827–32 – and partly at least by the same man – so that the painful work of recovery after 1832 had come to nothing, and it all had to be done again. The second time round, partly because there was no Peel to take the helm, the climb-back from oblivion would be a longer, trickier and much more effortful business. It would not have cheered Peel, as he nursed the bruised feelings with which he escaped from office, to know that Disraeli and Stanley would be the chief architects of Conservatism's eventual recovery and would therefore enjoy the fruits of Peel's work for the party in the 1830s. But then, if such a thing *had* been prophesied in 1846, neither Peel nor anyone else would have believed it anyway.

4

Wilderness Years, 1846–68

THE COLLAPSE OF the Peel government in June 1846 did not mark the nadir of Conservative fortunes, since it was only rather later, when the protectionists belatedly came to recognize that their split from the Peelites would be permanent, that they could begin to rebuild their party from its foundations, but it did begin two decades of Conservative impotence. Not until the death of Palmerston in 1865 did opportunities arise for putting Conservatism back into the centre of British politics; not until 1867 was the party able to seize the initiative and carry any important legislation of its own; and not until 1874 was there again a Conservative Party majority in the Commons.

The circumstances of Peel's overthrow meant that his late colleagues became an informal parliamentary grouping of their own rather than continuing to operate alongside his critics, and it was in deference to the nature of this split that one side (the Peelites) named themselves after a person, the other (the protectionists) after an idea – much as in similar circumstances the Liberals would split in 1886 into Gladstonians and Unionists. These Peelites were ready to cooperate – at least by abstention – to keep the new Whig government of Lord John Russell in office, rather than combine with the protectionists to re-establish a Conservative government, so deep was the hurt caused by the Corn Law debates. Stanley was the only former Cabinet minister to take the protectionist path, for all other established or rising front-benchers – men like Lords Aberdeen and Lincoln, Graham, Gladstone and Edward Cardwell – became Peelites and never again sat in a Conservative government. It was a more complex story down below: one Peelite first elected in 1847, Roundell Palmer (later the first Earl of Selborne), was to survive long enough in political life to return to his old friends via Liberal Unionism after 1886, and so found a dynasty of Conservative politicians who served the party through much of the twentieth century.

Stanley was therefore leader of the protectionist Conservatives by default. The party was strong in the Lords and still had over 200 supporters in the Commons, where Bentinck and Disraeli had seized the initiative by the vehemence of their attacks on Peel, but this was hardly the basis for a front bench that was either impressive to supporters or reassuring to the voters. Bentinck seemed unlikely to develop an appetite for long-term parliamentary attendance, once his enthusiasm for downing Peel had died away; Disraeli was distrusted (since he had only come to the protectionist position after trying every other stance, including radicalism, in his earlier career) and in any case, and quite apart from his ethnic and behavioural disadvantages in a party made up mainly of Protestant country gentlemen, he too still lacked the experience needed to lead effectively. The protectionists did not therefore have even the beginnings of an alternative ministry, once their front bench went off in a Peelite sulk. Outside parliament things were if anything even worse; Bonham, the chief organizer under Peel, simply departed with his master and took with him both the party's files and its funds, while local registration associations were so damaged by recent events as to have lost all effectiveness – in some places ceasing to exist altogether.

Bentinck's lead did not impress even his own followers, given as he was to apologizing to opponents when he (frequently) got his facts wrong in debate, and the poor tactics shown by both Bentinck and Disraeli in keeping up their attacks on Peel even after he had been driven from office created for some protectionists doubts about their judgement and comment on their lack of good taste. Beresford proved to be a hopeless Chief Whip, tactless and offensive in a post which demanded a flexible manner, and the country gentlemen therefore reverted to type by simply melting away from London once the hunting and shooting seasons began.

With the parliament of 1841 finally prorogued at the end of August 1846, Stanley had a few months of calm in which to consider his strategy. He chose to quieten things down in the hope of effecting a reunion with Peel's followers in the future, calling off Bentinck and Disraeli from their continuing attacks, and persuading local protectionists not to widen the breach by selecting candidates to run against Peelite MPs. He was quite successful in persuading the party to follow this low-key approach in the year that preceded the 1847 election, but the price for this was that they also had to soft-pedal the only issue that gave them a distinctive identity; and unless they opposed sitting Peelites, they would eventually have to face the electors with no means whereby they could turn their minority of MPs into a majority. Peel had declared that cooperation between the two Conservative factions was unthinkable since one would campaign for and one against the Corn Laws. As the permanence of repeal would be decided one way or the other by the MPs returned at the next election, by hoping to keep bridges open for a reunion after that election Stanley effectively sacrificed any chance he might have had of winning it. There was, though, little value in winning a majority of MPs if he still did not have the talent from which to form a ministry, while there seemed at least a possibility that Peelites would eventually rediscover a source of disagreement with the Whigs which would drive them back to the Conservative side, or that the passage of time would anyway heal the wounds of 1846.

It was in any case likely that rural voters' eventual choice between free trade and tariffs would be determined at the time of the election and in the context of the economic situation as it then was, but this was not at all hopeful for protectionists: bad harvests ensured that there were historically high food prices when the actual election was fought in the summer of 1847, and it was not at all practicable for candidates to respond by calling for policies that would actually push prices up further. Protection was again soft-pedalled and the party concentrated more on other traditional issues – the threat to the Church, pure anti-Catholicism and anti-Irishism, and the claim that Conservatives alone could defend the country against radical excesses. But these were all issues on which Peelites and protectionists took more or less the same line, while Stanley's success in limiting rival candidatures in the constituencies meant that there were in any case few places where the electors actually had a choice between a Peelite and a protectionist. Overall, the Conservatives lost about forty seats, but both factions lost in proportion to their previous strength; there were still over 200 protectionist MPs and 100 Peelites (though some new MPs were hard to categorize, not having committed themselves as their predecessors had had to do in 1846), which together made up a number only about equal to the number of Whigs and radicals, so that even the party's theoretical overall majority was lost.

The net effect was thus to confirm Russell's Whigs in office, where the tacit backing of the Peelites would ensure that they would win votes fairly comfortably. It would be four more years before Stanley was offered even a smell of office, and the protectionists therefore had to turn their thoughts to a long period in opposition during which free trade would become more and more firmly the new status quo, and more and more subsidiary elements of protection would be removed from the statute book. The zealots of protection were not yet ready to admit final defeat, having decided that the country's economic position during 1847 had ensured that their argument had not had a fair chance of winning, and so they determined to have (at least) one more try in 'normal' conditions. The commitments he had given in 1845–6 ensured that Stanley himself could hardly wean his party off the pure milk of protection, though their need of his services was so absolute that he alone might have got away with it if a determined effort had been made. In 1849 Disraeli did make such an effort, putting together a package of proposals that would widen the net of income tax (and so relieve landowners, who currently constituted most of the taxpayers) and provide cheap loans to farmers as an alternative system of agricultural relief, all of this in return for the abandonment of protection, but the backbenchers would not hear of it.

In part this refusal to ditch a losing policy was rooted in a desire for consistency of principle, for how would their denunciations of Peel look if they then adopted his ideas (which in the end is what Disraeli largely did, concluding that protection was 'not only dead, but damned', though only after a decent interval); in part it was felt that their abandonment of the Corn Laws would merely encourage Whigs in their further liberalizing of such protective devices as the sugar duties and the Navigation Acts; and in part they saw in the depression of 1848–9 (when protectionists won a number of by-elections in places such as Cirencester and Kidderminster) the seductive hope that the next general elections would be fought at a time when, unlike 1847, protection would have considerable appeal to country voters.

The decision to stick with protection in turn guaranteed that the split with Peel would remain open. Despite numerous peace-feelers and meetings intended to bring the party factions back together during the 1847 parliament, none ever had a realistic chance of success. When Peel died in 1850, and a major stumbling-block was removed, it was by then already too late, but the growing veneration for Peel's name that followed his death reinforced the Peelites' sense that they were guardians of the name and the legacy of an upright man of principle who had been unfairly brought down by the little men of 1846.

The protectionists now had to plan for a future in which they were on their own, while the Peelites gravitated increasingly from limited cooperation with the Whigs, via sharing in coalition with them in the 1850s, to fusing with them in the Liberal Party of the 1860s. One sign that

Peel's statue being unveiled at Bury and attracting an appreciative crowd,
18 September 1852.

the protectionists had recognized their isolation was that they increasingly referred to themselves once again as 'Conservative', the sole inheritors of the party and its tradition as well as the majority shareholders. They remained at a low ebb, with attendance unreliable, front-bench performances poor, and both whipping and organization erratic. The years in opposition after 1847 did, however, also mark one important advance – the gradual emergence of Benjamin Disraeli as an effective leader in the Commons.

Initially, Bentinck meant to remain in charge, even selling his racehorses as a public demonstration of intent, but he continued to depend heavily on Disraeli for support, advice and background material for his speeches, and somewhat surprisingly came to feel quite close to him in the process. Bentinck's amateurishness was, though, always a problem, and his rigid attachment to principle always a rock on which his leadership might break. This eventually happened in December 1847 when, with a fine disregard for others' opinions which was positively Peel-like in itself, he insisted on backing a Whig Bill for the removal of legal disabilities from British Jews, a liberal viewpoint that outraged his most bigotedly Protestant supporters. With his leadership repudiated, Bentinck resigned at once, though in fact his health was already failing and he was to die only a few months later.

Disraeli had until then been content to shelter behind Bentinck and to exercise influence through him, but he now made a bid to become Leader himself and was immediately rebuffed; it was still inconceivable to Conservative MPs that the party of the gentlemen of England should be led by an urban, literary-tradesman Jew, even if an Anglicized and Anglicanized one. For the 1848 session the party effectively had no Leader at all in the Commons, for decisions were taken at full meetings of MPs and whips were sent out on that basis, but this only led to an even poorer show in Commons debates since it was nobody's duty to do the necessary preparation.

The next solution was the triumvirate set up in 1849, whereby Disraeli would share leadership with the lightweight (but aristocratic) Marquess of Granby and with the experienced but colourless J. C. Herries, each of whom had already refused the office of sole Leader. Although this arrangement was highly insulting to Disraeli, implying as it did that he could not be trusted without minders, he had the good sense to accept it as a vehicle that would finally take him to the top, and then gave sparkling parliamentary performances which showed just how absurd it was to saddle him with such second-rate co-equals. Within weeks, Herries had withdrawn, and it was not long before Disraeli was effectively in sole charge, for the party acknowledged (as a Tory peer grudgingly put it when urging Stanley too to bow to the inevitable), 'we must of necessity choose the cleverest person we possess'.

Disraeli's rise had been subtly assisted by his association with the still-warm memory of Bentinck. He had written a two-volume life of Bentinck which both celebrated the late Leader and reminded readers of Bentinck's reliance on himself, and he then benefited from one of Bentinck's dying wishes, which had enjoined his family to set Disraeli up as a country gentleman, a bequest which allowed Disraeli to buy Hughenden Manor in Buckinghamshire and so become a landowner like other MPs (rather than the 'fancy little Jew' that Bentinck actually described him as to his father the Duke of Portland). This was always an unconvincing pose, but at least it showed that he was making an effort to mould himself to his party's expectations, and Disraeli himself knew just how vital it had been to his career: at the end of his life, he told a later Duke of Portland that he 'belong[ed] to a race that never forgives an insult and never forgets a benefit. Everything I have I owe to the house of Bentinck.'

Real harmony and affection were slow to follow the marriage of convenience between Disraeli and the Conservatives; he was not, for example, invited to Knowsley by Derby (as Stanley became when he inherited the earldom in 1851) until 1853, by which time they had already served a term in office together, and despite two decades of cooperation Derby never visited Hughenden at all.

The party, in rallying reluctantly to Disraeli, was not recognizing him merely as the cleverest among a lot of parliamentary duds; it had also scented his appetite for power and his determination to achieve it. For a man of such background, long denied access to the Commons, even to a hearing from other MPs, and to office, Disraeli's determination to climb to the top of the 'greasy pole' of politics was already well understood, but this was something that was now desperately needed if the 'Country Party' (as one front-bencher in defeatist mood again called the Conservatives in 1851) was ever to have its place at the court. Disraeli's flexibility of approach, expediency and sheer cynicism, all of which characteristics had slowed down his rise among Conservatives until 1848–9, were now assets that could be exploited in the party's service. By 1851, having at last given up on the idea of reunion with the Peelites, Disraeli was prepared to negotiate with the Whigs, with Palmerston, with radicals, even with O'Connell's Irishmen (who were scarcely likely to team up with the Protestant bigots on the Conservative benches, quite apart from the fact that Disraeli had had a famous trading of insults with O'Connell himself not much earlier), in the hope of making some deal that would unlock the gates of office.

Such desperate politicking came about in 1851 only because the Whigs had again split, as in 1834, and Queen Victoria invited Derby to form a government, but all of this came to nothing when no single Peelite would join a ministry committed to the reintroduction of protection, while Palmerston flirted with the Conservatives merely to strengthen his own bargaining position among the Whigs. Forming a Conservative government proved humiliatingly impossible, and the Whigs resumed their rule after just one week, though this setback did have one beneficial consequence: when the Whig Cabinet fell apart again in February 1852, Derby resolved not to risk another such humiliation and so accepted office without preparatory negotiations, forming a Conservative government which would be in a minority in the Commons but united on basic principles.

The team that Derby assembled was evidence enough of the depths to which the Conservatives had sunk. Disraeli, who had never previously held any office at all, had to be both Leader of the Commons and Chancellor of the Exchequer, while Derby and Herries were the only ministers with any previous Cabinet experience, and both the Home and Foreign Offices were occupied by men who seemed to be dangerously out of their depth. Of the new men appointed, one or two, like Spencer Walpole and Sir John Pakington, would in due course become reasonably reliable party workhorses and be called on by Derby again, while Lord John Manners would go on to serve in six successive Conservative cabinets, retiring (by then the Duke of Rutland) only in 1892, though the fact that a man of such social eminence never rose higher than Postmaster-General suggests that both he and others knew his limitations. When the list of appointments was read out in the House of Lords, the aged and now-deaf Duke of Wellington responded to each name with a puzzled 'Who?' and the first Derby ministry was thereafter irrevocably saddled with the nickname of 'the Who? Who? Ministry'.

Derby had only taken office on the assurance that he could have an early dissolution of parliament, so as to have a chance of acquiring a majority in the Commons, and he went to the hustings for that purpose in July. Unfortunately, the depression that had raised such hopes for protectionists in 1848 had now given way to boom conditions in which even agriculture was beginning to share, and it again proved to be a bad time to campaign for a reversal of the repeal decision of 1846. For the most part Conservatives campaigned on the old negative cries, which made little impact in Great Britain and may even have cost the party a few seats lost in Ireland. The overall result was much like 1847, with a small number of Conservative gains, but nothing like enough to challenge the Whig–Peelite domination of the Commons.

No government in the mid-nineteenth century accepted a verdict from the electorate without demur, and Derby tried therefore to soldier on, until Disraeli's budget of November 1852 became the point of no return. The idea behind the budget was similar to the plan that Disraeli had tried to sell to the protectionists in 1849 – financial support for agriculture and a widening of the groups sharing the burden of income tax – but it also contained financial unorthodoxies in the detail that opened him to spirited attacks from the Peelites, for whom sound money was an article of faith. The set-piece debate of 16 December, in which Disraeli carried the battle to the Opposition and received a lacerating counter-attack from Gladstone, therefore marked both the end of the phase in which Conservative reunion had seemed possible and the start of the rhetorical pyrotechnics through which Gladstone and Disraeli were to unite their two sides of the Commons over the next two decades. On this occasion it was Gladstone who had the votes already sewn up, and when its budget was defeated by 305 votes to 286, the Derby government resigned. Derby had been, as he later put it when describing both of his first two governments, 'a mere stop-gap until it should suit the convenience of the Liberal party to forget their dissensions, and bring forward a measure which should oust us from office'. After a rather undistinguished ten months in office – but scarcely in power – it seemed that no progress had been made, but the experience of office had in fact clarified the situation.

The logical response to the new parliamentary arithmetic was a coalition between Whigs and Peelites, and this was now formed under the Peelite Aberdeen, while to mark the finality implied by their cooperation with the Whigs in government, Peelites like Gladstone now resigned from the Carlton Club (where, thought Derby, 'they could not have escaped insult'). The Conservatives were the largest party in the Commons but isolated into an apparently permanent minority, and associated with a policy which was so out of touch with the public's current requirements that for two elections in succession they had hardly dared to advance their own case. The loss of the front bench in 1846 had deprived them of a generation of 'men of business' who could be put forward as capable administrators, while the loss of the party's core policy had thrown it back on its more basic prejudices, away from which Peel and his colleagues had been weaning it. Derby and Disraeli would have to attempt the same task in more difficult circumstances, for the party could not now be compensated for the sacrifice of its beliefs by the enjoyment of the fruits of office.

That they eventually triumphed over adversity was due mainly to Disraeli. When, in 1867, the party had governed successfully and kept the Second Reform Act afloat through a sea of difficulties, *The Economist*'s editor Walter Bagehot, one of the most acute political observers of the day, penned a column with the title, 'Why Mr Disraeli Has Succeeded'.

For Bagehot, though he himself had often written critically of Disraeli's lack of principle and want of scruple, his success could not be attributed to 'pure fraud'; it had come about rather because for years Disraeli had bided his time, absorbing a deep familiarity with parliamentary rules and tactics, and learning the way forward by trial and error. He did not have a mind like Gladstone's that revelled in foresight and forward planning, but he was quicker on his feet and had an unerring ability to make the best of any situation. He could speak woundingly whenever it suited him, but because he had 'the imperturbability of an apathetic man', he could not himself be wounded (which of course *really* irritated opponents). It was these talents that had enabled him to keep his party's hopes alive through more than a decade of hopelessness, and to seize his moment when it came.

The difficulty of Disraeli's task can hardly be exaggerated, for with the Peelite front-benchers gone for ever, the parliamentary forces of Conservatism consisted overwhelmingly of those whom Bagehot himself had called.

> the least able and valuable part of English society. They have neither the responsibilities and culture of great noblemen, and they have never felt the painful need of getting on which sharpens the middle classes. They have a moderate sort of wealth which teaches them little, and a steady sort of mind fit for common things, but they have no flexibility and no ideas.

However, Derby and Disraeli made a good combination for the task in hand: Derby's landed wealth inspired MPs' trust and respect (even though he himself was a liberal and open-minded man), while Disraeli could provide them with enough sport to raise their spirits as players in his team. They were also complementary in another sense, for even though there were times when Derby despaired of Disraeli's adventurousness and impetuosity, or when Disraeli was irritated by Derby's quiescence, they were both by temperament good party men who understood well enough that they had limited chances of success even if they pulled together, but none at all if they became separated.

The strategic problems in the period 1852 to 1865 were numerous. First, the franchise and boundaries of 1832 had strengthened the political centre by under-representing both big cities and rural areas, placing undue weight on small boroughs which were often still in the pockets of patrons, and the result was to keep both radicals and Tories away from power. In 1865 the average county member in England and Wales represented 3,335 electors, the average borough member only 1,477, a big disadvantage for a party which, like the Conservatives, did much better in counties than in boroughs (and something that explains in part why Conservatives were willing to take the very unconservative risk of changing the rules just two years later).

In the 1850s and 1860s, then, there were probably about as many Conservative voters as Whigs and Peelites, but they did not succeed in electing as many MPs. Second, the social and economic environment after 1850 would have been unpromising for any opposition grouping, for the steady industrial expansion of Britain's 'workshop of the world' decades produced seemingly limitless prosperity in which farming continued to share; and as the mechanization of farming released manpower, it was generally mopped up by expanding industries and growing towns, where the worst miseries of the earliest phases of industrialization were diminishing, and the social mood was more harmonious as a result. Between the last flowering of Chartism in 1848 and the recession of 1866 there was scarcely any visible working-class movement demanding greater equality or democratic reforms, and a correspondingly lesser role for the Conservatives to play as the party of resistance to revolutionary changes. Gladstone spoke of 'the general abatement of extreme views and an abandonment of impractical purposes' among radical Liberals too, while the presence of the reactionary Lord Palmerston at the head of Liberal governments for most of the decade after 1855 was another powerfully reassuring barrier to change.

The over-arching mood of contentment and political quiescence in this 'age of equipoise' was for years precisely the mood that governments most work for and hope for – and oppositions most dread. Since the years of prosperity coincided with the final shifts towards free trade, as evidenced in Gladstone's budgets after 1853 and Cobden's tariff-busting treaty with France in 1860, there was as strong connection in the public mind between prosperity and Liberal policy, a further problem for the Conservatives, who had now abandoned protection but found no distinctive alternative identity to put in its place. Only when all these parameters of the political debate shifted after 1865 did Disraeli have the chance for which he had been waiting.

In the meantime the leaders' main task was to keep the party active and to encourage its independent local activities (which national politicians were largely unable to influence in any case). The main reason for the Conservative Party's refusal to wither away in the heyday of Palmerston was the continuing vitality of its local roots; the continuing partisanship of squire and parson, if never enough to build a parliamentary majority, *was* always strong enough to keep Conservatism a major force. In 1853 the party's formal organization was still weak, but it did then begin a slow and steady recovery. A key moment was the removal of Beresford from the position of Chief Whip and his replacement after an interval by Sir William Jolliffe, a figure who could, like Fremantle, identify with the backbenchers and win their trust. Jolliffe, and his successor after 1859, Colonel Edward Taylor, moved back into the position that Fremantle had occupied, raising money, keeping records and acting as the main channel of communication between the leaders, the parliamentary party and supporters in the country.

A step forward came when in 1853 the detail of organizational work was farmed out to a firm of solicitors, Spofforth and Rose (Disraeli's solicitors, Derby still having only a distant interest in such matters). The deal that was worked out was that Spofforth would not be paid, so retaining the amateur status which would be of use in dealing with the party's elite, while Rose (more junior and therefore less 'nice' about such things) would be paid a salary by the party, though in practice Jolliffe, Spofforth and Rose acted together as an organizing team, and the firm's premises became in practice the party's first proper offices, though the Carlton Club again figured as its social and political crossroads. This seems to have worked well, and in 1859 Jolliffe raised some £50,000 for the election, more than was in the Liberal war chest, but it was still of strictly limited value, for all of it went on forty of the 401 constituencies (thirty-six of them boroughs, where Conservatives were weaker – and where money achieved more), which left the other 90 per cent to depend on their own resources.

Where advances were made in these years, as, for example, the first permanent Conservative Party structures to function in Manchester and in Leeds, they were invariably the result of local initiatives over which the national organizers had little or no control. At times these local advances were made even against the wishes of the national organizers, as the example of registration work shows. Liberal registration campaigns in the counties caused some rural Conservatives to demand the creation of a central body to coordinate and encourage such activity on their own side, but the national organizers simply failed to see the need to deploy scarce resources in areas that were already overwhelmingly favourable to Conservatives, and they may also have feared that a central body to represent county Conservatives would become another pressure group for agriculture, at a time when the party was finally living down memories of 1846. The registration effort in the counties went ahead anyway, through a private office set up by the Earl of Shrewsbury, and when a few county seats were lost in 1865 this did finally receive some official backing.

All this painful effort could achieve little until the party's strategic opportunity arrived, and that would always remain doubtful while Derby was at the helm, all too often leading the Conservatives in a way that suggested his own lack of faith in their future. In the three general elections that took place between his first ministry and his third (one of them an election which as Prime Minister he called himself), the party made little or no headway. In 1857 many seats changed hands all round, but the net result was only a Conservative reduction of about twenty seats, followed by limited gains in 1859 and further but equally limited losses in 1865. There was a small trend away from Conservatives in the counties and towards them in the smaller boroughs, probably no more than a return to normality after the town-versus-country polarities of the 1840s, but the most significant pattern was one of stability, for the lowest Conservative total of MPs in the period was 281 and the highest was 307, while at each election some four-fifths of the county seats were not even contested.

The electoral lethargy that this demonstrated, with the century's highest ever total of uncontested constituencies coming in 1859, when only two out of every five constituencies in the whole of the United Kingdom had a contest, suggests a quiescence in the party that went far beyond Derby's personal predilections. Many Conservatives in the constituencies looked on Palmerston as a man they were happy to see heading the government of their country, and with memories of Chartism still fairly fresh in their minds, they saw no reason to stir things up by unnecessary opposition. In these circumstances, the parliamentary politics of the time were of limited significance, but here again the party's performance contributed to its overall weakness. Derby and Disraeli had to do enough to show that their party was alive but not enough to convince supporters that they were being unnecessarily hostile to a popular government. This came hard to Disraeli, but (as Bagehot put it in 1868) 'for years he ... sat almost silent – never raising petty discussions, and confusing old people who thought a leader of Opposition ought to be always opposing, but watching day by day the course of events'. In fact he mixed this generally calm political style with brief but violent assaults on ministers, timed more for the needs of his own party's morale than for the issues then under discussion. The backbenchers would not have stomached any more active and continuous opposition during the Crimean War (1854–5), and were equally happy with limited opposition when Palmerston's domination was at its height in the early 1860s.

It was of course far more tricky to keep the front-benchers happy, for the prospect of an endless period out of power meant to them the loss of influence, salary and patronage. The period was therefore punctuated by mainly unsuccessful attempts to form Conservative governments when the Whigs fell out among themselves, and one effort in 1858 did succeed in putting the party back into minority office for a year. The first chance came with the failure to wage the Crimean War effectively enough, for although there was much feeling on the Conservative benches that the government should be supported in wartime, they could scarcely miss the opportunity that a bungled campaign and terrible logistical support offered to them. W. H. Russell, *The Times* journalist who exposed the war's mismanagement in his dispatches from the Crimea, was himself a Conservative supporter who later became one of the party's MPs. But although Conservatives voted in force for the motion that brought down the Aberdeen government, it was a radical who proposed it, and when Derby was then sent for by the queen and asked to form a ministry he gave up the attempt as soon as Palmerston refused to serve under him and advised the queen to send for Palmerston instead. The result was that Palmerston seized his opportunity, won the war, and reaped the popularity that followed.

Derby may well have thought that the sixty-nine-year-old Palmerston would not last long – he certainly would not have foreseen his staying at Number Ten until he was seventy-nine – but even allowing for that, the passing up of office in 1855 could only be taken to mean that the Leader of the Conservative Party did not feel that on its own it had enough talent to run the country during a crisis. This was a deeply damaging admission, and though the party as a whole seemed happy enough, the front-benchers gave Derby a hard time. When the next chance came, in 1858, he had no choice but to accept, for as he himself said, to refuse office twice in three years would be 'the signal for the utter and final dissolution of the Party', whereas even failure *in* office would do less harm (a pessimistic viewpoint characteristic of Derby by that stage). He told the queen that if he refused, 'the Conservative Party would be broken up for ever', and accepted.

The ministry of 1858 was slightly stronger than that of 1852, not least because those who had served before had learned at least a little from the experience, and a new generation of MPs had produced some promotable recruits anyway, including Derby's own son, and General Jonathan Peel (Sir Robert's brother). This time the party hung onto office for longer and managed to achieve more in the way of legislation, including a Bill that finally admitted Jews to parliament and one that reconstructed the administration of British India following the 1857 mutiny. This record was to an extent misleading, for none of the Bills which passed were party matters, and Disraeli conceded in private that 'everyone knows that all we did would have been done by our predecessors'. This was all that could be achieved by a ministry with no Commons majority, and it did at least give opportunities for the demonstration of basic competence, but once the other parties had patched up their difficulties they had no difficulty in evicting Derby from office and re-installing Palmerston. The 1858–9 Derby ministry was then followed by the period of greatest quiescence in Palmerstonian rule, during which opposition more or less ceased altogether.

It was, however, at this time, in the early 1860s, when all seemed most bleak, that the corner was being turned, not because of any party effort but because circumstance began to tilt back in the Conservatives' favour. The long-anticipated but long-delayed fusion of Whigs, Peelites and radicals into a single Liberal Party in the parliament of 1859 made some difference to the ideological temper on the government side of the House. A delayed effect of the 1832 franchise was now producing an influx of more nonconformist manufacturers who were keen on more rapid reform, while the demonstration of their rising status, and the rise of John Bright within their party and of Gladstone within the government, was giving them a focus for their aspirations. These aims included the eradication of traditional privileges in the state, and reform of the army, the navy, the legal system, education and the civil service, with questions asked even about the Irish Church and the Irish Union. More than anything else over the previous generation, Conservatives had suffered from having little to defend because nothing much was being attacked, but this would now change. As long as Palmerston remained to hold back this growing appetite for accelerated radicalism, then nothing much would develop, but when he finally died in 1865 Disraeli almost at once proclaimed that 'the truce of parties is over. I foresee tempestuous times and great vicissitudes in public life.'

The party's new opportunity was enhanced by the fact that the same period saw the first real cracks in the economic complacency of the mid-Victorian generation, for an economic downturn would both increase pressure from below for reform and increase the nervousness of the possessing classes – who also happened at that time to be the voting classes – about the desirability of making concessions. In short, the relevance of Conservatism was re-established, and especially so when Palmerston was succeeded as Prime Minister by the elderly Earl Russell, himself quite a radical in his younger days, and with Liberals in the Commons led by Gladstone, already the most forceful figure in the government and Russell's obvious successor when the time came. The contestants for the coming battle were lined up, and the battlefield would once again be parliamentary reform, though this time, because of Disraeli's superior footwork and his other parliamentary skills, it would be the Conservatives who would reap the benefit.

Further changes in the franchise had been talked about for twenty years by the time that Palmerston's death opened up the opportunity to do something about it, and there was no longer any great political benefit to be gained from harping on about 1832's 'finality' as a constitutional settlement, as both Russell and Peel had done in the 1830s; Disraeli had more cynically remarked that 'never' was not a word that should be found in the vocabulary of politicians. Large and rapid movements of population had over thirty years distorted the boundaries and seat distribution agreed in 1832, while the growth of a respectable and socially conformist 'labour aristocracy' of artisan craftsmen had rendered the franchise of 1832, heavily restricted to the upper and middle classes, more and more difficult to defend. When Gladstone spoke in 1864 of the right of such thrifty and responsible workmen to be brought within 'the pale of the constitution' he was using language derived from Irish history (when 'the pale' had been seen as the civilized, English settlement around Dublin, surrounded by the great mass of the Irish without) and in effect urging that the principle of 1832 be reapplied, that a further group of the besiegers be brought inside the constitution to help man its ramparts. Though he did not commit Palmerston's government, he spoke for most of the political nation in recognizing the necessity of some early action, and it was not therefore surprising that the Russell government of 1866 did indeed take up the issue of reform.

Reform had thus been talked about again for the best part of twenty years, and three rather moderate bills had already been introduced by previous governments in 1854, 1859 (by the Conservatives) and 1860, though none of these had passed. As their readiness to introduce a bill of their own during the second Derby Government had shown, Conservatives had learned one lesson from 1832: if there was an irresistible tide for change then they had better ride with it rather than drown in the process of failing to hold it back. As Derby had told the queen – always a reluctant reformer – since they had come to the conclusion that the issue could not long be ignored, they felt justified in taking it up and trying to settle it on their own terms. That did not of course mean that Conservatives had become converted to democracy, or to anything remotely like it, and it was only the party opportunity created by Russell's parliamentary weakness that led Conservatives to carry in 1867 a proposal more radical than any senior Whig, Liberal or Conservative had previously considered. As Robert Stewart has put it, 'if the disaster of democracy could not be avoided, there was another disaster which might: handing over to Gladstone of power and the credit for having brought democracy to pass'.

In the first phase of the crisis Conservatives played a predictable and conventional role, allying with the moderate Whigs to harry the Russell government when it offered its own bill in 1866, and then building a coalition of the more conservative MPs of all parties in order to wreck the bill and thereby force Russell and Gladstone out of office. On several key amendments the government lost to a combination of Conservatives and moderate Whigs, but Gladstone could not be persuaded to give up the effort, and the Liberal radicals were threatening to break up the government if it did postpone action by withdrawing its bill. Having lost control of the Commons (and never having had control of the Lords), the Russell government resigned at the end of June 1866, and the queen thereupon asked Derby to form a government for the third time. The opportunity was rather greater this time round, for the opposing party was now split from top to bottom (where in 1852 and 1858 there had merely been Cabinet splits which had barely reached down to affect the overall temper of the Commons), and so Derby's survival – let alone any success at which he might aim – would depend entirely on keeping open the divisions among the Liberals which had given him this third chance.

The Derby ministry now formed was once again a slight improvement on its predecessor, partly through the continuity of the now more experienced ministers of 1852 and 1858, partly through the arrival of some younger men like Sir Stafford Northcote, Gathorne-Hardy, Lord Carnarvon and Lord Cranborne (who as the 3rd Marquess of Salisbury was to be the Party Leader from 1885 to 1902). The party had in effect grown a new head to replace the one cut off in 1846, for after the Peelites left, no Conservatives of later generations had followed them. The Cabinet nevertheless still leaned heavily on Derby and on Disraeli, once again Leader of the Commons as well as Chancellor of the Exchequer. There was, though, a faction among the Conservatives, known as 'the Bath clique' after their leader Lord Bath, which had tried to remove Disraeli in 1860 and were soon to try again, so suspicious were they of his adventurous brand of Conservatism and his flamboyant manner (criticism of which was often in coded language that scarcely concealed the critics' anti-semitism). There was no commitment by the new government to take up reform as its own issue, and its apparent dependence on the votes of right-wing Liberals to keep it in office made it seem unlikely that it would do so. When the parliamentary session ended only six weeks after Derby returned to office, he was able from August 1866 to February 1867 to settle in, bide his time and consider his options.

The room for manoeuvre was not, however, as great as it might seem, for while reformers in the country had been reasonably patient up till now, the appearance and defeat of an actual proposal to extend the franchise stirred them up to greater activity (much as it had done in 1830–31), so that their campaign of petitions, demonstrations and processions had already made it hard for Derby to ignore the issue by the time parliament reconvened for the 1867 session. One influence in that direction which was much discussed through the autumn of 1866 was a series of 'riots' in Hyde Park at the end of July, disturbances in which few were injured and only minimal damage was done to property, but which did starkly demonstrate the limits to government authority if it were to be defied by mass working-class protest and if ministers were unwilling to use soldiers to keep order. These events have been much exaggerated in later accounts (notably by the poet and cultural critic Matthew Arnold in 1869 in his *Culture and Anarchy*), for they certainly did not frighten the new government into action it would not otherwise have considered, but they may at least have persuaded Disraeli to contemplate a bold course of action rather than a cautious one. He had already noted by the end of July 1866 that if Derby's Cabinet were to seize the initiative by introducing its own Reform Bill, it would achieve three benefits at once: it would remove the cause of outside agitation; it would 'cut the ground entirely from under Gladstone'; and it would 'smash the Bath cabal', since once reform had been settled there would be no big issues ahead to divide Conservatives one from another. We should not though forget that Derby had come to much the same tactical conclusion;

his son noted in March 1867 that he was 'bent on remaining in power at whatever cost, and ready to make the largest concessions with that object'. Disraeli without Derby could not have won the trick, and would not even have been able to bid high in the first place.

Early in the 1867 session Derby's Cabinet therefore decided to test the water in the Commons by proposing a series of reform resolutions, and when those went well it committed itself to a bill of its own, and to an ambitious one at that. Having consulted backbenchers, Disraeli reported to Derby his view 'that the bold line is the safer one, & moreover, that it will be successful'. This in itself was an awkward business which led to the resignation of three 'Bath clique' ministers, Cranborne, Peel and Carnarvon, who argued strongly that the bill now being proposed was too radical – or, as Carnarvon put it, explaining his opposition in classically conservative language, 'it may be good or bad; but it is a revolution'. It is clear, though, that in the spring of 1867 it was Derby and Disraeli who more correctly divined the wishes of Conservative MPs, which were that now that it had the chance their party should settle the issue for a generation and so remove the risk of something worse, more damaging in the counties in particular, coming from the Liberals. As the Lord Privy Seal put it a few weeks later, when the bill was becoming even more radical in the process of Commons debates, 'the Conservative Members seem disposed to accept anything and to think it is "in for a penny, in for a pound".'

Disraeli therefore offered the Commons a bill which would make all householders borough voters, a principle that went further than the Liberal bill of 1866 in the direction of enfranchising working-class voters, but which then hedged this apparent generosity around with so many obstacles of detail that the outcome would probably have been more restrictive even than Gladstone had intended. Once under debate, and with the party's chief objective being the passing of a conclusive measure – *any* measure – Disraeli had to get votes from whichever quarter of the Commons they were on offer. Since moderate Liberals were horrified by his proposals, he could mobilize a majority only by topping up the Conservative vote with the votes of radicals. In other words, having combined with the Liberal right to defeat Gladstone in 1866, he combined with the Liberal left to beat him again in 1867, and the only absolute in the process was that Disraeli would resist any amendment whatsoever that came from Gladstone himself, since any success would enable the Liberal Leader to reunite his party and re-establish his authority.

THE POLITICAL EGG-DANCE.

Disraeli nimbly avoiding the breaking of Reform eggs in a *Punch* cartoon of 1867.

The price of this strategy was the acceptance of a whole series of radical amendments which transformed a moderate bill into a near-revolutionary one, and at such a pace that the collection and analysis of statistical information could not at times keep up with the debates, so that it was often unclear what the precise effect of an amendment would be if it were passed. The most significant change of all, the vote to accept the Liberal MP Hodgkinson's amendment and so include all ratepayers in the borough electorate (whereas Disraeli had originally proposed a more restrictive test), added at least half a million potential electors to the registers – but it may well have been twice that number, so imprecise was the data on which the party's tactics relied. Faced with a choice between agreeing with Hodgkinson or losing his bill, Disraeli accepted the amendment, explaining to the House with colossal cheek that it merely gave strength to 'the principles we have been impressing on the House'.

He was able to keep his party behind the bill as it became steadily less restrictive because of the great speed with which he shifted direction to meet each new development as it arose, and because the Conservative backbenchers – enthused now by the thrill of the chase – were determined to get their bill through however much they actually disliked its provisions. Conservative critics like Cranborne found little support, not least because sitting MPs were now extremely reluctant to offend those who might soon be their constituents by being seen to vote against their enfranchisement. Cranborne himself gloomily noted that the real conservatives lost heart when their own leaders proposed such a bill, for they recognized at once that 'a strong Reform Bill would [now] be passed, whatever their views, and were consequently impressed by the danger of quarrelling with the new constituency, whose advent to power was assured ... Many thought the position hopeless, and submitted in silence to a disaster which seemed inevitable.' Although this is in its way a real tribute to Disraeli's tactical skills, it certainly underestimates his power to raise the actual enthusiasm of Conservative MPs with the momentum of substantial achievement after years in the parliamentary trenches.

When the bill reached the Lords, Derby's personal authority with the peers ensured it a relatively easy passage, and he was not ashamed to admit to the mainly Conservative membership in the Upper House that the calculation of party advantage had been among his chief motivations all along. He had 'upon former occasions ... occupied the position of a Minister upon sufferance', and he 'did not intend for a third time to be made a mere stop-gap'. He had therefore 'determined that I would take such a course as would convert ... an existing minority into a practical majority'.

There were indeed considerable benefits to his party in the detail of the 1867 measures that can be too easily overlooked in consideration of the massive extension of the right of vote in the boroughs, measures which more than doubled the borough electorate in England and Wales and tripled it in Scotland. First, the Conservatives had retained (against

Liberal pressure) the distinction between the borough and county franchises, and they had therefore been able to keep the electorate in their county strongholds far more exclusive than it would become in the boroughs; whereas one in eight of the population could now vote in boroughs, only one in fifteen could vote in the counties. The revised constituencies now created would also remove much of the urban overspill which had threatened to swamp some county electorates and place it back firmly within redrawn borough boundaries. The government's ability to control the redistribution of seats and the instructions given to commissioners who actually redrew the boundaries was also used to give twenty-seven of the new seats to the English and Welsh counties but only eleven to the growing industrial conurbations, while all the places that lost representation had been boroughs.

Eighteen sixty-seven was famously described by Derby as a 'leap in the dark', but if so it was at least a leap from a platform already known to be insecure onto one that might be more solid. The 1867 Reform Act initiated a new electoral balance which was unlikely to be worse for the Conservatives than that of 1832. It cannot, though, be seen as a Conservative leap of faith in working-class voters. There were certainly Conservatives who had detected (as the evidence of published poll books confirms) that those few working-class voters who already had the vote before 1867 were at least as likely to vote Conservative as Liberal, and they, like Gladstone, had seen heartening evidence of the patriotism and responsibility of British workers in the past two decades. Once the act was passed, they made serious efforts to bid for the votes of these newly enfranchised workers, both through organizational efforts and in the tenor of their speeches, sometimes with real success. But if that putative alliance of the Tory social elite with the workers did conform in some sense to Disraeli's cloudy rhetoric of 'one nation' as it had continued since the phrase was coined in the 1840s, there is not the faintest evidence that either Disraeli himself or Conservatives as a whole were motivated by such thoughts in 1867. They were spurred on above all by the hope of protecting their own traditional county seats (where the working class did not get the vote anyway), and 'dish[ing] the whigs' (as Derby honestly put it) by sowing discord among them and then unleashing reform in their borough strongholds. It was a backward-looking reform that, as it turned out, then forced the Conservatives to make big moves forward because of the opportunities they inadvertently discovered when it had been passed.

If Disraeli was the man who espied the Tory working man within the mass of the proletariat, as a sculptor divines an angel 'prisoned' in a block of marble (as his *Times* obituarist romantically put it in 1881), then he did not even take up his chisel until long after the Act of 1867 became law. In the meantime, though, the history of Britain and of the party itself was already being rewritten in order to use Disraeli's ideas from the 1830s and 1840s (as well as the 1860s) to appeal to the new voters, as the first annual report of the Metropolitan Conservative [Workers'] Association made clear in June 1868; the future choice would be between

> Conservatives who promoted the Factory Ten Hours Act or Liberals who persistently opposed those measures; Conservatives who have maintained peace and England's martial renown abroad, or Liberals who have truckled to every foreign Government so as, during Liberal rule, to reduce England to the condition of a fourth-rate power among the empires of the world; Conservatives who opposed as long as possible, and have always striven to modify, the Poor Law Act of 1834, or Liberals who promoted that oppressive measure; Conservatives who gave the working class the franchise, not as a favour but as a right, or Liberals who withheld it from them.

Disraeli neither liked nor trusted such organizations as the Metropolitan Conservative Association, but in the sheer bravado of such uninhibited, counter-factual electioneering there was the true Disraelian touch, and very apposite it was to prove in the new conditions.

There was no doubting that Disraeli could at once claim a greatly enhanced credit from the very achievement of passing the Reform Act, for his advice that the bold course would be the best had been stunningly vindicated by the outcome and his tactics in the Commons had been the real key to success. Bagehot told the readers of *The Economist* that it might not be a great bill, and probably was not even a very good bill, but there was no doubting that it was 'Mr Disraeli's Bill'. Derby was now sixty-eight and had been troubled by ill-health for some time. With the act passed and work on registration under way, he resigned in February 1868. Disraeli finally took his place at the top of the 'greasy pole' as both Prime Minister and Conservative Party Leader, though his final elevation was achieved more through the private manoeuvrings of the queen and of Derby himself than with the full-hearted consent of the Conservative Party. Since the party was in office, it was constitutionally proper for the queen to play this role (as George IV had done three times in the 1820s, though these were hardly favourable precedents for Conservatives), and she allowed herself the same rights on the Liberal side as late as 1894, but it is hard to resist the conclusion that the matter was handled so quietly in order to prevent the dissent of the snobbish, the elitist and the anti-semitic among Conservatives at the advent of such an outlandish figure as Disraeli at their absolute head. The queen herself recognized clearly enough what she had done, telling one of her daughters that 'Mr Disraeli is Prime Minister! A proud thing for a man "risen from the people" to have obtained!'

If all of this could easily be exaggerated, for Disraeli had by 1868 moderated considerably the manners of his earlier days, it remained true that he was a rank outsider in the ultimate establishment party, and continued to behave 'exotically' to his dying day. This was therefore the first occasion on which the party had truly surprised itself in its new Leader. It would do so again in 1911 and in 1975 – and on all three occasions it gave only limited consideration to just what it was doing in making its choice, except for the overriding consideration that it seemed to bring the enjoyment of power perceptibly nearer.

Perhaps it was appropriate that a supremely ambitious, demotic politician should replace an aristocratic statesman at the party's helm at precisely the moment at which British politics moved into a new age of campaigning, electioneering and politicking? It would thus fall to Disraeli to turn the promise of the 1867 act into actuality, and to convert a permanent minority position at last into a 'practical majority'. He had expressed the extent of his hopes in this direction at the height of the reform struggle in the previous April: 'There are, no doubt, breakers ahead, but I feel great hope of overcoming them, and of realising the dream of my life and re-establishing Toryism on a national foundation.' Whatever the rather different dreams of supporters of 'Tory Democracy' in later generations – not to mention their claims that Disraeli was their inspiration – this establishment of unchanging Toryism in real national power *despite* democratic reforms was where his own heart had always really lain. But could it be done?

5

Disraeli's Indian Summer, 1868–76

THE AFTERMATH of 1867 was a considerable disappointment: both before and after the replacement of Derby by Disraeli the final eighteen months of the 1866–8 Conservative government was one long, humiliating clinging-on to office on Liberal sufferance, followed by a general election on the new franchise which – rather than setting the seal on 1867 by proving a Conservative Party triumph – returned Gladstone's Liberals to office with an increased majority and a formidable reform mandate for Ireland. The following few years in opposition were just as disheartening for Conservatives, for Gladstone in full cry was bent on forcing through reforms of which they thoroughly disapproved, and was in most cases successful, while their own party could make only a weak and feeble resistance.

Nevertheless, beginning in 1871–2, a Conservative recovery then gathered head both in parliament and in the country, organization reached levels of sophistication hitherto unknown, the Conservatives' own confidence recovered with surprising rapidity, and the general election of 1874 proved to be both a smashing Conservative victory and the prelude to a triumphant period in office. Disraeli was thus able to crown his long career with the entirely unexpected pleasure of an apotheosis as a much-loved and highly respected national statesman. His life could thus be summarized by Lord Randolph Churchill as failure after failure after failure, followed finally by sudden and inexplicable triumph. Just as important in Disraeli's own mind, perhaps, was the fact that he was able to show in 1874–6 that the Conservative Party could govern as well as win power, passing legislation relevant to the post-1867 era of mass politics. It had returned to the heart of British political life, where it has remained ever since.

The problem in 1867–8 was that the main Reform Act which had been passed covered only England and Wales; similar bills for Scotland and Ireland now had to be prepared and fought through their parliamentary processes, and by a government which could no longer keep up the exhilarating momentum of the summer of 1867. Even after that, the lengthy processes of drawing up electoral registers on the new rules and preparing for elections on the new boundaries ensured that an appeal to the enlarged electorate could not take place before the end of 1868. Through all of this the government had to keep going without a majority and against a Gladstone burning to avenge his recent defeats. The decision was made to soldier on under these trying circumstances, and so give the Conservatives the chance to dissolve parliament and hold an election at a time of their own choosing. Continuing in office at all was possible only because the queen was now strongly in support of the Conservatives in general and Disraeli in particular (as she would continue to be for the rest of his life, if always through some personal effort of flattery, 'laid on with a trowel', on Disraeli's part), but this involved the acceptance of the continuous pinpricks of defeat in detail by the Liberal majority in the Commons, which would nevertheless not propose and carry a vote of confidence in order to remove the Conservatives from office; it was, as Disraeli himself put it, a case of 'no wholesale censure, but retail humiliation'.

Disraeli's Cabinet was only slightly different from the one that he inherited from Derby, though he did take the chance to bring in two capable new colleagues in Ward Hunt (taking his own place at the Exchequer) and the Ulster-born lawyer Lord Cairns, who became Lord Chancellor and was soon one of Disraeli's closest confidants. The problem was that Disraeli, as Prime Minister from February 1868, could not call on the same social authority or inspire the same general trust as Derby – even on his own side – whereas his provoking presence in Downing Street certainly stirred on Gladstone to greater efforts.

Gladstone's chosen instrument was the Irish Church, a symbol of the Anglo-Irish Protestant ascendancy and one largely unrepresentative of the Irish population. During 1868 he launched a powerful campaign for its disestablishment, with a view to reuniting his own party around a strong moral cause that appealed to the Whig traditionalists (who harked back to the religious politics of the 1680s in which some of their ancestors had lost their lives) as much as to nonconformist radicals, and he prepared for an election-winning appeal on this platform. It was not an issue on which Disraeli had ever specialized or was thought to be expert (and his much earlier description of the Irish Church as 'alien' to the Irish people did not help here), while without a positive lead it was unlikely that Conservatives would agree on a strong response. Some, like Lord Stanley (the former Prime Minister's son, who himself became Earl of Derby in 1869, and was beginning to drift into the Liberal Party now that loyalty to his father no longer held him back), wanted to compromise, declaring that the present constitution of the Irish Church was no longer morally defensible, while more orthodox Anglicans in the Cabinet like Gathorne Hardy saw any faltering in defence of Anglicanism as a breach of Conservative principles; Cairns was among those who saw Gladstone's move as a capitulation to Rome and a threat to the Irish Union.

Disraeli resolved to pull Stanley into line and play the Protestant card, though he then went further in that direction than was politically wise by articulating a strong anti-Catholicism himself. As the Commons passed during 1868 Gladstone's various resolutions, thereby approving his new policy, and when the 1868 election seemed therefore likely to turn on the Irish Church question, Disraeli inadvisedly went much further. The election address issued to his Buckinghamshire constituents, but aimed mainly at the rest of the country since Buckinghamshire would not have a contest, argued that the whole constitution was at stake, since the Church was so inherently involved with the monarchy, so that the 'ultimate triumph' of Rome over Canterbury would therefore be 'the supremacy of a foreign prince'.

This was all good, topical stuff, for in that generation both French and German politicians were also contesting the issue of the pope's Ultramontane authority in civil matters, but in Britain Disraeli's extravagant language entirely missed the target. Unlike the situation in the 1830s, there was now a readiness in the electorate to accept a degree of ecclesiastical reform, and Disraeli's anachronistic appeal to Protestant bigotry only opened him to ridicule. More seriously, the pinning of the Conservative campaign onto such an outdated and negative issue gave the impression that the Conservative Leader had nothing to offer for the future and that he did not understand how far the 1867 Reform Act had changed the parameters of politics, so completely had Gladstone wrongfooted him. *The Times*, hostile to Disraeli in any case but keen too to keep on terms with the coming man Gladstone, pointed out acerbically that Disraeli offered 'many promises to resist the policies of others, but no signs of any policy for the great Conservative party itself.'

When the election produced its Liberal majority, Disraeli resigned at once and so set a precedent as the first Prime Minister to quit office apparently at the behest of the electorate rather than of parliament or the monarch. But it was the Irish Church issue, rather than any thinking about the extent to which 1867 had changed the constitution, that persuaded the Cabinet to resign, and so to avoid the further humiliation of being defeated on Irish issues in the new parliament too, and on a Disraelian policy that many of his colleagues did not agree with anyway. When Gladstone then introduced his Disestablishment Bill in the 1869 session, and imperiously pressed it through the Commons, the Conservatives put up only a token, disorganized resistance.

They did not do much better when, in 1870, Gladstone moved on to attack the Protestant Irish ascendancy with a Land Bill too; the threat of a real fight if the Lords rejected the Land Bill soon vanished when even hawkish peers like the new Lord Salisbury (who as Viscount Cranborne had resigned from the Conservative government in 1867 and since then had written vicious polemics in the *Quarterly Review* about Disraeli's lack of principle) realized that neither the Church nor the Irish landlords had any stomach for a fight with the triumphant Gladstone, at least while he had most of Irish opinion and a Commons majority behind him. That defeat made Salisbury himself somewhat more of a careful politician than he had been as a younger Member (and so paved the way for his return to the collective leadership of the party), while over Ireland it led him to some significant conclusions – that the Protestant landlord class were not worth defending, that Conservatives must find a better line of defence for the Union than institutions already repudiated by the mass of the population, and that land purchase schemes to buy out absentee landlords were the only way of rebuilding an effective conservative presence in Ireland.

The overawing of the Lords by Gladstone in 1869–70 was completed by his high-handed use of the royal prerogative to enforce army reforms to abolish the sale of commissions (and thereby allow for a marginally more meritocratic recruitment system for the officer class). This proposal was seen by many Conservatives as an attack on the rights of property – serving officers had bought *their* commissions, so why should they not be allowed to sell them in due course? A 'Colonels' lobby', made up mainly of Conservatives, opposed the plan fiercely in the Commons. Gladstone's ingenious solution of introducing the reform without legislation did at least save the Tory peers from the choice between rejecting a bill with solid Commons support or surrendering another issue of principle, but it was also for them a dangerous precedent, though Disraeli was unsuccessful in raising a storm about the constitutional dangers posed by Gladstone's procedural device. After 1867 had widened the electorate, the peers were increasingly exposed when a Commons majority insisted on its mandate. They had begun to consider their own future position, structure and powers as a result, with the hawks averring that they might as well go down with a fight as vote for things that they did not like just because of the 'perpetual threat of extinction' if they did not. This was a dilemma dating back to 1832, but one that would run on right through to 1911, when these aristocratic bees were finally provoked into using their sting – and died constitutionally as a result.

In another sense, too, the Conservatives had spectacularly failed to learn the lesson of 1867, for they had not actually prepared adequately to face the new electorate that they had themselves brought into existence. It is possible to trace in 1867–8 some seeds of future organizational advances such as the National Union of (local) Conservative Associations, but these certainly did not flourish at the time and did not have either the support or much of the attention of the party's high command. Just as the real motivation in 1867 had been backward-looking and dominated by worries about the counties, so most of the organizational work done immediately afterwards was equally innocent of future developments. The main figures in electoral management for the party were Spofforth (who had taken over the lead role of Principal Agent from Rose in 1859), Monty Corry, who was Disraeli's political secretary from 1866, the Chief Whip Taylor, and the leader of county registration work Lord Nevill (dubbed by Disraeli himself 'the Grand Panjandrum of the Tories'). The lower-level work done by forward-looking borough organizers like John Gorst and H. C. Raikes was given a far lower priority, and organization in the counties continued much as if they did not exist.

Nevertheless, the passing of the 1867 Reform Act, and even to an extent the anticipation that it would be passed, had led to the creation of more active Conservative groups in the boroughs, and to the first organizations aimed at the newly enfranchised working-men voters. Raikes was selected by Nevill (who soon lost interest) to be the first promoter of a national body to coordinate such groups and keep them from going off at a tangent and causing the party embarrassment, though the work also attracted the attention of Gorst, a young barrister anxious to be a Conservative MP, and Edward Clarke, a future Conservative law officer. Despite these young men's enthusiasm, their proposal to launch a National Union of Conservative Associations in the autumn of 1867, with a grand demonstration at the Crystal Palace and a national conference, soon ran into trouble. They collided at once with the overlapping ambitions of the Metropolitan London and Westminster Association, which was aiming to combine all classes rather than to concentrate attention on one, and hoped to take the national lead in this work. This rival gained the ear of the party managers, upstaged the nascent National Union by taking over its Crystal Palace rally (which even then no party leader of significance could be persuaded to attend), and relegated the National Union to the secondary role of organizer of a poorly attended and scarcely reported conference.

The parliamentary leaders were anxious not to patronize working men's organizations too openly, lest they offend the middle class – which seemed a better prospect at a time when middle-class voters were rattled by the events of 1867 anyway. They were equally concerned not to allow too much room to these new Conservatives lest they ask for more; as one of them wrote: 'I trust ... that we shall not be like Frankenstein, & have raised a spirit that we cannot control!' The remarkably deferential tones of those working men who actually attended the first conference of the National Union and equivalent local bodies would have reassured them (had they been there to hear), and there would indeed prove over time to be no great danger from the National Union, created (as the mover of the resolution that brought it into existence put it) not to rival the parliamentary leadership, but to be its 'handmaid'.

With the National Union for the time denied official backing, and with the counties on which most party hopes still depended playing no part in it anyway, there was only inadequate preparation for the coming election. In the circumstances it is indeed remarkable that the Conservatives were able to do so well with the new borough electorate, winning some seats that had rarely if ever been Conservative in the past, and at least putting up a fight in all but twenty-seven English boroughs (whereas fifty-six had seen no Conservative candidate in 1865). But this was a testament more to the growing Conservative strength in the localities than to any central initiatives, for the £50,000 that the party could again afford to spend on the election from its central war chest was not sufficient to fund many actual contests. In any case, if the Conservatives fought more seats in 1868, so did the Liberals, and this meant that it was necessary to spend more time and effort defending ground already held, which dissipated the Conservative effort and ensured that their electoral advances were limited.

There were, however, two areas in which political events during the party's last eighteen months in office during 1867–8 looked forward rather than backward – or at least adapted older traditions to the Conservatives' present need, and these were the Abyssinian War and Disraeli's Edinburgh demonstration.

Once the British consul in Abyssinia and European missionaries had been imprisoned, the government demanded their release and full satisfaction from Emperor Theodore, and when his response was deemed inadequate, a British army of 12,000 men under Sir Robert Napier was sent into the heart of Africa – with the world's press taken along to witness a demonstration of British power. The operation went well enough and no British soldiers lost their lives in battle – though in the nature of such adventures it did cost the huge sum of £9 million. The missionaries were released, Theodore committed suicide when British troops approached his palace, and a more friendly ruler was installed in his place. At which time the government, having no wish to acquire the expense of keeping up such a distant colony, brought the troops home, where they were received as national heroes. Special medals were struck to commemorate the triumph and Napier became Lord Napier of Magdala, while, in celebration of this walk-over victory, Disraeli produced a height of patriotic rhetoric elevated even by his own dizzy standards.

The victory proved highly reassuring to the nation's rulers themselves, as evidence that they had not lost their willpower in the compromises and retreats of 1867. Such punitive expeditions were hardly rare for mid-Victorian Britain, though it was less usual for the crisis to be contrived and managed from London rather than by an expansionist proconsul on the imperial frontier. The whole episode had perhaps more in common with the Palmerstonian overreaction to such incidents as the Don Pacifico crisis of 1850, though even Palmerston had rarely looked outside Europe for flag-waving opportunities for domestic consumption. The Abyssinian War may be seen as a sort of transition between the gunboat diplomacy of Palmerston (which he had after all inherited from the Tories Pitt and Castlereagh) and the higher imperialism to which Disraeli himself was to give voice a decade later. It was therefore the first example of 'social imperialism', the use of British arms to win easy victories abroad – but to impress the voters rather than the natives. Disraeli assured a correspondent that 'it certainly cost double what was contemplated', but 'that is likely to be the case in all wars for wh[ich] I may be responsible. Money is not to be considered in such matters; success alone is to be thought of.' Here, then, began a theme of Conservative policy and a patriotic appeal to the nation that ran on right through to the 'Falklands factor' of 1982.

The idea that Disraeli should visit Edinburgh to receive from the Scots a Roman triumph similar to the one that Napier enjoyed in London was suggested when the reform crisis was coming to its successful climax. He was not the only Conservative Leader to go out to the provinces, for Prime Minister Derby enjoyed a banquet in Manchester, and even Cranborne was to be found appealing to the voters of Lancashire during the 1868 election campaign. Disraeli was not even keen to go to the Edinburgh rally, and had to be cajoled into it by Corry with assurances that 'a great and valuable demonstration and expression of good-will is in store'. It all came off successfully, though, on 29 October 1867, and once there Disraeli played up in grand style to the pomp of the occasion, both in the main event and at an evening rally of Scottish working-men Conservatives in the Edinburgh Music Hall. He assured his audiences that the Conservatives were 'the national party of England' (no nonsense about 'Britain' for Disraeli, even when addressing roomsful of Scots, but then he and Salisbury were shortly to launch the patriotic imperialism that would finally crack the near-monopoly that the Liberals had enjoyed in Scotland for years), and asserted that the party was a patriotic union of all classes under the nation's 'natural' leaders, a version of his Young England neo-feudalism now updated for the heyday of the empire and decked out in partisan clothing.

One motivation for Disraeli's trip north had been claims that Scotland was already ripe for penetration by Conservative candidates, but the 1868 election when it finally came proved otherwise, with Conservatives losing four Scottish seats, and returning only eight MPs against the Liberals' fifty-two. Something similar happened in Wales, where the Conservatives were reduced from eleven to eight, and in Ireland, where the reduction was from fifty to forty (though here the Liberals too were losing ground to Irish MPs intent on pursuing their own nationalist policy agenda). In England there was a smaller Conservative decline, and the party held 220 seats compared to the 225 of 1865 (though Liberals also fell away slightly from 246 to 243, so there was scarcely any net change between government and opposition). But the losses outside England ensured that Gladstone now had a Commons majority of over a hundred, and this at least contributed to the Conservative decision to yield office to him at once.

Within these results, and especially in England, the pattern was far more complex than the totals revealed, for while there were now twenty-eight more Conservative county members – mainly the result of additional constituencies recently created rather than any changes of actual votes, and so a vindication of Disraeli's 1867 strategy – in the boroughs the Conservative total was more than a fifth lower than in 1865, their lowest score indeed since 1832. Even this pattern of Tory success in the counties and weakness in the towns needs to be modified by the detail of individual results. In Lancashire, where Disraeli's Protestant campaign may have been most effective, the Conservatives took all eight county seats and twenty-four of the thirty-six borough seats, including a rare seat in Manchester and both seats in Salford. In the London area, too – a radical stronghold for over a century – there were spectacular advances: a seat was taken in the City of London (an early indicator of the financial classes' shift to the right) and there were signal victories in both Westminster and the highly urbanized Middlesex county constituency. Lord George Hamilton's victory over the radical wit Henry Labouchere in Middlesex – once the constituency of famous radicals like John Wilkes and Francis Place – was truly a sign that the railway revolution, the arrival of the genteel middle class in such areas as Ealing and Hammersmith, and the organizational efforts of an unusually able agent (the trainer of many Conservative agents to come, including the legendary Captain Middleton) would give the Conservatives rich pickings in the new suburbs, while the defeat of the Liberal philosopher John Stuart Mill in Charles James Fox's old Westminster city constituency by the newspaper wholesaler W. H. Smith (a recent convert both to Anglicanism and to Conservatism, but now ready to spend oceans of the proceeds of capitalism on a political career) seemed even more symbolic. Peel had long ago sought to bring capital and land together under the Conservative banner, and the arrival of Smith in the Commons as a Conservative MP, like the later crossing-over of Joseph Chamberlain in 1886, seemed clear evidence that it was actually happening. In the years to come, if not quite yet, London and Lancashire would be the keys to Conservative success.

Even at the time, these Conservative wins against the tide were seen as demonstrating the increasing vitality of local Conservatism in middle-class areas and in the growing conurbations. Gladstone's disciple John Morley wrote bitterly of the Westminster result as a 'coalition of true patricians, stuccoed patricians, and shopkeepers' – which was exactly the social alliance that would transform the London suburbs into a Tory heartland in the century ahead – while the *Fortnightly Review*'s analysis of Lancashire detected a similar tendency of employers to advance themselves socially by improving their rapport and electoral cooperation with the Conservative gentry. Other evidence of the same trend lay in the foundation of provincial Conservative clubs, and in the fact that the first daily Conservative papers to appear in Birmingham, Bristol, Leeds, Liverpool, Manchester, Newcastle, Nottingham, Sheffield and Southampton had all arrived in the past few years, signs both of capital locally available to the Conservative cause and of a sufficient readership to make the new papers viable.

But such developments remained patchy, and it would not be until the next wave of parliamentary reform beckoned in the 1880s that similar advances in the local party press would be seen in Bradford, Derby, Northampton, Norwich or Portsmouth, all places where the party was weaker. As this would suggest, it was smaller towns that were the Conservative problem in 1868, not least because the small print of the 1868 act had moved back within their boundaries many Liberal voters who had previously been swamped by the Tory county vote. All over the country, the force of the Liberal attack produced gains in such places as Exeter, Hereford and Canterbury – indeed cathedral England did not do at all well by the party that was trenchantly defending Anglicanism in Ireland – which together offset the much-discussed but numerically less significant Conservative victories elsewhere.

Once deprived of the balm and patronage of office, Disraeli's position as Leader came rapidly into question. For at the age of sixty-five it was not thought likely that he would even wish to slog through another full parliament on the opposition side, and the impact of his 1867 success had already faded from memory, displaced by more recent recollections of his poor management of the Irish Church and of the election. The death of the former Prime Minister Derby in October 1869 may both have weakened him (since a powerful colleague was no longer there to rally support) and at the same time ensured his survival, for the new Earl of Derby would have to be involved in any change of Leader, would be likely to be a strong candidate himself, and yet was so unsure about his own political future that he could never be counted on. Salisbury had meanwhile blotted his copybook by the vehemence of his recent attacks on the party and its policy; Gathorne Hardy and Stafford Northcote would not even contemplate taking the lead in the Commons while Disraeli sat behind them as a focus of disruption (and he, sensing the power that this situation gave him, refused even to think of solving their problem by accepting a peerage), so that most serious contenders were for one reason or another unavailable. Disraeli hung on, then, partly because there was no obvious alternative willing to challenge him, partly because his own powerful will had still not given up the hope of bringing his leadership and his strategy of 1867 to a triumphant success in the end.

Disraeli was, however, preoccupied with personal matters after 1868, including the poor health of his wife (through to her death in 1872) and his own return to writing (he published in 1870 his first novel since 1847, further evidence to his critics of an inappropriate, insufficiently serious lifestyle for a national leader). He had in any case formed the impression that the party needed a period of rest and recuperation after the excitements of 1867 and the disappointment of 1868, that it would be folly to attack a newly installed ministry like Gladstone's until it had exhausted its mandate and begun the process of antagonizing opinion for itself. He therefore argued that 'on our part there should be, at the present, the utmost reserve and quietness', which was hardly a strategy likely to strengthen his appeal to frustrated backbenchers. This position would only change when, in and after 1870, Gladstone's ministers ran into real trouble, initially over educational reforms which opened them up to attack from churchmen of every stripe. Since these changes ensured that Church schools continued to exist alongside new publicly funded board schools, and could even receive some income from local taxation to assist in their continued operation, the Conservatives voted for the Liberal bill, so allowing Disraeli to appear – as Peel had in the 1830s – as the statesmanlike supporter of a government against its own radical extremists. Civil service reform, the opening up of Oxford and Cambridge to non-Anglicans, and reforms in the army were all open to similar strategies, and in each case the Liberals offended some interest group that would now be likely to turn to Conservatives for future relief.

The Liberal attempt to reform liquor licensing was an even greater bonus, for it was in the first place an incompetent initiative that had to be withdrawn, and it was in any case resented by 'the trade' as an attack on their legitimate activities by Liberals, who were motivated by temperance and in some cases even by prohibitionism. As Derby put it, 'The whole of the liquor traffic', previously about evenly split between Liberal and Conservative in its political allegiance, 'has [now] thrown its weight into the Conservative scale', with a formidable effect on electioneering outcomes. In this sense the victory of the Tory brewer James Watney (over an aristocratic relative of the Liberal Foreign Secretary) in the East Surrey by-election of 1871 was as symbolic as Middlesex had been in 1868.

This result came not because the brewers made sure that Liberals were 'borne down in a torrent of gin and beer', as Gladstone exaggeratedly claimed in 1874 (though in a few places extensive 'treating' may have occurred), but because they offered financial assistance for all types of election activity, and because the social world of the pubs and clubs would increasingly become a local focus of Conservative identity to match the Liberals' support in the nonconformist chapels and the mechanics' institutes. Such support when once gained would prove lasting, reinforced perhaps by the Conservatives' rallying to save the breweries from nationalization during the First World War. Long after 1945 the drink industry would provide the Conservative Party's most reliable industrial funding, even though the threat to it from any other party had vanished long ago.

The value of such support in the long term was to an extent reduced by the introduction into law in 1872 of corrupt practices restrictions and of the secret ballot, which would over time make coercion impossible and bribery pointless, and which immediately worried the Conservatives' more traditional election managers in the counties (where the eviction of tenants who did not vote the landlords' ticket had been common practice, especially in Ireland). It was notable, though, that the newer breed of borough-mongers saw the secret ballot as an opportunity rather than a threat, and it seems likely that many middle-class defectors from Liberalism in 1874 were encouraged by the fact that their friends and relations would never now find out what they had done. Even though Disraeli strongly disliked secret ballots, this was a difficult reform to oppose, and the Lords once again duly gave way. The Ballot Act did nevertheless make a good target for Conservative speakers in 1872, and was used by Disraeli himself, when he contrasted 'all the pains and penalties of the Ballot Act' with the Liberals' alleged neglect of ordinary voters' true interests, such as their need for more sanitary living conditions. The Conservatives were derided by Liberals for concerning themselves with 'a policy of sewage', but this was a charge he gloried in, and he promised to continue with the approach, celebrating the pledge with one of the most dreadful puns in British political history, 'Sanitas sanitatum, omnia sanitas.'

This chimed in well with a curious incident in 1871, when Conservatives in the country and some younger Conservative front-benchers in the Commons came together to promote a more advanced social programme for the party, envisaging it in such grandiose language as a 'New Social Alliance' or a 'Charter' to be made between the party and the people. This owed something to the ideas of urban Conservatives who were genuinely worried about conditions in their areas and ready to envisage using state intervention as a solution, but it also owed a good deal to growing worries about working-class alienation and agitation (recently fired up by the bloodshed surrounding the Paris Commune of that year) and to the Conservatives' own need of something more positive to say in the boroughs than they had managed to find in 1868.

For a time, men like Northcote and Pakington, and the younger Viscount Sandon, who had his political roots in Liverpool, seemed so ready to discuss such revolutionary ideas that other Conservatives thought them to be flirting with socialism, and the press detected 'Mr Disraeli's flank march' to a position on Gladstone's left. Very little came of the whole affair, though almost all Conservative leaders who were consulted were prepared to back some part of the seven-point package of social policies under discussion. Hardly any (certainly not Disraeli) were prepared to deny their interest altogether, though many also followed Derby in pointing out the effects on trade and employment of too active a policy in these fields. Interest faded quickly, but the ghost of the 'alliance' of Conservatives and working men could be seen in Disraeli's big speeches in 1872; it may have helped a little in persuading urban voters in 1874 that the party was not hostile to their interests, and it provided a background from which the party did indeed draw some ideas when legislating in 1874–6. More broadly, it contributed to the persistent and historically crucial myth that Disraeli had since his support for Ashley and Oastler in the 1840s been a humanitarian social reformer, itself a key component in the shadowy concept of 'Tory Democracy' as it later developed. It was such things as this that persuaded the Liberal philosopher Frederick Harrison to the (to him) shocking conclusion, when reviewing the 1874 election, that 'there is nothing now exclusive about the Conservative party. It is, in the old sense of the words, just as popular and democratic as the Liberal party.' In so far as this was true, and 1874 certainly provided strong evidence of it, then it was because of Disraeli's success in interpreting events as showing that a long period in which the main issues had been financial and commercial had now come to an end. Social, constitutional and imperial issues would now be to the fore – issues on which his own party as effectively represented 'the democracy' as did the Liberals.

The final element that facilitated the Conservative counter-attack on Gladstone (and which the press thought to have persuaded Disraeli to 'wake up' early in 1871) was the new primacy of foreign issues in British politics after Germany's decisive victory in the Franco-Prussian War. Conservatives felt more secure on the diplomatic and military side than when discussing domestic policy and were equally confident that Liberals (and Gladstone) felt insecure in this area, as a poorly handled dispute with the United States over compensation for losses over the British-built Confederate raider *Alabama* seemed to demonstrate.

Disraeli welcomed some relief from 'the morbid spirit of domestic change', but more to the point he was among the first to realize how far the rise of Germany through wars of continental-sized mass armies had invalidated the traditional tenets of Palmerstonian international policy; 'the balance of power has been entirely destroyed, and the country that suffers most, and feels the effect of this great change most, is England.' Since no contemporary British politician, and certainly not Disraeli, contemplated Britain building armies on the Prussian scale, increasing concern about Britain's manifest future inability to intervene effectively in Europe could only be offset by the promotion of British prestige through activities outside Europe, where naval power and smallish garrisons could still control the scene. The shift of 1871–2 in Tory thinking about Britain's place in the world therefore followed on logically – but far more urgently – from Disraeli's 1867–8 rhetoric over Abyssinia. This had itself coincided with Prussia's earlier victory over the Austrians, when he had proclaimed that 'England has outgrown the continent of Europe. [Her] abstention from any unnecessary interference in [its] affairs is the consequence, not of her decline of power, but of her increased strength. England is no longer a mere European power . . . [and] she has duties devolving upon her upon a much larger scale.'

Nevertheless, Disraeli's burst of activity in 1871 did not last, and by July he was again convinced that it was too soon to strike Gladstone down, that 'our policy should be the utmost reserve'. This wisdom was again not universally respected, and in the following winter he faced the most organized revolt against his leadership in the parliament. A pre-organized meeting at Burghley House shortly before the 1872 session, attended by half a dozen of the party's senior figures (and with others signifying approval by letter), decided that the Leader must be made aware of the level of party discontent and invited to stand down. Once again, this plot foundered on the fact that Disraeli would not leave the Commons, while the popular choice, Lord Derby, would not take the leadership anyway, being by now unsure whether he was even in the right party. Within a few months this little incident would seem highly improbable, for during

1872 Disraeli finally did decide that the time was ripe, and launched the counter-attack that would carry him back into office.

An indication of the new mood was to be seen when in February 1872 Disraeli was cheered at a St Paul's service of thanksgiving for the Prince of Wales's recovery from illness, while Gladstone had a hostile reception. Disraeli's triumph was to be repeated at party rallies in Manchester and the Crystal Palace later in the year. In 1873 in Glasgow he had 'the greatest reception ever offered to a public man', as he himself modestly described it. The change was also to be seen in the gradual disintegration of the Liberal government, embarrassed by scandal and poor financial management, and divided especially over a scheme to create a non-denominational Irish national university. The Conservative success in by-elections which had been evident throughout the parliament now accelerated, with seven gains and no losses each year in 1872 and 1873; by the end of 1873 the party had made a new gain of twenty-three seats, eighteen of the captured seats coming in English boroughs, and had therefore restored its parliamentary position to what it had been before the 1868 election.

As in the 1867 trip to Edinburgh, Disraeli was a reluctant visitor to Manchester in 1872, hating such 'distant engagements' and being well aware that he would have to produce at least the semblance of a 'definite policy' if he accepted the invitation. Nevertheless, the cajolings of the organizers and the new mood of 1872 persuaded him to agree 'to meet the county and all the Boroughs of Lancashire'. There was a week of receptions, meetings with local dignitaries and parades of supporters, culminating in a grand rally on 3 April at the Free Trade Hall – irony of ironies, given Disraeli's protectionism in 1846! – at which Disraeli addressed 6,000 supporters for over three hours.

His main argument was constitutional, concentrating on the defence of the monarchy (currently under a rare republican attack from a few radicals, with Queen Victoria still withdrawn into a lengthy and invisible widowhood), but using this as the basis for the claim that only Conservatives could be trusted to defend *all* the national institutions. The crown, as interpreted by Disraeli, was the true protector of the liberties of the people, linked closely in that role with the House of Lords and the Church (both then coming under more official Liberal attack). He also spoke, though, of the need for a more positive social policy, calling for an active response to the report of the Royal Commission that he had himself set up as Prime Minister, for in such areas as sanitation 'no inconsiderable results may be obtained by judicious and prudent legislation'. However, the parts of his speech most appreciated by his audience were undoubtedly the polemical sallies directed at the 'exhausted volcanoes' of Gladstone's government, where 'not a flame flickers on a single pallid crest', and the cloudier rhetoric with which he concluded, hailing 'the cause of the Tory Party, the English Constitution, and of the British Empire'.

This masterly tying together of the party's traditional concern with constitutional issues and its newer interest in social reform and empire was reinforced when the same themes were celebrated in the terser speech that he delivered to the National Union on 24 June – though the fact that he went at all to the concluding rally of this sixth National Union conference, having refused to attend the first in the same location, may well have been more important than anything he said when he got there. At the Crystal Palace he explicitly claimed for the Conservatives the mantle of Palmerston, a Pittite-Canningite inheritance that had been lost to the party by Peel's apostasy and Palmerston's idiosyncrasies, so uniting old ideas of English patriotism with newer fashions for adventures outside Europe.

It was once fashionable for historians to detect a shift in Disraeli's view of external policy, between an earlier career in which he had once spoken of British colonies as 'millstones round our necks' and an apotheosis in which he became the prophet of high Victorian empire-building. In fact, each half of that apparent contradiction between the early and late Disraeli was exaggerated, for he had not wished to divest Britain of overseas possessions before the 1860s, and he certainly did not become committed to an especially active imperial policy afterwards. Disraeli did, however, sense a shift in both the public mood and the international circumstances and was as usual happy to play up to both. Hence Abyssinia in 1867–8, hence the rhetoric of imperialism in 1872, and hence the theatrical coup by which in 1875–6 he secured for Britain additional shares in the Suez Canal Company and then costlessly promoted Victoria to the status of Empress of India – so raising Britain's as well as its monarch's status among the European powers. Disraeli was in this sense very much 'the impresario of Empire', its unashamed apologist in a key period of international realignment, even though his own imperial policy was – as much as Gladstone's – cautious, inconsistent and generally determined by proconsuls on the imperial frontier whose adventurous and expansionist policies he usually deplored.

What was vital, though, for the Conservative Party was the extent to which the last fifteen years of Disraeli's career provided a basis on which it could once again claim to be the Pittite party of Britain's empire, prestige and greatness, a claim from which it would never again readily retreat. Whatever the realities of actual policy, some part of Salisburyite Conservatism's Second Jubilee jingoism, Bonar Law's exploiting of the Loyalist card in the 1910s, Churchill's playing to the imperial gallery in the 1930s and 1940s, and Margaret Thatcher's 'Iron Lady' identity in the 1980s were all rooted in the character that Disraeli claimed for Conservatives in the vacuum following Palmerston's death. Such myths shaped future ideas of the historical reality, and in this case determined many thousands of Tories' own views of what their party most represented. Those historians who have written most persuasively of the 'invention of tradition' in the same Disraelian generation, but confined themselves to the monarchy and the institutions of the state, would have found much the same phenomenon in the world of party had they looked.

For those who wished for a shorthand definition of the whole of Disraelian Conservatism, he set it out at the Crystal Palace as three interlocking principles: the 'maintenance of the empire of England', the preservation of the national institutions, and 'the elevation of the condition of the people'. This doctrine was cited approvingly by all his successors, up to and including Margaret Thatcher and John Major, and when the Conservative Party briefly considered the introduction of a national membership system in the early 1950s, it was these three Disraelian concepts that would have been placed on the membership card as the party's own version of Labour's clause four, the definition of what Conservatism meant. There was more than a little fuzziness about detail here, and Disraeli himself damagingly conceded in 1873 that his party was not ready for an election because it did not yet have a policy, but for most observers (and apparently for many electors too) that crucial gap had been filled in 1872.

These developments certainly ended doubts about Disraeli's leadership. In Manchester Derby hailed him loyally as his 'chief'; Salisbury discontinued attacks in the *Quarterly Review* (though he was not yet ready to offer actual support), while Carnarvon, as Salisbury's contact man, actually opened negotiations for their joint return to the fold. There was just one crisis still to be surmounted before an election: Gladstone, unexpectedly defeated on his Irish university scheme by an opportunistic alliance of Conservatives and Catholics, promptly resigned in March 1873. Disraeli was determined not to spoil his party's chances by accepting minority

THE CONSERVATIVE PROGRAMME.

"DEPUTATION BELOW, SIR.—WANT TO KNOW THE CONSERVATIVE PROGRAMME."
Rt. Hon. Ben. Diz. "EH?—OH!—AH!—YES!—QUITE SO! TELL THEM, MY GOOD ABERCORN, WITH MY COMPLIMENTS, THAT WE PROPOSE TO RELY ON THE SUBLIME INSTINCTS OF AN ANCIENT PEOPLE!!"
[*See Speech at Crystal Palace.*]

Punch on Disraeli's speech at the Crystal Palace, 6 July 1872.

office and further humiliations like those endured in 1868, but he had some difficulty at first in persuading all his colleagues of the wisdom of this course, and there were even ideas floating around about forming a coalition with disaffected Whigs. Gradually, his advice and his tactical skills prevailed, the Conservatives held together, and in the end it was Gladstone who had to limp back into office as a discredited man and then to govern for a further ten months while the situation deteriorated.

The evidence from the constituencies and from by-elections convinced most Conservatives that they could win the coming election, though Gladstone's bold dissolution of the 1868 parliament in January 1874, with the promise to abolish income tax, soon threw them into disarray and revived the defeatism (and the terror of Gladstone) of 1868–9. Neither Disraeli nor the party's election managers now expected to achieve more than a rough equality with the Liberals in the Commons, and they were consequently greatly cheered when actual results began to show a much better position.

This time the party was far better prepared for the fight, for if the years since 1869 had necessarily been marked by caution and reserve in parliament, they had witnessed a tireless cultivation of the party organization, in which Disraeli's 1872 speeches had played their part. The first necessity was to bring together the several different structures that had coexisted uneasily in 1867–8. The National Union, so ineffective that only six delegates bothered to attend its second conference late in 1868, was the first to be pulled into line, with the appointment as its new secretary of John Gorst, who had just lost his own parliamentary seat, and who now merged it with the Metropolitan Conservatives. In recommending that he also be appointed as Principal Agent to the party, the Chief Whip identified for Disraeli Gorst's three necessary qualifications: his gentlemanly status and manners (he remained unpaid), his legal training and his energy – a judgement which says much about the nature of the organization at that time. In 1870 Gorst moved the party's offices away from their old home in a solicitor's office and set up a new Central Office, to which the county organizers also moved soon afterwards, thus bringing all the organizing agencies together. Gorst got on well enough with the party leaders in parliament and with the county organizers and provided a personal link between the National Union and the party professionals. Although the National Union gradually became stronger, until it could bring together the mass meeting that Disraeli addressed in 1872 it was thought of mainly as a coordinating talking shop, and the professional managers took care to keep control of all financial matters, but it could still be useful in propaganda work and in convincing the local activists that they had a voice at the centre, a theme on which Lord George Hamilton spoke warmly at the fifth conference, held in Bristol in 1871 – perhaps the first to be a real success but also the first to be well attended by the party's social elite.

Gorst's real contribution, though, was that he set out to make a systematic attack on the boroughs, always the poor relation of Conservative activity before 1868 but the area in which most of the gains would have to be made if power was to be won. He now dealt with candidates in a more serious manner, keeping as before a central list of available men, but urging the constituencies themselves to be more active in finding suitable local candidates, striving to achieve a better match than in the past between candidate and vacancy, and getting work started well before an election was due. Detailed work over years in the annual revision courts could only be achieved at the local level, though this could have more effect than any methods of persuasion of voters already on the list; the Chief Whip had indeed told Disraeli in 1868 that once the registers were complete, 'we shall then be able to calculate with some accuracy what the result of the General Election will be', an exaggeration no doubt, but an observation containing an essential truth about late-Victorian politics all the same. If revision work could be exaggerated in its value, the fact that it was being pursued so actively did nevertheless demonstrate the vitality of the local bodies that launched these annual efforts, provided canvassing manpower, and mainly paid for the whole thing. It was only the response of such bodies in the bigger cities that enabled the party under Gorst's encouragement also to begin fighting local elections, valuable as training for parliamentary contests and for keeping the machine in annual trim. This new attitude to local organization gradually generated a new breed of agents, of whom W. H. Smith's Middlesex agent Wollaston Pym and the Exeter agent Joseph Gould were early examples, men who now did the job less as a profitable sideline attached to a legal practice than as a specialist profession in its own right.

Under Gorst's lead the party also took its first halting steps in serious management of the press. A press agency was purchased and used to circulate to supportive papers in the regions copies of speeches, reports of meetings and parliamentary sketches promoting the party's viewpoint. A similar cooperative effort and investment ensured that the London *Evening Standard* became a reliable daily supporter at the cheaper end of the market, and the *Morning Post* among what would later be called the quality papers, though neither could yet match the service given to the Liberals by the *Globe* and *The Times* respectively.

Gorst also unwittingly created another and less desirable precedent, for his later career was a considerable disappointment to him, producing only a long-term lack of preferment, increasing disillusion and eventual desertion of the party altogether. He was thus the first ambitious politician to devote his youthful energies to the party's organization in the hope that it would be an escalator to the top, and the first to find that the Conservatives were rarely grateful for such efforts, as Arthur Steel-Maitland in the 1910s, Lord Hailsham in the 1950s and Edward du Cann in the 1960s would all find out to their cost.

Gorst complacently noted after the election that active Conservative associations had been at work in sixty-five of the seventy-four constituencies that changed hands. It would be misleading, though, to suggest that organization was the basis of the 1874 victory, and Disraeli himself responded to his majority with the remark that 'no party organization could have caused this result', but it would also be foolish to underestimate it as a sign of the party's growing vitality and as a contributor to victory when it came. If the party's strategy and perceived identity were more important than routine organizational work like electoral registration, then it nevertheless relied on management of the press, leafleting and such party handbooks as *Hints for Candidates* to put its message across and to make sure that the party spoke with broadly the same voice throughout the whole country – as it had never done before. If the chief vehicle for the swing of about 7 per cent from Liberal to Conservative was middle-class resistance to Liberal reforms, then this was achieved at least in part because, as a Liberal despairingly put it, such voters 'read their *Standard* and believe the country will do well as it is'.

One small bonus in the 1874 results was in Scotland, where the disaster of 1868 was unexpectedly redeemed, and Conservatives again won a third of the seats. Ireland was again a bleak picture, with the party's share falling from forty MPs to thirty-three, and with now hardly a constituency outside Ulster and the Dublin area returning a Conservative, but this was to an extent offset by the fact that the Liberals suffered an even worse fate, being virtually wiped out in Ireland by the rising Home Rule Party. If that posed a major constitutional problem for the period ahead, and would unleash unprecedented parliamentary obstruction even in the 1874 parliament, it was also evidence of the complete failure of Gladstone's policy of conciliating Ireland through concessionary reform, a lesson from which Conservatives drew the moral that tougher resistance would have to be mounted if the Union were to be saved.

The 1874 results that really mattered were once again in England, where the Conservatives gained sixty-eight seats overall, fifty of them in the boroughs, to give Disraeli an overall Commons majority of about fifty and easily the best party showing since 1841: the veteran Duke of Richmond dazedly noted that he found himself for the first time in his long political life in a *majority* in the country. In part this reflected a further consolidation of support in Tory Lancashire, and another significant advance around London: Middlesex was now Conservative by a vote of over 70 per cent; three of the four seats were captured this time in the City; and seats were won in Chelsea, Marylebone, Greenwich, Southwark and Tower Hamlets. But if the Home Counties were now almost a Liberal-free zone, borough seats fell all over England in such different places as Kidderminster, Lymington, Oldham and Brighton. The trend noticed in 1868 had thus gathered head and delivered to Disraeli a great number of middle-class voters who were no longer sure that they wanted to be on the side of reform, as their own prosperity grew and as they perceived Liberalism more as a threat to their status than as a vehicle for their advancement. This tendency – especially when combined with the working-class voters whose own turn to the Conservatives owed more to the offer of an active social policy – would give Disraeli a difficult set of expectations to meet in office, but the very fact of a majority after years in the wilderness naturally attracted more attention than its perils did at the time.

In constructing a ministry for this purpose, Disraeli was anxious to respond to all such issues. Some posts could be filled merely by returning ministers to their posts of 1868 – for example, by sending Derby back to the Foreign Office – but Disraeli also hoped to bind up old wounds and, by incorporating some new blood, thereby recognize the forces that had swept him back to power. The key figure was Salisbury, who had brooded darkly away from the Treasury bench for seven years, but who after the party's 1874 triumph could no longer maintain his conviction that 1867 had been a tactical mistake for Conservatives as well as an unforgivable surrender of principle. Bringing him back proved a tricky business, for he and Disraeli had scarcely been on speaking terms for years, but Salisbury did not want to spend the rest of his public life without serious employment and had to swallow his pride and come in. He was returned to the India Office from which he had resigned in 1867, and his acolyte Carnarvon also returned to home base as Colonial Secretary. This was a vital moment in Conservative history, for it returned a future leader to the inside track, and even chastened him a little in the process.

More newsworthy at the time even than Salisbury's return was the symbolic offer of the Home Office to Richard Cross, a Lancastrian follower of Derby who was thought of as a middle-class representative in the Cabinet. At first he was the only one, though both Smith and Sandon (the latter scarcely 'middle class', but a man with a base in Liverpool and

PARADISE AND THE PERI.

"JOY, JOY FOR EVER! MY TASK IS DONE—
THE GATES ARE PASSED, AND HEAVEN IS WON!"
Lalla Rookh.

Punch on Disraeli's eventual return as majority Prime Minister, 28 February 1874.

an interest in social issues) also got there in 1877–8, when Sandon apparently greeted his new colleagues with the observation that it was all very fitting, for they were 'the people in fact who brought the Gov[ernmen]t into power'. This promotion of men of a non-landowning background was by most contemporary judgements a bold gesture on Disraeli's part, and when Smith attained the Admiralty he became the first Conservative Cabinet minister ever with personal experience in trade. Lord Randolph Churchill wickedly dubbed Smith and Cross 'Marshall and Snelgrove' (after the popular department store), while in HMS Pinafore (1877) W. S. Gilbert satirized Smith for having become 'ruler of the Queen's Navee' by keeping 'close to [his] desk, and never go[ing] to sea', and even Disraeli recognized the point by calling his colleague 'Pinafore Smith'.

Nevertheless, despite these symbolic appointments, the more overriding pattern in Disraeli's appointments was his exaggerated respect for aristocracy – though in deference to his own Jewish ancestry he tended to behave as if the D'Israeli blood was bluer even than that of the various dukes that he brought into office. He refused at first to have a single borough member at his Cabinet table, and over the years ahead he did very little indeed to give the new Lancashire and Metropolitan MPs the idea that they were regarded as equal partners in the governing party with the gentlemen who otherwise still packed the back benches. By comparison, he insisted that half his Cabinet be peers, and in 1878 he reacted to the promotion to Cabinet of Sir Michael Hicks-Beach by adding the inadequate (but feudally territorial) Duke of Northumberland, purely to even up the score.

If, as Disraeli's first biographer felt in 1888, all this meant that Disraeli had not grasped the scale of the social and political changes that he himself had lived through and helped to bring about, then this was hardly surprising. Disraeli was hardly alone among politicians in remaining attached to the ideas of his early manhood. He was at least luckier than Peel had been in that his slowness to adapt to new conditions did not bring him into conflict with the majority of his supporters, for on such social issues it is clear that most Tory MPs were still on the side of the aristocrats, and did not in the least resent in Disraeli his 'romantic penchant for the noble houses' of which Robert Blake has written.

For the future of the party, the key consequence of the promotion of Cross was that it denied the Home Office to Gathorne Hardy, who was shunted instead into the siding of the War Office (for which he was not well suited anyway), while Northcote got the Exchequer; in due course, when Disraeli went to the Lords, this left Northcote in pole position to lead in the Commons and then to emerge as the next Party Leader when he retired. However, though Northcote proved a capable Chancellor, he would also prove to have few of the talents needed for leadership, and especially to lack the power to inspire his followers which the more combative Hardy would probably have shown. Initially in 1874 a competent hand on the tiller and a policy of no excitement was just what the government planned in any case, so it is not surprising that Northcote was among its early successes, challenging comparison with Gladstone and even on occasion worsting him in debate. The 1874 session, abbreviated to under a hundred days by the January election and the business of getting the government into shape, was mainly uneventful and this was unlikely to cause complaint among the Tory MPs who had been regularly critical of the restlessness of Gladstone in office. Cross was also successful in showing his mettle over factory legislation, giving immediate evidence of his wish to satisfy the customers with a reduction of the permitted working hours of women and children, and surprising the radicals with his continuing readiness to steal their political clothes. Disraeli was far less wise to take over a plan by the Church of England to legislate for the putting down of ritualistic practices, a matter that was more contentious within his party than outside and which needlessly stirred up the last few weeks of the sitting in July and August. With the rising of parliament on 7 August, ministers resumed for the rest of the year the peaceful running of their departments.

There was, though, a fundamental strategic issue that the government had not yet faced up to, but which would have to be settled for 1875 and 1876. On the one hand the flood of middle-class voters who had come over to the Conservatives had done so in the expectation that they would put a brake on the legislative wheel of reform, and so restore 'Palmerstonian' quiet to domestic affairs after nine years of strenuous activity, while on the other hand there were working-class voters whose support had been conditional on a new programme of reforms. In Irish matters at least, Disraeli was determined on a policy of quiet, even to the extent that his Irish Secretary was not included in the Cabinet; in 1874 he refused even to visit Ireland, and though this was not perhaps the best response to the election results there, it did produce a short period of calm in which even the Coercion Acts did not need to be renewed, until further agricultural depression launched another period both of misery and of political violence at the end of the 1870s.

More broadly, though no Cabinet debate was ever conducted in such crude terms, it seems likely that ministers resolved their strategic problem by agreeing to social reforms in the first half of the government's life and then rather gratefully reached the conclusion that they had done enough. The fact that these reforms could then be used for generations to come as evidence that the party was still true to the legacy of Oastler and of Shaftesbury, and was deeply concerned about 'the condition of the people', says a great deal about the paucity of the competition in such policy areas from the Liberals, as do the unsolicited tributes to Disraeli's ministers from the TUC, from radical Liberal and Lib-Lab MPs, from trades unionists and even from Joseph Chamberlain, then just beginning his career as a reforming Liberal mayor of Birmingham. Such remarks as those from Chamberlain (who explained in 1875 that the Artisans' Dwelling Act had 'done more for the town of Birmingham than had been done in twenty preceding years of Liberal legislation') were pure electoral gold-dust, and were endlessly anthologized, quoted and referred back to by Conservatives in 1880 and for many years thereafter. As Richard Shannon has observed, 'never did a political party make, unwittingly, a more profitable investment in the future in half a dozen items of low-key legislation'.

Cross later recalled that he had been disappointed in 1874 to find that Disraeli had come into office with no practical ideas about social reform, though since he had been party to the discussions of 1873–4 it is hard to see how he could not have foreseen this, and Disraeli's choice of Cross himself for the Home Office and his steady support for Cross's plans during 1874–6 were the most that might reasonably have been expected. For the future, Disraeli might well bemoan the sheer tedium of such domestic legislation and the hours that he had to spend in the Commons in helping to get it through, but he did put in those hours, and he was also willing to use such opportunities as a speech at London's Guildhall in 1875 to explain to Conservative working men that their interests had not been forgotten and that relief was on the way.

What that relief was would depend more on Cross than on Disraeli, though, and he naturally drew on his own experience, on discussions conducted in opposition, and on his officials' advice. When Cross introduced the centrepiece of his 1875 programme, the Artisans' and Labourers' Dwellings Improvement Bill, he was anxious not to raise expectations too high (or indeed to offend those who did not want such schemes at all), urging the House 'not to imagine we are doing a magnificent and showy work'. The bill was a step on the road towards town planning and slum clearance, and as a precedent it was of the first importance, but its own provisions were limited in the extreme; town councils were given some powers to redevelop areas in order to improve conditions and to root out insanitary plague-spots, but the whole thing was permissive rather than mandatory, compensation levels were low (which guaranteed poor cooperation from existing owners, and limited aspirations from the councillors, who were mainly owners of property), and councils would anyway have to find the resources locally. In the hands of a Chamberlain, or of go-ahead councils in some parts of London, much could be done under the 1875 act, but elsewhere its impact was negligible. A Public Health Act was perhaps more successful, in that it was even less ambitious, pulling together and codifying years of legislation and thus providing a new statutory framework that would last for half a century – but at no cost at all.

Cross's other main thrust of policy was in trades union law, once again a reform with no financial implications – at least for government. The tangle of legal complexities left behind by Gladstone was stripped away, and to their astonishment the trades unions got almost exactly what they had asked for in the Employer and Workmen Act (which reformed and updated the main principles of employment law) and in the Conspiracy and Protection of Property Act (which legalized peaceful picketing, established the unions' immunities at law, and authorized the legal holding of union funds). There is no doubt that these were triumphs for Cross, who had taken a bold line, found that he had substantial press support, and bounced his measures through both the Cabinet and parliament. If Disraeli's claim that the legislation would 'gain and return for the Tories the lasting affection of the working classes' was pure fantasy, then it was at least supported by warm praise for the government from trades unionists themselves.

The 1876 reforms were already more timid and more reactive than those of 1875, and much time was taken up with responding to a backbencher's pressure to introduce safer practices in merchant shipping, for which the government in the end could claim only limited credit. The enthusiasm of the backbenchers was not all it might have been either, especially when votes coincided with race weeks at Ascot or Goodwood – still 'perilous' times for the lobbies (as a whip put it). Educational reforms were pressed through, retaining and reinforcing what was for Conservatives the key element of the 1870 Education Act, the provision of local tax support for Church schools, by making attendance virtually compulsory, and so filling empty places in voluntary schools with funded pupils. And, although there were efforts to push through improvements in later years – such as those made by Lord George Hamilton when entrusted with education after 1878 – in 1876 the programme of social reform effectively came to an end.

The petering-out of a programme so widely acknowledged to have been needed to reward recently converted Conservative voters is not easy to explain, and the lack of any such measures in the run-up to the election of 1880 was certainly unwise. Increased involvement in foreign policy crises and Irish obstructionism in the Commons certainly did not help, and the government might be forgiven for scaling down its legislative programme as a result, but then no major bills were lost through this filibustering process in any case. Disraeli's support was more fitful after 1876, but Cross and his colleagues do not seem to have had much left to propose, and they certainly did not put forward bills that were rejected in Cabinet for lack of prime ministerial backing. The truth seems to be that after 1876 the unambitious Disraelian agenda was complete, and the party simply had nothing much left to suggest when its own innate conservatism became more pronounced.

The increasing lack of direction on the home front was a testament above all to the failing grasp of Disraeli himself, never expected to last for long on health grounds after returning to the premiership and widely noted to be losing energy, seeming half-asleep at times and having to make great efforts by 1876 even to speak in Cabinet. By the summer of 1876 the problem could not be staved off for much longer, and in July Disraeli himself offered to the Cabinet the same choice offered to him by his doctors, which was between total retirement and his withdrawal to a quieter life in the Lords. Despite the queen's reluctance to lose even a part of Disraeli's leadership, there was no serious bid by Derby or Salisbury to take on the premiership (though neither commanded universal support anyway), and Disraeli therefore took the title of Earl of Beaconsfield and retired to the Lords, while Northcote duly took over the leadership of the party in the Commons that had been Disraeli's for twenty-nine years.

There seemed no reason to see this as denoting any great turning point, for the retirement of Gladstone had left the Liberals rudderless in the Commons as well – and Northcote was by no means undercast against the current Liberal Leader, the pedestrian Marquess of Hartington – while the Disraeli government's excellent start gave hope of a successful further period in office before another election need be fought. The summer of 1876 was, though, the beginning of a new era in British politics, when Gladstone swept himself back into contention by his Bulgarian and then his Midlothian campaigns, subsequently hurling onto the political agenda of the 1880s the even more dangerous issues of Irish independence. With the Disraelian agenda played out, the Conservatives would need to develop a new leadership, new allies and the new identity of 'Unionism' in order to deal with these threats. All the same, Disraeli's speeches of 1872 and the legislation of 1875–6 were a lasting bequest to British Conservatism, creating only a myth of a 'Tory Democracy' policy and an illusion of actual social reform, but these were myths that would inspire the generations to come more powerfully than most of the party's more concrete achievements had ever done. Few realities matter more in politics than the myths that a party can plausibly use to describe itself and what it stands for – providing of course that it really believes what it is saying. After Disraeli's 'Indian Summer', most conservatives *did* believe in their party's record in domestic policy.

6

Salisbury and Unionism, 1876–86

THE DECADE that followed Disraeli's retreat to the House of Lords as Earl of Beaconsfield was, in the Conservative Party, stormy, characterized by the increasing primacy of foreign, Irish and imperial issues, on which Conservatives at first spoke with an uncertain voice. This, together with the second and third comings of Gladstone in 1876 and 1879–80, produced a crushing and unexpected Conservative defeat in 1880, after which further internal party wrangling and an undeclared war for the succession following Disraeli's death in 1881 led to a further extension of the franchise by the Liberals in 1884 and a second successive Conservative defeat in 1885. That new franchise and the revised constituency boundaries that came with it, the gradual rise of Irish issues to the top of the political agenda in the 1880s, and the consequential attachment of many former Liberals to the Conservatives, were, however, the triple foundations on which Salisbury was able to achieve power again for the Conservatives in 1886, ushering in a fundamental political realignment to the Conservatives' advantage, and two decades of Tory dominance.

Between the end of the 1876 session and early 1878, and despite serious disagreements within his government and a violent attack on it by Gladstone from the outside, Beaconsfield managed to hold at bay a dangerous foreign situation, and then to crown it with a major diplomatic triumph. Derby was proving a vacillating Foreign Secretary who was in any case increasingly out of step with colleagues on other issues too, and palpably waiting for some event such as Beaconsfield's retirement to give him the chance to leave the Conservative government. This situation even increased Beaconsfield's reluctance to insist on his viewpoint, lest it give Derby the chance to resign on a clear issue of principle; looking back in

1880, he caustically remarked that 'why Lord Derby resigned [in 1878] is obvious enough. Why he did not resign before is the only problem that requires solution. I suppose it was too great an effort ever to form a decision which would relieve him from the necessity of deciding anything again.'

Derby's reluctance to take action in the Near East led him into conflict with Beaconsfield (whose interventions were sometimes bold, as over the audacious purchase for Britain of an additional block of shares in the Suez Canal Company, but rarely following a consistent line of policy) and with Salisbury (who had an overlapping responsibility for the Near East as Secretary for India, saw himself as a foreign policy expert anyway, and was itching to introduce some 'system' into British policy). Derby would do nothing to risk war with Russia, but while neither of Derby's critics within the Cabinet wanted a war, neither would be prepared to expose himself to a charge of weakness by running away from one either.

British policy had traditionally been linked to the defence of Turkey in order to resist Russian expansion towards the Mediterranean and the shortest route to British India, and the Crimean War of 1854–5 had been fought and won mainly for that purpose, but the increasing enfeeblement of Turkey at a time when the Tsar of Russia had good relations with his fellow emperors in Germany and Austria now put this policy under considerable strain.

The issue erupted into domestic politics when, in 1876, Turkish irregular soldiers massacred many thousands of Bulgarian Christians, whose nationalist aspirations posed a threat to continuing Turkish authority in the Balkans. At first the British government assumed that stories of massacres had been exaggerated (as local, pro-Turkish British diplomats assured them), and Beaconsfield dismissed rumours of massacres as 'coffee-house babble', but there then followed real panic when the truth became known and Gladstone came out of retirement to launch a moral crusade of outrage against the 'atrocities' committed by Turkey – and apparently condoned by British ministers. Assailed by this 'cyclone', the Conservatives managed almost to lose Beaconsfield's own safe seat in Buckinghamshire at the by-election that followed his elevation to the Lords. As in earlier debates following the suppression of the Indian Mutiny in 1857, and the putting-down of a rising in Jamaica in 1865, the Bulgarian debates of 1876 forced thinking men to decide between national self-interest and international morality. In the long run these debates probably hardened up the party of self-interest, and so paved the way for Unionism and for the next wave of British imperialism, in which some Liberals and most Conservatives found unsuspected areas of agreement. In the short term, though, the reappearance of Gladstone mainly rallied the parties along existing lines of loyalty, but at the same time detached from the Conservative side a number of its more religious-minded backers, and especially those high churchmen who had neither forgiven nor forgotten Disraeli's 1874 attack on ritualism.

It was possible, then, to survive 1876 mainly on the loyalty of Conservatives to a party under attack by the man that they most hated and feared – hence Beaconsfield's famous advice to a Tory waverer, 'Damn your principles. Stick to your party' – but this did not in itself provide the government with a policy. During 1877 the steam went out of Gladstone's campaign 'out of doors', while the government sought first to persuade Turkey to make appropriately apologetic and reforming gestures, so as to deprive Russia of an excuse for war, and then, when war came anyway, struggled to decide what Britain ought to do if Russia were to win.

These tangled debates led to the resignation first of Carnarvon in February 1878 and then in April of Derby too. But the main consequence of this was that Salisbury (who had already taken the lead in Near Eastern policy when sent to Constantinople to represent the government) now became Foreign Secretary and at last imposed a firm hand on British diplomacy. By then British 'jingoist' feeling against Russia among the population at large was almost out of hand (the very word 'jingoism' deriving from a music-hall song of 1878), and the prospect of Britain herself going to war seemed increasingly unavoidable.

The final act in the drama came when Salisbury and Beaconsfield went together to a congress at Berlin, called by Germany to enable the other powers to limit Russia's worrying advances at Turkey's expense. They revealed when they got there that Britain had now extracted from Turkey an acceptable reform programme which would be backed by a British alliance (for which Turkey had to surrender Cyprus to Britain), and the other powers had little option but to found their discussions on these new premises. The British negotiators therefore returned home in July 1878 proclaiming not only 'peace with honour', but also a great victory for Britain and the addition to the empire of a valuable base along the route to the empire. They were met with garlands of flowers at Charing Cross Station, and subsequently honoured in July and August with a banquet given by Conservatives in both Houses and a deputation of a thousand supporters from Conservative organizations out in the country.

Beaconsfield (who, Salisbury said, must now calm the jingoes 'in their own language ... [for] he is the only one among us who speaks it fluently') produced patriotic pride fit for these occasions, though Salisbury too urged the London crowds 'always to support a government which supports the honour of England'.

That last sally was a hit at Gladstone, who had denounced the granting of the title of Empress of India to Queen Victoria as distinctly unEnglish, and had recently gone on to accuse Beaconsfield of harbouring a Napoleonic – or at least Cromwellian – ambition to subvert English liberties through his ready use of the military as a support for his diplomacy. For his colleagues, the idea that the ailing and easily tired Beaconsfield was a dictatorial chief and a danger to anyone at all seemed laughable in the extreme, for in their view the real problem now was just the opposite – the lack of any real drive at the heart of the Cabinet. In their next two years in office, though, the Conservatives did not blench at the further use of British troops, and wars in Zululand and in Afghanistan, if started by expansionists on the frontiers, did nevertheless have considerable encouragement from London. The problem was that in both wars the early campaigns went badly and each produced in 1879 significant military disasters which cost the lives of many British soldiers. Both wars were won in the end, though at an even greater cost to the Treasury than Abyssinia in 1868, which in economically depressed times involved a recourse to tax increases as well as borrowing, and in any case the earlier defeats were not easily forgotten. At the 1880 election it was commonplace for Liberal candidates to denounce the cost of 'unnecessary' Conservative wars, thus taking the gilt off the almost costless diplomatic triumph of 1878; a popular Liberal poster depicted a British soldier being flogged by a Zulu, which directly undercut the Conservatives' Palmerstonian appeal to the patriotic voter. Not until Gladstone's apparent capitulation to Irish terrorists in 1882 and the death of General Gordon in the Sudan in 1885 would the Conservatives be able to seize back the patriotic card as their own. For the moment, even the propagandist activities of the 'Patriotic Association', founded in 1878 for 'the defence of the honour and interests of England, and the maintenance intact of the British Empire', could score few points in the party's favour, though such bodies would soon come into their own.

The victory at Berlin and the heroes' reception that followed seemed later to have been a missed opportunity to dissolve the 1874 parliament and secure a fresh term of office, but although it is clear with hindsight that Beaconsfield was not to have a better chance, it also seems likely that he would have won at best a bare majority had he taken such a gamble in 1878, so far were the forces that destroyed his majority in 1880 already at work. In Ireland these problems were both economic and political, but the main effect that Irish issues had elsewhere was the extent to which increasing obstructionism by Irish MPs in the Commons made the government – and especially Northcote as Leader of the House – seem impotent and ineffective.

In Britain, though, the issues were predominantly economic, for almost since its arrival in office in 1874 the Conservative government had had to face a worldwide collapse of food prices which had created a deep and seemingly intractable agrarian depression at home. Since this 'Great Depression' was an imported one – it arose more from the opening up of mass production in the western hemisphere's plains and prairies and from the introduction of modern transportation through railways, steamships and refrigeration, than from such traditional sources as poor harvests – there was little received wisdom about the course which a government should pursue, and no foreknowledge of the scale of the problem. Only in 1877–8, when the continuation of low prices for a third and fourth successive year underlined the impression that something quite unusual was taking place, did the Beaconsfield government begin to stir into action, and even then it was slow and ineffective. A bold plan from the Prime Minister to launch a massive voluntary relief programme with the royal family and the Cabinet at the head of the list of subscribers was welcomed by Salisbury and Cairns, but argued into the sands by Northcote, worried about setting such a precedent and by the danger that, if the government once accepted the responsibility, then when voluntary relief ran out there might have to be recourse to the taxpayer for further resources. An opportunity to take a moral lead and to deal with at least some of the symptoms of recession was thus lost, and the government stumbled towards the end of its life offering little to the rural areas on which it so depended for votes, except the bleak advice of the classical economist that wage reductions would eventually restore stability and equilibrium, and that no governmental action was either desirable or likely to be effective.

There was, though a secondary danger lurking behind this decision not to act: after years of prosperity, the depression of the 1870s reawakened many of the fears and hopes of the 1840s, and reintroduced the ghost of tariffs into Conservative politics. The demand that something must be done about rural distress was constantly around from about 1877, but there were also a few Conservatives by then prepared to say that protection had held distress at bay before 1846 and could do so again. Though when visiting Manchester's Free Trade Hall in 1872 he had cynically wondered how long it would be before its rafters rang with calls for tariffs, Beaconsfield now heard such mutterings with absolute horror, for a renewed party debate on protection would split Conservatism wide open and link the party once again with a vanished world of landowner privilege. In a word, it could destroy all that his mature political career had achieved in educating his party, for as he sagely told a deputation in 1878, 'in this country the interest of the consumer is stronger than the interest of the producer'. Protectionist feeling was therefore marginalized in the party by the refusal of front-benchers to have anything to do with its expression. Here again, protectionism's time would come soon, at least in the form of growing demands for 'fair trade' or reciprocity – the reintroduction of British tariffs against countries that imposed import duties on British products (which meant in practice almost everywhere).

In 1879–80 the government faced a further onslaught from Gladstone, whose two Midlothian campaigns attempted to rekindle the moral fervour of 1876 and who poured out remorseless invective against the government in general and 'Beaconsfieldism' in particular. Such efforts helped considerably to galvanize the Liberals for the coming election, though support was also liberally gathered in by the profusion of the promises which Gladstone and his supporters made to the various interest groups within the Liberal alliance. The Conservative leaders were not slow to follow the Liberals out into the provinces, and in the autumn of 1879 they too were stumping the country. The government's slackening central direction was indicated, though, by the uncertainty with which it approached even the setting of a date for the contest, and it allowed itself in the end to run on into its seventh year, and to hold a short pre-election 1880 session in which there was little business except an inescapable tax increase from Northcote, which was hardly the best start for any campaign.

This hesitation did not, however, reflect worries about the party's performance, for by-elections had gone better under Beaconsfield than for any full-term government in the last third of the century, with fifteen lost seats offset by ten Conservative gains. In the final months a near-win in Sheffield (a traditional radical stronghold from which little had been hoped, though this proved a poor pointer, for Sheffield was actually now swinging hard in the Conservative direction), together with good results in Liverpool and Southwark, seemed to promise a fair chance in the appeal to the people. When parliament was eventually dissolved in March 1880, the party managers had high hopes for the outcome, though there was some illogicality in this for – as Monty Corry kept pointing out – almost everyone expected seats to be lost outside England and it was hard to see where English seats might be gained to compensate for this.

The party organization itself had been neglected after the 1874 victory – but what winning party has not done this, at least to some extent? In the general management of the party, the whips had continued to direct patronage and nominations for honours towards their traditional county clients and mainly ignored their recent conquests in the boroughs, a subject on which Gorst waxed increasingly bitter. The party as a whole had probably not kept up with the continuing increase and movement of the electorate, but nor had it fallen away absolutely to its 1868 level, as some later claimed. At the top, the organization had come under the control of one of the worst appointees that the party has ever made, when the rather hopeless Scottish landowner W. B. Skene replaced the disillusioned Gorst as Principal Agent in 1877, but there is really no reason to suppose that this had yet had a very marked effect lower down – certainly not on the scale that Gorst himself was later to claim. What was very clear, though, was that the Liberals had reacted to defeat in 1874 much as the Conservatives had in 1868, by putting in a large effort to tighten up their own machinery, and their city caucuses in particular, and to that extent at least the Conservatives were relatively less well-placed in 1880 than they had been in 1874; this was a caucus-race that the Liberals would win and the Conservatives lose.

When the campaign began it was also clear that there was a gap of a quite different type between the parties, for Gladstone continued both his relentless campaigning, with its combination of a high moral tone and a package of policies aimed at pulling in the vote, while Beaconsfield chose an eccentric policy line and then did not press it very hard. The document that was effectively the Conservative manifesto was a letter from Beaconsfield to the Irish Lord Lieutenant, the Duke of Marlborough: it had to be issued in that form, since as a peer the Prime Minister no longer had electors of his own to 'address'. This ignored most of what the real campaign would be about (which was trade and agrarian depression, proposed Liberal reforms, recent wars and their cost) and concentrated instead on a powerful defence of the Irish Union, an issue that he had previously tried to keep out of politics altogether and on which he had taken no steps to prepare either his followers or opinion generally. As a prediction of the key issue of the near future, this was masterly, but as a contribution to the 1880 campaign it was completely off-message.

Outside England the Conservatives lost support, as had been feared, but on an unanticipated scale. Scotland, Ireland and Wales elected only thirty-five Conservatives, compared with the sixty-four of 1874 (and fifty-six even in 1868), and this in itself virtually guaranteed the loss of office. In England the story was not quite so bad but the swing to the Liberals was nevertheless very marked. Some of the advances of 1868 and 1874 were retained both in London and in Lancashire (despite Lord Derby's now coming out openly for the Liberals), but even in these areas there were losses too, and this time not only in the boroughs. In the wake of agricultural depression the party lost twenty-nine seats in the English counties and many country towns followed the trend. Overall, there would now be just 238 Conservatives facing 354 Liberals and sixty Irish Home Rulers, a shattering defeat by any standard and harder to bear when it had been so very unexpected. With hindsight, and with the experience of canvassing fresh in their minds, the Conservatives mainly attributed their discomfiture to economic factors: Beaconsfield told Salisbury that 'Hard Times' had been 'our foe and certainly the alleged cause of our fall', while Salisbury himself reflected philosophically that 'bad harvests & bad trade have done the most. I suppose a sick man may change his doctor, though the doctor may not be at fault.' Both Salisbury and Beaconsfield did, though, draw an important moral for the future too, which was that Gladstone's rampant Liberal majority could only now be restrained by the House of Lords, which must therefore be managed with exceptional care. This would prove to be Salisbury's real opportunity to come to the fore.

Defeat naturally involved a search for scapegoats. Some county MPs lamented the time wasted on seeking to woo the borough electorate with Cross's 1875 reforms, while a larger and more vocal cross-section of borough Conservatives attributed the disaster to the old guard of gentlemen who had failed to understand the vitality of political and social change in the party. For this last group, what was needed was a strong dose of 'Tory Democracy', and the giving of more influence to the lower ranks with more representational structures to provide guarantees. They received support and reinforcement in their arguments from Gorst, now rapidly returned to the post of Principal Agent as a reflex action after the party's defeat, and immediately taking up the cudgels where he had laid them down in 1877, battling against the whips and the 'old gang', who seemed to him to be rooted in the past. There was, then, a real fight for the future identity of the party in the years after 1880.

There were few who sought to hasten Beaconsfield's departure, not least because he alone seemed capable of holding things together and producing at least a chance of a victory like 1874, but the diminished authority that he enjoyed when no longer Prime Minister, together with his failing health, meant that in his last year he was a hands-off leader, and Conservatives began to prepare for what would happen when he retired or died, as soon he must. In the Lords, Beaconsfield continued to lead until he died on 19 April 1881, but effective day-to-day authority had moved to Salisbury, who therefore effortlessly became Leader in the Lords when Beaconsfield died.

In the Commons, Northcote continued to lead the Conservative MPs, as he had done since 1876, but made very heavy weather of it indeed; soon after the 1880 election he faced a devastating attack from the 'Fourth Party', a ginger group of just four MPs who devoted themselves to exposing his shortcomings, to humiliating him on every possible occasion, and in general to establishing the priority of Salisbury's claim over Northcote's when the party should resume office. Gorst's participation in this activity was the most resented (for as Principal Agent he was also responsible for the party machine and needed to keep on good terms with Northcote if undue friction was to be avoided); the young Arthur Balfour provided a link with his uncle Salisbury but soon detached himself from the group's activities anyway; Sir Henry Drummond Wolff provided some of the most imaginative grounds for embarrassing Northcote, but was really no more than a political lightweight. The real leader of the group was the brilliant, erratic, ambitious and utterly self-centred Lord Randolph Churchill.

Lord Randolph was intent on using the Fourth Party to destroy Northcote, so that he could lead in the Commons under Salisbury in the Lords, and he used every weapon that came to hand in order to advance that purpose, building bridges to the Tory Democrats in the party machine by using his own superb talent as a platform speaker to enthuse the provincial Conservatives. Where Northcote seemed dull, bureaucratic and pedestrian, Churchill was witty, rude and to the point, and in the early debates of 1880–81 Churchill and his friends used any issue that they could find in order to bring out that comparison in debate. Unfortunately for Churchill, once he had downed Northcote, he would come up against an even more ruthless rival in Salisbury, who would show from 1884 to 1887 the better judgement of the two, and who would eventually destroy

Churchill altogether, thereby establishing on secure foundations his own leadership of the party as a whole.

These personal battles disguised the fact that, at heart, the party had two available strategies to pursue after 1880, each of them relying on the known fact that Gladstone's own radicalism – reinforced by the input of such younger men as Joseph Chamberlain and by the radicalizing effect on them of Parnell's Irish MPs and their demands for Home Rule for Ireland – was loosening the bonds that tied to Liberalism the more traditionalist Whigs (and even some moderate Liberals who had never called themselves Whigs). Even in the 1860s it had been foreseen that a realignment might take place, by which these moderates would cross over to join the Conservatives and so create a conservative coalition with a much increased chance of controlling the Commons. Northcote, an instinctive consensual centrist, was always aware of such a strategy option and anxious at least to do nothing that would upset potential allies; his strategy seemed to receive reinforcement when such powerful Whigs as the Marquess of Lansdowne and the Duke of Argyll resigned from the Gladstone government in 1880–81, from a conviction that it was reforming too far and too fast. But the attempt to recruit such people involved a compromise of Conservatism's own traditions and identity, and it would certainly involve sacrificing the posts of potential Conservative ministers in any joint government, even perhaps the acceptance of a Whig prime minister such as Lord Hartington, and this would be hard medicine for the party to swallow. The alternative approach, always favoured by Disraeli, and also now by Salisbury and by Churchill (though at least partly because they did not believe that the Whigs could ever be relied on to act – the party had after all been waiting for them for over a decade by this time), was to rely only on Conservatives, especially those in the Lords, which would actually sharpen up the party battle-lines and so make any defectors come over on Tory terms. This strategic choice, not at all unlike the one that the Conservatives had to make again in connection with a declining Liberal Party in both the 1920s and the 1940s, lay behind most of the policy debates and the personal struggles of the 1880s.

In his final year Beaconsfield argued for a policy reminiscent of 1869, supporting the new government with the exception only of its 'violent proposals', though since carrying out such a tactic largely fell to Northcote in the Commons, already thought to be the very embodiment of such pusillanimity, it was Northcote who took most of the flak from discontented backbenchers. In the early debates over the admission or non-admission of the atheist Bradlaugh to the Commons, Churchill was already stealing Northcote's thunder and thereby removing the authority which would never return. Beaconsfield urged support for Northcote, though his arguments were not all that convincing; for who that remembered Disraeli's own youth would suspect him of truly backing a man who 'represents the respectability of the party', and especially when he added that 'I sympathise with you all, because I never was respectable myself'? Beaconsfield, perhaps dimly connecting the Fourth Party with his own Young England days, therefore gave them covert tolerance even while urging loyalty.

Nevertheless, the death of Beaconsfield just when the 1881 Irish Land Act was coming up for debate, the first great legislative struggle of the new parliament, did change things a good deal. His funeral was a time for an orgy of party sentimentality, for Conservatives certainly understood how much they owed to him for his own loyalty to his party over the past thirty-five years. His (allegedly) favourite flower and colour, primrose, were adopted as a party symbol, and the Primrose League, founded in 1884, would be a permanent, romantic reminder of his role and his importance. More significantly, the myth that was immediately created by Churchill and by other Tory Democrats from this veneration of their dead 'chief' was in itself a new political factor of the first order. Once safely dead, Disraeli became a democrat (which he had certainly never been) and a true believer in social reform (ditto). All this was a stick with which to beat the hapless Northcote (whom Disraeli had actually chosen as his successor) and a channel through which praise could be heaped on Salisbury (who had hated Disraeli for most of his political life). Such creative myth-making might at least have caused Dizzy some considerable amusement.

His absence did, though, cause an immediate political problem, for while it was easy enough to see who was the 'Leader of the Conservative Party' when it contained an ex-prime minister still active in politics and leading in either House, it was far from obvious who took precedence between Salisbury and Northcote when, after 1881, they led in the two Houses in uneasy partnership. Salisbury was senior in rank and the party's favourite, Northcote the senior in length of service and still backed by many Conservative MPs. Not since the 1830s had such a problem existed, and it was resolved in this case simply by postponement; Northcote and Salisbury would work together until office was achieved and the choice would then be the queen's. Northcote assumed that the queen's preference

STUDENTS ON THE MAKE.

Mr. F. E. Smith. "MASTER OF EPIGRAM—LIKE ME!"
Mr. Winston Churchill. "WROTE A NOVEL IN HIS YOUTH—LIKE ME!"
Together. "TRAVELLED IN THE EAST—LIKE US. HOW DOES IT END?"

[Mr. W. F. Monypenny's official Life of Disraeli has just been published.]

Disraeli as a hero for the young, *Punch* 1910.

for him, already indicated in 1881, would always hold good. His quiescence over the next few years, during which Salisbury first caught up and then overtook him in the palace's as well as the party's favour, was a major contribution to his eventual downfall.

The party's first battle without Disraeli's advice was a poor affair, for the staunch defiance of Gladstone in 1880 on Irish land issues faded rapidly when a far more radical bill appeared in 1881. Most Irish landlords decided that Gladstone could not be resisted and gave up their own fight; when many Conservative peers followed the same line of reasoning, especially amid government hints of another election if the Lords did not accept the Commons' view, Salisbury found himself with too few followers to maintain the contest, and so, as in 1869, Gladstone triumphed over the Conservative Lords. Salisbury drew from this an important lesson – that the use of the Lords' power of veto had to be used sparingly, and if possible should be used only when the government did *not* want an election on the issue under debate. The Lords' powers could thus be justified in a more democratic constitution as a sort of court of appeal from the government's Commons majority, which could choose to put contentious matters to the electorate. This strategy worked exceptionally well in 1884–5 and remained at the heart of Conservative strategy in the Lords, until the Edwardian period. Suitably modified after the Parliament Act of 1911, it evolved when Salisbury's grandson led the Lords after 1945 into 'the Salisbury doctrine', which stated that the House of Lords would only oppose in principle bills that did not have an explicit electoral mandate to justify them.

Without Beaconsfield's restraining presence, though Salisbury and Northcote continued to behave scrupulously towards each other, their supporters became less controllable, and both the Fourth Party and the Tory Democrats in the organization widened the area of conflict between 1882 and 1884. Gorst thundered that the party was now 'led by and in the interests of a narrow, oligarchic and landowning class, and that the people in whom the real Conservatism of the nation resides have no interest in the matter, nor are their interests ever consulted'. Such appeals had their effect in stirring into revolt the leaders of the larger boroughs (who certainly did feel neglected and patronized by the gentlemen who ran the party), and Churchill proceeded to use such disaffection as a means of seizing control of the National Union and then using it as a weapon against the 'old gang' who ran affairs through a central committee of whips and party managers. He was successful in the first aim, getting himself elected to the National Union's Central Council in July 1883 and then becoming chairman of its new Organization Committee in December, and he came near to dominating its 1883 and 1884 conferences with his oratory. He was, though, entirely unsuccessful in turning the

National Union into anything more than it had ever been in the past, a coordinating and talking machine. The whips refused absolutely to release party funds for separate National Union activities that would compete with those of Central Office, and at one time plans were even made for the eviction of the National Union from the jointly occupied headquarters. At this point loyalists in the organization, including many from the cities for which Churchill claimed to speak, began to rally to the party leaders (actually to Salisbury) and Churchill showed the brittleness of both his temper and his support when he resigned from the council as soon as it passed an adverse vote – with a vow to purge all those who had voted against him.

The danger was now obvious, and, with a real issue between the parties coming up in the Liberals' proposal to widen the franchise once again, Churchill and Salisbury moved to heal the breach. In May 1884 Churchill gave up all his claims on behalf of a more democratic control of party funds, policy-making and candidate selection, while Salisbury gave more shadowy assurances about future appointments to the management. Northcote was left stranded as a mere observer of events that he could hardly even influence. In the long run, perhaps the most important single part of the deal was one to which little attention was paid at the time: the acceptance by Salisbury that the just-founded Primrose League would be encouraged and accepted by the official party machine. The Primrose League had been Drummond Wolff's idea, a supporters' club for the party which would be constituted as a romantic celebration of Disraeli's youthfully feudal Young England days. It followed neo-masonic lines in having 'habitations' rather than branches, and knights and dames rather than members, with a hierarchy of grand masters, mistresses and chancellors reaching right to the top. Its activities were for the most part social, and operated in a doggedly deferential manner, but it would prove to be a crucial vehicle in attracting a mass membership to the party, and above all in giving an active platform on which Conservative women could participate during the last two generations before they had the parliamentary vote.

The 1883 Corrupt Practices Act, supported by MPs of all parties who were horrified both by the corruption and by the actual sums of money needed to get themselves elected in 1880, imposed tight spending limits which were by and large successfully enforced. This meant that, for a party containing as many rich men as the Conservatives did, far more was now available for spending on conventional party organization *between* campaigns (which also gave the emerging profession of party agents a big push forwards), but it also meant that an increased electorate could only be managed by the employment of hundreds of volunteer canvassers in every constituency. These the Primrose League existed to recruit, motivate and mobilize, and over the next generation it expanded to claim a membership well over a million, larger than that of all the trades unions affiliated to the TUC. Given the tiny or non-existent subscriptions demanded of members and the large sums contributed by the elite, the treats, outings, garden parties and bazaars at which the knights and dames were offered a chance to rub shoulders with their betters were an effective mechanism for socializing the masses into deferential attitudes. It was all, noted the Russian observer M. I. Ostrogorski in the later 1880s, 'a safe means of electoral bribery', but it was also, of course, all perfectly legal whereas actual bribery was not. 'Our greatest difficulty', a Primrose League organizer told Ostrogorski, 'is to keep them amused.' When chided about the vulgarity and snobbery involved in the League's appeal to the middle and lower classes, Lady Salisbury responded defiantly: 'Vulgar? Of course it is vulgar, but that is why we have done so well.'

Randolph Churchill thus casually abandoned in 1884 all those he had led into battle, but then there had always been a strong component of honest opportunism in his politics. He had on the public platform regularly asserted his commitment to Tory Democracy, but he had been able to define it only in cloudy terms, such as the statement that 'Tory Democracy means ancient permanent institutions becoming the instruments of far-reaching reform'. In private, when taxed by the radical W. S. Blunt, Churchill confessed that it was 'a question I am always in a fright lest someone should put it to me publicly. To tell the truth, I don't know myself what Tory Democracy is, but I believe it is principally opportunism. Say you are a Tory Democract and that will do.' In both the public bombast and in the private, disarming cynicism Churchill was indeed Disraeli's heir, if in nothing else. He did, though, come to play a posthumous part in carrying forward the Tory Democracy idea, for both his own son and Gorst's wrote books about it in the Edwardian period when, like Disraeli, he was safely dead and could not rise to dispute what was said about him: both Winston Churchill's *Lord Randolph Churchill* (1908) and Harold Gorst's *The Fourth Party* (1906) were acts of filial piety by sons who were by then Liberals, but they did allow later Conservatives to find consistency and principle in the Tory Democracy tradition where little had been visible at the time.

Those who really believed in the cause of Tory Democracy, like Gorst (who was once again removed as Principal Agent in 1882) were horrified by Churchill's betrayal, but many of the provincial Conservative leaders found plenty to satisfy them in the new regime that eventually emerged in 1884, with a true, businesslike professional whom they could respect as Principal Agent, Captain Middleton, a Leader whom they both admired and deferred to, and a reformed National Union structure that gave them more power in their own city machines to make up for losing the mirage of influence at the centre. The National Union reverted to being a regional and national talking-shop for those who enjoyed such things, though now much better managed by Middleton's network of area agents, each of whom was also ensconced as secretary of his regional National Union machine.

A party truce had been achieved just in time, for throughout 1884 Salisbury had to play a dangerous game of bluff-my-neighbour with Gladstone over the extension of the franchise. Radical Liberals had for years been seeking an opportunity to extend to the counties the more generous franchise provisions that the Conservatives had inadvertently granted to the boroughs in 1867, their ideal solution being the equalization of the franchise in town and country. Given their reliance on the counties, Conservatives were naturally very nervous about such a change, but by 1884–5 they also had their own agenda of electoral reforms which they planned to use as a bargaining chip in the process of legislation, and this revolved entirely around the distribution of constituencies. Conservatives would demand an end to the over-representation of Ireland (and to the under-representation of urbanized Ulster within Ireland), and, with the experience of the 1868 and 1880 voting in mind, many of them (including Salisbury) would no longer be unduly worried if the smallest boroughs were assimilated into the counties and suburban overspill placed back within town boundaries (which would then have to be more drastically sub-divided, broadly along class lines). Gladstone's hope was, therefore, to get his franchise extension without making promises about redistribution, while the Conservatives argued that an occupier franchise in the counties was fine by them, and quite consistent with what Disraeli had done in 1867 (which was scarcely true), but also pointed piously to the fact that in both 1832 and 1867–8 franchise and redistribution had been done concurrently, and so refused the one if they could not have the other. In practice, with a Liberal majority in the Commons, this meant that the House of Lords and its Tory Leader would need strong nerves, but in

Salisbury at the dispatch box, 1891, drawn by Harry Furniss (1854–1925).

Salisbury the party found that it had the man for the job. Disraeli had once explained to Salisbury's daughter (and later biographer), Lady Gwendolyn Cecil, that though they had differed on many things, they had been bound together by mutual respect for each other's decisiveness: 'You will find as you grow older that courage is the rarest of qualities to be found in public men. Your father is the only man of real courage that it has ever been my lot to work with.'

Salisbury offered indeed an exemplary display of courage in 1884, leading the Lords to a refusal even to discuss franchise before any deal had been offered about seats, ignoring the warning voices on his own side that said that the electorate would punish the party thought responsible for a deadlock, and equally discounting Liberal threats of an election (since he knew that the Liberals did not want an election before they had got their new franchise). On 8 July the Conservative peers, with some Whigs in support, refused Gladstone's Franchise Bill by fifty-nine votes, and Gladstone immediately upped the stakes by announcing an autumn session to discuss his bill again, before which the Liberals would whip up feeling in the country against the Lords. Salisbury, however, kept his eye on the ball, and when parliament reconvened in October the Conservative position remained unchanged, despite the withdrawal of Whig support and despite the urging of some on his own side that they should go for an election in order to avoid both franchise reform *and* new boundaries. It was, though, Gladstone whose stare faltered first, and when on 13 November he offered a deal on redistribution Salisbury immediately accepted. The franchise changes became law on 6 December, by which time redistribution was also very much under way.

The franchise changes now agreed were substantial, raising the total electorate of England and Wales by about two-thirds (though this masked a small increase in the towns while more than doubling numbers in the counties). Britain could finally be called a democracy in the sense that most men now had the vote, and the majority of electors were working class, though the survival of plural votes for graduates and the owners of property would limit the practical implications of such democratic principles until 1918. Registration remained a fiendishly complex process, and an even greater reward than before accrued to the party which could control the register and win elections on a low turnout – since sheer numbers now made it impossible to convert opponents by either bribery or coercion. Tight management and a low turnout would be the Conservative ideal of electoral management right through to 1918, though it would not in practice occur at any election after 1900.

The redrawing of the boundaries was cooked up in a straightforward deal between Gladstone and Salisbury, each flanked only by a few trusted subordinates (and with Churchill kept well out of these discussions by Salisbury), and then pushed through the Commons in the first half of 1885 as a joint proposal from the two front benches that could therefore be imposed on both Liberal and Conservative backbenchers; when it became law in June, Salisbury had most unexpectedly become Prime Minister. In those private negotiations Salisbury was as clear-sighted and determined as he had been over the tactics of the previous year, for electoral matters of this type were a subject on which he had long thought himself an expert and on which he was happy to trust his own judgement. He began with two key assumptions that were most uncommon in the politics of 1884–5. first, while most politicians thought of redistribution as a minor, technical issue, he was convinced that the new boundaries could in themselves make a very substantial difference to the damaging consequences he expected from the franchise extension; it was a 'vital interest to the party', and might make a difference of as much as a hundred seats. The second point was that both Salisbury himself and Sir Michael Hicks Beach (the ex-Cabinet minister who chaired the Central Office committee advising on redistribution) were among the few who supported the principle of single-member constituencies as the best way of ensuring that, within the tangle of urbanized counties and suburbanized towns, there would be a fair representation of minorities (so that, for example, a good number of farming seats would be retained). As in most cases where a strong-minded man who knows what he wants negotiates with others who have no fixed opinions, Salisbury achieved much of his personal agenda: the legal distinction between borough and county constituencies was maintained, but many county electorates would now contain small towns (a million voters moving from boroughs to counties) while larger towns would be extended to take in their outlying areas (so that even more voters were reallocated from counties to boroughs at the same time). There would be more seats allocated to the counties, but an even bigger increase in the representation of the rapidly growing conurbations, including the tripling of the number of MPs elected by Greater London to sixty-four, nearly a tenth of the entire House of Commons.

Although Salisbury's primary objective was defensive – the hope of preventing large Liberal majorities which could act as Gladstone had done in 1868 and 1880, and so restoring something of the tranquillity of mid-century politics – the effect was to be quite different. The electoral changes of 1884–5 helped instead to pave the way for a new period of Conservative dominance and (as Richard Shannon puts it), 'as a matter of aids and pressures towards Conservative adaptation piecemeal to a new order of politics, the Redistribution Act of 1885 is second to none'. This was substantially because in the period since 1868 the rapid growth in the size of the middle class and its move in a conservative direction had dramatically altered electoral possibilities. Salisbury himself had noted this in his frequent references to the 'villa Toryism' that he observed in such places as Maida Vale (on the route he took back to Hatfield House from Westminster), and his harping on the need for his party to organize it effectively.

While the total working-class population rose between 1850 and 1880 by 15 per cent, the overall number of middle-class people rose in the same period by 300 per cent; there was even an actual increase of 690,000 in the *upper* middle-class group who earned between £150 and £1,000 a year. And the growth went on; over the decade to 1891 there were increases of 20 to 30 per cent in such occupations as clerks, bank employees, shopkeepers and other 'white-collar' trades. Such rising social groups now had property of their own to defend, and suburbs of their own to protect from outside incursion – suburbs that were usually Tory seats after 1885, whether they were in London, Birmingham, Liverpool, Leeds or Sheffield. The 1885 boundaries, therefore, by giving it separate representation, enhanced the influence of exactly that group that had passed in large numbers from a commitment to Liberal reformism to a growing satisfaction with the status quo which fitted more easily with Conservatism. These were the voters that the future Lord Curzon listed in 1887 as 'young men of the middle and lower classes, clerks, apprentices, shopkeepers, mechanics, and artizans, who at each succeeding election are found enlisted in larger numbers in the Conservative ranks'.

In order to reap the full benefit that was available to the party from these changes in the electoral rules, Salisbury also steered into office a new management team. Rowland Winn, horrified by the passing of the old county order that he knew so well as the member for North Lincolnshire, stood down as Chief Whip and was replaced by his deputy, Aretas Akers-Douglas, who would hold the post for ten years. Akers-Douglas had learned his politics in the more urban county of Kent, and was well integrated into the party's Westminster elite through such contacts as Lord Cranbrook (formerly Gathorne Hardy). He appointed as Principal Agent Captain Middleton, the agent for West Kent and a former naval officer who already had years of professional experience among the new breed of agents in the field. Akers-Douglas and Middleton helped to calm the machine down after the excitements of 1880–84. They also gradually established the tightest overall management that the party had ever had in its electoral organization, but in a way that did not (as Gorst had done) challenge the autonomy and authority of the politicians at Westminster. The National Union was now indeed a 'handmaid' to the party as promised in 1867, while the constituency associations by and large flourished, discreetly prodded towards a more professional basis of continuous organization by Middleton's men out in the regions.

Their opportunity was likely to come soon, for the Gladstone government had been breaking up for months, and the strain imposed on it by the death of General Gordon at Khartoum in January 1885 was to prove mortal. There had been earlier setbacks – as, for example, when, in the first Boer War, Britain had suffered a humiliating defeat at Majuba in 1881, and when Gladstone's 'treaty' with the Irish leader Charles Stewart Parnell at Kilmainham gaol in 1882 had opened the government to severe criticism. But Gordon's death was on another scale altogether as an imperial disaster, and the intensity of public criticism proved impossible for a weak and divided Cabinet to withstand. The Lords passed a strong vote of censure, and in the Commons (with the Irish MPs now quietly sidling up to the Conservatives in the hope of playing off Liberal against Conservative in a coming constitutional auction) there seemed a chance of passing a similar motion; Northcote's muffing of that chance with a tired and half-hearted attack on Gladstone removed any final chance that he might become Prime Minister.

There remained, though, a strong sense that change would come soon, with Liberals now anxious to escape office anyway. Tory discussions with the Irish, which the headstrong Churchill did not even bother to conceal, eventually produced the majority which defeated the government on 8 June 1885. It was only then, when Gladstone's resignation was followed by the queen's summons to Salisbury rather than himself, that Northcote grasped the weakness of his position. It then rapidly became even weaker, for Churchill refused to serve in any office at all if Northcote was not pushed up to the House of Lords (and on other occasions Churchill also tried to evict Richmond, Manners, Carnarvon and Cross). With Churchill's reputation what it was among the party rank and file, Salisbury had to bow resignedly to his main demand and edge Northcote first away from the second position in his government and then out of the Commons, until to general relief Northcote himself solved the difficulty by taking a peerage (as Earl of Iddesleigh) and only a purely honorary post.

Salisbury's first ministry followed on fairly close from Disraeli's 1874–80 team. He retained the Foreign Office himself – indeed taking it was one of his few compensations for the less attractive post of Prime Minister. Apart from Churchill, who became Secretary for India, having only entered the Commons in 1880, most were familiar faces, for every living survivor from the Cabinet of 1880 was accommodated. After the past few years Salisbury wanted no rogue elephants rampaging around the back benches to disturb his minority government. There were, though, even during its mere six months in office, troubles enough on the inside, arising both from Churchill and from Irish policy. Churchill had soon irritated most of his Cabinet colleagues with his arrogant, interfering and domineering ways, while at the same time disappointing his followers on the outside. It was an unstable situation, and some ministers were already saying in 1885 that they must strive to keep Churchill until the next election but would not be unhappy to see him go afterwards.

Irish matters were one of the areas in which Churchill meddled, keeping open a personal line to Parnell and discussing with him options that were not part of the government's policy, but Salisbury seems to have been happy enough with this, for he was expecting defeat at the coming election anyway, and any deal that might deliver Irish votes to the Conservatives in English and Scottish constituencies seemed worth exploring. The real problem came from elsewhere, and did not explode until much later. Unlike Disraeli in 1874, Salisbury knew well enough that he must have an active Irish policy, and he was content to accept the extensive new programme of land purchase which was being hatched by Lord Ashbourne, Irish Lord Chancellor and (most unusually) also a Cabinet minister in his own right. Salisbury also had back in his Cabinet Lord Carnarvon as Lord Lieutenant of Ireland, and here he exercised insufficient control over a minister with grand plans of his own. Aware that the government needed Parnell's cooperation, and remembering his own earlier successes in colonial constitution-making, Carnarvon began to believe that the Conservatives should themselves offer devolution to Ireland, plans that he then unwisely broached with Parnell himself (and even more unwisely did so without a witness, contrary to Salisbury's explicit instruction). When he heard of this, Salisbury attempted to put a lid on things, informing neither the Cabinet nor the queen of what had transpired, and no doubt reflecting that it was only until the election, now just beginning, that he needed to keep Irish MPs sweet in any case. In the long term, there was no question whatsoever of any senior Conservative supporting Carnarvon's ideas, for even Randolph Churchill made it very clear that Home Rule for Ireland was entirely unacceptable.

In the short term Salisbury's tactic worked well enough, for Parnell sensed that his hoped-for auction was going well, and in order to provoke the Liberals into a higher bid he did indeed urge Irish voters to back Conservatives at the 1885 election. In the longer term, though, the idea that Conservatives might carry Home Rule as their own proposal percolated through the political world, encouraging both Parnell and Gladstone first with a false expectation and then with grounds for claims of betrayal when their hopes were dashed. This was not a good basis for opening constitutional debates that would determine the future both of the Union and of British politics. But all of this would necessarily be shaped by the result of the 1885 election itself, for which campaigning now got fully under way.

Given the extreme delicacy of the party's position on Ireland, which would clearly be the most pressing matter to come before the new parliament, Salisbury had some difficulty in pulling together a platform on which his party could fight. He fell back therefore on a formula which had many times served the party well in the past – the idea that the Protestant tradition was in danger from Liberal and Irish reformers. This threw out hints to those disposed to listen as to the party's likely stance when, in the following year, Ireland's future could be seen as one in which Home Rule would bring Rome rule in its wake, but it did not explicitly reject Irish overtures in a way that would have repulsed Parnell's proffered good offices with the English electorate. When Gladstone refused to rule out disestablishment of the Scottish Church in all eventualities, Salisbury neatly reinforced his argument that the Church[es] were in danger by going on about the question of disendowment, and so related the issue less to religion than to education, which worried the disestablished Catholics as much as the established Anglicans and Scottish Presbyterians. If there really was an Irish vote for Conservative candidates in mainland constituencies in 1885 (which was far from ever being proven), it may well have derived more from Salisbury's tactical skills than from Parnell's advice.

The party organization had at least recovered from the relative malaise of 1880–85, and in one area at least it was breaking important new ground. 1885–6 was the period in which Central Office as a publisher of high-quality works of reference first came on the scene, in particular with the first edition of the *Constitutional Year Book* (an invaluable almanac of political facts, but also a source of partisan material for party politics – 19 April was duly celebrated for the next half-century as 'Primrose Day. Lord Beaconsfield d., 1881' and 24 February helpfully recalled as the date on which 'Mr Gladstone's Irish Coercion Bill passed, 1881') and with the first substantial edition of *Campaign Notes*, precursor of the famous *Campaign Guide* series which began in 1892. This was both a beneficial resource for Conservative candidates and MPs in general – especially those facing the traditional Liberal cry that Conservatives were 'the stupidest party' – and a sign of a far more bureaucratically professional approach at the centre than in the hand-to-mouth days of Gorst in the early 1870s.

Conservatives had, though, few solid grounds on which to base predictions of the results in 1885, for both boundaries and franchise were new, as were many candidates to the areas in which they were standing, since numbers of county Tories had fled to new suburban seats for safety, and there was the added complication of Parnell's influence, generally reckoned to be worth twenty-five seats. The results when they came were therefore both a relief (since the worst fears of the effects of the franchise extension were not borne out) and a disappointment. The Conservatives returned to Westminster with 250 MPs, only a dozen more than in 1880, so they had surmounted the sea of electoral changes without disaster but made up so little ground that they were still eighty-four seats short of the Liberal total. Still further losses in Ireland (leaving Ulster and Dublin University as the only electorates supporting Conservatives) and tiny gains in Scotland and Wales were offset by gains in England. The most important arithmetical fact was, however, that Parnell's Irish Party had eighty-six seats and therefore held the balance of power, and with it the opportunity to make and break governments.

Within this overall pattern there had been an electoral revolution in Conservative support in England, for now they held for the first time in recorded memory a majority of the borough seats but had done so badly in the counties that they held only 100 seats there to the Liberals' 122. Some Conservative candidates benefited from their support for fair trade in northern cities and the radical Liberals' campaigns to extend smallholdings to agricultural labourers had a big impact among the new rural voters (by then anyway distressed by ten years of rural depression), but the major influences seem to have been a further consolidation of middle-class backing for Conservatives (which gave them a strong regional hold over London's borough seats and the nearby urbanized counties) and the effect of moving voters back and forward across constituency boundaries so that hundreds of thousands of former county voters now lived in suburban constituencies and the depleted rural electorates were tilted to the Liberals by the accession of new reserves of radicalism from the small towns submerged into them. The effect was that many county seats that had been Conservative since the 1830s now had Liberal MPs, old county families were humbled all over rural England, and a whole generation of knights of the shire were forced into retirement (so that even when the seats were won back a year later it was new men, if sometimes sons of the defeated MPs, who returned). The parliamentary party had received such an access of commercial and industrial new blood and such a haemorrhaging of traditional sanguinary supplies that it would never be the

| Churchill | Salisbury | 6. The Home Rule Card Game. Parnell | Gladstone | Chamberlain |

The Home Rule Card Game in a cartoon of 1885 showing Parnell awaiting the end of the four-handed game between Churchill, Salisbury, Gladstone and Chamberlain.

same again; the revolution predicted ever since Hamilton and Smith's token victories in 1868 had now come about.

Salisbury, who had on principle never approved of the way in which the last three elections had been followed by immediate ministerial resignations, decided to meet the new parliament, though it was clear that Parnell's only real option for the use of his balancing vote would be to install Gladstone in office and extract from him an Irish Home Rule bill, for which he would expect to have the substantial majority behind it provided by Liberal and Irish MPs. The only way to prevent this would be for the Liberals to break up as a party and a coalition of Conservatives and Whigs be formed under either Salisbury or the Whig Leader Hartington, so creating a majority to *stop* Home Rule. Despite Churchill's enthusiastic buccaneering in that direction, and Salisbury's more cautious approaches, the Whigs were even now reluctant to move. In the meantime, the Cabinet now formally told Carnarvon that it was 'not possible for the Conservative Party to tamper with the question of Home Rule', and he therefore resigned on 23 January 1886, though since the government fell only four days later this was too late to matter much.

Carnarvon's departure, linked with election defeat, did, however, clear the air, for Conservatives could now return unequivocally to the policy that they almost universally preferred, which was one of resistance to Irish Home Rule. Salisbury therefore declined to have anything to do with Gladstone's hopeful offers to support a Conservative bill (saying of the Grand Old Man that 'His hypocrisy makes me sick'), and left the Liberal Leader with no option but to turn him out and take the responsibility himself. The six-month poker game in which no major British politician behaved very cleanly was over, and the real battle could now commence. That it would be a battle with no holds barred was indicated by Churchill now dangerously taking up the cause of Ulster as a rock on which Home Rule could be smashed; he informed Gladstone through an intermediary that 'I should not hesitate ... to agitate Ulster even to resistance beyond constitutional limits; that Lancashire would follow Ulster, and would lead England'.

Gladstone's neat footwork ensured that Salisbury was defeated on an agricultural rather than a specifically Irish issue, but this nevertheless resolved the deadlock by releasing the Conservatives from office and freeing them for their campaign of resistance. Against Gladstone's threat of a breakdown of order in an Ireland denied Home Rule, Conservatives theatrically promised a breakdown if it were passed. On 22 February

Churchill played the 'orange card' in public (characteristically expressing the private hope that it would prove the ace of trumps and not the deuce), when he told a cheering crowd of Protestants in Belfast's Ulster Hall that they should go beyond the 'lines of what we are accustomed to look upon as constitutional action'. In May he was even more defiantly proclaiming that 'Ulster will fight and Ulster will be right'. Salisbury was careful not to let Churchill get too far ahead; he lauded Churchill to an audience of Conservatives for his 'brilliantly successful effort to rouse the Protestants of Ulster to a sense of their danger'. Churchill also skirmished ahead of the main force in offering cooperation with the Whigs, and was the first to give public currency to the possibility that a new party could now emerge: 'might not we call it the party of the Union? Members of that party might be known as Unionists.'

Within a few days of Salisbury's resignation of office, the refusal of most Whigs to serve under Gladstone suggested that a realignment of parties was indeed coming at last, and by mid-February 1886 the Conservative whips were in secret discussion with the Whigs about a possible mutually beneficial electoral pact if Gladstone were to call another election after Home Rule had been defeated in parliament. The resignation from the government on 26 March of Joseph Chamberlain, rootedly opposed to a Home Rule bill which sacrificed English interests, and anyway infuriated by Gladstone's refusal to keep him informed, opened up the chance of a wider deal and a bigger catch; for it was at once recognized that the hard-nosed Chamberlain, if once committed, would at least make a more reliable ally than the proverbially slippery Whigs. As a leader of opinion in provincial business circles, he would now fit in on the Conservative side of the House as he certainly would not have done a decade earlier. In 1937, the year in which Chamberlain's younger son became Conservative Leader, the historian Robert Ensor was famously to argue in the *Spectator* that the Unitarian screw-manufacturer Chamberlain's crossing of the floor had been a symbolic moment in British social and political history, which indeed it was, but it could hardly have happened if the Conservatives had not recruited many of the business classes already (as the 1885 election had shown), thus putting Chamberlain in danger of being behind rather than ahead of the times.

The Commons began on 8 April 1886 three months of epic but three-sided debates about Home Rule, culminating in the rejection of Gladstone's bill on 8 June by 343 votes to 313; the majority was made up of 250 Conservatives and ninety Liberals (of whom about two-thirds were

THE MEETING IN THE ULSTER HALL, BELFAST

Drawing of Churchill addressing an Orange meeting in Belfast, February 1886.

Chamberlainites and only a third true Whigs). The Conservative case in those debates was straightforward: that there was no satisfactory compromise between Union and full independence for Ireland, that the interests of the empire did not allow for Irish independence, and that Home Rule would thus have to be faced down, by coercion if necessary. It was a political stance in which Salisbury and his front-bench colleagues were entirely unapologetic, and it was one that ensured that Liberals who came over to them in these debates would have to make a clean break on the principle, rather than voting against their fellow-Liberals only on a procedural technicality. Its strong articulation of the overriding claims of the (British) national interest, notably in economic terms when applied to Ireland's interest in setting up tariffs against English and Scottish goods, helped to complete the transition of the possessing classes towards Conservatism, signalled by the strong support that the party henceforth enjoyed in the City of London, and in such weathercocks of financial interest as *The Economist*. It was also a stance that appealed strongly to the emerging force of intellectual opinion which, shaped and encouraged by W. H. Mallock, A. V. Dicey, Sir Henry Maine and J. R. Seeley (whose *The Expansion of England* was vastly influential here), saw Britain's imperial mission as a manifest destiny and Ireland as a test-case of imperial willpower. As the historian – and former Liberal – W. H. Lecky had put it in 1883, 'it is curious to see how Irish affairs *turn us all into Tories*'.

Having defeated the Gladstone government, its opponents absolutely had to win the election that now followed or lose all credibility, and here the debating tone lowered a good deal. The same arguments used in the Commons were mobilized in the politer areas, but a good deal of old-fashioned anti-Catholic and anti-Irish campaigning also came into its own, as did more uninhibited music-hall language about the empire. Salisbury's injudicious comparison of the Irish to 'Hottentots', as an uncivilized people not yet ready for self-government, fell into that category, since it directly linked Ireland to empire, as did his invitation to the Irish to emigrate *to* the empire if they did not like the United Kingdom. Individual Conservative candidates in their own constituencies were frequently even less restrained.

The election's outcome was expected to turn on the extent to which a workable electoral pact would enable the Conservatives and their new allies to pool their support. Since April 1886 the allies had been appearing on the same platforms, while the nucleus of a Liberal Unionist organization was already being formed, and by the end of May Salisbury had

The Marquess of Hartington, later eighth Duke of Devonshire, drawn by Sir Francis Carruthers Gould (1844–1925).

promised not to run candidates against any Liberal Unionist who actually voted against the Home Rule Bill. This pledge proved difficult to carry out, since local Conservatives now had the bit between their teeth and sensed a chance of winning, but it was at least arranged that no Conservative who broke ranks would get a front-bencher to speak in his support. In the event, the Liberal Unionists had almost a free run in Scotland and Wales, while only five Liberal Unionists faced Conservative candidates in England – and this cost the alliance only a couple of seats – though one of those threatened had been Lord Wolmer, prospective Liberal Unionist whip and Salisbury's own son-in-law.

In any case, the sweep of the vote at the election turned out to have less to do with electoral deals in the constituencies than with the broad national picture. The appearance of the massively reassuring Lord Hartington and the entirely unexpected Chamberlain supporting Conservative candidates, against a Gladstone campaign that entirely missed the real point, was far more significant in the end. Gladstone appealed on traditional lines to the moral 'masses' to support the grant of Home Rule against the selfish refusal of the possessing 'classes', failing to see that at least a million and a half electors now thought of themselves as the subjects of such rhetoric rather than its object. The Liberal surge of 1885 in the counties fell away, possibly in part because the 1886 election was at harvest-time, but more likely for the more generalized national reasons discussed above, and thirty-eight English county seats were recaptured by Conservatives. Since they also made a net gain of twenty-six in the boroughs the balance of the new parliamentary party confirmed the change of 1885; half the net borough gains were in the emerging imperial capital, London, where there were now fifty Conservative MPs out of sixty-four, and the patrician Salisbury wrote amazedly that middle-class 'London is really the base of Tory principles'.

With the electoral tide bringing Conservative and equivalent Liberal Unionist gains in Wales and Scotland (where the Liberal Unionists had brought over the backing both of the *Scotsman* and of the *Glasgow Herald*), Conservatives had 316 seats in the new parliament to the Liberals' 190, while the Liberal Unionists' seventy-nine helpfully neutralized Parnell's eighty-five. The Liberal Unionist balance had reversed, for there were now twice as many behind Hartington as Chamberlain, and this in itself – as well as the rivalry between them – shaped the formation of the next government. Salisbury, who was willing enough to take the Foreign Office and escape the strains of supreme command, invited Hartington to become Prime Minister, but the crafty Whig recognized well enough that the likeliest effect of this would be to drive Chamberlain and his radical followers back to the Liberal Party (which he might well then capture), while both factions of the Liberal Unionists could be content for their different reasons to back Salisbury. Chamberlain reached the same conclusion, and this ensured that Salisbury returned to Downing Street, setting up a Conservative minority government which at least ensured that few hopeful Conservatives would have to be sacrificed in the process of selecting the team. He had, though, guarantees of outside support from the Liberal Unionists, much like those that the Peelites had given to Whigs in 1847 and again in 1855. That historical analogy was much noticed at the time and boded well for a future fusion. In 1886, as earlier, the hardening of party divisions in an actual election campaign would make difficult any later reunion of parties on the old lines, while the habit of Unionists working together in the lobbies in the future would keep Liberal divisions open, creating the likelihood of a Conservative–Liberal Unionist merger in the future, just as had occurred between Whigs and Peelites in the 1850s.

Salisbury had plenty of problems to surmount when he returned to office in July 1886 – Lord Randolph Churchill, who was unlikely to be satisfied in any post he could be offered; Joseph Chamberlain as an unexpected ally and a potential backer of Churchill's political intrigues; Ireland to govern after its hopes of Home Rule had been snatched away; and an untried voting coalition to sustain him in the lobbies for years ahead. Not until the end of 1887, by which time Liberal reunion had failed to materialize, Ireland had proved to be surprisingly governable and Lord Randolph had wantonly destroyed himself, could Salisbury even begin to relax.

He had nevertheless stamped his leadership on his own party and achieved something crucial in the great political face-offs of 1884–6 that set the seal on the life's work of Derby and Disraeli since 1846: he had – if often uncomprehendingly and without enthusiasm even for his own successes – 're-established Toryism on a national basis', and he had turned a permanent minority into a practical majority.

7

The First Summit: The Hotel Cecil, 1886–1900

BOTH THE 1886 PARLIAMENT and the Unionist alliance lasted for much longer than anyone had foreseen at the outset, for Gladstone, though already seventy-seven in 1886, refused either to retire after the destruction of his Irish policy or to modify his commitment to Home Rule for Ireland. Hartington had agreed that his Liberal Unionists would support Salisbury's Conservatives in office, provided that by their lights he governed sensibly, but also 'so long as Gladstone lives'. While this undertaking could hardly have been enforced for the twelve years that then ensued until Gladstone did finally die, the fact that Gladstone kept the Irish issue alive until he at last retired in 1894 meant that 'Unionism' remained in being for long enough to become a natural habit rather than an alliance of mere convenience.

This long-term cooperation led eventually to the complete merger of the Liberal Unionists and Conservatives in 1912, but in the meantime Liberal Unionists occupied a halfway position. In Oscar Wilde's *The Importance of Being Earnest* (1895) John Worthing answers a question about his politics by denying that he has any, for although he does not want 'to put the asses against the classes', he is a Liberal Unionist. Lady Bracknell reassuringly responds, 'Oh, they count as Tories. They dine with us. Or come in the evening, at any rate.' That final sentence perfectly captures the situation, for social convergence between the former rivals was even in 1895 only half-achieved, and right up to 1912 political cooperation continued to be hampered by the fact that the Liberal Unionists could still not be members of the Carlton Club. This was not simply a matter of Conservatives snobbishly refusing to admit ex-Liberals as their equals, but just as much about Liberal Unionists being unwilling to surrender all that their previous careers and ancestral traditions meant to them. As late as 1909, when Lords Lansdowne and Devonshire (by then respectively Unionist Leader and whip in the Lords) were caught in a downpour in Pall Mall, Lansdowne indignantly refused even to enter the Carlton for shelter, and they trudged on, getting steadily wetter, until they reached the portals of the impeccably Whig Brooks's Club in St James's, where they could dry off under the approving stare of a portrait of Charles James Fox.

But if the Whiggish Liberal Unionists were not for at least a generation to forget their past, reliance on their support did nevertheless alter the circumstances within which Conservative policy was made. These Whigs had spent the previous quarter-century obstructing radical policies from the Liberals and they were no less conservative an influence when they changed sides. 'Tory Democracy', as a Disraelian legacy articulated by Lord Randolph Churchill and a number of minor, mainly provincial functionaries in the National Union, never really amounted to much as an actual programme, but its chances of getting anywhere after 1886 were in any case reduced by the negative impact that Hartington's followers had on policy, at least as much as by the early downfall of Lord Randolph himself.

In principle, the negative effect of gaining Hartington's Whigs ought to have been offset by a radicalizing influence on the Unionist alliance coming from Joseph Chamberlain, but in practice this never quite happened. In the first place, Chamberlain seemed far more likely to return to the Liberals than did Hartington, and the further move of the Gladstonian Liberals in a radical direction in the later 1880s did not place any barrier in his way as it did for Hartington, but the continuing debates over Ireland (in which Chamberlain took delight in taunting his former colleagues) ensured that he remained a Unionist through to the end of the 1886 parliament and beyond. When addressing the Conservative National Union in Birmingham in 1891 (both the place and the speaker highly significant in themselves), Chamberlain confirmed that he no longer hoped for Liberal reunion and would therefore conduct his political future entirely within Unionism. By then, Churchill's fall had removed any leverage that a Churchill–Chamberlain alliance could have exerted for Tory radicalism (though even this was more hypothetical than real, for they were as much rivals as natural allies) and the rise of Arthur Balfour to the pole Unionist position in the Commons filled the vacancy to which Chamberlain could otherwise have aspired, though Chamberlain and Balfour were careful to work together and remain always closely in touch.

Concessions had to be made in order to retain Chamberlain's block of seats in the West Midlands and his appeal to nonconformist opinion everywhere. He was realistic enough to see that his room for manoeuvre was limited, and to ask only for a little at a time and not to complain too much if he did not usually get it, but a degree of resentment did nevertheless build up. When, in and after 1895, Chamberlain refocused his own career on imperial and international issues on which he could appeal more widely to Unionist opinion, he increased his influence generally, but not in ways that enabled him to press on the party such domestic initiatives as old age pensions. The net effect of the accession of the Liberal Unionists was thus to reduce the temptation on Salisbury's Conservatives to opt for adventurous domestic reform programmes – not least because it was difficult to secure agreement among the even more disparate group of allies that the Unionists now were. The cautious Salisbury was unable as Prime Minister even to achieve much for his own pet scheme: improvements to working-class housing. The Housing of the Working Classes Act of 1890 did, however, mark an advance on Cross's Act of 1875 by giving local councils limited powers for the compulsory purchase of land, and it stands as witness to the (easily forgotten) generously paternalistic side of Salisbury's patrician politics.

The 1886 government was thus a Conservative government, but one which would operate in unusual conditions. The key decision related to the post to be offered to Churchill, a man who was already (as Lord Carnarvon noted) 'a rival that can compel, or thwart, or drive, or hold back'. In practice, though, all worked out easily enough at first: Churchill became Chancellor of the Exchequer and Leader of the House of Commons (from which position Hicks Beach bowed out happily enough in order to take the Irish Office), but with Churchill's ambition to be recognized as the party's second man so easily achieved, he did not have much excuse to bargain in the allocation of other places. It therefore became mainly a traditional Conservative Cabinet, containing such men as Cross, Cranbrook (ex-Gathorne Hardy), Iddesleigh (ex-Northcote) and Smith, all loyalists who had served under Disraeli, and with little recognition through the appointments of the changing character of the parliamentary party. Salisbury himself, whose combined tenure of the premiership and the Foreign Office had led to criticism of a lack of grip by the government as a whole in 1885, was compelled to cede the Foreign Office to Iddesleigh. A key appointment for the future was Salisbury's nephew and former political secretary Arthur Balfour, who became the first Conservative

Arthur Balfour drawn by Harry Furniss.

Secretary of State for Scotland in August 1886 and was promoted to the Cabinet in the same post in November.

The real character of the government was, however, settled not by appointments but by the way in which it weathered its first crisis four months later in December 1886, and by the reshuffle that followed. From the start Randolph Churchill seemed as restless in office as he had been in opposition, picking unnecessary fights with colleagues, interfering in their departmental business, and given to grand pronouncements that could be self-contradictory. He was convinced that he would not live long

– as indeed was his son Winston, with much less justification – and so behaved (to adapt his own words about Gladstone) like a young man in a terrible rush. He seems to have modelled himself on a mythic impression of Disraeli's larger-than-life political style, missing the central fact that Disraeli's 'outsider' exoticism could not be plausibly imitated by a duke's son, and that so much of Disraeli's posturing was anyway carefully thought out in advance. As Lord Derby put it, Churchill's 'eccentric and outrageous utterances ... are with him outbreaks of his real nature, whereas with Disraeli they were carefully calculated for effect.' In Lord Randolph's case, all of this meant that some of his colleagues already suspected the increasing instability of mind which was to lead to his eclipse and then to his early death in 1894.

The problems gathered when Churchill began in October to strike out in speeches to Conservatives in the country with a personal political agenda, much like Chamberlain's 'Unauthorized [Liberal] Programme' of 1885. Although the party organization published these speeches as if they were official statements by the government, they were widely perceived by colleagues and by the press as the opening shots in a campaign to displace Salisbury and seize the premiership, reviving the use of the National Union as a pathway to advancement, as he had tried to do in 1883–4. Churchill's Dartford programme included advanced proposals for social legislation – for example, through facilitating the provision of allotments for rural workers, reform of Church tithes, and an extensive new system of local government. He was soon complaining bitterly about the refusal of his colleagues to carry out these plans boldly enough, but it was his parallel call for retrenchment in public expenditure that led to real political crisis, not least because it was the only part of his programme that fell directly to the Chancellor himself to carry out.

In November 1886 the anticipated clash came over army expenditure, partly because that just happened to be an area in which necessarily early decisions would test Churchill's determination, partly because the War Secretary W. H. Smith seemed to Churchill both a soft target and a man whose defeat would weaken the Prime Minister. By 20 November Churchill was telling colleagues melodramatically that the army's financial requirements meant that 'the Govt. are proceeding headlong to a smash and I won't be connected with it', while he also cultivated relations with Chamberlain in an openly threatening manner. But he now quite outrageously overplayed his hand by sending Salisbury an insulting letter of resignation; he himself had thought of it only as a threat and therefore had not even consulted his intended ally Chamberlain about the tactic, but he ensured that *The Times* published the story, which left him no chance to back down. As Balfour reminded Salisbury, Churchill had failed to find a 'Tory Democracy' ground for resignation, on which he might well have stirred up feeling out in the country and found common ground with Chamberlain, and had resigned instead as a Chancellor trying to starve the army of funds – hardly a popular Conservative cause in any generation. Salisbury was not a man to be browbeaten so inexpertly, and in any case the rest of the Cabinet was behind him to a man; as Smith wrote, 'it was really Salisbury or Churchill: and if Salisbury had gone, none of us could have remained ...' Salisbury therefore called Churchill's bluff by accepting his resignation without further debate or negotiation.

The only minister to resign with Churchill was the Under-Secretary at the Colonial Office, while out in the country the party was at first stunned but rapidly rallied to Salisbury with the encouragement of some astute management of the press, while the National Union, now firmly under the control of Middleton and Akers-Douglas, made hardly a sound. Chamberlain correctly deduced that Churchill had ruined himself and refused to come to his aid, though the fear of their possible future cooperation remained a factor in many minds right through until Churchill's health finally collapsed in the early 1890s.

Salisbury again made the gesture of inviting Hartington to take the premiership, but received the same response as in July 1886, after which he buckled down happily enough to re-form a Conservative team without Lord Randolph, but with the knowledge that Hartington had now gone a little further than in July by urging at least one Whig to come directly to his aid. The ex-Liberal Admiralty minister G. J. Goschen, who had parted company with Gladstone as early as 1880, took Churchill's place at the Exchequer and proved a sound and respected finance minister, while Salisbury took the much bigger gamble of appointing W. H. Smith as Leader of the Commons, where he proved more than adequate after a rather sticky start. Salisbury also took advantage of the unexpected chance to edge Iddesleigh aside and take back the Foreign Office for himself, and shortly afterwards replaced Hicks Beach (whose health was poor) at the Irish Office, by promoting Balfour to that high-profile position after only a few weeks in Cabinet.

After this dramatic start the second Salisbury government had a far less exciting life, but it cannot be said to have been a particularly successful one, for although it was supported by a solid majority in both Houses on any question relating to Ireland, and on most international and imperial issues too, it proved to be very difficult indeed to mobilize that majority in support of a distinctive domestic policy. It was largely for this reason – and because Ireland and the Union were the government's entire *raison d'être* – that Balfour's success as Irish Secretary was so significant, so that when Smith died in 1891 it was Balfour who succeeded him as Leader of the Commons and, because he was still only forty-three, as Salisbury's heir apparent too.

Balfour's success was all the more welcome because it was so unexpected. Hicks Beach, a far more experienced politician, had not fared well in his few months dealing with Ireland in the immediate aftermath of the failure of Home Rule, and Salisbury's appointment of his nephew to begin 'twenty years of resolute government' seemed a desperate throw. Balfour had the image of a dilettante philosopher, with the nickname 'Pretty Fanny' deriving from his elaborately courteous and languid public manner, so that Irish Nationalists, who were already mobilizing much of Irish opinion in open defiance of the government and in a rent strike against the landlords, were convinced that they would eat the new Chief Secretary alive. But Balfour had a willpower and a determination that were entirely belied by appearances, and he soon acquired in Ireland itself the new nickname 'Bloody Balfour'. He withdrew at once the authority that Hicks Beach had given to his officials to keep working on compromise schemes for devolution, and declared that all policy would be subordinated to the restoration of the government's authority; police and the military were given stronger backing and gradually the processes of the law took their toll, with increasing numbers of jury-convictions taking place as the months went by. A tighter closure system was needed to curtail Commons debates on a tough Crimes Bill, but the Unionist alliance proved equal to the occasion, and Balfour acquired the additional powers that he needed to face down opposition.

By April 1888 his toughness was already showing sufficient success to prompt the National Union to give him a special celebratory dinner, and Salisbury himself wrote that his government was 'infected with the spirit of Arthur Balfour and very much disposed to vigorous measures'. By this time the Parnellite 'Plan of Campaign' had fallen apart and Parnell himself had come under attack in *The Times* for alleged complicity in murderous activities several years earlier; though the government as well as *The Times* lost credibility when it appeared that these charges were based on forgeries, the Unionists once again rallied in the parliamentary debates that followed,

"UNITED IRELAND." Saturday, September 17th, 1887

GOVERNMENT BY MURDER.—FRUITS OF THE COERCION ACT

BLOODY BALFOUR (to Policemen) : " Well done, boys. That's a good day's work."
CHORUS OF POLICEMEN : " But look at our heads ! They are not as hard as Tipperary blackthorns."
BLOODY BALFOUR : " Never mind : don't hesitate to shoot."

An Irish Nationalist view of Balfour's Irish policy, 17 September 1887.

with Chamberlain well to the fore. Parnell never again fully re-established the authority he had wielded in Ireland between 1880 and 1886, and his involvement in the O'Shea divorce case and subsequent death in 1891 then left his movement split and leaderless for a decade. Already by 1889, though, defiance and violence in Ireland itself had receded, and the number of recorded political crimes was lower than it had been even before the agrarian disturbances of the early 1880s, so that the emergency measures themselves could be scaled down in 1890.

Balfour was less successful in the positive half of his 'heavy policing and light railways' policy for Ireland. He had promised to be 'as relentless as Cromwell' in acts of repression, but not to make Cromwell's mistake of neglecting the redress of real grievances once order was restored. The upshot was that reform of Irish local government was delayed, as was the creation of an Irish university, and not until 1891 did he produce a substantial land reform, the Irish Land Purchase Act, which in any case had the bureaucratic effect of reducing rather than increasing the number of tenant purchasers compared to previous years. There were minor successes in economic amelioration through the Congested Districts Act of 1890, by which public funds were invested in railways and other forms of infrastructure necessary to widen the occupational base in areas where agriculture could no longer support the population. The net effect of these reforms was, however, all rather limited; enough to satisfy tender-minded British Unionists that they were doing more than just repress the Irish, but nowhere near enough to convert the mass of Irish opinion away from its scepticism about the Union.

Defence and foreign policy could also be claimed as reasonably successful policy areas, except that Salisbury preferred to treat diplomacy as such a confidential personal preserve at to leave few grounds for claiming anything at all. None the less, he was widely praised for the skill with which his diplomacy was conducted in such activities as the Mediterranean Agreements that freed Britain's hands for the last round of colonial expansion in Africa, and for the openly imperial framework within which he set his policy, a development that recognized both the nature of Britain's actual economic interests in the world by 1890 and the domestic political marketplace within which such imperialist bodies as the Primrose League now operated.

In defence, for the first time since the unification of Germany in 1871, Britain began to reorganize its forces in recognition of the changed European balance, and to commit far more money to the Royal Navy as a result. Attempts to improve the coordination of defence planning as a whole failed because of the entrenched opposition of the Admiralty, and had to await the next bout of military reforms after the Boer War, but this in itself largely reflected the fact that in that imperial age the navy was by a long way the country's most important defence force, and that the government had not the slightest intention of allowing the army to plan for participation in a European war (from which the navy could in principle insulate Britain anyway).

The Naval Defence Act of 1889 committed an additional £5 million a year to the building of warships, and set out statutorily the objective that the Royal Navy be as strong as any two other navies combined – the 'two power standard' that operated (if with some modifications) right through to 1914. With the benefit of some active campaigning in the press and the country by the First Lord of the Admiralty, Lord George Hamilton, this was another popular policy of which the party could thoroughly approve, even if the price was to be an accumulating public expenditure problem, and the frustration of the army with its second-priority status.

Domestic policy was, however, a much less impressive matter all round. Central Office could put together in 1892 only a barely adequate list of 'working-class legislation' – a Mines Regulation Act in 1887, a limited Allotments Act, a Truck Act which excluded agricultural workers from the ban on payments in kind, a very limited Shop Hours Act in 1892 – and was correspondingly grateful for Chamberlain's endorsement of the party in 1891, as deserving 'the credit for almost all the social legislation of our time'. Even these limited reforms could be achieved only when the party leaders pressed for them very hard against the dead weight of party inertia – pressure exerted partly because of fears that Liberals would exploit Unionist inaction, partly too from the great anxieties created by riots in the West End of London in 1886 which suggested a deep undercurrent of social unrest that ought to be appeased.

Among Conservatives in the parliamentary party, though, there was often a feeling that social reform was being promoted to appease Liberal Unionists like Chamberlain, and the almost complete failure of the government's legislative programme in both 1887 and 1890 reflected that feeling. When successes were achieved – as, for example, over the creation of county councils in 1888 and an extension of educational provision in 1891 (which Central Office optimistically proclaimed to be 'free education brought within the reach of almost every family in England') – Conservative MPs still resented the extent to which the reforms had had a Liberal as well as a Conservative input, as when educational reform reflected Chamberlain's concern for the nonconformists.

To many Conservatives, the ending of centuries of tradition in county government by quarter sessions and the introduction of democratically elected councils was a wholly unconservative scheme, and they were not much mollified by the election in most places of precisely the sort of people who had governed the counties as magistrates for years. The London County Council was a particular bone of contention, for a unified authority covering such a large proportion of the total English population was scarcely 'local' in the normal sense of the word, and Salisbury himself was keen to see its powers broken up by the creation of a second tier of genuinely local boroughs, but this proved impossible to do by agreement and the final stage of reform had to await the Liberals.

Nevertheless, the single most important outcome of the 1886 parliament was that as it drew to a close the Unionist alliance remained intact. The Liberal Unionist and Conservative parties were now planning to fight another election in tandem; it was this continued cooperation that denied

Gladstone, still crusading for Home Rule, an independent Liberal majority in 1892 and so saved the Union for a generation (or, from the opposite viewpoint, ended the last chance of reforming Anglo-Irish relations peacefully). The Unionist parties did not, however, approach the 1892 election with a great deal of confidence, for by-elections since 1886 had produced a net loss of twenty seats and the early results in elections to some of the new county councils (particularly in London in 1889) had also been disappointing.

These were, though, years in which quiet organizational consolidation was taking place, in the National Union (which by now supervised the organization of most counties as well as the boroughs), among the local constituencies, in the trend towards better-paid and more professional agents, and in the steady advance of the Primrose League's membership and propaganda work. There was also a growing membership of a roster of London clubs which by the end of the century offered Unionists a choice of eight alternatives, each carefully graded socially from the mighty Carlton at the top, through the Junior Carlton for younger men and the City Carlton for financiers, down to the Conservative Club (which aimed to provide a London base for provincial party leaders) and the Constitutional Club, which at Middleton's insistence admitted even the paid professional agents. Beyond this network in the West End there was a local network of political clubs which included both the elite meeting places of city bosses in places like Leeds and Liverpool and the hundreds of street-corner drinking dens (often named after either Disraeli, Salisbury or the Queen, or with an imperial theme) right across the country – but especially in Lancashire, where there were literally hundreds of them.

The Russian observer M. I. Ostrogorski, who researched British politics in the late-1880s for *Democracy and the Organisation of Political Parties*, which he published in 1902, saw the clubs and the Primrose League as a gigantic machine for political socialization, the means by which Unionist organizers brought ordinary voters into their networks of influence by providing relief from their drab, workaday lives, and then used these social contacts to promote their political objectives. Middleton was anxious to ensure that such a widely disparate range of activities did not get out of control, and therefore promoted the formation of an Association of Conservative Clubs, of which all these bodies – from the Carlton Club in Pall Mall (as it then was) to the roughest working men's drinking room in Blackburn – would be in membership. The ACC was actually run by a committee provided entirely by the elite London clubs, and its organizers were paid by and situated in Central Office, but by offering such useful practical help as a cheap stocktaking and accounting service, printing facilities, advice on the organization of social events and so on, the ACC was able to retain contact and promote political causes in the hundreds of clubs that were especially important in working-class constituencies.

All this activity did not come cheap, and it proved to be an enormous benefit to the Conservatives that after the Irish crisis of 1885–6 so many of the owners of property were now on their side of a deep party divide; commercial and financial men in particular were to be seen in increasing numbers on the Unionist side in the Commons. The party fund for 1892 was over £100,000, as much as had been raised in 1880 for a campaign which cost far more, while the Liberal Unionists had themselves built up an even larger sum. But in order to pay the bills for regular organizational efforts the party managers were now having regular recourse to the exchange of cash contributions for peerages and other honours, a sphere in which the Conservative and Liberal Unionist whips were especially careful to avoid clashes. One effect of this – which Salisbury at least deplored, but accepted philosophically as another of the necessary concessions to contemporary politics – was the growing tendency for men with great commercial wealth to end up in the Lords, a final stage in the Peelite process by which land and capital gradually fused into a single British elite. The 'beerage' had joined the peerage, in the Upper House and in county society too.

The Conservative Party in the 1890s was thus an infinitely more formidable electoral machine than it had been even in 1885–6. The 1890s were, as Lady Salisbury put it, 'the classic period of Conservative electioneering', and in view of what followed, the regime of Akers-Douglas and Middleton would long be looked back to as a golden age of party efficiency and effectiveness. Growing professionalism was demonstrated as much as anything by the publication from 1888 onwards of the fortnightly *National Union Gleanings* (later *Gleanings and Memoranda*), which summarized in great detail and with statistics, footnotes and bibliography the most recent events in British politics from the Unionist viewpoint, a gold mine both for speechwriters and friendly columnists at the time and for historians ever since.

For all Salisbury's aristocratic aloofness, he was the one of the party's leaders most aware of the value of this side of politics (which he conceded to be 'a necessary condition of the new state of things'). He routed much patronage through Middleton – or at least acted only after taking his advice, was always ready to see him for party business and was himself a regular visitor to Central Office, where (as Balfour's secretary later wrote) the Prime Minister 'would sit in long intercourse with his Chief Agent, studying reports from constituencies, and cynically discussing the merits and demerits of aspirants for honours and promotions'. It was a lesson that Balfour himself might with profit have learned from his uncle, for this was now a world in which such things could be neglected only at a party leader's peril.

The 1892 contest was nevertheless one that the party did not expect to win, in part because no party had ever won successive elections since the 1867 Reform Act, but also because their reading of the situation showed them a Liberalism revived since 1886 – the 1892 campaign produced the second lowest number of uncontested seats of any election between 1832 and 1900 – and an electorate which was, as in 1880, worried about economic matters on which the Unionists had little unitedly to say. The 1887 National Union Conference had caused something of a stir by passing a resolution calling for fair trade, and Salisbury, himself sympathetic to the idea of retaliatory tariffs, had encouraged the advocates of tariffs to take their campaign out into the country and win over public opinion. They had not yet done so to any great effect, for the weight of half a century of public opinion was all against them; as Disraeli had remarked, in Britain 'protection was not only dead but damned'. In the meantime, the National Union had been more carefully managed than in 1887 in order to ensure no repetition of that year's debate, which had alarmed the Liberal Unionists, still strongly committed to free trade.

There were thus many Conservatives, now including quite a number from industrial areas, who had grave doubts about the country's basic trading policies, but despite an indiscreet speech from Salisbury himself describing 'a war of tariffs' as taking place, their views were smothered in the approach to the election, lest the Liberals should be given the chance to claim that Conservatives favoured higher prices; memories of 1846 cast a long shadow. One Conservative junior minister, Walter Long of the Local Government Board, attributed his own defeat in Wiltshire to the Liberals' use of the 'dear bread' cry, for 'the labourers are an ignorant lot & swallowed it whole'. He was not alone in that view, for after the election Chamberlain – with consummate irony in view of what was to come – complained to Balfour that 'Lord Salisbury's unfortunate allusion to fair trade cost us a dozen seats in the counties.'

Unfortunately for Unionists in 1892, while Gladstone remained commit-

HERCULES AND THE FARMER.
(Old Fable—Modern Version.)

HERCULES-SALISBURY *(quoting from recent Speech at Brighton)*. "I AM CONSCIOUS THAT WHEN THE GOVERNMENT HAS DONE ITS BEST, EVEN IF THE GOVERNMENT WERE ABLE TO ADOPT THE ROMANTIC DREAMS OF SOME ESTEEMED FRIENDS AMONGST US, THEY WOULD ADVANCE BUT A VERY SMALL DISTANCE IN DIMINISHING THE SUFFERING WHICH THE HAND OF PROVIDENCE HAS INFLICTED——". BRITISH FARMER. "O LOR!"

Punch on Salisbury's equivocal response to the agricultural depression, 30 November 1895.

ted to Home Rule as a first priority, he was reticent about the form of self-government that he would propose, and his party's Newcastle Programme of 1891 provided a catalogue of other reforms which Liberals could offer to different interest groups, and which ensured a disparate localized campaign rather than the one-issue referendum-like campaign of 1886.

Unionists lost ground in their London and Lancashire strongholds but in both cases held on to the majority of their seats, and Chamberlain managed to retain most of his 'Grand Duchy' of Birmingham, while there was even a swing to the Conservatives in Yorkshire. Wales and Scotland, though, provided worse news – as they always did in bad Conservative years at that period – but in every area the Liberals failed to win enough contests to point to a parliamentary majority of their own, which would enable them to introduce Home Rule without prior bargaining with the Irish MPs (bargaining which would in itself encourage the Unionists in the Lords to reject Home Rule).

Overall, 268 Conservatives (down by forty-eight) and forty-seven Liberal Unionists (down by a more worrying thirty-two) faced 274 Liberals and Lib-Labs and eighty-one Irish Nationalists. The differing sizes of constituencies allowed the Unionists to claim that they had a majority, perhaps as high as 40,000 votes, if all the British constituencies were aggregated (though the few uncontested seats complicated this), and here too was a ground for further obstruction of Home Rule by the Lords.

In general the party reacted to its defeat – and to the Liberals' failure to win a real victory – with relief, and the fact that Unionism now had a weak Home Rule ministry to face was in any case encouraging. In the dying days of the second Salisbury ministry, after the election but before parliament met and installed Gladstone in office, the Unionist parties thus came closer together in discussing the final Queen's Speech, which was certain to be defeated and therefore had more to do with the future than with immediate legislation. Agreeing on policy was far from easy, and Chamberlain's ambitious plans were not adopted, but the discussions did reveal a Liberal Unionist willingness to join the next Salisbury government as full members, confirming the prospect of moving on eventually to a single, fused party.

In the short term, Salisbury's resignation of office in August 1892 was important in giving ministers a long-delayed chance of recuperation while Gladstone struggled with the impossible task of bringing about Home Rule without a majority, but in the longer term the convergence of the

Unionist parties was of greater significance. Once Commons debates on Home Rule began in April 1893, Chamberlain took the lead in attacking the bill – it suited both Conservatives (since it demonstrated the breadth of Unionism) and Chamberlain himself (since it raised his star appeal to Conservative backbenchers) that it should be so – while both Salisbury and Balfour returned to the hustings at rallies in Ulster and in Dublin to demonstrate the strength of Irish resistance to the bill. Irish votes ensured that Gladstone's bill was bound to pass the Commons, as it duly did by majorities of around forty votes, but only after debates in which Unionist speakers had intervened to great effect and after a guillotining procedure that meant that most of it had not been discussed at all. The Unionist preponderance in the Lords was by now enormous, and for the summer debates great efforts were made to bring up as many backwoodsmen as possible in order to secure the biggest possible majority – though Salisbury was careful to ensure that, as in 1886, it was actually a Liberal Unionist motion that would be passed. On 8 September the bill fell in the Lords by 419 votes to forty-one and the party organized extensive autumn celebrations to mark the 'saving of the empire'.

So far, so good, for Conservative leaders correctly divined that Gladstone would not be able to persuade his Liberal colleagues to take on the Lords with a proposal to change the constitution itself over an issue on which the British electorate was thought to be predominantly Unionist, and the usual autumn campaign of speeches around the country in 1893 concentrated on reminding voters of the perils of Home Rule in order to keep that issue, rather than the role of the House of Lords or other, more popular Liberal policies, in their minds.

With Gladstone's sulky recognition that Home Rule could not for the moment be further pressed, and the Liberals' move into areas of social policy, Unionists became more nervous. Worries about the appeal of Liberal policies on agriculture had Conservative MPs once again thinking about their rural bases and wondering whether they should themselves offer a more radical policy to the agricultural labourers, much as they were to do – and equally inconclusively – in 1913, when another and more powerful Liberal government presented the same threat. There were also fears that the Liberals were deliberately highlighting their problems with the House of Lords, giving up bills altogether rather than let them pass after being heavily amended in the Upper House. This was another forerunner of the tactics of post-1906, as was the Liberals' tendency to promote their social objectives through such budgetary means as increased death duties, prompting Salisbury in 1894 to assert (but not actually to apply) the Lords' right to reject even a Finance Bill. But these were in 1893–4 only short-term and limited concerns, for from the failure of Home Rule onwards the Gladstone–Rosebery government was visibly riven by internal disagreements on policy, priorities and personality, and was unlikely to be a threat for long to anything but itself.

The greatest worry was simply that by hanging on to office into 1894–5 the Liberals would persuade British voters to forget Home Rule and so make it more difficult for Unionists to play their winning card when another election finally came. Meanwhile the allies prepared for the day on which they would come together in office, with Chamberlain, as in 1892, urging the compilation of an ambitious domestic programme of the type that he advocated at the National Union Conference in November 1894 – old age pensions, shorter shop hours, employer's liability for industrial injuries, restrictions on immigration, and arbitration machinery for labour disputes. These proposals were once again publicized in Central Office literature with a view to their voter appeal, but Chamberlain never came near to getting Salisbury's agreement to such ideas either in principle or in detail. For all their awareness of Chamberlain's increased importance to Conservative electoral fortunes, the party's leaders still found him and his preferred policies too hard a pill to swallow; as Balfour wrote privately, 'Joe, though we all love him, does not completely mix, does not form a chemical combination with us.'

There now came a rare episode of social convergence. When Chamberlain was at last invited to Hatfield for Christmas 1894, formal agreement to serve together in office was finally achieved; shortly afterwards Balfour told the Primrose League to expect 'a permanent union of the two sections of the party'. Even this was a gain that had problems attached, for not only would Conservative MPs complain of excessive Liberal Unionist influence on policy, they would now also complain about the 'good Conservatives' who would have to be sacrificed to find places for them at the Cabinet table. When Rosebery's government was finally harried out of office in June 1895, this became a practical rather than a hypothetical matter, though the likelihood of an immediate election gave Salisbury's Cabinet-making an urgency that pre-empted his usual leisurely approach.

This time Salisbury made no suggestion that the Duke of Devonshire (as Hartington had now become) should be premier, and all issues of importance were settled at a single meeting between himself, Balfour, Devonshire and Chamberlain. The Liberal Unionists would have four of

LEFT *Arthur Wellesley, 1st Duke of Wellington with Sir Robert Peel* by Franz Winterhalter.

ABOVE *Lord George Cavendish Bentinck* by Samuel Lane, c.1836.

LEFT *Edward Stanley, 14th Earl of Derby (1799–1869)* by Frederick Richard Say, 1844.

ABOVE The most popular engraving of Benjamin Disraeli, based on a photograph by Mayall.

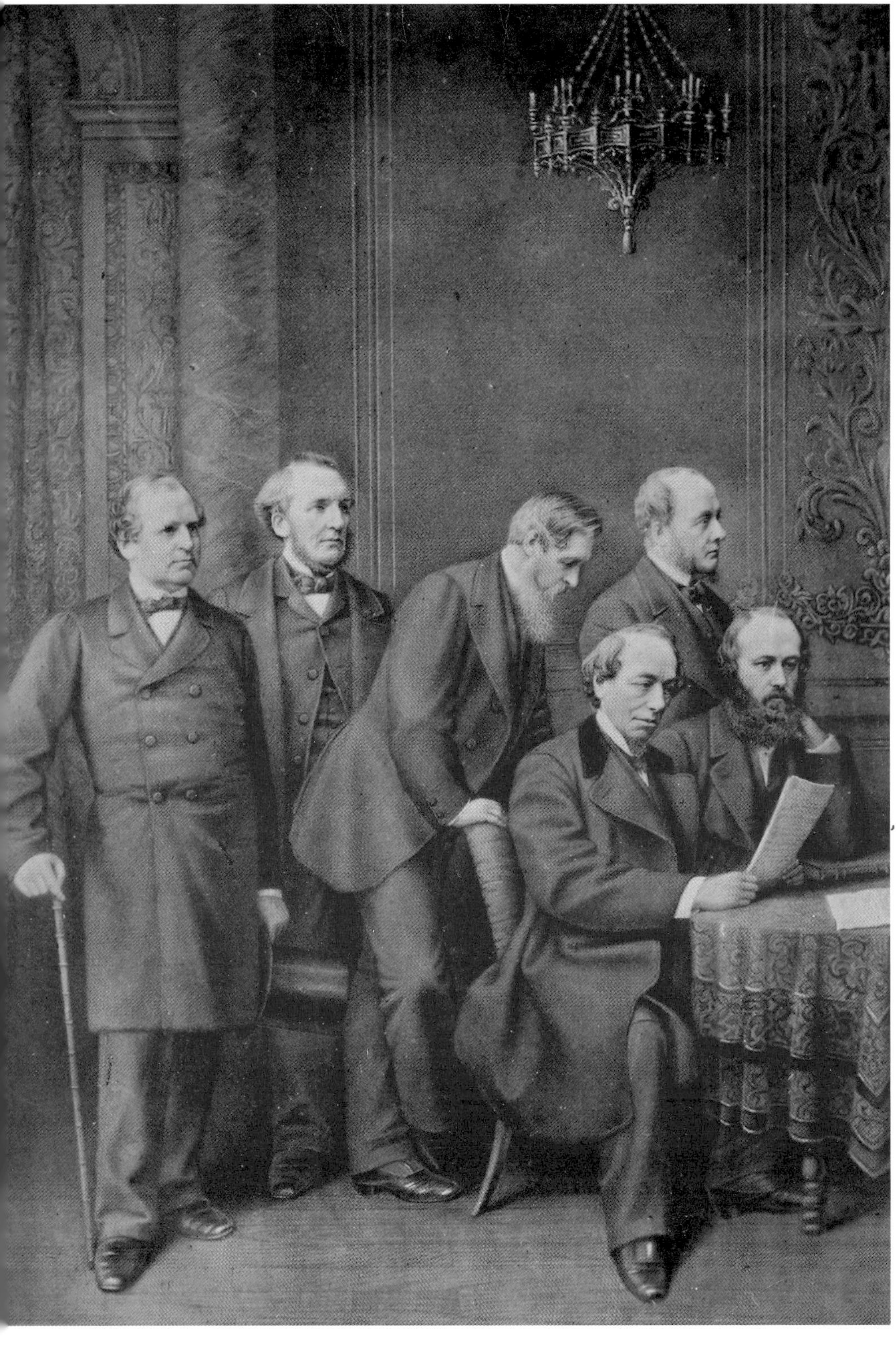

OPPOSITE Members of Disraeli's 1874 Cabinet photographed c.1876: (from left to right), the 15th Earl of Derby, Lord Cairns, Sir Stafford Northcote, Disraeli, Gathorne Hardy, and the 3rd Marquess of Salisbury.

RIGHT Lord Randolph Churchill in 1874.

BELOW *Arthur James Balfour and Joseph Chamberlain on the Front Bench* by Sydney Prior Hall, 1902.

Andrew Bonar Law addressing a Rally of Unionists at Blenheim Palace on 29 July 1912.

Andrew Bonar Law and J.C.C. Davidson leaving the Carlton Club after the meeting that overthrew Austen Chamberlain as Conservative leader, 19 October 1922.

Stanley Baldwin greeting photographers outside the Caxton Hall, before a meeting with his Party critics, 1930.

Stanley Baldwin recording a newsreel film in the gardens of No. 10.

Stanley Baldwin is given a presentation book by Neville Chamberlain on his retirement in May 1937.

OPPOSITE Winston Churchill speaking at Walthamstow on 4 July 1945, during the General Election campaign.

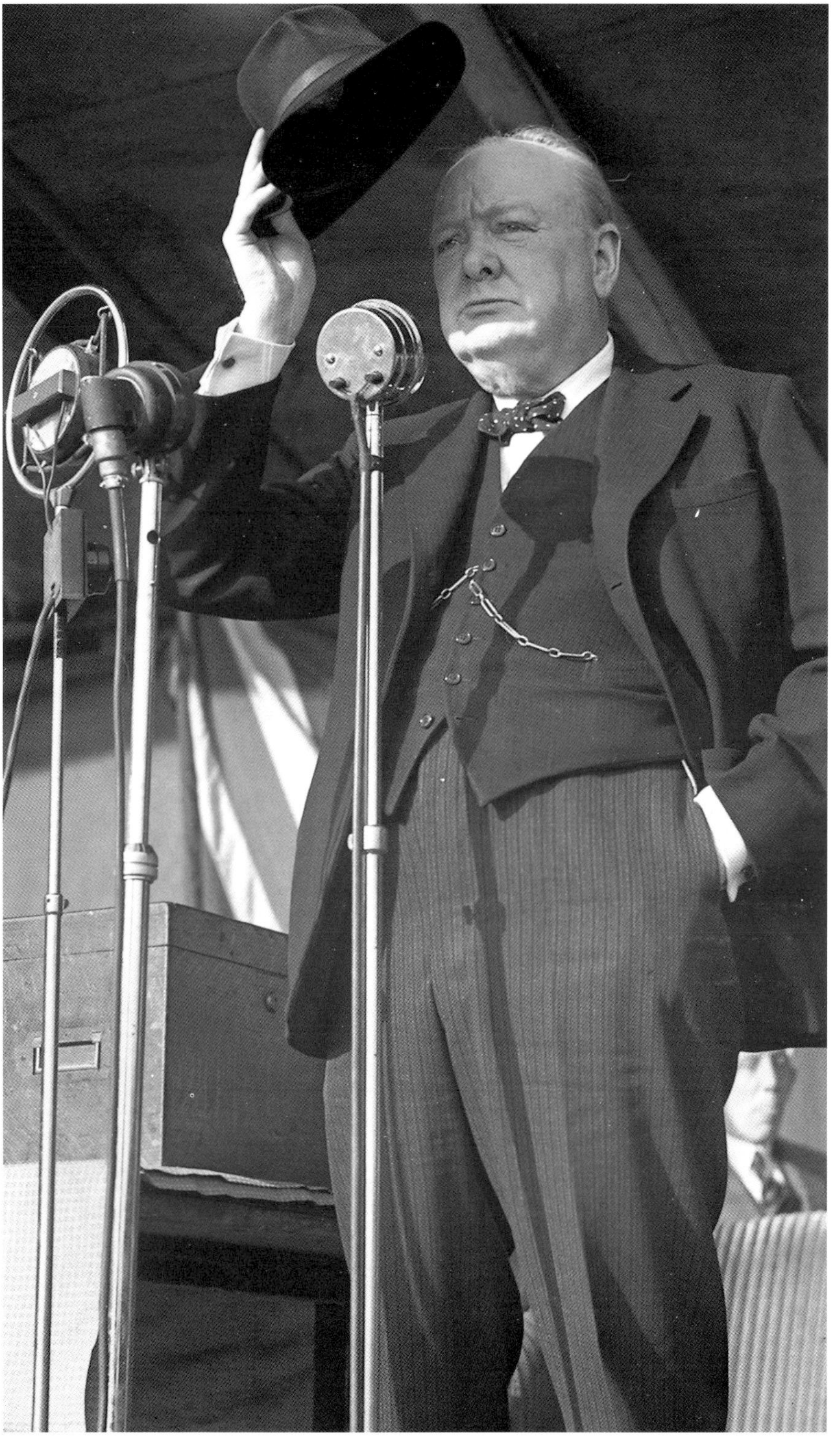

Harold Macmillan helping to launch *The Right Road for Britain* at the 1949 Conservative Party Conference.

Members of Churchill's shadow cabinet shortly before the 1950 General Election, including, (from left to right), Harold Macmillan, the 5th Marquess of Salisbury, Harry Crookshank, Lord Woolton, Sir David Maxwell Fyfe, Anthony Eden and R.A. Butler.

the eighteen Cabinet posts and a comparable share of the junior positions, but this generosity prompted them to take relatively junior posts which would excite the least Conservative jealousy. Salisbury again occupied the Foreign Office and Balfour was again Leader of the Commons, while Chamberlain turned down the Exchequer in favour of the Colonial Office, where his increasingly imperial outlook would enable him to attract rather than repel Conservative MPs. Apart from the coalition aspect, which naturally attracted most attention, appointments were traditional, with Cross prominent among the returning veterans. On the eve of the dissolution Salisbury argued in the Lords that his government would aim to 'mitigate the misery which attends on the vicissitudes of this changeful time and to lessen the sorrows that attend the lives of many millions of our fellow creatures', but confusingly he also promised to make no 'revolutionary changes' and to avoid 'ambitious programmes'. Expectations were raised and fears calmed by this approach, but it was not a basis for a programme that could be promoted in office.

Prospects for the election looked increasingly good, for by-elections produced a crop of gains and the LCC elections went much better in 1894 than they had done in 1889, promising well in a key electoral battleground. This time, the fall-back of the Liberals was marked from the start, for no fewer than ninety-two English constituencies failed even to produce a Liberal candidate, and across the country as a whole the outgoing government put up a half-hearted performance, while Unionists campaigned confidently on the themes of Home Rule, the empire and the need for a return to strong government. Gains were made all across the country, including sixteen in London and another sixteen in Lancashire, over thirty in the English counties, and even eleven in Scotland and six in Wales. Overall, the new parliament would have 341 Conservatives (just a majority in their own right) together with seventy Liberal Unionists, facing a mere 177 Liberals and eighty-two Irish, a government majority, with Irish support, of no less than 176.

The victory seemed to crown a decade of efforts by Akers-Douglas and Middleton, who were duly lauded for their work. Akers-Douglas had joined the Cabinet as First Commissioner of Works, but Middleton stayed on as Principal Agent until retiring in 1903, encouraged no doubt by the £10,000 testimonial presented to him in 1896 by a grateful party. Nevertheless, although Akers-Douglas continued to take a fatherly interest in organizational matters, 1895 did mark some slackening of the party's enthusiasm in the field of organization, for his successors as Chief Whip,

Sir William Walrond (1895–1902) and Sir Alexander Acland-Hood (1902–11), were neither of them men of the same calibre. The parliamentary link with the organizers had already weakened when Balfour replaced Smith as Leader of the Commons in 1891, while Salisbury's increasing age and remoteness reduced practical connections at the top too. In any case, the very scale of the victory of 1895, especially when repeated in much less promising circumstances in 1900, encouraged a degree of complacency, a conviction that the machinery would always be able to deliver the goods, which together with a reluctance to keep up the pressure of innovation would leave the Conservatives with a less than satisfactory organization by 1910.

Salisbury himself found it hard to explain the trends of his political lifetime, for such Conservative dominance in the 1890s defied all the pessimistic, disintegrationist and class-conflictive predictions that had been his stock in trade ever since 1866–7, when he had defied Disraeli over the extension of the franchise; 'the result has turned out exactly the other way', he confessed in 1895. Since he did not even pretend to understand the forces that had brought about this desirable but baffling outcome, he was hard pressed to know how his government should react to it, and only too ready to take refuge in a comfortable caution and an overriding concern with foreign policy. In the complacent atmosphere of 1895–9, in which the country luxuriated in the assurance that it was not just isolated from European entanglements but 'splendidly isolated', and in which the Queen's Diamond Jubilee of 1897 provided an excuse for weeks of jingoistic flag-waving, such an approach by the Prime Minister was not particularly out of step, but as preparation for the crises that would follow after the turn of the century it was wholly inadequate. It might well be politically 'a time of slack water', as Salisbury himself put it in 1897, but this did not encourage the party to prepare – or even to keep a careful look-out – for reefs ahead.

Most crucially, the complete defeat administered to Irish Home Rule in 1893, which was then in effect confirmed by the electorate in 1895, exiled Home Rule from the realms of the politically practicable. The Liberal Prime Minister Rosebery had already confessed that Irish aspirations could not be met unless English voters were first convinced, and no further Liberal attempt to bring forward Home Rule would be made until the Irish again held the balance of power in the Commons after 1910. This meant that for a generation politics would return to something more like the normal situation as it had been before 1886, and that the main purpose that had brought the Unionist parties together could no longer act as a focus of their cooperation, the cement for their prospective fusion. It was no accident that it was the revival of Home Rule in 1910–11 that provided the final spur for the Unionist parties to merge in 1912. In the meantime, though, it was not at all clear what it was that the Unionists ought to do together in government.

In principle at least, the easiest area to deal with ought to have been Ireland itself, for here the complete defeat of Home Rule seemed to have provided the breathing space for an alternative policy, and one on which the coalition partners could agree. The new Irish Secretary Gerald Balfour explained that the government would like 'by kindness to kill home rule', a phrase which could just as easily have applied to his brother Arthur's policy before 1891, but which it was impolitic to explain so bluntly. Nationalists were outraged by the suggestion that Ireland could just be bought off, and Irish Unionists by the implication that the Nationalists would get much of what they wanted (short of Home Rule) in order to keep them quiet.

In practice, Gerald Balfour could be less tough on political dissent now that the extent of crime and disorder was falling in the later 1890s, and therefore more opportunity to pursue the other half of the Unionist package. But he was far too lightweight a politician for so sensitive a post and proved unable to do anything much with dynamism or determination. Land purchase, reinvigorated after the slowing down following the 1891 act, and the introduction of democratic local authorities in the Irish counties in 1898 (ten years after England and Wales) were both brave reforms, but they increasingly antagonized Unionists (especially when most of the new county councils acquired Nationalist majorities which then reinforced the infrastructure of the Home Rule Party all across southern and western Ireland). A general bill creating two new Irish universities was rejected by the Cabinet simply because they could not see how to get Unionist MPs to vote for such concessions to Irish Catholics. With the Union no longer apparently under threat, Unionists were not easily persuaded to take advantage of concessionary measures that might just have persuaded some Nationalist Irishmen that the Union could have real benefits to them personally. Perhaps such a prospect was never more than chimerical, as the growing interest in such non-economic symptoms of Irishness as Gaelic-speaking seemed to indicate, but it is certainly true that the uncertainty with which the Unionists approached Irish policy after 1895 did not maximize whatever chance there might have been for reaping the benefits of Arthur Balfour's earlier years of 'resolution'.

On more general domestic issues the parliament of 1895 tended to repeat the experience of 1886–92, with Unionist MPs mutinous in several sessions and with numbers of bills withdrawn (as was a proposed educational reform in 1897) or so weakened in the process of production through Cabinet and subsequent legislation as to make them seem grudging and inadequate, as was the Working Men's Compensation Act of 1897. To a large extent this stemmed from the fact that the alliance of Anglicans and nonconformists, countrymen and town-dwellers, industrialists and aristocrats who sat on the Unionist benches did not share a core belief of what their party was actually *for*, so that once they were denied Liberal bills to oppose – and especially when denied the defence of the Union itself – they found disciplined and collective action in pursuit of a common cause to be almost impossible. Rating tax concessions to ameliorate rural depression infuriated MPs representing urban taxpayers; educational protection for Church schools irritated nonconformists and Erastians alike; rural Conservatives objected to the time and energy spent on yet another reform of London's local government in 1899; and the exclusion of farm workers from the plans for employers' liability seemed to many to be a disgraceful concession to a vested party interest. Was the party to be seen simply as a spokesman for property and privilege – and if so could the organization continue to deliver working-class votes in the time of increasing industrial antagonism which would lead to the creation of the Labour Party in 1899–1900? Or were the ghosts of Disraeli and Lord Randolph Churchill (as well as the actual presence of Joe Chamberlain) to be propitiated with social reforms which the propertied would have to be made to swallow for their own protection? These were not choices that Salisbury's Cabinet was encouraged to make by the Prime Minister, and the party therefore continued to face both ways and to invite criticism from both flanks.

There was enough in the legislation and administration of 1895–9 to provide Central Office with adequate electioneering material, but little to satisfy those with a real ambition to see the Conservatives respond dramatically to the growing perception that the country was in industrial, agricultural and commercial decline. Such frustrations, dammed up for years, were to explode into the tariff controversy of 1903, when the party's most frustrated politician, Joseph Chamberlain, finally gave a dramatic lead. Tariff reform, though, also owed something to the perceptions of related crises in the empire and in public expenditure. Even without a more advanced social policy, and before the great strains imposed after 1899 by the Boer War, the 1890s witnessed a steady growth of public expenditure as the demands of an increasing population on education and the social services took their effect, and to this problem Unionists felt obliged to add increased military spending too, when Germany began threateningly to build a fleet of battleships.

As in 1886–92, Salisbury's conduct of British foreign policy won widespread praise, and the facing down of France in the Fashoda affair of 1898 without the need for war was rightly seen as one of the country's greatest diplomatic triumphs. Yet although Salisbury kept jealous control of diplomacy as before, he could not remain unchallenged on imperial matters once Chamberlain was at the Colonial Office and pursuing (particularly in South Africa) an unashamedly expansionist, 'pushful' policy in the pursuit of British economic interests. Increasingly, Unionists contrasted Chamberlain's confident policies in the empire with Salisbury's necessarily more careful approach to European diplomacy, and Chamberlain emerged from that comparison with an enhanced reputation, though he was careful never to challenge Salisbury in any way or to break the solidarity of the Cabinet in public.

Although he was far from sharing Chamberlain's growing interest in tariffs, the young Winston Churchill recognized a fellow-activist and found him spell-binding, a clear contrast with the other Unionist leaders, as he later recalled in *Great Contemporaries* (1937):

> At the time when I looked out of my regimental cradle and was thrilled by politics, Mr Chamberlain was incomparably the most live, sparkling, insurgent, compulsive figure in British affairs. Above him in the House of Lords reigned venerable, august Lord Salisbury, Prime Minister since God knows when. Beside him on the Government Bench, wise, cautious, polished, comprehending, airily fearless, Arthur Balfour led the House of Commons. But 'Joe' was the one who made the weather. He was the man the masses knew. He it was who had solutions to social problems; who was ready to advance, sword in hand if need be, upon the foes of Britain; and whose accents rang in the ears of all the young peoples of the Empire and of lots of young people at its heart.

Chamberlain was in fact practising what he had preached to the radical Liberal Sir Charles Dilke in 1892, which was to 'be as radical as you like.

Be Home Ruler if you must. But be a little Jingo if you can.' As the Salisbury government's domestic policy seemed so hesitant, it was on its foreign and colonial policy that its reputation increasingly came to rest, with benefits conferred by the Jubilee in 1897, by Fashoda in 1898 and by 'victory' in the Boer War in 1900. In effect this meant that more and more of its fortunes also came to depend on Chamberlain.

The combination of reliance on international policy for the impression of a government in control of affairs, and of the 'pushful' determination of Chamberlain to do something dynamic, produced in South Africa both the humiliating Jameson Raid of 1895 and the Boer War of 1899–1902. Years of steady pressure on the Boers by Chamberlain – and by his representatives in South Africa – produced a situation by 1899 in which Boers could choose only between fighting and submitting, either of which course was expected to lead to the advance of British control over their territories. The careful cultivation of the press by Chamberlain himself, particularly in the case of the new mass-production *Daily Mail* (which had just become the first paper to exceed a million copies a day, precisely by highlighting such jingoist stories as Boer 'persecution' of British settlers), built up a public opinion in Britain within which there would be little room for any retreat when the moment of crisis came; with the advance perception that this was a testing moment for the future of the empire, the Conservatives as well as the Liberal Unionists were behind Chamberlain almost to a man. When war came in October 1899 only two Unionist MPs out of 428 spoke against it, and so far were they working against the grain of party opinion that neither was still an MP by the end of 1900.

The course of the South African War of 1899–1902 fell into three distinct phases, and the politics of the war need to be seen in much the same way. First, there was a short period in which the Boers proved that their irregular soldiers could inflict humiliating defeats on the flower of the British army, culminating in 'Black Week' in December 1899, in which three British armies were defeated in succession and actual loss of the war briefly stared the government in the face. This was a great shock to Unionist opinion, though the resolution of Balfour and of the War Under-Secretary George Wyndham in the face of these setbacks helped to steady things, as did the reflection that, as Chamberlain himself put it, the Boers were after all 'of Teutonic race' (unlike the easier victims of most colonial wars). There were, however, scapegoats to be found among those who had been responsible for military planning, and army reform continued to be a central objective of the party right through to the loss of office in 1905.

The second phase was more cheerful, covering the first half of 1900, in which the resources of the empire were finally mobilized under Lord Roberts's command to defeat the Boer field armies, raise the sieges of Mafeking and Ladysmith, and capture the Boer capital Pretoria in June. To a large extent this restored both the morale and the reputation of the government, and although a snap dissolution in the summer was avoided as being somewhat obvious and out of keeping with the mood of the country, this phase did nevertheless provide the backdrop to the 'khaki' election held in October, in which the government was comfortably re-elected. At that time there was scarcely anyone in Britain who foresaw that the third and final phase of the war would last until the middle of 1902, with a messy two years of guerrilla warfare reducing the entire British empire to apparent impotence at the hands of a few thousand farmers and thus administering a second shock to the government and the electorate. Meanwhile, the massive cost of the war – running at something like five times the level of peacetime military expenditure – went on and on, added about a quarter to the National Debt, and brought to crisis point the existing problem of the public deficit and how to finance it.

The shortness of the first defensive phase of the war, and the fact that the Liberals were so divided on the fact of war itself as to be unable to exploit the British army's poor showing, helped to limit the political damage, while the support for the Boers of Irish MPs who saw them as fellow-strugglers against British imperialism did much to unite the Unionists. By-elections, which had produced eleven net losses since 1895, changed course for the better as the tide of war turned, and once Mafeking was relieved – the moment for a mass outburst of patriotic relief – a government near the end of its fifth year was bound to consider whether to dissolve parliament. Interestingly, those in the party who opposed an election often did so in the hope of avoiding a repetition of 1895, an election in which little positive was on offer in a negative campaign and which could therefore produce only a relatively unsatisfactory government afterwards. Nevertheless, the temptations gradually became irresistible, and the claim that the Boers would not give up their fight so long as they might hold out for a 'pro-Boer' Liberal ministry (claims that only an election could scotch) gave the dissolution some national as well as party justification. However, when the 1895 parliament was eventually dissolved in September 1900, the keynote of the appeals issued by both Salisbury and Balfour was the need for continuity and a renewed majority to complete the victory in South Africa. On this occasion Chamberlain was too much involved in the war himself to offer a more positive programme for domestic consumption, and when the campaign got going, he 'played it down low to the man in the street' (as the socialist writer Beatrice Webb put it) with the best of them, banging the imperial drum and taunting pro-Boer Liberals with being traitors. Ever since facing Gladstone in gladiatorial contest in the Commons over Home Rule in 1893, Chamberlain had realized that his sheer combativeness had a strong appeal to Unionists led by the cool Salisbury and the elegant Balfour, and in 1900 this tactic reached its climax.

It was a highly one-sided campaign, for the Liberals, divided and leaderless for much of the period since 1895 and now deeply embarrassed by their divisions over the war, could put up little real resistance. Over a third of all constituencies were uncontested, and the overwhelming majority of these returned Unionists – 138 in England alone – while the turnout in constituencies that did have contests fell somewhat, another favourable circumstance for the Conservatives. Just how tight was the organizers' grip on an election fought in such a low key is borne out by the fact that the party lost sixteen of the seventeen seats that Middleton thought most vulnerable and captured all nine on his list of targets. Unionists had only to keep banging on about the war and otherwise keep the temperature low to win a considerable victory – and this is exactly what happened. There were unusual victories in some dockyard and arms-manufacturing areas, a few losses in Wales, where nonconformity rejected the war, but the vast majority of constituencies that went to the poll produced results remarkably like 1895. The only real exception to that pattern was in Scotland, where Unionist representation rose from thirty-one to thirty-six and the Liberals held under half of the Scottish seats for the first time since modern electioneering began in 1832. Scotland's military involvement in the war perhaps accounted for some of this, but so too did more generically imperial feeling in such places as Glasgow, where the Unionists now held all seven seats, one of those gaining a Liberal seat (on a 10 per cent swing) being the local ironmaster Andrew Bonar Law. Overall, this produced a combined Unionist tally of 402 and an overall parliamentary majority of 134.

This was both impressive and in its way surprising, for the politicians' folklore that the electorate would by swinging the pendulum to prevent any government from becoming its own successor had been deeply ingrained since 1867. Salisbury, always a man to expect the worst, was dazed by his second successive landslide, though relieved that the electorate had given him clear authority for the prosecution of the war to a finish. Unfortunately, the fact that the election – and the majority achieved – had rested so much on the circumstances of the war as it stood at the time of the campaign meant that it was again hard to see how the government should now react domestically. There were those who argued – much as others would do in 1931 and in 1983 – that the Opposition had rendered itself unfit for office and that the government did not therefore have much of a mandate for anything. And since the government itself had scarcely asked for one except in the context of the war the essential problem of 1895–1900 would remain.

It was in any case unlikely that the seventy-year-old and increasingly detached Salisbury would wish to change the habits of a lifetime and espouse a dynamic domestic policy, as some of his party critics were demanding, but if there had been any doubts then the way in which he reshuffled his government after the 1900 election certainly dispelled them. Pressure from colleagues who felt that he was no longer up to the task of doing two major jobs compelled him to give up the Foreign Office, though the choice of the patrician Whig Lansdowne to succeed him was in itself an indication of his lack of concern for feeling in the broader party, where all too many Unionists felt that Lansdowne (as War Secretary) should be held responsible for failing to prepare the army adequately for the Boer War and were horrified that he should now be promoted. Much the same was true of Gerald Balfour, who had to be moved from the Irish Office, but somehow managed to acquire a Cabinet place at the Board of Trade (about which he knew next to nothing and where he made a very poor showing). The majority of ministers remained in the same posts, including both Balfour and Chamberlain, and those promoted reflected the same aristocratic and family preferences. While Salisbury had, both in 1886 and 1895, been widely but quietly criticized on the back benches for doing little in his appointments to recognize the changing character of the party, he was now openly accused of nepotism. Of the five new Cabinet ministers, one was Salisbury's son-in-law and another a nephew. The premier's eldest son joined the team as Under-Secretary at the Foreign Office, and as Salisbury's younger sons Lord Hugh and Lord Robert Cecil also reached the House a bright ministerial future was confidently predicted for them. Cross hung on in Salisbury's government right through until 1900 largely because nobody like him had been brought forward as a replacement, and because Salisbury, unlike Disraeli, was unwilling to take a chance with the unproven – unless they had the right background, breeding and character.

Both at the time and since, the 1900 reshuffle has seemed a missed opportunity, though it may well be that the real missed chance was for Salisbury to bow out in triumph and leave others to look forward to the new century, for he himself was unable to grasp either the extent of the problem or the way in which his 'Hotel Cecil' regime was now viewed from his own party's back benches. 'Hotel Cecil' was a shorthand that came to represent the dominance of the Cecil family in Unionist politics, and more broadly the aristocratic, gentlemanly ethos that Salisbury represented in a party that was becoming the political vehicle of industrialists and bankers, men who after highly successful careers of their own were increasingly unhappy at being treated as less deserving of political office than such as Gerald Balfour. A columnist in the *National Review* complained that Salisbury was still making appointments as if 'England was the only Colonial Power and only great manufacturing commonwealth', while through the mordant pen of its editor Leo Maxse that journal wrote with increasing insistence of the impossibility of continuing for much longer with 'the old gang'. The young Unionist journalist J. L. Garvin wrote that Salisbury was 'utterly out of touch with the nation that has just returned him to power', and pointed out that his party could not indefinitely postpone the giving of authority to its only real star, Joseph Chamberlain. In the next generation Garvin, Maxse and Chamberlain were all to be at the heart of the convulsions that would overtake Unionist politics – convulsions which Salisbury's increasingly lethargic leadership had done little to prevent.

The final problem that the reshuffle of 1900 presented as the party faced the new century was in the succession. Salisbury would not retire until the war ended in South Africa, but Balfour was undoubtedly going to be his successor, since he had led the party in the Commons for a decade, with considerable distinction. Conservative MPs, despite their admiration for Chamberlain, would never have accepted him – the only real alternative – as their leader; in 1906 Walter Long, claiming to speak as always for the English squires in the party, explained bluntly that Chamberlain could not be Leader because 'the Conservative Party ... will not be led by a bloody radical', and in 1911 he was still referring to all that Chamberlain stood for as 'Birmingham and Co.'. But if Balfour offered hope for the future as a younger and far more open-minded man on policy issues than Salisbury was by 1900, he also represented at the same time a great degree of continuity with 'the old gang' and the Hotel Cecil's way of doing things that would continue to arouse criticism. He himself had an aloofly aristocratic strain which the opening up of his private papers has presented in far less appealing light than his uncle Salisbury's. Balfour was not at all averse to sneering behind their backs at rising provincial and suburban party men and their villas, 'with their vineries and pineries'; he wrote of an industrialist with civilized traits as a 'rara avis', and described a week spent among supporters in his Manchester constituency in 1886 as 'loathsome but necessary'. In the Edwardian generation in which the party would finally have to deal with the aspirations of the party men that Chamberlain represented, Balfour's touch would not turn out to be much more secure than his uncle's had been in widening the social base of the Hotel Cecil. Though he had played a crucial role in converting the party opportunity that Disraeli had created into actual power, and achieving thereby twenty years of Unionist domination of British politics after 1886, Salisbury and his 'old gang' had been unable to keep up with the pace of change, unable and indeed unwilling to keep their party facing towards the future. And for that there would be a terrible price to be paid.

8

Drifting, 1900–1914

DURING THE TWO YEARS between the general election victory of 1900 and Salisbury's retirement in 1902 the Unionists' position remained steady enough on the surface, while underlying problems gathered. These can conveniently be categorized as deriving from the continuing war in South Africa, from the ferment within the party over financial, economic and imperial policy which the Boer War had unleashed, and from the foundation of the new Labour Party and its move towards an alliance with the Liberals. But over and above all of these things, the death of Queen Victoria after sixty-four years on the throne reinforced the pre-existing *fin de siècle* sense that the new century required a more dynamic politics than Salisbury's 'slack water' caution had recently offered. There were problems aplenty for Edwardian Unionists, but (as Harold Macmillan's Conservatives were also to discover in the early 1960s) none was more difficult to meet than this sea-change of cultural mood, which would penalize the old regime simply for having had its twenty-year dominance of Britain, and for its association with things past when there was a new national appetite for looking forward.

The country's failure in the Boer War both caused and reinforced this change in mood, for after the enthusiasm of 1900 came a grim campaign against the civilian Boer population which drove the army into repressive policies that were popular neither at home nor abroad. Even 1900's 'khaki' election drew attention in its nickname to the fact that this was already a mud-coloured modern war rather than a scarlet-and-gold imperial triumph, and that downbeat aspect became steadily more pronounced as the months went by. It was increasingly difficult to deny the questions that had already surfaced in 1899 – questions about the whole fitness and competence of Britain for her imperial role, once it proved impossible for 'the Empire on which the sun never sets' to subdue a small farming people without having to have recourse to what the Liberal Leader called 'methods of barbarism', which besmirched the high moral tone that most Britons liked to associate with the empire – and even these repressive methods did not prove to be either quick or effective. Since Britain's imperial role as the governor of hundreds of millions of subject peoples had always to an extent depended on a claimed moral superiority, on self-confidence and on bluff, the Boer War administered a severe shock to all of these, and offered a blinding glimpse of a future in which hundreds of millions of Indians and other subject peoples would follow the example of the few thousand Boers.

After the Boer War, then, it became impossible to ignore underlying issues about Britain's international future; a coming retreat or a lengthy battle to hold on to colonies in revolt had at least to be contemplated – campaigns which would require the regular use of unlimited armed force and much money too. These questions would be, right through into the 1960s, very hard issues for Conservative politicians to deal with. In the short term, the new realism about Britain's place in the world produced in 1900 a temporary consideration of rapprochement with Germany which came to nothing, and then in 1901–2 an actual alliance with Japan to limit Britain's over-extension as a world sea-power. This fitted in well enough with the Conservatives' navalist, 'blue water' traditions in international policy, but it also marked a turning away from Salisbury's policy of avoiding entangling alliances with other powers. This shift of outlook also marked the beginning of a diplomatic revolution towards Britain's wider participation in Great Power alliances, with Balfour's government signing in 1904 the entente with France that ended Britain's isolation in Europe, but which was also to draw Britain into the First World War in 1914.

There were more direct short-term lessons from the Boer War too. The army had clearly proved inadequate in training, weaponry, generalship and logistic support, and the Unionists committed themselves to a root-and-branch reform programme, though in view of the vested interests involved and differing opinions as to what should be done, this in itself proved divisive and difficult.

Beyond the army, the physical inadequacy of a high proportion of the volunteers who came forward as recruits, especially in such urban areas as Manchester, created for a generation filled with the ideas of Charles Darwin – and imbued too with the bastard version of those ideas, the racially based 'social Darwinism' – deep fears of the deterioration of the race itself. These worries were reinforced by such social investigators as Seebohm Rowntree and Charles Booth, whose systematic research into poverty showed at just this time, and with convincing statistical detail, how far many urban workers' diets made the bringing up of healthy children a near impossible task. One reaction to this was to turn to policies of social reform – for example, through subsidized school meals and medical inspections, or through old age pensions (which would have the effect of relieving working people of the need to support aged parents at the same time as feeding children) – and the decade before 1914 therefore became one in which 'national efficiency' would be pursued by active social policies, a political dynamic that powerfully challenged Salisbury's pessimistically lethargic political stance. The Balfour government's appointment of a committee to investigate physical deterioration and of a Royal Commission on the Poor Laws were two examples of this concern, but an advanced social policy would run against the grain of Unionist's innate caution and would offend many in the party because of its cost, for an existing public sector deficit could only be brought further into crisis by increased social expenditure.

There was, though, an alternative and even more radical Unionist response to the perceived physical and military crisis of decline, one that appealed to quite a wide spectrum of party opinion. This was compulsory military service, which would give the country a large pool of trained and fit men ready to fight a future war even on a European scale. The demand for such a policy would grow steadily as Britain's alliance with France developed and as relations with Germany continued to deteriorate. The National Service League came into existence under the leadership of Lord Roberts, the hero of Afghanistan and South Africa, and with the pen of Rudyard Kipling as its most powerful weapon. Many Unionists no doubt read with much pleasure such propaganda works as Kipling's short story 'The Army of a Dream', in which he fantasized about a future Britain with a militarized, disciplined and bronzed manhood enjoying themselves in weekend soldiering that was much like a grown-up version of the recently founded Boy Scouts (which stemmed from very similar ideas). But to accept the levels of compulsion called for by the National Service League was quite another thing, for this could well prove to be a very unpopular policy in a country that had had no tradition of conscription since the hated naval press gangs of the Napoleonic era, and a lively tradition of disliking and distrusting the army that went back to Oliver Cromwell. The Unionists did not therefore give any corporate backing to the National Service League. Many were in any case more actively involved in the rather older Navy League, and Unionist leadership of both of these bodies did not help in maintaining a united front. If in 1902 the Boer War had been for Kipling 'an imperial lesson' but one that 'may make us an Empire yet', he was already by 1904 despairing at the inability of democratic politicians to tell the public hard truths that the national interest demanded.

The overriding sense of crisis that the Boer War created brought into focus at the same time a growing fear that the British economy was in dangerous decline and the empire in danger of falling apart, issues that had a close relationship at a time when so much of Britain's trade was with the empire. As the country which had industrialized first, Britain was bound eventually to lose its overwhelming preponderance as a manufacturer and a trader in manufactured goods, once such countries as Germany, France and America got into their industrial stride, but the steady fall in Britain's share of world trade in key areas like steelmaking was both an economic and a strategic worry nevertheless. Here, too, Germany seemed to pose a threat to Britain's future, and in the 1890s there were increasing concerns about the penetration of British markets by goods labelled MADE IN GERMANY – concerns that were whipped up, along with other xenophobic causes like Jewish immigration, by such as the mass-circulation *Daily Mail*. After 1900 the same fears continued, and were reinforced by understandable suspicion of Germany as a naval rival which also had a formidable army, and by invasion scares and spy fever in which Germans were invariably cast as the potential threat, with the popular press again taking the lead. Tariffs obstructed British access to the domestic markets of her main trading rivals, and there seemed therefore every reason to concentrate on the imperial trade, which would at least be taking place among friends, but here too there were already tariff barriers to be encountered in such places as Canada, which would be likely to be replicated and increased as the British Dominions became more conscious of their autonomous futures. Demands for changes in trading policies therefore took two directions: suggestions that 'fair trade' required that Britain should also introduce tariffs, at least against those who placed tariffs on British goods, a retaliatory concept that allowed for an imagined future in which reductions all round could then take place; and, concurrently, demands for a tighter economic union within the empire which aimed to encourage political as well as economic convergence. Chamberlain, as Colonial Secretary since 1895, had mainly promoted this second idea, much as Salisbury had quietly favoured the first, and in 1897 he had already floated the idea of reciprocal trading arrangements at a meeting of colonial prime ministers. The shock administered to the empire by the Boer War, all too often derided by his critics as 'Joe's War', only underlined the force of such thoughts in his mind, but tariffs also offered him the opportunity to press on with social schemes such as old age pensions, investigated by the Salisbury government in 1900 and found to be a desirable objective, but thought just too expensive at that time.

The final contribution of the Boer War to the Edwardian crisis in which Unionism found itself was financial. Thirty-two months of war obliged the government to raise armed forces that had not been needed on a similar scale since 1815 and had such financial implications as to force increases in income tax: the basic rate went up from eightpence in the pound (3.3 per cent) in 1898 to 1s. 3d. (6.3 per cent) in 1903, thus nearly doubling in five years. Even in 1905, when the Unionists lost office and the war was three years over, income tax was still 50 per cent higher than it had been in 1898. Beyond that, the Chancellor, Hicks Beach, had to introduce in 1902 a temporary corn duty, as a money-raising device rather than an instrument of trade policy but nevertheless an innovation which gave the party's fair traders considerable encouragement. In urging his colleagues to face up to the need to cut expenditure, Hicks Beach offered them the grim alternatives of either income tax at permanently high rates (which he expected to cause serious political and social instability) or higher indirect taxes (which would, he thought, open the way to tariffs, which he abhorred). Both free traders and tariff reformers could already foresee the two sides of the argument to come, and the parting of the ways could not now be long delayed

There was one other issue of substance only slightly linked with the war which came to a head while Salisbury remained Prime Minister and which added further pressure on the finances, and this was educational reform. Though a broad extension of secondary education was consistent with national efficiency doctrines, the decision to act owed more to the tangle of uncertainties about Church schools left by the government's failure to legislate effectively in 1896 and by subsequent judgements in the courts. The 'Balfour' Education Act of 1902 was so dubbed because it was the Leader of the House who took the initiative in steering the bill through the Commons, so winning himself a signal parliamentary triumph just before his uncle retired and the new king summoned him to Downing Street.

The act clarified the situation and provided a solid, legal basis for the investment of public funds in secondary education through both board and Church schools, with the county councils taking over from separately elected school boards the supervision of the state sector. This sensible administrative measure ran into considerable trouble with nonconformists, though, for it was seen by them as extending public funding of sectarian education. This caused predictable upsets with the Liberal Unionists which reminded Conservatives of Chamberlain's origins at an inopportune moment in his career. Far more seriously, it also occurred when the nonconformist churches themselves were undergoing a religious revival and ensured that the fruits of that revival would feed political Liberalism, especially in Wales, where in many areas Anglican schools were seen as an alien intrusion. The Liberal Party's recovery of momentum in the new century derived, then, both from new social issues like poverty and the policies needed to remedy it, and from the unexpected return to relevance of its favourite old issues of free trade and religious education.

In another area, though, Unionists were not keen to step forward with legislation in order to reverse or amend decisions in the courts, and the failure to act in industrial relations may have been the most costly mistake of all. After their defeat in 1906 – though not before, when they could hardly even imagine the political cost of their inaction, and were anyway engaged in other debates nearer to hand – Unionists recognized that their government's antagonizing of organized working-class opinion had encouraged the formation of a Labour Party in 1900, and so placed themselves at a severe disadvantage in bidding for working-class votes, especially when the new Labour Party formally linked its fortunes to the Liberals.

The problem arose from an implicit alliance between employers, increasingly grouped into active bodies like the Engineering Employers' Federation, and conservative lawyers who had a substantial foothold within the government. This reactionary alliance looked for a lead to Lord Halsbury, who after five years as Solicitor-General under Disraeli was for seventeen years Lord Chancellor under Salisbury and Balfour. Employers, increasingly conscious of their need to reduce costs in order to export into an ever more competitive world market, and locked into conflict with the growing, mass-membership 'New [Trades] Unions', resorted to lock-outs and the use of blackleg labour to reduce union power, but they also took to the courts to fight test-cases on trades union immunities. Lawyers like Halsbury, who saw the immunities granted by the trades union legislation of the 1870s as an affront to their entire concept of law and its place in society, and who were anyway developing an increasing willingness to use judge-made law in the defence of the rights of property-owners, argued that circumstances had changed radically since Disraeli legislated in 1875 and that the courts must act appropriately. As a result, litigation that generally reached a final judgement only in the House of Lords, as did the crucial Taff Vale case in 1901, systematically eroded the unions' powers in industrial disputes. It is doubtful whether the average trades unionist understood that the 'House of Lords' as a judicial tribunal was different from the legislative body in which so many employers now sat as peers, but since these legal judgements were so political in character the distinction was anyway more theoretical than real.

A party which now so broadly represented the owners of property, and which in its best theoretical writing in the latter part of the nineteenth century had actually made a virtue of the fact and insisted on the need to amend the laws to protect property more firmly, was hardly likely to resist this trend with a Disraelian proclamation of the rights of workers. Ministers like Chamberlain were certainly unhappy about the class-war attack on trades unions in which they had been made unwilling accomplices, but Halsbury was an extremely difficult colleague who would brook no opposition. When the Prime Minister received complaints about the number of right-wing Unionists appointed by Halsbury to the judicial bench, he sheepishly admitted that in the most-criticized cases the nominations had been his own rather than the Lord Chancellor's anyway. Salisbury was content to proclaim the government's neutrality in such matters and to assert the sanctity of due legal process. But if neutrality meant inaction, then it also meant siding with the employers as their lawyers steadily reduced trades union immunities, for only a government decision to legislate could have overruled the courts.

It is hardly surprising, then, that the trades unions, already coming under the persuasive influence of socialists in their ranks, should have concluded that they must take independent political action, and that once they had a party in being it was likely to be Liberals rather than Unionists who would seem better allies. The Taff Vale judgement, and the government's refusal to offer its legislative reversal, was followed by an acceleration of trades union affiliations to the new Labour Party which made it financially viable, and shortly afterwards Labour and the Liberals formed an electoral pact which aimed by the tactical voting of their respective followers to eject a large number of Unionist MPs from parliament. As

Joseph Chamberlain's son Austen wrote in 1910, by which time Unionists had two elections' experience of Liberal cooperation with Labour,

> the combination of the Liberal and Labour Parties is much stronger than the Liberal Party would be if there were no third party in existence. Many men who would in that case have voted for us voted on this occasion as the Labour Party told them – for the Liberals ... The existence of a third party deprives us of the ... 'swing of the pendulum', introduces a new element into politics, and confronts us with a new difficulty.

The Liberal and Labour allies could raise the political temperature and bring to the poll many voters who had previously stayed at home, so creating exactly the electoral circumstances that Unionist organizers had always feared. That difficulty was the party's greatest single problem in the Edwardian period, and it was largely a self-inflicted one, though it is hard to see how a regime constituted as Salisbury's had been could in practice have acted differently.

By the time that Salisbury was succeeded by Balfour in July 1902 – a remarkably uneventful succession in which once again only limited changes were made to the government – the party had therefore moved significantly away from the comfortable world in which the parliamentary majority of 1900 had been achieved, though by that stage Unionists had only lost two seats at by-elections in two years (one of them an Irish seat where the reason for victory in 1900 had been a mystery anyway) and had gained one from the Liberals in return. The twenty-five losses and single gain of the next three years indicated how much more quickly the slide in the party's fortunes took place under Balfour than under Salisbury. There was a loss of half a dozen seats even in Balfour's first year, before the real party crisis erupted with Chamberlain's dramatic announcement of his conversion to tariffs in May 1903.

Balfour's easy succession was accompanied by a formal courtship of Chamberlain, who was both informed of Salisbury's resignation in advance and consulted before Balfour accepted the premiership, but Chamberlain seemed reluctant to use his authority to force a wholesale reconstruction of the government – for example, by demanding the Exchequer, vacant because of Hicks Beach's insistence on retiring with Salisbury. Perhaps Chamberlain felt that he could manage Balfour better by not irritating him at the start, and anyway wanted to remain in the Colonial Office in order to develop the imperial aspects of his developing support for tariffs, but in any case this proved to be a bad mistake for two reasons. First, it allowed Balfour to place at the Exchequer C. T. Ritchie, a former 'fair trader' who had now recanted his views and would prove to be a defender of free trade, filled with all the enthusiasm of the convert; this was a classically Balfourian tactic of playing off one side against another, but would prove an even bigger problem for him than for Chamberlain. Second, the acquiescence of Chamberlain in this appointment meant that no reconstruction of the government as a whole took place – the *Spectator* described the 'half-hearted and perfunctory patching which has taken place in lieu of remaking'. Balfour was content to carry on mainly with Salisbury's ministers rather than stamping the team with his own image (much as Eden would do on succeeding Churchill in 1955, also with disastrous consequences).

The effect on the party was much like that created by the failure to reshuffle and promote new faces in 1900, except that Balfour did not enjoy the unchallengeable personal authority of his uncle, and so he began as Prime Minister very much on the wrong foot, and entered the political crisis over tariff reform in 1903 with a party already in poor heart. When challenged for his failure to bring forward new men, Balfour responded that he did not feel that able alternatives existed, a remarkable comment on a party that had something like 800 members in the two Houses. His brother Gerald retained his place, while the ineffective St John Brodrick was merely moved from the War Office to the India Office; Lansdowne, whom Balfour himself only thought 'better than competent', retained the Foreign Office. The 'Hotel Cecil' character of the regime continued too, and when the new Lord Salisbury joined the Cabinet in 1903, he found no fewer than four of his relations already there.

An added problem was that Balfour's own characteristic insouciance, now reinforced by the acquisition of the premiership, did not go down at all well with some sections of his party, for Balfour was generally thought to lack both real beliefs and heart. As Lord Curzon (admittedly a hostile witness) later put it,

> Balfour with his scintillating intellectual exterior had no depth of feeling, no profound convictions ... no real affection. We all knew that, when the emergency came, he would drop or desert or sacrifice any one of us without a pang, as he did me in India, as he did George Wyndham over Ireland. Were any one of us to die suddenly he would dine out that night with undisturbed

composure, and in the intervals of conversation or bridge, would be heard to murmur 'Poor old George'.

Curzon could not know when he wrote that private assessment that when Balfour had returned in 1923 after being consulted by the palace as to whether Curzon or Baldwin should become Prime Minister, he would reply to his hostess's question, 'And will dear George be chosen?' with the sad (but perfectly composed) reflection that 'Dear George' would not – for he himself had advised the king to send for Baldwin.

The *Morning Post* decided in 1902 that Balfour's witty answer to a hostile parliamentary question on naval efficiency was all very well in its way, but that while it 'would have made the fortune of a contributor to *Punch* ... [it would] confirm the belief, already not uncommon, that the element of dilettantism is stronger than it should be in the traditions and practice of a British Government'. The *Spectator* found in Balfour the same lack of 'a certain hardness of temperament', and the *National Review* merely redoubled its attacks on 'the old gang' and insistently portrayed Balfour himself as a gentleman amateur who was simply too unserious a figure to lead a party professionally in the new century's world of democratic politics. That last charge was to be repeated throughout Balfour's nine-year leadership of Unionism, but it derived much of its credibility from the detached air that Balfour himself cultivated and refused to change. He was a difficult man to get onto the public platform to inspire the party faithful, he rarely read newspapers and so often could not grasp the urgency with which colleagues were demanding action. He evinced none of his uncle's interest in organization, and he communicated with both party and colleagues through a loyal and selfless political secretary, Jack Sandars, who (it was generally thought) protected his master too determinedly from hard truths and difficult decisions. As Balfour increasingly struggled to maintain control of a split and mutinous party, his own style would be for some a provocative obstacle to loyalty and discipline. As the *National Review* put it in 1910, linking the attack with a reference to the Leader's own favourite pastime, 'the old game between the ins and the outs may be very amusing – like lawn tennis – but after all it is only a game. It is not business.' But then, given Balfour's patronizing view of businessmen in the party, it is not likely that 'business' would have been a word he would ever have wanted to be applied to him and his ways.

Apart from tariffs, the Balfour government had to face a number of problems not of its own making but which nevertheless gave the cumulative impression of a regime drifting out of control. In South Africa the process of normalization after the war was sullied by the local authorities' approval of a scheme to import and employ indentured Chinese labourers, but on terms and conditions that allowed the Liberals to denounce it as 'Chinese Slavery' and to link the scheme with the nascent Labour Party's claims that the government was indifferent to workers' rights. Since the High Commissioner in South Africa was Lord Milner, an imperial hero for Unionists despite his responsibility for starting the disastrous Boer War, he could not be disowned by the government, and so the issue dragged on painfully into the election campaign, when Liberal posters depicted Chinese coolies being flogged by British soldiers (a neat variation on the images that had embarrassed Disraeli in 1880).

In India an epic battle of wills between the Viceroy Lord Curzon and the Commander-in-Chief Lord Kitchener almost paralysed Indian government for a time and drove ministers to distraction, before Curzon's eventual resignation in a huff in 1905; his return did, however, provide in due course a reinforcement to the front bench. Over Ireland, the Chief Secretary George Wyndham finally persuaded the Treasury to release adequate resources for land-purchase loans and pushed through a generous scheme in 1903, but in the process he antagonized many Irish Unionists who once again saw generosity as appeasement. Wyndham was a popular man among the Tory squires but a less than effective minister, and when it was discovered that his civil servants had been preparing plans for devolution of power to Ireland the resultant outcry forced his resignation in March 1905. Among other consequences, this embarrassment prevented the Unionists from mounting an effective campaign against the Liberals on Irish issues in the 1906 election. Army reform, nonconformist hostility on education, 'Chinese slavery', antagonizing the trades unions, India, Ireland – the issues on which Balfour's team were under attack made a formidable list.

However, there is little doubt that even these issues were secondary to tariffs in producing the gradual disintegration of Unionism that took place between 1902 and the end of 1905. It seemed at first that the Balfour Cabinet had nerved itself to take decisive action, for in November 1902 it resolved with just four dissentients that the new corn duty would be retained as more than an emergency measure, now that the war was over, and that it would not be levied on imperial produce, so making possible a scheme of imperial preference, something with which the Colonial Secretary would be able to bargain when dealing with colonial premiers in conference. Chamberlain departed for a tour of South Africa with the conviction that his key battle had been won, and while under the influence of Milner's 'kindergarten' of young imperial dreamers his convictions became considerably more fixed. Unfortunately, though, the four dissentients included the Chancellor, Ritchie, and the Liberal Unionist Leader the Duke of Devonshire. In Chamberlain's absence, Balfour failed to hold the Cabinet line, allowing the free traders to believe that the issue remained open. By the time Chamberlain returned to Britain in March 1903 Ritchie was planning a budget in which the corn duties would be repealed, and the free traders had been working together for four months and so established the bonds of mutual loyalty that Balfour himself felt to amount almost to 'a cabinet in a cabinet'. The Prime Minister could scarcely allow his Chancellor to resign over his first budget, and so the policy line was shifted; it was now agreed to end the corn duty, but also to have a full-scale debate on tariffs in the summer. Ritchie then widened the gap by denouncing in his budget speech in April 1903 not just the corn duty but all thought of taxes on food, a speech which the pro-free trade *Spectator* thought to have marked the 'final and, we believe, except in time of war, irrevocable relief of the bread of the people from taxation'.

Both sides had now won one victory, but the party was dangerously split. The fifteenth of May 1903, when Chamberlain was to speak in Birmingham and Balfour to receive in London a deputation of agricultural protectionists, would be vital for future unity. In matters of hard detail they both said much the same thing, but the tone in which they spoke and the future that they envisaged was dramatically different. Balfour allowed grudgingly that there *might* be a corn duty if a general fiscal scheme could be agreed, but scarcely mentioned the empire as relevant to the debate, while Chamberlain blazed a fiery speech of imperialist conviction in which the current debate embraced the entire future of the British as an imperial people and from which only one outcome would be acceptable to him. The impact on Unionists was enormous, partly because of the inescapable comparison between Balfour and Chamberlain that 15 May created: the *Morning Post* thought that Balfour's speech had been 'a policy of vacillating shilly-shally' which was 'not very creditable or honourable in a political sense. To throw a back somersault may be an accomplishment of a kind, but it is not very dignified.' In contrast, the paper thought that Chamberlain had displayed 'a breadth of view and magnanimity of spirit that had not been visible in our public life for perhaps a whole generation.' In a word, Chamberlain offered an end to the drift of Unionism that had been increasingly resented ever since 1886 by those who wanted a more constructive policy. Without either of them intending it, the impact of Chamberlain's speech meant that he and Balfour were for three years locked in undeclared combat for the control of the party; it was a combat in which all the enthusiasm was on Chamberlain's side but all the resources of the incumbent Leader on Balfour's.

Within days, Chamberlain's supporters had launched a Tariff Reform League to lobby for his views, followed shortly by a Tariff Commission to research the economic detail of a tariff policy, and by efforts to seize control of the party machinery with supportive motions at both the National Union and the Liberal Unionist Council. This provoked the free traders to set up their own organization, the Free Food League, which slogged it out with the TRL in the constituencies but for the most part lost these local battles fairly heavily. By the end of 1904 the TRL had gained control of almost the whole of the Unionist press for Chamberlain's views, it had raised a substantial fund for propaganda work, and it had effectively won the backing of the party in the country. It was against this background of a party slipping over to his main rival for leadership that Balfour had to operate for the rest of his premiership.

Between May and September 1903 Balfour struggled to keep his Cabinet together in impossible circumstances, conscious of the fate that had befallen both party and Leader in 1846, and determined not to be 'another Sir Robert Peel'. It was a forlorn hope, for complex negotiations resulted only in the resignation both of Chamberlain (who wished to free himself for a full-scale campaign in the country, with Balfour's apparent encouragement) and of the four free trade ministers (who would not accept even a Balfour compromise on fiscal policy). He therefore lost both wings of his Cabinet, but then had to re-create the split in the reshuffled government by appointing new ministers from both factions in order to balance the conflicting groups on the back benches; Austen Chamberlain became Chancellor of the Exchequer (bound by Balfour's compromise on policy) but this was offset by the simultaneous promotion of Lord Derby (son of Disraeli's minister who had defected to the Liberals and grandson of the Prime Minister), whose local connections in free trade Lancashire made him a convinced free trader himself. Regional Tory magnates like 'Eddy' Derby did not acquire the title 'King of Lancashire' by riding roughshod over their subjects' wishes, but to colleagues their timidity when faced with Lancashire rebellions often looked like innate weakness.

Harold Macmillan was later to remark caustically that 'the Stanleys have been running away every since the battle of Bosworth'.

Balfour therefore had to operate for his last two years as Prime Minister with three factions in his Cabinet: tariff reformers, free traders, and a middle group personally loyal to him and desperate to bridge a deepening split, while the real leaders of the two factions had been freed to carry on the battle out in the country. For Balfour himself, as Austen Chamberlain put it, 'protection was not a dogma but an expedient, and its expediency was to be judged according to the need of particular cases', while for both tariff reformers and free traders it had become the first article of political faith. The result was that both groups of true believers blamed Balfour for the worsening split, and hardly anyone actually believed in the increasingly tortuous compromises that he hammered out. Austen Chamberlain told Balfour in 1904 that his compromises involved 'further disunion, a prolongation of the present uncertainty, a controversy over, and therefore a hardening of our views . . .' From the other side, the free trade *Spectator*, whose views Balfour had struggled so hard to keep from being driven out of the party altogether, was equally unforgiving: 'Mr Balfour's tactics may be very clever, but they have ruined the Party. It is idle for his defenders to say it is all the fault of Mr Chamberlain . . . Not until the Party is purged of Balfourism as well as Chamberlainism can it be re-established on a firm basis.'

In the party as a whole it was the free traders who, conscious of losing the battle, widened the breach further, when Devonshire urged voters in a by-election at Lewisham in December 1903 not to back a 'whole-hogger' tariff Unionist. This licensed the more numerous tariff reformers to claim that the free traders had broken party ranks and it was thus fair game for them to attack the free traders themselves in their own constituencies. Over the next few years the free trade minority found life very hot for them in the constituencies. As a result some, like the young Winston Churchill, defected to the Liberals, some simply retired rather than fight such an uphill struggle, and some, like Balfour's cousin Lord Robert Cecil, fought an increasingly desperate battle to save their careers. By the end of 1910 Lord Hugh Cecil was virtually the only one of the core group of tree traders still in the Commons.

December 1903, when the Unionists held the Lewisham by-election even against Devonshire's advice to the voters, was perhaps Balfour's last chance to dissolve parliament and have even a theoretical chance of winning an election, and he might well at least have limited the Liberal

THE MAN ON THE RAFT.

Balfour adrift between Hartington and Chamberlain in *Westminster Gazette*, 20 January 1904.

advances to the extent of putting the balance of power back with the Irish and so restoring the happy (for Unionists) circumstances of 1892–5. His decision not to dissolve at that point owed much to concern with national policy – the entente with France was under active discussion and he was developing plans to improve artillery procurement for the army – but it was a party opportunity that would never recur. From the start of 1904 the tide of by-election disasters was relentless, and when Balfour finally resigned office in December 1905 – the last British Prime Minister ever to quit office without either defeat at an election or humiliation in a confidence vote in the Commons – he could only hope for a Liberal split over Cabinet-making which would wipe out memories of the Unionists' own divisions. When the Liberals quickly reunited on the promise of office and dissolved parliament for an election in January 1906, even this transparent tactic backfired. Reading 'all recent signs and portents' on the day Balfour resigned office, the *Morning Post* predicted that there would be a Liberal and Labour majority of about 140 seats.

By this time the Unionists had opponents who were raring for a fight, and the fact that now only five Unionists were returned unopposed (compared with thirty-two seats where no Unionist dared to run), and that many Unionist candidates put in a late appearance even where there were contests, demonstrated the low morale of the party and the extent to which organization had run down since 1900. Increased turnout almost everywhere was also bad news for Unionists, who had traditionally done well in low polls and lethargic contests. Most Unionist candidates gave prominence to fiscal reform in their own campaigns, but it was easy for the Liberals to show how far their promises failed to match up to an agreed party programme. Attempts to play the Irish card were effectively stymied by the Liberals' promise not to introduce Home Rule during the next parliament, and the attempt to campaign on anti-socialism after early results showed Labour gains was not much more successful. On the first day of polling in the vital Lancashire boroughs several seats were lost; in Manchester Balfour lost his own seat and Winston Churchill was returned to the Commons as a Liberal. The scale of the disaster was in the end much worse even than the *Morning Post*'s prediction, for 245 seats were lost compared with 1900 and only 157 Unionists elected. No Unionist at all won in Wales and only ten out of seventy in Scotland, but in England too seats were lost in every region. Even in the party's strongholds of southern England and London the party retained only sixty-four seats to their opponents' 180.

The scale of defeat left Unionists in a state of numbed shock, now at last seeing the effect of Labour's intervention. While the depleted size of the party in the Commons facilitated the rise of new men on the front bench like Andrew Bonar Law and F. E. Smith, and the loss of safe as well as marginal constituencies cleared out a whole generation of backbenchers who were generally replaced by younger and abler men when seats were won back in 1910, in the meantime the relative weight of the Lords in Unionist politics was increased, with serious consequences.

Balfour had been defeated along with three other Cabinet ministers, but Chamberlain was re-elected at the head of a parliamentary party now consisting mainly of tariff reformers, while the arrival of a Liberal government bent on funding social reform through direct taxation gave tariffs an even greater appeal to Unionists as an alternative source of government income. All this suggested that the leadership could now be seized by 'Birmingham and Co.', but once again Chamberlain, conscious of the deep distrust felt for him by Tory squires like Walter Long, held his hand. Balfour found a more agreeable haven than Manchester as MP for the City of London and on his return to the Commons he negotiated a new compromise with Chamberlain, the 'Valentine compact', which, when confirmed in an exchange of letters on 14 February 1906, stated that fiscal reform 'is, and must remain, the first constructive work of the Unionist Party'. This seemed finally to commit Balfour beyond further wriggling, and to rule out any further use of what Chamberlain himself had recently called 'the Balfourian policy of delay and mystification'. Chamberlain would be able to hold Balfour to the new line, enforce it on the few remaining free traders and the party would fight the next election unitedly in pursuit of the full tariff policy. That prospect fell through, though, when in July Chamberlain himself, worn out by three years of vigorous campaigning, suffered a serious stroke during his seventieth birthday celebrations in Birmingham. He lingered on until 1914, transmitting instructions to his followers through Austen, and always deferred to as a lost leader by tariff reformers and imperial-minded Unionists, but the mainspring of the crusade for tariffs had gone, and Balfour had fortuitously recovered his room for manoeuvre.

As a result of this, the next four years in opposition were years of further wrangling over tariffs and free trade, during which the most dedicated tariff reformers worked ceaselessly to seize control of the party from Balfour and to destroy his supporters. It proved relatively easy to seize the National Union, and to remove the Balfourian 'old gang' influence over its regional and local structures by breaking the formal link with Central Office. Henceforth each county was an independent entity, electing its own organizing secretary who would have no direct connection with Central Office, while the National Union Executive resolved to take direct control over propaganda and run it as an uninhibited campaign for tariffs. Balfour, though, through the Chief Whip he appointed, retained control of Central Office, of the subsidized party press and of the party funds. This was a perfect recipe for institutional confusion, overlap and inefficiency, and as a result the organization and morale deteriorated much further after 1906 even than before.

None of this would have mattered greatly if the party had pursued a clear policy in response to the Liberal government's legislative programme, or worked out a positive response to the Liberals' more advanced ideas of social reform and to their increasing frustration with the House of Lords. Balfour encouraged the Lords to act much as in 1892–5, though the Liberals now had a much clearer democratic mandate, and he even stated imperiously in 1906 that 'the great Unionist Party, whether in power or whether in opposition, should still control the destinies of this great Empire', a promise he could only redeem by regular use of the Lords' veto powers. His basic tactic was to wreck in the Lords any Liberal bills dealing with purely party ideas like licensing and education, but to let through popular social reforms and bills associated with Labour (such as accepting the reversal of the Taff Vale judgement, for which Unionists now got no credit among trades unionists anyway). To an extent this worked well enough in 1906 and 1907, stoking up great frustration among Liberal MPs, but no effective work was done to prepare the party for a coming constitutional crisis over the power of the Lords, into which the Liberals were increasingly driven by Balfour's own tactics. In 1907-8, when an economic downturn and a popular demand for quicker naval building to meet the German threat was added to these other difficulties, the Liberals seemed to be at a low ebb. The Unionists swept into control of the London County Council (which they held until 1933) and both Unionists and Labour took Liberal seats at by-elections – seven Unionist gains coming in 1908. A particularly sweet triumph came when the deserter Winston Churchill lost his Manchester seat in the by-election that followed his promotion to the Cabinet, the *Daily Telegraph* screaming in a triple-decker headline, WINSTON CHURCHILL is out, OUT, OUT!' Labour gains in Colne Valley, Jarrow and Sheffield even persuaded some local Liberals that they had backed the wrong horse, and that they should now be allying with Unionists to hold back socialism, so that discussions of local government pacts (prefiguring those that would emerge after 1918 and provide Unionists with an important platform for their anti-socialism) took place in such places as Sheffield and Newcastle.

This hopeful situation was, however, swiftly blown away by the new purposefulness that Asquith gave to Liberal politics when he succeeded the ailing Campbell-Bannerman as Prime Minister in 1908, and by the new Chancellor of the Exchequer Lloyd George. Old age pensions, for which Chamberlain had lobbied for so long, were now introduced by the Liberals and (since they were non-contributory) naturally evoked a wave of gratitude across the land, but this merely accentuated the crisis in public finance which naval building had been creating. In 1909 Asquith and Lloyd George took decisive action to solve all their problems with one bold stroke, exploiting a tactical opportunity that Balfour had presented by exposing the Unionists' flank on the constitutional issue. Lloyd George's 'people's budget' proposed a decisive hiking up of redistributive taxation, and would therefore if implemented prove that both social reform and naval building could be financed without tariffs. The incorporation of social programmes into a financial measure meant that the Lords would either have to acquiesce in the drastic diminution of their powers by allowing such a blatant case of 'tacking' or start a constitutional crisis by rejecting a finance bill for the first time in centuries. Worse even than that, the crisis would begin with the Unionists on the wrong foot, opposing a popular social measure and apparently doing so in defence of vested interests like landowners (who would pay higher taxes if Lloyd George got his way). This was the Robin Hood scenario of a Chancellor seeking the votes of the poor in order to carry out a scheme to soak the rich, something Unionists had dreaded ever since the advent of working-class voting, and which they were to fear even more with the rise of Labour towards national power.

In the short term the Unionists could battle against the budget in the Commons and in the country, for which purpose a special Budget Protest League was created under Long, and in these hectic defensive actions a degree of party unity was re-established. But the real question would only arise when the Liberal majority carried the bill and passed it on to the Upper House. It seems likely that Balfour and Lansdowne (leading the Unionists in the Lords) would have recommended rejection of the budget anyway, having got themselves into a tactical position from which they had no retreat, but the situation was again taken out of their hands by Lloyd George. In speeches at Newcastle and at Limehouse, Lloyd George launched a verbal attack on the Tory peers – describing them, for example, as a useless group chosen randomly from among the unemployed – which angered them so much that they needed no encouragement to vote down the budget by 350 votes to seventy-five on 30 November.

In principle this was much like the massive defeat that the Lords had inflicted on Home Rule in 1893, but in every practical sense the tactical advantages were now reversed; the point at issue was popular with the British electorate, as Home Rule had not been, and this meant that if the Liberals dissolved parliament and achieved a new mandate, either alone or with their Labour and Irish allies, then they would not only be able to carry their redistributive budget but also go on to settle scores with the Lords too. In this debate, the fact that the Lords had a constitutionally respectable case for throwing out a contentious measure for which the government had never sought a mandate tended to be overlooked, and it would not figure greatly with an electorate convinced that the Lords' real motives were more to do with the defence of class interests.

In its actual outcome, the result of the January 1910 general election made the tactical situation as bad as it could be for Unionists, for the Liberals lost their overall majority and could now continue to govern only on Irish MPs' votes, which ensured that battle would be rejoined with the Lords as the prelude to achieving Home Rule as well as the budget. Tactical incompetence in the handling of the Lords' veto in the years 1906–9 thus meant that in 1910–11 the Unionists had to concede not only the 'people's budget' but the veto power of the Lords too, and with that the prospect of the entire Liberal programme going through in the following years – Irish Home Rule, disestablishment of the Welsh Church, land reform, restrictive liquor licensing, the abolition of plural votes, and the entire list of Unionist nightmares for generations past. The ensuing crisis, as the diehard Lord Milner put it in 1914, 'altogether transcends anything in ... previous experience and calls for action which is different, *not only in degree but in kind* from what is appropriate in ordinary political controversies'.

None of the Liberals' objectives were conceded without a fight, and from 1910 to 1914 the Unionists were in a constant state of warfare against Liberals which did indeed go well beyond the norms of parliamentary rivalry, because most Unionists were convinced in their hearts that the Liberals had done a cynical 'log-rolling' deal with Labour and the Irish to destroy the historic constitution of Lords and Commons. When the Parliament Act of 1911, which replaced the Lords' power of veto with a limited delaying power, stated in its preamble that it was an interim measure pending the reconstruction of the Upper House (a pledge that Asquith's government made no effort to redeem), Unionists considered that the historic constitution was in suspense and that they were therefore justified in using all manner of 'unconstitutional' means to halt the Liberals' further legislation, especially when it touched on such organic matters as the Irish Union.

The January 1910 election showed a considerable Unionist recovery from the debacle of 1906, for they scored by a very long way their highest ever vote on the franchise introduced in 1884 (almost matching Liberals and Labour combined in the popular vote, when allowance is made for uncontested seats), but 112 of the 116 seats regained were in England, and even in the key battleground of Lancashire the Unionist advance was blunted by Liberal and Labour cooperation in industrial constituencies. As Austen Chamberlain now argued, the Lib–Lab pact prevented the swing of the electoral pendulum far enough in a Unionist direction to bring them even near to power.

In the immediate aftermath of their defeat the Unionists conceded that the budget must pass, and the Lords now let it through unamended, but this was too late to satisfy the government and its allies, and the debate moved on straight away to the constitution. A brief hiatus occurred in the party dogfight when the death of Edward VII in May 1910 enforced a truce to allow George V to play himself in without undue pressure on his constitutional powers. During this truce there were secret discussions in an attempt to settle outstanding matters of contention between the British parties and so prevent Irish MPs from holding them both to ransom; there was even a brief, foredoomed attempt to form a Grand Coalition of Liberals and Unionists to deprive Irish and Labour MPs of control of the House, but the tribal passions of 1909 were much too fresh to allow for any deal which the front benches could sell to their angry followers on either side. The new king now requested a second election, so that he would not have to overrule the Lords by the creation of several hundred Liberal peers unless the people had very specifically voted on that policy. This meant that in December 1910 the electors were consulted again in an even more explicitly 'Peers v. People' contest than January's had been.

The Unionist leaders at last saw the reefs ahead of them, and in a desperate effort to divert the course of events most of them were prepared to throw even tariff reform overboard in order to save the rest of the cargo. In the hope of winning some key marginal seats in free-trade Lancashire, Balfour announced in mid-campaign that he would agree to submit tariff reform to a referendum if the Liberals would do the same with Home Rule – an ingenious device, since Unionists could reasonably hope to win at least one of the referendums, while the offer to consult the people had anyway a veneer of democracy about it – but it was the very obviousness of this ploy that ensured that the Liberals would have nothing to do with it. Balfour's tactic was denounced in any case by the more extreme tariff reformers in his own party, prompting from Derby the exasperated 'Damn these Chamberlains! They are the curse of our Party and of the country!' Since the Unionists were in the event more embarrassed by Balfour's tactic than the Liberals, it may be said to have rebounded on its perpetrators, and although it had received backing from most of the front bench as a stunt worth trying, it was Balfour who received most of the blame when it did not work, for his reputation just could not stand another cynical reversal on this same policy.

When the December 1910 election produced a parliamentary balance

PUTTING A GOOD FACE ON IT.

LORD LANSDOWNE. "SAY THIS HOUSE IS BADLY CONDUCTED, DO THEY? AND MEAN TO STOP THE LICENCE? AH, BUT THEY HAVEN'T SEEN MY COAT OF WHITEWASH YET. THAT OUGHT TO MAKE 'EM THINK TWICE."

Punch on the peers' attempt to stave off the 1911 Parliament Act, 19 April 1911.

almost exactly the same as in January – except that the Liberals had gained in the process a clear mandate to end the Lords' veto – Balfour's days at Unionist Leader were clearly numbered. The *National Review* mounted an explicit 'Balfour must go' campaign. The tariff reform zealots who gathered in such secret factional organizations as the 'Reveille' and the

'Confederacy' began to work for the same outcome. Finally, the Halsbury Club – which celebrated the peers' final defiance of the Liberals before the Parliament Act passed with the Unionists in the Upper House split three ways (rebellions in which even some front-benchers joined) – proved to be the final straw. Warned that the coming National Union Conference in Leeds in November 1911 would witness formal attempts to have his leadership disowned by the party activists in public session, Balfour decided to bow out rather than go on fighting an impossible battle. Though the decision had probably been made two months earlier, he announced that he was resigning on 8 November 1911.

In one important area, though, the Unionists' third successive defeat in December 1910 had a more immediate effect of a positive kind. After two campaigns in one year, Unionist MPs were well aware of defects in the party organization, and in any case the Unionist press took up the matter in a big way in January 1911. There had been criticism ever since 1906, but after the way in which his opponents had taken over the National Union in that year Balfour and his secretary Sanders would not hear of any changes to the Chief Whip Acland-Hood or to the Principal Agent Percival Hughes, for both had stood loyally by the Leader and so absorbed much of the party's discontent. In the rest of the party there was a broad consensus that these men had to go in order to allow the machine to be modernized. and generally made more efficient; as the young MP Leo Amery told Bonar Law, nothing could be done until Acland-Hood was 'poisoned or pensioned'. When a meeting of half a dozen front-benchers at Hatfield House resolved that they could wait no longer for action, and Curzon delivered to Balfour their collective view that something must be done, the Leader had to give ground.

A Unionist Organization Committee was set up under the chairmanship of the veteran organizer Akers-Douglas, and with nine others representing all the various groups and organizations within the Unionist alliance. It proceeded both thoroughly and expeditiously, taking evidence in writing and verbally from dozens of witnesses and sending Balfour its interim recommendations as early as March. Although there was no intention of conducting a witch-hunt, as soon as relevant questions were asked, the avalanche of criticism convinced the committee that drastic changes were needed. Local parties needed to go over to a more permanently active organization under full-time professional agents, the regional structures needed to be rearranged to end the chaos introduced by the feuds of 1906, more money must be raised, and the party's relations with the press needed a complete overhaul. But the core of the report was about the inadequacy of Central Office's accommodation, management and financial control, and of the system by which the party as a whole was managed. The key recommendation was that instead of management through the Chief Whip, there should be a tripartite division, with a new Chief Whip responsible only for the Commons, a Party Treasurer engaged full-time in the collection of funds, and a 'Party Chairman' who would need to be 'of Cabinet rank' and who would run Central Office and the organization in the country. This was deeply embarrassing to the Leader, but the award of a peerage to Acland-Hood in the 1911 Coronation Honours list opened the way for the appointment of a new team without actually sacking the 'old gang', and Balfour then accepted the report in full, as did the National Union in the autumn. It took some adroit tactics to persuade some front-benchers to agree to Arthur Steel-Maitland as the first Chairman, for he was relatively junior, and both a tariff and a social reformer, Milner's ex-secretary and MP for a Birmingham constituency. Balfour made him only 'Chairman of the Party Organization' (as the title of the post has remained ever since) rather than 'Chairman of the Party', and explained that he would have to earn the Cabinet status that had been talked about earlier.

Nevertheless, once Balfour had gone, and with the connivance of his successor, Steel-Maitland actually did the job that the Unionist Organization Committee had proposed rather than the one to which Balfour had appointed him, and made the party chairmanship the pivotal position that it has remained. He was an enthusiastic activist, improving and expanding Central Office's accommodation and staff, setting up an effective press bureau which offered Unionist newspapers advance copies of key speeches, getting candidates for nearly all constituencies actively in place by the end of 1912, and bringing together in coordinated action the 'legion of leagues' – the numerous pressure groups which had previously thought the party organization to be too hopeless a body with which to work. With Central Office encouragement, and with the assistance of a huge endowment fund raised by the new Treasurer – over £600,000 by 1914 – the district agents were able to intervene regularly to gee up the constituencies and the party was able secretly to subsidize a varied and wide-ranging roster of Unionist newspapers. Every aspect of party activity felt the new broom of the Steel-Maitland regime. Though the First World War intervened before another election could take place and test the worth of these reforms, the party was to see their benefit in its electioneering in the 1920s and in a basic party management system that continued from 1911 until the Maxwell Fyfe period of reform after 1945.

None of this was likely to have happened without a change of leader, for, quite apart from the actuality of Balfour's lack of concern for such things, the perception that he took no interest was in itself a crippling handicap to his party managers; the *National Review*, after detailing the failings of the organization in January 1911, concluded that it had happened 'simply because our Leader is not a practical man and takes no interest in practical affairs, which accordingly drift into inferior hands'. This would have changed in November 1911, whichever of the available candidates had become Leader, for all of them had a record of deep prior involvement in organizational matters, but the fact that the party chose a provincial businessman undoubtedly helped in the practical adoption of the doctrines of managerial efficiency in the organization afterwards.

How, though, had the parliamentary Unionists – despite the recent arrival of industrial MPs still mainly composed of landowners, ex-officers and lawyers – come to choose a businessman in the first place? Lloyd George's view after the contest was that 'the fools have stumbled on the right man by accident', and this gets pretty close to the truth. When Balfour resigned, there were only a few days to go before the Leeds Conference, at which the Leader would have to speak, and events therefore moved very fast. By Friday 10 November it was already clear that the two front-runners were the colourless Austen Chamberlain (backed by the party officers and whips, Liberal Unionists, tariff reformers and the imperial wing) and the choleric Walter Long (backed by Balfour loyalists and English county members). Each had the support of almost half of all Unionist MPs, but – like Hailsham and Butler in 1963 – each was also strongly opposed by the other's followers, so that neither looked like a uniting choice. The leader of the Irish Unionists, Sir Edward Carson, had also considered standing but received too little early support, and the only alternative was therefore the fourth candidate, Andrew Bonar Law, who also had too little support to win a vote but refused just to stand aside like Carson. In this stance, in which he was encouraged by his devoted friend and supporter Max Aitken, a Canadian newspaperman and Unionist MP, the future Lord Beaverbrook, Bonar Law showed his own ambition and his often-hidden confidence in his own abilities. He had the advantages of being a Conservative rather than a Liberal Unionist, a man with Ulster roots who would stand well in the Irish debates to come, a tariff reformer less extreme than Chamberlain, and a man who had earned much credit for abandoning his safe seat and going off to Manchester in December 1910 to spearhead the attack on Lancashire marginals – and costlessly, for Derby found him another safe seat as soon as he failed to win in Manchester.

With the whips actually preparing papers for a ballot at the party meeting due two days later, and with almost everyone involved feeling that such a mechanically democratic procedure would be, as Long put it, 'a degradation' of the party, Chamberlain resolved the deadlock by offering to withdraw in Bonar Law's favour if Long would do so too; and once that offer was made, Long could hardly refuse. On 12 November Bonar Law was therefore unanimously elected as a healing leader, the *tertium quid*. The avoidance of a divisive contest produced great relief, and the whip Robert Sanders wrote in his diary that 'the meeting separated in great content with the Conservative Party all round'; his fellow-whip William Bridgeman noted that 'I never thought so highly of our party till now ... & we all parted with the feeling that "we were jolly good fellows" & so we really are.' It was this healing spirit which at last allowed fruitful negotiations for a Liberal Unionist–Conservative merger to take place, so that the long-term allies finally became one party in 1912 and Austen Chamberlain had at least the consolation of becoming a member of the Carlton Club.

It was recognized at once that the party of the 'Hotel Cecil' had made a bold and surprising choice in entrusting its fortunes to a man who looked, sounded and was by background a Glaswegian ironmaster. Long spoke of the succession crisis as the swansong of the country gentlemen's domination of the party, and a Unionist friend told Lord Milner after hearing Bonar Law's Leeds Conference speech that 'a new era of political life has dawned for England, the old aristocratic school is practically swept out of it'. Many compared the choice made in 1911 with the rise of Disraeli – as they would do again when the party made the equally bold choice of Margaret Thatcher in 1975.

Bonar Law himself immediately adopted a quite different style from the one that had been on show under Salisbury and Balfour, putting himself at the head of the party's wilder spirits rather than trying to rein them in, and earning himself much enthusiastic support by the sarcasm and rudeness which he applied to Liberal ministers in the House. This 'new style' of escalating confrontation in British politics should, though, be traced back to earlier in the year, for it was the high church aristocrat Lord Hugh Cecil and his 'Hughligans' who in June 1911 first reduced the

Commons to a state of disorder, and it was the diehard peers in the Lords who that same summer raised the emotional temperature of the debate to such heights that a party leader must either follow them or go under like Balfour. Bonar Law's alleged dictum, 'I am their Leader. I must follow them', indicates something of the deliberation with which his choice was made, as does his reported remark to the Prime Minister in February 1912, 'I am afraid I shall have to show myself very vicious, Mr Asquith, this session. I hope you will understand.' In such attacks on the Liberals as he made during the Marconi scandal of 1913, in which he was quite ruthless in leading his party to the exposure of corruption by Lloyd George and other ministers, and in three years of debates on Irish Home Rule, Bonar Law consciously chose (as his Chief Whip put it) 'to employ the bludgeon as well as the rapier'. Even if this approach was indeed purely artificial, he was nevertheless rather good at it, and the party loved it. What Opposition would not?

Bonar Law had, though, to deal first with the same incubus that had eventually destroyed Balfour – tariff reform – for Balfour's offer of a referendum, when not taken up by the Liberals, had left Unionist policy in a state of limbo. Bonar Law himself had no doubt that he wished to revert to the full policy of tariffs, food taxes and imperial preference, in which he had been a believer for years, and he and Lansdowne (who as leader of the Unionist peers was technically his co-equal, since neither had been Prime Minister) resolved to face the issue head on by reverting to the full tariff policy of 1906. The shadow cabinet was persuaded to back the policy, despite reservations in the usual quarters, and after a longish delay the policy was announced by each of them at the end of 1912. Once it was publicized there was an outcry in Lancashire, expertly stage-managed by Derby even while he was protesting loyalty to his leaders, and Bonar Law and Lansdowne had either to retreat or see their policy openly repudiated by an important and populous area of the National Union, in which lay many marginal seats. Bonar Law's own instinct was to stick to his guns on policy and to resign, but the great impact he had already made in reviving party morale and momentum in his first year made other Unionists most reluctant to let him go. Eventually almost all Unionist MPs signed a document urging him to stay on with a revised policy, a signal compliment that he could scarcely ignore (and which such a loyal party man as Bonar Law would be unlikely to discount anyway). In January 1913, then, both he and Lansdowne confirmed that their belief in tariffs was as strong as ever, but, because of the importance of other issues which might be lost through a party split, he promised that tariffs would not be introduced by the next Unionist government without a second election – a variation on the referendum idea that Balfour himself had offered in 1910, but one that did not rely on Liberal cooperation. The resolution of this problem by a reversal of the leaders' course without apparent loss of face 'reminds one', as John Vincent has put it, 'how a chess-player's skill may avert the fate of Peel'.

There was in January 1913, therefore, another collective sigh of Unionist relief, which cleared the decks for the main event, the battle against Home Rule inside and outside parliament. This was always a strange, charade-like process (except that the dangers lurking in all possible outcomes made it a battle in deadly earnest), for the Parliament Act of 1911 settled in advance the timetable of events, and the failure of the parties to compromise in 1910 had set the scene for extraordinary bitterness and for charges and counter-charges of betrayal of the national interest. The Liberals only had to introduce their bill in three successive sessions and carry it in the Commons – which was no problem for them – and it would then become law in 1914, whatever the Lords said or did, while the next general election was not due until 1915 unless the Unionists could use Ulster's resistance to Home Rule as a means of forcing an earlier dissolution. The Unionist majority in the Lords could reject the bill, and the party in the Commons and in the country could rant and rage, but they could do nothing to stop the new legislative machinery. They therefore felt themselves driven, in the context of their core assumption that the constitution was in suspense after August 1911 until the Liberals restored some form of bicameral constitution, to admittedly 'unconstitutional' acts, suborning and encouraging the armed preparations of Ulster Protestants to resist the law, pressuring the king to intervene with his prerogative power to overrule his ministers, and at least considering (if not actually carrying out) threats to licence mutiny in the army.

These were desperate measures for a party that still at heart believed in loyalism and discipline, but which had convinced itself that the Liberals had seized power unfairly and had to be stopped from wrecking the state and the empire by any means that came to hand – even by civil war if nothing else worked. Bonar Law believed that he was in an eyeball-to-eyeball face-off with Asquith and that his nerve would hold out longer, that (as he put it) Asquith was 'in a funk about the resistance of Ulster', for he knew that Liberals would find it quite impossible to compel Ulster Protestants into a united Ireland when Ulster was making its case on the same ground of self-determination as that advanced by the Irish Nationalists to whom Asquith was deferring (but whom many Liberal nonconformists did not trust in the slightest). And when taxed with the lengths to which he was going, Bonar Law's response was always to challenge the Liberals actually to fight an election on Home Rule and to promise that he would abide by the result, an offer that Asquith was bound to refuse (since both knew that the Unionists would most likely win such an election). This at least gave the Unionists some democratic colouring for their extremely undemocratic actions. In the meantime, embarrassment about Unionist activities could be covered by such declarations as Bonar Law's about the government in 1914: 'they have become revolutionaries, and becoming revolutionaries they have lost the right to that implicit obedience that can be claimed by a Constitutional Government.'

This campaign did, though, succeed quite remarkably in its own terms, for by the end of 1913 the king had been moved sufficiently to urge his government to negotiate with the Commons minority – a quite unique event in British peacetime history – and in the spring of 1914 this scenario was repeated, with talks actually taking place at the palace. The questioning of orders by army officers instructed to move into Ulster to protect supply and munitions dumps suggested that the officer class, with which Unionism had strong links, would indeed refuse to lead military enforcement of Home Rule and in 1914 this offered the Liberals some very hard choices. The problem for Bonar Law was that, having managed to get Asquith to the negotiating table, and then wrung remarkable concessions from him – so that in 1913–14 the same option of partition was being debated which eventually emerged as the settlement of 1920–21 – he was unable to clinch a deal. By then his style of leadership and the excitement of such absolutist political campaigning had led the Irish Unionists, always a difficult group to manage, into such an intransigent frame of mind that they would not accept any negotiated deal. Many British Unionists supported their diehard stance and would anyway refuse to abandon their Irish allies.

As the day came nearer on which Home Rule would become law and civil war was likely to follow – an outcome prevented in the event only by the outbreak of the First World War in August 1914 – Bonar Law was still waiting for Asquith's nerve to fail first. At the start of 1914, as he bluntly told the king, Bonar Law thought that the government 'must either submit their Bill to the judgement of the people, or prepare to face the consequences of civil war', but his private view, communicated to a

Scottish editor, was that the fact that Asquith expected to lose an election meant that he might well 'go straight ahead and land the country in something like disaster'. Though he was quite capable of synthesizing anger for public display, neither in public nor in private did Bonar Law ever waver from his coolly calculating, bridge-player's view that the avoidance of such a disaster was entirely the government's responsibility once it had started on its course towards Home Rule without popular (British) support.

Bonar Law had told Asquith bluntly that if Home Rule produced a bloodbath in Ireland then this could only help Unionists in British constituencies in a general election, which was plausible enough in itself, but the allocation of blame would presumably have much depended on the precise circumstances in which the final slide to uncontrollable civil disorder took place (as it was to do in actuality in 1919–20). It remained possible until the end that Asquith would pull off an Irish settlement that Unionists would at least have to tolerate and then fight an election on the more mundane issues of domestic policy. When Asquith introduced on his own government's responsibility a bill to compromise on Home Rule in the spring of 1914, this eventuality came decidedly nearer. This was a far from welcome situation for Unionists, for their united campaign on Home Rule had papered over some difficult cracks in their own party on other matters. There was a wing of the party, receiving considerable encouragement from Steel-Maitland at Central Office, which wished to see more emphasis on the social reform policies which had flourished under the auspices of tariff reform, and which worked with the Unionist Social Reform Committee under F. E. Smith's chairmanship to produce practical proposals. Serious research was done, detailed proposals were developed which can be traced forward to the work of Conservative ministers in the 1920s, but it was difficult to get Bonar Law's active interest or commitment to such ideas while his attention was focused on Ireland and on the absolute need to keep the party united for that fight. The USRC quoted a great deal from the writings and speeches of Disraeli and Lord Randolph Churchill, and so helped at least to re-create the idea that the Unionists were a reforming party after the arid years of Salisbury and Balfour, but it was far more tricky when it came to actual policy for the future. When the USRC considered, for example, the setting up of wage boards to fix agricultural labourers' pay, the farmers and MPs from rural areas raised a storm and the party backed off rapidly, as it tended to do whenever any proposal threatened a vested interest that was already

THE TRIANGULAR TEST.

Liberal Whip. "MY COW, I THINK." Labour Party Leader. "MY COW, I THINK."
Unionist Candidate (milking). "MY CHANCE, ANYHOW."

Punch on the advantage to the Unionists of three-party contests, 10 July 1912.

supportive, and – at least until a further threat from the Labour Party persuaded the owners of property that they should make greater concessions – this left the Unionist Party in much the same difficulty as it had been when in office before 1905.

Where, then, were the Unionists placed when war broke out in 1914? Since 1911 the organization had been transformed and steady work in the registration courts had raised the party's chances in many constituencies, particularly in rural areas and small towns. There had been steady gains in local government elections, so that most major towns and politicized counties were now, like London, under Unionist control. By-elections had produced so many gains that by the outbreak of war Unionist MPs numbered almost as many as Liberals and Labour combined, and the range of different types of constituencies that had been gained, both in straight fights with Liberals and in three-cornered contests when the Lib–Lab pact broke down locally, suggested an optimistic prospect in the coming general election. Against that, the party was dependent on events in Ireland which it had lost the power to control or even to influence to any great extent, and it was still far from solving the problem created by its growing support from the owners of property when it had also to appeal to the working class for their votes. As long as the Liberal–Labour alliance held and the Labour Party was restricted to junior status in British politics, this strategic problem was likely to remain. Only the First World War would unexpectedly provide Unionists with the solution they had for so long been seeking without success.

It was while the politicians were actually waiting to pay their respects to the king after the failed Buckingham Palace conference on Ireland that a newspaper was brought in, containing the news of Austria's ultimatum to Serbia and the likely outbreak of a European war. There would thus be no election for some time – for more than four years as it turned out – and by then the political landscape at Westminster would be almost as hard to recognize as the village of Passchendaele was after the battle of 1917. Bridgeman wrote in his diary even on 10 August 1914 that 'everything fades into distance & flees from memory with the War in full swing'. The certainties of 1912–14 vanished into the gunsmoke, and Bonar Law himself told a Party Conference in 1917 that he could not offer them any informed view of the party's future, for 'we are looking into a fog'.

9

Clambering Back, 1914–22

SINCE THE BEGINNING of the century some Conservatives had warned in increasingly urgent tones about the likelihood of a European war in which Britain would be fighting against Germany. For since the Boer War had administered such a sharp jolt to the Diamond Jubilee complacency of the 1890s, right-wing writers and politicians had warned of a coming Armageddon in which Britain's unpreparedness for a modern war would be dramatically exposed. That lesson, as Rudyard Kipling put it, would be all too easy to read once war came, for burning coastal towns would ensure that 'light ye shall have for the lesson, but little time to learn'.

There had been periodic invasion scares throughout the nineteenth century – hardly surprising in a country which maintained only a small army mainly scattered around the world in colonial garrisons – but, with vivid memories of Napoleon, the feared invader had usually been French. Once Kaiser Wilhelm II's naval power was flaunted, though, all of this changed. It was a Liberal Irishman who penned *The Riddle of the Sands*, which in 1903 sparked off the Edwardian obsession with invasion and espionage, but it was mainly Conservatives who followed this up with further publications in the same vein. The *Daily Mail*'s William Le Queux wrote several such books, generally in sensationalist tone, and when his *The Invasion of 1910* was serialized in the *Mail* he happily followed editorial instructions to re-route his hypothetical German invasion of England so as to take in as many Home Counties towns as possible, both to frighten their inhabitants, and incidentally to bump up regional sales of the *Mail* in the process. Conservative readers were undoubtedly much influenced by reading such scare stories.

There was, therefore, a wave of anti-Germanism sweeping over Edwardian Britain, manifested in spy fever (much of it ludicrous and absurd to later readers), in popular distrust of Germans in such harmless domestic occupations as waiters and barbers, in exaggerated fears of German diplomatic initiatives, and in occasional invasion panics. This hysteria affected Britons of every class and party, but it is hardly surprising that the Conservatives, already in a lather about the twin threats to the empire from free trade and Irish Nationalism, should have become particularly keen to appear as Britain's best defenders against an actual threat from abroad. Nor is it surprising in that decade of party disintegration that it was the Tory diehards, both in parliament and in the press, who made much of the running, or that the party leadership, overwhelmed by its domestic priorities, should lend only half an ear and hardly any voice at all to the stridently patriotic demands that were emerging from behind them.

Conservatives could therefore just about legitimately claim that they had shown more foresight than Liberals before 1914 with regard to the defence needs of the country. As Prime Minister, Balfour had initiated the reforming thrust of British defence policy which characterized the period, setting up in 1904 a permanent Committee of Imperial Defence with a professional secretariat (the forerunner of the Cabinet Office), and hanging on to office into 1905 partly in order to ensure that the army had placed firm orders for more modern artillery before it became the responsibility of Liberal ministers. As the Opposition after 1906, Conservatives pressed and cajoled Liberal ministers to continue with the process of military reform, and were, for example, instrumental in forcing the government to speed up the building of battleships. Tory speakers like Admiral Lord Charles Beresford, MP (who represented at different times both naval Portsmouth and munitions-making Woolwich), addressed Navy League meetings around the country and endorsed the strident cry for more Dreadnought battleships, 'We want eight, and we won't wait.' This was a stance that followed on directly from the party's policy in the 1880s, when Beresford himself had been Fourth Sea Lord at the Admiralty under Lord George Hamilton. Such pressure became less necessary when the belligerent Winston Churchill went to the Admiralty in 1911, but Tory MPs (led this time by the young backbenchers Samuel Hoare and William Joynson-Hicks rather than by elderly admirals) shifted their criticism to the Liberals' neglect of a much newer weapon, the aeroplane. In personal activity, too, Conservatives were often willing to back up with their time and their money the beliefs about the nation's peril that they voiced in parliament and on the platform. Tory MPs and their local supporters were very regularly active in the Yeomanry and the Territorials, and in uniformed youth organizations which imparted both drilling and military ideas into the boys of the period and so prepared the way for the patriotic recruiting of 1914.

In all these ways, then, Conservatives had had, in the decade before 1914, a good pre-war, and could reasonably point to their prescience when some at least of their warnings came true. If Liberals eventually paid the political price for failure to prepare Britain before 1914 for a war on the scale that the First World War eventually became, then that was possibly only because some of the alternative approaches had been mapped out in advance of the war by their opponents.

Much of this Tory concern for national security was no more than the strategy that any party in opposition would have been tempted to adopt in the deteriorating international circumstances of the period before 1914. In their internal political arguments over the coming war, though, Conservatives may be said to have failed to grasp the nettle of national defence just as surely as the Liberals, and with rather less ideological justification. The most active advocates of a more militaristic posture for Edwardian Britain were in fact deeply unhappy with the Conservatives' flabby response to their key demand – national service. This was, indeed, why so much Edwardian effort had to go into such voluntary forms of training as the Boy Scouts. Supporting military reorganization for greater effectiveness, weapons expenditure to improve the firepower of the professional forces, more and bigger battleships for home defence, and such new technology as air power were all relatively easy options; and the effect of all these policies on national taxation was in any case seen by Unionists as a timebomb that would tick away under free trade finance – at least until the Liberals went for more redistributive taxation to finance their defence programme (as well as their social policy) in and after 1909. But to go further and back the National Service League in its call for compulsory military training risked alienating voters at precisely the time at which the crucial battles were going on over Lloyd George's tax plans, the House of Lords and the Irish Union. It seems clear that Unionists had no great personal objection to the idea of conscription, and that some at least saw its benefits in social as well as military terms. Others might well have been more in favour but for the fact that the army itself was at best neutral on the issue of compulsory service, preferring as it always had a small, professional force that would be less committed to running permanent training camps for the semi-skilled. Nevertheless, it is clear that it was electoral tactics at a difficult time, rather than any more principled attitude to the army, that ensured that conscription never became a clear party cry before 1914.

Even when the war came, this political dilemma still remained a tactical difficulty, for the short war that almost all expected in 1914 would have been followed by an election due in 1915 and the electors might be expected to give short shrift to a party which had called for compulsory service while the flow of volunteers was still providing all the recruits that the army could cope with. From the middle of 1915, by which time the Unionists were sharing in ministerial office anyway, that problem vanished as the likelihood of an early election receded and the flow of volunteers slowed. Henceforth it was the Conservatives who pressed constantly for conscription (which could now be justified on the additional ground of fairness to the hundreds of thousands who had already joined up from personal choice), it was Liberals and Labour MPs who held out against it, and it was a Liberal Prime Minister, Asquith, who gave way only an inch at a time and thus acquired the reputation of doing too little and too late. It was only in that middle period of the First World War, then, that the Unionists' pre-war campaigns for defence readiness came to fruition; only then that they could begin to reap the political benefit from a claimed farsightedness before 1914.

Whatever their prophecies on defence policy, it is clear enough that Conservatives were no more aware than Liberals that a great war was actually coming in the summer of 1914. Bonar Law's eyes were fixed on Ulster and on the parliamentary tactics and the military implications of Home Rule's likely passage into law later in the year, and there is little sign that other Conservative leaders had any greater awareness of the diplomatic crisis of July 1914 until, like the Liberal Cabinet, they were swept along by events in the week that took Britain into the Great War. When Lord Crawford (until recently the party's Chief Whip) left London on 23 July 1914 for the Wagner festival at Bayreuth, he worried that he might miss *Das Rheingold* if the government were to dissolve parliament in order to solve the Irish impasse. As it happened, he only just managed to hear the whole of Wagner's 'Ring' cycle before rushing back to London – but his 'adventurous' return journey had nothing to do with Ireland; rather it was undertaken to avoid being interned in Germany as war was breaking out.

Conservatives may have had a slightly less complicated view of the implications of a Franco-German War than Liberals (for whom the invasion of 'gallant little Belgium' by the 'wicked Hun' provided a welcome pretext for involvement in a morally justified war), and were thus a shade more likely to accept war's inevitability in the final days of peace, but the difference was at most a small one. In the cases of tough-minded Liberals like Churchill and Lloyd George, with whom Conservatives would increasingly identify over the years ahead, the difference was non-existent. This, then, gave an indication even in the summer of 1914 of the extent to which the war would loosen old attitudes and allow new combinations of men and of measures.

As far as the unfinished business of Edwardian England was concerned, on the other hand, the gulf between the British parties was as wide as ever. Once Britain went to war, Bonar Law argued that in the national emergency party politics should be suspended and he offered unqualified Conservative support for any measures needed to fight the war to a finish. That pledge was given in the heat of excitement in August 1914 and in the expectation of a short war, and was soon regretted, not least because Asquith and the Irish MPs who kept him in office had no intention of freezing the Home Rule issue in the delicate state in which it was then poised. Asquith therefore carried on with the parliamentary timetable that derived from the 1911 Parliament Act, forced his Home Rule Bill through into law in the autumn of 1914, and bowed to the situation created by a party truce (and also to the desire not to provoke Ulster's resistance in wartime) only to the extent of proposing and carrying a motion to suspend the act's implementation until the war's end. Unionists were outraged by what they saw as the cynical manipulation of the wartime party truce to complete the legislative processes of a partisan Liberal measure. They were entirely unimpressed by Asquith's desire to get out of his procedural impasse one way or the other and by his even greater need to keep his Liberal-Irish majority intact, now that it was the basis of a war ministry. Bonar Law made a final impassioned speech on what he saw as yet another Asquithian act outside the spirit of the constitution, and then led his party in a demonstrative walk-out from the Commons in which all available Tory MPs took part. Lord Selborne, a Tory diehard, had explained to his wife only a few days earlier that he would 'never believe that Asquith is capable of playing such an infamous trick on us as to pass these bills during a truce of God ... until he does it', and he was therefore one of many Unionists who would never forgive Asquith when his hopes were dashed. William Bridgeman likewise wrote in his diary that 'the behaviour of the Gov[ernmen]t about Home Rule is abominable', and even several months later, in late November 1914, he was still rumbling on about 'treachery ... They are incapable of honesty or truth ...'

However – and this was crucial both for the war effort and for the future of the Conservative Party – a dignified public protest and a great deal of private moaning was as far as it went. While Bonar Law's pre-war strategy had seemed on the verge of success in early 1914, and had engaged the king and elements of the army in moves that would have negated the will of parliament, this tactic had always depended on Asquith's uncertainty as to how far the Unionists would go in the direction of gun-running, civil war and the treasonable encouragement of dissent in the armed forces. With the outbreak of European war, there was no question whatsoever of Unionists pursuing any of these tactics further, and Asquith was rescued from the 'blue funk' over Ulster that Bonar Law had earlier detected. It was now Bonar Law who had lost the strength of his tactical position, for the postponement of Home Rule's implementation even for a year provided him with a new dilemma: if the war was short then it would presumably be victorious, and this would enable the government to campaign in a 1915 election on issues that would not be likely to centre on Ireland (as they would have to have done in a peacetime election in 1914–15), while a longer war would produce a steadily lengthening period in which Home Rule had been on the statute book, after which it would be ever harder to reopen the main issue. The longer the war, whatever its eventual outcome, the less willing the British people would be to contemplate a prolonged military struggle to hold down Ireland or to embark on a civil war in which parliament was defied by one of the British parties.

So, quite apart from the mistreatment of Ireland in wartime, the Easter Rising of 1916 and all that it ushered in, and the rise of Sinn Fein to eclipse the old Irish Nationalist Party by 1918, even Unionists could soon begin to perceive that the First World War was effectively terminating any possibility of retaining the Irish Union. When the flood of war ebbed in 1918 and politicians fixed their eyes once again on Ulster's parish boundaries as a possible partition line between North and South – what Churchill later called 'the dreary steeples of Fermanagh and Tyrone' – most Unionists had come to accept that their battle was now for Ulster alone. When Ulster's place within the United Kingdom was guaranteed by the Government of Ireland Act in 1920, most Unionists seized this security with both hands and soon afterwards let the rest of Ireland go, with an audible sigh of relief. This was still an extremely painful wrench for a Unionist Party which, as its very name demonstrated, had since 1886 placed the Irish Union at the heart of its self-assigned identity, but it was also a development that withdrew the bulk of the party from a cul de sac within which there had been no room for a three-point turn in order to face the modern world. That relieved majority of party opinion excluded, of course, embittered southern Irish Unionists, forerunners of Indian princes, Kenyan white highlanders, southern Rhodesians and other colonial elites who were to experience the same shock of betrayal later in the century, for, as the more farsighted had argued at least since 1886, Southern Ireland was indeed the harbinger of that which was to come in the rest of the empire. It was perhaps not entirely coincidental that the coalition government that brought about British withdrawal from most of Ireland without losing many Tory supporters in 1920–21 was in the same years making significant moves towards Indian self-government too; this also produced Tory objections, but it did not produce resignations or the level of resistance that could have stopped the process, as Conservatives had still hoped to do over Ireland in 1914.

Back in the autumn of 1914 the Conservatives' embarrassment over Ireland had derived largely from the unlimited and largely one-sided liability imposed on them by their backing for the war effort, a backing that scarcely faltered throughout that most terrible of wars. One Conservative peer, Lord Lansdowne, in a letter to the press in 1917, made one of the few open appeals by a British statesman for a negotiated, victory-less peace with Germany, but the chorus of outrage from his own party, then assembling for a rare wartime Party Conference, showed how unrepresentative a figure he was by that time and on that issue. The outcry 'excommunicated' Lansdowne from Tory society, as he himself put it, and removed him altogether from public life. He was replaced as Leader in the Lords by Curzon, a hard man on all issues relating to the war and one who never seems to have faltered in his commitment to a fight to the finish. Far more typical than Lansdowne were the regular activities of the Unionist War Committee and the Unionist Business Committee in the Commons and the Association of Independent (sic) Peers in the Lords, backbench ginger-groups which unrelentingly urged ministers to get on with fighting the war more effectively, at whatever the cost in blood and treasure.

Tory tradition had not been as hostile in principle to state intervention as had Gladstonian Liberalism, whatever was implied by Edwardian debates on social policy, and in the campaigns of men like Lord Randolph Churchill and Joseph Chamberlain the more advanced of them had already advocated a much-extended role for the state in British domestic policy.

The party had in any case espoused for half a century before 1914 a robust patriotism of *realpolitik* which had left it mystified by Liberal scruples about Ireland, about colonial expansion and about defending Britain's Turkish allies even when they behaved as badly as they had done in 1876. That 'my country right or wrong' approach now dictated the subordination of all preconceptions to the nation's need in this total war. The same patriotism was practically reflected in the party machine's active involvement in recruiting campaigns, and later also in War Savings and War Aims movements (on which it spent tens of thousands of pounds of the party's own money), and in the personal service in the armed forces of over a third of all Tory MPs and an equivalent number of the party's employees. Bridgeman thought in November 1914 that 'it has been a very high trial of the patriotism of Unionists to support [the Liberals] through all on (sic) the War. But we have certainly done it wholeheartedly, going on [speaking] tour[s] with little-navyites, traducers of the army, & peace-at-any-price men, to raise recruits & explain the war to the people.' For some, then, merely agreeing to share a platform with the hated Liberals was a form of sacrifice for the war effort.

Conservatives acquiesced readily in much higher wartime levels of expenditure (and therefore higher taxes too, for which Bonar Law became personally responsible when in 1916 he went to the Treasury), huge military commitments, censorship and social control, public direction of industry and agriculture, and the extension of state control across the whole of society. These were all things that were entailed by Britain's prosecution of her first industrial war in Europe, and if in 1916 the Conservatives did finally draw the line and refuse to sanction the nationalization of their old allies the brewers, this was a rare exception to the rule. They were indeed frequently to be heard lamenting throughout the years 1914–18 that the nation and its resources had not been more effectively mobilized and that governmental activity was inadequately vigorous. It was typical of this mood that a man always seen as the ultimate hard man on the Tory benches, the Irish Unionist Sir Edward Carson, was one whose party reputation rose dramatically in debates in which the backbenchers' virility test for leaders was their readiness to subordinate everything to the war. It was also significant that listed among the Conservatives whose standing increased as the war went on were Lords Milner and Curzon, men who had never yet quite lived down their stormy periods at the head of proconsular governments, in South Africa and India respectively, but who were perceived after 1914 as tough-minded men who had again come into their own in a national and imperial emergency. If Britain in wartime had to be governed much like a colony, then the Conservatives had more than their share of ex-colonial governors, and when Lloyd George formed a small War Cabinet in 1916, Milner and Curzon occupied two of the five seats, a decision that generated widespread Conservative approval even though it necessarily meant that more orthodox Tories had to be left out.

The party's front-benchers in 1914–15 were uneasily aware of the vulnerability of their position, so long as backbenchers were demanding a more vigorous prosecution of the war, but the party remained in opposition and a party truce required abstention from factious criticism. In November 1914 Curzon complained to Bonar Law that 'we are expected to give mute and almost unquestioning support to everything done by the Government ... They tell us nothing or next to nothing of their plans, and yet they pretend our Leaders share both their knowledge and their responsibility.' Long pointed out that 'there has been no coalition – personally I do not favour it, and I doubt its success', but this meant that Liberals went on being party men while Unionists could not complain without incurring the charge of dividing the nation in wartime. As Curzon also put it, 'the Government are to have all the advantages while we have all the drawbacks of a coalition.'

Unionists could reconcile these conflicting pressures only through an actual coalition – by themselves taking a share of responsibility for the war – though in practice it was more a case of wrenching responsibility from the faltering Liberal Party than accepting it when offered. A crisis in May 1915 over the inadequate supply of shells for the army (which was in effect a surrogate debate for failings in the whole supply side of the war machine), and a public battle over naval policy after the First Sea Lord resigned, allowed Unionists to force their way back into office, but at that stage it was only as junior partners in an Asquith government in which Liberals continued to hold almost all the key posts. In choosing his new colleagues, Asquith expressed his own views on the relative merits of the Unionist leaders by sending Bonar Law to the wartime backwater of the Colonial Office while putting his more patrician predecessor Balfour in the key department of the Admiralty. The Unionists were therefore still obliged to avoid public criticism without gaining much actual power, but their disappointment was at least offset when they forced the renegade Winston Churchill out of the Admiralty in 1915 as one of their prices for coming in at all. In view of Churchill's later war service to the Conservatives themselves this was in itself ironic, but it also demonstrated how far pre-war antagonisms still continued; they would do so in the case of Churchill's relations with his former (and future) party for a long time after 1918 too.

This halfway house to power lasted for eighteen months in 1915–16 and was a tense time; as ministers, the Tory leaders now sat with the Liberals on the government benches in parliament, while the rest of the Conservatives faced them from the opposition side. The war continued to go badly throughout the period of Asquith's coalition, with military disappointments at Gallipoli, Loos and in the naval battle of Jutland, a major military disaster on the Somme in July 1916, and gathering gloom all round, with steadily lengthening casualty lists and increased losses of merchant shipping to attacks by submarines – setbacks for which Conservatives now had to take their share of blame. There was some grim satisfaction to be gained from forcing conscription on still unwilling Liberals (and indeed also from the deepening disillusion that such decisions produced in the Liberal Party). There was also encouragement to be gained from the way in which the unusually strong Liberal front bench of 1914 was gradually falling apart under the strain of war. Unionists now forced Churchill out of the government altogether, but, conversely, Unionists were also partly responsible for the wartime rise of Lloyd George, previously their party's chief devil-figure among Liberal radicals, but, now that his standing as 'a man of push and go' was at the nation's disposal for war service, respected as the man for the job.

In the end, this unstable combination could not hold through years of war, and Unionist backbenchers became steadily more discontented during 1916. In a tense political crisis in December Asquith was ousted and Lloyd George became Prime Minister in his place. Both Bonar Law and Edward Carson played a key role in the discussions that preceded these events, and it was Bonar Law's refusal of the premiership for himself and his party, and his commitment that the Unionists would serve instead under Lloyd George, that resolved the crisis in Lloyd George's favour and forced a bewildered and humiliated Asquith out.

Despite the competitive rhetoric of the platform, Bonar Law and Lloyd George had developed a warm personal regard across the Cabinet table, perhaps recognizing in each other kindred spirits from lower social backgrounds than were common in the higher ranks of either party in that generation. Bonar Law had modestly decided that a Lloyd George government with full Conservative backing would be best able to prosecute the war and maintain the backing of parliament and the country for the war effort, whereas a Bonar Law government would never gain the united support of the Liberals. For the next two years, as the Liberals gradually split irrevocably into Lloyd Georgian and Asquithian factions riven by mutual antagonism, the reliable voting support of the Conservatives kept Lloyd George securely in office. Bonar Law became effectively the second man in the government, managing the Commons majority that rested mainly on Tory votes, as well as being Chancellor of the Exchequer and the only conventional Unionist Party politician in the War Cabinet. More widely, the party's leading lights now shared office on a more equal basis than in 1915–16, with three Tories in the five-man War Cabinet, and held a major share of other ministerial posts too.

However, Unionists continued to have reservations about the wartime coalition – both about the veracity and political reliability of its ethically challenged premier and about the continuing Liberalism of other ministers like the radical Christopher Addison. A diehard minority was always grumbling about these and other matters (relations with the military, for example, on which issue most Conservatives were more disposed than was Lloyd George to give the generals a free hand). On domestic issues such as electoral reform, and the future of Ireland and of the Welsh Church, suspicion of Lloyd George because of his radical past remained a constant factor. Nevertheless, the Unionists remained a loyal bedrock that carried the British government through the last two gruelling years of the war, and they were therefore well-placed in 1918 to claim a share of the credit for ultimate victory. When the fighting eventually ended in November 1918, an election could not be long delayed by an eight-year-old parliament, and Unionists were indeed anxious to have one while their old rivals the Liberals remained split into two increasingly irreconcilable factions.

By November 1918, though, the electoral battleground had been transformed in several ways in comparison with the way in which it would have figured in a peacetime election in 1914–15. Most obviously, the long debate over extensions of the franchise (to women for the first time, but also more widely for men too) and changes in the electoral rules had finally been resolved in a behind-doors party deal in the 1916 Speaker's Conference, and then implemented as the Representation of the People Act, 1918. This fourth reform act was larger in its sweep than any of its predecessors of 1832, 1867 and 1884 had been, and enfranchised far more new voters in its provision of votes for all men over twenty-one, irrespective of wealth, class or housing tenure, and most women over thirty. The British electorate of 1918 numbered 21.4 million voters (compared with the 7.7 million of 1910) and, since it was also eight years since a general election had been held, the normal processes of deaths and ageing came into account to an unusual extent: more than three-quarters of the electors of 1918 had never cast a vote for any party at all in a national election. It truly seemed as if old loyalties would now count for nothing and there would be everything to play for in the contest for power in the post-war world.

With tighter control of election expenses, a much easier system of electoral registration, state payment of returning officers, and elections in which all contests would be on the same day, and in which almost all adults would be allowed to take part, the modern British electoral system was coming to birth in 1918. Despite the Tories' effective modernization of their party machine between 1911 and 1914, and the very fact that changes in the law and in constituency boundaries in 1917–18 had got the local parties back into a state of electoral readiness for the 1918 election, the party that had traditionally won elections on a strategy of high expenditure and tight manipulation of limited electorates could only look to the future with extreme foreboding. There was therefore quite a mutinous mood in the party as a whole over these sweeping reforms, to which its parliamentarians had agreed, and a good deal of detailed work was done in order to limit the damage that was anticipated from the Representation of the People Act. Despite their commitment to the war and to the Lloyd George government, the Conservatives had not taken their eye off the ball of electoral self-interest as they were to do in 1944–5, and so during 1917 they geared themselves up to write favourable details into the small print of the legislation. With effective party whipping (sometimes so effective as to wreck the whipping of the government that the party actually supported), victories were won on many highly technical issues – often on small votes in committee rooms or in the middle of the night on the floor of the House – which helped considerably in moderating the effect that the act eventually produced. For example, rules for redrawing constituency boundaries were revised so as to ensure the continuation of exclusively agricultural constituencies (and local spadework when the commissioners got to work in each county saw that this was effective in practice as well as in theory – for example, in Cheshire, where the local Conservatives' own proposals were substituted for the commissioners' original plan); spirited defence efforts in the lobbies ensured the continuation of hundreds of thousands of businessmen and women as plural voters for another generation, while the increased number of university constituencies ensured second votes for a larger number of graduates too – all of this in an age in which farmers, business voters and university graduates were all overwhelmingly Conservative by inclination.

Such efforts demonstrated Conservative concern, and the package of amendments that were secured during the bill's passage ensured that the party's position in parliament was stronger than it might otherwise have been in some of the tight contests of the two decades to come. It is almost certain, for example, that these technical amendments to the 1918 act were enough to deny Labour a parliamentary majority in 1929 and may even have been sufficient to make the Conservatives the largest rather than the second party in 1923–4, with important consequences for tactics in a hung parliament. With his known preference for such restrictions of the 'fancy franchise' type, Disraeli would have been proud of his successors' work in 1918, and in paying as much attention to boundaries as to the franchise they were also following the example of Lord Salisbury in 1884–5.

All the same, the main effects of this fourth reform act were more sweeping in scale than anything that could be achieved by such technical restrictions, and were broadly either neutral between the parties or favourable to the Conservatives in any case. The advent of a mass electorate – something that at last deserved to be considered as approximating to democracy – was, despite the Tory worries of the time, to prove no great barrier to the party's campaigning for victory. For in the period from 1918 to 1939 the Conservatives won five very large parliamentary majorities and no other party ever won a majority at all. Women's suffrage would require a complete restructuring of the voluntary side of the Conservative Party in order to allow for the existence and representation of women's branches, and a revamping of electoral campaigning too – a new world towards which some of the more misogynist local activists advanced only with fear and loathing, sacrificing their all-male worlds of smoking concerts and drinking clubs slowly and with much regret. But women voters proved on balance to be an advantage rather than a disadvantage to Conservative candidates: opinion polling evidence has demonstrated this clearly and consistently over the past forty years, and there is no reason whatsoever to think that this was not already as true of 1918–39 as it has been since 1945.

More broadly, the forward-looking campaigning reforms of the Edwardian period did indeed turn out to be a precedent, showing that

Conservatives could campaign more uninhibitedly than Liberals before a less discriminating, less interested and less educated electorate, while such older campaigning ploys as the patriotic celebration of nation and empire were to pay as many dividends with a democratic electorate as they had done when Disraeli offered them to the first Tory working men voters of 1868. And, finally in this context, the acquisition of the vote on a more or less equal basis by the working class, by at least accelerating if not actually causing the final rise of Labour to major party status in the 1920s, would frighten many propertied people away from Liberalism and towards a more determined and stronger party of resistance. Just as the 1867 franchise change had unlocked the electoral system of 1832 under which Conservatives had scarcely ever won, and the 1884 changes had pushed things a stage further, so the 1918 reforms completed during the 1920s the process by which most owners of property gravitated to the right in the anxieties of self-interest occasioned by a British Labour Party now bidding for real power – and actually holding office as His Majesty's Government in 1924. For the generation that had seen a weak socialist government under Kerensky give way to Lenin's Bolsheviks in 1917, with all that followed in terror, civil war and confiscation of property, it was relatively easy to exaggerate the fear of British Labour and to see Ramsay MacDonald as a 'British Kerensky' who would simply prepare the way for a much more dangerous British Lenin, a fear that most Conservatives shared – but did not much regret when it drove thousands of middle-class voters in their direction.

In one final way, the changes of 1918 set up an electoral balance in which the Conservatives were the natural majority party, and that was, as in 1884–5, shaped more by boundaries than by franchise, a technical issue that historians have often underestimated in their analyses of the higher profile and more ideologically driven debates over the franchise. Since the last changes in parliamentary boundaries in 1885 the adult population had risen by about two-fifths, there had been major shifts in its regional distribution, and a significant increase had appeared in the social stratification of British housing between the different classes. 1918 therefore became the first of many redistributions of seats in which the parliamentary boundary commissioners chased the population around the country in their objective of creating constituencies of approximately equal size, each stage (until the 1990s) providing a Conservative bonus as the growing middle-class suburbs generated an unanswerable case for a bigger share of the parliamentary seats. In 1918 these boundary changes probably netted the Conservatives about thirty seats overall compared with the position before the war, which – even if nobody at all had changed their vote and the new voters had been divided just like the old – would have placed them ahead of Labour and the Liberals combined when compared with the elections of 1910.

An accidental bonus of even greater weight was the triumph of Sinn Fein in most of Ireland in 1918, the refusal of its MPs to take their Westminster seats, and the creation in 1921 of the Irish Free State without representation at Westminster. This complete *defeat* for all that Unionism held dear nevertheless removed from the Commons some eighty MPs who had kept non-Tory governments in office in 1885–6, 1892–5 [1892–5] and 1910–15, and who had never been Tory allies except for one brief and unconvincing flirtation in 1885. Meanwhile, because six counties of Ulster remained in the United Kingdom (as Unionists were determined that they should), most of Ireland's remaining MPs took the Conservative whip as they had done for the past two generations and so helped to sustain Tory majorities – indeed making and keeping Churchill Prime Minister almost by themselves in 1951–5.

The net effect of all these changes in the boundaries of the United Kingdom and of the parliamentary constituencies within it between 1918 and 1921 was that there would be over a hundred fewer anti-Conservative MPs and thirty more Conservatives in the Commons than in the Edwardian period, a massive shift in the parliamentary arithmetic that would last at least until the boundaries were reviewed again (which would not be until 1945–8, by which time another war would have remade the political balance in any case).

Beyond this, there was not just a positive Conservative balance in the electoral system that emerged in 1918; there was also a phalanx of safely Conservative seats that could hardly be lost even in a bad year, so effectively was the party's vote distributed across the new constituencies. There were some 200 suburban, agricultural, seaside resort and small town constituencies that were effectively unlosable at a general election. With a total of 615 MPs in the Commons and a fragmented party system of at least three parties emerging from the war and the peacetime Lloyd George coalition, these safe constituencies would be a strong base from which to launch a bid for a governing majority, a crucial footing from which to persuade ex-Liberal voters that only a Tory government would be able to protect them from the socialist alternative.

Much of this safety net was visible only with hindsight, when a number of actual elections demonstrated how the new system worked in practice, but one reason for the Conservatives' reluctance to recognize their strengths in the post-war world was their own fear of Labour. For while, since 1906, it had been common form for Unionist candidates to emphasize the socialist implications of Labour's pact with the Liberals, the limitations of Labour's advance before 1914 both blunted the effectiveness of this as a campaigning argument and reduced the conviction with which Unionists themselves could act as if they believed in what they said. The by-elections of 1911–14 demonstrated after all that in three-party contests, even in mining seats that would soon become its heartland, the Labour Party could not manage even to rise to a single second place, and the many Conservative gains in those contests showed the opportunity offered by the weakness of Labour – strong enough to challenge the Liberals but still too weak to replace them.

All of that changed in the latter half of the First World War. In part this arose from the war itself, given the extent to which it forced the government to accept the aspirations of the labour movement to be consulted on a wide range of industrial, economic and social issues, and the fact that from 1915 onwards Labour shared in office with the other two parties and thereby gained a credibility denied to it even by its Liberal allies before 1914. The extended franchise of 1918 certainly added at least some natural Labour supporters to the electoral register, even if we now know that the change was not as entirely beneficial to Labour's advance as historians once thought, and the new boundaries added to the representation of the heavy industrial areas as well as of the suburbs. Most importantly, though, through its experience of the war, and of the Russian Revolution that ratcheted up the expectations of socialists all over Europe, Labour in 1918 believed it could win power, developed a fully socialist programme to put before the working-class voter (as well as a constitution that allowed intellectuals to play a role too), and seemed in every way the coming force in British politics. Stanley Baldwin told Conservative supporters in 1924 that 'there is a vitality in Labour at present in the country' and went on to tell his followers that 'unless we can share a vitality of that kind we shall be unable to conquer'.

Just what form that Labour vitality would take was much more difficult to say, not least for Conservatives, whose inside knowledge of trades unions and socialist societies was to say the least limited. It was therefore easy for them to see events in Russia – the breakdown of order, the violence and civil war, and the assassination of the monarchy along with many others among the rich and powerful – as the sign of things to come. A Leeds conference in 1918, at which British trades unionists (among them even the phlegmatically moderate Ernest Bevin) resolved to set up workers' and soldiers' soviets on the Leninist model, with branches in every urban and rural district in England and Wales, did nothing to reassure those of a nervous disposition on the political right. When the end of the First World War in November 1918 was followed by revolutions in a wave across much of central Europe, occasioned as much by the fact of national defeat and wartime deprivation as by socialist ideology (though this was hardly clear at the time), it was natural for Tory pessimists to foresee that the contagion would spread in Britain's direction. And when wartime unrest in British industry produced some extraordinarily violent scenes on 'Red Clydeside', in Sheffield and elsewhere, it was easy to foresee that the difficult transition from a war economy to peacetime would only increase the revolutionary potential that the police perceived already to exist on the left.

This was the background to the unlikely decision of the Unionists to keep Lloyd George as Prime Minister for a peacetime government when the Great War came to an end, but this was an outcome that owed something to accidents of timing as well as to strategic choices. Earlier in 1918, when a major British defeat in France in March demonstrated that the war was going as badly as it had ever done and defeat was staring the Allies in the face, parliamentary unrest had naturally given the government some uneasy weeks; in particular, a censure debate in May 1918 had produced the first organized attack on Lloyd George by disaffected Liberals since Asquith's fall from power eighteen months earlier. Nearly all Conservatives took much the view that they had taken in 1916 – that Lloyd George was the man to prosecute the war, and that they did not want Asquith back, whatever the merits of the case he was advancing in this actual debate – and they therefore solidly voted down the Liberal motion, but the episode did give the government a severe fright. Since the new franchise was at last through into law, the government would soon need to hold an election, and it therefore now began planning to get from the new electorate a specific mandate to wage the war to a finish, whatever it might cost. Talks began for an electoral deal between supporters of the Lloyd George government which would allow them to crush the anti-war MPs (and in the process the pro-war critics of their actual policies) at the polls. These talks produced a broad agreement by which Unionists would have a free run in half the constituencies and

Lloyd George Liberals in a quarter, with the rest left for minor parties and to allow for the possibility of Asquithians rejoining the government later. This was a deal which, when once made, was hard to unstitch, and especially so when the tide of the war then changed dramatically in the summer of 1918, and so quickly that the Allies were clearly heading for an unconditional victory in the autumn. By late October the pact that had been planned for a war election was being considered instead for a victory election, for the same purpose of crushing the coalition's critics on the left. But in another important sense the motivation was now different, even if the arithmetic and the potential players in the game remained much the same. The purpose of an election would now be to grab a majority from a grateful electorate in the very moment of victory. This would thereby provide a five-year breathing-space in which the non-Labour parties could put the country back onto a peacetime economic footing, and enable it to 'stand the racket' (as a Tory MP put it) of expected Labour unrest at the same time.

The war duly ended in November, and the momentum towards an election proved unstoppable, but when Asquith again proudly refused to serve under Lloyd George an even greater electoral opportunity was opened up for the Unionists. Apart from a few strongholds like Wales, the Lloyd George Liberals simply did not have a political machine able to support a national election campaign, and their Leader was pushed to find more than 150 candidates in any case, so his share remained about a quarter of the British seats while the Unionists were free to attack almost all the rest. They were also freed, by Asquith's own decision, to attack Asquith and the other Liberal leaders outside the government and, by defeating them while in alliance with Lloyd George, to open the Liberal split still wider. The details of a policy agreement with Lloyd George proved to be more tricky, but the Unionists now held most of the cards and so gained most of what they wanted, including promises not to coerce Ulster into an independent Ireland and even to consider tariffs as an economic weapon. Lloyd George had effectively been captured by the Unionists, and in their private correspondence the party's leaders showed that they thought they could now use him as Joseph Chamberlain had been used after 1886 – immediately to discredit his former colleagues and in the longer term to bring his followers into their own party. In the first of these objectives they were entirely successful, in the second only partially so.

In the general election of 1918 Unionists did very well indeed, winning a clear parliamentary majority on their own and a huge one when their Liberal allies were included; the Asquithian wing of the old Liberal Party was almost destroyed, and many of the Lloyd Georgeites owed their survival to Unionist votes. A government could therefore be formed with an unassailable majority in the Commons, which was then able to ride out some extremely tense economic and political disturbances during the period of demobilization and post-war reconstruction. If a revolutionary situation really did exist in 1919, which is on the face of it doubtful, despite the panic-stricken reports submitted to the Cabinet by the police and apparently believed when read there – 'red revolution all round', as a Cabinet secretary described one meeting – then it certainly did not exist by 1921. By then the bubble of the post-war boom had burst, the heat had gone out of labour disputes with the onset of mass unemployment, and, since the formation of the British Communist Party in 1920, the revolutionary left had begun to be quarantined off from moderates in the Labour movement and were as a result losing their ability to influence events. Time gained by winning in 1918 therefore produced exactly what it had been intended to achieve: a limiting of what was seen as the most dangerous problem of the hour, the Labour threat.

All that was negative about Lloyd George's post-war coalition thus worked well enough, except that once it *had* worked so well the negative case for a coalition government ceased to be relevant, and their diminishing fear of revolutionary socialism eventually made many Tories rather lukewarm coalitionists. On the other hand, all that was positive about coalition was an intensely messy failure, mainly because the government was constantly veering between the contradictory policies of its Liberal and Conservative members, and because the deteriorating economic situation both landed it with a reputation for incompetent management and limited the resources available for other policies too. Liberal plans to extend educational, housing and other social provisions were largely shorn of their effectiveness by the Conservative MPs' assumption that such things were inherently unaffordable in a time of financial stringency, and almost all of the government's Liberal agenda was therefore a casualty of expenditure cuts after 1918. Any backsliding among Conservative MPs on the issue of holding down public expenditure would be ruthlessly penalized by attacks from the maverick Conservative press, in which the *Daily Express* and the *Daily Mail* in particular were assuring their readers that taxes were unnecessarily high (which was not hard to believe for a generation which had seen income tax rise fivefold in five years). Beyond even this continuous sniping, a pressure group largely formed under the auspices of the same newspapers, the Anti-Waste League, ran candidates against the Conservatives in four 1921 by-elections and received significant support from middle-class voters. As a result of this outside attack, it was largely Conservative backbench pressure that enforced the appointment of a committee of businessmen to make even more drastic economies in public expenditure in 1922.

The Conservatives had an equally frustrating time with their own policy priorities, despite their inclusion in the agreed manifesto of 1918. Empire development turned out to include a policy on India that involved an increased sphere for native self-government. Liberals were as capable of blocking Unionist proposals for tariffs as Unionists were of vetoing Liberal initiatives, so that a Safeguarding of Industry Act was passed but then rarely actually applied to the relief of British industry against cheap foreign goods; when, in a rare case, Baldwin, President of the Board of Trade, managed in 1921 to get a proposal through to protect British manufacturers of fabric gloves, it was only by threatening to resign, which was hardly a tactic that could be repeated as each new category of imported goods came up for discussion. The coalition government proved entirely unwilling to tackle the composition and powers of the House of Lords, one of the highest Unionist priorities ever since 1911 and especially so now that they feared a Labour majority in the Commons; but Liberal ministers who had fought for the 1911 Parliament Act had no wish to disown it within a few years of its passage. On another contentious issue even Unionists who felt some relief about the end of fighting in Ireland were racked with guilt over the desertion of southern Unionists and still inclined (at least in public) to blame this too on the Liberals.

In all these ways, then, the very structure of the Lloyd George coalition negated any positive achievement, and as its premier was constantly forced to shift his ground in order to keep his mixed team together, his personal reputation for consistency declined too. As its maximum five-year term proceeded, speculation about the coalition's future became increasingly fevered.

In 1920 scrapping between factions within the government persuaded both teams of front-benchers to contemplate a 'fusion' into a single party. Lloyd George was always keener on this idea than Bonar Law, and when it failed as a result of Liberal resistance and before it had even been formally put to Conservative MPs, Bonar Law was mightily relieved, as he told Balfour:

> The result ... will probably be not to attempt any real fusion of the Parties but to get cooperation, something on the lines of the Liberal Unionists and Conservatives in the early days. This will be difficult to arrange and will certainly not be efficient, but personally I am not sorry at the turn events have taken. I do not like the idea of complete fusion if it can be avoided, but I had come to think, as you had also, that it was really essential if the Coalition was to continue ... As a Party we were losing nothing and, since the necessity of going slowly in the matter has come from L.G.'s own friends, I do not regret it.

In practice, cooperation after early 1920 was extremely *in*efficient, so that after the Irish treaty produced an apparent political triumph there was an attempt late in 1921 to produce fusion by compulsion, or at least a stay of execution for coalition government. The idea was for Lloyd George to call a snap election, in which everyone on the government side would have to campaign together to save their seats and which would at the least provide another five years during which the two groups would become more habituated to working together. It was notable that this time it was articulate and determined Unionist hostility that left the idea dead in the water, with the Party Chairman, Sir George Younger, taking the lead by running a press campaign to head off what he (and many other Tories) saw as a threat to his party's identity and independence.

By this time the official party leadership was less responsive to such upsurges of loyalism from below decks (one front-bencher famously spoke of Younger as 'the cabin boy' who was usurping the role of the party's officers), largely as a result of Bonar Law's retirement through ill-health in March 1921. Austen Chamberlain succeeded as the Leader without a contest, his rival of 1911, Walter Long, being by now out of the running as a result of his own declining health and his retreat to the Lords.

At the meeting that elected Chamberlain, his proposer E. G. Pretyman, MP, spoke with pride of the fact that Conservatives had no need actually to elect a leader, since the best man would always 'emerge'. Chamberlain was, though, a Leader with a very different view of his role from that of Bonar Law, and had become since 1916 a convinced, indeed an ideological coalitionist. This derived from two distinct motivations: first, Chamberlain had an intense sensitivity to ideas of political honour, hierarchy and loyalty (stemming at least in part from his recognition that his father Joe's reputation had always been that of a political wrecker motivated by personal ambition), and he was unwilling now to cast off and then treat as enemies those Liberals who had sat around the Cabinet table with him since 1916. Other Conservative ministers, Balfour and Birkenhead (the former F. E. Smith, now Lord Chancellor), for example, were also keen supporters of the idea of coalition if for slightly different reasons; their natural centrism and their belief in government by 'the best men' (among whom they naturally counted themselves) had been held in check by Bonar Law's partisanship, but they now found a Tory leader who would apply no such restraint. As the lower ranks of the party grew more mutinous during 1922, with diehards threatening to oppose in their constituencies any MP who backed Lloyd George, with the Unionist press taking sides in a partisan way, and with the National Union becoming increasingly convinced that the parliamentary leaders had lost sight of their responsibility to look after the party's collective self-interest as well as their own, Chamberlain and his closest advisers became more short-tempered, more inflexible and more imperious in their conviction that they alone knew what was best.

The second reason for coalitionism in 1922 was also a reason for Chamberlain's obduracy and arose from a slightly different version of that fear of Labour that had motivated much Conservative tactical thinking in 1918. By 1922 the threat of industrial unrest had receded, Labour's moderates were resuming control of their own party after the wartime upsurge of radicalism, Communists were being excluded from the mainstream labour movement, and even on the international scene the threat posed by a Bolshevik government in Russia no longer seemed so frightening. This did not, however, remove the Labour threat so much as divert it into parliamentary channels. Labour's more moderate leaders had always aimed at taking power by legal, parliamentary means, and by-elections in 1921–2 showed that Labour candidates were running strongly.

Almost all Conservatives shared this diagnosis of the problem and wanted to make decisions about their party's future status in that context, but that is where agreement ended. Chamberlain's conviction was that unless Conservatives united with any available Liberals to oppose the Labour threat, then Labour would win enough seats to take power, and he was therefore prepared to argue for concessions to Liberals to avoid any splitting of the anti-Labour vote. Tory diehards and party loyalists on the other hand argued that the shackling of their party to an unpopular Liberal Prime Minister, whose post-war career had been one long catalogue of compromises and policy reversals, would in itself threaten Tory chances of holding seats against Labour opponents – not least because it prevented Conservatives campaigning with conviction for policies in which they really believed. Some thinking Conservatives, like Baldwin within the government and Lord Salisbury on the outside, argued that it was immoral to seek to unite all property-owners on one political side in order to deny influence to the labour movement for ever, and that it would anyway be counter-productive, since it would in the end encourage working-class voters to back Labour in ever larger numbers and so vote it into power.

These various and contradictory reactions to an agreed problem presented the Conservative Party in 1922 with a difficult tactical choice. It could try to ally with the Liberals or it could seek to go it alone, smash the Liberal *Party* and challenge Liberal voters then to support Tory candidates in order to keep Labour out. In the end it was the second of these alternatives that was preferred, but less as a rational choice than as a Pavlovian lurch towards saving the Conservative Party's identity and its unity. As 1922 proceeded it became clear that the Tory diehards would not accept another period of coalition in any circumstances, and that this would in itself ruin Chamberlain's preferred strategy because it required a united party to pursue it. In the autumn of 1922 the coalitionists sought once again to force the Conservative Party into a renewed period of coalition, and this time Chamberlain took a high line with his followers and threatened to quit if they would not follow him. His opponents at the crucial party meeting at the Carlton Club on 19 October 1922 were not for the most part trying to end coalition there and then, and few of them probably had sufficient confidence to abandon all thoughts of a coalition in the future either, but the overwhelming majority of Conservative MPs were not prepared to accept the inflexible lead of a man whose strategy was closing off all alternative options and at the same time committing them to five more years of a government that few of them now respected, and within a strategy that seemed at the least problematic. By 185 votes to 88, Conservative MPs rejected Chamberlain's advice, and he therefore carried out his threat, resigning on the same day, as did Lloyd George as Prime Minister.

Although this was clearly a rebellion in which a wide range of middle-of-the-road backbenchers took part as well as diehards, the final decision was made possible only by the disintegration of collective responsibility by the Unionist front bench during 1922. Baldwin and Curzon, together with other juniors and former ministers like Derby, had already deserted

Lloyd George and Chamberlain before 19 October 1922, and the reappearance of Bonar Law as a potential new leader, as legitimator of the party revolt, and as a prime minister in waiting, completed the process. After the Carlton Club vote Chamberlain was still backed by thirteen Conservative ex-ministers (including nine of Lloyd George's Cabinet), all of whom now signalled their continuing dissent from the decision that the party had taken by their refusal to serve under a new Conservative prime minister. In this sense, the Carlton Club vote was indeed, as Baldwin's parliamentary private secretary J. C. C. Davidson suggested to a journalist as he made his way into the meeting, 'a slice off the top', but the fact that another top slice was available was an important part of MPs' calculations as they sharpened their knives.

Recognizing that something quite out of the ordinary was going on, Bonar Law did not accept the king's invitation to form a government, but asked for and was given time to explore the party situation further; a similar strategy was followed in Alec Douglas-Home's opposed succession to the premiership in 1963. From Lloyd George's outgoing Cabinet, Curzon and Baldwin would be available, and other opponents of Chamberlain's coalitionism included the Party Chairman and his deputy, the Chief Whip, several former Cabinet ministers and the majority of the under-secretaries. Further investigations indicated that about half even of those who had voted with Chamberlain had done so more from loyalty to the incumbent Leader than from support for his strategy, and would not make any further waves once Bonar Law was restored to his former place. On this reading, the Tory coalitionists now sulking in their tents were seen to be a group of all chiefs and no Indians; Bonar Law's soundings therefore soon convinced him that he could more or less reunite the party in government, and he kissed hands on 23 October as the first Conservative Prime Minister for seventeen years, heading the first party government of any sort for seven.

In effect, though, since the 1918 parliament was dissolved within less than a week, it would be for the electorate to ratify or abrogate the decisions so far made. With a normal party election unexpectedly under way and with the saving of their own seats now their primary concern, the coalitionist Conservatives made few disruptive noises over the next few weeks, and a Liberal Party fighting as two separate factions could not impress the electorate as a real alternative either. On 15 November, then, the electors returned 345 Conservative MPs in a House of 615, thereby registering in the first normal, peacetime election since 1910 the strengths that Conservatives had in the new electoral system of 1918. The climb-back to power from the shattering defeat of 1906 had been a slow one, much more prolonged, contentious and difficult than recovery was to be from the comparable defeat of 1945. But the three-party struggle that 1906–10 dimly foreshadowed, and which emerged in full vigour during (and partly as a result of) the First World War, had held up the resumption of normal party activities for years past. It was with some relief that Tories now turned to the more familiar territory of two-party debate, even if the major party opposite was now Labour rather than the Liberals. Their assumption of a complete return to partisan normality would prove to be more than a little premature, but the 'great recovery' of the party in 1922 (as Younger put it) did indeed indicate the beginnings of one of its strongest historical periods, not least because the fall of the Lloyd George coalition, partly on his advice, had shot into unexpected prominence the man who would encapsulate the next period of Conservative history, Stanley Baldwin. Within a few years Tories gathered in Conference would be affectionately and gratefully singing along to a new version of Al Jolson's greatest hit, a version that from the fertile pen of Waldron Smithers, MP, ran, 'Climb up on my knee, Stanley Boy!'

10

The Second Summit: Baldwin's Party, 1922–29

BONAR LAW'S REAL ACHIEVEMENT as Conservative Leader was to keep the party in the political game at the highest level throughout the period in which Edwardian three-party politics and then the Great War removed all the certainties, to prevent any section of importance from splitting off more than temporarily, and finally to recall it to its independent identity in 1922 when the siren voices of anti-Labour coalitionism threatened to destroy both unity and coherence. These were vital successes which suggest that Bonar Law should be included in the pantheon of the party's greatest leaders, for without them there would have been no solid base on which his successors could build. It is quite conceivable that the Conservatives rather than the Liberals might have fragmented and lost faith in their party's future in the difficult decade of the 1910s; the Liberals would then have become the chief anti-socialist party while the Tories were remorselessly squeezed by the British electoral system's denial of a fair share of seats to any party that achieves less than 30 per cent of the vote, with Liberals and Labour then assiduously explaining to electors that a Tory vote would be a wasted vote which could not elect either many MPs or a government. There certainly seemed to Tory contemporaries a real possibility that events could develop in that depressing way, and Bonar Law's apparent success in halting the process was reason enough for his veneration among Tory politicians and activists when he died in 1923.

Conceivable such a process may have been, and naturally dreaded by Conservatives themselves, but not perhaps likely. For Liberal decline had much to do with social change and its expression in political attitudes as well as with miscalculations, the personal feuds of politicians, and their tactical errors. The taproots of Tory strength in the agricultural counties and the better-off suburbs remained solid even in their wilderness years after 1906 and were then given even greater leverage by the 1918 changes in the electoral system. In inter-war Britain the Conservatives had a favourable wind, for the Lib–Lab alliance which had obstructed them since 1906 was no more, and elections were there to be won by the party. It is unlikely, though, that Bonar Law would have proved to be the right man to head the next stage of Tory recovery. In the 1922 election he did achieve a signal personal triumph, but this was in uniquely favourable circumstances: Labour was on the rise but not yet ready to challenge for a parliamentary majority, the Liberals were split and fighting among themselves, and the electorate was all too ready to accept as premier an honest man of limited communicative powers after six exciting years shaped by Lloyd George's flashier talents. As Baldwin later said of 1922, the electors at breakfast opened their newspapers and read that Lloyd George had disparagingly said that Bonar Law was 'honest to the point of simplicity', and they had turned to each other and said, 'By God, that is what we want.' And since Bonar Law removed almost everything controversial from his party's manifesto, justifying this with the argument that the country needed a period of 'tranquillity' and consolidation after thirteen years of incessant innovation, he invited the voters to ratify the overthrow of Lloyd George without having to say much about the alternative that he would pursue if elected. The large Conservative majority produced in that 1922 election was Bonar Law's only answer to his critics who said that he had no policy, but it was not an answer that would have lasted for long.

Bonar Law's success in 1922 was achieved, then, as to an extent all his achievements were, by negativism, and it would take a Party Leader with very different skills to reap the full benefits of the party's post-war opportunity. The Bonar Law government after November 1922 soon ran into deep difficulties; it remained united around the key point that had brought it into existence, the refusal to form alliances with Liberals, but this kept Austen Chamberlain and his friends in semi-detachment from their party's front bench, and the government was in any case united on little else. Bonar Law by this stage of his life was even more gloomy and taciturn than in his prime, his natural pessimism deeply underscored by the loss of two sons during the recent war, and probably by tiredness and failing health too. He exerted no strong pull in any particular direction, and as a result of this his six months as Prime Minister were characterized by internal wranglings, policy failures and the mounting unpopularity reflected in by-election defeats: there was, for example, a terrible muddle over rent decontrol, following which the Minister of Health lost his own seat at Mitcham, one of three seats lost in just four days in March 1923. It was a respectable government, in which a number of the key figures of the next generation – Neville Chamberlain (now able to emerge from the shadow of his half-brother Austen), Philip Lloyd-Greame (later Cunliffe-Lister, and eventually Earl of Swinton), Samuel Hoare, William Joynson-Hicks and Edward Wood (later Lord Irwin and eventually Earl of Halifax), among others – were finding their ministerial feet for the first time, but it lacked stars and effective communicators, a factor given added poignancy by the visible presence of Austen Chamberlain, Birkenhead and Balfour on the sidelines. It was fortunate both for the party and for Bonar Law's reputation that this limbo did not last for long, terminated in May 1923 by his enforced retirement due to the cancer that killed him only a few weeks later.

With the most talented and experienced front-benchers exiled from office since October 1922, and therefore unable to come forward for the leadership, the party did not have an easy choice. Curzon, a party workhorse and a man of Cabinet rank for a generation, was (in his own mind at least) the obvious successor, but this was problematic because of his olympian, exaggeratedly aristocratic manner and style. He was given to upsetting colleagues with such remarks as 'No gentleman takes soup at luncheon' and 'A gentleman never wears a brown suit in London', and was hardly the natural choice for a party just learning to cope with the arrival of democracy. The same argument had a narrower, constitutional relevance too, in the fact that he sat in the House of Lords, where the Labour Opposition was hardly even present. Although it was only twenty-one years since Salisbury had led his government from the Upper House, that had been when the Houses were still theoretically co-equal, as they remained until 1911, and when there remained a Liberal peerage to whom he could be accountable. Now even many Tories asked – and this question surfaced at the palace among other places – whether the country could be led from the Lords at all. Since peers did not until 1963 have the right to give up their peerages and continue or resume careers in the Commons, there was thus a half-century in which they remained prominent in Cabinets without the chance to rise to the very top.

The only serious alternative to Curzon among the Cabinet's commoners was Stanley Baldwin, who had only two years' experience of the Cabinet, had merely been Bonar Law's reluctant third choice for the Exchequer six months earlier, and had not exactly covered himself in glory since, prompting among other things the Bonar Law government's greatest internal crisis when he blurted out to the press a confidential detail of financial policy on which the Cabinet had not yet agreed. On the positive side, Baldwin had had fifteen years in the Commons during which he had become a popular and respected figure, he had been competent in junior office, and he had been one of the most compelling of the speakers who had at the Carlton Club urged the abandonment of Lloyd George in October 1922. Without a change, he had argued, 'the old Conservative Party' would be 'smashed to atoms and lost in ruins' by the 'dynamic force' that Lloyd George offered; privately, the Baldwin circle referred to Lloyd George as 'the goat', a soubriquet that simultaneously celebrated Welshness, sexual prowess, and the reputation for having dirty habits. Already fifty-five when he made that speech at the Carlton Club, Baldwin had expected that it would end his political career, though when the party unexpectedly took his advice it became instead a springboard for fifteen years of high office.

Bonar Law gave no formal advice to the king when he resigned in May 1923 – though he may have known of the unofficial document that was sent to the palace by a group of Baldwin supporters and which was said 'practically' to represent his view that Baldwin should succeed him. Balfour and Salisbury, the party's elder statesmen consulted by the king's secretary, supported Curzon and Baldwin respectively. The tide of pro-Baldwin letters that flowed into Central Office leaves little doubt, though, that the party out in the country welcomed Baldwin, as a player rather than a gentleman leader for a new age of democratic politics. When the king took the same view and summoned Baldwin to office, Curzon was deeply affronted at coming second to 'a man of the utmost insignificance', not perhaps grasping that this very fact was (and would continue to be) Baldwin's real appeal to the Conservative Party.

The choice of Baldwin was, then, a fortuitous one, arising from the dearth of other candidates and the impossibility of choosing the only available alternative, but it would prove to be one of the best ever made for the party's future shape and development. Baldwin remained Conservative Leader for the fourteen years until he retired in 1937, during which he was Prime Minister three times and deputy premier with a Tory majority at his back in the Commons for a further four years. During that time he succeeded in giving his party a characteristically personal flavour, shaping a policy and a campaigning identity that guided the party for half a century, and developing a particular style of Conservative politics that may be traced through to R. A. Butler and Harold Macmillan, to Iain Macleod and Robert Carr, and to Chris Patten and John Major in the next three political generations. The mixing-up of Baldwin's historical reputation with bitter post-war arguments about the origins of the Second World War meant that not all of these were keen to acknowledge their political ancestry, but the clearing of the dust and the lengthening perspective of time, together with the efforts of revisionist historians since the late 1960s, allowed the correction of the record, so that for Major and Patten no such denial was necessary.

Baldwin did not, however, shape the destiny of his party in any of the usual ways, for he was no great legislator, no political thinker at all, no international strategist, and not a particularly talented administrator either. There is scarcely a statute – with the possible exception of the Government of India Act of 1935 – that can be unequivocally attributed to his input and his support. He became notorious for his lack of systematic thinking, and indeed his characteristic political conduct went so far towards becoming a self-parody of his own lack of philosophical thought in later life that historians may even be in danger of exaggerating the fact. He showed no great interest in diplomatic matters, made few international contacts, was on occasion brought in to meet visiting statesmen only to forget the purpose of the meeting, and at least once announced when foreign policy was reached on the Cabinet agenda, 'Wake me up when this is over' (another probable moment of self-parody, later seized on by historians of Appeasement to wreck his good name). Unrelentingly hardworking colleagues like Neville Chamberlain found Baldwin a constant trial, for he could not be persuaded to read the papers in advance of a meeting, relying more on instinct than on briefing or research, and he lapsed into long periods of apparent inactivity when his fairly shallow reserves of nervous energy gave out. As lobby correspondent for the *Morning Post*, William Deedes witnessed Baldwin's last speeches as Prime Minister in 1937, recalling the apparently random scraps of notes from which he drew inspiration for a powerful and successful appeal for the ending of a coal dispute in the week of the Coronation, the impact that his moral appeal had even on determined Labour opponents, and the nervous prostration induced by such successes.

It is not, therefore, surprising that colleagues tended, at least at first, consistently to underestimate Baldwin and to ask themselves despairingly

Baldwin's homely features, as drawn by David Low, *New Statesman*, 4 November 1933.

how he could possibly have become and remained their Leader. Curzon's reference to his insignificance was insistent; Balfour once called him 'an idiot'; and Austen Chamberlain often vented similar remarks *de haut en bas*, as when he lamented that the talented men in Baldwin's 1924 Cabinet had 'so uninspiring a Commander in Chief'. Birkenhead thought that he typified the 'second eleven' that had gone in to bat when their international-class betters had been ousted in 1922, and Churchill, when playing chess and urging his opponent to develop his pawn-play, cried, 'Come on F.E. [Smith], bring out your Baldwins!' And yet Baldwin was able to survive the intrigues and the contempt of all these cleverer men; he regularly outmanoeuvred them at the highest level, and – what is more – he was also generally able (like Clement Attlee on the Labour side in the 1940s) to lead them as a team and to get the best out of them.

The reason for this was that Baldwin had something which – at least in private – all these men knew that they had not got in the same measure: an ability to communicate which made him both a shaper and an interpreter of opinion *par excellence*. Even when commenting on the quite unnecessary election defeat to which Baldwin had led them in December 1923, Balfour could see that the campaign, Baldwin's first as Prime Minister, had also demonstrated the emergence of a new star of the hustings on whom the party would be able to trade for years ahead; Churchill (though adding that 'I cease to be astonished at anything') accepted after a Baldwin triumph in the Commons in 1925 that 'Nous avons un maître'; and, even while lamenting the frustrations of actually working with the incurably 'lazy' Baldwin in office, Neville Chamberlain had to concede that his leader did 'provide something vital in retaining the floating vote'.

Baldwin's importance, therefore, lay in the most ephemeral of the political arts, the cultivation of mood, performance on his feet and the judgement of issues as to timing and practicality. While he paid much attention to advice from the professionals and was prepared to subject himself in the field of communications to preparation and even rehearsal, he was undoubtedly fortunate that the period of his career at the top coincided exactly with new technology that he was perfectly equipped to exploit. The use of electric amplifiers to enable large crowds actually to hear political speeches at open-air rallies became common only in the 1920s, and this enabled the party machine to gather huge crowds not just to see a political heavyweight in action and to have a good day out at a party fête, but actually to hear and absorb his message. In 1927 72,000 people gathered from all over eastern England to hear Baldwin speak at Welbeck Abbey, but the size of the crowd was a cause not for party complacency but for an internal enquiry which sought to explain why it had been so small. Big outdoor rallies had, of course, existed since the birth of participatory politics in Britain, but it seems unlikely that more than a fraction of the people who attended such meetings as those conducted by Gladstone in Midlothian in 1879 ever heard much of what was said, compared with those who read about it later. At rallies strategically placed around the country, and with the annual Party Conference visiting every region twice during Baldwin's leadership (each one climaxing in a

Leader's rally), the activists could truly feel that they had been close to their man. For those more distant, Baldwin's speeches were also made available by the party organization on gramophone records and were published commercially in six volumes of books, an exposure to the publishing market greater than for any other twentieth-century politician except Churchill (who anyway had to wait until his triumphs in 1940 before he was able to hit the speech-reading public with prose on Baldwin's scale).

These were no more than adaptations of traditional methods, but more modern techniques achieved even more. The BBC began radio broadcasting just five months before Baldwin first became Prime Minister and his career at the top exactly coincided with the rise of radio as a major medium of national communication. Already in 1924, Baldwin's election broadcast was being hailed as the work of a master of the medium, not only in its own right but in comparison with the inappropriate efforts of Lloyd George and the Labour Leader, Ramsay MacDonald. Heeding good advice from the BBC's general manager, John Reith, Baldwin had a special talk written for the radio, took his wife with him into the studio (Mrs Baldwin brought her knitting, which gave a real 'homey' atmosphere to the occasion), and then spoke quietly and directly to listeners as individuals, exactly the approach that best paid off in the new medium. He was soon so accomplished a radio performer as to be invited by the BBC to give concert-interval talks on non-political subjects as well as broadcasting as his party's spokesman, and he thus perfected the folksy manner required for the 'fireside chat' long before that approach was commonplace. One of his trademarks in the creation of atmosphere during radio addresses was to strike a match, and so convey the impression of a calm, relaxed pipe-smoker, at ease with the microphone (and therefore with the listener too).

Baldwin's pipe was a visual trademark too, and he was occasionally to be seen before mirrors with it, rehearsing the best angles and gestures. The suppliers of his favourite tobacco – which, typically, was the unfashionably provincial 'Dr Gale's Glasgow Presbyterian Mixture' – placed his name on the lid of their tins ('as made famous by the Rt. Hon. Stanley Baldwin') and placed an appropriate quotation from one of his speeches on the inside ('My thoughts grow in the aroma of that particular tobacco'), a form of sponsorship for mutual benefit that seems redolent of a much later age (and was indeed to be repeated in Harold Wilson's association with Erinmore Flake in 1964). All of this was a gift to the cartoonists, who thus gave Baldwin a sharp political image as soon as he became so unexpected a premier in 1923, when scarcely any voters can have known much about him. The pipe figured prominently in early silent newsreels and film cartoons of Baldwin, and in many newspaper photographs of the time too.

But it was the opportunity to put together his speaking skills, his voice and his visual image when sound newsreels appeared in 1930 that completed the process. Cinema was already by then a mass medium with an extraordinary degree of penetration of the adult population, and this provided an able performer with an unprecedented opportunity. When he first spoke on sound film, for a British Movietone News item entitled 'Mr Baldwin Speaks to the Conservative Party' early in 1930, he was quite certainly heard as a living person within a couple of days by more electors than had ever been able to view him as a personality in his career to date, and quite probably by more than had ever seen Disraeli perform in the whole of his fifty years in public life. Over the next decade Baldwin was regularly on the newsreel screens, unveiling statues, speaking at meetings, commenting on public events and giving a few minutes to the cameras when arriving from or departing for foreign travel. Since newsreels would allow partisan political comment only during general election campaigns, in a system open to all parties on a theoretically equal basis like the later party political broadcasts on television, these 'non-political' appearances built up Baldwin as a personality rather than as a party man, but they did add immensely to his authority when he pronounced on political issues later. And to supplement this exposure in a way that it could control itself, the party built up from 1927 a large fleet of its own cinema vans which drew larger attendances than more traditional speaker meetings; the vans' touring programmes generally contained a film speech by Baldwin, shot and edited so as to look and sound just like a newsreel. For such occasions Baldwin could effortlessly deliver what his Party Chairman Davidson called 'inimitable little speeches so free from party bias that you felt that the dangers [of socialism] seemed all the greater as no allowance had to be made for partisanship'.

Baldwin was thus the first British politician ever to become truly familiar to the voting public, with his personal gestures, his accent and intonation, his favourite phrases and his political vocabulary all instantly recognizable. Much of this was fortuitous, in that his career happened to coincide with the years in which this new technology first existed, but it also depended on his awareness of the opportunity and on his recognition of the impact that he would make by using it for his party. To a large extent this would depend on what the public actually heard and saw in Stanley Baldwin, and what message he chose to put over. In other words, this was the point in British politics at which the medium and the message became inescapably intertwined. Here no amount of advice from seasoned professionals could have done the trick, for what mattered most was the fact that the Baldwin that came across on the radio and on the screen was the real thing. As a public speaker he eschewed elaborate language or complicated syntax, and both as a writer and as a performer he avoided rhetorical flourishes and literary references. It would be unduly patronizing to say that Baldwin thought in sentences rather than in paragraphs, but that observation does capture something central to his mode of address, and explains why he was able to tailor his normal manner so easily to the limited time-slots offered by the studios, where an entire broadcast would be five minutes long and a more routine news item limited to two or three sentences. His ability to say complex things in a lucid, simplified manner presented audiences with no obstacles to their understanding and – in the manner of the later soundbite – presented few problems to newsfilm editors either.

Much of this makes Baldwin sound like a media performer, which is in part what he did become to the great benefit of his party, but it should not be assumed that this was a performance for the cameras which presented a fundamentally false image of the man. For Baldwin was an essentially moral, honest man, a convinced and practising Christian with a strong sense of the duty that that position imposed on a man in the secular world. By the end of the First World War, for which he was too old to fight but which left him with an overwhelming awareness of the sacrifice that others had made, Baldwin was a conviction politician – not so much in terms of a specific programme as because he saw the necessity for healing, emollience and calm – and he believed after 1923 that he had, as the country's leader, a personal vocation to promote these causes: 'There is only one thing which I feel is worth giving one's whole strength to, and that is the binding together of all classes of our people in an effort to make life in this country better in every sense of the word. That is the end and object of my life in politics.' He detected no particular gulf between himself and his socialist opponents, recognizing that many who joined the labour movement were motivated by 'a perfectly genuine and altruistic feeling', the wish to 'bring about ... a better condition for his fellow-men – with more equality of opportunity, and giving to them a better chance of enjoying more education and more of the good things of life'. When such people were in bitter conflict with his government during the General Strike of 1926, Baldwin confessed that 'Everything I care for most is being smashed to bits'.

His own motivation in politics was succinctly set out in a speech on the same issues in March 1925, when he stated that 'We at any rate shall not fire the first shot. We stand for peace. We stand for the removal of suspicion in the country. We want to create an atmosphere in a new Parliament for a new age, in which the people can come together ... Give Peace in our time, O Lord!' The readiness to see good in the other side, and the overriding desire to avoid conflict, gave Baldwin a strong appeal to the people as a whole, but frequently placed him in dispute with his own MPs, whose diehards at least were quick to view him and his policies as 'semi-socialist'. Such reactions were held in check as much as anything by the quite remarkable talent that Baldwin had for judging public opinion, or at least for grasping what the Tory part of it would and would not stand for. His skills as a communicator on behalf of the party derived to a large extent from this instinct, for he had (as Neville Chamberlain put it in 1937), 'a singular and instinctive knowledge of how the plain man's mind works'.

Perhaps this was because Baldwin was, and prided himself on being, a plain Englishman himself. Bonar Law's accession to the party leadership in 1911 had marked a new approach not only because he was a provincial, a businessman with no pretensions to landownership and gentility, and a man with limited formal education, but also because he was the first potential Prime Minister of Britain to seek the post on the ground of his representative rather than his exceptional status. Socially, the next three Tory Leaders, Austen and Neville Chamberlain and Baldwin, all came from the same world of provincial business – and all three of them from Liberal Unionist rather than Tory backgrounds so far as their own families went – though each had come from later generations of industrial wealth than Bonar Law, had more typical educational backgrounds for Tory leaders and spoke with more conventional parliamentary accents too; indeed, Baldwin's progress via Harrow to Cambridge, and his ownership of a country estate in Worcestershire, as well as an accent suitable even for the BBC when access to the microphone was so jealously guarded, seemed hardly a step away from the traditional elite. But in the way in which he made his claim for office, he more resembled Bonar Law than any of the Chamberlains ever did, and he thus behaved very differently from most of his Cabinet colleagues in the 1920s. Baldwin was in truth a modest man – on one occasion while Prime Minister and the most famous face in the country, he quite seriously introduced himself to the daughter of an old friend with the words, 'You won't remember me, but . . .' – and he approached the electors with modesty, asking for their votes as a man much like themselves, 'the man you can trust', rather than as a *leader* with exceptional personal gifts.

In the European world of the totalitarian dictators of the 1930s, this grounding of Baldwin's appeal in the very ordinariness and representativeness of English provincial life was in itself a contribution to the case for democracy, at a time when it was most under threat. When, in a newsreel broadcast of December 1936, he pointed to the horrors of Nazism in Germany, Fascism in Italy, Communism in Russia and civil war in Spain (which, characteristically, he thought in Burkeian terms to be the worst of the four evils), and contrasted all this with the unexciting world of British parliamentary government, Gaumont British News cannily entitled the interview, 'Premier Takes Stock, Finds Britain Best'. Britain was, said Baldwin, the custodian for the whole world of democracy, liberty and progress, but he rapidly corrected himself so as to claim that Britain actually stood for 'ordered liberty' and 'ordered democracy', so avoiding the charge of carrying even democracy to the logical limits of the enthusiast.

Baldwin was unusual in that interview in speaking so highly of 'Britain', for it was much more usual (despite his mother's Celtic blood) for him to talk of 'England'. For Baldwin's claim to representative Englishness was grounded in a particular vision of England and the English that he regularly and insistently articulated. It was a characteristic of the age, this rediscovery of 'deep England', involving people from right across the political spectrum and manifesting itself in George Orwell's essays, in the series of Shell guides to the English counties, and in the rise of the National Trust, but nobody contributed more to the idea that 'England is the country, and the country is England' than Baldwin. His first book of speeches contained one, appropriately delivered to the Royal Society of St George in 1924, entitled 'On England', words which were also chosen for the book's title; his final volume's title claimed that Baldwin had been *An Interpreter of England*. Baldwin had assured his listeners in 1924 that 'the English are at heart and in practice the kindest people in the world', and 'a brotherly and a neighbourly feeling which we see to a remarkable extent through all classes'. This was reassuring stuff for the majority of his audience, but it also meshed in directly with the type of politics that he wished to pursue, and its idealism went down extremely well in a post-1918 democratic age that was (as Lord Salisbury told Baldwin himself) 'panting after ideals'.

Baldwin's Conservative Party thus geared itself up for a more democratic time, 'a new age', by opening its ranks to a wider participating membership than the party had ever known before. The growth of membership was not uniform across all constituencies in the 1920s, for it was in just this period that Labour so consolidated its class appeal to a wide swathe of heavy industrial and mining seats that they became almost no-go areas for Conservative organizations. But in the suburban, rural and mixed constituencies that made up the bulk of the country the Tory membership flourished as never before. Its expansion was to be seen in actual numbers, in activity at social events, in zealous participation in the business of the constituency associations, and in such new practices as the rotation of office-holders and the fixing of meetings for evenings and weekends (which demonstrated that the party no longer belonged only to the rich and the leisured – those who, said Baldwin, 'never did a hand's stir' of work for themselves and believed that Conservatism consisted only of '*Coningsby* and county cricket').

It was the party's ability to tap the subscription income of a large individual membership, as well as donations from industry and the wealthy, that enabled the organization to indulge in the technical innovations already described, as well as maintaining the more traditional forms and methods of campaigning – posters and leaflets (printed in larger numbers in the 1920s than ever before or since), canvassing on the doorstep and in the streets, and meetings addressed by the candidate and other speakers. It was also characteristic of Baldwin that he went out of his way to endorse that side of the party's life, for he had done it all himself, as he told the 1928 Party Conference, to the obvious enjoyment of those present:

> I have had forty years' experience of Politics, most of it in the rank and file. There is nothing I ask you to do that I have not done myself. I have marked off polling cards. I have addressed envelopes (laughter), and I have shepherded the last batch of voters from the public house (cheers, and laughter). I gained my experience in an old borough and there is nothing that you can teach me.

This was the internal party version of the Baldwin appeal to the electors to send him back to Downing Street because he was just like them, and could therefore govern on their behalf as a national leader who embodied what English nationality was all about; as he put it in 1935, 'I ask you to trust me – and I think you can trust me by now.'

However, there was another area of party innovation in Baldwin's time in which he had no particular interest and for which he could claim little credit, but which was equally significant in the long run, and this was the professionalization of policy formulation. Here the key figure was Neville Chamberlain, an MP only since 1918 and a Cabinet minister only from 1923, but by the late 1920s already a key party figure and Baldwin's obvious heir-apparent. If Baldwin provided the inspiration, the tone and the communicative skills, Neville Chamberlain provided the perspiration and was the executive arm of this phase of party history.

Chamberlain shared in many of Baldwin's social objectives and like Baldwin devoted much time to party as well as to government in his own order of priorities; it was notable that he had come out against coalition in 1922, even though trying to stay loyal to his half-brother, the Party Leader. Such was the lack of available talent that Chamberlain was already Chancellor of the Exchequer in the later part of 1923, a post he held again for six years in the 1930s, but on the party side it was the year in opposition in 1924 that really brought him to the fore. As a result of shared office under Asquith and Lloyd George since 1915, the party was in 1924 fully in opposition for the first time in nine years, and with another election bound to come soon. Following precedents like the Tariff Reform League and the Unionist Social Reform Committee of the Edwardian period, Baldwin was persuaded to set up a small Policy Secretariat to act as his private office, to review policy options, and to draft a full-scale policy document for the party as it now reunited after years of division. Chamberlain rapidly became the front-bencher who took the greatest interest in the secretariat's work, and it was Chamberlain who drafted the document that the shadow cabinet approved and published in June 1924. *Looking Ahead: Unionist Principle and Aims*, which was the basis on which the party's manifesto was drafted in October and was then the blueprint for five years in office when the election was won, was in effect the first comprehensive policy document that the party ever produced. Within his own main field of interest, when he went to the Ministry of Health after the election, Chamberlain was well enough prepared to present the Cabinet at once with a list of twenty-five proposals for implementation over the next five years, twenty-three of which were eventually put through. Conviction here worked alongside party self-interest, for Chamberlain was convinced that 'unless we leave our mark as social reformers the country will take it out on us hereafter', but without policy preparation in advance such a reflection would have had little chance of being followed by evidence of productive action.

Once in office, some of these lessons were forgotten, and those like the novelist MP John Buchan, who in 1928 urged the Conservative Party to keep up a constant process of policy research and political education, could make little headway. With the approach of the next election in 1928–9 the construction of the manifesto was a more haphazard, amateurish and inefficient process than in 1924, but this time the lesson was truly learned. A Conservative Research Department was set up later in 1929 and after a short transition this too came under Neville Chamberlain, who was appointed its chairman in 1930 and retained the position until his death ten years later.

The CRD ensured that in the 1930s the party was well prepared for debates on tariffs and other such complex issues, that the shadow cabinet (or Tory ministers when meeting to discuss matters politically) had a mechanism for minute-taking and chasing up the implementation of its decisions, that MPs would have professional briefing and their backbench committees reliable secretarial support, and that planning for future manifestos would be taking place well ahead of the next campaign. Under the aegis of Neville Chamberlain, then, the CRD made itself a permanent part of the Conservative Party machine, and since Chamberlain himself was both a workaholic and a stickler for detail the CRD also developed working habits of that kind; when Frank Pakenham married Chamberlain's own niece, his fellow-CRD staffers petitioned the chairman for time off to attend the wedding, but they were allowed to attend the service only on condition that they were back at their desks for the afternoon. The CRD also developed early in its life what was to be another of its roles, the giving of opportunities to bright, young future politicians: in the 1930s a key CRD figure was Henry Brooke (later in Harold Macmillan's Cabinet), much as the 1924 secretariat had included Robert Boothby and Geoffrey Lloyd, both of whom had already become ministers by 1940, and the post-war CRD would employ Iain Macleod, Reginald Maudling and Enoch Powell – and many other future ministers in later years.

It would, however, be difficult to carry through in practice both the inspirational lead of Baldwin and the businesslike methods of Neville

Chamberlain, not least because in each case their moderate policy preferences conflicted with those of many Tory MPs, and so the actual record in the 1920s was indeed fairly mixed. Baldwin's first government in 1923 was in fact something of a fiasco, for only five months after becoming Prime Minister he was personally responsible for a misdirected initiative that set his government slithering by December 1923 to election defeat four years before the end of its normal term. Baldwin had inherited from Bonar Law a renewed pledge not to introduce tariffs without previously consulting the electorate, but by the summer of 1923 he was convinced that only tariffs would prevent a further slide into depression in British industry and a continuing rise in unemployment. He therefore explained his views to the Party Conference in Plymouth in October, and since a Prime Minister could hardly announce that a policy was necessary and then not actually do anything about it, he found himself at once in conflict with Bonar Law's pledge and driven remorselessly into an election for which the party was neither ready nor united. The 1923 election campaign was one of the party's unhappiest, as candidates in neighbouring constituencies regularly contradicted each other, as the leaders made up policy as they went along and as Liberals reunited and revived in defence of their most sacred article of faith. The outcome – loss of the Conservatives' Commons majority but retention of the position of largest party – demonstrated just how strong the party's position was under the 1918 electoral system, for a worse scenario than the 1923 campaign was hard to envisage, and yet the party had only just lost and nobody else had won.

Once Baldwin had got over the initial shock of rejection by the people with whom he so closely identified, he refused to contemplate any deal with Asquith or Lloyd George, or any change of policy either, until the Liberals (the third largest party) had taken the only step available to them and installed MacDonald's Labour Party in minority office. This sequence of events achieved what the past year in office had failed to do: it reunited the Conservatives by forcing Austen Chamberlain and his supporters to rejoin the ranks; it accelerated the collapse of the Liberal Party (which incurred the onus of putting Labour in, and then eventually also had to turn them out); it encouraged anti-socialist Liberals like Churchill to move to the Conservatives (in his own case, to 're-rat', as he later put it); and it gave a breathing space in opposition during which policy options and Baldwin's personal appeal to the voters could be sharpened up along the lines already described. At the same time, even Labour's halting and unimpressive first year in office gave the Conservatives a considerable

THE RECRUITING PARADE

The Conservatives' 'anti-sosh'[ialist] campaign, with Beaverbrook and Rothermere looking after the banner, wins over Churchill, from the *Star*, 7 October 1924.

boost as the strongest party of resistance to socialism. When MacDonald gave diplomatic recognition to the Soviet regime and tried to organize a large loan to Russia (even though the Bolsheviks had repudiated all pre-1917 international debts), the gap between Labour and the Communists became more blurred – or at least could be more easily blurred by anti-socialists in their quest for votes.

This 'red card' was played with a vengeance in the 1924 election campaign, which culminated in the *Daily Mail*'s publication of the 'Zinoviev letter' – a letter purporting to have come from Moscow to the British Communists and urging them to prepare for bloody insurrection. Historians have been arguing ever since as to whether the 'red letter' of 1924 was or was not a forgery (and if so, by whom), but there is no doubt about the impact that it made at the time, or about the masterly use that Central Office made of it in the last days of the 1924 campaign (including, almost certainly, leaking it to the *Mail* in the first place, after the party itself had acquired it in mysterious circumstances from the Foreign Office). While it did not in itself create Baldwin's large winning majority, the Zinoviev letter's publication fitted in extremely well during a campaign in which anti-socialism was already rampant, a mood that extended from Conservatives and the *Mail* to Liberals and quality newspapers too. Winston Churchill, then in transition between Liberal and Conservative and standing at Epping as an 'Anti-Socialist Constitutionalist', told his constituents even a fortnight before the Zinoviev letter appeared that, 'spellbound by the lure of Moscow, wire-pulled through subterranean channels, Mr Ramsay MacDonald and his associates have attempted to make the British nation accomplices in Bolshevist crimes.' The Tory Duke of Devonshire might be claiming that Labour took its marching orders from Moscow, and Curzon that MacDonald was the secret slave of the Communists, but Lloyd George was saying very much the same, and even *The Times*, after reviewing Labour's plans to build more power stations, added the beautifully delicate smear that 'some such project was dear to Lenin'. Baldwin, using just that reputation for non-partisanship that could be so deadly in a real street fight like this, told a meeting at Southend that 'it makes my blood boil to read of the way in which Monsieur Zinoviev is speaking of the Prime Minister of Great Britain today. At one time there went up a cry "Hands off Russia!" My word! I think it is time that someone said to Russia, "Hands off England!"'

In October 1924 the Conservatives finally reaped the electoral benefit of the 1918 Representation of the People Act and the fall of the Liberal Party, winning the biggest single-party victory of modern times. The Tory vote turned out in force and many Liberals clearly backed Conservative candidates too, so that the party won about half the total vote and 419 seats out of 615. Just as crucially for the future, the Liberal decline to a mere forty seats in the new House of Commons signalled their irreversible descent into minor party status, from which the electoral system would make it ever more difficult to mount a credible recovery. It was premature to write off the Liberals altogether, for the next election in 1929 would show that they retained the ability to wreck the Conservatives' chances and let Labour back into office, even if they no longer had the capacity to gain many seats themselves. On a medium-term view, though, 1924 showed clearly enough that the new polarity of Labour against Conservative was the wave of the future. Baldwin spoke of this as the way in which things had been shaping for some time, if coming to a much quicker fruition than he had expected: now Labour's moderates must eliminate the Communists from the political mainstream and the Tories absorb the Liberals, and 'we shall have two parties, the Party of the Right and the Party of the Left'. For this strategy to work, of course, Labour's moderates would need to continue to receive the tacit backing of such men as

Baldwin in their own inner-party battles, and the Conservatives would need to avoid provocative action which could re-radicalize the left.

Cabinet-making in 1924 allowed the rifts of the past to be visibly healed, with Austen Chamberlain's appointment to the Foreign Office and Churchill's return celebrated in his appointment as Chancellor of the Exchequer. Party loyalists and former coalitionists, tariff reformers and free traders, were now all back in the same team, and under a Prime Minister who showed considerable skills as a peacemaker in the early months in which these former antagonists were testing out each other's strengths and willpower. For the next five years Baldwin's government offered a stable administration with very few ministerial changes and a creditable legacy in the pursuit of peace in Europe and social reform at home (for which the Chamberlain brothers could together claim much of the credit).

Baldwin's personal agenda had a more mixed outcome, for in the field of industrial relations in which he mainly interested himself there was the 'Red Friday' climbdown from confrontation with the miners in 1925, the defeat of Britain's only general strike in 1926, and then, from 1927, both a revanchist Trades Disputes Act aimed at reducing trades union power and a new mood of cooperation in industry that dramatically reduced labour disputes both in regularity and in scale. Initially, Baldwin had to fight a series of battles with his own party to persuade it not to use the large majority acquired in 1924 for vindictive and partisan causes. He was convinced that this had been a 'national' win for the Conservatives, and that to fulfil the wishes of the voters they must act in accordance with national interests rather than the party's own. In 1941, when looking back on this period, Baldwin explained to a friend that 'I tried hard in those confused years immediately following the [First World] War to get a reorientation as it were of the Tory Party and in Disraeli's words to make it national, i.e. to give it a national rather than a party outlook.'

In 1925, therefore, Baldwin persuaded the Cabinet and Tory MPs to pull back from legislation to limit trades unions' political activities, although such legislation had been a Conservative priority ever since 1913; a few months later he backed down from a confrontation over the coal industry by renewing a government subsidy, so buying a further nine months in which a dispute between owners and workers could be resolved without a strike. This was deeply unpopular with Tory MPs and with the party in the constituencies, where fear of Labour was still a deeply held view. To an extent their scepticism was answered by the government's creation of effective emergency machinery to face the crisis if it should still come (and even

THE PRACTICAL VISIONARY.

Punch on Baldwin the peacemaker, 28 March 1925.

Baldwin later explained his avoidance of a fight in 1925 with the words, 'we were not ready') ⁓me Office enlisted thousands of middle-class volunteers in a⁓ for the Maintenance of Supplies, which helped to keep ⁓ the General Strike eventually took place, and in the meantime probably also mopped up the excess energies of many of the diehards. Baldwin could win the arguments of 1925 by courageously appealing to his supporters not to do what they believed was right, simply in order to avoid conflict (a strategy which echoed Peel's *Tamworth Manifesto*), but he also showed a much clearer perception of the moderate reality of British Labour than most of his colleagues: 'Many are now in the ranks of Labour who ought to be with us, for there are no more crusted Tories in England than many of those who sit not only on the back but on the front bench of the Labour [Party] today.'

However, when the immediate upshot was not the 'peace in industry' that he had called for but the General Strike of May 1926, the mother and father of all British industrial disputes until the miners' strike of 1984, Baldwin's peacemaking position was undermined and his policy wrecked. Neither the miners nor the mine-owners would fully accept the compromise deal offered by a government commission, and with the TUC backing the miners a great battle could no longer be avoided. The 'General Strike' (technically a lock-out of the miners, accompanied by a large-scale sympathetic action by other unions under TUC leadership) began on 3 May 1926 and lasted for nine days: 2.5 million men combined in a historic show of class solidarity, frightening the TUC almost as much as it frightened property-owners and contributing to their decision to call it off. The miners stayed out alone until starvation drove them back to work in the autumn.

Despite grumblings about him on the backbenches, Baldwin's will to win the dispute was absolute, and he used his communicative skills to great effect in radio broadcasts, which aimed to rally supporters around the country and to keep up their morale. Within the government itself he was successful in preventing hawkish ministers like Churchill and Birkenhead from making provocative shows of strength with the military, which might well have escalated the basically peaceful events of May 1926 into a dangerous spiral of violence. It may also be right to conclude that the moderation that he had personally shown in advance of the fight was an asset to the government in persuading moderate opinion in the country that the strike must be defeated unconditionally, as it duly was, and he was later frequently to point back to 1926 as another example of the instinctive English preference for moderation, even when the country had been on the brink of social disaster.

Baldwin thus gained much credit for the defeat of the General Strike. None the less, the fact that it had taken place despite his peacemaking efforts to head it off could not be seen as anything other than a setback for his policy. On the trades union and Labour side there was a rapid recognition that the strike had been a terrible mistake, entered into by unrevolutionary men who had neither thought through what they were doing nor prepared for a fight in order to win it (as the government certainly had done). As a result they scaled down their readiness for conflict in the years ahead, concentrated their movement's attention on parliamentary action rather than industrial disputes, and entered into more productive talks with the employers in the search for common ground and a less embattled future. None of that could save Baldwin, however, from the political setback that his policy had met with, and as a result his government carried in 1927 just the type of partisan anti-trades union act that he had persuaded it not to put forward in 1925. Just when Labour was resuming its drive for power by parliamentary means, and as Lloyd George was scenting the chances of a Liberal revival based on the mounting levels of unemployment, the Conservatives in effect abandoned the centre ground of 1924–5 and lurched both to the right and towards confrontation. Baldwin, his own moral and nervous energy sapped by the battering of 1926, seemed unable to fight more than a few delaying actions and to slow down his party's march in a direction of which he heartily disapproved.

The last two years of Baldwin's 1924 government were therefore a time of internal division and poor tactics. The right won the battle for trades union legislation and another Cabinet fight which ended by terminating diplomatic relations with Soviet Russia, but younger MPs from the left of the party defeated on Baldwin's behalf an attempt to restore the undemocratic powers of the House of Lords lost in 1911. All of these were proposals motivated by an exaggerated fear of British socialists as revolutionaries, a view from which Baldwin had largely failed to wean his party. Most crucially for the long-term future, but at a considerable cost in lost support from some Tory MPs, Baldwin succeeded in carrying forward a non-partisan policy over India in the teeth of right-wing attacks. Finally, in battles that cut across these left-against-right divisions as the economy sank into torpor and the end of the parliament approached, there were renewed disputes about tariffs and a gruelling Cabinet brawl between Churchill and Neville Chamberlain over a reform of local government structure and finance. Even the extension of voting rights to women between the ages of twenty-one and thirty, more or less promised by Baldwin in 1924, was bungled in the implementation and now seemed more like a grudging necessity than an act of generosity for which gratitude might be forthcoming from the new voters.

No new Zinoviev Letter appears in time to save the Conservatives' 1929 campaign, *Evening Standard*, May 1929

When seeking re-election in 1929, the party thus had no unifying theme except the 'Safety First' fear of Labour (which was not particularly frightening in any case since its move back to moderation following the General Strike). Baldwin's very real achievements in office had been tarnished by recent disputes; most crucially, the centrist position that he had seized with his 'national' appeal in 1924 was impossible to sustain in the light of his own government's recent policies, while his success in encouraging Labour back to the democratic path had removed much of the need to vote for him as a moderate. The outcome was much as might have been expected, and was in any case foreshadowed by Liberal gains in by-elections over the previous two years. With the electorate substantially increased again by the equalization of the franchise, the Liberal vote almost doubled (but there were still only fifty-nine Liberal MPs, so far had that party's credibility now sunk), while the Tory vote scarcely rose at all. Although the Conservatives outpolled Labour by a third of a million votes, Labour was easily the largest party in the Commons and MacDonald again became Prime Minister.

With hindsight, 1929 seemed a good election to lose, for the Wall Street Crash came only a few weeks after Labour returned to office and its international ramifications wrecked all attempts to restore the British economy and to hold down British unemployment levels until a very slow recovery finally began in 1933. With a longer perspective, too, it is possible to see that there was comfort even in the actual election figures, for in the unpromising circumstances of 1929 the Conservatives had retained the largest voting block and had hung onto enough seats to deny Labour a real taste of power, while non-socialist voters were unlikely to go on supporting Liberal candidates who did not win but whose very candidature let Labour take seats on a split vote. Baldwin's leadership would be more under attack now that he had lost the patronage powers of a premier and the opportunity to shape the political agenda that could be exercised only from Downing Street, but the underlying basis of his standing in the country had not been lost, and this would be available to the party in its campaigning and its policy choices for another eight years. What would have seemed truly unlikely in the summer of 1929 was that Baldwin, the arch anti-coalition man of British politics in the 1920s, would spend the rest of his governmental career in a National Government organized as an anti-socialist coalition, or that he would find it to be the ideal vehicle through which to practise his particular brand of Conservatism.

11

The Centre Holds, 1929-39

THE 1920s had confirmed the Conservatives' status as one of the two major parties, with all the advantages that that implied under Britain's voting system, and suggested that, for the time being at least, they were the stronger of the two. But the elections of 1923 and 1929 had also shown that there was enough residual loyalty to Liberalism to allow Lloyd George to accumulate a respectable vote – in 1923 it had still been almost 30 per cent of all votes cast – and so damage the Conservatives' prospects. By 1929 Liberal support, even in a good year, was down to less than a quarter of the national vote (despite their running an excellent, well-financed campaign, and fielding the largest number of Liberal candidates at any election between 1910 and 1974), but that still meant that there were more than 5 million Liberal votes to be bid for, as and when their party's decline was resumed. It is also clear that Liberalism's recoveries of ground in 1923 and 1929 had coincided with moments at which Labour had seemed relatively moderate and the Conservatives rather less so, as a result of their unconsidered raid on the electorate for a tariff mandate in 1923 and their lengthy catalogue of illiberal policies between 1926 and 1929. In order to reap the full benefit of Liberal decline, and to continue to deny Labour office with a majority in the Commons, the Conservatives would need to recreate the coalition at the polls that had succeeded so effectively in 1924, when (as Baldwin put it in a speech in 1925) 'the number of Liberals who voted for us at the last Election ran into six figures, and I should think we polled more labour [working-class] votes than the other side'. They would need, in short, to show that they were a party fitted to govern the nation as a whole and in the national interest rather than just to pursue in office their own partisan agenda.

The party's greatest asset in moving back to that centre ground was Baldwin himself, though by 1929 there was also a distinct wing of the party that cheerfully followed his lead and even urged him to go further; Robert Boothby, Duff Cooper, Anthony Eden, Harold Macmillan and 'Rab' Butler (the first four veterans of the 1924 parliament, the fifth elected for the first time in 1929) were just a few of those who saw in Baldwin a champion of the brand of caring Conservatism which both fitted in with their own moral predilections and gave those' like Macmillan, who sat for industrial constituencies, a reasonable chance of holding their seats. Macmillan and Duff Cooper were both among the moderate Tories who had been defeated in 1929 when so many northern and Midlands marginals had been lost, while the more reactionary members entrenched in their South of England strongholds had lost very few of their own numbers. The arithmetical balance within the parliamentary party was therefore more adverse to Baldwin in the 1929–31 parliament than before, at precisely the moment at which he had to draw his party back towards the centre, and during a period in which Labour's moderate performance in office would make it harder and harder to portray British socialism as a Bolshevik threat to civilized life and the ownership of property.

Baldwin had a further handicap, though, which irritated his admirers as well as his detractors: his inability to put on a convincing performance as a leader in opposition. He was temperamentally unsuited to the assumption of a veneer of righteous indignation when attacking MacDonald's Labour government, especially when it was actually doing things of which he approved – and these were frequently also things that he had himself done, or would like to have done, when in office over the previous five years. He remained on friendly terms with Labour MPs, employed his sharpest words for critics on his own side, and in general did little that would raise the spirits of his own supporters and give the Tory Opposition a comforting sense of momentum. Duff Cooper, remembering the eighteenth-century origins of such concepts as the 'whipping in' of the backbenchers, later wrote of these years that 'Mr Baldwin never showed game, and when he saw [his parliamentary] hounds hunting his first instinct was to call them off. His love of peace could easily be mistaken for indolence, and his desire to be fair to his political opponents could be represented as secret sympathy with their views.'

The battles with the party's right wing therefore carried over from office to the years of opposition, except that Baldwin was now deprived of many of his active, younger supporters, and of the discipline of patronage that had at least kept his ministers on a tightish leash before 1929. The personal nature of these attacks was brought out by the extent to which Conservative politicians mounted a personal drive to get rid of J. C. C. Davidson, an outstandingly successful party organizer who had been Baldwin's appointee as Party Chairman since 1926. There was no real doubt that the party organization itself was as well-financed as ever before, and as extensive in its range and professionalism as it was ever to be, so the attack on Baldwin's chief organizer could only be construed as a surrogate for attacks on Baldwin himself, not least because Davidson was a personal friend as well as a political confidant of the Leader. For several months Davidson endured such attacks, until eventually the conviction that his continuance in office was actually harming Baldwin (an impression that Baldwin's silence did nothing to refute) led to his resignation in May 1930. Davidson thus drew the fire on Baldwin's behalf for one of the two years in which the party was out of office, and by doing so he may indeed have saved Baldwin from dismissal, but in the second year the target was inescapably Baldwin himself. This was so not least because Neville Chamberlain was the new Party Chairman. Chamberlain was scrupulously loyal to Baldwin while in that post, but, as almost everyone's first choice to succeed the Leader, he gave the impression of being a leader in waiting, especially as he ran Central Office with visible authority and did many of the political jobs that a more aggressive leader than Baldwin would have done for himself.

A further sign of the depth of hostility to Baldwin from his party opponents can be seen in their readiness to conspire with the leaders of the Conservative press, and in particular with the maverick newspaper barons Lords Beaverbrook and Rothermere, in order to force their views on the party. There was nothing new in the involvement of Conservative politicians with the owners and editors of the daily press, for *The Times* in the 1880s and the *Observer* in the 1900s had each played active parts in the inner workings of the party, the *Morning Post* and the *National Review* had been at the heart of the diehard assault on Balfour, and Beaverbrook's own *Express* had been largely acquired with party funds in the first place; when Beaverbrook tried so actively to rock the boat in the early 1920s, the Party Chairman, Younger, reflected that 'when I think how much money [Central] Office has put into that gutter print it makes my blood boil'. What was new in 1930 was the scale of influence that press barons aspired to, now running empires of papers which reached into towns all across the land and with flagship titles with unprecedentedly large circulations: Beaverbrook's *Daily Express* and Rothermere's *Daily Mail* had a combined circulation of about 3.5 million copies daily; compared with a total sale of under half a million copies for *The Times* and the *Daily Telegraph*, which generally took a more helpful (to Baldwin) line. Even this last group did not ensure solid support in the quality press read by the party's higher command, for the *Morning Post* (then still much read by the official and service class) was as hostile to Baldwin as any paper on the political right. Moreover, the direct involvement which their proprietors took in the editorial policy of the mass-circulation papers ensured that no news that contradicted their proprietors' current views would ever appear – a huge influence on public opinion when there was still little radio or television news to offer alternative sources of information. As Baldwin himself put it in a 1931 speech, 'the papers conducted by Lord Rothermere and Lord Beaverbrook are not newspapers in the ordinary acceptance of the term. They are engines of propaganda for the constantly changing policies, desires, personal wishes, personal likes and dislikes of two men.' So in 1930 the *Mail* and the *Express* offered a particular interpretation of recent by-election results to suit their current campaigning line, and when Central Office issued briefings that gave a much more pro-Baldwin slant on the same events the news never appeared in most papers and was never therefore read by most party members.

It suited Baldwin and his defenders to treat Beaverbrook and Rothermere as if they were simply an inseparable pair of terrible twins, but while they were in part responding identically to the competitive demands of the newspaper market and shared a rabid, unthinking anti-socialism that led them to see Baldwin as unacceptably weak for a Tory leader, their differences were much more important – and their inability to stick together for long in any campaign eventually undermined their influence altogether.

Beaverbrook had been a Conservative MP and close friend of Bonar Law, he was to be an effective minister in Churchill's 1940 government (as he had already been under Lloyd George), and he was undeniably a serious political figure in his own right – even if his occasional dreams of the premiership owed more to fantasy than to realistic calculation. His political identity was still much related to his Canadian birth and to his continuing economic interests there, and his agenda in the debates of 1929–31 therefore revolved substantially around the question of empire trade (as it would continue to do right through to the *Express*'s implacable hostility to Britain's joining the European Economic Community in the early 1960s). This set of policy options had been in the Conservative mainstream ever since 1903 and appeals to the true faith of tariffs and

"WANTED, WITHIN NINE MONTHS respectable obedient 'Tin God' to take over job now held by Baldwin. Must be able to pick trouble and smash Trades Unions. Good publicity for right applicant. Suit of armour provided. Unique opportunity.— Welsh not barred. Apply PLOT PRESS"

"SITUATIONS VACANT."

Rothermere and Beaverbrook against Baldwin, *Star*, 11 August 1925.

imperial preference therefore struck a deep chord in many Tory hearts, with moderates as well as diehards.

Rothermere, on the other hand, was a more undiscriminating defender of extreme right-wing causes, an admirer of Mussolini and for a time the main press supporter of Sir Oswald Mosley in his British Fascist campaigns; his political views were generally regarded with contempt by all Tories except those bidding for personal support from his newspapers.

But, despite these differences, Beaverbrook and Rothermere had much in common, for both were birds of a very different feather from the journalists and editors with whom Balfour had dealt in 1910 or Lord Randolph Churchill in 1887, and it was a clear sign of their mutinous desperation that the anti-Baldwin right were prepared to fish in such murky waters for allies against their party's duly-appointed Leader.

Apart from the personal antagonism against Baldwin himself, accentuated no doubt by the extremely poor fist that he was making of the job of leading the party in opposition, the serious attacks homed in on two issues: tariff reform and India. The first of these was one on which the right did not differ much from the Leader on policy objectives; Baldwin had after all been a tariff reformer all his life, and his 1923 election gamble had been one of the most courageous – if also one of the most foolhardy – attempts to bring in tariffs in the thirty-year history of the debate. But Baldwin could see clearly enough that a tariff policy would both split the party and alienate the Liberal voters that he had to win back. The argument about India was a much more fundamental divide over principles, in which both sides more or less accepted the other's analysis of what was at stake. Over tariffs the issue was timing and tactics, and here Baldwin's favourite gambit of delay eventually paid off and allowed him both to keep his party together and not to put off potential Liberal support. Over India, the issue dragged on for seven years as an open wound in Conservatism, and poisoned relations at the top (for example, between Baldwin and Churchill, with the critical consequence of keeping Churchill out of office until war came in 1939). The debate did, though, produce in the end a liberal solution of the type that Baldwin had sought, and so did not result in the loss of the centre ground of political life; indeed, it made ever clearer Baldwin's success in keeping his party there. Tariff policy was a battle mainly over by the time that the National Government was formed in August 1931, but the Indian issue was not settled until 1935, by which time Baldwin had taken over direction of the National Government himself, and it almost certainly could not have been dealt with in this way unless the National Government had first been created.

The tariff debates were thus ones in which Baldwin steadily gave ground between 1929 and 1931, moving first to a position in which he promised a far more active use of retaliatory safeguarding to prevent dumping of cheap foreign goods on the British market, then to the repudiation of all previous pledges about referendums or second general elections before tariffs would be implemented, and finally, by early 1931, to the full policy of imperial preference, including even the food taxes that it had been so hard to get the electorate to accept in 1910 and in 1923. The pace in the debate was forced throughout by Baldwin's critics, but his crablike progress back to the full Chamberlainite programme ensured that the party did not lose touch with the trend of informed opinion outside. The deepening world recession meanwhile turned many traditional free traders into protectionists, so that by the time the party had completed its move in that direction, most of the Labour Cabinet had moved almost as far towards protectionism, a lifelong free trader like Churchill had reluctantly accepted that tariffs could not now be avoided, and even a section of the Liberal Party was beginning to cohere around Sir John Simon and preparing to ditch its most scared economic tenet.

The international financial blizzard that had blown unemployment up to unprecedented levels in Britain had discredited earlier orthodoxies (much as relative economic decline was to do for a later orthodoxy in the 1970s), and the Keynesian alternative was still rejected as theoretically unproven by the Treasury, by most politicians and businessmen, and indeed by most economists too. Tariffs thus became for many the only positive policy on offer at a time when it was obvious that some drastic action was required. Baldwin may have been unduly cautious in moving with this sudden shift in informed opinion, but it was probably better for his party to seem to be a step behind than a step ahead of the trend. As a result, Baldwin could envisage an election in 1931 in which a tariff policy would not be the incubus to both party unity and the pursuit of former Liberal voters that it had been as recently as 1929. As the country's finances slid into a desperate deficit, Baldwin told his followers that 'economy and tariffs' were the twin ingredients of the Conservative recipe for dealing with the crisis.

On India, on the other hand, Baldwin showed courage and conviction and refused to budge an inch, despite the very real distress that his policy caused to more traditionalist Tories – though there was of course nowhere else for these imperial-minded Tory voters to go, so it was unlikely that this division would produce any great electoral liability. In office before 1929 Baldwin's government had had to deal with the timetable for further reform of the Indian constitution set down in 1919, and was confronted with evidence of rising Indian support for both Gandhi and the Congress Party, each in their different ways showing a determination to bring British rule to a speedy end. Baldwin had no intention of seeking to hold down India by force once it was clear that there was no real consent. There would be no repeats of the Amritsar massacre of 1919 which had so discredited British rule among enlightened imperialists (though the

Morning Post had even then reacted by raising a subscription to reward General Dyer for his bloodily repressive actions) and he was equally determined that India should not become a political football between the British parties as Ireland had been since the 1880s, with terrible consequences for both countries. He therefore sent out as his Viceroy in 1925 Edward Wood (appointed Lord Irwin at that time and later the Earl of Halifax by inheritance of the title). Wood was from a landed Tory family and was a lay pillar of the Church of England, so he was not in principle unacceptable to the traditional Tories, but he was also a close friend of Baldwin and shared both his Leader's general political stance and his idealistic convictions about India.

Baldwin offered staunch support for Irwin's liberal policy in India, both as Prime Minister and then from 1929 as Leader of the Opposition, and he also sought to build a cross-party consensus in support of that policy at Westminster. A strong constitutional commission was set up under Sir John Simon, and since it was at work when the 1929 general election came about, Baldwin also intervened to ensure that Simon was not opposed by a Conservative in his Yorkshire constituency, deeming his Indian work to be of national importance. He duly supported the Simon Commission in its report, which recommended the setting up of responsible government in the Indian provinces as a first step towards internal self-government. He acquiesced in the necessity of releasing Gandhi from prison and beginning negotiations with him in the hope of generating Indian support for such a compromise policy, and he refused to criticize even Irwin's unilateral declaration that British policy was now aimed at the ultimate self-government of India. Neither Irwin nor Baldwin expected to see the British leave India altogether for decades ahead, but their readiness publicly to accept the ultimate loss of Britain's most prized overseas possession was a key moment in Conservative history; it would be another quarter-century before the lessons of Ireland and of India would begin to be applied to the rest of the colonial empire, but from this time on the clock was ticking. The party leadership also signalled this in more symbolic form by accepting the 1931 Statute of Westminster, which formally marked the transition from 'Empire', with all its connotations of power and prestige, based wholly on Britain, to 'Commonwealth', which implied a family of equals among which Britain would simply be the first.

The Tory right-wingers who had already called Baldwin a 'semi-socialist' when he sought to keep the peace with the trades unions in 1925 were outraged by all of this, and especially by his willingness to see the might and splendour of the British empire sitting down for open-ended discussions with a 'malevolent fanatic' (as Churchill described Gandhi). Since the Indian issue came to a head when MacDonald was already Prime Minister, they could do little to retard the policy, which was broadly supported by Labour and Liberals as well as by liberal Tories, but they anticipated an unforgiving fight in the lobbies when legislation was eventually needed to implement any Indian deal.

Baldwin's position was at its weakest in the winter of 1930-31, when the tariff issue had not been quite settled, and when the growing unease about India was added in. Churchill, for example, formally left the front bench — for nine years as it turned out — only late in 1930, but at once launched into an assault on Baldwin that employed his strongest language (which was of course saying a good deal). The real threat came when the press lords managed to link the two right-wing causes through a United Empire Party which would challenge Conservative candidates at the polls. In several by-elections this UEP, with the backing of both the *Mail* and the *Express*, humiliated official Tory candidates and unsettled many MPs with its threat to put up opponents next time against any sitting Tory who backed Baldwin and his policy.

Under this challenge to the party as an organization (which led, for example, to a falling-off of subscriptions), morale began to buckle and Baldwin's support to crumble. Front-benchers asked themselves whether morale would ever recover unless a new start was made, and Central Office reported that many members in the constituencies were equally doubtful about Baldwin's future value, the General Director of Central Office even advising in writing that Baldwin would have to resign before the party could be reunited. Eventually, early in 1931, Baldwin (privately reflecting that leading the Conservatives was roughly equivalent to 'driving pigs to market') almost made up his mind to resign, even though by then the battles on the tariff side of the debate were almost over, and it was only a series of accidents, and the recognition, even by front-benchers like the Chamberlains who now wanted a new leader, that they could not be *seen* to act at the dictation of the 'yellow press', that saved Baldwin's own bacon. Instead he came out fighting, found a platform for a contest with the press lords that he was almost bound to win, in a by-election at St George's, Westminster (as safe a seat as any in England), and was then rather misleadingly credited with seeing off a threat to British democracy. The sinister forces of unelected press proprietors, he now said, had aimed at 'power without responsibility, the prerogative of the harlot through the ages'. The opportunity was accidental, the victory largely bogus, and even the famous phrase was not Baldwin's own but coined for him by his cousin Rudyard Kipling, but the outcome was none the less of seminal importance. The St George's by-election of March 1931 confirmed Baldwin's moderate leadership of the Conservative Party at its most vulnerable moment, and just before it turned out to be vital that the party retain a moderate regime in order to profit from the opportunity given by the August 1931 financial crisis.

Over the last few months of the Labour government of 1929–31 Baldwin stirred himself to a more vigorous denunciation of Labour, which produced some pained responses from MacDonald, so unexpected was it. This may in part have been due to Baldwin's awareness of how narrow had been his survival (and therefore the survival of those policies he most cared about), but it clearly also had something to do with the perception, which Baldwin shared with the rest of his party, that Labour's tenure of office was drawing to a close and that an election would come soon, for which the party must be united and active. Conservatives believed that Labour in any case thoroughly deserved to come under spirited attack for its ineffective handling of the economy. From his fastness in the CRD, to which he had retreated from Central Office when Baldwin was confirmed in the leadership, Neville Chamberlain prepared for debates in which Labour was impaled on a series of ever more difficult hooks of financial policy. Chamberlain was also developing closer relations with the Simon Liberals, even promoting an electoral pact that would produce a parliamentary majority for tariffs, whichever party won the coming election, and he was warily awaiting the moment to strike MacDonald down.

The crisis, when it eventually came in August, took almost all the participants by surprise, and Baldwin was rarely even in the country during the critical weeks, leaving the conduct of the party's strategy and tactics entirely to Chamberlain. The outcome – a National Government in which the Conservatives agreed to serve under Ramsay MacDonald as Prime Minister – was also a situation that they had neither worked for nor foreseen (they had after all expected the collapse of the Labour government to result in a general election which they would win). The depth and rapidity of the financial crisis in August (which scared many rentier Tories to the core and led them to abandon all their preconceptions), the opportunity both to get Labour ministers to take responsibility for sweeping cuts in public expenditure and also to damage Labour almost terminally by the split that this would create, and the call to the nation's service put to Baldwin in the end by the king and the Liberals – these were the factors that together swept all before them. Baldwin therefore agreed, without consulting even the shadow cabinet, much less Tory MPs in general, to join an emergency National Government under MacDonald, with the objective of taking crisis measures to save sterling and rescue the economy from chaos. No Conservative of any significance opposed the decision, and most applauded it warmly. The Conservatives had certainly lost the chance to win a party majority at an early election, which would have ensured a Conservative government under Baldwin for years ahead, and it seemed to have got in return only a minority share of office – four seats out of ten in the August 1931 emergency Cabinet – but it had also achieved a tactical opportunity both for the party and for its Leader of the sort that comes but once in a lifetime. And even at the moment of the National Government's all-party formation, Baldwin assured his followers that their party remained free to campaign for tariffs as the real solution to the country's economic problems.

Within weeks the National Government's claim to all-party status had been removed by the declaration of opposition to its existence and its policies by the overwhelming majority of Labour MPs and by the Labour Party as an organization, a parting of the ways made irreversible by the expulsion of MacDonald and his Labour ministerial colleagues even from membership of the party they had helped to create. This in turn meant that the government had only a small and uncertain Commons majority, an unsteady foundation on which to build a programme of national economic recovery; it also turned MacDonald into a hostage in his own government and into a man thirsting for revenge on his recent colleagues. The case for an early election therefore became overwhelming and Liberal ministers' resistance was fairly easily brushed aside.

In November 1931, as in 1918, the parties with whom the Conservatives were allied had no real mechanism for the mobilization of a national majority. MacDonald's 'National Labour' Party did not exist at all in the constituencies (having only twenty potential candidates, all of whom would depend on the votes of their former enemies if they were to survive), and the Liberals had fallen away badly since 1929, so that they too now failed even to contest more than a quarter of the constituencies. If the National Government were to win the election it would have to be by Tory efforts at the hustings, and this obvious fact gave the party's strategists a great deal of leverage; it was easy enough to allow MacDonald and his friends a free ride back to the Commons, for most of them sat for seats that Tories could not win anyway, and at least *some* price would have to be paid for having them denounce the Labour Party up and down the land to the general benefit of Conservative candidates. But, on Chamberlain's advice, the party was much more discriminating when it came to dealing with the Liberals: few Tory candidates were put up against Simonite Liberals who would support tariffs, but Tories stood against other Liberals wherever there seemed a chance of winning the seat. The result was that of forty-one Simonite Liberal candidates, thirty-five were elected (many of them on Tory votes for which they would need to show their gratitude), while only thirty-seven other Liberals were elected out of 119 candidates. Conservative electoral tactics therefore drove a further wedge into a Liberal Party already perilously close to another deep split, and largely determined which 'Liberals' were in the new parliament.

Overall, with the Tory and Liberal votes united behind a mainly Conservative slate of candidates, and with MacDonald (as well as general revulsion at Labour's desertion of office in August) adding some former Labour voters too, there was a massive government victory. Even if Liberals other than Simonites are excluded (they still in fact supported the government but would soon leave), the government won over 60 per cent of the national vote and 521 of the 615 seats; 473 of these winners were Conservative, the biggest number won by any party in any British election, and there were such unusual local patterns as seven Tory wins out of seven in Sheffield and an equivalent clean sweep in Manchester. In the post-election reshuffle that set up a National Government of a more normal size and character, the Conservatives took a majority of the places, and when the free trade Liberals left the government in 1932 they were replaced either by more Conservatives or by Simonite National Liberals.

In return for this landslide victory, the Conservatives had made no policy concessions whatsoever; the government parties agreed to fight the election asking for a 'doctor's mandate' to do whatever was necessary for economic recovery, and each partner therefore continued to promote its own platform of policies. Tariffs and the need for economy therefore figured prominently in the Conservative campaign, as Baldwin had said that they would six months earlier, and, even without the added support of the Simonites, the election therefore produced a huge majority for tariffs as well as for Conservatism more generally. Within a few weeks the government had introduced an emergency tariff and, after a lengthy Imperial Economic Conference at Ottawa in the summer of 1932, a full programme of tariffs with imperial preference was carried into statute, with Neville Chamberlain as Chancellor proudly proclaiming the fulfilment of his father's dream. This process inevitably led to the final departure of the independent Liberal ministers from the government, though it was not until a year later that they took the logical step of moving to the opposition side in the Commons as well. That parliamentary situation facilitated the gradual convergence of Simonites and Conservatives, in which the habit of working together throughout the 1930s did gradually produce a sense of being on the same side (as it never had quite done for Conservatives and Liberals under Lloyd George). The Simonites maintained a separate organization both nationally and in their constituencies until 1947 (as indeed they had to if they were to continue to pull in Liberal votes for Tory candidates as well as for themselves), and there were sometimes prickly inter-party discussions, but for most Simonites there was no avenue of retreat back to Liberalism after 1932 and therefore a steady drift into the Tory embrace.

This process could only take place because the National Government was not simply a Tory government in disguise, despite the overwhelming Conservative majority in both Houses which could have instituted a pure Conservative government at any time. In its inner workings the government worked as a team, almost irrespective of which party particular ministers belonged to, and MacDonald was no figurehead as Prime Minister, except perhaps after about 1934, when age and increasing querulousness took its toll. When Conservatives suggested removing MacDonald before he was good and ready to retire, Baldwin firmly made it known that the supplanting of MacDonald would lead to his own resignation at the same time. Until he accepted the premiership again at MacDonald's own insistence in June 1935, Baldwin was even urging MacDonald to stay on; his broadcasts regularly paid 'all honour' to 'the Prime Minister, the pilot who did not desert the ship' in 1931, and there is no reason to doubt the sincerity of his view. In part this reflected the fact that, as Baldwin's friend the Cabinet Deputy Secretary Tom Jones nicely put it, 'this being second and not first suits him perfectly'. He did not have the ultimate responsibility, with all the strain that was entailed in the loneliness of command; nor did he have to concern himself with the details of every policy area and could concentrate instead on what he did best: communicating on the government's behalf with the nation, managing the day-to-day business at Westminster, jollying along MPs, and being constantly in the lobbies, the smoking rooms and the Commons chamber.

Baldwin was no doubt reassured in this managerial role by the fact that the sheer size of the victory of 1931 ensured that his party now held all the marginal constituencies (and quite a few that would be regarded as safe for Labour in normal times too), and these were often occupied by members who were extremely well aware of their vulnerability next time round. The balance of the much-enlarged parliamentary party had shifted back towards moderate centrism in 1931, just as it had shifted the other way in 1929, and although about eighty seats were lost at the next election in 1935, this still left over 400 MPs, mostly sitting for the same seats that had produced a similar majority and a similarly moderate parliamentary party in 1924. Harold Macmillan, whose support Baldwin had lacked in the parliament of 1929–31, was not only safely back in the House after 1931, but was again sitting for Stockton-on-Tees and very conscious of the sort of policies that were needed to ensure both the welfare of his constituents and the prospering of his own career as its Member. Duff Cooper had not returned to Oldham, but had, by winning Westminster St George's on Baldwin's behalf in March 1931, become even more closely associated with the fortunes of his Leader.

As well as benefiting from this mood on the backbenches, Baldwin could assure his party that it was necessary to pursue a centrist political stance in order to keep National Labour and Simon's National Liberals content. In this sense, what emerged in and after 1931 on the broad front of domestic policy was a cross-party consensus much like that which had steered Indian policy before the National Government had been created. This was exactly the 'national' and non-partisan (though overtly non-Labour if not actively anti-Labour) stance that Baldwin had sought to achieve in 1924–5 from the Conservative position alone, and which had crashed to ruins in the aftermath of the General Strike. Afterwards Baldwin constantly referred back to 1931 as demonstrating that responsible people of all parties had united to put country before party, and that it had been 'the acid test of democracy' – a test that British democracy had triumphantly passed just when democracies across the rest of Europe had been falling from grace. The party now broadly accepted this 'national' prescription, partly because the National Government did indeed seem to provide a steady bulwark against both the economic threat that had surfaced so frighteningly in 1931 and the anti-democratic extremisms of Fascism and Communism.

It was in any case hard to reject a Leader and a strategy that had been so resoundingly successful at the polls and which had even in 1935 won for the party the second biggest election victory ever: 54 per cent of the national vote and 432 MPs in a House of 615. For Conservatives whose first priority lay in keeping the parties of the left away from the levers of power – and such people existed in that as in every other generation – that overriding sense of the party's electoral security in a dangerous decade was in itself a powerful vindication of Baldwin, while others who had in 1931 worried about the safety of their savings and their investments could draw similar comfort from the solidity of the National Government's vote and the orthodoxy of its policies.

The opportunity that this opened up can be seen in the carrying – if only after a long struggle – of the Government of India Act of 1935. Baldwin quite deliberately played the issue long, demonstrating through laborious sittings of a Joint Select Committee of both Houses that all alternative policies had been fully investigated before introducing an actual bill (though he had also ensured in advance, through its composition, that the Select Committee would come up with an acceptable recommendation). On one occasion overly clever management of the proceedings threatened to disrupt progress, when Churchill discovered that evidence from Lancashire was being pre-cooked with the Secretary of State, Sir Samuel Hoare, before actually going to the committee, but his violent denunciations of Hoare mainly had the effect (as did most of his speeches at that time) of antagonizing moderate opinion and reawakening on the Tory benches the distrust of Churchill himself that had been dormant since his return in 1924. Most Conservative backbenchers saw Churchill's crusade over India as a form of revenge for his exclusion from the 1931 government and for Baldwin's pointed reminders that the world had moved on somewhat since the Second Jubilee of Queen Victoria in 1897 (when Churchill had last seen India for himself and formed the views that lasted him a lifetime), especially when Baldwin and Hoare had fun at his expense by quoting back at him liberal speeches on India that he had himself made when serving under Lloyd George. When Churchill declared in a mood of high principle that his watchword would be 'fiat justitia, ruat coelum' ('let right prevail, though the heavens fall'), Leo Amery mischievously offered an alternative, vernacular translation: 'if I can trip up Sam [Hoare], the government's bust'.

Recognizing their numerical weakness in parliament – even in the Lords – the diehard Conservatives, organized in the Indian Empire Society, took the fight to the party outside, where there was rather more dissent, especially in southern English rural constituency parties which often had ex-

Nazi Movement—Local Version

The impact of Churchill's Indian campaigning on his reputation, *Daily Herald*, 30 March 1933.

officers and retired colonial civil servants among their elected association officers. Time and again the National Union Executive sided with Baldwin against the diehards; this was different from its attitude during the previous coalition in 1918–22, mainly because the rules had changed: until 1930 the Executive had been elected by the Annual Conference and so tended to include a disproportionate number of hard-liners with national reputations created by a record of fiery speechmaking, but after 1930 it was based on indirect election through the area federations, and as a result it now contained far more local worthies with an eye to the electability of their own local candidates in a coming election, and a generally more loyal and unity-based attitude to the party. This development matched to a large extent the way in which the 1922 Committee had also changed: it began as a small dining club of new members in 1922 and moved on to be a ginger group of active backbenchers, but in the early 1930s it became a body that included all Tory MPs who were not ministers, with a whip attending each meeting to keep it in touch with the party leaders, and with ministers occasionally in attendance to explain policy issues and answer questions. Thus it was less a focus for discontent, as most backbench committees had been in the past, than a platform on which the majority could advertise their loyalty and conformism.

Nevertheless, the diehards had plenty of backing among the rank and file. An impromptu debate on India at the Party Conference at Bristol in October 1934 produced a near tie between pro-government and antigovernment forces, with scenes of considerable disorder greeting the news that the government's policy had been endorsed by just twenty-three votes. The leadership had been caught unprepared by the breadth of discontent voiced at Bristol, but both sides now prepared carefully for a special Central Council meeting in December. The government was defended in debate by four ex-Cabinet ministers, including Leo Amery, who could hardly be called either an anti-imperialist or a semi-socialist, and by a carefully balanced cross section of National Union area dignitaries, while the diehards also had three former Cabinet ministers. Since the debate boiled down very rapidly to a call for party unity and loyalty to Baldwin on one side, against a plea not to abandon the empire on the other, and produced a vote of about three to one in Baldwin's favour, it may be said that the Central Council decided to put party before empire. After this, although the parliamentary processes were a long story of hard pounding, there was no doubt of the outcome, and Baldwin was able to use the parliamentary debates as a means of raising the argument back onto the moral level at which it had begun, after several years of low politicking in between. Shortly afterwards, in June 1935, Baldwin replaced the now-ailing MacDonald at the head of the government and thus became Prime Minister for the third time – leading what was by now a mainly Conservative 'National' Government.

The comfortable re-election of the National Government in November 1935, almost as soon as the India debates ended, was testament to the value of restoring party unity and morale. But the government's success in 1935 also owed something to the continuing disarray of the Labour Opposition, which, as in the 1980s, took a considerable time to recover from the loss of office, and also to the government's actual policy outputs. The domestic programme of the government was held together by Neville Chamberlain, whose tenure of the Exchequer from 1931 to 1937 provided an object-lesson in the use of the Treasury to dominate all areas of departmental policy. When the Tory ministers met ahead of the 1935 election to plan their party's electioneering and their contributions to the National Government's manifesto, the meeting took place at the CRD with Chamberlain effectively in the chair, and with his CRD's policy briefs shaping most of the discussions. As he himself had noted privately when taking on the CRD chairmanship in 1930, 'I shall have my finger on the springs of policy.' At the heart of domestic policy – not only because it suited Chamberlain's personal views, but also because the way in which the government had come into existence in 1931 more or less demanded it – was an unshakeable orthodoxy in the management of finance. Budgets were resolutely balanced, and only when both the economy and the public finances showed, in about 1934, clear signs of recovery from the catastrophe of 1931, were earlier cuts in expenditure cautiously reinstated. This contributed to the relative harshness of the way in which unemployment assistance was administered, with the hated means test at the centre of a menu of demeaning and intrusive measures that were deeply resented in working-class circles (and for which the party would pay heavily at a later date).

However, a Chamberlain-driven government would never be content simply to administer the systems of relief and await an economic upturn, for, as he once confessed in a family letter, 'I cannot contemplate a problem without trying to find a solution.' The National Government, therefore, like the Baldwin government of 1924–9, had a respectable record of modest social reforms, often incremental advances on previous initiatives and codifying measures but of value none the less, and testament to the generous spirit that was not often enough associated with Neville Chamberlain in the image of him that was abroad after 1940. Among other measures, the National Government set up the London Passenger Transport Board, improved safety measures in road and rail transport, provided for free milk in schools, tightened factory legislation, ran the first national slum clearance campaigns (replacing about a third of a million dwellings in 1938), introduced holidays with pay for some 10 million British workers, and authorized small advances in pensions. These policies provided MPs with a solid diet of policy achievements to take even to their working-class electors when seeking a renewal of their support.

Perhaps more important than legislation, though, was the positive side of the British economy in the 1930s, owing at least something to the recovery of business confidence after 1931–2 (which itself depended on financial orthodoxy at the Exchequer) and to the low interest rates that then applied throughout the decade: bank rate was at a steady 2 per cent from 1932 to 1939 and was therefore lower than at any time since the beginning of the century - or at any time since 1950. Real wages for those in work rose steadily – and those in work always exceeded those out of work by a huge margin even in the depth of the depression, especially in the Midlands and the South. The many who in the 1950s and 1960s argued that no government could ever win an election in a time of mass unemployment had completely forgotten what actually happened in the 1930s (and they could not of course foresee what would happen in the 1980s either).

The widespread increase in disposable income led to spectacular increases in the purchase of such luxury goods as cars, telephones and radio sets. Above all, the cheapness both of land and of money provided the perfect conditions in which a housing boom could take place: one and three-quarter million new houses were built in the five years before war came in 1939, most of them for purchase, so that home-ownership became a realistic aspiration for a steadily widening middle class; whereas only a tenth of families had owned their own homes in 1919, almost a quarter did so by 1939. The benefits of such policies had some effect on the whole country, but were undeniably more likely to be enjoyed in the South and the English Midlands than in the North, Scotland or Wales; there was in effect a boom economy in such places as Oxford, Coventry and the London suburbs, alongside the dispiriting persistence of unemployment and depression on Tyneside and on Clydeside. From the viewpoint of the National Government, the accidental correlation between the prosperous areas and the regions that elected most of its Tory supporters was an important component of its political strength. It may well be the case too that the prosperity of the South blunted the edge of those campaigns against the government on India and on Appeasement which also looked for their main support to those prosperous regions.

It should not be assumed, though, that the National Government had an easy passage through the 1930s, effortlessly sustained by the support of a grateful people, for such was far from the case. In 1933–4, with the persistence of high unemployment and the suddenly widespread fear of a future war when Hitler came to power and the last chance of international disarmament collapsed, the government could scarcely hold a seat at a by-election, and all of Baldwin's cheerleading talents were required to keep the lid on the ferment that this caused at Westminster.

An insensitive administrative amendment to the public assistance schemes in 1934 caused uproar and a new upsurge of violence, partially orchestrated by the Communist Party but also attracting a mass of unorchestrated working-class support in the depressed areas. In the mid-1930s there were the activities of Mosley's British Union of Fascists to add to the trouble on the left, engendering a new worry through their indoor violence practised at Olympia in 1934 and their outdoor violence on display in the East End of London. This climaxed in the anti-Fascist demonstrations which produced the Battle of Cable Street in London in 1936, though in this case rapid action by the government (easier to take precisely because it *was* a National Government with strong democratic credentials) soon restored order to the streets.

Also in 1936 came the abdication of Edward VIII, skilfully handled by Baldwin in a way that avoided public discussion of the issue until it was almost settled, again a strategy that would simply not have worked unless the king himself, Dominion leaders, and the British Labour Opposition had all had a rooted belief in his good faith. That crisis also provided another example of Churchill's lack of judgement and of his limited backing among Conservatives in parliament, for it was the only occasion in his long career on which he could not even persuade the Commons to listen to him. There were far more Conservatives who were in the end glad to see the troublesome young king go, and thus take with him both his unconventional ideas and his political unpredictability, than would rally behind Churchill's romantically Cavalier view of the modern monarchy.

Finally, as the decade drew to a close, there was the diplomatic and military prelude to the Second World War, far more divisive in Conservative circles than anything before 1914, which occasioned some of the toughest whipping, the earliest spin-doctoring, and the most determined attempts to discipline MPs through their constituency parties, that is yielded by a study of the history of the Conservative Party. Even Churchill himself had to fight off determined attempts to have him de-selected by his constituency party in Epping, just a few months before war broke out and he rejoined the government.

Nevertheless, despite all this sound and fury, the fundamental basis of the National Government remained strong throughout the peacetime

1930s. In 1935, despite its acute unpopularity only months earlier, the government won a huge victory at the general election. It seems clear that while there were considerable protests against its policies, it was in no real danger of being replaced by Labour at any time between 1931 and 1939, and, with the further decline of the outside Liberals, Labour was now the only alternative on offer. With Baldwin as Prime Minister from 1935, it was headed by the most popular politician of the age, while, under Neville Chamberlain after 1937, it acquired a leader who gave it more drive and direction after the relatively flaccid period of Baldwin's final years. Although further seats were lost in by-elections after 1935, they were not lost on swings of a size that threatened to remove the government's overall majority. As the next general election (due in 1939–40) drew near, neither Labour nor Conservative politicians expected that it would produce a change of government.

Nor was the National Government one that had run out of steam as it approached its third term, for Chamberlain's tenure as Party Leader and Prime Minister had given it renewed momentum. In the party, the last years of peace saw enquiries into the state of the organization in London and among younger voters, producing proposals that were not implemented only because the Second World War came first (but which in the second case prefigured the type of structure which emerged as the Young Conservatives after 1945). The party was also being urged to push ahead with a reform of candidates' financial relations with their constituency associations, in this case a reform generally attributed to 1949.

On the policy front, the CRD was hard at work on a manifesto for a peacetime election, and the surviving correspondence suggests that this might have included the introduction of family allowances and the extension of health cover to the dependants of those in the National Insurance scheme. A more general extension of pensions was considered but turned down on grounds of cost, but that proposal might well have resurfaced in 1940 if war had been averted and the defence costs of rearmament had been scaled down. These were not huge or bold initiatives, but they did include quite a bit of the agenda picked up and made his own by William Beveridge in 1942 and then returned to the Conservatives on the rebound. Had it been able to fight a peacetime election on such a programme in 1939–40, the party had an excellent chance of hanging on to that middle opinion which its 'national' stance had entitled it to claim in 1924, 1931 and 1935. So far at least, the centre was holding very well.

12

War and Aftermath, 1939–47

THE ENTRENCHED party position in British national life that Baldwin and Neville Chamberlain had built up in the 1920s and 1930s collapsed rapidly and well-nigh completely under the strains of the war that broke out in 1939. The cohesive group of front-benchers which had sustained them in office were scattered to the four winds in the upheaval that both produced and was worsened by Chamberlain's fall. The reputations of those leaders themselves were retrospectively annihilated in the search for scapegoats for British unpreparedness in 1940, while the new leaders of their party stood by watching – if not indeed cheering on the critics. Moreover, all the comfortable certainties of the inter-war years on the domestic front – a political agenda defining what was and what was not practical politics that had largely been set out and limited by the Tory leaders themselves – vanished in the midst of the Blitz, evacuation, military defeats, wartime economics and the planning of the huge task of post-war reconstruction. Since the party was so closely associated in the public mind with a political world viewed by 1945 as irredeemably finished and done with, the task of making the Conservatives seem relevant and supportable would have been a formidable one, even if approached with vigour, flexibility and determination by a united party. But the Tory hierarchy of 1940 to 1945 did not approach it in that frame of mind, focusing its collective effort instead almost exclusively on the temporary phenomenon of the war, which would never be the electorate's main interest once the fighting came to an end.

The Conservative Party as a whole did not therefore engage effectively during wartime with the issues that most concerned the people whose support it needed to retain. It lost as a result the opportunity to influence the way in which the debate about post-war Britain was taking place, and it paid a heavy price for this neglect in the 1945 general election. This was a mistake that it had not made in 1914-18, when the party had entered into the war in an assertive frame of mind and never lost sight of its own future interests, even while giving support to wartime Liberal prime ministers and making real sacrifices for the national war effort. Indeed, that collective involvement with the Great War had been one of the well-springs from which Baldwin's 'national' rhetoric and his personal sense of vocation sprang, and the war experiences of Captains Eden and Macmillan helped to motivate their own political careers in the next generation too, engendering a caring paternalism that derived directly from their experience of life in the trenches of the Great War. In 1939-45, though, Churchill's fixation with the war meant that the party neglected the domestic political situation and its leadership showed but limited interest in the future, suggesting (when the issue was confronted at all, which was but rarely) that there would somehow be a lengthy political pause between war and peace during which politicians would then turn about and engage with the future.

Conservatives once again had an excellent war record in 1939-45, but this was on the war fronts alone, while after about 1942 it was a good record on the home front that would really have paid dividends for the future. The party was no doubt cheered up in 1945 when the Party Chairman asserted that it had lost power only because 'we went to the war' – a statement that was both literally and metaphorically true – but this still provided no guidance as to what Conservatives should do next, in the aftermath of an election defeat almost as large as the victory of 1918. After 1945 Conservatives would have to try to rebuild the political coalition of middle opinion that had sustained the National Government in the 1930s, and they would have to earn again the trust of middle-ground voters. Moreover, because conventional wisdom asserted in the later 1940s that the Second World War had been a watershed beyond which the past had become a foreign country in which the essence of things had been done differently, they would have to rebuild their past approach while proclaiming at the same time that all was new. And, to make the task even harder, they would have to perform the trick while continuing to be led by Winston Churchill, the Conservative who had contributed most to the catastrophe of 1945, who had no wish whatsoever to restore the reputations or the strategies of his predecessors, and whose own political mentality derived more from the 1910s than even from the 1930s. That this formidable target was squarely hit, with the Conservatives catching up with Labour by 1950 and then overtaking it in the 1950s, says a great deal about the deeper strengths of British Conservatism, about the ability of younger members to force the pace of reform even when the Leader was uninterested or downright hostile, and about the party's most fundamental characteristic – its tendency to subordinate all other considerations to the drive for power.

The new fault-lines that wrecked the party in wartime had been visible long before Britain and Germany went to war in 1939. Some traditional Conservatives from military and service families had, like Winston Churchill and Viscount Cranborne (the later Lord Salisbury), been in the forefront of the opposition to the Appeasement of Nazi Germany. Both Anthony Eden and Duff Cooper (each rather more typical of Baldwinian 'New Conservatism') had resigned from Chamberlain's government over foreign policy, and Harold Macmillan on the back benches had been one of Chamberlain's sternest critics. In the youngest party generation, Edward Heath, who would thirty years later come to epitomize moderate, middle-class Toryism, began his political career in 1938 working with such as Macmillan against the official Conservative candidate, Quintin Hogg, in a by-election in Oxford that turned on Appeasement and produced the extraordinary slogan, 'A vote for Hogg is a vote for Hitler'.

What was absolutely clear from 1933 to 1939 was that foreign affairs must occupy a central position in British political life as they have rarely done, to the considerable disadvantage of Baldwin and Chamberlain, each of whom had a much better feel for the domestic side of things. From the early 1930s onwards there were nagging worries about Japanese expansion in the Far East, threatening Hong Kong, Singapore and other imperial possessions in the region as well as requiring additional naval expenditure. From 1936 to 1939 the Spanish Civil War deeply divided British opinion, and the government's policy of keeping clear of both sides came under heavy criticism because it effectively facilitated General Franco's Fascist overthrow of an elected government. In 1936, too, Mussolini's Italian invasion of Abyssinia (and in 1939 of Albania too) placed the British government under pressure as a result of its hesitant leadership of democratic opinion against the aggressor.

However, these relatively distant events provided mainly a backdrop to the far greater threats posed by Nazi Germany once Hitler seized power in 1933. In 1936 Britain and France reacted feebly to Germany's militarization of its western border (forbidden by the 1919 peace treaty but essential if Hitler was to embark on adventures further east), and this was followed by the absorption of Austria into the Third Reich in 1938 and by attempts to absorb the German-speaking Sudetenland border areas of Czechoslovakia later in that year, facilitated by Chamberlain in his efforts to 'appease' at the Munich Conference. But while these crises of 1936 and 1938 could just about be seen as being about Germans exercising self-determination, the dismemberment of Czechoslovakia (even before the Nazis took over the rest of the country in March 1939), and the subsequent threats to Poland which did eventually start the war in September 1939, were quite inescapably a threat to the balance of European power by Britain's enemy of only twenty years earlier. Even though, as Chamberlain poignantly remarked at Munich to his PPS, the future Prime Minister Alec Douglas-Home, it was no part of a prime minister's duty to involve the country in a war that it could not win, it increasingly became a question of when Britain would confront Nazi Germany rather than if she would do so.

The 1930s arguments over defence and foreign policy therefore opened up entirely new divisions in the party that cut across the traditional lines of left and right, traditionalists and moderns, Baldwinian 'scuttlers' and imperialists. In the short term this assisted Chamberlain in retaining the support of his party for Appeasement, since his foreign policy critics were united on nothing else. The most vocal critic of all, Winston Churchill, was not trusted even by most Tories who did share his views on armaments and diplomacy, so that when Eden and Duff Cooper left the government in 1938, each was careful not to associate himself too closely with Churchill, lest it damage his own credibility. But this fragmentation greatly reduced their leverage, and even into the spring of 1939 the Conservative Party's loyalty to Chamberlain remained overwhelming, a fact that is less surprising when it is borne in mind that this was likely to be an election year and one in which the only alternative, a Labour government, would be at least as uncertain as Chamberlain on rearmament; even at that late stage Labour was still voting against compulsory military service. And even if the Labour Party was more ideologically opposed to Hitler than the Tories, and gradually coming round to the need for armaments, it had its own blind spot in its inability to see Stalin for what he was, a failing which made its cooperation with Conservative critics of Chamberlain even more problematic.

Nevertheless, whereas Baldwin's leadership on these dangerous issues had been characteristically indirect and instinctive, moving only alongside the glacial shifts of public opinion much as Franklin Roosevelt was doing in the United States, Chamberlain saw rather the need to use his position of leadership to drag his party and country out of the path of a major war. To adapt a later footballing analogy much used by Harold Wilson when Prime Minister, where Baldwin had seen his role as that of a deep-lying sweeper, Chamberlain wanted to be at the same time the manager, the midfield playmaker *and* the striker for his own government team – and he had an unhealthy tendency to involve himself in writing the match reports through his press secretary too. He therefore forced the pace in his efforts to secure a peaceful understanding with Hitler, he took great risks with his own reputation by involving himself so personally in the last phases of Appeasement, and he continually talked up the chances of peace in his speeches (even when he knew that the odds were not good) as a personal contribution to the trust and harmony that he was desperately trying to achieve; the silencing of his party critics was thus in itself a part of his foreign policy. Nor did he underestimate the risks involved in that process, for he privately wrote just after the Munich crisis that if all of this eventually went wrong then Churchill would win the later debates with his argument that war with Hitler had been inevitable all along and should therefore have been confronted earlier.

Downing Street had received persistent warnings from the military top brass that Britain would lose a war with Germany, at least until late 1938, and even after that date there was equally downbeat advice from the Treasury, which said that the country could neither win a short war nor afford a long one; Chamberlain therefore could not deal in the easy certainties that were available to anyone out of office. In terms of Britain's real interests, his struggle was to keep her out of a war which would probably – and in the event did – wreck her economy, her imperial position and her world role, so there was far more to be said for Chamberlain's foreign policy than was appreciated until long after the event; but, in terms of his own position and that of the party he led, he was taking another huge gamble. In the immediate aftermath of the Munich crisis of 1938, when there still seemed at least an outside chance that his gamble would succeed and he therefore proclaimed 'peace for our time' with more assurance than he probably felt, the wave of public relief occasioned by the escape from war enabled him to consolidate his position and to make life in their constituencies extremely difficult for critics like Churchill. But by upping the stakes he had also made his future entirely dependent on the outcome of events that he could neither clearly foresee nor determine, and on the whims of a man whom even he himself had privately described as 'a mad dictator'.

When in 1939, then, first with Hitler's final destruction of Czechoslovakia in March and then in the Polish crisis that brought Britain into the war in September, all that Chamberlain had been trying to do could only be seen as having crashed into ruins; when, as he himself said on the outbreak of war, 'my long struggle for peace has failed', the basis of his hold over public opinion began fatally to erode. He was soon claiming that delaying the start of the Second World War through the Munich settlement would turn out to be Britain's best hope of victory; the two-year interval before 1940's battle of survival had been a vital one, enabling the country to catch up in the armaments race. As he told the National Union in June 1940:

> After the Munich agreement, the Labour Party were relieved that we had escaped war. Now they want to know why we did not call Hitler's bluff. If we get through this war successfully, then it will be to Munich that we shall owe it. In the condition our armaments were in at that time, if we had called Hitler's bluff and he had called ours, I do not think we could have survived a week.

As an intellectual argument this had much validity, and, given the Royal Air Force's narrow margin in 1940, it is indeed hard to see that Britain would have fared better in 1938, but this shifting of his ground was unlikely to impress a public that remembered well that he had defended Munich at the time not as a valuable breathing space but as 'peace for our time'.

In the first months of the war there was some rallying to the government, and at least a veneer of party unity was restored by the reintroduction into office of Churchill and Eden. Beneath that surface, though, the disappointments of the 'Phoney War', in which Britain stood passively by as first Poland and then Finland were destroyed, seriously damaged the government's prestige. Conscious that victory could come only in a long war, for which economic resources would need to be carefully husbanded, Chamberlain still sought to avoid too abrupt a transition to a war economy, but this earned him the reputation more of a half-hearted warlord than of a careful planner. Among Tories only Churchill's reputation rose during this 'bore war', partly from a real zest for conflict that few of his colleagues seemed to share, partly from his being at the helm of the one armed service that easily outgunned its German equivalent (so that the navy alone won clear victories in the first year), and partly because he managed quite brilliantly to remain loyal to Chamberlain but at the same time to convey the impression that he would do the job far better than the incumbent. Years earlier Baldwin had reflected that keeping Churchill out of office might prove to be in the long-term interest of the country, since it would keep him fresh and, if war did come, untainted by any recent responsibilities of office and of failure. While this was by no means Baldwin's only intention in marginalizing Churchill in the mid-1930s, the upshot was pretty much as he had foreseen.

When boredom and frustration were followed in 1940 by the humiliation and fear caused by military defeat in Norway (for which Churchill was substantially responsible, but for which Chamberlain got most of the blame) and then even more seriously in France and Belgium, the slide in Chamberlain's fortunes turned into a collapse. He failed, much like Asquith in 1916, to take the only advice that might have saved him, which was to reconstruct his government far more drastically than in 1939, and give real executive authority over the war to his chief rival. That drift of events should not, however, be exaggerated, for far more Tory MPs still backed Chamberlain than opposed him; when he was in due course supplanted by Churchill, it was Chamberlain who was cheered to the echo from the Tory benches on his next appearance in the House and Churchill whose first speech as Prime Minister was received with Labour cheers and Tory silence. Nevertheless, the number of critics had grown substantially, many of them now the younger MPs who were themselves in the armed forces and who returned periodically to the Commons to bemoan the lack of equipment, training and pre-war preparation in their own units.

In the 'Norway debate' on 7 and 8 May 1940 Chamberlain's attempt to use the peacetime party mechanisms of whipping, and his personal appeal to the loyalty of his 'friends', struck exactly the wrong note in a House profoundly worried about the threat to the national interest. About a hundred government supporters either voted with Labour or abstained, and although the government comfortably won the vote, the size of the rebellion and the bitterness of anti-Chamberlain speeches from his own side made his fall inevitable. Even Chamberlain's admirers recognized that Labour must be brought into office, as in 1915–18, mainly because of the benefit this would produce in encouraging trades unions to cooperate in the war industries, but Labour still categorically refused to serve under Chamberlain, as much as anything because of his known contempt for them. Long before, Baldwin had unavailingly advised Chamberlain that he really should not give the impression that he looked on Labour as dirt, while Chamberlain's own Chief Whip now commented that his personalization of policy disputes 'engendered personal dislike among his opponents to an extent almost unbelievable'. This factor alone would have sealed his fate as a war minister seeking to unite the country, once Conservative MPs failed to sustain him with a united party of his own. What was far less foreseeable was that Chamberlain was succeeded by Churchill rather than by a safe party man such as Halifax, the other obvious candidate in May 1940. This happened in part because Halifax had doubts about his own ability to do the job in wartime, so that in the key meeting he failed to seize the helm as he could certainly have done had he wished, partly because Churchill himself, secure in the belief in his moment of destiny, played his own hand with steely determination.

There was some irony, then, in Chamberlain's being succeeded by Churchill, a man whose attitudes on domestic policy had far less in common with Labour's than Chamberlain's own, and who had in sections of the community been seen ever since 1910 as an anti-working-class warrior. Nothing more clearly demonstrated how far the national emergency had transformed the political landscape, but it was far less clear how long this would last, and Chamberlain at least continued to harbour the illusion that after a shortish war he might be able to return as Conservative Prime Minister and resurrect the politics of the 1930s. For a time at least that hope was given credibility by the continuing importance within Churchill's government of Chamberlain himself, for whom Churchill had a great respect – far more indeed than he had ever had for Baldwin. When Chamberlain died in October 1940 and Churchill paid a warm tribute to him in the Commons, occasioning polite surprise from friends who had thought them deadly foes, he privately confided that he could not have summoned up such sentiments in the case of Baldwin. Even after the war Churchill continued to apply this distinction, denouncing Baldwin with far greater venom than he applied to Chamberlain in his *War Memoirs*, and, when refusing even to join in a tribute to the dying Baldwin on his eightieth birthday in 1947, adding the comment that it would have been better for the country if Stanley Baldwin had never lived.

Chamberlain remained Deputy Prime Minister into the autumn of 1940, chaired meetings in Churchill's regular absences on military business, and, as chairman of the Lord President's committee, both took many domestic burdens off the new Prime Minister's shoulders and kept his finger on the pulse of government business as he had previously done from the Treasury and from Downing Street. More significantly yet, he remained

THE TASKMASTER

A view of Churchill from the left before 1940, *Sunday Worker*, 8 August 1926.

Leader of the Conservative Party, so that Churchill (like MacDonald in 1931–5) led his National Government without having control of any significant part of its voting support in either House. This suited Churchill well enough, for he wished in 1940 to be a 'national' leader, unlimited and uncommitted by too strong a party association, but Chamberlain seems in any case not to have offered to stand down. It was inconceivable that the Conservatives in the Commons would have overthrown him in his party role in favour of the 'rat' of 1904 who had 're-ratted' in 1924 but had even so been distinctly unorthodox in his Conservatism ever since.

However, when Chamberlain contracted cancer in the autumn of 1940 and soon afterwards died, this presented a situation in which Churchill's detachment from his own party could not be maintained. Despite his own continuing reluctance, Churchill did not dare risk the party leadership falling into the hands of someone other than himself, for it would probably have gone to a younger rival who would be less amenable to cooperation than Chamberlain and who, if the war went badly, would be well placed to strike down Churchill and take the premiership. Churchill therefore became the Party Leader in October 1940 and, despite grumbles on the back benches about the future of the party under such an egotist, the whips were able to stage-manage a party meeting that handed the job to him without any other candidate being nominated, and without even the threatened call for an elected deputy who could remind him of his duties to the party (as had been predicted in the press). In his speech of acceptance Churchill actually asked rhetorically whether he was in fact a Conservative at all, and gave a somewhat clouded answer in which his lifelong Toryism was equated with 'the maintenance of the enduring greatness of Britain and her Empire and the historical continuity of our Island life'. This drew applause from his assembled supporters. It had obvious relevance to one of Disraeli's three great principles outlined in 1872, to the national mood of 1940 and to the basis on which Churchill had supplanted the Appeasers at the head of the party's affairs. But it had little to do with the basis on which the Conservatives' campaigning strength had rested for the previous twenty years.

Over time, the balance of influence swung steadily away from Churchill's critics and the limited room for political manoeuvre that he had enjoyed in the summer of 1940 was expanded. Firstly this arose from Churchill's ruthless use of the premier's power of patronage both to promote those who owed their positions to himself, and to exile from influential office most of those whose loyalties were to Baldwinite and Chamberlainite traditions. Packing Halifax and Hoare off as ambassadors to Washington and Madrid respectively was one visible part of this strategy, though, as with most of Churchill's wartime appointments, these were not hard to justify in their own right and were both in the end rather successful. Patronage was, though, handled with cunning by a Prime Minister who knew well enough that he needed both to keep potential critics occupied and to show all wings of the party that they could hope for promotion while he was Leader. R. A. Butler's removal as junior minister at the Foreign Office (where Churchill thought him insufficiently committed to the war) was achieved by promoting him to the Board of Education, which was thought (but in Butler's hands did not turn out to be) a backwater in wartime. Another Chamberlainite, Oliver Stanley, who, when returning from military service in 1942, seemed poised to give a lead to Tory critics of the premier, was instead made Secretary of State for the Colonies (another wartime backwater).

Despite such subtleties, the long-term effect of Churchill's appointments to office was to remove by stages most of the party loyalists who had served under Chamberlain, and to replace them with longstanding cronies of his own with similarly patchy records of party loyalty. Beaverbrook and Brendan Bracken were obvious examples, but something of the same character applied to Amery, Eden and Duff Cooper too, to long-term mavericks like Harold Macmillan and Robert Boothby, and to Labour ministers, Liberals and men of no party at all. It was thus characteristic of the Churchill government that the coordinating domestic role that Chamberlain played in 1940 was given first to Sir John Anderson (a former civil servant with no party attachment) and in 1943 to the Labour Party Leader, Clement Attlee. The crucial post of Minister of Reconstruction, responsible for all post-war planning, went to another non-party minister, Lord Woolton. Meanwhile, a large number of posts with high visibility on the home front went to Labour stalwarts like Herbert Morrison, all of whom emerged from their war service as experienced administrators and who when taken together made up a very credible front bench for a future Labour government. By comparison, although Conservatives had been in office ever since 1931, the team that Churchill assembled when the war ended in 1945 contained very few with extended Cabinet experience and a fair number who were scarcely known at all to the voters. In the five years after the summer of 1940 the cohesive Conservative front bench of the 1930s more or less vanished.

In the same five years the reputations of those who were ousted from office suffered a retrospective character-assassination of a viciously polemical type. This characterization of Chamberlain and his colleagues, as hard-faced capitalists who cosied up to Fascist dictators while enforcing unacceptably tough social measures at home, had begun with such peacetime efforts as the Left Book Club's *Tory MP* and the satirical film *Peace and Plenty* (which depicted the umbrella-toting Chamberlain as Hitler's actual puppet). However, it received its greatest impetus from the book *Guilty Men*, written by a group of Beaverbrook journalists in the summer of 1940; this added the topical charge that the Appeasers had criminally neglected the country's security through their failure to rearm fast enough, their reluctance to bring Russia into the European balance against Nazism, and their credulous readiness to believe their Fascist friends' assurances of peaceful intentions. *Guilty Men* was followed by an ever-lengthening shelf of such books as the war went on, including *Your MP* (by 'Gracchus', a characteristic Roman pseudonym chosen to denote its author's public spiritedness – and in the process usually to conceal a long Labour-supporting past as well), which listed the votes given by MPs in several key foreign policy divisions of the past but wrenched quite out of context the significance of those votes.

These books had a mass sale – and a wide circulation in public libraries that would not previously have stocked such polemics but which did so now, to feed the wartime public's voracious appetite for political reading matter. They were reinforced by the continuous drip-feed of articles of the same type in all the mass-circulation newspapers – but particularly in the left-leaning *Daily Mirror*, now the biggest circulation British paper, in the *Express* and the *Mail*, both of them keen to exorcize their own support for Appeasement by now avidly joining in the search for scapegoats, and in the popular new medium of photo-magazines like *Picture Post* (which portrayed the Conservatives in 1945 as 'anti-Russian, anti-Irish, anti-French, anti-American [and] anti-Resistance', and therefore a threat to world peace and stability). The Tory MPs of 1945, wrote 'Gracchus', were 'still, in spite of any changes, the sort of person who could believe what he did believe in 1935 or in 1938, and the sort of person who could in May 1940, the month of defeat, vote to keep Mr Chamberlain in power'. Against this tide of vitriol, much of it pure fiction and all of it highly misleading, there was little point in showing – as Quintin Hogg did in his *The Left Were Never Right* – that Labour's record on rearmament in the 1930s was even worse than the Conservatives', or that so many Tory MPs had fought and fourteen had died in the 'People's War'. Whatever the facts, such defensive writings were almost invariably seen as special pleading by an establishment that was on the skids.

The historical image of the 1930s as a time of continuous economic crisis, universal deprivation and despair, with the added ingredient of a ruling class that betrayed the nation's interest for shallow personal – or at least dubious political – motives, was a gross misrepresentation of the decade through which the country had just passed. But through the force-feeding of such continuous propaganda, this became for twenty years the dominant folk memory of what the poet W. H. Auden now called, in accordance with the emerging orthodoxy, 'a low, dishonest decade'. The party that had run the country in those 'years that the locust hath eaten', as Churchill himself later biblically dubbed the 1930s, suffered a calamitous collapse of its own collective reputation and self-respect in the process. And while Churchill had, in 1940, responded to Chamberlain's plea that he discourage the type of personal vituperation indulged in by such friends of his as Beaverbrook, once Chamberlain had gone there was no longer any barrier to the tide of abuse. When Beaverbrook sought later to deny his share of responsibility for the mood of 1945, pointing to his strong support for Churchill and his supporters in their campaign for re-election, he was roundly told by the Party Chairman that once he had given space for years in the *Express* to the writings and cartoons of Michael Foot, David Low and J. B. Priestley, 'no whirlwind campaign of a few weeks can undo the long-term anti-Conservative work of these men'.

The contribution of the Tory *Express* and *Mail* and their associated papers – in a sense the revenge of the irresponsible harlot of Fleet Street for Baldwin's victory over it in 1931 – did not of course create the mood of 1945, for it is clear that the *Mirror* and the other big-selling titles of the left and centre would have argued such a case anyway, and to considerable effect. But flanking fire from normally supportive papers seemed to confirm the more predictable attacks from the Conservatives' natural opponents, and the lack of any mass-circulation media outlet coming reliably to the Tories' defence ensured that critical messages became accepted as the truth. It would be fifty years before the Conservative Party once again had such a bad press to contend with.

Actual experience of the war reinforced the same process. The egalitarian spirit that emerged during the time of invasion fears, mass evacuation from the cities and sheltering together against the Blitz in 1940–41, and the policies pursued in order to wage war more effectively and to secure popular support for war sacrifices, offered new perspectives on much pre-war experience. By 1941 unemployment was almost non-existent and the government was driven even to conscript women in order to keep the munitions factories going. In the same year Britain's first budget on Keynesian lines was introduced by – of all people – Chamberlain's acolyte Sir Kingsley Wood. By 1944, under the influence both of the desire to reward the British people for their war sacrifices and of the growing acceptance of J. M. Keynes's economic principles of demand management of the economy, and also in order to respond to the growing demand for equality of sacrifice and for a fairer share of the nation's resources, all parties in the Churchill government had agreed to pursue the objective of 'full employment' after the war. This decision alone cast a very sinister light on the policies of Baldwin and Chamberlain before 1939, when they had been the political spokesmen for an orthodoxy that said that unemployment was simply beyond any government's ability to control. So, in sum, just when polemical propaganda induced a collective national amnesia about the good side of life in the 1930s, the very real working-class suffering of that decade was made to seem entirely unnecessary. The scapegoats for the failure to rearm would also now be the men held responsible for the pre-war recession, for malnutrition and for the means test.

The invalidation of the Conservatives' collective past both at home and abroad was rendered far more serious by the party's failure to plan with effectiveness for the future. At the local, campaigning level, the Conservative Party almost ceased to exist under the stress of a six-year war. Insistent circulars from Central Office urging the continuation of at least a skeleton organization in the constituencies were scarcely even read or debated by local parties that could not manage to get quorate meetings anyway; membership fell away, subscription income was lost, offices were closed, agents' employment was terminated, and the ability to project a political message entirely evaporated. An increasingly elderly residue of activists railed ineffectively against the left-wing bias that they perceived in the BBC and the Army Bureau of Current Affairs, but no effective propaganda was done for Conservative thinking in order to offset the leftward slide in public opinion. There were, as the Birmingham Chief Agent put it, 'lots of sevenpenny Penguins but no Tory books', and the party organization was in no state to fill the void.

At Westminster, almost all Conservatives were well aware of the extent to which the war had made a new approach to policy inescapable. Even Chamberlain himself, the Conservatives' social policy expert for twenty years, wrote to his sister in 1940 that the sight of evacuees from Birmingham had opened his eyes to things he had never previously known to exist – and which now shocked him deeply and made him thoroughly ashamed of his ignorance. As early as 1940 the National Union had set up machinery which would try to keep party thinking alongside the new trends of thinking that the war had unleashed. With enormous significance for the future, a new body, which became in 1941 the Post-War Problems Central Committee, with representatives of local parties and Tory MPs as well as those from the National Union, was put under the chairmanship of R. A. Butler. The choice of Butler was in fact indicative of the low priority given to policy work, for he was in 1941 merely a second-rank minister in an unprestigious domestic department, a man who had neither the Party Leader's ear nor his backing in case of trouble, and he was certainly not the first choice for the job. In the circumstances, the PWPCC in general and Butler in particular achieved a good deal, though these achievements had more significance for the future than for the Conservative Party during the war. The fact that Butler took charge of the PWPCC, with the lawyer-MP David Maxwell Fyfe as his deputy and like-minded younger men such as Henry Brooke among its members, would place them in pole position for the more serious task of rewriting party policy after 1945, while the casual decision of 1940–41 set Butler up as the party's policy impresario for almost a quarter of a century.

Despite the distractions of wartime, the virtual disappearance of the CRD and the lack therefore of any back-up machinery for policy research, the PWPCC conducted a detailed review of party policy and published reports on a wide range of issues – for example, on industrial policy in 1943. The reports were linked where possible with discussion teams of ordinary party members organized as 'onlooker groups', and provided some of the material for a series of *Signpost* booklets which the party produced in the hope of refuting the charge that it had no ideas on policy. In his own field, Butler could be more adventurous, bearding Churchill in his lair to insist on introducing a major education bill (which the premier characteristically thought to be a distraction from the war), sticking to his guns when the whips became nervous about divisive religious opinions on the bill's detailed clauses, and seeing it through triumphantly as the 'Butler' Education Act of 1944, which provided for a generation the statutory framework for a vital public service. It was a characteristic piece of reconstruction planning in its derivation from much non-party as well as political opinion, but a rare example of wartime reconstruction planning actually brought to fruition before 1945. It was also unique in being a wartime legislative achievement unequivocally due to the efforts of a Tory minister, and its insistent citation on the hustings by Tory candidates in 1945 was evidence both of its real importance and of their lack of any other usable ammunition for the same constructive purpose.

This was largely because the PWPCC entirely failed in its broader ambition of constructing a comprehensive post-war policy for the party. In part that reflected the real difficulty of getting anything agreed in the conditions of the wartime party – where the standing-down of the activists

THE BUTLER'S DREAM

"It came out of my head."

Punch gives Butler due credit for the Education Bill, December 1943.

for the duration had a far more drastic effect on normal procedures than on the Labour side, where conferences, regional and local meetings went on much as usual, as did recruitment of members and much party campaigning. Just as important, though, was the lack of interest at the top in post-war policy in general, and in particular in anything that might divide the party and the nation. Churchill proclaimed in a broadcast as late at March 1943 that it was simply too early to talk about policy – though he also mendaciously claimed that he had a five-year plan for domestic reconstruction ready to announce and implement when the time came.

Even in the last year of the war he seems to have envisaged that between war and peace there must be an interlude in which all-party government would continue under his leadership, during which the troops would be demobilized, the economy returned to something like normality, and policy planning only then begin for the next phase, a concept that entirely ignored the public's understandable wish, after six years of war and privation, for an indication in detail of what they could expect next.

In all of this, Churchill was in any case influenced by two factors that weighed on his mind but had considerably less influence with others. First, he invariably thought of 'the war' as including all theatres, and anticipated battles against Japan going on into 1946–7, so that even in early 1945 the problems of peacetime seemed reassuringly far off into the future. And second, he continued to hope, in spite of all evidence to the contrary, that he would not have to return to party politics at all; rather that, as in 1918, there would be a continuation of wartime cooperation into the post-war parliament, at the end of which he would be able to retire as a national hero, amidst universal love and admiration. None of this was very seriously thought out or explained in detail to the party that he led, for the good reason that he did not see any urgency in it anyway, but also because the actual waging of the war and his increasing concern about post-war Europe took up all his time and energy. When his own government produced detailed proposals on post-war health policy, he had no time even to read (let alone to absorb properly) the implications of such dramatic reforms, and he therefore took refuge in increasingly petulant assertions that it was all too soon. Occasional suggestions as to the need for a detailed policy from such colleagues as Anthony Eden, Churchill's acknowledged Conservative deputy and his designated heir from 1942 onwards, fell on deaf ears. Eden himself was too busy with the Foreign Office and the management of the Commons to keep up such a line of attack for long, and Churchill would not give real authority to anyone who was less pliable than Eden, and who might either limit his own future choice of policy options or, by developing a distinctive Tory policy at all, reduce the chances of all-party coalition when the war came to an end.

Churchill therefore abdicated as Party Leader from the position of policy supremo that Chamberlain had occupied in the 1930s. Having abdicated, he then left the throne vacant rather than allow the appearance of any possible rival to his own authority. Without a lead from the top, much of Butler's policy work was doomed, for none of it had either authority or official backing. This was demonstrated when little of the PWPCC's work saw the light of day in the 1945 Conservative Manifesto, which owed far more to inputs from government than from party; this meant that the Labour Party could claim in 1945 to be co-heir to everything the Tories said and did, though they also had their own more advanced policy position, while the Tories had nothing distinctive at all but their Leader. The lack of a dynamic lead on policy-planning was made far worse by the fact that, even when future policy choices could not be avoided, there was still no strong lead, and as a result the party marched off in several directions at once, giving a distinctly poor impression of itself to the voters. The moderate MPs organized in the Tory Reform Group, the right wingers who were beginning to fear the drift of Tory policy to the left under the People's War banner, and the soft centre who simply sought in vain for a party line to toe, all manoeuvred uncomfortably in 1943–5 for the right to express the Conservative viewpoint.

That fragmenting pattern emerged over post-war trading policy, on post-war planning for housing and land use, in a debate on equal pay for men and women teachers and, in a particularly contentious case, on the wages paid to workers in the catering industry. In each case the impression given was either of a party irredeemably split or of a patched-up compromise in which the party eventually said what the electors seemed to want to hear, but said it without either conviction or the appearance that some of them would go on saying it once the restraints of wartime had been cast off. The great test case for reconstruction planning was debate on the Beveridge Report of 1942, the comprehensive document on post-war social and health policy on which a party response could simply not be avoided. As we have seen, the Conservative Party had in 1939 discussed offering of its own volition some of the reforms that now came onto the agenda through Beveridge, and it had not shied away in the 1930s from such debates (though its characteristic response of that time – that sound finance prevented many desirable things from being done in practice – had been to an extent invalidated by the vast wartime expenditure on arms). The party offered no evidence to the Beveridge Committee and so lost any opportunity to be linked in advance with its approach. When the report was published, Churchill, with only half his mind ever on the issue, allowed his government's official response to be grudging and half-hearted (in comparison with Labour's warm endorsement), while Tory backbenchers, given no real cue, argued on both sides of the case. Tory Reform Group MPs were for full acceptance of Beveridge (though spoiling their case somewhat by openly arguing that electoral tactics were part of their reason for doing so); right-wingers were for a 'sound finance' response to limit the harm that advances in social policy would do to the post-war economy, and against any endorsement of principles that facilitated what would later be called a 'dependency culture'.

These 1943–5 arguments on post-war policy framed therefore – on both sides – much of the Tory debate on social policy as it was to run for the next half-century, and they were already being given a new edge by the use of arguments derived from the writings of Friedrich von Hayek, whose *The Road to Serfdom* appeared in Britain in 1944. Hayek's book was welcomed by some Conservatives in high places, including the Party Chairman Ralph Assheton, who even tried to use part of the party's scarce ration of paper to secure a 1945 reprint of Hayek for the election, and who sent copies to colleagues, including Churchill. The rhetoric of freedom that Hayek offered both typified and reinforced the Tory right's response to totalitarianism abroad (whether of the left or the right) and to the massive extensions of state power in wartime Britain too, while Churchill's use of such language as 'serfdom' in 1945 suggests that he was not immune to these influences himself (though he had almost certainly read only a summary and not the book).

In the medium term Hayek's basic premise – that the public could and must be mobilized against dangerous, unnecessary forces of state control – would be a significant influence on Conservative strategy after 1945, culminating in the 1951 slogan 'Set the People Free', though this was a tactic that the party would almost certainly have worked out for itself when in opposition and confronted with a Labour government bent on 'planning' for the foreseeable peacetime future. In the long term, Hayek would resurface in the 1970s, when his brand of economics became suddenly fashionable and his political ideas were therefore read again with more attention. In the short term, though, the philosophical support that his book lent to obscurantists of the Tory right like Assheton simply made it more difficult for the party to stay in touch with a public which in 1945 did not regard *British* state intervention as either sinister or malign.

The Conservative Party therefore emerged from the Second World War without a coherent front bench, without an organization in the country ready and able to fight an election, and without a policy on which to fight one either. Whatever Churchill's claim on the nation's hearts and minds for his activities since 1940, his stewardship of his own party had been an unqualified disaster. The enormous danger that this implied had been demonstrated by wartime opinion polls and other such surveys, all of which had from 1943 predicted a Labour election victory (though such sampling of public opinion was still primitive in the extreme and therefore easy to ignore), and by wartime by-elections since 1942, in which support for non-Conservative candidates and unconservative domestic policies had been deafeningly endorsed right across the land. Some shrewd observers who had spent the war on the home front and had kept their ears to the ground could see the danger that this scenario presented. Butler, for example, argued unavailingly for a better definition of policy, for efforts to revive the organization and for delay before a general election. Such arguments cut little ice with the party leaders, mainly because of the universal assumption that victory would transform the electorate's views, that Churchill would be triumphantly returned to power by the grateful voters, and that those candidates who backed him would be swept in on his coat-tails. Conservatives who forgot what had really happened in 1918 (when they had themselves had a strong leader, an active organization and a clear party identity, as well as Lloyd George as a war-winning ally) made an all too easy equation between the equivalent moments of victory, but since Labour MPs and most independent commentators also expected a Churchill sweep to victory in 1945, Tories may perhaps be forgiven for falling into the same trap.

Irritated by Labour's refusal to stay in his all-party team once the European war ended in May 1945 (and by the departure of most Liberals too once Labour had gone, in order to protect their own party's continued independence), Churchill carried on for two months with a caretaker government of Tories and Independents. Erroneously believing that his best chance now lay in a quick election, he secured a quick dissolution, with polling on 5 July and the results to be declared three weeks later when the votes of servicemen around the world had been collected.

In the event, the 1945 campaign was an affair from which few Conservatives emerged with much credit, and the party as a whole marched unsuspectingly into its greatest defeat since 1906. In view of the terrible tactics that the party employed, it is perhaps worth pointing out that if opinion polls were correct then the party would have been defeated by an even greater margin six months earlier. As the war drew to a close and an election neared, some rallying of the Tory vote probably took place, either from fear of a Labour government as the possibility seemed actually to materialize, or from the almost invariable recovery that governments have enjoyed after mid-term unpopularity. In either case, this suggests that the 1945 campaign as such may not have made much difference to the outcome, except in so far as it may have hastened or slowed down the Tory recovery and so changed the actual margin of Labour's victory – and on that hypothesis there is virtually no verifiable evidence on which to base a judgement. The problem was considerably complicated by the attenuated state of the party organization. Few local parties could do much more than publish and deliver literature, and as a result of the near-universal lack of canvassing Central Office was flying blind throughout June and July 1945 anyway: even after all the votes were cast in this Labour landslide, Central Office and its area agents continued to predict a Conservative win, but this was based more on wishful thinking and the wing-and-a-prayer school of reasoning than on any analysis of evidence.

In the absence of Tory infantry out in the localities, the party's campaign therefore consisted overwhelmingly of an artillery battle in which the big guns fired off barrages at the national level and hoped to be fully and favourably reported in the media. Much of the campaign revolved around big public meetings, touring motorcades and speeches, and the newly significant medium of BBC radio. The Tory press to an extent rallied – if with the limited effectiveness that is referred to above, in view of their earlier conduct. The big-circulation papers like the *Express* may even have been counter-productive in their rediscovered partisanship – for example, by reporting Beaverbrook's own increasing fantasies about the horrific form of a possible Labour government rather than the more sober campaigning of such men as Eden and Butler. But even some staunch Tory allies of the past like *The Times* could not bring themselves to endorse the party once they had seen and reported Churchill's own campaign. For whatever Churchill's failings as Party Leader in the past, and however much or little the campaign may have mattered anyway in 1945, there is little doubt that what he now did had a negative influence on the Tory vote. And it is worth emphasizing that such seasoned campaigners as Leo Amery and the Chief Whip, James Stuart, expressed that view very forcibly during the campaign, and long before they anticipated that there might be a defeat to explain away.

In his public appearances, Churchill was greeted with wild acclamation, understandable enough in view of his service to the nation since 1940, but dangerous in the extreme as an influence on the judgement of a man never noted for his modesty. He was convinced that his reception proved that he would be returned triumphantly to power, hardly even hearing the muted asides of his secretary, Jock Colville, who thought that the cheers would have been useful for predictions only had it been a presidential election (which is more or less the way in which Churchill conducted himself anyway, with 'National' far more often on his lips than the word 'Conservative'). Towards the end of the campaign, clear in his view that he had the public's backing, Churchill reminded voters in a broadcast that he could remain Prime Minister only if they voted for 'his' candidates – the actual word 'Conservative' still not being used. It was, however, one thing for Baldwin to campaign for a 'National' Government in 1931, or even in 1935 (when at least there were still politicians from other political groups in his Cabinet), but for Churchill to claim to be head of a 'National' Government in 1945 was the sheerest effrontery, and the fact that the Labour and Liberal half of the nation was ranged against him in organized, effective and patriotic opposition gave the lie to his claims in any case.

Churchill therefore set out to argue from his first election broadcast onwards that Labour had deserted the nation by refusing to stay in his government (a rather pale version of Baldwin's much more plausible allegation of the 'desertion' of office by Labour in 1931), and that in any case the national interest would not be served by the return to office of socialists who would divide the country on ideological lines – again a recasting of Baldwin's reiterated theme that 'Conservatism unites, socialism divides'. But if that theme had worked well for a Conservative Leader who was (and was seen as) an emollient, non-partisan healer, it sounded very odd indeed on the lips of a politician generally seen as confrontationist, belligerent and partisan. These were popular memories of Churchill from before 1939 that Labour sedulously revived in the minds of voters as the 1945 campaign went on (if with great care, given Churchill's real personal popularity), but Churchill in any case provided them with perfect ammunition from the present, when he denounced as threats to democracy and freedom the same men who had loyally served with him for the past five years. The reports of the Mass Observation surveys had already shown for some years that the British people were quite capable of feeling intense gratitude to Churchill and at the same time not wanting him as post-war prime minister, and the campaign he fought can have done nothing to remove such deep-seated doubts about his *future* value. Since his failure to carry out even the most basic tasks of the Party Leader since 1940 had left the party exposed now to an election in which his personal vote was its only major asset, his failure to exploit that one asset

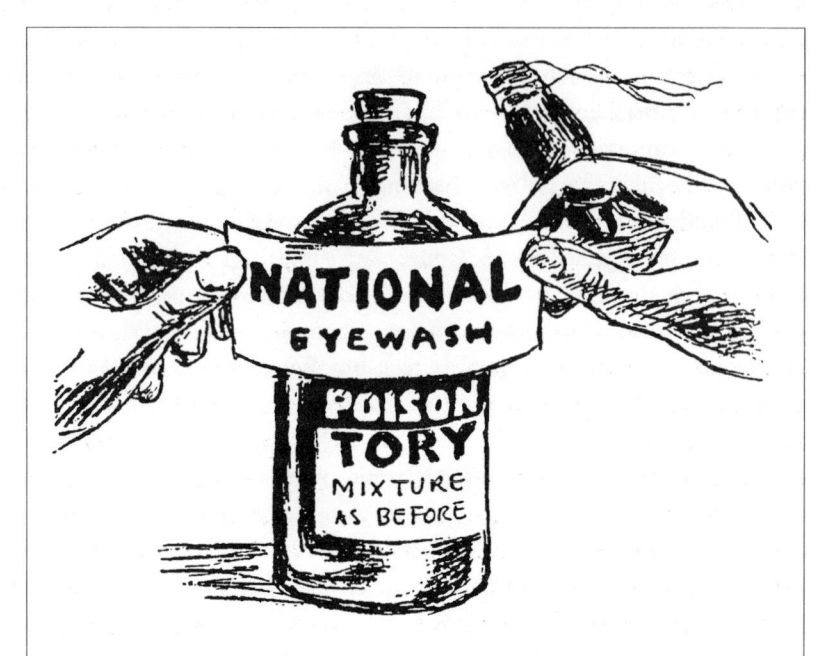

Don't judge by labels

Remember what

CHURCHILL

said . . .

"We know what to expect when the Tories return to power—a party of great vested interests, banded together in a formidable confederation; corruption at home, aggression to cover it up abroad; the trickery of tariff juggles; the tyranny of a well-fed party machine; sentiment by the bucketful; patriotism and imperialism by the imperial pint; an open hand at the public exchequer, an open door at the public house; dear food for the million, cheap labour for the millionaire."

—*Winston Churchill speaking at Dundee in 1908.*

Labour leaflet in the 1945 campaign, attacking Churchill's 'National' credentials and bringing up his past to embarrass him.

sensitively during the campaign was the self-inflicted final nail in his party's coffin.

In the event, the combination of the world war and its effects, the retrospective blackening of pre-war Tory governments, and the counter-productive campaign of 1945, managed to fire up Labour voters with greater determination and to alienate from Tory candidates the ex-Liberals and middle opinion in general which had backed Baldwin and Chamberlain in the 1930s. Indeed, *The Economist* felt bound to point out in its analysis of the 1945 results that, while Churchill might be an incomparably greater international statesman and war leader, he could still take elementary lessons in party management from Baldwin. In 1945, just as in 1929 when the party had last managed so signally to alienate the middle-ground vote, Conservatives got about 40 per cent of the national vote. The difference was that by 1945 the continued decline of Liberalism, and the Labour Party's greater success in identifying itself with the popular mood, meant that 40 per cent for the Tories produced not a hung parliament but a Labour landslide. Fewer than 200 Conservative and National Liberal MPs held their seats in 1945, though that rose to 213 once various independent and 'National' candidates had later taken the whip.

This parliamentary force, halved in size since 1935, faced not only a Labour government but one with a majority of 150 and a hugely ambitious programme to carry, a programme on which the Tory MPs would be able to make little impact. By the end of the 1945 parliament, then, the landscape really would have been altered, for by then there would be a much increased public sector in industry, full-scale peacetime economic planning, and just the expansion in social and health provision on which Tories had already fallen out in 1943–4. If the Conservatives' policy problems had seemed acute in 1944, then surely they would now get worse? This perception, as well as the generalized gloom incurred by such a violent turn of the electoral tide, generated much Conservative depression in 1945. Churchill himself, reminded by his wife that all clouds had silver linings, replied that in this case the good side of his defeat was very effectively disguised, and he turned down the king's offer of the Order of the Garter on the grounds that it would be an unfitting honour now that the electorate had given him the order of the boot. For the first year after defeat in 1945 Churchill shared his party followers' doubts as to whether a Conservative Party had any future whatsoever in Britain.

Despite the carry-over into opposition of the biggest single difficulty of the past five years – Winston Churchill as Leader – these doubts soon turned out to be groundless, though it was largely in spite of Churchill rather than because of him that the party achieved its remarkable comeback from the 1945 catastrophe. The first issue raised by defeat for the Conservatives was indeed Churchill's own position as Leader, for no other Conservative Leader had ever so loftily ignored the party's interests, led it to a shattering defeat and survived to tell the tale. On the other hand, it was also clear that the two-fifths of the electorate that had stayed with the party in 1945 felt gratitude to Churchill and affection for him in rather larger measure than the other three-fifths, so that any stage-management of a change of Leader would have to be carefully handled. At the early stage, it was possible to believe that the problem would solve itself, for it seemed likely that the seventy-year-old Churchill, exhausted by his war services and now from time to time quite unwell too, depressed by electoral defeat, bored as he always had been by opposition, and anxious to write his *War Memoirs* in order to defend himself 'before History', would bow out of his own accord. Under this reasonable impression, the party's other front-benchers missed their only chance to force the issue, for once Churchill returned refreshed from his holiday and from the triumph of his 'iron curtain' speech in the United States, in the spring of 1946, he never again seriously intended to quit while he was fit (in his own assessment) to do the job. He would from time to time hint to Eden that he was going to hand over soon, but this was more a case of his masterly playing on Eden's personal loyalty to him than a serious statement of intention, and in the party manoeuvrings of the later 1940s Churchill demonstrated both his ruthless determination to stay on and his readiness to treat as disloyalty any suggestion to the contrary.

When the front-benchers as a team tried to edge Churchill aside in 1947 he simply refused to go and challenged them to overthrow him by a public coup – an inconceivable scenario for the national hero of 1940, now increasingly admired and loved for himself as he aged. There were in any case considerable advantages to be derived from Churchill's continuing leadership – his continuing personal appeal to at least some of the voters, his burgeoning international reputation deriving both from his war record and his great post-war set-piece speeches on foreign policy at such places as Fulton, Zurich and Strasbourg, and the benign, Victorian presence that he offered to the party faithful, a comforting reassurance while so much modernization of the machinery and of policy was going on.

Churchill was therefore suffered to remain Party Leader, but effectively on terms that both he and his colleagues could accept – if for opposite reasons. Churchill had no intention of being active in the leadership; indeed he still did not really wish to be a party leader at all, and he was determined to spend more of his diminishing reserves of energy on his memoirs and his international career than on the dull round of parliamentary debates and party management. This effectively maximized his value to the party while reducing his capacity to do it harm in terms both of identity and of policy as the party reins slipped out of his hands in 1946–7 while he was busy with the other priorities in his life. As a result of his regular absences from the Commons and from many of the more important meetings of the Opposition, the rest of the front bench reclaimed their party from his grasp, did what was necessary to make it once again electable, and in the process developed a feeling of team loyalty that had not existed since 1940. Harold Macmillan, a permanent rebel in the 1930s and a minister outside the mainstream who owed everything to Churchill in 1940–45, was a full member of a normal party front bench by 1949. If this owed something to the changes in policy which led some columnists to see the Conservatives moving in 1947 to what Macmillan had called in a book title of 1938 *The Middle Way*, it also owed a great deal to the habits of collective action in the shadow cabinet, to the fact that a Labour government had the effect of reminding Tories how much they had in common, to the exposed position that the Opposition occupied when in such small numbers in the Commons, and to the shared conviction that working together was the only way in which the party would recover from 1945.

Churchill wanted the Opposition to pursue almost exactly the strategy that he had followed as Prime Minister (and indeed had wished to pursue at least since he served under Lloyd George and backed the idea of a centre party in 1920); the Conservative Party should offer itself as the heir-general of his wartime government, continuing to back the agreed policies of 1943–5 and avoiding where possible new policies that would alienate in particular Liberal politicians and their voting support. He would thus brand Labour as the deserter from the national unity of 1940–45. In the aftermath of defeat Churchill wanted (again as in 1920) to ditch the very name 'Conservative' and adopt instead some umbrella title, such as 'the Union Party', to which Liberals would be able to offer support without apparently selling out to their ancestral enemies. That initiative died away rapidly when it became clear that neither the 1922 Committee nor the Party Conference would countenance any termination of their own party's nominal continuity and integrity. In much the same way, the shadow cabinet talked out various Churchillian suggestions for appointments to key offices, so effectively reminding the Leader of the Opposition that his patronage would now need to be dispensed with consent. Eden's proposal to make his own close supporter Jim Thomas the Party Chairman was rejected, but so was Churchill's suggestion of Macmillan (not yet in 1946 trusted by the rest as anything but a Churchill stooge), and the compromise choice of Lord Woolton emerged instead. When a new Chief Whip was needed, the rest of the front bench seem to have insisted on the promotion of Stuart's deputy, Patrick Buchan-Hepburn, not exactly welcome to Churchill as a former Chamberlainite, but an appointment that – if after a longish delay – went ahead all the same. Perhaps the key difference of opinion came over responsibility for policy matters, where Churchill's nominee, his son-in-law, the hawkish Duncan Sandys, failed to get shadow cabinet approval, and the responsibility therefore fell back on the much more moderate Butler (who proceeded to steer things in directions of which the Leader did not greatly approve). The return to prominence on the front bench of other Chamberlain loyalists such as Oliver Stanley, while some of Churchill's closest supporters like Beaverbrook and Bracken were lapsing into relative inactivity in party affairs, again emphasized the return to party normality after 1945.

The strategic objective of a centrist block was still being pursued, though, by Churchill, and with unrelenting determination, in his aim to negotiate a new alliance with the Liberals. The first part of this exercise was relatively painless, and in 1947 the National Union formally merged the Conservative and National Liberal parties after sixteen years of cooperation. But while this might avoid some duplication of effort and improve the coordination of campaigning, it did not of itself produce a single extra MP or vote for the party. The real objective was wider, and Woolton expressed the hope that it would lead 'the Liberals throughout the country [as well as] the National Liberals to become our allies'.

The strategic choice was much like the one in which the party had been involved in the 1920s; in order to do any sort of deal with the independent Liberals, the Conservatives would have to make concessions, perhaps on policy and certainly by standing down in some constituencies in favour of Liberal candidates. Churchill saw no problem with the first of these, stressing the continuities of his own career since his Liberal days – continuities that were far less visible to everyone else – and the common anti-socialism of the Liberal and Tory traditions, and he constantly

"WHAT LIBERALS COULD RESIST US NOW?"

Low on Conservative efforts to woo the Liberals, *Daily Herald*, 10 February 1950.

preached the need for an electoral pact. But – again as in the 1920s – a Conservative Party that could see little sign of Liberal vitality at the grass roots (and which on its own side was just then experiencing a huge revival of membership and activity) was not at all prepared to make the concessions that would have made a Lib–Con pact viable. With the exception of a couple of northern towns, Bolton and Huddersfield, no pacts could be negotiated, and the parties fought each other for votes; in 1950 the electors were to show clearly enough what they thought of the relative merits of the two non-socialist parties by annihilating the Liberals at the polls. Partly as a result of this factor, Conservatives were able almost to remove Labour's majority in 1950 and to secure a majority of their own in 1951 (for which, see Chapter 13).

Churchill returned to the fray in 1950–51, urging a renewed effort to negotiate a pact, but this time Butler and Woolton secured the backing of the National Union to face down even the Leader's threat to resign if he did not get his way. In 1951, without a pact and desperately short of money, the Liberals could put up no more than 109 candidates, and most former Liberal votes went to the Conservatives without their having had to make any formal concession in return. In 1953 Butler reminded Churchill how far the absence of Proportional Representation had aided that strategy, since 'a good deal of middle of the road opinion which now votes Conservative in the absence of an effective middle party would under P.R. transfer its allegiance to the Liberals'. This process uncannily replicates the strategy debates of the 1920s, with the same outcome and with Winston Churchill for the second time on the losing side. He was not, of course, a man to be so easily thwarted, and on becoming Prime Minister again in 1951 he offered the Liberal Leader Clement Davies a Cabinet post, a gesture which could well have had more than formal significance for both parties' future identities had not the Liberals turned him down. With plans for a centrist political identity rejected by Liberals as well as Tories, then, Churchill padded out his 1951 Cabinet with men of goodwill but no particular party allegiance (as in 1940), and for a time he tried to keep the Conservative Party machine at arm's length from Downing Street, until a series of public relations disasters necessitated a reversal of course. He was thus, by about 1953, whether he liked it or not, head of a normal Conservative Party government, and one which did not even pretend to be anything else.

This turn of events was only made possible because of the nature of the policy review which the Conservatives carried out in and after 1946–7, and which enabled them to appeal to moderate voters in 1950–51 from a very different position from the one they seemed to occupy in 1945. In the first place, partly to avoid increasing the distance between parties and so wrecking his claim that it was Labour that was dividing the nation, Churchill did not want any serious work at all done on party policy, though this preference also derived from his conviction that oppositions could only lose votes by detailing their policies in advance. He was determined too that he would not spend his own time on what he saw as an essentially wasteful exercise, and did not intend to allow anyone else to do it for him, lest it commit a future Churchill government in advance in ways that he did not like. That negative policy strategy was effectively overthrown by an increasingly subversive response from the party, both among MPs and peers and in the constituencies. So clear was this by the time of the Party Conference of October 1946 that Churchill's only viable response was to bow to the demand and allow work to begin on party policy, though his press release did then cheekily claim that the Leader had been planning this for some time.

The Industrial Policy Committee set up under the chairmanship of Rab

Butler in 1946 has a good claim to be regarded as one of the key moments of Conservative Party history, something akin to Peel's drafting of *The Tamworth Manifesto* with which Butler, Macmillan and others often compared *The Industrial Charter* even while they were working on it. The committee contained three future Tory Chancellors of the Exchequer (with another as its assistant secretary), as well as several businessmen, and a careful balance between different sections of the party, ranging from Oliver Lyttelton (whom Butler considered to be a 'city shark') to David Eccles (whom Churchill's friend Brendan Bracken described in 1948 as 'that semi-socialist'). The committee's remit from the shadow cabinet, drawn up by Butler himself and not debated in much detail, allowed it to range over the whole field of economic, regional, industrial relations, and (because of the financial issues involved) social policies. Its process of operation was in three phases: research (for which it was serviced by the reviving CRD), drafting and education, and it may well be that the third was the most vital in the long run. The committee considered extensive evidence submitted to it and interviewed dozens of witnesses, both in London and on various regional visits, and it rested its conclusions solidly on what it saw as the practical experience of people who worked in industry themselves – it took in other words a defiantly untheoretical approach. Once the drafting began on a single document intended to cover such a wide range of issues, it became clear that it must also be short on detail; it would be what Butler later called 'impressionistic' in its use of the broad brush rather than the fine-nibbed pen or the camera in its construction of a post-war Conservative image. Collective drafting enabled the document to have in it something for everyone in the party, while also ensuring that the dominant tone was the one that the most influential committee members, like Butler and Macmillan, were determined to produce.

The Industrial Charter thus contained surprisingly positive statements for a Tory document when it came to discuss trades unions, and it implicitly accepted that the energy and transport industries nationalized by Labour would almost certainly remain in public ownership; and, despite worries about future costs, there were no clauses in the document that could be read as indicating any Tory readiness to abolish the National Health Service then just coming into existence. In the long-term context of Tory policy, this was not especially revolutionary, for even public ownership had never been ruled out in principle by Tory governments, and in the 1930s there had been Tory-led experiments, such as Imperial

Airways, which could now be cited as precedents. What was new in the actual industrial policy clauses of *The Industrial Charter* was that its tacit acceptance of much of what the Attlee government was doing was accompanied by the drawing for the first time of a line in the sand, beyond which the Conservatives would not go. The 'mixed economy' might be acceptable, but moving by stages to a fully socialist economy would not be, and this one parliament of Labour action would define just how mixed the economy would be. That drawing of a new battle line in domestic policy, which effectively separated the Labour and Tory parties for the next thirty years, was in itself of great significance. Much as Peel had tacitly accepted in 1835 the reforms of 1830–34 but vowed to resist further changes, so Butler and his colleagues did the same thing in 1947, digging in just ahead of Labour's current programme rather than counter-attacking to recover lost ground. 'We were,' wrote Butler later, 'out-Peeling Peel in giving the Party a painless but permanent face-lift, and the more unflamboyant the changes, the less likely were the features to sag again.'

When the philosophical mood changed in and after the 1970s, and state intervention went out of fashion, this Butlerian tactic could variously be presented as a wimpish form of domestic appeasement or as a devilishly clever plan to lull socialism into a sense of false security before launching the great Thatcherite counter-attack. It was neither of these – for both such interpretations were unhistorical in the extent to which they ignored the actual mood of 1947. Rather it was an honest (if sometimes desperate) attempt to reapply the practical traditions of Conservatism to a political landscape in which most of the mileposts had been swept aside by the flood tides of the war and the 1945 election. And although it was no sort of deep-laid tactic – rolling with the socialist punch before counter-punching, as Michael Fraser later liked to put it – it was certainly a necessary concession to the agenda of the day if the Conservatives were ever to win back office and the opportunity to begin once again redefining the political agenda on their own terms.

Educating their own party was therefore of great importance for the policy-framers of 1946–7, for the 'impression' that Butler sought to make – of a party now up to date with recent political change but emphasizing at the same time the continuing vitality of private enterprise and political freedom – would be ruined if the Conservatives did not wholeheartedly endorse *The Industrial Charter*; for they had certainly not endorsed such policies when offered to them in 1944, and when advanced in 1945 they had been advocated with such a lack of conviction as to inspire widespread disbelief. The shadow cabinet now accepted the document with the enthusiastic backing of Eden in the chair; his politics had never embraced the hard-shelled defence of property at all costs and he had become very uncomfortable of late in the company of some of the party's more right-wing industrialist MPs, a faction sometimes half-affectionately known to the likes of Eden as 'the forty thieves'. Whatever their earlier differences in the confidentiality of the committee room, the members of the Industrial Policy Committee now took their document out collectively to the party, endorsing it in big speeches and constituency meetings over the next few months, and apparently securing overwhelmingly favourable party reactions in advance of the Party Conference due in October 1947 at Brighton. The growing membership of the party clearly felt that this was a message with which the party recovery could be continued, with which more members and voters would be won over from Labour. Much of the debate seems to have taken place in exactly that self-interested party context rather than on issues of political and economic principle: the conviction that a campaign actually to reverse Labour's 1945 programme would merely encourage the public to vote in another five years of radical socialism in 1950 was a powerful reinforcement of such tactical reasoning, and one that appealed even to those Tories who most disliked what Labour was already doing. It is only fair to add that the younger generation, who had been so strikingly absent from party deliberations in 1943-5, were inherently more sympathetic to *The Industrial Charter* than their predecessors and elders, not least because they too had been through the war experience in the forces, which had done so much to shape and popularize Labour's 1945 programme in the first place.

At the Party Conference in October the right fought a doomed attempt to defeat or delay the new policy approach, but were outwitted tactically by its supporters, entrenched both widely across the party and in its high places. The key amendment to approve *The Industrial Charter* as a clear statement of the party's policy (rather than just to note it for further debate, as the nervous framers of the conference agenda had suggested) was moved by Reginald Maudling, both the party candidate for Barnet and one of the CRD staffers who had worked for the original committee. Faced with hysterical calls to vote down the amendment in order to 'save the Conservative Party and England', the Conference preferred Maudling's more balanced language and approach; hundreds voted for his motion and only three against, so that the *Charter* was emphatically approved.

In the Conservative Party, though, policy could still only be made by the Leader, who had neither attended the Conference debate (as was normal for all Party Conferences until 1965), nor been present when the shadow cabinet had endorsed the policy in the spring. It was very likely in fact that Churchill had still not fully read the document, and he certainly jibbed at endorsing it in the terms offered to him (again by Maudling) for a paragraph in his rally speech that would close the Conference week. But when told that this was what the party had voted for, Churchill acquiesced with the words 'in that case leave it in'; and if he read that particular paragraph without enthusiasm – a practice he often employed when obliged to read words that were not his own – then he did none the less read it, and thus authoritatively described *The Industrial Charter* as 'the official policy of the Party', language he had never applied to anything published by the PWPCC.

From this point on, much detailed work needed to be done before the party had what in CRD parlance came to be known as 'a white fish document' (a policy statement that covered all possible questions for an election campaign, including the future of the white fish industry), but the framework of an approach was authoritatively in place and the course set. The party's policy famine that had existed since 1940 was over; it had both insisted on maintaining its historic identity and on developing an up-to-date policy stance, and together these strategic decisions would enable Conservatives, in the 1950s as in the 1930s, to seize the middle ground and to win and hold power. It would also follow fairly logically from this that the framers of *The Industrial Charter*, such men as Butler, Macmillan, Eccles, Heathcoat Amory and Maudling, would be the ones who would have to deliver the goods domestically for the party in the generation to come, for the acceptance of *The Industrial Charter* gave a substantial boost to their careers as well as to their policy preferences.

13

'Post-War', 1947–57

AT THE END OF the twentieth century historians and politicians still lazily refer to everything since 1945 as 'post-war', a syntactically correct but increasingly unhelpful concept, for, since only a small minority of living Britons have any memory of the Second World War and few of the liveliest political issues of the 1990s can now be traced usefully back to 1945, it is not much more helpful to see contemporary Britain as 'post-war' than to describe it as 'post-Florence Nightingale'. But for one generation after the social and political convulsions of 1940–45, the boundaries of British politics were indeed shaped by the war experience, and it makes little sense to analyse the way in which Conservative politicians functioned in that post-1945 era without asserting first the centrality of the Second World War in their thinking – its origins, its political direction and implications, and its international fall-out. Having had a 'good war' in that widely understood sense – and having learned the widely perceived lessons of the war too – became an important criterion for prospering in the post-war world, both for the Conservative Party as a whole in its political battles with Labour and for individual Tory politicians pursuing their own careers.

The presence of Winston Churchill as Conservative Leader right through to 1955 ensured not only that the war remained central to Conservative thinking, but that the party's record on Appeasement in the 1930s also remained a live issue in political debate. One of Churchill's chief objectives after 1945 was to 'justify' himself 'before History', and if that meant bruising some important figures in the party that he now led then so much the worse for them. He therefore laboured mightily for almost ten years after 1945 on his six volumes of *War Memoirs*, the first two volumes of which set out as the literary orthodoxy for more than twenty years his own view of the 1930s and the early months of the war, a story in which many old scores could be settled. Baldwin, Neville Chamberlain, the whips and the party machine, and by implication the bulk of parliamentary Conservatives too, were all branded as 'Appeasers', as Churchill gave that word its over-easy association with cowardice and spinelessness as well as with unwisdom. Since he was writing only about foreign and defence matters, the domestic constraints within which Conservative leaders in the 1930s had had to make those policies received little attention, and the real domestic achievements of the Baldwin and Chamberlain era of Conservatism were hardly even mentioned.

Churchill therefore completed the process that the writers of *Guilty Men* and other such polemics had begun during the war years. As a result, the Conservative Party became thoroughly ashamed of its recent past and determined to show that it had purged all such influences from its current thinking. Sir Keith Joseph admitted, decades later, that when he was a young man his party had 'found it hard to avoid the feeling that somehow the lean and tight-lipped mufflered men in the 1930s dole queue were at least partly our fault'. There were a few Conservatives of the next generation who battled against this defeatist tide – as, for example, Iain Macleod was to do in writing the biography intended to rescue the reputation of Neville Chamberlain – but it was always an uphill struggle, involving the tricky task of confronting the party's greatest asset on his home ground. Most Conservatives were happier to knuckle down and accept the new orthodoxy, which stated that 1940 had marked both the end of 'twenty years of shame' and the dawn of 'Churchill's day', as Alan Bennett summarized that new orthodoxy in his play *Forty Years On* (1968).

In theory at least, Conservatives were freer to challenge the parallel domestic myth, peddled by the left rather than by Churchill, which was that Britain between 1919 and 1939 had been one long period of depression and deprivation, the leaderless, 'locust years' of the century in which nothing positive had been aimed at and nothing worth mentioning had been achieved. This was to say the least a gross misrepresentation of the 1920s and 1930s, what a Tory pamphlet of 1947 called 'the lie about Tory misrule' before 1939. As Labour first had to tighten rationing and controls when the war ended in 1945, and then fell into a period of savage austerity in 1947, there were openings for Conservatives to exploit in order to defend their pre-war record. At a detailed level, it could be shown that even the unemployed of the 1930s had enjoyed a better diet than the average men and women had to survive on in 1947, and in that year the party also mounted a full-scale exhibition, 'Trust the People', in which the most elaborate charts and diagrams explained how prosperous and well-fed Britons had been before 1939, compared with their experiences under Attlee, when they had to 'shiver with Shinwell and starve with Strachey' (as a Conservative slogan had it). None of this seems to have made much difference to the popular view, and in the early 1950s there remained in industrial areas a deeply ingrained conviction that a Tory return to power would bring about mass unemployment, the means test and the dole, fears that contributed in 1951 to the largest-ever Labour vote. Not until revisionist historians got to work in the 1960s did the reputation of inter-war Britain begin to recover, and even then it was only the younger generation who were receptive to a more balanced view; in Britain's coalfields, Tory candidates were still occasionally spat upon in the 1960s by older miners with vivid memories of the 'Slump'.

To a large extent, the Conservative Party therefore tacitly drew a line under its own past, made little attempt to save the reputations of Baldwin and Chamberlain, and stressed change rather than continuity both in its own affairs and in its policy. But for all that, the 1930s and the war remained embedded in its own collective mind as a talisman. Churchill survived as Party Leader after the defeat of 1945 largely because his front-benchers had not the heart to ditch the man that most saw – for all his faults – as Britain's saviour in 1940, and because in fighting off challenges to his leadership Churchill demonstrated exactly the mixture of resolution and bloody-mindedness that had made him such an asset in his 'finest hour'. As he aged, he was increasingly loved and admired by the party rank and file, and even in opposition between 1945 and 1951 he was able to stage a series of international successes that sailed him straight back into the 'statesman' class while most of his younger challengers seemed becalmed as mere politicians. Even in those international successes his claim on the world's attention was based on the view that he had been uniquely far-sighted in the 1930s and the saviour of freedom in and after 1940. They did, though, keep him constantly in the public eye, and ensured that he remained on close terms with the world's leaders, no small advantage to the Leader of an Opposition so heavily outnumbered in the Commons.

For most of the time, though, Churchill did not use this weight and reputation in any party cause, for he spent far more time on his memoirs and his international jaunts than he did on the affairs of the party that he led. While ready to fire with both barrels whenever there was a confidence debate or a big party rally, and rarely missing debates on India (which continued to fascinate him during its last battles for independence), he rarely put in the time or endured the drudgery that were needed to keep up the party's end in detailed legislative debates on nationalization and welfare reform. In effect, the leadership of the party in the Commons fell to Eden because Churchill was usually not there, and it was Eden too who chaired most of the business meetings of the shadow cabinet and most detailed discussions of debating tactics – at least until 1949, when Churchill sensed that the approach of an election gave party debates a greater relevance to what he might have to do if re-elected to office.

The party was therefore not actually led by Churchill after 1945 any more than it had been led by him during the war, but with the crucial difference that in peacetime and in opposition other hands could seize the tiller of party authority rather than leaving the vessel to drift with the tide and swing in the wind. Churchill was simply not present often enough to exercise even the veto power of an absentee landlord on the development of the party estate, and he was certainly not able to ensure the appointment of his favourites to the key positions among the tenancy.

Perhaps the most serious way in which the war remained a current factor in the party was in the extent to which it blighted the later career of Anthony Eden, who became de facto Deputy Leader when, in 1942, Churchill advised the king that he should turn to Eden if Churchill failed to return from one of his wartime missions abroad. The party had not been consulted about this development, and the ageing Churchill himself soon regretted the nomination of a successor, but it was a decision that, once made, could scarcely be revoked. When Churchill went to the United States in 1946, Eden was informally appointed Conservative Leader in his absence, and those front-benchers who unavailingly urged Churchill to retire at about this time all assumed that Eden would take his place. This was, though, the weakness of their position, for Eden, who had a strong sense of personal honour (much like Austen Chamberlain, whose PPS he had been in the 1920s) and whose career had been for better or for worse yoked together with Churchill's in 1940, could not bring himself to do anything that might seem ungrateful or unduly ambitious. Churchill ruthlessly exploited the younger man's reluctance to push him out, and when Churchill and Eden visited Washington together in 1952, the Prime Minister took to referring to Eden in front of his American hosts as 'the remainderman', a cruel jibe that exactly reflected the fact that Eden's future depended on his own death or retirement – and that Eden was not at all enjoying the lengthy period in waiting.

When Churchill had a stroke in 1949, the shadow cabinet concealed the fact rather than use it as an unmissable opportunity to install Eden in his place, and when the same thing happened to Churchill as Prime Minister in 1953 (with the added complication that Eden was at that time seriously ill too), the seventy-eight-year-old Churchill once again survived as Leader. In part this reflected not only Eden's hesitations, but the jockeying for position lower down, a politicking that owed at least something to memories of the war. Until he died at the age of only fifty-four in 1950, the third man in the party after Churchill and Eden was Oliver Stanley, who enjoyed the triple advantage of having been in Chamberlain's Cabinet, in army service, and then a member of Churchill's wartime Cabinet too. After 1950 things were much less straightforward. In the vacuum at the top created by Eden and Churchill's simultaneous indisposition in 1953, Rab Butler acted as Prime Minister since he was Chancellor of the Exchequer and therefore the senior minister in the Commons, but Lord Salisbury took over the Foreign Office, and elaborate (and almost certainly unconstitutional) plans were made to make him acting Prime Minister if Churchill should die, solely to keep Butler out and hold the place open for Eden on his return. The reasoning behind this was that in 1938, the year of Munich, Butler had been Chamberlain's man as Under-Secretary at the Foreign Office and he had toyed with the idea of a compromise peace with Germany in 1940. In contrast, Eden and Salisbury had resigned rather than appease the Fascist dictators (or at least that is what they now claimed, though the actual reasons for Eden's resignation in 1938 were far more ambiguous). When Eden himself retired after the Suez crisis of 1956, the contest for the succession between Butler and Macmillan was again widely reported in these terms, with the defeat of Butler interpreted as a sign that the Conservatives would not have an 'Appeaser' as their Leader. The truth was again more complex, for Butler had done more than enough during the recent Suez crisis to inspire anew a widespread lack of respect in the party, while Macmillan had at least tried to stand up for British power and prestige in the Middle East; at the least, recent events had reinforced earlier attitudes to both men, and arguably it was by then the recent events that mattered most.

As time passed, the question of having had 'a good war' was less of an issue in practice (though the press continued to say otherwise, and for older backbenchers it could still matter in their assessment of their leaders). In the next battle for the party succession, in 1963, Macmillan backed first Quintin Hogg and then Lord Home (both strong supporters of Chamberlain in 1938, while Home had actually been at Munich himself as Chamberlain's PPS) in order to keep Butler out of Downing Street but, in his personal assessment of Home, Macmillan convinced himself that if only he had been the right age then he would have fought like a hero with the guardsmen of 1914. If resistance to Butler still owed something to perceptions that he was in some sense weak, this derived by then mainly from the party's experience of him since 1945.

For Macmillan the story was more positive, for the war years and Churchill's patronage had enabled him to develop from a maverick backbencher – the Tory Tam Dalyell of his day – into a man who understood and was fascinated by the exercise of ministerial power, and who had shown himself to be rather good at it. In opposition after 1945, as one of the first defeated Tories to return to the Commons at an arranged by-election, Macmillan began to show evidence of a formidable ambition, and to relocate himself in the centre of the party as it was being reconstructed. He worked hard at the day-to-day business of the Commons, he bombarded Churchill and other colleagues with helpful advice, and he put himself about to speak at regional party events and so get himself known. His moustache was trimmed, his clothes became more traditional in cut and in style, he waved to crowds (often without even waiting for them to wave at him first); the rounded glasses and uneven teeth that had been his trademark in the 1930s both vanished. In the place of the earnest young man who had liked to give his colleagues lectures on economics emerged a debonair charmer with an elaborately aristocratic and 'Edwardian' insouciance. Although Macmillan was not among the first group of Conservatives summoned to office by Churchill in 1951 – a fact that caused him agonies of disappointment – his eventual post as Minister of Housing was both evidence that he was already seen as an executive achiever and the opportunity for executive action on which his later career would be based. Even that opportunity came partly because Churchill remembered that in 1941 Macmillan had been an enthusiastic butcher of red tape at Lord Beaverbrook's wartime Ministry of Supply.

It was mainly in foreign and defence matters, though, that the war experience became the virility test for post-war Conservatives, and here the real victim was certainly Eden. His resignation from Chamberlain's government (actually as much to do with pride and vanity as with any disagreement over policy) had retrospectively been seen, not least by

Churchill in his bestselling *War Memoirs*, as the final moment at which Chamberlainite Toryism lost touch with what was best in the party's traditions. During the war and afterwards, Eden was constantly in disagreement with Churchill over foreign and defence matters. He regretted Churchill's increasingly anti-Russian stance, his contempt for post-war France, his courting of the Americans, and his apparent support for a 'United States of Europe', all of which Eden saw as over-sensationalized and under-researched pieces of political buccaneering that should not be the basis of a proper foreign policy. But the onset of the Cold War ensured that in most of these areas events had by 1951 vindicated Churchill rather than Eden.

With the party's return to office in 1951, Eden was more sensitive than Churchill needed to be to charges from the more hawkish Conservative MPs that British policy towards Russia and towards independence movements in the colonies was insufficiently robust. As Foreign Secretary between 1951 and 1955, he now preferred a tougher line with Russia than Churchill was pursuing, but he was also trying to continue the difficult task of matching British commitments around the world to the reduced resources with which Britain had emerged from the war, while Churchill more irresponsibly asserted that even as an empire in decline Britain could 'punch above our weight' because of the quality of its statecraft. Against insurgency in Malaya and in Kenya, the Churchill government took strong action that ultimately proved successful – in Cyprus equally strong action failed only later in the decade – but these were all colonies in which Britain at that time intended to stay on for some years ahead. The crux came with the withdrawal of British troops from Egypt in 1954, and in particular from the Suez Canal zone. Egypt was a country which had never been a formal part of the British empire, never a colony of settlement or an important economic asset, but it was one which, because of the Desert War and the Battle of Alamein, evoked the most acute memories of 1939–45. Because British withdrawal came in the face of Egyptian nationalist demands that would have been resisted in earlier years, this could all too easily be portrayed as a new example of 'appeasement' from weakness and lack of willpower.

Churchill, who was himself hesitant about military withdrawal from Suez (growling, for example, that he had not previously known that Munich was in Egypt), eventually came round to support the idea on the idiosyncratic ground that such conventional bases would be useless anyway if the next war was – as predicted – a nuclear one and hence over in minutes. He rallied to Eden's support and put his own wartime reputation on the line at a meeting of the 1922 Committee in order to pull the backbenchers into line. That crisis of 1954 was, though, the moment at which the Conservative right started to move away from the front bench's international policy, a development that would lead on in due course to resistance to decolonization, to opposition to joining the EEC when Britain applied in 1961 and in 1970, and more generally (through the activities of the Monday Club) to the repeated allegation that British ministers knew only how to retreat when British interests were challenged abroad, a grumble that went on until given the lie by the Falklands War of 1982 – and then resurfaced in the Europhobia of the 1990s.

In the short term, the vehicles for this viewpoint were the Suez Group of backbenchers in the Commons, including such rising young men as Julian Amery and Enoch Powell as well as backbenchers who had little hope of personal preferment but plenty of kinfolk and business interests in the empire. The same line was taken by the League of Empire Loyalists, which made up in vigour and in vitriol what it lacked in numbers, and was influential mainly through the backing of the weekly magazine *Time and Tide*. For all of these people, the scapegoat for Britain's withdrawal from Egypt (as a symbol of 'retreat' in general) was not Churchill but Eden, a diagnosis that seemed to gain confirmation from the regular attacks on Eden by Churchill's journalist son Randolph – attacks that became entirely uninhibited as soon as Churchill finally retired and Eden became Prime Minister in 1955.

Eden therefore reached the top with a known specialism in foreign affairs (and a widespread assumption that he did not know the domestic side of the business anything like so well), but with a gut feeling entertained by many in high places that he could not be trusted to take a firm line in a crisis. His early months were spectacularly unlucky both at home and abroad, for a popular budget and a quick election victory in April–May 1955 led on only to an early credit squeeze, a series of damaging strikes and international setbacks in the Middle East. By the end of his first year as Prime Minister, Eden was having to announce repeatedly that he was not going to resign, the result of press speculations that such announcements failed to quell; he was being sniped at increasingly by the Suez Group and other backbenchers in his own party, and even Tory papers were becoming openly hostile. Early in 1956 an editorial in the *Daily Telegraph*, after reminding its readers that Eden tended when speaking to strike his fist into an open palm in order to emphasize the point he was making, remarked that in practice his premiership had lacked 'the smack of firm government', a phrase that was widely recycled and repeated because it so neatly summarized what was already being said. It was said just about as often that Eden was also inadequate as a successor to Churchill, that he was simply not up to the top job.

Such attacks only increased Eden's personal sense of isolation and his conviction that he was the subject of attacks based on malice and jealousy, but they also made him ever more determined to prove himself worthy by taking action that would confound his critics. The catalyst came when Egypt's Colonel Nasser, after a complex negotiation with the United States failed to win him foreign aid, nationalized the Suez Canal Company in order to raise the needed resources himself. The legality of the issue was complicated, for the canal was owned by an international company based in Paris, with a substantial British shareholding dating back to Disraeli's celebrated purchase – and was therefore a central part of the myth of Tory imperialism. In any case, the legalities rapidly sank from view as Britain and France, the two countries which made greatest use of the canal and which depended on it for oil supplies and other trade, sought but failed to get American help for immediate action, military or otherwise, which would make Nasser give back the canal.

Almost all analyses of the Suez situation referred back to the Second World War for points of reference. Eden simply saw Nasser as a new dictator who must be stopped if the west was to avoid the mistakes that had led in the 1930s to world war, and even the Labour Leader Gaitskell, who eventually denounced Eden as a warmonger, initially compared Nasser with Hitler, remarking that 'we have seen it all before'. When the British and French forces invaded Egypt in November 1956 it was noted – proudly – that the invasion fleet was larger than had been used on D-Day in 1944, though since the earlier bombing attack lacked the formality of a declaration of war Pearl Harbor in 1941 might have made a better comparison.

As the months dragged on between July and November (months eaten up by extraordinarily duplicitous American foreign policy), the Suez Group's hawkish position was taken up by an increasingly wide cross-section of Conservatives, and at the Party Conference in October the demands for early and decisive action were almost universal. Against that, Eden was striving not to part company with the Americans, on whom western Europe's defence now really rested, and to carry with him a Cabinet that included not only the endlessly hesitating Butler and other less senior ministers who were threatening resignation if armed force was used, but a few, like Macmillan, who were threatening to leave the Cabinet if it was *not* (and asking provocatively what the late war had been *for* if Britain was now going to surrender spinelessly to such minor powers as Egypt). Under such pressures, Eden did indeed fail to live up to the demands of the post, drifting into a policy that matched the Americans for duplicity but had much less chance of success. Britain and France came together to fight in 1956 – as they had not done in 1936 or in 1938 – but ruined the point of what they were doing by lying about their cooperation with Israel. The hope was that the reluctant United States would back Britain once a shooting war started, but in the event the American administration – outraged by the deception involved and ignoring its own responsibility for what had happened – did everything possible first to stop the invasion from succeeding, and then to ensure that Britain and France had to withdraw in circumstances in which their humiliation was as public as possible.

Two junior ministers resigned from Eden's government, but it is clear that more than one in the Cabinet was wholly out of sympathy with what he was doing and stayed on only to avoid splitting the country and the party during a war. Once his policy had failed, and with his health in ruins anyway, Eden took his doctor's advice and went to the West Indies to recuperate, a retreat that his critics saw as a final sign of his weakness, a desertion of his post (as a constituency activist wrote in to Central Office) that Churchill would never have contemplated. Butler's temporary responsibility for managing Britain's Middle Eastern retreat while Eden was away did not do his future prospects much good either, while Macmillan's footwork over the same weeks was exemplary, but the likelihood was that the crisis itself rather than its aftermath had already given Macmillan the air of a decisive commander and Butler the reputation of a wobbler. When Eden resigned office in January 1957, shortly after returning to London, and thereby forestalled moves that would almost certainly have driven him out anyway, Macmillan was fairly decisively chosen by the Cabinet to succeed him.

The inheritance did not seem to be a very positive one, and neither Macmillan himself nor most of his ministers expected the new government to last for more than a few weeks. The country had after all suffered a major international humiliation as the result of a policy over which no Cabinet minister had resigned (and most of the same men continued to serve under Macmillan – who anyway had more personal responsibility for Suez than anyone except Eden). At home the economy was in recession, the party in open revolt, the Liberals picking up Tory votes at by-elections and a new challenge to the established parties beginning to appear on the right. It seemed indeed a damnable inheritance that Macmillan had so avidly schemed to acquire between November 1956 and January 1957, and scarcely anyone then foresaw that he would prove to be one of the greatest party leaders of the century, that he would lead Conservatives to a landslide victory thirty-three months later, and that he would initiate policy reviews that would truly mark the end of 'post-war' continuities in defence and foreign policy, and to a large extent at home too. The room for manoeuvre that allowed Macmillan to do these things arose from a recovery on the domestic side of the party's history since 1945 – a recovery that had seemed in its way just as unlikely as Macmillan's prospering did in 1957. For while paying lip-service to the idea that 1940–45 was a watershed in Britain's political life, in the party's own affairs and in the domestic policy that they put before the country, the Conservatives had quietly reconstructed a good deal of continuity with the despised 1930s, and here too it would be the Macmillan period after 1957 that truly marked the beginning of the new.

The most directly controllable aspect of a party recovery from the shambles of 1945 would be the 'restoration' of the organization (as experienced party hands like R. A. Butler were always careful to call it, rather than a revolution, a renewal or a fresh start). The key figure here was one who owed no exclusive loyalty to either the Chamberlain or the Churchill/Eden factions of the party before 1940. Lord Woolton had assisted in Chamberlain's preparations for war before 1939 (for which he had received his peerage) and had also held office under Churchill, but he did not actually join the Conservative Party until after its 1945 defeat. In his own background he fortuitously represented two different strands of what would be the party's public identity in the post-war years, for as a young man on Merseyside he had devoted much time to social work, and he had then gone on to become one of the leading managerial figures in the retail trade. As British Conservatism after 1945 had to make the case for capitalism with a human face, and as it had to work at 'the rendering of the traditionalist régime respectable in the eyes of the prosperous working class which it had begotten' (as Butler later put it), then Woolton offered a very acceptable public face as Party Chairman through from 1946 to 1955, so popular indeed that Churchill himself became jealous and tried (but failed) to fire him in 1952.

Woolton had, though, little to do with the development of actual policy, and had been chosen more for his presentational skills than for what he represented. His business career had demonstrated formidable organizational talents, and his wartime period as Minister of Food had shown not only further evidence of this in the public sphere, but also his quite remarkable ability through radio broadcasting to put across the ideas behind his policies and to mobilize support for them. When Macmillan called Woolton 'the great salesman' he was paying tribute to far more than his background as a shop manager, for he also recognized powers of communication and inspiration that would now also be at the party's service. His more popular nickname in the party, 'Uncle Fred', suggests the widespread affection that he was also able to generate through the genially bluff persona of a self-made man.

Directly, Woolton built up the numbers, training and calibre of the headquarters staff at Central Office and in regional offices around the country, he added a broadcasting department to older communications activities, and he both improved existing facilities at Abbey House in Victoria Street (to which Central Office moved in 1946) and built up a fund over time to allow the building of a purpose-built Central Office in Smith Square (eventually opened in 1958). Under Woolton the central party organization reached a pinnacle broadly comparable in numbers and technical expertise to the position that Davidson had built up by 1929.

In order to accomplish these tasks, Woolton (like Davidson) also had to be a consummately successful fundraiser, and this he pursued along two parallel tracks. At one level, and in a secrecy that was barely penetrable even forty years later, the Conservative Board of Finance which had been established at the end of the war sought large donations from wealthy individuals and from industry, an operation that produced something like half of all the money that Woolton spent but to which he directed practically no public attention. The Labour government's nationalization and planning programmes, and the general perception among British industrialists that they would fare better under a Conservative government, were both vital here; for these influences produced a growing conviction that capitalism would have to invest in its own fight for survival, partly by helping the Conservatives with money, partly by forming front organizations such as Aims of Industry and British United Industrialists, which both channelled further money to Central Office and conducted poster, leaflet, letter-writing and press advertising campaigns of their own. The steel industry, sugar refiners like Tate and Lyle, and the road

Anti-nationalization campaigning on every sugar packet, c. 1949

hauliers were particularly active in fighting Labour, shoulder to shoulder with the Conservatives, and the net effect was a big increase in the capacity of the Conservatives themselves to fight Labour with literature, stories in the press, films, and all the other arts of the political campaign.

Little public attention was directed to this by the party, for an open alliance with capitalism in precisely the generation in which many working-class voters were deeply suspicious of Conservatives as a class enemy would be to give Labour too big an advantage. Since Conservative Party accounts were not then published – and would not be in the future, even in the most basic form, until the late 1960s – the party's actual dependence on industrial contributions could not be analysed by anyone outside the Party Treasurer's office, but attention was also diverted by the continuous highlighting of the other side of the party's fundraising. As soon as he became Chairman, Woolton superintended during 1946–7 the recovery of the party's mass membership from its wartime collapse, and then drove onwards to achieve further increases until it reached its highest ever level at the end of the decade. By 1952 there were 2.8 million Conservative Party members in England and Wales, and well over 3 million in total when Scotland was added in, easily the largest number of individually subscribing members that any political party in Britain has ever managed to have on its books. While the safer Conservative seats always had the largest totals – so large indeed that in parts of the Home Counties and the London suburbs a third of all the Tory voters were also annual subscribers – such enormous national totals could only be achieved with large numbers of members in industrial areas too, only the coalfields stubbornly resisting this surge in Tory membership. Why, though, did they join? In part no doubt because in those grey years of austerity the newly revived and extremely active local Tory branches offered a social opportunity that faced little competition; in part because the austerity itself (when continued for years after the war) generated both among middle-class voters and among workers with aspirations to social mobility a belief that they deserved better, and that the Tories would give it to them; and in part certainly because with 'Churchill to lead us and Woolton to feed us' (as a local Tory slogan had it in Yorkshire) the party's leaders did indeed exert a strong attraction to join them in their anti-socialist campaigning.

There were important direct advantages from such a large membership, for it both ensured that the party would be fully represented in the various national and local communities, councils and voluntary organizations at every level, and also provided manpower for elections and other party campaigns (especially from the keen and sometimes hyperactive Young Conservatives, a new movement launched in 1945, which had itself attracted over 200,000 members by 1950). All of this reduced the damaging impression that in 1945 the party had represented only a narrow sectional interest, but it also produced a lot of money, for even with a minimum party subscription of half a crown (12.5p – where there was a minimum at all), 3 million subscribers collectively put up a lot of money. In practice the average was well above the minimum and subscription income was anyway approximately doubled when these same members attended the party's thousands of garden parties, bazaars, coffee mornings and strawberry teas.

Woolton therefore celebrated this huge outpouring of voluntarist effort (what a Party Treasurer shortly afterwards called 'the best money that we have politically') and refused to explain how much of the party's actual expenditure it covered. In 1947 he enthused over 'money ... being subscribed in half crowns, five shillings and guineas. Old age pensioners had sent a few pence in stamps, saying that their present living conditions were intolerable.' At the lower level, the healthy finances of the constituency parties allowed most constituencies to become self-supporting –

which was a good reason why too much attention paid to industrial contributions at the centre would anyway have been misleading, for constituencies collectively spent far more than Woolton did at the centre. As a result the party could once again recruit a large band of trained and skilled career agents; by 1950 almost all winnable constituencies had a full-time agent, and in strongholds like Birmingham, where something like seventy party employees covered thirteen constituencies, a very tight organization indeed had been restored. Since there was a near complete redistribution of constituency boundaries in 1948, and postal votes were introduced in the same year (providing a substantial bonus to well-organized local parties – perhaps a big enough bonus to explain the Conservative election victory in 1951), this was an era in which local organizational activity paid measurable dividends.

Reform of the rules also played its part, though once again continuities were ignored and novelties stressed in a party keen to be seen to have cut adrift from its past, a process which came together in the 'Maxwell Fyfe Report' of 1949. This covered two main areas, both financial: the payments by candidates to their own local associations and the contributions that the associations themselves paid to the centre. In each case what happened in 1949 was the adoption of rules to force the most reluctant constituencies to do what some had begun to do before 1939 and many more had moved towards during and since the war. The change in rules about candidates had come about largely because wartime taxation had drastically reduced the number of rich men who could afford to water their constituencies lavishly in the hope of getting elected, so that reliance on rich men became increasingly dangerous as well as out of keeping with the temper of a more democratic era. Building on past good practice, the Maxwell Fyfe Report (which became compulsory for all constituencies once the National Union's Central Council had approved it in 1949) laid down that no candidate could pay more than a token amount to his own local party, none could pay his own election expenses, none must be asked to contribute to local charities and good causes, and no financial discussions at all must take place with potential candidates during an actual selection process. In parallel with this, a new system of quota payments was developed, whereby the constituencies would between them contribute about £200,000 a year to the central funds (each local association paying a share calculated by a complex formula which took account of the differing strengths of the Tory vote in each area). The burgeoning local memberships therefore had to take on two additional responsibilities financially: both the full cost of looking after their own local organizations and campaigning, and a share of the cost of Central Office, a spur that ensured that they would have to remain active in fundraising in the years ahead.

In each case, the new rules were not quite universally observed in practice, though infringements of the candidates' rules were few and constituencies that paid nothing at all to 'quota' when the scheme had been going for a few years were also relatively rare. What had happened was a tilting of the balance, so that what a few, progressive constituencies had long practised now became the expectation of all and the practice of nearly all for the future. It should perhaps be emphasized, though, that whereas these new rules applied in England and Wales and were paralleled by similar changes in Scotland, no change of the financial arrangements took place in Ulster, where Unionist candidates remained mainly responsible for financing their own very expensive campaigns, right through to the point where relations between Conservatives and Unionists were severed in the 1970s.

The net impact of these changes had as much to do with public relations as with practical activities, for the wider membership and the quota system helpfully obscured the overall balance of fundraising, and both the mass membership and the new selection rules provided excellent opportunities to argue that the Conservatives had once again become a 'national' party along Disraelian lines, representative of all the classes and communities in the nation. The truth was that the social character of the parliamentary party changed only very slowly, but the arrival in the Commons in the first election after 1945 of an especially talented 'class of 1950' – and especially 'the premier cru of that vintage' (as *The Economist* put it), the One Nation Group founded by such younger and relatively unprivileged MPs as Iain Macleod, Edward Heath and Robert Carr – seemed to clinch the argument that Conservatism had become less of an exclusive club of the rich and aristocratic. Some of these 'new' men had, like Macleod himself and Reginald Maudling, already fought seats and lost in 1945, and most had been selected for winnable seats in 1947–8 before the Maxwell Fyfe rules were applied, but they seemed nevertheless a powerful symbol of all that had changed in the party since 1945, and scarcely anyone described all of this as the culmination of trends that had begun long before the war.

Despite all the misleading hype, these developments did mark a difference, for the party which had in 1940 moved a step backwards up the social ladder in putting itself under a man born in Blenheim Palace (and who would in due course be succeeded in turn by a scion of the Durham gentry in 1955, by the Duke of Devonshire's son-in-law in 1957, and by a Scottish earl in 1963) was now moving back in the broadening direction that Bonar Law's selection as Leader had indicated in 1911. It would be another generation before the class of 1950 made it to the top of the party, and not until 1965 that the first man from a background comparable to Bonar Law's again became Leader. By that time many of the new men had become as indistinguishable as had Edward Heath himself from the more traditional Tory establishment, whether in their accents or their behaviour, and it was the further changes in the social character of the party that were already by then happening lower down that produced the 'peasants' revolt' that overthrew Heath himself in 1975 and unleashed the real social revolution that then followed. Along that road 'Maxwell Fyfe' was a milestone, though the number of miles yet to be travelled was appreciably greater than was understood at the time. There was also a less-noticed development brought about by the changed financial relationship between candidates and their local supporters; as MP for Ashford, William Deedes detected 'a subtle change' on the part of his Tory supporters, who demanded more of his attention now that they were paying the piper.

In retrospect, one final area of organizational reform in the 1940s which fitted particularly well into the idea that the party had crossed a social divide after 1945 was on the policy side. Here apparent continuity masked a major change, for the Research Department re-created in 1946 bore little resemblance to the tiny team of four graduate staff that had existed in the 1930s. Initially, there were now three separate units, a library to service other sections and back up campaigning by Central Office, a secretariat to provide front-benchers with the professional support which would come from the civil service when the party was in power, and a research unit to do longer-term thinking about party policy. In practice these never worked independently and in 1948 they were merged into one reconstructed Research Department, which aimed to fulfil all three functions, but in practice was rarely to find the time or the opportunity for longer-term forward thinking. The staff consisted in 1948 (and continued to do for long afterwards) of about two dozen full-time graduate research officers, a mixture of career professionals and aspirant politicians; the launching pad that it provided for the careers of Macleod, Powell and Maudling ensured that its theoretical status as a forum of 'backroom' research would never adequately describe its function, for all of these (and others) were extremely pro-active both in writing briefs and speeches for their seniors and in debating issues and policy documents as they emerged.

The effect of this, especially when translated via the class of 1950 into the parliaments of the 1950s, was to raise the intellectual calibre of official Conservatism. This was far from accidental, for the CRD set out to publish some of its work as 'Third Programme efforts' (writings aimed, like BBC radio's arts channel of the time, at 'the egghead vote'). It commissioned Quintin Hogg to write the influential Penguin Special *The Case for Conservatism*, it ensured that policy documents were factually accurate and rigorously thought-out by able minds, and it worked with the new Conservative Political Centre, and after 1950 with the Bow Group too, to give thinking Conservatives a focal point within the party machine. Many of those involved on this side of the party understood well that before 1945 the party had become isolated from the 'intelligentsia', whose opinion-forming influence greatly exceeded its own voting power, and they were determined to tilt this balance of ideas in the party's favour. For a generation it became fashionable in British universities to support the Conservatives – as it had certainly not been in 1945. Where Macmillan and his cronies in the 1920s had been tolerated condescendingly by backbench colleagues who could barely understand their wish to read and to write books on political issues, the intellectual dimension of Conservatism in the 1950s was welcomed by many and at least tolerated by the rest.

None of this could have helped much in the party's recovery from 1945 if the content of policy had not also been perceived to have changed in the aftermath of election defeat. For it was as a move towards the political centre that the Conservative policy review was mainly reported, and with R. A. Butler at the heart of the operation as chairman both of the Research Department and of the party's Advisory Committee on Policy and Political Education it is hard to see how it could have been otherwise.

Whatever its content, *The Industrial Charter* of 1947 was undeniably a public relations success of the first order. It received a broad welcome right across the spectrum of the press (except for a few growls from the *Daily Express* – but, as Macmillan pointed out, the opposition of Lord Beaverbrook was almost a badge of approval for Tories after what he had done to their party in the recent past) and it sold huge numbers of copies within a party desperate for evidence that the policy vacuum of 1939–45 had been filled. As a 'Charter' (a word apparently coined by Macmillan even before the Industrial Policy Committee got to work), it was marketed as something akin to a social contract with the British people, and hence a document of more than ephemeral significance. When the Party Conference nervously but overwhelmingly approved it in October 1947 and Churchill grudgingly then gave it the stamp of official approval, a decisive step back towards political credibility had been taken. Later Conservative policy documents (notably 1949's *The Right Road for Britain* which, as the continuity of titles suggested, led straight to the 1950 manifesto, *This Is the Road*) put flesh on the bones, but, right through to the 1951 election, *The Industrial Charter*'s approach remained the key to understanding what the Conservative Party offered. It seems clear that the winning of so many ex-Liberal votes in 1950 and 1951, without which the party could simply not have recovered power, owed a good deal to the general perception created in and through *The Industrial Charter* – that Conservatives were now moderate, interested in the nation as a whole, and up to date.

In office after 1951, much that the *Charter* had made explicit remained central. It had, for example, promised 'a stable level of employment', but in the prosperous 1950s that pledge was not hard to carry out; by the 1955 election unemployment had never exceeded half a million insured workers, a fraction of the figures for the 1920s and 1930s. The weapons to achieve this desirable objective would be derived from Keynesian economics, which the *Charter* had explicitly endorsed even while Labour was still more committed to physical planning. In government, the use of these similar weapons by Gaitskell for Labour and Butler for the Conservatives led some to identify a consensual 'Mr Butskell' (as *The Economist* described a composite all-party Chancellor of the Exchequer) who had effectively taken economics out of politics. This was at the least vastly overstated, for the use of similar tools never implied that the parties were working from the same political designs, and even in 1952 Gaitskell was horrified by Butler's attempt to move towards free exchange rates (a gambit that scared the Cabinet too, and thus had to wait another twenty years). The *Charter* paid a warm tribute to the trades unions' 'great and vital part to play in industry', and when Churchill returned to office after 1951 there were actually fewer strikes and fewer workers on strike than under Attlee. This was an objective largely achieved by the increasingly criticized tactic of settling disputes at almost any price in order to ensure industrial harmony, but it was a success none the less when it is recalled that Labour had in 1950–1 predicted the certainty of industrial anarchy if the Conservatives returned to power.

The *Charter* did not deal directly with the social services, but other party statements offered pledges in much the same spirit. Conservatives were highly conscious of the popularity of the new National Health Service – the principle of which did indeed derive from joint work between the parties in wartime, work that was itself in part a moving on from more cautious developments under Neville Chamberlain – and they were therefore happy to claim a share in its paternity. It would, though, have been a very different scheme in detail – more selective and more voluntarist – had the Tories won in 1945 and carried it into law. And despite the public support offered to most of what Aneurin Bevan now did in order to bring the NHS to birth, the Conservatives backed the British Medical Association's campaign against an enforced role for doctors in the new structure (another use for the party's growing 'freedom' rhetoric), worried privately about the escalating costs that arose precisely because the NHS *was* so popular, and rejoiced (though quietly and amongst themselves) when in 1951 Labour was forced to make the first breaches in the principle of free provision. It is quite clear, though, that the Conservatives' real preference, as in other social policies such as pensions and education, was for a greater degree of selectivity than they wished to explain to a public taught to associate the concept with the snoopers and the means test of the 1930s.

With the party in power after 1951, and especially when Iain Macleod became Minister of Health in 1952, Conservatives were still very careful about what they said and did, but in practice new emphases and different nuances soon began to appear. The actual principle that would be applied, as Macleod had agreed with his friend Enoch Powell, was to ask of any social service why it should be provided *without* a means test. Over time, though the change was frequently disguised within increases in social spending that years of affluence allowed, Conservative administration of social policies diverged from what they had inherited from Labour, but always stealthily and in ways that prevented Labour from claiming plausibly that any great principle had been abandoned. Social policy can usefully stand as a paradigm for the policy review as a whole, for it had produced by the mid-1950s a practical policy that owed something to Labour's input but something too to the reassertion of older Conservative traditions from before 1939. Over time, the balance in the package would swing back more in the Tory direction, as it became tactically less difficult to resist Labour claims that Tories would actually abolish the NHS and the other social advances of the 1940s, and as it anyway became more difficult for any party to expand provision without facing hard choices about public expenditure and levels of taxation.

On industry as such, *The Industrial Charter* can be seen as demonstrating the party's theoretical commitment to the case for a mixed economy, partnership with the trades unions and state responsibility for public welfare that had been emerging by accretion under all parties for the previous twenty years, but which the Conservative Party had never considered in principle – not least because it had had no full-scale policy review at all since 1924. It has thus often been interpreted in that way by historians who believe that the Tories moved towards a left-leaning 'consensus' after 1945. If some on the Tory right lamented all of this as 'pink socialism' barely distinguishable from the fully blown red variety of Attlee and Bevan, they, like later historians, tended to miss the point that, by setting down the party's principles more clearly than before, Butler's team had not only endorsed the interventionist ideas that Macmillan had been peddling for years but had also endorsed the free enterprise ideas articulated on the Industrial Policy Committee by Oliver Lyttelton and Oliver Stanley.

The nature of this facing-both-ways stance becomes clearer when it is related to the way in which the party developed its industrial policy in relation to Labour's nationalization plans. Little more than token resistance was put up to the taking into state ownership of coal, electricity, gas and the main transport industries, each ruined by years of underinvestment and all of them industries whose owners were happy enough to accept the embrace of the state. But it was only on such pragmatic grounds that the party accepted new state industries (while generally criticizing compensation terms, new management structures and reserved ministerial powers of direction). As effectively the Party Leader in most debates, Eden consistently resisted the argument from the Labour left that state ownership was a public good in itself. In that sense the Tories had scarcely moved on since they had themselves pragmatically taken coal reserves under the wing of the state in the 1930s, but the actual existence of the majority Labour government with a lengthy shopping list had changed the leverage that such a pragmatic approach could have. For in deciding in the same years *not* to support the proposed nationalization of road haulage and of iron and steel, when proposed from the left, and in edging towards the idea of introducing competition for the first time in broadcasting, the Conservatives were also committing themselves to capitalism more clearly than they had ever done before. The battlegrounds chosen had more to do with the industries which themselves chose to fight than with any real party decision at all, but, since these tended to be the profitable ones whose owners had no wish to give up their shares, competition and profitability – the essence of capitalism – emerged in practice as the line that the Conservatives found themselves defending against the future encroachments of the state. The principles that emerged from debates on the floor of the Commons thus converged with the detail that accrued after the principles of *The Industrial Charter* had been agreed, and it makes little sense to analyse one without the other.

The Tory front bench therefore refused to contemplate denationalization of the monopoly industries that had made up most of the Attlee government's programme, but they did commit themselves explicitly to the return both of road haulage and of iron and steel to private ownership. Both those industries contributed heavily to the Tory campaigns and fought hard for their own survival, as did sugar – so hard indeed that Labour gave up its nationalization plan before it was even implemented. Detailed collusion with the City and with the industry ensured that the Conservatives were already well furnished with plans for denationalizing steel when they returned to power in 1951. The defence of the 'mixed economy', as it emerged from both *The Industrial Charter* and from parliamentary debates and political commitments to allies, was thus defined along a line in which the Conservatives (and industry itself) chose to fight; steel became the no man's land of the nationalization debate for thirty years, the symbol of a free enterprise system to which the party was now clearly committed but Labour far from clearly opposed.

The fact that broadcasting was now figuring in these same internal party debates (for, under pressure from his own party, Churchill refused to back Attlee's proposal to renew the BBC's monopoly in 1950 and reserved his position if he became Prime Minister) demonstrated another element of the policy alignment that was in itself hardly new but extremely popular among Tory MPs of all shades. This was the weight which the party now gave to the rights and demands of consumers – who were of course also voters. To an extent this tactic was one which any Opposition would have been likely to pursue in the austere aftermath of a war which had necessitated draconian rationing and unprecedented state controls over ordinary people's lives. Restrictions which had been acceptable in wartime soon palled when they went on (and in some areas of rationing even increased) after 1945. But even when not mentioning explicitly the Tory record from the 1930s, Conservative attacks on the Attlee government reflected a similar approach to the consumerist one that their predecessors had pursued.

Conservatives therefore pushed hard for a relaxation of rationing, and in the process discovered too a belief that competition rather than state organization would be more efficient in encouraging actual production, as well as in generating the public good of greater personal freedom through widely distributed market decisions. This may well be seen as a ruthless exploitation of Labour's problems during terrible years of reconstruction and shortages, problems that any government would have had to face in order to build up exports before consumption and to keep sterling afloat when it again became internationally convertible. To that extent, the Conservatives were fortunate that they were out of power after 1945, and that their return to office coincided with the lessening of those structural problems in the economy, so that rationing could indeed be phased out in the early 1950s without massive problems either for Britain's trade or for her currency. It did also represent, though, a genuine clash of philosophies in which both Labour and Conservatives diverged from their *wartime* compromises when working together in government – as, for example, over egg production, an area of food supply that had virtually no relevance to sterling or to the export trade: Labour's view was that state control (if necessary with batteries of regulations and frequent intimidatory prosecutions to prevent evasion) was both fairer and more efficient than the open market, while the Tories argued (and after 1951 proved, through its implementation) that the abolition of controls would encourage production, increase consumption, cut prices and end both the black market and the need to prosecute ordinary citizens for using it.

By articulating such views fiercely and continuously, and by allying with both producer groups like farmers and consumer groups like the British Housewives' League, the Conservatives put Labour under a good deal of pressure before 1951 and set out their stall for a policy success in office afterwards. Even when Labour bent towards a less interventionist philosophy and initiated its own 'bonfire of controls' (partly because they had become genuinely converted to a more flexible form of economics than physical planning controls, but partly too because Tory-led consumer resistance was too uncomfortable to confront without such bending), socialists of that generation could not compete with Conservatives – and would hardly have wanted to – in an auction of consumerist rhetoric which culminated in the Tory election slogan of 1951, 'Set the People

Free'. When Labour believed that 'the gentleman from Whitehall really does know better what is good for people than the people know themselves', as Douglas Jay argued once again in 1947, then it was fair game for the Conservatives to 'trust the people' (thereby following a Disraelian piece of advice) and so reap the benefits in their votes.

Housing provided an even better example of the same divide opening between the parties. In 1945 electors had told those who surveyed their opinions that housing was their first priority for post-war action, but such was the negative memory of pre-1939 that the Conservatives, who had governed during the great 1930s housing boom, gained nothing at all from that public mood, and in a badly fought campaign did not stress housing policy anyway. For both good and bad reasons Labour did not deliver the goods – forgivably because priority was placed on industrial investment before private consumption (and housebuilding would have had a big impact on trade, through wood and steel imports among other things), more ideologically because the Minister, Aneurin Bevan, was strongly committed to keeping a forest of controls, licences and allocations, which discouraged any builder but those in the state sector from risking capital on actually building houses. By 1950 the crisis had worsened dramatically, for in addition to the destructive effects of the war, the marriages surge of 1946 and the baby-boom of 1947 had greatly increased the number of families seeking a new home. Tory candidates returned from the 1950 election convinced that their party must have a more definite policy. At the Party Conference eight months later the housing debate was a heated one, and (almost for the only time in party history) the advice of the platform, the considered view of the Advisory Committee on Policy and the caution of the Research Department's professionals were all swept away in half an hour by insistent demands from the floor for a specific pledge to build at least 300,000 houses a year.

Having given the pledge (which Labour ministers not only denounced as irresponsible, since it did not concede the subservience of housing policy to the needs of the economy, but also as impractical and unachievable), the Conservatives had now to plan its implementation, for their denunciations of Labour failure would soon come back to haunt them if Tory ministers did no better. Detailed work was done by the Research Department in the last year of opposition, and it was soon recognized both there and by MPs who specialized in the area (like Ernest Marples, who as an accountant had worked for private builders before 1939 and who would be a junior housing minister from 1951) that the best way forward was to re-create the decontrolled market that had built so many houses in the 1930s, and indeed in the Edwardian period too.

Macmillan, Marples and the industrialist Lord Mills at the Housing Ministry therefore set out in 1951 both to use the resources of the state, by quickly channelling money to local authorities for large-scale building schemes which could be launched at once and so re-house large numbers with minimal delay, and at the same time to abolish controls and licences wholesale, thus encouraging the speculative builder to commit his capital and build houses for sale. The resulting success was handled with characteristic flair by Macmillan when he visited the young couple moving into the 300,000th house completed in 1953, with the entire national media present to tell the country the good news. As the debates of 1950 had indicated, this was not a costless achievement, for to get the resources for such massive investment in housing Macmillan regularly had to face down the Treasury's calls for cuts in his programmes in the national economic interest. He succeeded in doing so only because the premier backed him throughout, conscious of housing's position in the paternalist tradition of Toryism, which to him at least Lord Randolph Churchill still epitomized – Winston Churchill still talked, misty-eyed, of helping the humble worker to own his cottage – but conscious too of just how many votes were involved in this policy area's high visibility.

During the thirteen years that the Conservatives were in office after 1951 a quarter of the entire population was rehoused and the proportion of families who were home-owners doubled again to almost half, so bringing what had previously been a middle-class lifestyle within the reach of affluent working-class families for the first time. Politics were important here as well as purely social effects, for, as Woolton put it in 1952, halting the drift towards large council estates would also 'remove in some measure the herding of more people into these huge ... Council housing areas, which become predominantly socialist in political outlook'. What John Turner has called 'social gardening' – the tendency of governments to conduct their domestic policy in a way that improves the political landscape for their party's long-term electability – was scarcely invented in 1951; Herbert Morrison's professed aim to 'build the Tories out of London' by creating council estates in marginal constituencies in the 1930s was a particularly fine earlier example, but the consumerist Tories of the 1950s had nevertheless now found a social Rotavator made politically of solid gold.

Despite all of this – and not least because the electorate in 1950 and

COUNTING HOUSES: ...'299,998, 299,999'

Vicky on Macmillan's need to succeed as Housing Minister, *Daily Mirror*, c.1952.

1951 could not foresee the subsequent Conservative successes in office – the actual recovery of power was a steep, uphill task. No by-election was gained by the Conservatives from Attlee's Labour government (though this much-quoted fact was actually misleading, for after 1946 no seat fell vacant that would prove to be marginal in post-war conditions) and although hundreds of seats were gained at local elections, and most cities and counties had Tory administrations by 1950, morale remained shaky. The main problem was Labour's insistence that the Tory leopards had not changed their spots since the slump, so that a new Tory government would abolish the free Health Service, restore mass unemployment, demolish the new public sector of industry and turn industrial relations into a permanent battleground. Without actually winning power, there was nothing that the Conservatives could do to disprove such claims, given all the more weight by the fact that most Labour MPs fervently believed what they were saying. In 1950 and 1951 Labour increased its vote by 2 million over the score that had already produced the 1945 landslide, reflecting both working-class satisfaction with what Attlee's men had done in office and a widespread fear of the alternative. Tory recovery would need to generate an even bigger increase in their own vote, as indeed it did, by 2.7 million votes over the same six years. This indicated something of the enthusiasm, especially but by no means exclusively middle-class, that the efforts of Woolton and Butler had together generated since 1945.

Apart from enjoying the natural benefits that accrued from a better organization, new constituency boundaries and postal votes (which together explain about half of the Tories' net recovery of seats between 1945 and 1950), Conservatives could only go on explaining their newly defined policies and concentrate on negative campaigning against Labour. In the 1950 election the party's recovery was a solid one, with eighty-five seats won back and Labour's overall majority cut from 146 to six, and though Labour still remained in office it could clearly not survive a whole parliament with such a fragile lead. Hence the energy now devoted to the housing pledge, desperate Churchillian demands for deals with the Liberals, attempts to harry the Labour government to death by endless all-night sittings, and the even more unbridled rhetoric of freedom and consumerism. In 1951, largely because the disappearance of Liberal candidates forced even more non-socialist electors to turn to the Conservatives, a further twenty-three seats were gained and Churchill returned to office. His majority was only seventeen (though he proclaimed defiantly that 'a majority of one is enough' and had in fact no real trouble in the Commons in the next four years, except over the Suez withdrawal of 1954), but the fact of being back in power did provide the vital chance to show that Conservatives would do what they had promised.

As Macmillan wrote in his diary shortly after the 1951 campaign, Labour had fought on the electorate's fear of the Conservatives, a fear that could now be dispelled, and this provided the party with the opportunity to fight next time (and, as it would transpire, on the two occasions after that too) on a positive Conservative record and on the threat to choice and freedom now posed by Labour. The Tories would now be able to fight on fear of Labour, but only if their own share of the electorate felt as comfortable with the Tory record as Labour voters had done in 1950–51. The tactic would be, as the 1959 slogan had it, 'Life's better under the Conservatives. Don't let Labour ruin it.' When that tactic had its first post-war outing in 1955, during a time of national prosperity following a period in government in which Butler at the Exchequer had lowered taxes and at the same time raised public expenditure on social services, the Tory vote held up well. Labour's vote, on the other hand, fell away from its 1951 zenith (and has never reached that zenith since), for Labour voters – or at least enough of them – had finally had their 'memories' of the 1930s moderated by happier, and more recent experience of Conservative government. Only then, as Butler put it in a private note to his Research Department staff after Eden's 1955 election triumph, had the ghost of 1945 been exorcized and only then had the party 'destroyed the myth that 1945 represented the beginning of some irreversible revolution'. Although, as the economic recession and the Suez crisis of 1956 showed clearly enough, the party in office could still face terrible troubles, 1955–6 did nevertheless mark the return from 'post-war' to a more forward-looking normality.

14

The Third Summit: Macmillan's Party, 1957–65

THE GENERAL ELECTIONS of the 1950s and 1960s, and the results of surveys undertaken by opinion polling organizations and social scientists (which were done only for the first time in this period and so offered contemporaries new ways of understanding the deep currents beneath the electoral surface) both showed that 1945 had not initiated a long-term period of Labour dominance. Rather it had begun a time in which Labour and the Conservatives would have approximately equal voting support and in which the contest for national power would therefore be keen. Where between 1918 and 1939 the Conservatives had been the dominant force, and would be again when Labour's fortunes declined precipitously in the 1970s, in the heyday of Harold Macmillan there was a continuous contest for power between two roughly equal rivals, while there was no third party strong enough to confuse except briefly the main issue.

However, 1945 did usher in a new class balance as well. Labour had only very limited middle-class backing, but continued in the 1950s and 1960s to enjoy the support of about two-thirds of the working class (itself then the overwhelming majority of the nation), and especially of those employed in heavy industry (a number then higher than ever before or since), living on council estates (then increasing in size even more rapidly than were private estates for owner-occupiers), and in membership of trades unions (also proportionately at an all-time high). Such constituencies as Dagenham in East London (car workers), Merthyr Tydfil in South Wales (steel workers) or Hemsworth in Yorkshire (miners) were typical of the cohesive, one-class communities that provided Labour's safest seats. In trying to break down such citadels of Labourism (where – it was joked – votes for Labour were weighed rather than counted, and instead of canvassing the party went out with a whistle to call in the faithful to vote), Conservative candidates had a very tough job indeed.

By comparison, the Conservative vote was more evenly spread both socially and geographically: about four-fifths of the middle class voted consistently for Conservatives (the middle class was itself around a third of the electorate), but outside the suburbs of London and the larger cities this vote dominated few actual constituencies, and was for the most part thinly spread right across the country. In order to win – as ever since 1867 – the Conservatives therefore needed to attract and hold a large proportion of the working-class vote too. In the 1950s they could expect to win about a third of all working-class votes, but because of the great disparity in the size of the classes this third of the workers contributed half of the total Tory support at the ballot box. Because this social mix in the Tory vote was less geographically concentrated into the areas of heavy industry than was Labour's more socially narrow support, Conservatives won their seats right across the country. In 1955, for example, Eden's Conservatives won half the seats (and half the votes) in Scotland, and a respectable two-fifths of the seats in London, the Midlands and the North of England; at the opposite extremes were Wales, where the Conservatives could win only six seats out of thirty-six, and the South of England outside London – the party's heartland ever since the 1830s – where 163 out of 206 were won; if Ulster is excluded then half of all the Tory MPs came from that southern region. In the thinking of the time, Ulster would not of course have been excluded for any purpose at all, for the alliance of Ulster's ten Unionist MPs with the Conservatives was unequivocal and unquestioned; Ulster had provided most of Churchill's parliamentary majority in 1951 and would deny Labour a decent majority in 1964.

This overall, unchanging alignment of the electorate was more significant than the relatively small shifts between successive general elections which determined who governed for the next five years – shifts to the right that produced three successive Conservative wins in 1951, 1955 and 1959, and thirteen years of Conservative government during which the party's share of the national vote fluctuated only between 48 and 49.7 per cent. Partisan stability was matched by the highest ever level of membership of the parties, historically high levels of turnout at elections, and a strong degree of partisanship shown by the electorate when asked by opinion pollsters whether they felt that they 'belonged' to any particular party or whether they felt it mattered to them who won elections. This deep and continuing fissure in the electorate casts in itself an interesting light on the historians' description of the 1950s and 1960s as a period of cross-party consensus, for if such a thing really did exist then it effectively went unnoticed by 20 million electors. Political commentators might gradually come to see the party battle as a 'bogus dilemma', and the Liberals might ask of Edward Heath and Harold Wilson in the 1960s the question 'Which twin is the Tory?' but most of the electorate seemed clear enough in their own minds that there was both a real distinction and one that mattered to them, far more so than would be the case when political loyalties loosened and swings between the parties accelerated after 1970. (That is precisely when 'the post-war consensus' is supposed to have ended, on the traditional view, so perhaps it is time that the British people were re-admitted to the historians' view of post-war Britain?)

This pattern of voting and this distribution of Tory support in the 1950s and 1960s had a number of implications for party strategy. First, it produced a large number of marginal constituencies that would change hands on a small swing of national opinion, a number greater than in either the 1930s or in the 1980s, and this in itself made for general election campaigns on which much seemed to turn. These marginal constituencies – small towns like York, Darlington, Exeter or Gravesend, the socially mixed sections of the conurbations, and county seats where boundaries arbitrarily enclosed industry with agriculture – could be appealed to only by a national campaign that would itself appeal across the classes to the entire national electorate. Considerable effort had therefore to be made to ensure that the electorate did not lapse again into thinking of the Conservatives as a socially narrow ruling group as in 1945, an endless campaign in which the party organization and local government electioneering could play its part, if never quite so successfully as under Lord Woolton.

Already by the time of the recruiting campaigns of 1958 and 1962-3 the Conservatives had lost much of the ground they had gained in the 1940s. The 1958 campaign in particular came as a shock, for, even with the party back on the upswing under Macmillan by then, it proved impossible even to replace the large numbers of members who had died, moved or resigned since 1952. No national figures were published in 1958, so embarrassing would they have proved to be, for even after great efforts to fill the gaps the total was still some half a million down since 1952, and the losses were disproportionately in the industrial areas that the party had to be seen to represent if it were to justify its claim to be a national, cross-class party. By 1962 the Conservative membership had just about halved in ten years, and, with the Macmillan government then in the toils, it proved impossible to do much to repair the damage. The decline in numbers then stabilized for a period, with a total party membership by 1970 of some 1.5 million, still above pre-war levels but only half of the size of 1952, and with remaining members more concentrated in the safer seats where their impact would be relatively limited, both as fighting troops at elections and as an advertisement for the social character of the party itself. In part this decline took place only because the Conservatives were victims – like most other voluntary organizations – of the success of their policies in other fields, for the mass-ownership of cars, televisions, foreign holidays and the like was as much cause of the party's numerical decline as was any overtly political factor. Some comfort was to be had in the fact that when a Labour government was returned in 1964, both the Tory membership and the efficiency of the party machine in general recovered some lost ground.

But even without a membership decline, the party's success in an age of mass communications would predominantly depend on the image and the actuality of its national policy, as was indicated by its increasing concentration on television and on a press that was more and more dominated by a small number of national titles. The national poster campaigns of 1957–9, in which young families, technicians and teachers beamed out at passers-by over the slogan 'You're looking at a Conservative', were one manifestation of this strategic situation. Conversely, the pit into which the party fell after 1960, derided for its 'grouse-moor image' as a landowning, aristocratic elite, while young homeowners struggled with inflation, unemployment and rising mortgage payments, showed all too clearly the dangers of getting it wrong.

Opinion research conducted by academics, and, after 1959, opinion polls commissioned by Central Office, showed that the working-class voters who defied the dictates of 'their' class to vote against 'the working-class party' had many things in common, but fell into two broad categories. On the one hand there were those pragmatic voters, claiming to be free of ideological baggage though frequently exhibiting classic traits of individualism, who reported that they judged the parties on what they had actually done for them and their families. The years of Tory affluence in the 1950s (especially when compared with austerity under Attlee in the 1940s, however unfair that comparison might be) would reinforce such judgements, though this type of support might just as easily melt away in bad times, as to an extent it did after 1959. In practice, some such pragmatists took a longer view, seeing in the new grammar schools of the 1944 Butler Education Act or in the chance to move to New Towns and new suburbs from the inner cities a vindication of their key belief that Conservatives actually managed things better for those with rising social aspirations. On the other hand, there were those whose ideology was worn on their sleeves, electors who accepted the idea of a ruling class, and who often saw their own role as naturally subservient to those born (or at least able and educated) to rule, whose leadership was linked with the prestige of Britain's world role, the empire and all that Churchill still symbolized of Britishness during the quarter-century after his finest hour. These people too could easily be alienated by Tories in office, by the faltering international policy that led to Suez or by the confusions that decolonization, the ending of Britain's imperial era, and the onset of coloured immigration all produced. But whatever the personal and familial flavour, all of these working-class Conservatives denied the centrality of class in their lives, sometimes by placing their focus of identity below that level, on family and individual betterment (many of these claiming in fact that they were not 'working class' anyway), sometimes by placing their loyalty neither on class nor family but on the nation as a whole. The openings were certainly there to be exploited by the party within these thought-worlds, but together they constituted a package of aspirations that was hard to deliver over the long and difficult years in office after 1951. They would be even more difficult to satisfy when the overall level of economic growth faltered and the colonies had gone, as Edward Heath discovered as Prime Minister after 1970.

Despite appearances, however, and the reality of the relative stability of the 1950s in comparison with what came afterwards, the electoral situation was not a static one, for the electorate were already showing limited signs of the dynamism that would produce extreme volatility two decades later. The class alignment of the electorate reflected both inherited relationships within industry and the existing patterns of housing and community that arose from earlier decades of speculative building and of party control in the local authorities, but these were changing both of their own accord in response to the marketplace and with discreet steering from Whitehall. Sociologists found, for example, that when families lived in overwhelmingly one-class districts in East London the predominating ideology of labourism brooked little resistance, so that Labour actually scored a higher vote in such places than even the national class pattern would have indicated; but when the same families moved out to leafy suburbs they tended to absorb different life expectations altogether and voted Labour in smaller numbers than the national average. When entirely new working-class communities were created in New Towns like Harlow and Stevenage, their existence as communities without historical class identities that derived from industrial tradition (and the fact that these New Towns tended to have light – and lightly unionized – rather than heavy industry) produced a much more open-minded attitude to political loyalties. In 1959, foreshadowing much that would come later in the century, the Conservatives won the contests in most of the first generation of New Towns, demonstrating (as Lady Davidson, widow of Baldwin's Party Chairman of 1926–30 and herself a veteran of many contests in Stevenage, put it) that 'the New Town people are not Socialist. We hoped that the people that came to the new towns would become the backbone of our [Conservative] party', and they had now done so. Essex and Hertfordshire man was already beginning the march to the right.

A more general debate of the same type also surrounded Macmillan's win with an increased majority in 1959, and particularly in the light of what was seen as his unashamedly materialist appeal to the electorate to return him to office in order to continue to provide them with what he called 'the silent, the Conservative revolution' of continually rising standards of living. Did this third Conservative victory mark the permanent unlocking of Labour's hold on working-class loyalty, and did it mark the onset of a trend which would eventually doom Labour to irrelevance in a successful capitalist economy? Had Keynesian methods, in other words, provided the secret by which British Conservatives could provide long-term affluence and short-term election booms which would guarantee them a theoretically endless period of power? Academic research stubbornly failed to find voters who would admit to having changed their votes for such reasons (though as research then and since has only rarely found voters who admit *ever* to changing their votes for any reason at all this was not entirely surprising), and when Macmillan's government ran into trouble in 1962–3 and Labour then won in 1964, the memories of 1959's 'affluent workers' being steadily 'embourgeoised' into Toryism faded rapidly from the mind. But it is now clear that 1959's 'affluent workers' represented the tip of a large approaching iceberg of politically unaligned voters. The mistake was to assume that their detachment from Labour implied a new attachment to the Conservatives – a natural mistake in a world of generally fixed political loyalties and only two strong parties –

when in actuality they would simply swell the pool of electoral pragmatists, floating voters and increasingly cynical abstainers, with no fixed loyalties at all.

Macmillan was in 1957 an ideal Party Leader to preside over this period of transition, for his own complex personality embodied much that these different groups of electors wanted from a Conservative government anyway. Having come from relatively humble origins, he was proud to display in Downing Street a painting of his ancestral Scottish croft as visual evidence of his own 'log cabin to White House' roots, and of the unobstructed openings to men of talent that a meritocratic Toryism seemed to offer. Reflecting these roots, he could affect a vulgar populism with neither blushes nor regrets. But Macmillan was also an Etonian who had served in the Grenadier Guards and owed his original entry into politics to the Duke of Devonshire, whose daughter he had married. Since 1945 Macmillan had cultivated the bearing and the manner of speaking, the cynical detachment and the raffish charm of a late-Victorian Whig, though in deference to his actual generation this was more often described as 'Edwardian'. He developed indeed such a skill in concealing his own feelings behind an increasingly pervasive mask that even friends found it difficult to tell the act from the reality. As a backbencher told the Chief Whip, Edward Heath, on hearing Macmillan speak as the new Prime Minister in January 1957, 'What a pity that now we have the most intelligent Prime Minister of the century, he has to conceal his intelligence from the public for fear that they will suspect it.'

In another field in which art must conceal art, Macmillan made himself a successful television performer by sheer application and practice. The number of households with sets was increasing rapidly and in 1959 for the first time a major part of an election campaign was fought on the new medium; by 1964 almost all households would have sets and most of the electorate would tell pollsters that they now received most of their news about politics from television. Although Eden had both in 1951 and in 1955 made much-praised election broadcasts for the party, Macmillan was the first British politician actually to understand the significance of the new medium. It was a medium that he hated and feared so much as to be physically sick before important interviews, and he frequently referred to the television studios as the 'modern torture chamber', but he none the less mastered it – as his climaxing solo broadcast during the 1959 campaign demonstrated. In the pursuit of power, there was probably no torture that Macmillan would not resignedly have undergone.

This was far from the Macmillan of 1939, for as a young man he had been happy to be seen more as a theorist than a practitioner, a book-learned specialist in industrial and economic policy, converted early to Keynes (whose books the family firm of Macmillan published) and unfashionably committed in Chamberlain's Conservative Party to greatly increased state intervention. When he wrote *The Middle Way* in 1938, he was seeking to demonstrate a democratic alternative in economic policy to the totalitarianism of both Fascism and Communism, but, if this placed him at the centre of the British political spectrum in the 1930s, he seemed therefore on the extreme left of Conservatism. It was thus easy to view Macmillan's move to the Conservative front bench in the 1940s and its espousal of some of his pre-war ideas as a shift by the party in his direction rather than the other way round. The *Daily Express* reminded readers of *The Industrial Charter* of 1947 that Macmillan 'once wrote a treatise called *The Middle Way*. This is the second edition.' As a rising and ambitious politician, Macmillan was the last person likely to deny the apparent connection, and he later wrote of 'great satisfaction and some little pride to me. For the leaders of my party . . . had now accepted the policies for which I had striven in the past.'

This view – and especially the *Daily Express*'s hostile version that it was a shift to the 'left' – ignored a good deal of evidence that pointed in different directions. First, Macmillan's move to the front bench owed much to Churchill's patronage and to his own record as anti-Appeaser in the 1930s, but hardly anything to his views on economics, while his survival as a party leader after 1945 (when other Churchillian protégés fell back) involved Macmillan's own willingness to accept and advocate the whole run of party policy – whether he agreed with it or not – as he had never done before 1940. Second, *The Middle Way* – one of the many much-quoted but scarcely ever read books in British political history – was not just making the case for collectivism, so as to allow Tories to steal the socialists' clothes, but was also a book that advocated 'the greatest possible measure of freedom' alongside economic regulation, precisely because it saw all forms of *socialist* interventionism as 'a narrow-minded conception of life . . . [that] would merely prostitute social efficiency for the pursuit of reactionary ends'. Macmillan's combination of the rhetoric of freedom and the practice of regulation did therefore fit in with *The Industrial Charter*, but only if the *Charter* itself is seen in the way described above, as the importation of Tory principles into current practice rather than the simple acceptance of Labour's leftist approach. And since (if Butler is to be believed) Macmillan bored stiff the other members of the Industrial Policy Committee of 1946–7 by actually reading to them long extracts from *The Middle Way*, the convergence was far from accidental.

Macmillan did, though, bring to the party leadership in 1957 another piece of intellectual baggage from before 1939 that was more influential than any of this theory. As MP for Stockton-on-Tees (1924–9 and 1931–45), he had witnessed at first hand the consequences of economic depression both on the local economy and on the human spirit of the unemployed and their families – and also indeed on the popularity of Tory MPs, who seemed to have stood by and allowed the depression to run on for years unchecked. His core belief after 1945 was that neither the country nor his party should allow such a thing to happen again. As a Keynesian he believed that recessions were avoidable, and if that meant taking risks with inflationary pressures to avoid the greater threat of deflation, then so be it. 'A little inflation never hurt anyone' was a favourite Macmillan saying, but the real implication was that *de*flation had caused a great deal of hurt. As he told a junior minister who joined his government during the recession of 1962, 'Poor old Treasury, they will plunge us all into a slump.' As a Tory paternalist, he asserted fiercely the duty of the nation's rulers to facilitate the best possible living standards for ordinary people, much as his generation had in 1914–18 striven as junior officers to look after their men in the trenches. He would bring to this task both determination and courage, for as his fellow-Grenadier (and himself another Tory front-bencher) Harry Crookshank was fond of reminding people in the early 1950s, Guards officers of 1914–18 had used the phrase 'as brave as Mr Macmillan' when they wanted to denote a special act of coolness under fire.

Macmillan could therefore bring to the task of reviving his party from the trough in which he found it in January 1957 both a foreign policy record and an aristocratic bearing that appealed to the deferential Tory voter, and an approach to domestic policy which attracted the more pragmatic Conservative who looked for evidence of economic competence and social caring. He could also bring to the task political skills and formidable willpower that hardly anyone had known him to possess before he became Prime Minister. As a result, he was able to hold his Cabinet together through difficult early months during which a further major resignation from the government took place, and gradually to show MPs and the party in the country an impression of coolness at the top which trickled down to inspire confidence in ministers, MPs and finally the party at large.

There have been few more impressive examples of inspirational Tory leadership from the top than the turning around of the party's fortunes by Macmillan in 1957. By the summer, the Suez fiasco was safely astern and from then on the public seemed in no mood to listen to Labour's regular attempts to rake over the coals of a national humiliation. Macmillan had recognized indeed that the best way to deal politically with such a national humiliation was to refuse all apologies, enquiries and witch-hunts, and then to ignore the issue altogether by highlighting other things in his speeches and in the party's campaigning. The Anglo-Americans relationship, which had reached its post-war nadir over Suez, was re-established as a connection of some warmth, Macmillan having enjoyed since the war a good personal rapport with President Eisenhower, who was himself happy to bury the past now that Eden had gone. A joint television broadcast from Downing Street by Macmillan and Eisenhower on the eve of the 1959 general election, during which neither even mentioned the Middle East, was nevertheless a quite intentional demonstration that the problems of Suez were over and that Britain's premier was once again respected internationally. That last perception also owed something to Macmillan's extended tour of the Commonwealth in 1958 and to his reception in Moscow earlier in 1959 – though in that case the public relations impact owed more to his appearing before the cameras of the world wearing a gigantic white fur hat (long before such photo-opportunities became the norm in statesmen's travel plans) than to anything said to or by Nikita Khrushchev. By that time he was so lauded by his followers as to provoke his sour depiction by Vicky of the *Evening Standard* as 'Supermac', a cartoon character of supreme improbability, but Tory supporters then adopted this as their own catch-phrase anyway.

Political success in the international sphere derived also from the relatively low temperature of colonial policy as the empire drew to a close. Soon after becoming Prime Minister Macmillan had commissioned a profit-and-loss survey of each British colony, but he offered little to the public debate as a result of this until the 1959 election was safely won, so that, with only limited exceptions in the more economically developed areas of West Africa, British colonial power was still being consolidated rather than wound down. Nor did Britain move on in these years from the halfway house to Europe inherited from Eden, in which Britain had

"I TOLD YOU THIS SORT OF STUFF WILL FETCH 'EM BACK INTO THE OLD CINEMA...."

Vicky on the appeal of 'Supermac' in 1958. Hailsham is the doorman saying, 'I told you this sort of stuff will fetch 'em back into the old cinema', *Evening Standard*, 17 November 1958.

worked for freer trading (and created the European Free Trade Area to encourage this) but rejected all the elements of supra-nationalism implied by those seeking to build a European 'community'. Macmillan had himself been a committed pro-European earlier in his life, and would be again before long, but none of this was allowed to disturb the even tenor of politics before a difficult election.

Only in one aspect of international policy were tough issues tackled at this time: in relation to defence. Duncan Sandys's 1957 White Paper sought to apply as a lesson of Suez the principle that Britain must never again fight a colonial war without American backing, and as a result it initiated a shift back to the small, volunteer armed services more traditional in British policy than the compulsory National Service forces employed since 1939. The country's main contribution to the global Cold War was now made through an enhanced role for nuclear weapons. Parts of this package irritated service chiefs, and many sections of left-wing opinion were horrified into public demonstrations by the nuclear issue, but few likely Tory voters had reservations, and the ending of conscription (though not finally implemented for several years) was a major step forward for a party that had promised to 'set the people free'.

One unforeseen factor in ending conscription was the increasing shortage of manpower, a shortage that produced new social strains when British public sector employers actually organized coloured immigration in order to find more employees. Immigration as a political issue began to surface from the mid-1950s, and certainly caused excitement among Conservatives in parts of London and the Midlands (especially after 1958 brought Britain's first real race riots and a Fascist campaign to exploit the issue), but this too was kept off the legislative agenda until after 1959.

With most other issues deflected or postponed, the party knew well enough that the drive to retain power would hang mainly on the performance of the economy, and here there was a trial of strength of considerable importance. As his Chancellor of the Exchequer Macmillan appointed Peter Thorneycroft, a natural choice since he had specialized in economics and had had five years at the Board of Trade. At first the difficult economic inheritance ensured that the Cabinet was united behind a tough policy. When Macmillan spoke in July 1957 at Bedford, he reminded the British people that 'most of our people have never had it so good', not in order to ask for voters' gratitude or to appeal to their base, materialist instincts (as *The Times* and the bishops suggested when criticizing the speech) but to warn them that the good times might not last, and that inflation now posed a serious problem which must be tackled. By the autumn of 1957, though, with the government now halfway through its term and Conservatives continuing to do worse in by-elections, opinion polls and local government contests than in 1951–5, Macmillan was increasingly in conflict with his Chancellor. By then, as would happen again in 1962, the Prime Minister was convinced that the Treasury (which he had ever since the 1920s suspected of over-emphasizing currency exchange rates in its economic thinking) was unduly delaying the moment at which reflation should take place and thereby risking a recession deeper than was either desirable or necessary. The crunch came over public spending for 1958–9, which would almost certainly be the last full year before an election: the Chancellor wished to contain spending within the current year's cash limits, but this alarmed almost all other Cabinet ministers, who wanted to see it relaxed, for both electoral and policy reasons. Though the gap narrowed as discussions went on, this difference of approach was never likely to be susceptible to compromise, though impeccable behaviour by all involved ensured that nothing surfaced in the press until Thorneycroft and his entire Treasury team of ministers then resigned at the start of 1958.

In the short term, the problem was easily contained. Macmillan departed for his world tour with the airy (if rehearsed) observation that these were just 'little, local difficulties' when compared with peace, war and the future of a multi-racial Commonwealth. He found both a more compliant and a more growth-orientated Chancellor in Derick Heathcoat Amory – who had himself converted from Liberal to Tory after reading *The Middle Way* and then been one of the centrist framers of *The Industrial Charter*, while Thorneycroft had been kept off the 1946 committee in view of his maverick tendencies even then. In that generation in which Lord Kilmuir (the former David Maxwell Fyfe) spoke of loyalty as the Tories' secret weapon, the party indeed rallied loyally to limit the fall-out from these 1958 resignations, even after they contributed to a particularly humiliating by-election defeat at Rochdale (at which the Tory candidate came third in a seat won in 1955), the defeat coming in the first-ever televised contest. In the memoirs and the memories of those involved, Thorneycroft seems to have greatly overplayed his hand – a strategy attributed by some to the malignly uncompromising influence of his Financial Secretary, Enoch Powell – and it was often recalled that when the Chancellor had extracted most of what he wanted from the Cabinet he had eventually resigned over a mere £50 million out of government spending of about £6 billion. But when Powell later emerged as the chief Conservative exponent of the alternative approach to economics eventually called 'monetarism', and when Thorneycroft himself was rescued from retirement and made Party Chairman by Margaret Thatcher when she became Leader in the full flood of monetarism in 1975, these events of 1958 acquired a different significance. The Cabinet in 1957–8 was not making a choice for or against 'monetarism' and all that it later came to imply, for much of that concept did not exist even for academic economists until a decade later, while the lesser version known as economic 'Powellism' was not expounded in any detail until Powell's own first book on the subject appeared in 1965.

What was, however, at stake in 1958 were alternative priorities between public expenditure, inflation and taxation. Since returning to office in 1951, the Conservatives had been uniquely fortunate in that a period of economic growth, for which they could claim some if not all of the credit, had co-existed with the final running down of the war economy, with its stock-piles and state apparatus; they had therefore been able to lower taxes and at the same time fund desirable social programmes, particularly after the Korean War ended in 1953. With the economic downturn of 1955–7, during which the Conservatives came under heavy attack from middle-class supporters because of continuing inflation, the avoidance of difficult choices became impossible, and in 1957–8 the Conservatives in office decided in effect that public expenditure would not be further lowered and that it would therefore have to be funded through economic growth, and failing that through either taxation or inflation. As Powell was fond of pointing out later, between 1951 and 1957 the state's share of British national income fell steadily, while in 1958 it began again the insistent rise that has characterized much of the century. If this seemed later like special pleading for his then favourite cause, and if critics could and did point out that Powell as Minister of Health – and indeed his ideological descendants Keith Joseph and Margaret Thatcher too (at Health and Education respectively) – had all been big spenders themselves, there was still no denying Powell's figures. The Tory Party did indeed decide in 1958 to prioritize public spending over its other policy objectives, even if at the time it still seemed that Keynesianism would make such a choice temporary and relatively cost-free.

Under Heathcoat Amory the shift from Thorneycroft's policies was not rushed, but the change of direction was significant. Successive reductions in credit controls accumulated to a doubling of total consumer credit between 1957 and 1960, which certainly stimulated the economy, and these efforts were crowned with a substantial tax cut in the 1959 budget; where the standard rate of income tax had been 48 per cent when Churchill became Prime Minister in 1951 and 42 per cent when Eden was re-elected in 1955, Macmillan called the 1959 general election with the standard rate below 39 per cent. When placed alongside the other successful outputs of domestic policy and the avoidance of difficulties abroad, Macmillan could thus appeal both to the deferential and the pragmatic working-class Tories and to the middle-class taxpayers, each section of the Tory voting coalition finding things in his record to draw them to the polling booths.

With the party itself also rebounding into an upswing under the joint lead of Lord Hailsham, an ebullient, flag-waving cheerleader as Party Chairman, and of Lord Poole as one of Central Office's best ever fund-raisers, morale was high by the time the election came in the autumn of 1959. The party had also moved into a new dimension by running, long before the campaign as such, a coordinated and professional public relations appeal to the electorate. As a result of Poole's efforts, almost half a million pounds could be spent in poster and press advertising over the two years before the election, firstly to reinforce the impression that the party was representative of the country as a whole and then to ram home the consumerist message that continued prosperity required another Tory term in office: 'You're having it good. Have it better.' Opinion polls showed that the combination of the record itself and the advertising and speech-making that had insistently drawn it to voters' attention had produced a strong link in voters' minds between Conservatism and the concept of affluence. When the Tories' campaign television broadcasts in 1959 were criticized at a strategy post-mortem, an MP remarked that the key was that 8 million more families now actually *had* televisions than in 1951, and that in this case the very existence of the medium was more important than the message that it conveyed; the public's perception of the Tory record in office was the factor that had really mattered. What was true of television sets was equally true of homes, cars, telephones, washing machines, and foreign holidays – all luxuries enjoyed only by the rich in 1950.

In these circumstances, and with Labour in disarray for much of the period between 1955 and 1959 anyway, it was highly unlikely that the Conservatives would lose. Despite some mid-campaign wobbles and poor television communication (largely the result of over-preparation which created a lack of spontaneity), Macmillan was duly returned as Prime Minister in October 1959 with a majority increased to a hundred. This was the first time in well over a century that a party had increased its number of MPs at four successive elections, and the first time ever that an incumbent government had been re-elected twice. The Area Agent from the North West concluded that 'the Conservative theme that "Life is better under the Conservatives" was a winner. Conversely, the Labour theme that only the few had benefited for the mass of the people were poor was not believed because it was not true.'

In principle, and with Labour deeply disheartened by its third successive rejection, there seemed no reason why Conservative government could not go on for ever, and academics began to research just that possibility. Professor Samuel Finer speculated on whether democracy could survive if one party always won the elections, while the sociologist Mark Abrams asked, 'Must Labour Lose?' In 1960 Tory popularity increased even further, with yet higher poll ratings for the party and for Macmillan than in 1959 and with a by-election gain from Labour in a Yorkshire marginal, but this was exactly when things began to go badly wrong, when the fit

'Well, gentlemen, I think we all fought a good fight . . .'

Trog on Macmillan and affluence, *Spectator*, 16 October 1959.

between what Macmillan had to offer and what the electoral situation demanded began to go askew.

The equation changed from both ends. On their part, Macmillan and his staff became dangerously over-confident, and in doing so the careful balance of his pre-1959 appeal was lost, much less attention being paid to the spadework that had produced the triumph. There was the promotion of more peers and too many Etonians into his Cabinet, presenting an image underlined by frequent press and TV pictures of ministers banging away aristocratically at the grouse on Scottish moors; there was also less fastidiousness applied to the distribution of honours. Macmillan's own cod-senile 'act' became ever more exaggerated – even supportive MPs took to calling him 'the old actor manager', and referring to 'Edwardianism with a touch of the Donald Wolfits' – so that the demotic, caring young man of 1938 was more and more difficult to recall; even the dynamic Minister of Housing of ten years earlier seemed a different person altogether.

What made this retreat by the Prime Minister into a parody of his former self rather more serious was a cultural change in the opposite direction within both the media and the predilections of elite opinion.

This shift towards the celebration of youth, merit and modernity over experience and tradition, as the affluent fifties were succeeded by the 'swinging sixties', took many forms, ranging from the new centrality of beat music in mass entertainment to the worldwide impact of John Kennedy as American President. But the factor that most impinged on politics in Britain was the new freedom to lampoon the nation's rulers, as variously evinced by the popular review *Beyond the Fringe*, by the newly founded *Private Eye*, and by BBC television's programme *That Was The Week That Was*. British satirists were mainly themselves from privileged backgrounds, and time was to show how even-handed they could be between the parties, but because a distinctly backward-looking Conservative regime was in being when they sprang upon the scene it was the unrepresentative outdatedness of Conservatism that became their first major target. Since slackening economic growth rates produced in the same years a growing pessimism about the effectiveness of inherited attitudes, even Conservative newspapers rapidly found themselves carried along by this same cultural wave.

The problem was exacerbated by the public's increasing boredom with long-serving ministerial faces, an entirely new phenomenon of the television age, and by the fact that 'events, dear boy, events' (as Macmillan himself liked to describe the chances of political life) offered both satirists and newspapers a series of stories that showed the government in a very bad light. Macmillan remained a potent communicator on the government's behalf, but many of his senior colleagues in the second half of his premiership were liabilities, at least in that respect. Lord Home, whose promotion to the Foreign Office in 1960 had prompted the *Daily Mail* to tell Macmillan to 'stop making a fool of himself', was an extremely able Foreign Secretary, but one who in the domestic political context did little to disprove the *Sunday Express*'s view that he was an 'unknown and faceless earl'. Selwyn Lloyd, who replaced Heathcoat Amory at the Exchequer in 1960, made a poor impression in television interviews, inspiring little confidence in the government's economic policy, and Macmillan himself thought that he lacked personality on the public platform. Henry Brooke, Home Secretary from 1962, seemed peculiarly accident-prone, but showed in any case an illiberalism in his discretionary decisions that opened him to regular criticism as the cultural mood shifted in a liberal direction. The second man in the government, R. A. Butler, was also slowing down after more than twenty years of uninterrupted front-bench service, disheartened by Macmillan's determination not to make way for him at the top. The party's reputation for competence, on which much of its pragmatic vote rested, would not easily survive the continuous battering that this central team received in the media.

This problem became far more marked when, in 1962, the Vassall spy scandal led to the unnecessary resignation of an innocent minister, and a judicial enquiry then imprisoned for contempt two journalists who would not reveal the sources they had used for their stories (sources that probably never existed anyway), so that the press, scenting an attack on its constitutional freedom, became more hostile and ready to exploit the next scandal when it arose. The Profumo affair of 1963 would have rocked any government, for the involvement of the War minister with a prostitute who was also sleeping with a Russian diplomat, Profumo's initial lie about his innocence in the Commons, and the sleazy, amoral world of the rich and famous publicized by subsequent enquiries when his lie was eventually admitted, were stories far too juicy for suppression or self-censorship even by Tory papers.

For a time in the summer of 1963 it seemed possible that all this might even bring down the government, so wide-ranging was rumour and innuendo about who had been involved in covering up what. Macmillan's eventual survival in a Commons censure debate was only achieved by proving his honesty at the cost of impugning his own judgement. Butler thought that Macmillan, 'partly due to age and decency of living', had indicated 'that he is out of touch with some of the underground so ably canvassed and represented in the daily press'. There could scarcely be a more damaging position to be in during a period of changing social attitude. For many provincial Tories, far removed from the mores of 'swinging London', Macmillan had responsibility for a decline of moral standards and might indeed have encouraged it by his 'never had it so good' materialism, while for others he was at the same time too old and too out of touch to work out what was going on under his nose.

Macmillan was far too tough-minded and resilient a politician to take this battering without mounting counter-attacks, and it remains true that he was not overthrown by his critics inside the party and outside. Although the Profumo scandal damaged his own nerve and morale, it was only ill health that forced his retirement in October 1963, and had he not mistakenly assumed that he was very ill indeed he would probably have gone on to win the election of 1964. The party, after all, came within 1 per cent of winning in 1964, despite the divisive leadership crisis that Macmillan's retirement provoked and despite being led by a successor who was poorly

Anthony Eden with Conservative candidates for Kent constituencies at a Rally in the Dartford football stadium, 1951, those pictured include William Deedes (third from left), Anthony Eden (sixth), Edward Heath (ninth), and Margaret Roberts (tenth).

Sir David and Lady Maxwell Fyfe campaigning in Derbyshire, 1950.

ABOVE Peter Rawlinson (standing for Hackney South) in a characteristic 1950s Conservative campaign.

LEFT Lord Hailsham ringing the Conference chairman's bell at the 1957 Party Conference in Brighton.

ABOVE Harold Macmillan entertains President Eisenhower *and* television cameras in Downing Street, just before the 1959 General Election.

RIGHT Harold Macmillan at Burch Grove House in 1960.

R.A. Butler is applauded after his speech at the 1963 Conservative Conference by, amongst others, three other contenders for the Party Leadership, Lord Hailsham, the 14th Earl of Home, and Iain MacLeod.

Sir Alec Douglas-Home, apparently unimpressed with his own television image in 1964.

Edward Heath lauded after his first Conference speech as Leader of the Party, by (left to right) Peter Thorneycroft, Reginald Maudling, Sir Alec Douglas-Home, Michael Fraser and Edward du Cann.

Edward Heath's Cabinet in the garden of No. 10, including, (left to right) Lord Carrington, Sir Keith Joseph, William Whitelaw, Margaret Thatcher, Edward Heath, Anthony Barber, Robert Carr, Sir Alec Douglas-Home, Peter Thomas, Gordon Campbell and Jim Prior.

Edward Heath and Sir Keith Joseph, apparently not enjoying one another's company, in the autumn of 1974.

Kenneth Clarke's wedding in 1964 brings out in force the future 'Cambridge mafia' of the Thatcher-Major Cabinets, those pictured include Michael Howard (second from left), John Selwyn Gummer (third), Kenneth Clarke (fourth), Leon Brittan (fifth) and Norman Lamont (seventh).

John Major campaigning from a soapbox in Cheltenham in March 1992, on his way to winning the General Election.

A Labour poster – Major and Clark as Laurel and Hardy, May 1996.

> "WONDERFUL JOB, SIR! THE PUBLIC WAS GETTING A BIT BORED WITH THE SAME OLD FACES..."

Evening Standard, 13 July 1962.

suited for the campaigning task in hand, while Macmillan himself, had he survived, would have led a more or less united party and deployed the skills that had been so effective in 1959.

For Macmillan had – for all the increasing appearance of aristocratic remoteness – approached the 1959 parliament in a highly professional manner. At the outset, foreseeing the problem that the 'time for a change' argument would pose when the Conservatives reached the end of their third term, he had set up several enquiries which would provide fresh policy material for the last year of the parliament and for a manifesto. These initiatives produced among other things the Robbins report on higher education, the Buchanan report on urban traffic, and the Willink report on the police service. He had also fully grasped the need to bring fresh faces into his government. In 1962's 'night of the long knives' he was indeed a butcher who left far too much blood visible on the Cabinet room's carpet, but this was mainly because a leak to the press caused a panicky acceleration of what was to have been a slow process aimed initially at removing the uncommunicative Selwyn Lloyd from the Treasury. As William Deedes (who joined the Cabinet as a result of that crisis) has put it, 'what Macmillan had intended to be a leisurely game of shuffle-board on deck became instead a race for the lifeboats'.

The thinking behind 1962's reshuffle, apart from the need to ditch another Chancellor who was slow to reflate an ailing economy as an election approached, was to bring the meritocratic 'class of 1950' up to the senior posts in the government. The changes would add the middle-aged Macleod, Heath and Maudling (and even younger 'beavers' like Keith Joseph and Edward Boyle, as Macmillan dubbed them) to the older generation of Macmillan, Home and Butler in a team intended to demonstrate the union of vitality and experience. As before, this mixture derived its real logic from the complexities of Macmillan, a man who could be reassuring with Home and dynamic with Heath at one and the same time. It remained very much Macmillan's government, however rattled its leader may have been at times by the increased criticism of all that he stood for – and his diaries show that beneath the urbane surface the supposedly unflappable Macmillan often did get very rattled indeed.

The central thrust of policy for this new Cabinet would be a drive to reorganize and modernize Britain to seize a historic opportunity, for this was also the moment at which Macmillan's biggest strategic gamble also reached its critical point. Soon after the 1959 election victory he had begun to put the pieces in place for a reorientation of Britain's international policy, sending the liberal Macleod to the Colonial Office to accelerate Britain's exit from Africa and putting the Europhile Heath as second man at the Foreign Office to lead negotiations for British entry to the European Economic Community.

Macmillan never seems to have seen the European Free Trade Area as much more than a bluff, and when the original six members of the EEC ignored the bluff and continued with their statebuilding plans for western Europe, at precisely the time in which Britain's trade was increasingly in that direction and her economic growth rates failing to keep up with most developed economies, he now simultaneously abandoned EFTA and the empire with a remarkably tough-minded lack of sentimentality. He did not, though, envisage that Britain's European identity involved any stepping down of her relationship with the USA (and despite a difference in age Macmillan got on extremely well with President Kennedy, to whom he was connected by marriage) or any reduction in the world role of sterling as a reserve currency. With hindsight this could be seen as a recipe that invited European (or at least French) scepticism about the depth of Britain's change of heart, but at the time this was a point scarcely heard in British debates – and certainly not from within the government. In this, as in much else, Macmillan's generation of Tories was a prisoner of the international framework within which Churchill had delineated Britain's role after 1945, in which Britain's centrality to world affairs would be ensured by the intersection in London of the 'three circles' of Europe, the Commonwealth and the Special Relationship with the USA, each circle linking Britain to different friends but none of them limiting her room for manoeuvre in the other two. This had already been a dangerous delusion when Churchill put it forward in the 1940s, but only after the 1960s were British prime ministers to realize the extent of the fallacy.

The move towards Europe had to be handled with subtlety, for it could wreck the party if either the agricultural interest (for which Butler was a key figure, having represented an Essex rural seat since 1929) or the Commonwealth lobby managed to seize the party's attention and win majority support for their views. The Macmillan government did not therefore apply for Britain to join the EEC; it merely initiated discussions as to what the terms would be if she *did* apply to join. This helped to reduce opposition within the party, but it also meant that supporters and ministers could not expound the full case for joining in case the talks failed, and that sceptical Europeans had further reasons to doubt Britain's sincerity. Since Heath's Brussels talks over agricultural and trading terms (needed to reassure potential Tory sceptics) took a very long time to conclude, this placed the central core of the government's international policy in limbo for the whole of 1962 and left the possibility open throughout that time of eventual failure throwing the government off course. In the autumn of 1962, with agriculture reassured and reasonable terms achieved for New Zealand butter and other Commonwealth commodities, and with Labour now coming off the fence to oppose entry to the EEC, Macmillan edged nearer to a full commitment to Britain's membership, not least because it offered the chance to portray a wide gap between the parties, graphically demonstrating the modern outlook of the Tories; for Labour 'a thousand years of history books', as Butler pithily summed up the argument, 'for us the future'.

Unfortunately, and for reasons that had little to do with Britain or the detail of her application, in January 1963 France vetoed British entry to the EEC and persuaded her five partners to accept her view, so wrecking the entire stance on which Macmillan had focused the second half of his premiership. The Research Department's director, Michael Fraser, mournfully noted in 1964 that Europe 'was to create a new contemporary political argument with insular Socialism; dish the Liberals by stealing their clothes; give us something *new* after 12–13 years; act as a catalyst of modernisation; give us a new place in the international sun. It was Macmillan's ace and De Gaulle trumped it.' After a few weeks of shock in January 1963, when Macmillan wrote in his diary that 'all our policies at home and abroad are in ruins', the government gradually decided to stick to its modernization policies, asserting that France would not be able to keep Britain out of the EEC for ever and that it therefore still behoved the government to prepare for the day of entry. Although that stance was itself knocked off balance by the Profumo scandal only a few weeks later, it remained the official Conservative position right through to the loss of power in 1964; in effect it then remained the position under Heath until Britain did join the EEC in 1972. But the rhetoric of modernization, when shorn of its immediate justification and excitement in a European future, was a cold doctrine – especially for Conservatives who might be expected to (and often did) prefer the old to the new anyway. Plans to rationalize the railway system, to modernize local government into larger units (especially in London, where the new Greater London county swallowed many reluctant suburbs), to make industry more competitive, to restructure health services, and to extend educational opportunities were all proposed and implemented, but each plan produced a degree of lukewarmness, some of them outright hostility, from ordinary Conservatives. The Buchanan report on *Traffic in Towns* produced an even more hostile response, suggesting as it did restrictions on the private motorist's rights of access (which no government has yet faced up to even a third of a century later, though the number of vehicles has more than doubled in that period).

The final example of this modernizing thrust in action came after Macmillan himself had retired, when Heath, during the Home government, pressed through – almost literally over the bodies of many Tory MPs and constituency activists – the abolition of Resale Price Maintenance. In Britain's competitive, bracing future, younger Conservatives like Heath saw no room for such restrictions on the market and on trade, but for Tory shopkeepers who correctly foresaw their destruction by supermarket chains, or for villagers who feared the loss of their local shop, the brave new world offered only cold comfort. The party's historic role as the protector of propertied interest groups and of rural, traditional Britain rested uneasily alongside this hearty espousal of the new and more modern consumerism, though as long as the 'Edwardian' Macmillan remained in charge it was easy to miss the significance of the party's change of direction. 'Modernize with Macmillan' was after all the real heart of his domestic policy as well as a satirists' joke.

The period 1961–2 also involved a bold initiative of a modernizing type in economic policy, when Macmillan steered through his Cabinet the creation first of a National Economic Development Council and then of a National Incomes Commission, each of them bodies on which representatives of industry and the trades unions would meet under the government's chairmanship in order to hammer out – it was hoped – agreed economic objectives to which all would then be committed. There were precedents for this in mechanisms of the First World War years and in discussions of the later 1920s, in collaboration during the Second World War and in the three-man Council on Prices and Incomes set up by Thorneycroft. There had also been an explicit commitment to collaborative approaches in *The Industrial Charter* (though it was reticent on actual mechanisms), and it was consistent with the generally friendly relations with the trades unions enjoyed in practice since 1951. But what Macmillan intended was bolder than any of these precedents, and when dignified with his title 'the New Approach' seemed to promise an important step forward. His most important motive was the need to secure collaboration across industry in order to achieve higher rates of growth, with the 'indicative planning' of Gaullist France the obvious model to follow, so as to gear up Britain for the opportunity that free trade in Europe would offer. In the upshot, the NEDC and NIC proved useful for the exchange of views but never came near to persuading the unions to accept wage restraint in a time of inflation or the voluntary modernization of industrial working practice. Soon after they came into existence, the government had plenty of other problems to contend with which ensured that these bold new approaches dropped beneath the surface of the main political debate.

These 'corporatist' moves of 1961–2 did, though, have important implications for Conservatism, both at the time and later. By seeking to re-enlist the trades unions as a partner in government, Macmillan's Cabinet effectively surrendered the alternative strategy of enforcing modernization on industry (and especially on industrial relations) on its own and on parliament's authority. Although the main drift of Tory policy towards the unions since 1951 had been one of 'softly, softly', there were by the early 1960s quite a number of Conservatives who saw the unions as the major obstacle to effectiveness in industry, and who, losing hope of the unions ever putting their own house in order, now called openly for legislation – as, for example, the CPC, Conservative lawyers, the Advisory Committee on Policy and the new Monday Club were all doing by 1963. There were also signs that the unions had forfeited the admiration of the public and the press that they had enjoyed during the war years and soon afterwards. That change was indicated by increasing suspicion of Communist subversion after ballot-rigging was proved among the Electricians, and at another level by such popular films as *I'm All Right, Jack* (1959) and *The Angry Silence* (1960), or by ITV's situation comedy *The Rag Trade*, in which a shop steward's whistle and the parrot-cry 'Everybody out!' added a new tag to the language.

Reform by compulsion was no longer as unthinkable as it had been for Churchill's government in 1951, and would at least have been a modernizing gesture of which Conservative voters would have thoroughly approved. Such thinking went, though, entirely against the grain for Macmillan and his successive Ministers of Labour, who continued to see trades union leaders as people to be supported by the government against their own unruly members, rather than be undermined by attacking their organizations from the outside. Rank and file demands for trades union reform were therefore marginalized by the party leaders and from 1962 became impossible anyway – at least until the NEDC and NIC had been given a chance to show what they could do. In all of this thinking, instinctively seeing the unions as partners rather than rivals or enemies, Macmillan had little difficulty in retaining the backing of Edward Heath, himself Minister of Labour in 1959–60, and Heath would retain in the back of his mind much from his experience under Macmillan even when the party's policy seemed to move on after 1964.

The party therefore spent the summer of 1963 nervously but resignedly awaiting Macmillan's decision either to retire or to pull himself and the party together and launch a campaign for a fourth term in office. After unusual hesitation and self-doubt, he finally decided that he would announce during the party's Blackpool Conference that he would fight the next election as Leader, only to find that he needed an urgent operation in the actual week of the Conference. Self-dramatizing to the end, Macmillan imagined himself perishing under the surgeon's knife and gave too little attention to the management of what would happen next. Butler was put in temporary charge of the government (though since he had done this from time to time ever since 1953 that hardly amounted to much). Home delivered the Prime Minister's bombshell announcement of his resignation to the party assembled in Blackpool, but Macmillan also

"If you ask me it's not a new tablet we need but a new Moses"

Daily Express, 20 February 1963.

thereby asked his party gathered in Conference to begin the 'customary processes of consultation' prior to choosing a new leader. There were two problems with this: firstly there actually were no 'customary processes', only a bundle of precedents which were mainly of considerable antiquity and which relied on the palace rather than the party for their activation anyway (as in 1923 and in 1957); and secondly Macmillan had chosen no successor who could 'emerge' as smoothly as Balfour, Chamberlain and Eden had done in 1902, 1937 and 1955. Since 1957 he had variously considered Hailsham, Home, Maudling and Macleod as possible successors – though not Butler, who was thought most likely by the majority of outsiders – but he had never stuck with one favourite for long.

The result was that the 1963 Blackpool Conference erupted into something like an American convention, with activists cheering their favourites and booing (or at least remaining ostentatiously silent) after speeches by others, with badges and banners proclaiming different candidates, and with the actual successors competitively briefing the press (except for Butler, who was so anxious not to do the wrong thing that week that he did none of the right things either) and seizing every opportunity to make news.

One effect was that many in the party resolved never to allow anything like this to happen again, a view that received powerful reinforcement from the events of the following week in London; this would be the last time that a Tory leader would be chosen without a properly verifiable election. In the short term, though, the week at Blackpool did destroy the hopes of the candidate that Macmillan himself was at the time supporting, Lord Hailsham. As Party Chairman before 1959, Hailsham had done much to revive morale, offering plenty of photo-opportunities by his habit of bathing in the sea each morning and publicly eating giant sticks of rock during the compulsory autumn week by the seaside, and securing a huge public relations success in 1957 when ringing the Conference bell to symbolize the knell of Labour's hopes. The mix of intellectual calibre and campaigning vulgarity that Hailsham offered was thus as close to the Macmillan style as was on offer from any candidate, but it was the vulgarity rather than the intellect that now stuck in the mind in the media circus that Blackpool had become, and this created a widespread belief among other Tories that Hailsham must not get the job that he all too obviously craved. Watching all of this on television in his London hospital, Macmillan resolved to 'switch peers in midstream' and back Home instead of Hailsham when the real battle for the succession moved to London.

In view of the outcome, there was much ink later spilled over who did what in that third week of October 1963, and the opening of private and government papers has still not settled all the matters in dispute. What is clear, though, is that Macmillan managed, with full Cabinet support rather than through some sort of conspiracy, an extensive exercise of consultation involving Tory MPs, peers, constituency activists and the National Union, and that the result of those consultations when given to the queen at the end of the week supported his recommendation that Home become Prime Minister, as the man best able to unite the party and the government. The problem was akin to that of 1911, for the front-runners, Butler and Hailsham, each had implacable opponents as well as a solid block of supporters, while as third man Home attracted less support but far less hostility too. The whips and organizers who conducted the various soundings seem to have perceived early on that Home was their best chance of a compromise choice that most Tories would support, and to have behaved accordingly, marginally misrepresenting some and entirely misreporting others in order to 'make a majority' for Home. But there is no reason to doubt their conviction that any other candidate would have been more divisive. Their problem was that making a majority in this way was divisive anyway, whoever actually won the prize as a result.

Macmillan ignored last-ditch efforts by the other candidates to stop

"Fight over the leadership! What fight over the leadership?"

Cummings of the *Daily Express* on the leadership contest of 1963.

the Home bandwagon, and on his advice the queen only invited Home to see if he could form a government (she being well aware of Conservatives' continuing doubt about the processes and the outcome). But the fact of Home's visit to the palace and his subsequent occupancy of Number Ten inexorably brought most of the doubters over to his side, and despite the fact that all the other candidates and about half the outgoing Cabinet now backed Butler against Home, Butler failed to make a fight. As a lifelong servant of Conservatism, Butler had imbibed its core tradition of loyalty. As a history undergraduate he had made a special study of Peel's government of 1841. When a journalist wrote in the 1950s that if Butler, like Peel, was called upon to split his party then he would never do it, Butler had read the passage and commented, 'It's true you know'; and he remarked soon after the 1963 leadership crisis that Peel's 'betrayal' of his party in 1846 was 'the supremely unforgettable lesson of history' for Conservatives. Butler therefore characteristically agreed to serve under Home, as did most of the rest of Macmillan's ministers, but from a combination of highmindedness and frustration both Iain Macleod and Enoch Powell refused to join. This ensured that October 1963 did not quickly fade from the memory, for Macleod and Powell represented a social type of Conservative far removed from Home's own, and both their presence on the backbenches and their writings over the next year ensured that they remained a highly visible sign that Home had in actuality failed in the task for which he had been mainly chosen, the ability to deliver party unity.

Personally, Sir Alec Douglas-Home (as he now became on renouncing his peerage and returning to the Commons at a by-election) was as popular a man as any Tory leader has ever been, honest, trusted and utterly devoid of personal animus or 'side', and he did indeed achieve a great deal in a short time by pulling the party together and by almost winning the 1964 election against very long odds. But the fact that he was a major Scottish landowner and patrician (as even his new Commoner name proclaimed), representative of exactly the old ruling class that was increasingly derided as out of touch and unmodern in the 1960s, gave him an uphill task when bidding for ordinary people's votes in competition with the carefully preserved Yorkshire vowels of Harold Wilson. Sir Alec could proclaim defiantly that he was for 'the modernization of Britain' and that his party was 'busy designing a programme of policies for that purpose', but the very fact of his being Leader, as Butler laconically put it, 'spoilt the image of modernization'. His frequent stumbles over the names of colleagues, or over details of his own government's policy – his Party Chairman later recalled that even 'his supporters were nervous for him before every appearance he made at the dispatch box' – and his inability to project a sense that he understood how the other 99 per cent lived, only confirmed these instinctive impressions. They would have been even more nervous had they known (as his brother later recorded) that Lady Home had to prompt the Prime Minister as they left the plane on each foreign visit with such reminders as 'Peking, Alec, Peking, Peking' (lest he should address the first microphone with the words 'I'm very happy to be back in Montreal . . .')

The main strategy for dealing with this difficulty was the foregrounding of the government's two most important movers and shakers, Reginald Maudling at the Exchequer and Edward Heath at a new super-department

'Well Enoch, there goes our last chance to get into the technological age'

Powell and Macleod regret the choice of Douglas-Home, *Guardian*, October 1963.

of Trade, Industry and Regional Development. It was for this reason that Heath's battle with the shopkeepers over Resale Price Maintenance had to be pushed forward despite its divisive effects on the party in an election year, for with Douglas-Home in Macmillan's place and Macleod stubbornly outside, the government had to try even harder to achieve the same reputation for drive. Yet with Douglas-Home fronting for the party on television, this would always be a losing battle, for nothing in his previous career had prepared him for the ordeal that he now had to undergo before the cameras, and he never managed to become more than a barely competent performer on what was now the main medium of political communication. His appeal rested largely on the realistic appraisal that he was a much better than average gentleman-amateur in politics, motivated more by duty than ambition, and therefore a definite contrast to many of his own ministers and to Harold Wilson; Douglas-Home versus Wilson would be, as David Frost summarized it for viewers of *That Was The Week That Was*, 'dull Alec against smart Alec'. Baldwin had traded successfully on just such an image, and Douglas-Home anyway had undeniable appeal to deferential Tories, while his straightforwardness proved to be a powerful asset in itself in getting over the aftermath of Profumo. But none of this was likely to win back the party's reputation for competence on which the more pragmatic votes depended.

Here much would rely once again on the economy, and here again the task was more difficult than in 1955 or 1959, for the record was more mixed. The very fact of a second recession in 1961–2 after a second election year boom in 1959 induced cynicism, and the slowness of recovery in 1962 reduced the party's electoral fortunes to a lower ebb than in 1957, with a Liberal surge climaxing at the Orpington by-election of March 1962, the first (but by no means the last) solidly middle-class suburb to desert the Conservatives since 1945. By 1963–4 the threat was again from Labour, but the Liberal vote did not revert to the low level of 1959, and in fact Labour took some seats as a result of Conservative defections to Liberal candidates, as they would do across the country in 1964. The eventual recovery of the economy helped to produce an unsteady and late Conservative revival in the last year of the parliament, but, as a result of such unrelated matters as Profumo, RPM and the leadership issue, the economic and the electoral cycles were no longer well synchronized. Chancellor Maudling's wish to hold an election in the spring of 1964 could not be granted, for Tory improvement in the polls had been too slow, and by the time the Labour and Conservative parties were about level in the autumn the economy was already overheating and it was difficult to proclaim an unequivocal message of economic success.

Nevertheless, the overall record of thirteen years was a good one. Few if any of the fears that Labour had exploited in 1950–51 had materialized. The housing boom had continued after 1955 and almost 4 million dwellings had been completed; the number of cars on the road had tripled (as had domestic car production), the number of telephones had doubled, the number of televisions had risen twentyfold. Conscription had now finally ended, and there had been no military operations of significance since Suez, while apart from a brief winter upsurge in 1962–3 unemployment had remained low – certainly well below inter-war levels. Over the whole period average earnings had risen more than twice as fast as prices. Over time, the erosion of class barriers that improved lifestyles promoted would provide new Tory opportunities, but in the short-term the economic legacy narrowly failed to win back enough of the votes lost in the doldrums of 1962–3. In the general election of October 1964 the Labour Party actually won fewer votes than in 1959, but the much greater fall in the Tory vote (significantly affected by those who had gone to the Liberals) generated sixty-one lost seats and an overall Labour majority of five.

In the harsher world of opposition, Sir Alec proved even less suited to the role of Leader, for, like Baldwin in 1930, he was loath to abandon policies that he had believed in when in government or to attack Labour for continuing with them. He also lacked the bite that an opposition's leader needs in order to gee up his troops and he was hurt by the party's increasingly critical tone. He stayed on long enough to authorize the first stages of a policy review, to ensure that there would be no leadership vacuum if Wilson called an early second election, and to give his authority to the adoption of a formal system for electing the Conservative Leader – so that no future Leader would have to endure, as he had done, taunts that he had got the job only by a 'fix'. But his heart was never in the job after October 1964 and he increasingly delegated the actual tasks of opposition in the Commons to Maudling and Heath. With the first difficult session in opposition over and with party criticism mounting, he resigned without either fuss or rancour in July 1965 – though characteristically he then loyally served under his successor for another nine years.

The party had been formally reunited when, in reaction to election defeat, both Macleod and Powell rejoined the front bench, though in Home's allocation of portfolios he had promoted younger men too, and in the retirement from active politics of Rab Butler in early 1965 there was a recognition that the slog of opposition involved a further move towards the next generation. The decision of Hailsham and (more reluctantly) Thorneycroft not to challenge for the leadership when it fell vacant reflected the same sense that youth must take the helm. Macleod's decision not to stand reflected the view that his rocking of the boat in 1963 was still too recent, while Powell's failure to attract more than a handful of votes when he stood in the contest showed that his free-market alternative to Macmillan's 'new approach' to domestic policy had as yet only minimal backing. The choice therefore came down to Heath or Maudling, who reflected a similar social basis of Conservatism, had similarly Macmillanite policy preferences, and had had broadly parallel careers since reaching the Commons in the class of 1950. It was thus a choice more between styles than content, and one in which the result reflected the professional seriousness with which Heath's men prepared and organized, compared with Maudling's more casual approach to promoting himself. Nevertheless, the fact that in July 1965 almost all Tory MPs voted for either Heath or Maudling, neither of whom had been seriously mentioned during the last leadership contest in 1963, indicated the extent of the move forward, a move that would have seemed wildly improbable back in 1951 when Churchill had last led the party back to power. With Heath, and then his successors, Thatcher, Major and Hague, the Conservative Party was once again moving down the social scale after a quarter of a century of leadership entirely by men who might by birth have qualified for the top job even in the nineteenth century. Now, as the *Sunday Mirror* put it, there would be 'a new kind of Tory Leader – a classless, professional politician who has fought his way to the top with guts, ability and political skill'. Having tried the combination of tradition and modernization that Macmillan embodied, and then the more backward-looking Home, Conservatives now opted unequivocally for the unashamed modernization implied in 'the rise of the meritocracy'.

15

Conservatives for a Change, 1965–74

PARTY LEADERS elected when their parties are in opposition suffer many handicaps, but not the least of these is the extent to which they are chosen in reaction to whatever the government of the day happens to be doing at the time. In dismissing all candidates for the party leadership who were over fifty and in preferring Edward Heath to Reginald Maudling, Conservative MPs were consciously seeking to lose the out-of-date, out-of-touch and amateurish images that had haunted their party over the past few years, but they were also seeking someone who could match (and preferably beat) Harold Wilson in debate. Heath's more abrasive manner and his humbler origins thus made him in 1965 marginally the stronger candidate than Maudling, and he duly obliged by unleashing his deeply felt contempt for Wilson in their twice-weekly duels in the Commons, exchanges that reached a depth of rudeness not employed by Conservative front-benchers since Bonar Law's 'new style' of 1912–13 and one that was unlikely to have occurred under the more relaxed Maudling. It was no coincidence that Heath was the first Conservative Leader since Bonar Law chosen when his party was out of office, for, like Bonar Law, he too faced a lengthy period during which the lack of a prime minister's authority and patronage made it difficult for him to impose his will on his party, and in which virulent denunciation of the government had to play its part in papering over the cracks on his own side.

Since his elevation to the leadership was followed only eight months later by a big Conservative defeat in the 1966 election – and hence the certainty of another full parliament out of office – Heath's first five years were the second longest continuous period that any Conservative has had as Leader of the Opposition in the twentieth century. This prolonged and

"If you can keep your head when all about you . . ."

Daily Telegraph, 17 October 1967.

depressing period was punctuated by regular calls for him to step down by people on his own side, by battles with colleagues who were only reluctantly persuaded to pull together, by opinion polls that stubbornly failed to register approval of his performance as Leader (though the party itself was miles ahead of Labour in the polls, and both local and by-elections confirmed its dominance without interruption from the summer of 1966 through to the end of 1969), and by media assessments of his failure to put across the party's case. For, despite the circumstances of his election to the leadership, Heath neither was nor wanted to be very good at the tasks required of opposition, and his energies were always directed more towards what he would do with power than to winning it in the first place. His Opposition was aptly dubbed a 'government in exile', while his record as Prime Minister has been interpreted as that of 'a civil servant manqué', even an 'anti-politician', happier with administration than with politics.

To understand these apparent anomalies, it is necessary to place the mature Heath in the context of his earlier career. He had indeed come to the top from lower down in society than most of the class of 1950 with which he was usually linked, for while they had for the most part come from upper-middle-class professional families, Heath's father had been a building craftsman and he had personally experienced in the 1930s the rough side of unemployment and poverty. He had, though, upwardly progressed through grammar school, Oxford, a wartime commission in the elite Honourable Artillery Company and genteel journalism on the

Church Times, before he entered the House of Commons in 1950; he had also acquired an accent and a passion for racing yachts and serious music that set him well apart from most others who had shared his Kentish origins. This made the real Heath an uncomfortable fit with the representative status as meritocratic man that he had also by then acquired. At one level his rise had left him with a set of fixed opinions that he never lost. From his father's experience he was left with a deep fear (for others rather than for himself) of the social and spiritual effects of economic recession, much like Teesside's effect on Macmillan. From the later 1930s (when he had, even as an undergraduate, denounced Chamberlain's appeasement policy at the Oxford by-election of 1938) he became a staunch believer in deterrence and in the need for strong defence forces, and from the war years he acquired, like so many junior officers of the time, a belief that such a European war must never be allowed to happen again, a commitment that made him an ardent advocate of British participation in the European movement towards integration. After 1945 he became a popular speaker on the Conservative circuit and a gregariously popular candidate for the new suburban constituency of Bexley on the Kent–London border. Once in the Commons he was known as an effective parliamentary debater and a convivial man with many friends.

Thereafter, and somewhat mysteriously, during his nine years in the Whips' Office in which he rose to be Chief Whip between 1955 and 1959, the Heath character changed considerably. Many rising politicians serve for a short time as a whip – it is to all intents and purposes a necessary first step on the ladder and invaluable training in the rules of the House – but few spend almost the whole of their first political decade in the self-denying abstinence from public-speaking and in the obsession with management and unity that must characterize the whip's daily life. There is no doubt that Heath's rapid rise within that private world showed him to be a very good whip, and it was generally acknowledged that he almost saved the party by limiting the damage over Suez in 1956, so much so that Macmillan could not bring himself to move him on for another three years. There is no doubt either that he formed between 1957 and 1959 a close working relationship with Macmillan, with whom he dined on the evening of Macmillan's arrival at Number Ten, or that their working relationship relied on similar approaches to political issues as well as on mutual respect. When Heath finally escaped from the Chief Whip's office, he was soon placed in the key position of European negotiator on which Macmillan's whole strategy would depend. When Macmillan stood down,

Heath was one of the ministers who supported Home's succession and the one who benefited most when it succeeded, for, with the shortage of younger, dynamic ministers that followed the loss of Macleod and Powell, he was vital to the government's public image. Even the rough ride that he gave to the party over Resale Price Maintenance was turned to his advantage as evidence of his determination and drive, and in opposition from 1964 his spirited campaign as shadow Chancellor to expose Labour's faltering start in office provided the final evidence that projected him to the leadership.

Throughout this – as a whip, as Macmillan's protégé, and as Douglas-Home's chief lieutenant – Heath had risen on the inside track, and despite his earlier origins on which so much comment touched, he was effectively the establishment candidate in 1965. When, a few years later, the Central Office strategists discussed with him ways of 'selling' him as a political personality, they found him fastidiously resistant to the idea in general (because it was 'the sort of thing Wilson would do'), but especially hostile to any party campaign that dwelt on his background and on his rise from obscurity. At the end of the 1964–70 period of opposition, the dilemma was solved more by good luck than by a change of approach, for his international yachting success in the Sydney to Hobart race in 1969 allowed him to be promoted as an international highflyer without much mention of the point of departure. The truth seems to be that Heath was sensitive about his social background in a way that contrasted sharply with Harold Wilson's (mainly fictitious) accounts of walking to school barefoot, or with the way in which Margaret Thatcher, John Major and William Hague would all use their origins as the focus of a populist appeal in the years to come.

In other senses, too, Heath had moved from the ardent political campaigner of 1950 to a very different figure by the mid-1960s. He had withdrawn from former friendships – at least among politicians, and he kept his remaining personal contacts forbiddingly private – and he was now widely regarded as remote and insensitive, a man who neither initiated warmth nor welcomed it in others. He was also a man with a steadily decreasing fund of small-talk and a reluctance to spend those diminishing reserves on political colleagues, missing out therefore on the costless benefits that a party leader can acquire by his words of encouragement and congratulation, pats on the back for a speech well made, and all the other little gestures that lubricate social (and especially political) life. As Prime Minister, this would show in the curtailment of the use of the honours list (an area where he could with profit have followed Macmillan's generous example) and in the steady increase in the numbers of Tory MPs whom he had unintentionally insulted or irritated by some brusque remark.

Above and beyond this, there was now for Heath a fascination with the minutiae of the policy process that not all were likely to share, a belief that what the party stood for was so obvious that it barely needed to be spelled out, and perhaps (as Enoch Powell was later to put it) a lack of confidence in discussing large ideas which did not inhibit him in matters of detail. Increasingly, therefore, Heath's public-speaking became bogged down in detail, resembling lectures more than political addresses, offering a wealth of evidence in support of his viewpoint but often at the same time failing to express clearly enough what that viewpoint actually was and why he had adopted it in the first place. As his political secretary Douglas Hurd put it, when describing Heath as Prime Minister, 'Mr Heath believed that people deserved the evidence, and, by God, they were going to get it. Sometimes it made for hard pounding.' Nor was it easy to attract his attention to the necessary preparations for public speaking; his Party Chairman noted, on a visit by the Leader to the Conservative Local Government Conference in Weston-super-Mare, that Heath 'read out the text of a speech written for him by his staff apparently without rehearsing it or even reading it through'.

Public relations advisers sought vainly to pierce this wall of pedestrian oratory, but only in the context of 1970, an election year (when even Heath could hardly object to being 'packaged' for the voters), did they have much success, and as soon as he reached Downing Street he eschewed even these limited advances and reverted to type. When, in the winter of 1973–4, he sought re-election, there had been little pre-planning for a prime ministerial campaign and there was even now no turning away from the priority of governing, and he thus allowed his party to drift into an early election for which Conservatives were less well-prepared than the Labour Opposition. As Edward Pearce recently put it, after reviewing Labour's own terrible performance in the early 1970s, 'the ability of Edward Heath to lose to this demoralized, split, intellectually-distressed band of non-brothers remains one of the great negative achievements of British politics'.

Heath was able to behave in this resolutely 'anti-political' manner partly because his party to a large extent shared his own belief that Wilson had demeaned the premiership by being *too* political, and insufficiently concerned with running the country, but partly too because he had few colleagues able to challenge him from a position near to equality. The jump to a new generation in 1965 had to a large extent left older Conservatives feeling that their day had passed while, of the men in Heath's own age group, his Deputy Leader Maudling was temperamentally unlikely to face down a determined Heath (and was to be forced out of politics by a scandal in 1972), Enoch Powell left the front bench over immigration in 1968, and Iain Macleod, who was still working his passage back to loyalty after 1963, died immediately after the 1970 election. By 1972, then, and to an extent long before then, nobody on the front bench had a weight remotely comparable to the Leader's, and he was receiving little or no advice to which he would have to listen.

The problem was accentuated by Heath's patronage within the party and on the front bench. It would be quite wrong to suggest that he packed the shadow cabinet, and after 1970 the Cabinet, with 'yes men' from his own Macmillanite wing of the party, but it was certainly the case that when Powell departed in 1968, or Edward du Cann left the party chairmanship after a spat with Heath in 1967, he did not exactly go out of his way to find like-minded replacements. Du Cann had been appointed by Douglas-Home as an independent-minded chairman not especially close to the then Leader, but he was succeeded at Central Office by Anthony Barber, Peter Thomas, Lord Carrington and finally William Whitelaw, all perfectly reasonable appointees but also all men who had a strong personal loyalty to Heath. Like Davidson under Baldwin – and most unlike Woolton under Churchill or Hailsham under Macmillan – the Party Chairman became Heath's representative to the party rather than the other way round. On the policy side, Heath retained personally the chairmanships of the Research Department and of the Advisory Committee on Policy, making no colleague the 'policy impresario' that Neville Chamberlain had been under Baldwin and Butler under Churchill, Eden and Macmillan. When he had to delegate some of these tasks on becoming Prime Minister, the men he chose were again his faithful followers rather than colleagues of an independent turn of mind. The channels of party communication were predominantly one-way, and when, for example, the ACP became highly critical of the Heath government in and after 1972, there was little sign that ministers were listening to what it was saying or changing anything as a result of its critical 'advice'.

Little of this was obvious at the start, for when Heath became Leader he had already embarked (as Douglas-Home's lieutenant) on the most comprehensive and businesslike policy review that the party has ever mounted, a review into which all sections of the party were drawn as participants. The sheer effort that went into that review mopped up much of the party's surplus of energy, and, at least until the main lines of the review had been published in full detail by about 1968, gave a very real impression of positive activity.

There was, though, a problem inserted into the process by its timing that flawed it from the start, and particularly because it accidentally reinforced Heath's own preference for deciding detail over discussing principles. Just because Labour had won such a small majority in October 1964, the Conservatives had to react very quickly to their defeat, in case a second general election came upon them before they were ready. This 're-forming under fire' (as the Party Chairman, Lord Blakenham, put it) dictated the shape of the policy review and its urgency. When numbers of policy groups were up and working by the early part of 1965, most of them – and all those dealing with high-profile policy matters – had been instructed to produce at least an interim report by the following summer. Most managed to meet this ambitious target, and the first fruits of the review, across the whole range of policy, duly appeared as the document *Putting Britain Right Ahead* in the same month in which Heath became Leader of the party. This was then fed very soon into the manifesto on which the party fought the 1966 general election, exactly as had been intended. But when the party lost that second election by a hundred seats, it had to embark on a full parliament with a package of policies so new that they could hardly be ditched, but so specific that there was little room for reconsideration. In some areas, such as trades union reform, more work after 1966 did provide a chance to refine details of policy and in that case to sound out trades union leaders as well (though in the event neither exercise proved to have been especially helpful when it came to implementing the plans in office); in other areas, like local government reform, the party could after 1966 move into new areas as a result of the actions of the Labour government and the march of events. But for the most part, even where much more detail was added later, the essential policies on which the party had to fight in 1970 were the ones that had been developed at the gallop in the spring of 1965 and published in July of that year.

With dozens of different groups each considering its own policy remit – such a hive of activity that on busy days there were several groups meeting at the same time – it would have been impossible for overlaps and inconsistencies to have been avoided, for there was little initial guidance from the shadow cabinet before the groups got going. Completed group reports then had to be dealt with by the shadow cabinet in batches, so tight was the timetable for publication before the 1965 summer recess. Since at this time most groups were headed by shadow spokesmen who had themselves been ministers only a few weeks earlier, they were unlikely to propose the abandonment of everything that they had been doing in office. In the key area of policy towards Europe, Heath was so sure that there must be continuity of policy that he did not even set up a review group. Since this had been the driver of so many other domestic policies during the Macmillan/Douglas-Home governments, the key assumption remained that the rest of the policy package must provide means for modernization so as to enable Britain to enter the EEC competitively, without that assumption ever being properly re-evaluated.

In some areas this freedom from the restraints of office to pursue policy detail without a review of principles did not cause undue difficulty, and policy developments on housing finance and on taxation (both rather technical matters) did indeed lead forward to substantial reforms that the Heath government was able to make in office. Even there, though, there could be problems when the consideration of technical changes impinged on more philosophical areas of the party's identity and purpose. The taxation reformers, for example, were keen at least to consider the introduction of higher capital taxation, even of new taxes, in order to make room for cuts in taxes on earnings and consumption. This was an approach that fitted well enough with the modernizing, meritocratic ethos which Heath was supposed to represent, in which high retained earnings for the most able were seen as entirely justifiable, while windfall inheritances that derived from the accidents of birth or from mere speculation were thought to be legitimate targets for the taxman. It was this sort of distinction that led CRD staffers to describe some of Heath's speeches as amounting to the statement, 'Blessed are the pacemakers', for he did tend to dwell repeatedly on the importance of incentives for highflyers and on the disproportionate effect that their enterprise could have on the lives of ordinary citizens. But when the ACP got wind of these taxation plans – critics describing them emotively as a 'wealth tax' (which was not quite right, but did recognize the basic approach) – and the reformers' ideas were seen to conflict with the party's duty to defend property (and the propertied among its best supporters), the whole approach was rapidly and unceremoniously jettisoned. Forced to decide whether they were set to become a 'party of earners' rather than a 'party of owners', a principle that had never been directly raised before, the Conservative leaders decided that they did not dare alienate either group. Taxation plans that dealt with technicalities were fine, but anything that made significant shifts in the overall tax burden was to be avoided, and the shadow cabinet decided nervously that if Labour now introduced such capital taxes then the Conservatives would just have to vote against them.

In other areas, too, decisions on individual cases produced some odd bedfellows in the new Tory package. Opposing Labour's plans to nationalize iron and steel in the Commons, Anthony Barber took a pragmatic and cooperative line and refused to commit the Conservatives to the future denationalization that Churchill had promised on the previous occasion. And when a policy group under free marketeer Nicholas Ridley proposed a wholesale programme of privatization even among industries that Tories had left in the public sector between 1951 and 1964, the shadow cabinet suppressed the report and Heath personally ensured that it did not surface as party policy. And yet at the same time, the plans that Peter Walker was making as Environment spokesman included the sale of council housing to tenants, and the denationalization of the government travel agency Thomas Cook's and of the public houses in Carlisle (run by the state since the First World War). Heath's justification for such apparently inconsistent approaches was – much as moderate Labour had argued ever since Anthony Crosland's *The Future of Socialism* (1956) – that ownership arguments were old-fashioned and irrelevant, when what was needed now was the best management suited to each particular case, consumer-orientated for genuinely competitive services and state-directed for monopolies.

Increasingly, therefore, effort went into methods and techniques rather than into policy content, and when Heath promised in 1970 'a quiet revolution in government', he referred more to the way in which Whitehall was managed and organized than to policy outputs. Much research was done into government practice abroad and into management methods within industry, and as a result the Heath government was ready, when it took office in 1970, to set up a Central Policy Review Staff (the 'think tank') to provide busy ministers with a non-departmental long-term review facility, and such methods as programme analysis and review to ensure regular reconsideration of the effectiveness of policy delivery and of value for money. Within a few months in office new super-ministries for Industry and the Environment had been created to improve managerial coordination at both the political and the administrative levels, building on Heath's own experience in 1963–4. Finally, and with a substantial input from David Howell's Public Sector Research Unit (if with more scepticism elsewhere), new technology and a modern managerial vocabulary were promoted as essential both to the image of the Conservatives as a modernizing party and to the success of a Tory government as manager of the nation.

When *Private Eye* took to lampooning Heath as the managing director of 'Heathco', a man drowning in his own management-speak but entirely unable to motivate his workforce, they were commenting not only on his platform style but also on the preference for method over ideas that seemed to permeate much of his front bench. A *Telegraph* columnist had spotted just this problem when reviewing *Putting Britain Right Ahead* in 1965. Colin Welch quoted Heath himself saying in the introduction to the document that 'what men and women want, quite rightly, is not theories but results in terms of more dependable service and better performance', and commented that 'this sounds, blunt, businesslike, British stuff. Yet even in this fog-enveloped island there must be grey pedants who suspect that theories and results are closely connected, that wrong theories will produce wrong results . . . ?' Along much the same line, the CRD director wrote to a predecessor two years later and urged him to 'write to Ted sometime and tell him that the public want to know where he wants to go just as much as how he means to get there'.

Heath was unimpressed by such reasoning, and in 1966 the party fought the election by making 131 specific proposals that were only loosely woven into a programme, and on the slogan 'Action not words' (though even Sir Alec – hardly the party's greatest theoretician – gently wondered 'if "ideas" ought not to be brought into it'). As polls showed, the attempt to put across so many detailed plans rather than a few coherent themes meant that hardly any of it got across at all, and, as Iain Macleod remembered in 1967, 'at the last election the Conservative Party manifesto had contained 131 specific promises. This was far too much to put across to the electorate, and the net result was that everybody thought we had no policy.' To an extent, better marketing to emphasize policy priorities would solve the problem for 1970, but the uncertainties at the heart of the programme remained. The result of waiting for principles to emerge from the detail was that what emerged was almost bound to be (and was) identical to what had motivated the party in office between 1960 and 1964 – modernization and Europe – but that the implications of sticking to this and trying to implement it a decade later were never faced up to. More important for the future unity of the party, neither was the fact that some Conservatives were by 1970 beginning to reject the corporatist, interventionist weapons that had been Macmillan's choice of methods with which to modernize Britain.

There was, though, one very clear exception to this general pattern, and that was the party's policy for the trades unions. Within a few weeks of the loss of power in 1964 the front-bench consensus that had marginalized calls for trades union reform was swept aside and a study group under the ex-Chancellor Viscount (formerly Derick Heathcoat) Amory decided on a bold initiative to modernize industrial relations law by instituting a legally enforceable code on trades unions which would make production-stopping wildcat strikes and demarcation disputes a thing of the past. Such a commitment appeared in *Putting Britain Right Ahead* and remained central to the party's thinking about industrial and economic policy until Margaret Thatcher succeeded in breaking the power of the unions in the 1980s. The original framers of the policy, coming, like Amory himself, from the consensual traditions of the war generation, did not envisage pitched battles with the unions of the sort that happened in the early 1970s and again a decade later, for they believed in their power to win trades unionists to support their new approach (which opinion polls showed to be popular even among union members). They also believed in the respect for the authority of parliament which would lead trades unions as organizations to accept changes in the law once made (a view that was reinforced by discussions with the union leaders between 1966 and 1970), and in the crucial importance of an electoral mandate as authority to carry out the proposed reforms. It scarcely seems to have occurred to the party's successive shadow spokesmen, or to their policy group colleagues, that those who ran the unions were changing in their own political outlook as a result of a significant swing to the left among union activists, that what union members said to opinion polls or the unions' national leaders said privately to Conservatives would be of little value if confrontation occurred, or that the unions might simply defy the authority of parliament and its electoral mandate. Even when Wilson's Labour government produced, in 1968–9, a similar package of reform proposals, the Conservatives criticized them for being half-hearted rather than backing them as a step in the right direction, and then rejoiced at the unions' defeat of Labour's blatant attempt to steal their most popular policy rather than recognizing in Wilson's failure a warning for themselves.

However, although the framers of this new direction in Tory policy did not either want or expect a battle with the unions, they did see what they were doing as having revolutionary importance for Britain's future. When Heath proclaimed on entering Downing Street that 'we were returned to office to change the course of history of this nation, nothing less', he was surely thinking of trades union policy as being at the head of the list of his objectives, but it was an objective that he expected to achieve by persuasion and encouragement (the new Industrial Relations Bill did after all include numerous benefits to the unions intended to sweeten the pill) rather than by fines, imprisonments, strikes, lock-outs, demonstrations and battles in the streets. The target was a hugely ambitious one, for, above and beyond the detail, Heath and his colleagues believed (like Thatcher's team in the 1980s) that the unions had become since the war the main obstruction to efficiency in industry – by, for example, perpetuating over-manning and other such lazy practices – and that the real objective of the reform was to reverse that trend, give power back to managers and so unlock Britain's potential for growth.

These bold proposals were undeniably popular with the public, and as the party gave more and more attention to marketing them once the full detail was published as *Fair Deal at Work* in 1968, they were widely recognized as a distinctly Tory policy, particularly after Wilson's very public failure to steal the issue in 1969. However, the package acquired a secondary importance as time went on, for on other economic issues the Conservative Party in opposition was less united, so that trades union reform had to make up for various other gaps in the programme. Most crucially, the Conservatives under Heath failed to deal coherently with the issue of price and wage inflation. In office, before 1964, they had used wage and price controls as tools of economic management, and in particular as a means of keeping export prices competitive, but there had been, even in Macmillan's Cabinets, those, like Powell and Joseph, who did not in their hearts believe that such control of the market system would ever be effective, and others who saw such things as acceptable only in emergencies. In opposition the party voted solidly against Wilson's wages and price controls of 1966 and thereafter. They generally justified their votes more by the rhetoric of freedom and their general doubts about government policy than by anything specific to price and wage levels, for within the shadow cabinet there was simply no agreement about what the Conservatives should do. The most recent Tory Chancellor, Maudling, was a strong believer in interventionist methods and was backed by other former ministers, but the shadow chancellor, Macleod, was more instinctively a free marketeer than an interventionist, and had his own supporters in the team, while Powell (at first by ranging outside his own policy brief and from 1968 from outside the front bench altogether) was flying the flag of unlimited economic liberalism with increasing force and fervour. Heath's solution to this unbridgeable gap was to ensure that the Economic Policy Group, which he chaired personally rather than placing Maudling under Macleod or vice versa, spent all its time on tax matters and hardly ever got round to economic policy.

Nevertheless, the rising rate of price inflation as the 1966 parliament drew to a close was too tempting a target to ignore, and this was therefore a stick with which Tory spokesmen increasingly beat Labour. When the 1970 campaign began, Heath correctly predicted that prices would be the biggest issue over the weeks ahead, and his party certainly made every effort to exploit Labour's poor record, though they were rarely able to offer much of an alternative policy of their own. A prospective government that was desperate to achieve a higher rate of growth, both for its inherent advantages and as a basis for entering Europe, was therefore driven more and more into proclaiming that its key policy for restraining inflation was its reform of the unions' bargaining power at law, rather than through legal control of their members' wages.

The BBC's Ian Trethowan has recalled in his memoirs how the 'dangerous hole in the Tory economic policy, the absence of any clear idea how they were going to deal with the inevitable pressure on incomes', was handled by Heath when questioned by friendly journalists such as himself:

> Heath (and Macleod too) tended to dismiss such questions rather impatiently by saying that one should look at 'the policies' as a whole, and they would automatically encompass the problem of incomes. Some of us did not see how this would happen and, when the gap in the policies was so cruelly exposed by the first miners' strike [of 1971–2] and the Government's ignominious defeat, the emperor was seen in this area to have no clothes.

The party's professional policy advisers were well aware of the problem, recognizing that the need for unity and the demands of party management had had to be given a higher priority than facing up to hard policy choice. The party files are littered with their warnings of what this might bring in its train.

At the last minute the tactical problem was solved in two ways in the early months of 1970, first by an agreement among shadow ministers that could no longer be postponed on what they would *say* about prices (since they still could not agree what they would do), and second by the intervention of an outside force which promoted a routine policy weekend at Selsdon in South London into a major breakthrough to (false) policy coherence. On Macleod's advice, shadow ministers agreed that they must at least seem to be decisive, and therefore to say in the manifesto for the approaching election that they opposed price and wage controls and would not introduce them in office; if, he cynically added, it was necessary to have such things later, then it would be explained at that time that the circumstances had changed. This enabled the party to campaign enthusiastically against Wilson's policy over the next few months and was the basis for some very unguarded language by Heath himself which he must have bitterly regretted soon afterwards: 'we have always been opposed to compulsory wage control. We opposed it in the House when the Bill was going through, and we are opposed to it and we will not introduce it.'

The Selsdon Park conference of January 1970 merely confronted shadow ministers with decisions already taken at previous meetings and asked them to approve the overall programme that had accumulated, thus clearing the decks for an election. But re-publication of these commitments in successive press releases in just a few days, and the fortuitous early concentration on law and order (which had hardly even been discussed in the meeting but was trailed to the press as a lead issue for the Sunday papers), certainly reinforced the idea of bold and tough policies in the offing. The conference itself was – again fortuitously – a big public relations success in a slack week for news, but its greatest importance was that it provoked an invaluable Labour counter-attack. Harold Wilson denounced 'Selsdon Man' (a neat shorthand phrase which implied prehistoric barbarism as well as middle-class exclusivity) as a systematic throwback to a less caring, less civilized age. This was an attack which, when picked up in the press, can have done little to enhance Heath's aim to present his party as modern, but did make his policies seem far more coordinated than they had ever done before. And since the Labour government and Wilson himself as Prime Minister had been massively unpopular for three years by this time (and were recovering only a fragile credibility during 1970), to be denounced from that quarter as offering something completely different was no bad thing at all for Tory chances at the election. Both the internal bargains and the externally imposed impression of policy coherence lasted through to the election in June, but did not of course solve the basic problem.

The reality of 'Selsdon Man' was rather different. The 1970 Tory package certainly did contain more 'economic realism at election time' (as a CRD staffer put it) than had been usual, and the language in which Heath talked of 'the great divide' and the need for 'a new style of government' implied anyway that he was offering an unusually substantial shift of direction, as he continued to claim over the year ahead as Prime Minister. But while there truly was a dimension of radicalism in the Tory programme on a whole range of technical issues, and in the central (but for the time being doomed) domestic target of weaker, tamer trades unions, there was also a fatal ambiguity on the economy – which is what, then and later, Selsdon was thought to be mainly about. By 1970 journalists and financial columnists could already see that the Conservative Party spoke with two distinct voices on economic matters. Some were moving towards the free-market view that the Institute of Economic Affairs had been pushing since the later 1950s and Powell more politically in his speeches and writings since 1964; these were proclaiming views that seem more characteristic of later decades – for instance, when Keith Joseph proclaimed that capitalism had not failed in Britain, since it had not yet been tried, or when he called for government to let more firms go bankrupt in order to improve opportunities for the rest. Others, like Peter Walker, took a more traditional view, seeing an important role in job-creation for the agencies of the state, for regional policy and for public investment in industry.

It was generally thought that Heath was in the latter camp by instinct, but his speeches in 1970 certainly did not convey that impression. He was of course forced to articulate opinions for the whole party and to accentuate, as oppositions always do, the things that distinguished them from the government, but, as a result more of his speeches in 1970 than of his actual policies, Heath raised expectations among younger Conservatives entering the Commons in 1970 of a freshness and toughness of approach to which he was never very deeply committed. Heath did not complain about Joseph's provocative speeches on industry, but nor did he make him the minister responsible for industry (which Joseph had been shadowing). Ironically, when Macleod's death forced a reshuffle only a few weeks after the new government was formed, Heath turned for a new Industry minister to the non-political former industrialist John Davies, who promptly began making very Joseph-like speeches, emphasizing his refusal to save 'lame ducks', and the need for industry to 'stand on its own feet' rather than be 'bailed out' by the Treasury. Heath did not restrain Davies in this choice of words, but nor did he rely on him very much for advice on industrial policy when the going got rough in 1972.

There is some tragic irony in the fact that Heath – the most puritan of all recent Tory leaders in relation to the black arts of public relations, and one later regarded as insufficiently responsive to his party's needs in that field – should in 1970 have got himself into a position in which he was advocating, or at least tolerating, policies that in his heart he disliked and distrusted, but which his party demanded of him and which his public relations men then promoted with reckless enthusiasm. It was, though, the inescapable consequence of a policy review that leapt into detail before settling on underlying principles, and it would, in 1972 and afterwards, expose him to increasingly bitter taunts from other Conservatives who actually agreed with what he had proclaimed on their behalf in 1970, accusations that he betrayed in office what he had said in order to get there. This was at most only half-true, for Heath scarcely ever bothered to conceal the fact that the choice between alternative methods in economic policy was entirely secondary to the need to maintain economic growth and increase national competitiveness. If the chosen weapons were to fail, then he would without sentiment discard them in favour of others. Tories who believed (as Angus Maude had argued in 1966 in the *Spectator*, and got himself sacked by Heath for saying so) that 'a technocratic view [was] not enough', would not prove to be so flexible in their thinking.

In this context, the problems that the Heath government faced and the violent party reaction that followed its humiliating fall in 1974 become easy enough to understand. The actual circumstances of the 1970 election did, though, contribute a final dangerous ingredient. Despite the fact that Conservatives rode high in the polls throughout the years 1966 to 1969, their lead was always heavily reliant on Labour's failure in office and its consequent unpopularity. When the Labour record improved somewhat at the end of the term, the Tory lead crumbled, and by the spring of 1970 the parties were again neck and neck. Since Wilson had the timing of the election at his disposal and was generally deemed the master-campaigner of the age, Tory morale plummeted too, and when the election was called and Labour's position in the polls continued to strengthen, there were few Conservatives either in the party or in the press who expected anything other than a third Labour term. With hindsight, the omens were actually more mixed, for the national polls never settled into a stable pattern after years of wild fluctuations (always a sign of their unreliability as predictors); polls taken in marginal constituencies mainly predicted a Tory win, 1970's local government results had been better for Conservatives than had been generally reported, and local Tories who studied canvass figures had cause for cheer there too. None of this made much impact against the headline message of the national polls, and as a result – at least until the news turned against Labour in the last week of the actual campaign – only Heath seems to have consistently behaved as if he thought he would win (and even his own staff did not know if this was conviction or just a brave front). As a result, when Heath did win on 18 June 1970, securing a Tory majority of thirty, much of the credit went personally to him, and there is not much doubt that he saw it that way himself.

In the next few years, as Heath withdrew increasingly into his prime ministerial shell – by 1973 into a sort of Downing Street bunker from which he rarely emerged to meet outsiders – he forgot the sophisticated media campaign to which he had grudgingly submitted in 1970 and remembered rather that he had won by straight-talking to the people; imagined indeed that he had a sort of personal line to the electorate which could by-pass party, press and public relations people, a line that he could reopen as and when he needed it again. In view of the general opinion that Heath had scored a historic personal triumph in 1970, his personal authority as Prime Minister was substantially reinforced at much the time when he would have benefited from being brought down to earth and forced to listen to just those party and media people who were soon bemoaning his government's failure to explain what it was doing with any effectiveness – but who were generally unable to attract the Prime Minister's attention.

In the later Conservative historiography of the 1980s it was fashionable to portray Heath's government as insufficiently committed to anything, forgetting its pledges at the drop of a hat and lacking the guts to 'tough it out' as the Thatcher team did in and after 1981. To those who before 1981 said crudely that Thatcher was just another Heath, if a 'Heath with tits', her admirers would respond with equal directness that the real truth was that she was 'Heath with balls'. Or, as a *Telegraph* cartoon presented the same idea in February 1975, Thatcher as Lady Macbeth had seized the daggers labelled 'Tory policy' from the hesitating Heath/Macbeth with the words, 'Infirm of purpose! Give me the daggers!' However, that analysis ignores all too much of the evidence. Thatcher's rhetoric and programme in 1979 were not at all unlike that offered by Heath in 1970, but it was underpinned by an intellectual and media consensus behind her policy that Heath never enjoyed in his first two turbulent years in office, and it is far from clear whether the often pragmatic Thatcher would have 'toughed it out' in 1981 if she had attracted no support whatsoever in the press for what she was doing – and faced, as a result, electoral annihilation.

Thatcher herself chose not to resign from Heath's government, though she was certainly uncomfortable with some of its later policies, and nor did other later Thatcherites, which suggests that in 1972 things were not as clear to them as they were to be ten years later – when among other things they would have, as a chart to steer by, the example of the Heath government's failure.

Most significantly, the Heath team had and deserved to have a remarkably good reputation for actually carrying out its promises from 1970 (as contemporaries who did not have the benefit of hindsight tended to point out), and even those who criticized its reversals of course in 1972 tended also to recognize that these were tactical reversals carried out in pursuit of the same strategic objectives – growth and competitiveness. Policy pledges that were successfully implemented included joining the EEC, tax reforms, housing finance, restructuring of local government and of the machinery of government, and of course the Industrial Relations Act of 1971. The fact that a number of these policies failed to deliver their anticipated benefits (as did the changes in government machinery, for example) may imply a lack of judgement by their framers, but it does not remotely amount to 'the systematic inversion by the Heath Government . . . of every pledge and principle on which it came to power' (as Powell later claimed).

There was one policy area which did not conflict with pledges made in 1970 but which nevertheless marked 'too sharp a curve' (to use a favourite phrase of Lord Randolph Churchill's) for some Conservative supporters and eventually ran the Ulster Unionists right off the Tory road. With the steady deterioration of political conditions in Northern Ireland in the 1960s, Heath had kept his party firmly behind the Labour policy of pressing civil rights reforms on Northern Ireland's Unionist government as a means of heading off increasingly violent street protests. When troops were sent in during 1969, the Conservatives again backed the Labour government, but Maudling, as Home Secretary from 1970, was then unable to stem the decline into further violence and was increasingly frustrated by the divided control of security between Belfast for the police and Whitehall for the army.

Westminster was held responsible for the overall situation by world opinion but had had since 1920 no clear right to interfere in detail in Northern Ireland's domestic arrangements. Eventually, in early 1972, the government grasped the nettle and abolished Northern Ireland's devolved parliament and government, initially as a temporary measure, with a new post of Secretary of State for Northern Ireland (William Whitelaw) added to Heath's Cabinet. As a tough response to violence this dramatic reversal of fifty years of policy occasioned little Conservative resistance, especially when it enabled the army to get a better grip on the situation later in the year. It did, though, mortally offend Ulster Unionists, who saw only a betrayal of a century of Conservative commitment to their cause; the two parties drifted apart at Westminster, and although no final constitutional breach had been made by 1974, the Unionist MPs would never again take the Conservative whip. Heath's commitment to the national interest, as he saw it, over a partisan supporter-group, was to cost him power in 1974, and the lack of a dozen or so Unionists' taking the party whip to offset declining Tory support in Scotland and Wales was to damage Conservatism in the parliamentary arithmetic right through to John Major's difficulties in the 1990s.

The case that 'U-turns' in policy in 1972 amounted to a betrayal of the hopes of 1970 has to rest, then, on a few specific policy areas, though these were all matters about which Conservatives felt far more deeply than they did about technical matters of taxation law or the internal machinery of government: specifically, immigration, intervention by government in industry, and wage and price controls. The immigration issue raised the smallest furore outside but may have been as important as anything to Heath's Tories themselves. Ever since 1959 this had been a dangerous pitfall for Conservative leaders, for while the party's right wing, now coherently and articulately organized in the Monday Club (which reached the pinnacle of its numerical strength and influence in about 1970), and the mass of the rank and file in the constituencies, took a very tough view of the need to control coloured immigration, there were always principled liberals at the highest level, like Macleod, Edward Boyle and Lord Hailsham, who made the adoption of a harsh policy impossible to pursue. Increasingly there were also local Tories who saw that in areas like Bradford an anti-immigrant stance would cost them votes, even if elsewhere it could win them for the party.

Hesitatingly, and too late (said the hardliners), the Macmillan government moved after 1959 towards the idea of immigration controls, and in 1962 imposed quotas on entry from each Commonwealth country, though

"But what if this hurts me more than it hurts him?"

Powell kept out of the Conservative campaign, *Daily Telegraph*, 1 June 1970.

MPs on both the left and the right of the party voted against the measure for opposite reasons. In opposition from 1964 things became more difficult, because the advocates of hawkish policies became angrier, convinced that there was collusion between Labour and Tory front benches to conceal the long-term population effects that even controlled immigration involved, and because the race relations machinery that Labour set up in 1965 (as the price of getting Labour MPs to back its own policies for restricting entry) presented Tories with a new range of difficult choices. The need to deal with the illegal white supremacist regime in Rhodesia added a further dimension to race politics at home – and made debates about sanctions against Rhodesia an annual tribulation for Heath. Explosions came in 1967 and 1968, firstly when the eviction of Kenya's Asians prompted Labour to admit these greatly disadvantaged former British subjects, but only on a restricted basis after criticism from Tories like Powell and Duncan Sandys (who, as a Tory minister, had actually given those Asians the right to come to Britain in Kenya's constitution, which was the reason that Macleod and Boyle gave for not voting with the rest of the party to keep them out now).

The second explosion came when, in 1968, Powell took off the gloves in the internal debate and made in Birmingham a speech which was reported as predicting 'rivers of blood' in British streets if immigration continued, though his own choice of words had been a little more careful. 'We must be mad, literally mad, as a nation', he asserted, to allow any further immigration. Powell regarded this simply as the summation of what he had been saying more quietly for years, a duty imposed on him by the need to speak up for his Wolverhampton constituents, and quite consistent with shadow cabinet policy, but almost every other shadow minister thought it so inflammatory as to arouse racial hatred. He was sacked from the shadow cabinet, though there was little doubt that his views rather than Heath's more liberal approach represented those of the mass of Tory voters and activists (and a large number of Labour voters too, as was evidenced by the thousands of dockers and meat-porters who marched on the Commons in his support). Central Office received sackfuls of hate mail, while over 100,000 letters poured in to Powell, mainly taking his side of the argument. With the Monday Club now active in the constituencies of some liberal Tory MPs, Heath had to give some ground – accepting, for example, that money could be made available for voluntary (but not compulsory) repatriation, and entry controls further tightened. Though the highest post he had occupied had been Minister of Health, and he had sat for only sixteen months in the Cabinet, Powell now became a major political figure in his own right, credited with a huge personal following. In the 1970 general election, despite his awareness that he was now well out on a limb and unlikely to be offered a job if Heath became Prime Minister, he urged people to vote Conservative, and the big swings to Tory in his homeland West Midlands – which contained concentrations both of immigrants and of illiberal white voters – showed that influence at work.

The similarly large swings away from the Conservatives in the same area, when Powell – for reasons to do with Europe rather than race – urged people to vote Labour in 1974, only confirmed Powell's influence, and may have done enough in the region's marginals to determine the national result, and so to remove Heath from Downing Street. Noting the news of Heath's fall, Powell rejoiced, but his 1974 treason was something that his party would not forget, and although he was to enjoy a second parliamentary career as an Ulster Unionist, his influence in Tory politics after February 1974 was over. Even when his economic ideas became Tory orthodoxy, his reputation on race and his desertion of the party itself ensured that for years very few Conservatives acknowledged his paternity rights over their ideas.

Powell and the Tory vote, *Sun*, 18 June 1970.

In office, Heath sought to downplay the immigration issue, but a new eruption of the East African Asian problem – now more acute when it arose in Uganda, in view of the bloodthirsty nature of the Amin regime there – brought out his liberal instincts and ensured that he deeply offended his party. Once again, Britain relaxed controls for good liberal reasons that derived from the country's tradition of giving asylum to political refugees, but for many Conservatives this was simply another abandonment of solemn pledges given by Heath in 1970. In the complaints that reached the top of the party from the constituencies in 1973, there were often generalized moans about the failure to carry out promises, and more specific complaints about reversals of course over economic policies. But at the top of the list, or (as some put it) 'the final straw', was often the way in which the Ugandan Asians issue seemed to demonstrate a party leadership which had no regard for the views – and the prejudices – of ordinary members and voters.

The reversals of course on economic policy were not so comprehensively denounced within the party, not least because the alternative to changing course in 1972 had been rocketing unemployment and unacceptably large increases in prices. During 1971, a year in which much of the government's attention was directed towards putting the Industrial

Relations Act on the statute book and then trying unavailingly to implement it without making martyrs out of trades unionists, ministers tried to maintain friendly links with union leaders but found that the rhetoric of battle subsumed all attempts to stay on good terms. Meanwhile, delay in reflating the economy following the harsh measures that Labour had taken at the end of its term ensured that unemployment would rise (briefly touching the psychologically important barrier of one million early in 1972) at the same time as prices were soaring. After decades of 'stop-go' Britain seemed to have moved into 'stagflation', theoretically impossible in Keynesian thinking and involving at the same time the disadvantages of both the 'stop' and the 'go' phases of previous economic cycles.

This phase reached a climax with a bitter strike for higher wages by the miners in the winter of 1971–2, a dispute in which the Cabinet did indeed decide to 'tough it out', as they had already done with a somewhat easier enemy, the postal workers, and so send a signal to the rest about the need for wage restraint. That strategy failed miserably when it became clear that coal stocks could not be moved around the country to keep industry and power stations working without pitched battles on the streets, and that the police were neither psychologically nor logistically ready for such battles. The damage to the government's morale and prestige was increased when the miners, sensing their power as the government caved in, would not at first even accept a settlement close to what they had been striking to achieve. The party's own national trades unionists' committee deprecated 'the refusal, even abdication, of the government to show itself willing to govern during the recent miners' strike' and went on to complain of 'a serious lack of political judgement', while from within Heath's private office Douglas Hurd wrote of 'the Government . . . now wandering vainly over the battlefield looking for somebody to surrender to . . .' Heath announced gloomily that the country *must* find a better way of settling disputes – and set out himself on a very different path.

Meanwhile the government also acted swiftly to curb rising unemployment. This was feared not only for electoral reasons – it was generally argued by those who neither remembered the 1930s nor foresaw the 1980s that no government could win an election with a million unemployed – but also because unemployed workers were seen by technocratic modernizers like Heath as a massive waste of human and economic resources. The policy of letting competition rule the day and allowing industrial lame ducks to drown had already taken a dent from specific interventions to save first Rolls-Royce (on grounds of its strategic importance as a maker of aero engines) and Upper Clyde Shipbuilders (on the less defensible ground of embarrassment arising from a workers' occupation of the yards). This shift of emphasis would now be generalized, principle developing from practice rather than the other way round.

The change also owed something to Heath's considerable irritation that, although (as he saw it) he had created for industry since 1970 the conditions it had asked for, it had responded by taking quick profits and raising prices rather than by investing in future production. He was rapidly coming to the conclusion – rather remarkably for a Tory leader – that industry could not be left to manage its own affairs, and that if it was so left it would only display what he shortly afterwards called 'the unacceptable face of capitalism' (a remark that all too many Tories found quite horrifying). After rapid discussions by groups of civil servants reporting directly to the Prime Minister, and with virtually no input from the Treasury, which would have to find the money, a new Industry Bill was promised during debates on the 1972 budget, and carried into law shortly afterwards. This set up machinery (not entirely unlike that only recently dismantled by the same government) to inject huge sums of public money into industry in order to promote competition and investment, while the government arrogated to itself unprecedented powers of direction and regulation for the same purposes.

Although Britain's actual entry to the EEC in January 1972 was the 'driver' of this policy change, an argument that helped to restrain criticism in the Commons, many Tory MPs, and some junior ministers too, voted for the 1972 Industry Bill only with a heavy heart. Although only a few backbenchers actually voted against it or abstained, others voiced their criticisms and made it clear that they would not back such 'socialist' measures in anything other than a national emergency, as even the chairman of the 1922 Committee felt obliged to explain. The gulf between front- and backbenchers was widening dangerously, even though effective whipping ensured that the government was in no danger of actually losing votes. Backbenchers also indicated their irritation in other ways: they elected critics of government policy and sacked ministers like Nicholas Ridley to key posts on backbench committees in order to ensure that dissident voices were heard, and in November 1972 even fired a warning shot directly across Heath's bows by electing as the new chairman of the 1922 Committee one of Heath's most implacable critics, Edward du Cann, sacked by Heath from Central Office and apparently still bent on revenge. The minutes of the Advisory Committee on Policy and the correspondence files of Central Office show just how dangerous this gulf was becoming, how critical of the government the party became during 1973.

The third area of policy reversal was, though, the most dangerous of all. The move from a hands-off policy on prices and incomes to detailed control by force of statute did not merely antagonize both Tories who did not like such policies in principle *and* trades unionists who felt that they would suffer from their consequences. It also placed the government's credibility entirely at the mercy of a future challenge from a powerful union, a challenge which, if it was as determined and successful as the miners had been in 1971–2, could invalidate the new laws and leave the government bereft of authority, much as the trades unions as a whole had already wrecked the Industrial Relations Act. Heath did not therefore at first leap back to the controls that Wilson had used, but tried instead a move to the looser mechanisms that the Conservatives themselves had tried before 1964. The union leaders and industrialists were invited to join a partnership to run the economy, with the government ready to concede this time much greater powers to the tripartite bodies now proposed. It was also prepared (tacitly at least) to abandon the Industrial Relations Act, the flagship of its 1970 reforms, in order to promote a new mood of cooperation, but with the proviso that industry must agree to voluntary price restraint and the unions to a wage freeze. The first of these was achieved and actually took place for several months, but binding cooperation with the unions was a quite different matter, and the union leaders – who had only just emerged from the trenches of battling with the government – were unsure to what extent the government's change of heart was genuine, and aware that they could probably not persuade their followers to deliver on any deal they might make.

When these talks broke down, Heath accepted that the problem remained one which the government must deal with and went instead for legally imposed controls on wages and prices, but in order to demonstrate that this alternative approach was fairer than the one he had denounced before 1970 the new Conservative variety of intervention would have to be more detailed. Ministers and civil servants would gradually become embroiled in the minutiae of relativities between different groups of wage-earners, and in such micro-levels of control as fixing the price per mile charged by London taxis and the differential increases allowed in the rents of furnished or unfurnished flats. For a time the policy worked well enough, first as a freeze and then as a programme to allow only small increases, and it did succeed in lowering the rate of inflation from the peak of 1972, but after the demonstration of union power between 1968 and 1972 this was always a bluff that was likely sooner or later to be called.

The union that administered the death-blow to the policy and to the government was once again the National Union of Mineworkers, with whom Heath had in any case less room for manoeuvre, since Tory MPs were not likely to accept a second humiliation from the same quarter, and the presence of a Communist vice president in the union led them to suspect that political subversion as much as earning power lay at the heart of the miners' decision to take on the government again in 1973–4. The situation had changed since 1971–2, though, in the sense that 1973's Arab–Israeli war and the success of the Arab oil cartel in raising prices internationally had placed a much greater emphasis on such alternative fuel sources as coal. Heath had tried in advance to avoid a confrontation, framing the details of the current phase of his pay policy specifically so that the miners would benefit from the small print, though the government had also laid in larger coal stocks and planned for their distribution in case a strike did take place. In the event, the government's inability to *say* that the miners would benefit disproportionately from its policy, and its refusal to believe that the other unions would not exploit any hole that the miners made in their anti-inflation strategy, led it inexorably into another fight that it could not win. Coal stocks again proved inadequately mobile for a fight with the miners right through the winter, when oil supplies were unreliable and inordinately expensive, and the imposition of a fuel-saving three-day working week and of restrictions of broadcasting hours (in order both to save fuel and to make the public feel that the government was fighting their battle) failed to shake the miners' resolve for a fight to the finish.

The bluff had been called, and the Conservative government had only two alternatives. Either it could pay whatever it cost to get the miners back to work, so living to fight another day and gradually reducing the country's dependence on coal as it became more expensive (which is in effect what the Thatcher government was to do from 1979 to 1983, before its big showdown with the miners in 1984–5), though Heath himself would very likely have been overthrown in the process by Tory MPs furious at a second successive defeat by the same enemy. Or the Prime Minister could appeal for support from the people in the hope that a specific electoral mandate would overawe the miners where all other arguments had failed. Unfortunately, the idea of a snap election was talked about for several weeks before it was eventually tried in February 1974,

7 February 1974

'Just you come down this instant — or I'll ask the electorate who owns the building!'

Guardian, 7 February 1974.

and the main stumbling block was Heath's own reluctance to descend further into the confrontationism which he expected an election to produce. He may therefore have missed his best chance by delaying, but even when persuaded that he had no alternative way forward, he did not then embark on the sort of election campaign that would alone have justified such a crisis appeal to the people.

Asked what he would actually do if he won, Heath had to argue that the miners would respect the wishes of the people (a view that miners' leaders naturally refused to confirm), but he soon afterwards referred the miners' case to arbitration, so rendering it unclear what the electors would now be asked to vote on. And when Conservative candidates launched into an uninhibited anti-leftist campaign, alleging Communist subversion by an enemy within (which was also the line taken by one – but only one – party television broadcast), Heath called off his hounds, worried that he would not be able to govern after the election if he raised the temperature too much during the campaign. He certainly did expect to win, partly because both published and privately commissioned opinion polls suggested this, partly no doubt because he had such a strong level of support in the press and in his party for the stand that he was now reluctantly taking.

But although Heath had called the shortest legally possible campaign of only three weeks before polling day, in the hope of keeping it focused on his 'who governs?' appeal to the voters, it was quite impossible to fulfil that central strategic aim. Newspapers anxious to avoid boring their readers could not just go on reporting on twenty successive front pages Heath making the same speech everywhere he went, and nor could broadcasters (obliged by their corporations' charters to promote political balance) refuse to report that the other parties saw this as a bogus election appeal, urging rather that the voters concentrate their minds on the Tory record when deciding whether to give them five more years. Gradually, inexorably, the issue on which the election had been called faded from sight, and this became instead an election on the unusual issues of jobs and prices, and one in which the government's record would be the chief determinant of the vote.

Unfortunately for Heath, he had called his snap election at a time when the government was not particularly popular and its record neither widely understood nor appreciated, as disastrous local government results in May 1973 and three parliamentary seats subsequently lost to the Liberals at by-elections demonstrated clearly enough. In 1974, because of the special

Daily Telegraph, 18 January 1974.

circumstances surrounding the government's central domestic policy objective, the Conservative Party went to the country without waiting for the recovery that usually follows on from mid-term disaffection, and without preparing either the party or the country for the basis on which an electoral appeal would be made. Finally, the bitter circumstances in which the campaign had been started and the way in which some candidates at least fought it throughout may have turned off some moderate voters and persuaded them to abandon both Tory and Labour extremes and go instead for the easier option offered by the Liberals (whose vote rose dramatically in the last week of the campaign). 'We were clobbered', said the Party Chairman, 'by the head-under-the-bedclothes vote' – by those who, when offered a real choice, decided to go for neither stark alternative.

Whatever the cause, the Conservatives found themselves on 1 March 1974 with more than a million fewer votes than in 1970, and with thirty-three fewer MPs. They had actually scored more votes than Labour but won fewer seats. In a parliament in which nobody had a majority, while it was not clear who had won, it was obvious enough who had lost. When Heath asked the electorate, 'Who governs?' they in effect replied, 'Well, not you, anyway.' Desperate attempts to patch together a deal with the Liberals on the basis of shared policies on Europe, defence and wages policy could not in any case produce a Commons majority and failed when the Liberals turned them down on 4 May. More half-hearted discussions with the remaining Ulster Unionists (who if they had still been taking the Tory whip as in every other parliament of the century would have made Heath easily the leader of the largest party and therefore Prime Minister) succeeded only in widening the breach between London and Belfast, and a century of party cooperation thereby came formally to an end.

Heath yielded office to Wilson, having now lost two of the three elections he had fought as Party Leader (three out of four after a further defeat in October 1974). Now even many loyalist Tory candidates were returning from the hustings with the absolute conviction that the party simply could not win with such a poor communicator as its chief spokesman on television. The twenty-eight-week parliament of 1974 (which was expected at first to be even shorter) allowed no opportunity for either a full-scale leadership crisis or for much of a policy review, but it provided the final catalyst for the party's subsequent changes both of leader and of direction.

Back on opposition, Heath reappointed most of the same faces as his shadow ministers, but took care once again to keep such free-thinkers and arguers as Keith Joseph away from sensitive areas. As a result of this, and of Heath's renewed refusal to allow the shadow cabinet to debate alternative economic philosophies, Joseph linked with Thatcher and with advisers from outside the party to create the Centre for Policy Studies as an advocate for what were now being called 'monetarist' views. In the summer of 1974 he made a series of big speeches in which he detached himself from almost all previous practice – in proclaiming, for example, that 'governments cause inflation' (rather than trades unions, as the party's candidates had only just been arguing in the election campaign). With a strong following wind in the press and respectable backing for such ideas now among academic economists (and a great deal of support from the party's younger candidates too), Joseph was blazing an important trail, though one that would reach no particular destination until after the October 1974 election.

Heath had little time for such matters, but he could in any case have had no truck with them for another reason: the abandonment of twenty years of consensual economic thinking would hardly have fitted with what was now his own strategic priority – the creation of a centrist government of national unity. That had been the logic both of his attempts to turn

A Man For All Seasons

Morning Star, 1 October 1974.

embattled industrialists and trades unions into partners in 1972 and of the attempt to cut a deal with the Liberals in March 1974, but it soon became an explicit policy objective to which he committed the party (if never quite spelling out the answers to such questions as who would join such a combination and who would lead it). One disadvantage was that it opened up Conservatives to charges of inconsistency when the confrontationism of February had already become a call for national unity by the summer. The strategy seems to have had short-term success, for in October, though the party's overall vote fell again, Conservative voters rallied impressively in the marginals and almost denied Labour a majority for a second time in one year, partly at least because Heath's more centrist and less confrontational stance had won back some voters who had gone to the Liberals in February. But for activist Tories, such a strategy smacked more of defeatism and betrayal of all that their party stood for than of good tactics, for it implied that the Conservatives did not have the will or the capacity to govern alone, and that once the election was over Heath would bring into his team MPs that the party had recently been trying to keep out of the House altogether. As in earlier days of coalitionism, this was a poisonous brew when discussed by a party used to enjoying power on its own terms.

Had the strategy won back even a share of power (and so denied it to a Labour Party thought by Tories to have gone entirely to the Bennite left), it might have seemed worthwhile, but when the party lost more seats in October and was now faced with a full term in opposition again, it was more often added by Tories to the list of Heath's misjudgements, and by some was now cited as evidence that he was not really a proper Conservative at all.

The party therefore returned to Westminster in October 1974 in a decidedly unhappy state, with a beleaguered Leader bent on the defence of a policy stance that some other Tories had now rejected. At the least they wanted promises that the policy would be re-examined, and Heath refused to concede even this: the question of the party leadership and debates about policy issues therefore became inextricably intertwined. In girding itself in the autumn of 1974 for the difficult task of throwing out for the first time a leader who had actually been elected to the post, the party prepared at the same time to take a much bigger leap in the dark than even that eventuality implied.

16

Thatcherism: The Way Up, 1974-87

DESPITE THE VERY REAL PROBLEMS that surrounded Edward Heath after the Conservatives had lost the October 1974 general election, his position as Leader was still a strong one, for his loyal supporters occupied all the key positions of party management – William Whitelaw as Party Chairman, Ian Gilmour as Chairman of the Research Department, Humphrey Atkins as Chief Whip, Lord Carrington as Leader in the Lords, and Heath's own former speechwriter Michael Wolff as the General Director (effectively chief executive) at Central Office. There was no formal way of forcing a contest for the leadership unless Heath himself triggered one by resigning (which he was certainly not about to do), for residual scepticism about the very idea of choosing a leader by election had ensured that the rules adopted in 1965 had set no term limit on the Leader thereby chosen, and made no provision at all for the periodic confirmation of his authority. In any case, there were few members of Heath's front bench who were prepared even to urge Heath to stand for re-election, let alone to tell him to retire from the leadership altogether, and scarcely one who could envisage standing against him if he did offer the party a chance to confirm or withdraw his mandate.

This reluctance derived in part from the very genuine respect that Heath had inspired among almost all colleagues for the way in which he had operated as Prime Minister, in part from the ingrained belief in the party that in a crisis the team should stick together – that, as Lord Kilmuir had put it in 1961, and every textbook on British politics repeated ever since, loyalty was a peculiarly Tory quality, the party's 'secret weapon'. Perhaps, though, it was also because the ambitious among the shadow cabinet had also concluded that anyone who played the part of Brutus was unlikely to become the next Caesar: 1911, 1923 and 1963 had all been Tory succession crises in which the over-confident had paid the penalty for their presumption, and the only blip that had impeded Heath's own succession to Douglas-Home in 1965 had been the moment when the press had alleged that Heath had a hundred backbench supporters ready to strike down his Leader. As Douglas-Home's triumph in 1963 seemed to have shown, the party thought that the job should only go to someone who did not seem over-anxious to get it, much as the Speaker of the Commons was traditionally dragged to the chair after a decorous 'After you, Cecil – No, after you, Claude' contest.

As a result of this, Heath's front-bench team as a whole became even more detached from the party in the Commons and in the country, a trend that had begun in 1972–3 but which was far more dangerous when the Leader did not have the authority and media exposure of the premiership to offset disintegration below stairs. For beneath the surface there had now developed a widely held and dangerous assumption that the party simply could not win elections under Heath, and that it must have 'anyone but Ted' if it were ever to govern again in the foreseeable future. Among those whom Heath had insulted or offended over the years this mood was espoused with joy and discussed in public from October 1974, while among those who admired him or who at least wanted to continue with his centrist political approach there were quiet but insistent warnings to the whips that a change must come – but should be well-managed in order to maintain unity and decorum. The critics only reinforced Heath's resolve to stick in there and fight it out with the party's right wing, while the well-meaning supporters would have had to be far more insistent in order to achieve their aim of an orderly transition to a Heathite regime under Whitelaw.

Heath made this problem much worse by at first refusing to give any ground at all, insisting that he would stay on and offering neither policy concessions to his critics nor a more responsive manner of conducting himself as Leader to his friends. After witnessing a typically insensitive Heath performance among a group of senior backbenchers, Jim Prior asked them gloomily, 'What *can* I do with him?' When the officers of the 1922 Committee (re-elected eight months earlier) added their voices to the call for an early leadership contest, Heath (whose own election was now ten years old) refused even to meet them to discuss the issue until the parliamentary party had confirmed them in post. Even Heath's strongest supporters were outraged by this high-handed behaviour, implying that the Leader in effect owed nothing at all to his followers in return for their allegiance, while they owed to him an unquestioning loyalty; a back-bencher received an ovation from the 1922 for pointing out that the party leadership was a leasehold rather than a freehold. This was not what the 1965 rules said, even if it was certainly what MPs wanted to hear in 1974 – though, in view of the small number of Tory Leaders over the previous century who had actually retired of their own volition, it might well be argued that on the historical record he had a point. Heath never did have the gift for viewing his actions as others saw them, but this was an especially gauche gesture, and (partly as a result of his insulting remarks) MPs now voted to maintain the critics' hold over the executive of the 1922, while his arch critic du Cann was returned unopposed as its chairman, news that was received with an ovation when it was announced to the backbenchers.

Heath now *had* to be seen to meet his critics, but with their authority enhanced and his own diminished, and the result was announcements that the rules for election would be rapidly revised and updated, and that there would then be an early contest at which Heath confirmed that he would be a candidate. Rule changes went through a committee under the party's elder statesman, Alec Douglas-Home, and were jocularly christened 'Alec's revenge' by those who still thought that Heath had connived at forcing out his predecessor in 1965. Two changes of substance were made, though neither of them had much impact in 1974–5. First, an unqualified system of annual re-election was introduced (unlike Labour's system, which at that time forced its leader to seek re-election only when the party was in opposition). This provision would make it possible to have three or four contests before another general election could come in about 1979, and would have made it difficult for Heath even if he had won in 1975, as it was to do for Margaret Thatcher when Prime Minister in 1989 and 1990. Subsequent amendments to the clause did not really change things, and John Major had to submit himself voluntarily for re-election when his authority was eroding in 1995. The second change was more technical, raising slightly the threshold of votes required to win by defining it as a proportion of the whole electorate rather than just those who voted (which in effect counted abstentions as votes against, and so would make the unenthusiastic re-election of an incumbent less likely).

The new rules were formally endorsed by Heath, and had already received the approval of Tory MPs and of the National Union, whose representatives had sat on the Douglas-Home committee. A first contest was set for early February 1975, and Heath announced, in an admonitory tone that suggested that he had still not grasped how far MPs disliked his methods of operation, that he would stand in as many ballots as it took to get him elected and then serve, however small his majority (though this was also a tactic designed to maximize his first ballot vote among those who thought he would win anyway and so wanted it over as quickly as possible in order to limit the damage).

The problem with this as a means to an orderly transition was that most of the shadow cabinet immediately lined up to announce that Heath had their support, and it was not at all clear how there could be the serious contest that the party was demanding unless Heath was faced by an electable opponent. Around Christmas 1974 candidates seemed to be disappearing much faster than they were declaring themselves. First, Keith Joseph withdrew from the fray after a speech he had made on social policy had strayed into the sensitive area of the eugenic control of population and so generated a chorus of press hysteria – SIR KEITH IN 'STOP BABIES' SENSATION shrieked the *Evening Standard*. Then du Cann decided after long hesitation that he would not stand either, apparently because of complications that might (and soon did) arise in his business career, while consideration of others who had remained outside the Heath team, such as Christopher Soames, did not get far.

This left the field free for Margaret Thatcher, who had entered the race only when Joseph withdrew and very specifically to articulate their shared economic-liberal viewpoint. Implacable critics of Heath like Airey Neave gradually – though at first reluctantly – grouped themselves behind her candidature; Neave became her very effective campaign manager and a close friend until his assassination by Irish republican terrorists in 1979. The almost universal assumption was that she would lose the contest heavily, for she was not even in the top half of the shadow cabinet on seniority, and she had sat in Cabinet for less than four years, and only in the 'woman's post' of Education Minister. Heath, by contrast, had been in the Cabinet when she first entered the House, and yet was still only fifty-nine to her fifty in terms of age. Furthermore, her supporters included hardly any of the front-benchers whom the press and broadcasters routinely consulted, she was backed by none of the Tory daily newspapers (though the *Spectator* had become so critical of Heath that at least one weekly did back her), and both campaign teams were telling all questioners that Heath was comfortably ahead – his own campaigners because they saw this as a way to roll his bandwagon over Thatcher at the first attempt, hers because they wanted Heath's reluctant backers to think hard about a future in which he had been comfortably re-elected.

Thatcher did, though, campaign superbly in January 1975, speaking and writing in a way that conveyed the impression of a born communicator, with clear convictions and a gift for expressing them lucidly (no small matter, given the prevailing party view of Heath's failings). For a key article on her policy instincts in the *Daily Telegraph* just before the first ballot, she had the assistance of another of Heath's foes, the professional writer and ex-journalist Angus Maude. That article showed that she recognized, as Heath seemed not to when he also gave his views in the *Telegraph*, that carrying on with more of the same was not a valid response to losing two elections in eight months. She conveyed a definite readiness to espouse new solutions to what she as well as Heath diagnosed as acute national problems. What those solutions would be was less clear, but she did not disguise the fact that her heart lay in more right-wing policies than the party had mainly pursued under Macmillan and Heath, or that she was convinced of the need for the monetarist approach to economics which Powell had been urging since the early 1960s and Joseph more urgently over the previous year. Precisely what it was in that package of attitudes that most appealed is unknown and unknowable (since it was a secret ballot, and many MPs never declared either their vote or their reasoning), but it is clear that the widespread sense of failure in the national political economy current in the mid-1970s, itself given sharp focus by the humiliating fiasco in which the Heath government had ended, had at least neutralized MPs' confidence in traditional approaches, while the sense of the party's own crisis that was equally abroad opened the way for a more adventurous Conservatism too.

No analysis of where the Thatcher regime came from makes any sense without an understanding of the prevailing despair within which the political nation and the Tory Party were each wallowing at the time of her arrival – despair that would broadly continue until the Falklands War and the economic recovery of 1982–5. In 1974, as her future Foreign Minister (and critic) Francis Pym was to put it, 'amidst the shambles and doubts of that time, here was one person who could articulate a point of view with conviction'. What it was that she actually believed in may then have been less important than the fact that she passionately believed in something *positive* and was prepared both to say so in ringing tones and to convince MPs that it could be achieved. To the question increasingly posed by commentators, and which would be the title of the CPC's Party

LADY M: "INFIRM OF PURPOSE! GIVE ME THE DAGGERS."

New Statesman, 31 January 1975.

Conference lecture in October 1975, 'Is Britain Governable?' Thatcher both by her manner and by her confidence offered a resounding 'Yes', when all too many Tories were muttering 'Don't know'.

On the first ballot Thatcher won 130 votes, eleven more than Heath, who immediately stood down. Since the press and their informants had almost all expected Heath to win, this result produced almost universal astonishment. Having expected nothing of great interest to take place, the Central Office press department was not even manned on that evening, with the result that the world's press had to make do with a telephone line which was answered only by the Polish nightwatchman on duty in Smith Square. Over the next week Heath's supporters (and his critics too) had just seven days to stop a Thatcher win on the second ballot, and although Whitelaw, Prior, Geoffrey Howe and John Peyton all tried to mount campaigns, it was too late for them to seem anything other than belated and negatively divisive candidates. There was now much party comment on Thatcher's 'courage' in risking everything by standing in the first ballot, while her second-ballot rivals were easily (if quite unfairly – since they had been motivated mainly by loyalty to Heath) seen as cowards who had only now come forward to profit from the opportunity that she had created. This time the Tory press was all for her, buoyed up by the Tories' exhilarating opportunity to become the first British party to elect a woman as its Leader. The Thatcher campaign had all the momentum, and though on the second ballot she lost some moderate supporters who had voted for her simply in order to get Heath out and open up a real contest, she more than made up for this with new supporters who now saw her as a strong leader who could unify the party. There is no doubt either, from the National Union's soundings in the constituencies – which had backed Heath on the first round – that she was now the local Tories' choice too. She won 146 votes on the second ballot, a clear majority of the 277 Tory MPs, while Whitelaw in second place got only seventy-nine. So Margaret Thatcher became Party Leader on 11 February 1975, and held the post for fifteen years and nine months, a term longer than that enjoyed by Disraeli (thirteen years), Bonar Law (eleven), Baldwin (fourteen), Churchill (fourteen) or Heath (ten), and exceeded in longevity only by Lords Derby (twenty years) and Salisbury (seventeen) during less turbulent, less democratic times.

The initial task of reuniting the party after a contentious four months was rendered possible by Whitelaw's acceptance of the deputy leadership under Thatcher and his success as a broker in persuading almost all of the outgoing front bench to stay on. Of Heath's senior shadow ministers, only Peter Walker and Geoffrey Rippon refused to serve and only Robert Carr was sacked by Thatcher, but Heath's own retreat into a public huff (growling, with echoes of de Gaulle in the 1950s, 'I'm in reserve') guaranteed that there would be limits to how far reunification could go. There has been something of a conflict in the autobiographical memories as to whether he was actually offered diplomatic or European posts (and if so how many, and when), but in any case Heath clearly preferred to remain free 'to speak out on the great issues', and thus to rock the Thatcher boat from the outside. Not for him – or indeed later for Thatcher either – the loyal correctness with which ex-Party Leaders had acted in the past: Balfour, Neville Chamberlain and Douglas-Home had each resumed the role of supportive lieutenants after stepping down; Austen Chamberlain and Anthony Eden had at least kept reasonably quiet after they were overthrown; Macmillan had accepted (if with some regret) that 'old actors should retire from the scene'; and Baldwin had promised in 1937 that 'once I leave, I leave. I am not going to speak to the man on the bridge, and I am not going to spit on the deck.' The captain of the yacht *Morning Cloud* did not follow that naval advice very closely.

Sunday Express, 6 May 1975.

Thatcher was imaginative in filling the vacancies created by these departures, bringing back both Soames and Peter Thorneycroft from the period before Heath's leadership, and Angus Maude, whom Heath had sacked from the front bench a decade earlier. She also courted du Cann and sought his advice, though without giving him employment, and so both avoided making a dangerous enemy and signalled her recognition of the importance of the 1922 Committee. As well she might, for, as Robert Blake has pointed out, it was the backbench Tory MPs alone who had made her the Leader by their support on the first ballot, and had the electorate been either widened to include Tory peers and the National Union (as in 1963) or narrowed to the front bench (as in 1957), then Heath would surely have been able to hang on and defeat her challenge.

In actual appointments, though, it was clear that the Thatcher leadership would be a very different one from Heath's, both in the shadow cabinet and in the party. Thorneycroft went to Central Office as Party Chairman, where he remained an avuncular presence, extremely popular with the activists, until the autumn of 1981; he could provide a new Leader both with experience to compensate for her own relative lack of exposure to the party machine in the past, and with trenchant support for her economic views in a key post in the party communications network, at least at first. One of Thorneycroft's first decisions was to sack Michael Wolff, a confidant of Heath's and the first non-agent to occupy the top professional post at Central Office since the 1920s (when it had also been unpopular with the party's career professionals). Under Thorneycroft the official machine was once again put in the hands of the career agents, and this ensured popularity in another influential quarter of party opinion.

Keith Joseph took over the chairmanship of the Advisory Committee on Policy and broad responsibility for the development of policy, with the like-minded Maude as chairman of the Research Department, while Joseph and Howe (as shadow Chancellor) jointly worked on the key area of economic policy, on which probably they alone in the shadow cabinet fully shared the new Leader's views.

By the summer of 1975, then, all the key levers of the party machinery were in the hands of those who had been out of favour under Heath. Although the Research Department was not purged of its Heathite staff and remained under the direction of the moderate Christopher Patten right through to the 1979 election, the price was a reduction of its influence in the party. It had already lost the effective monopoly of research advice when the Centre for Policy Studies came into being in 1974, and the addition to this of the Adam Smith Institute, the Selsdon Group, the Conservative Philosophy Group, the *Salisbury Review*, the Freedom Association and the Middle Class Alliance threatened to recreate the 'legion of leagues' which had existed before 1914, except that this time all these new 'think tanks' shared the similar objective of pushing the Conservative Party in a more economic-liberal and less *dirigiste* direction, a trend with which the Leader heartily agreed. The CRD was therefore still the official machinery for servicing shadow ministers and MPs, but was kept at arm's length by some of its clients, and when Patten entered the House himself in 1979 his old department was merged into Central Office and so lost the semi-detachment which had been so valuable in generating dispassionate advice to the party over the previous fifty years.

It was necessary for Thatcher and her closer supporters to operate in this way if they were to keep the direction of affairs in their own hands, for Whitelaw's very success in bringing round most of the Heathites to serve under Thatcher meant that she sat in her shadow cabinet surrounded by those who did not much agree with what she was trying to do (which was no doubt part of what Whitelaw had intended), while some of those that she had brought in herself, like Soames, soon proved anyway to be more Heathite than those they had replaced. There were three strategies adopted for evening up the balance, which would otherwise have ensured that Thatcher won few votes in her own shadow cabinet, and indeed after

1979 in her Cabinet either – bilateralism and personal initiatives by the Leader, the avoidance of specific commitments, and the promotion of broad principles of traditional Conservatism.

The first of these was purely personal, deriving its effect from Thatcher's ability to dominate most of her colleagues in bilateral discussions (and this ensured that there were lots of bilateral discussions, where in other circumstances decisions might have come to the shadow cabinet as a whole). She was able to mobilize considerable force of personality and conviction in these private conversations, sometimes exploiting in particular the reluctance of men of a certain class and age to fight back when attacked by a woman. She was invariably backed in tight corners by Whitelaw, who both developed a warm personal regard for Thatcher's abilities after 1975 and regarded it as his duty to work always for unity. If the Leader threatened unity by her methods, it was the Deputy Leader's task to move towards her and bring his friends with him.

An example of Thatcher's personal initiatives concerned the question of race relations and immigration, on which the party remained very hot and bothered, and the neglect of which seemed to be giving an opening to the far right National Front, then beginning to score significant votes in by-elections. As shadow home secretary, Whitelaw himself had to produce a more restrictive policy on entry controls, working assiduously on the entry statistics and collaborating on matters of detail with his junior spokesmen, the backbench committee and the Leader (who had thus already edged the policy somewhat to the right). At the moment at which the package was to be announced early in 1978, and with an eye on a key by-election due shortly in North Ilford (where opinions on race were known to be well to the right), Thatcher on 30 January effectively gazumped her own spokesman and Deputy Leader by calling for yet tighter controls and – far more controversially – also spoke emotively about the British people's fear of being 'swamped' by an alien invasion, much the sort of language for which Powell had been sacked by Heath in 1968.

None of this had been cleared with colleagues in advance, but once it had happened Whitelaw's only choices were between resignation (which would have been entirely out of character) and rallying to his Leader to limit the damage. The Research Department had only a few weeks to invent a policy consistent with what the Leader had now already said, and Whitelaw then presented it for approval as *his* policy at the party's Central Council in March. The Leader had thus by-passed all the normal procedures in which she might well have been outvoted, but in the process she had given the party what it wanted and contributed at least something to the by-election gain that finally removed Labour's parliamentary majority (in a contest where the NF now fared badly).

If at first her colleagues attributed these personal initiatives in policy-making to inexperience, they gradually realized that (as Prior later put it) 'it was her way of making certain she got her way', and they even found it hard not to admire the political skills and streetfighting determination that such an exercise demonstrated. But there was in any case no real mileage for ambitious shadow ministers in obstructing a Leader who was pandering to the party's baser instincts, even though it ran completely against the way in which party leaders had invariably operated on such sensitive issues since Baldwin's time. The regular use of such tactics in less sensitive areas enabled Thatcher to punch well above her weight in the development of policy.

The overall nature of the policy review was in any case dramatically different from that of 1964–70, not least because of the consensus that the Heath government had been *over*-prepared and over-committed when it took office in 1970, a mistake that almost all shadow ministers were happy not to repeat. There were therefore once again lots of policy groups meeting and absorbing much of the party's excess of energy, a process that Patten described (on a Maoist analogy from the Chinese Cultural Revolution) as encouraging a thousand flowers to bloom. There was, though, and quite deliberately, only the most haphazard procedure for culling these flowers and arranging them, so that even chairmen of groups often did not know after they had completed their reports whether they had the Leader's blessing. A good deal of valuable preparation for policy in government was made, but by leaving the exact status of most reports unclear, the freedom of action of a future government remained unrestricted.

More of the Opposition's time and energy than in 1964–70 was taken up with actually being the Opposition, and in the context of a failing Labour government with a crumbling majority this was perhaps as good a use of front-benchers' time as any. During the Callaghan government of 1976–9 the Conservatives were able to exploit the humiliating dictation to Britain of an economic policy by the International Monetary Fund; the failure of the government to get its devolution plans through the Commons and its subsequent failure to get Scots to vote for a later version in sufficient numbers to bring them into force; a Lib–Lab pact that kept

Callaghan in office but which enraged anti-socialist Liberals much as it had in 1930; a major confrontation with the trades unions in the 'winter of discontent' of 1978–9, which wrecked once and for all the Labour claim to be able to get on with organized labour better than Conservatives; a new twist in the Cold War which required additional defence expenditure and a new generation of nuclear weapons, always better ground for the Tories than for Labour; and finally, in 1979, the first confidence debate to bring down a government since 1924, forcing a general election when Callaghan least wanted one.

It required continuous application by the Opposition to hammer home all of these points, and it was a situation in which not too much attention need be paid to the Tory alternative, though, as in 1970, the Conservatives' opponents helped out through their counter-attack. At home, the Labour Chancellor Denis Healey called Thatcher the 'La Passionaria of Privilege' after she had defended a reduction of taxation on the better-off, while abroad, the Soviet press denounced her as 'the iron lady' of the west for her anti-Communism. Both of these were epithets that did her no harm at all with Tory voters. More generally, Labour asserted that Thatcher stood for greed, privilege and an uncaring 'devil-take-the-hindmost' approach to British society, so considerably widening her distance from their own self-image at precisely the time when Labour's popularity was at an all-time low. There was everything to be said, then, for the Conservatives avoiding those detailed domestic policy commitments which would offend some interest group or other, and concentrating instead on winning power without explaining in every particular how it would be used. The success of this strategy can be seen in the fact that when the Conservatives actually won power in 1979, commentators on the campaign stressed over and again how few promises they had made, and how little they had actually committed themselves to in the process.

This strategy would only work if the party did indeed win power, and winning in 1979 was therefore vital for Thatcher's approach as Leader, but victory did then enhance her position, just as it had Heath's in 1970. In one area her readiness to go for broke was already apparent to the close observer, and that was in matters constitutional.

Conservatives had been especially depressed in 1974 – not just by the loss of power, but by the fact that Labour had gained office (and in October a parliamentary majority) with under 40 per cent of the vote, but then governed as if it had a mandate for policies which were actually more left wing than those of the more broadly supported Labour

Daily Telegraph, 26 April 1979.

governments of 1945 and 1966. Heath's reaction had been to seek a coalition, or a government of national unity with majority support, while other Conservatives increasingly wondered whether they should opt for a change to the voting system to prevent anything like 1974 happening again. A voluntary organization called Conservative Action for Electoral Reform mobilized Conservative sympathizers for proportional representation, and through the activities of the all-party Hansard Society tried to make links with other parties to bring about their objective; in the Commons a third of Tory MPs voted for PR to be used to elect a Welsh Assembly (for how else would Tories win seats in their weakest area in the UK?) They did not, however, support PR for European elections, expecting to do well under the traditional system, which suggests that, for many, their conversion to PR was at best pragmatic – if not outright cynical. At the governmental end of the mandate spectrum, several senior Tories fulminated against the Labour government's arbitrariness and castigated Callaghan as an 'elected dictator' rather than a democratic politician representing the national will. Lord Hailsham, Heath's Lord Chancellor and the party's chief legal affairs specialist, called for a fundamental change in the constitution, with the introduction of a Bill of Rights to entrench restrictions on the right of parliament to legislate in ways that affected individual liberties.

But although such initiatives had a broad attraction to Conservatives in opposition, and were tolerated as policy speculations like much else on the Tory side at that time, neither of these ideas came near to getting official approval, for Thatcher expected to win power, probably anticipated the need to use the doctrine of a mandate based on the support of less than half the voters, and wanted the power of parliament left untrammelled for her own future use. When support for PR in the party seemed to be growing dangerously, a motion calling for its introduction was selected for debate at Party Conference, purely so that it could be thrown out (a well-night unprecedented tactic for Tory leaders to employ). Angus Maude replied for the platform to a debate in which the supporters of changes in the voting system had made most of the running, but made a blistering attack on 'insouciant' reformers who would cast aside centuries of practice for an untried and as yet unspecific alternative. He asserted that in Britain PR would allow the minority Liberals always to choose who governed, since they would always hold the balance of power, and finished with a thunderingly Tory declaration that power was not merely a reward handed out on grounds of fairness after a quinquennial political beauty contest, but a weapon to be seized by the strong and determined, and then used without restriction for the good of the country. It was noticeable that Thatcher led the ovation when Maude sat down, and the Conference duly obliged her by voting down the motion. In power after 1979, nothing more was heard of Conservatives introducing either PR or a Bill of Rights, even though Hailsham was for eight years Thatcher's Lord Chancellor.

There was a similar going-for-broke in the retreat from a Conservative commitment to devolution, another area where the party interest in constitutional reform had been no more than skin-deep. Back in 1968, and purely in response to the sudden appearance of the Scottish National Party as a seat-winning political force, Heath and his advisers had issued the grandly titled (but barely considered) Declaration of Perth, promising to bring more responsible government to Scotland, and a commission under Sir Alec Douglas-Home had laboured to produce a plan acceptable to Scottish Conservatives. However, the crumbling of the SNP position in Scotland at the 1970 election, when it won no seats at all and fewer than 5,000 votes per candidate, removed any incentive to act, and the Heath government neither introduced devolution nor even promised much in February 1974. But the election of February 1974 produced a surge in support for all third and minor parties, and within Scotland the SNP was now a bigger threat to Conservative seats north of the border even than in 1968. By October 1974 the party was once again offering devolution in Scotland, though this did not prevent the loss of four Tory seats to the SNP, which also seemed poised to take more of the mere sixteen Scottish seats that the party still held.

The decline of Conservatism in Scotland was a long-term phenomenon to which the SNP merely added the final push. In 1959, when Macmillan had increased his overall majority, less-affluent Scotland swung to Labour and five seats were lost, and from then on the Scottish electorate began to shift in stages away from the Conservatives. Battles between the gentlemanly middle-class Unionists of Edinburgh and the tougher capitalist Unionists of Glasgow certainly did not help to prevent a steady decline in organization, membership and activity on the part of Scottish Tories. The party was all too often seen by Scotsmen (as a private survey for Central Office in 1968 had already made clear) as 'a bastion of foreign (English) privilege', and associated in the public mind only with lairds, landowners and the rich, people whose instinctively Unionist sense of personal identity cut them off from the mass of their countrymen. Despite this situation, already much worse by 1975 as a result of further organizational neglect and of the failure to deliver on devolution plans which most Scottish Tories had not wanted anyway, Thatcher seems to have decided in 1975 that there was little to be gained from being the fourth most devolutionist party in Scotland (since Conservatives were less enthusiastic than Liberals, SNP or Labour) and that it made more sense for her to appear as the only defender of the Union. This involved ditching the party's lairdish Scottish leadership, which was too committed to the previous line. Instead Thatcher relied for advice on the more populist Teddy Taylor, whose long-term survival as a Glasgow MP seemed to show what could be done by a more Thatcherite type of Unionism (though the loss of Taylor's own seat in 1979 was rather to disprove this and begin a further slide in the party's Scottish position). In the short term, there was much to be gained from exploiting Labour's own divisions over devolution; the Conservatives could claim to be the only party that campaigned unitedly for a 'No' vote in the 1979 devolution referendums in Scotland and Wales, and (when those referendums killed devolution for a generation) the only real defenders of Scottish and Welsh interests within a United Kingdom. In 1979 the Conservatives gained three seats in Wales and seven in Scotland on the back of that strategy, but in both cases it was to prove a false dawn once local resentment of 'English' domination then reasserted itself. Even before 1979 Rab Butler had rather theatrically explained to his Leader that whereas Mary Tudor had died with 'Calais' engraved on her heart, Margaret Thatcher's heart would bear the word 'Scotland', a prophecy disproved only to the extent that Thatcher herself fell before the Scots wreaked their final revenge on Thatcherism in 1992 and 1997.

Despite the bold espousal of some difficult causes, the confrontation at Conference over PR was nevertheless highly untypical, and more usually the thousand flowers were allowed to bloom without either tending or weeding. This approach worked only because on broad domestic strategy the inner Thatcher group did move their party over quite a bit, and thus created the strong impression that – despite the lack of detail – a Conservative government would do things differently both from Callaghan and from its own predecessors, always a vital thing for an opposition to achieve. This involved some fairly bloody debates in shadow cabinet, for, as Heath had already found, core economic policy could not be decided in bilateral deals with individual shadow ministers. The Thatcher supporters were assisted here by the fact that the tide of elite opinion, which had begun to move their way in the early 1970s, flowed with increasing force after 1975, both within Britain and internationally. It was only in 1974 that Hayek was awarded the Nobel Prize for Economics, and in 1977 that it went to Milton Friedman, but by then there was a respectable body of academic opinion supporting their monetarist views, and their approach had captured the Treasury (which then infiltrated them even into the Labour government during the International Monetary Fund crisis of 1976), the main financial institutions and most of the serious press. Much as in 1949–51, the Labour government found itself having to react to an increasingly rightward drift of opinion, which the Conservatives had certainly assisted in bringing to birth but for which they could not claim absolute paternity; as in 1949–51, this development moved the national political debate onto ground where the Tories were far more comfortable than Labour, just as the Tories of the right wing were more comfortable than the Heathites. Tory Keynesians, fighting their rearguard action against libertarianism and neo-liberal economics in 1977–9, were in fact defending a citadel most of whose garrison had laid down their arms and gone home.

In one area, in any case, the shadow cabinet's hawks were entirely happy to pursue a doveish line, and that was on industrial relations, for in the first four years of the October 1974 parliament the Tories had to cope with the same problem as in 1973–4 – a general assumption that they would again turn trades union policy into a battlefield; only Labour's own failure to manage the unions in 1978–9 neutralized this difficulty. As shadow spokesman Thatcher appointed Prior, who was as anxious as anyone not to repeat the mistakes of 1970–71, and who therefore committed the party only to the most moderate programme of legislation; some of Labour's more extreme extensions of trades union powers would be reversed, and ballots would be required before strikes, but the rest of what Heath had tried to achieve in the Industrial Relations Act was quietly ditched. This was entirely tactical, for a 'softly, softly' approach did not (and was never meant to) imply any retreat by Conservatives anywhere on the party spectrum from the conviction that they must sooner or later reduce union powers. It made sense to go slow and to take it in stages (as had not been done after 1970), if only to reassure sceptical voters, but Prior's apparent success in keeping to a moderate line also in the meantime conveyed the mistaken impression that Thatcher would be controlled by wiser counsels.

For the look of the thing, and to demonstrate the different face of Tory policy in outline if not in detail, the walls of traditional orthodoxy had nevertheless to be breached and the citadel taken. This came about with an exercise a little like that which had in 1947 produced as an 'approach document' *The Industrial Charter*, and it was again as much presentational and educational as to do with research and writing. The process had actually begun in 1974–5 with the speeches that Joseph had later published as *Reversing the Trend*, a title that succinctly summarized his argument that thirty years of increasing state intervention ought to be followed by a period in which the pendulum should be swung back the other way. This was indicative of the predominant current of thought among Thatcher's closest advisers, and was highly influential in party circles. It promised to open a Pandora's box of party expectations, with the centre of political gravity ratcheted back to the right, whereas – most Conservatives felt – it had moved ineluctably leftwards ever since 1945. This whole way of approaching economic policy was irresistibly appealing to many in the party who but barely understood any of the economics involved (but grasped easily enough that it made lower public spending and lower taxes a respectable position to take up), for it promised to keep them in control of the political agenda for years ahead rather than having to be content merely with slowing down the movement in a direction of which they thoroughly disapproved.

While such optimistic tones were to be found in the speeches of Joseph, Howe and Thatcher in 1975, they spoke only for themselves in their rejection of thirty years of past practice – spurning of course seventeen years of Tory government in the process. *The Right Approach*, published in October 1976 and endorsed by that year's Party Conference, was the first attempt to make the new way of thinking actual party doctrine. It was very visibly a compromise – almost a treaty – between Joseph and Howe on the one hand and Whitelaw and Prior on the other, and edited with some intellectual gymnastics by Maude. It did not go as far as the party's economic spokesmen would have liked, but it did none the less mark a shift in their direction. The somewhat more detailed *The Right Approach to the Economy* (1977) then moved the party's own ratchet a whole notch further in their anti-statist direction, so that in 1979 Conservatives could, as in 1951, talk of rolling back the state and of a holiday from legislative interventionism. Thatcher would not, though, allow even this favourable slant to party policy, signed by five of her senior colleagues, to come out actually as a shadow cabinet document, and it duly appeared instead under the CPC imprint, with the usual disclaimer stating that it did not necessarily reflect the views of anyone in the party but its authors.

The Keynesians thus conceded a great deal without getting any bankable commitment in return, partly in order to stay on board and influence later policy, partly because they, like most politicians at the time, were entirely convinced that the responsibility of office would 'tame' Thatcher, much as it had forced a reversal of course on Heath. Prior later wrote that 'I assumed that quite a bit of what Margaret claimed we would do was Opposition rhetoric which would be moderated by the realities of government. I failed to recognize, however, that the mood of the country had changed during the 1970s and it was ready for a more radical move to the right than in 1970.' That is a useful reminder that experienced observers of the scene entirely failed to read the runes correctly before 1979 – indeed before 1981 in some cases – for most of those columnists who most avidly celebrated 'the Thatcher revolution' in the mid-1980s had still been predicting in 1978 that she would be 'just like her predecessors' if she became premier. Nor was she even immune from such assumptions herself, remarking in a rare moment of self-doubt during the 1979 campaign that 'I shall be remembered as the woman who was allowed one go – to lead the Party to defeat.'

Semantics and tones of voice were important in such economic policy-making, in the general impression they gave about who had won the argument. The punning use of 'right' (as meaning both correct and non-left) had first been applied to a Tory document in *The Right Road for Britain* (1949), though its presentation by Churchill had suggested that in that case the party would mainly put right what Labour had done wrong. In the same sense, Heath's 1965 statement was originally to be called 'Putting Britain Right', until Reginald Maudling pointed out that after thirteen years of Tory government and only a few months under Labour it would be embarrassing if people were to ask who had put Britain wrong; the title thus became *Putting Britain Right Ahead*, which (appropriately for Heath) suggested only momentum and acceleration rather than any particular direction. But with *The Right Approach*, both the language of the document and its presentation by Thatcher made it quite clear that 'right' was now to be juxtaposed with 'left'. As Ian Gilmour recalls the 1979 campaign, 'when she said, "This is my faith and vision. This is what I passionately believe", she was evidently not referring to the careful compromises enshrined in the manifesto.'

In the shadow cabinet argument more or less came to an end in 1977 – though there was a late spat in the autumn of 1978 when they could not agree (again) on attitudes to an incomes policy; no commitment was given either way, and both sides of the shadow cabinet gratefully agreed to postpone determination of what would be done after the coming election until it had actually been won. The Conservatives therefore officially moved far enough in a monetarist direction before the 1979 election to convey a clear impression of having a different and more right-wing approach than that of the unpopular Labour government, but without saddling themselves with burdensome and awkward detail about the ways in which their policies would be executed. It was overall an impressive piece of political management by the shadow cabinet's minority, and one that kept party disagreements well within bounds during the years out of office. The proof would come, though, entirely in the implementation.

Callaghan was forced eventually into an election campaign in April–May 1979, opting for the longest possible campaign, at least partly in the hope that the less experienced Thatcher would trip herself up with a gaffe of some sort. She had, however, committed herself as soon as she became Leader to a far more public-relations orientated approach than her predecessor's, and had undergone extensive training from professionals in the arts of public speaking, broadcasting and communication in general (lowering her voice about half an octave in the process of acquiring a more 'caring' tone for the microphone). The party organization under Thorneycroft had recovered ground and members lost during the Heath government, and the near-bankruptcy of the party after two general elections in 1974 had been turned around. This allowed a bigger and more sophisticated public relations campaign run by the gifted but so far hardly known Saatchi and Saatchi Company, leading the way forward towards modern electioneering as both the 1959 and 1970 campaigns had done, but with the main emphasis on negative campaigning against Labour's record. An effective theme was 'Labour isn't working' (nationwide posters which showed a long snake of the apparently unemployed queuing for benefit – though they were really Young Conservatives, in the last generation in which there were enough of them actually to stage a crowd scene).

During the campaign itself Thatcher conducted herself professionally, though her refusal of a head-to-head debate with Callaghan indicated the caution of her advisers, convinced that victory was in the bag if nothing risky was attempted. As indeed it was, for on 3 May the Conservatives raised their vote by more than 3 million over the disastrous showing of October 1974, and now led Labour by the largest voting margin enjoyed by a government since 1945 (though one that would be exceeded in all of the next three contests in which the Tories were the incumbents). The margin in seats was less dramatic, but a majority of forty-three guaranteed a full parliament in which Thatcher could now – indeed must – show her true colours.

Policy implementation under a Leader who favoured bilateralism over full meetings of front-benchers (the number of Cabinet meetings was soon halved) would depend heavily on who was put in which post. Thatcher had to make extensive use of ministers who shared little of her outlook on life, some of them in such senior posts as Whitelaw at the Home Office, Carrington at the Foreign Office, Heseltine at Environment, and Pym at Defence, and she even surprised many by bringing back Peter Walker for Agriculture. But she took great care that only those individuals who were 'one of us' (an increasingly used litmus test of the true-blue believers) should be in the key economic posts. Howe became Chancellor, backed by the former Powellite John Biffen as Chief Secretary and the rising ex-financial journalist Nigel Lawson as Financial Secretary, with Joseph at Industry, David Howell at Energy, and John Nott at Trade.

The only unreconstructed Keynesian at the economic heart of the government was Prior at Employment, where the tactical objective remained much as in opposition. Arguably, indeed, the tactics now went a stage further, for Thatcher had declared that she would need two full parliaments for the 'turning round' of Britain, and she was determined not to be blown off course during the first few years, as Heath had been, by trades union resistance. Prior was therefore operating with full Cabinet support in maintaining friendly relations with the unions and jollying them along to accept his reform programme in easy but relatively uncontentious instalments (and there was even some success in persuading trades unionists that they ought not to make Prior's position too difficult lest he be replaced by a more Thatcherite minister whom they would find much less acceptable). On pay policy, the government used the overall control of public spending as a crude tool to control the pay of its own employees, and broad economic policy rather than detailed interventionism to influence pay bargaining elsewhere. In politically sensitive areas, the government took a highly pragmatic line (much as Churchill had done in 1951, when he too came into office against a public perception that Tories would fight battles with the unions). The miners in particular found their annual pay rounds easier and less contentious than under Heath, for the lack of a formally announced pay policy and of legally enforceable restrictions allowed the government to buy them off each time without either a public fight or too obvious a loss of credibility. In 1981 the government intervened to force the Coal Board to withdraw a programme of pit closures and adjusted the board's cash limits to allow uneconomic production to continue instead, rather than face a strike. As Baldwin had said of concessions to the miners in advance of the General Strike of 1926, 'We were not ready': only after the strike of 1984-5 wrecked both the union and the industry did this earlier phase seem to the miners to be a period of fattening them up for the pot. Thatcher's own core belief was indicated clearly enough, though, by her reply to the backbencher who suggested at that time that care was needed to avoid alienating moderate trades union leaders: 'There is no such thing as a moderate trade union leader' (a response apparently delivered with her bright blue eyes positively blazing with conviction).

But if the Thatcher government avoided many of the pitfalls of 1970-72, it still managed to find itself during 1981 in a position not unlike the one which Heath had faced in mid-term. Howe's 1979 reductions in income taxation at the standard rate (down from 33 per cent to 30), in the top rate (down from 83 per cent to 60) and in tax on unearned income (down from 98 per cent to 75) all sacrificed government resources

"HOME, JAMES, AND DON'T SPARE THE HORSES!"

Sun, 11 February 1980.

on a big scale. Even if they were to be successful in yielding higher returns through increased incentives and faster growth, there would be a delay, as there would also be before – if ever – government spending could be reduced. The gap was plugged by a large increase in value added tax, initiating the strategic shift from taxing incomes and property to taxing consumption and charging for services which was underpinned by the government's market philosophy, but which in the short term raised prices significantly. So did the new government's decision to continue for a time with a large programme of index-linked pay settlements, which bought time in the avoidance of industrial disputes but carried forward and reinforced inflationary pressures. When another worldwide increase in oil prices was added to this brew in 1980, the rate of inflation raced away, and the headline rate reached 15 per cent in the middle of that year. Since unemployment was also rising rapidly, reaching 2 million in 1980 and passing 3 million (where it stayed for five years) in 1982, the 'stagflation' of 1972 had returned with both halves of the equation worse than ever before.

The government did, though, have two advantages that its predecessors had not enjoyed, one entirely fortuitous and one of its own making. The arrival onshore of the first significant quantities of North Sea oil and gas at exactly this time – it was in June 1980 that Britain first became a net exporter of oil – cushioned the country's trade from the recurrent balance of payments crises that had crippled previous Chancellors in their efforts to promote stable economic growth, and made possible the adoption of tough policies to stabilize the domestic economy without unacceptable consequences for the currency. Sterling had been set free to float by Barber in 1971, but Howe's abolition of controls on capital movements now added considerably to the net benefit that oil production was producing in freeing British domestic policy from international pressures. All the same, by 1980 Britain was suffering its worst economic recession since the 1930s, and the impact on manufacturing industry in the Midlands, North, Scotland and Wales was (as in the 1930s) particularly severe.

Faced, then, with heavy pressures both on unemployment and on inflation, Howe as Chancellor and Thatcher as Prime Minister had to pick their priority target. Unlike all previous post-war governments (and certainly not believing, like Macmillan, that a little inflation hurt nobody), they decided to target inflation. The 1981 budget would therefore administer additional deflationary medicine to an economy in which production was already plummeting; steel production, for example, which had fluctuated at about 20 million tons per annum in the 1970s was just 15.5 million tons in 1981 and 13.7 million tons in 1982. In these circumstances there was acute discontent among the Heathite 'wet' members of the government, grim resolution among the 'dries'. These were now popular epithets in the economic vocabulary, distinguishing the sound money men from the inflationaries, which had been current in the 1940s and which now resurfaced as Keynes went out of fashion, though 'wet' now also had unmistakable connotations of 'wimp' when employed by Thatcher herself at this make-or-break time for her government.

The 'wets' could do little to hold back the tide of policy, grasping far too late that they had underestimated Thatcher's willpower all along, and they now paid the inevitable price for mounting ineffective opposition from within. As junior ministers of the 'dry' persuasion proved themselves, Thatcher had less and less need for their more uncooperative betters, but she displayed remarkable cunning in picking them off one or two at a time. Norman St John-Stevas was sacked in January 1981, Soames, Mark Carlisle and Ian Gilmour in September (Gilmour repaying the compliment

Housewife Thatcher hangs out Jim Prior to dry, c. 1981.

by telling the assembled press that the government was going full-steam ahead towards the rocks). Prior, refusing a transfer to Northern Ireland, was faced down and told in effect 'Northern Ireland or nothing', at which he accepted Northern Ireland in the hope that he could achieve something positive through his emollient political presence in Belfast, and that by staying inside to argue he could at least ensure that the 'wet' voice continued to be heard. The outcome was different, for he often missed London meetings in order to keep up with his Belfast job, and was anyway removed altogether in 1984.

Whitelaw, Walker, Heseltine and other 'wets' were able to survive and achieve policy successes in their own areas (for example, Heseltine's interventionist investment initiative in Liverpool following 1981's unemployment-driven riots there), but the promotion to the Cabinet of Norman Tebbit, Nigel Lawson, Cecil Parkinson (now Party Chairman) and Leon Brittan to replace those who had been sacked had tilted the balance of the Cabinet decisively in the Prime Minister's favour by 1982. She had also discovered in the contests of 1980–81 a new tool of political management: the use of off-the-record briefings by her press secretary, Bernard

Ingham, to undermine her colleagues and keep them on their toes. Meeting Ingham before he had moved to Number Ten, Tory backbencher Sir Anthony Meyer had already thought him to be 'a tough, genial but unscrupulous Yorkshireman ... the sort of chap I would rather have on my side than against me'. All too often, headlines such as BATTLING MAGGIE UNDER ATTACK FROM WETS would miraculously coincide with the days on which ministers had tough choices to make. Then, after the Cabinet had both agreed a policy and unanimously deplored such leaks to the press, the next day's accounts would follow remorselessly along the lines of the *Sun*'s story on public spending cuts in October 1980: 'Premier Margaret Thatcher routed the "wets" in her Cabinet yesterday... She waded into attack ...'

From September 1981 onwards the Thatcher Cabinet slid remorselessly downhill: it no longer resembled so much an engine of government as a court in which the switchback progress of the favourites, 'who's in and who's out', was the favourite topic of an endless speculation, fuelled by the behind-the-hand observations of Ingham. It would be years before this came to matter very much, but the seeds of destruction were certainly sown during the government's earliest crisis in 1981. It might just be added that the idea that the Tories were uniquely loyal and gentlemanly in the way in which they behaved towards each other had always been something of a myth (as its originator Lord Kilmuir himself found out when Macmillan sacked him without warning just after he had spoken glowingly of loyalty as the 'secret weapon' of the party). Nevertheless, the deliberate undermining of colleagues by the Party Leader herself, and the second-guessing of her views and intentions by ambitious juniors that soon began to follow, was a distinct move downhill in British – and Tory – political ethics, and it was a shift that did the lady herself no real good in the longer term. By 1990, when Thatcher was in deep trouble with her party, her backbench critic Julian Critchley was joking that *dis*loyalty was now the Conservatives' secret weapon.

All of this was possible largely because the Prime Minister herself had acquired by 1981 a stark reputation with the Tory activists and with the electorate. With the public at large, as opinion polls showed, she had an unusually sharp political image, admired by those who thought her plucky and determined, hated with rare ferocity by those who thought that the same qualities added up to dogmatic narrow-mindedness, and with a large proportion of the country's intellectual elite in that second category. In the party, though, her readiness to fight issues out with a lead from the front, to speak up for the attitudes and prejudices she shared with ordinary members, and to appeal to the party faithful on the populist agenda that her predecessors had disdainfully thought to be beneath them, was extremely popular. At the 1981 Party Conference she received a huge and noisy ovation for her courageous declaration that despite the economic crisis there would be no going back: 'You turn if you wish. The Lady's not for turning.' This was a classic and carefully thought-out soundbite for the television news, but it was also a multi-layered statement of principle, which phonetically compared her positively to Heath and his 'U-turn'. More often the populist appeal was rather less subtle, as when Prior's successor as Employment Secretary, Norman Tebbit, reminded the (largely employed) Tory delegates at the same Conference that in the 1930s his unemployed father had got on his bike and found work, rather than sitting around and waiting on the state.

The proverbially moderate Rab Butler had once caustically remarked that those 'dry' Tories who talked airily of the need to create 'pools of unemployment' should be thrown into such pools and forced to swim for their own lives. But despite the part played by the 'Labour isn't working' campaign in winning power in 1979, it was now the large pool of unemployment that existed – and grew rapidly – during Thatcher's first term that provided Tebbit with the opportunity to move on from Prior's tentative start to a more determined attack on union powers and immunities. As their members feared for their jobs in a recession-hit economy, the unions were in no mood to fight purely political battles, nor indeed to confront the government and the employers over pay claims either. The government was therefore able to go onto the offensive against the unions, demonizing them in speeches from 1981 onwards and thereby once again playing successfully to their own partisan gallery. They could also make trades unions seem virtually irrelevant, for at the same time Tory ministers completely abandoned decades of identifying the union leaders as partners in national economic management; there would be 'no more beer and sandwiches at Number Ten', no more late-night deals to stave off strikes, no admission, indeed, that the union leaders had anything at all to offer the nation. As the number of trades union members fell – partly the effect of deindustrialization during the two 1980s recessions and partly the effect of unions that could do less than in the past to look after their members anyway – the government screw continued to tighten, while privatization of the utilities distanced many individual unions further from contact with Whitehall than they had been since 1914. By the time of Thatcher's retirement in 1990 the number of union members had fallen by almost a third since she had arrived in Downing Street, unions' legal rights had been trimmed back almost to the position of the Taff Vale judgement of 1901, and their once-feared ability to make and break governments was so entirely a thing of the past that even Labour leaders could envisage snapping their fingers in the union leaders' faces – a far cry from the 'winter of discontent'.

It was, however, in international affairs that the populist agenda most obviously came into its own during the first Thatcher term, for, first over Europe and then in the South Atlantic, Thatcher was able to mobilize a degree of xenophobia that did no harm at all to her support at home. She had voted in support of all three of Britain's applications to join the EEC, and as a minister had actively supported the decision to join in 1972. When she became Leader in 1975, one of her first major tasks was to lead the party through the referendum held by the Wilson government to seek endorsement of its renegotiated terms for entry, and in this she had again shown herself quite ready to back the pro-European cause, though it was true that even then she left most of the campaigning to those who were more enthusiastic. Once in office, though – perhaps resenting the fact that in European meetings she had to spend time listening to her equals rather than monopolizing the discussions and steering them in her preferred direction – she rapidly moved in a more sceptical direction. At first she was confronted with a consolidating period in the life of the EEC, with few new initiatives, but as her government sought ways of controlling public expenditure to facilitate tax reductions, her attention was increasingly fixed on the size of the British contribution to the Community budget, set in more affluent times and becoming burdensome as the British economy shrank. Her almost obsessional campaign to get back a proportion of 'our money' was received with incredulity and embarrassment both at home and abroad. Her very use of the possessive pronoun already suggested an instinctive lack of European-mindedness which would increase over the years, but the determination and sheer bloody-mindedness with which her campaign was pursued enabled her to achieve a £1.8 billion rebate on Britain's contributions, a signal personal success against most Foreign Office advice, and a very exploitable issue with the British electorate. Europe was increasingly to be an issue that Thatcher could turn to in order to retain voter support back home.

It was, however, the entirely unforeseen invasion of one of Britain's

Thatcher takes on the EEC *Daily Telegraph*, 30 April 1980.

few remaining colonies, the Falkland Islands, by Argentina in April 1982 that allowed the maximum exploitation of Thatcher as the defender of the national interest against enemies within and without. If not foreseen, this was certainly a self-induced problem for the government, for the Foreign Office had botched the pre-war diplomacy and so convinced the Argentinian military that Britain would not fight, and a defence review's decision to withdraw the only ship that the Royal Navy kept on the Falklands station had confirmed that impression. In that sense, the government was lucky to suffer no greater setback than the resignation of Foreign Office ministers, and when later investigations and enquiries showed that blame might well have been more widely shared it was far too late to matter. In the short term, the nation reacted in outrage to its biggest humiliation since Suez, especially since it was at the hands of a nasty military regime which had barely recovered from a ferocious suppression of dissidents in its own backyard, and was indeed suspected of invading the Falklands mainly to distract attention from its record at home. Herein, though, lay the Thatcher government's opportunity, for there was scarcely anyone in British public life prepared to oppose the dispatch of armed forces to rescue the Falklanders from an imposed, alien, neo-Fascist regime; in leading the country through such a 'good war', though it presented huge risks, Thatcher herself gained enormous advantages too. It also gave her the chance to show how far the credit earned by being a loyal American ally and cold warrior could be cashed in during Britain's time of need, for her personal friendship with President Reagan helped enormously, first to win and then hold American support, without which the war simply could not have been won.

That analysis may be unduly cynical, for after all Thatcher and her ministers shared in the national mood, and, for a politician whose departmental experience had been limited to Education, she mastered the military, naval and diplomatic structures and issues with impressive skill and nerve. There was some dissent (both then and later, though not within the Tory Party) when the sinking of the cruiser *General Belgrano* seemed also to torpedo a final chance of avoiding war, but the critics both ignored the military realities in their allegations and seemed to have little effect on popular opinion anyway. British losses, incurred when first HMS *Sheffield* and then other warships were sunk, and when poor tactical planning by local commanders led to heavy casualties at Bluff Cove, only consolidated support behind the government, and it was the government that reaped the benefit when the war ended in a complete British victory. The Falklands incident was now more often contrasted with Suez than compared with it, and Thatcher was even held by some admirers to have exorcized the ghost of 1956, to have ended a quarter of a century of British retreat. Street parties held to celebrate the end of the war were conducted on the pattern of 1945, Dame Vera Lynn sang 'The White Cliffs of Dover' for the official victory concert, and it was noted that the patriotic songs at 1982's Last Night of the Proms had a quite different emotional pull on their young audience. That October, 'Land of Hope and Glory' was also played by the organist before the final session of the Conservative Party Conference, and enthusiastically sung by those present, just before they gave Margaret Thatcher her most ecstatic reception yet.

Conservative enthusiasm in the autumn of 1982 owed something to the fact that in the opinion polls the party was now a long way in the lead, while in 1980 and 1981 it had been far behind Labour (and even, for a time, in third place). The 'Falklands factor' certainly played its part in that political recovery, but it had begun before the war and owed quite a bit to the modest economic recovery that was also taking place in the South of England at that time. The government had, in other words, come through a time of mid-term unpopularity, as most recent governments had done, though the lowest point at mid-term had been deeper than for most because of the scale of the recession and because a new party had been founded, mainly by defectors from Labour's lurch to the left (the Social Democrats, founded in 1981 and soon allied to the Liberals). The Liberal–SDP Alliance had heavy backing among the non-political and in the press (not least for its sheer novelty value) and won some spectacular by-election successes from both Labour and Conservatives in 1981–2, but it was always going to have a tough time keeping up its momentum, and as the economy recovered it tended to be the Tory defectors who returned home, the Labour ones who stayed with the SDP. By early 1982 and before the Falklands War, the Tory performance was already back on the rise.

It was tempting for Thatcher to dissolve parliament and go for a new mandate in the immediate aftermath of victory in the South Atlantic, but this would almost certainly have been a mistake. Press critics were already worrying over the triumphalist, 'Rejoice, Rejoice!' quality in Thatcher's reception of good, military news – though it seems unlikely that this fastidiousness ever affected the typical voter. An election did not therefore come until a year after the war ended, by which time the 1979 parliament was already four years old, and no special reason had to be offered for a dissolution. The extra year was, though, vital in allowing the economic recovery to gather force, and though it was still much stronger in the Midlands and the South than in any other region, this did allow the Conservatives to benefit from the 'feelgood' factor in areas where over half the population now lived – and where far more than half of the Tory MPs had to get re-elected. Three million unemployed seemed a difficult matter for the government to explain away, but that still left some 26 million who were *in* work and benefiting from some rapid increases in wage rates and a level of consumer credit which doubled in the two years before the election (and would double again in the four years before the next election came in 1987).

In another area, careful planning and accident coincided to provide a substantial widening of ownership within the economy, a piece of 'social gardening' that was only just beginning to pay political dividends. The sale of council houses had been pioneered by local government Tories, mainly in Birmingham, but was now a governmental objective for which a legal 'right to buy' and substantial discounts and inducements were offered in 1980. By 1983 somewhere over a third of a million council houses had been sold to their tenants by the Thatcher government, implying well over half a million more mini-capitalists whose level of dependence on the public sector had already been transformed.

The privatization programme was a good deal more fortuitous, and had barely got going by 1983. Despite some limited experiments under Heath with the sale of Thomas Cook's and British Rail's hotels, the public sector in 1974 was rather larger than in 1970, and was much larger again by 1979 after the interval of Labour government. In the first place, the privatization exercise was a purely financial one, with the Treasury selling off small industrial assets in return for small sums of money, though even this had raised about £1.5 billion by the 1983 election and thereby contributed to the lowering of taxes. By then, the government had also begun to scent a more political opportunity too, for the sales of Cable and Wireless and of Amersham International in 1981 had begun to tempt new investors into the market. This process, with the extensive promotion which briefly made 'Tell Sid' a national catch-phrase and offered substantial discounts for customer-purchasers, would transform the operation from 1984, when British Telecom went on offer and overnight created hundreds of thousands of new shareholders, yet more mini-capitalists with a stake in anti-socialist politics. Although many purchasers sold almost as quickly as they bought, between 1979 and 1993 the proportion of all British adults owning shares rose from 7 to 21 per cent.

Labour councils' reluctance to process requests to purchase their housing stock and Labour's general opposition to the running down of the public sector – even a reluctance to say whether these former state assets would be compulsorily reacquired or not, and if so at what price – provided golden opportunities for the Conservatives to seek votes among these new classes of owners. To such people, Thatcher seemed vindicated when she reminded them in 1983 that in 1979 'we offered a complete change of direction – from one in which the state became totally dominant in people's lives'.

This was clearly foreshadowed in the 1983 Conservative Manifesto, which, while offering no retreat on core economic policy, also showed clearly enough that the government had not lost its appetite for radical change or for attacking the party's enemies. Without much advance trailing or consultation, the manifesto committed the next Conservative government to further trades union reforms, to the taming of excesses in local government (where Labour's swing leftwards had created some easy, 'loony left' targets) and to the abolition altogether of the upper tier of government in London and the Metropolitan counties, overwhelmingly

Labour-held since their creation (by Conservatives) in 1963 and 1973 respectively, and, in the case of the Greater London Council, since 1981 the national flagship of the Labour left. These would provide, alongside a prolonged struggle with the miners in 1984–5, a series of set-piece battles in which opponents occasionally won the headlines but the government was bound to win the wars, generally to the delight of its supporters in both the party and the press. Such battles also kept the Labour Opposition in a state of division and embarrassment and ensured that the government retained the political initiative.

The campaign for the 1983 general election was not a taxing one, for the chaotic state into which the Labour Party had fallen since 1979 – shedding moderates to the SDP and led by Michael Foot, who offered a pathetically easy target for Conservative attacks – and the falling back of the centrist third force too during 1982 ensured that only one party could win. The actual campaign was fought on a low key by the Conservatives, more conscious even than in 1979 that they could only lose support by raising the temperature. In the end they more or less retained their 1979 share of the vote but benefited from a more divided opposition to increase their number of MPs to 397 (the largest number the party had had since 1935) and gain an overall majority of 144 (which was then the largest majority since Attlee's in 1945).

For the two years after that 1983 victory, then, with a huge Tory parliamentary majority, with the subjugation of the miners and the defeat of the local government left occupying most of the headlines, and with Labour concerned mainly with its own internal battles and the Liberals once again divided and despondent, and with the Conservatives usually ahead of – or at least broadly level with – Labour in the monthly polls, the Conservative government completely dominated British political life. From this pinnacle the only way forward was down.

17

Thatcherism: The Way Down, 1987–97

IN 1987 Margaret Thatcher led her party to a third successive general election victory, thus ensuring it a continuous period in office comparable with that of 1951–64 (except that on that earlier occasion the three victories had each been won under a different leader). Thatcher would now comfortably outlast all previous twentieth-century premiers, and historians had to delve back to the pre-reform career of Lord Liverpool between 1812 and 1827 (and before that to Pitt the Younger, Henry Pelham or Walpole) to find a prime minister who had survived for longer. In 1989, the tenth anniversary of her original installation as premier, both party celebrations and press comment attributed to her a predominant share of the credit for her party's recent success. The Party Conference chant of supporters after her October speech was 'Ten more years!' and, in response to insistent questioning about her future intentions, she replied airily that she had hardly yet even begun, and that she intended to go 'on and on'.

Although Conservatives had lost a few seats in 1987 compared with the landslide of 1983, she still enjoyed an overall majority of a hundred and was in no danger of failing to get through the Commons any legislation she chose to put forward (though the Lords could sometimes be more of a problem). Political scientists were beginning to describe this – much as in 1959–60 – as a new stasis in British politics, a situation in which a decline in the link between class and voting had opened the way for the Thatcher government to build a new voting coalition that could sustain it in office for as far into the future as anyone could see. Whereas the pioneers of the Labour Party had believed in the 'inevitability of gradualness' and that time was on their side, the prevailing cultural

'My specialist subject is British Prime Ministers, 1979–1988.'

The Times, 10 May 1987.

assumption in the later 1980s was that social and economic change was steadily reinforcing the right rather than the left.

This was not especially clear if the criterion was to be expressed support for key Thatcherite policies, for opinion polls stubbornly refused to find that a majority of voters had moved away from their traditional support for welfarism, a free health service and public support for the underprivileged; though it is only fair to add that such support did not prevent the same voters from demanding the extremely Thatcherite objective of lower taxes at the same time – much as the peasants of Third Republic France had been said to have their hearts on the left but their wallets on the right. In 1983, 1987 and especially in 1992 the hope of more tax cuts was almost certainly crucial in subduing some electors' continuing centrist doubts about the Thatcher team's other domestic programmes. For a politician as wedded to the doctrine of the electoral mandate as was Thatcher, it did not after all matter very much what the electors *thought* about policy, provided that enough of them went on voting Tory in general elections, for even the most sophisticated electoral system (and Britain's was certainly not that) cannot weigh up the feelings that lie behind actual votes cast.

The assumption that Thatcherism was the social wave of the present (and presumably therefore of the near-future) relied on the accumulating evidence that working-class voters were in the 1980s more open to the Tories and more suspicious of Labour than at any time since the 1920s, as a consequence both of actual social change and of the Labour and Tory parties' policies. Specifically, survey evidence showed that there were now in effect two working classes: at one pole were those in the North or Scotland or Wales, still living in council houses, members of trades unions, and working in the public sector or in manufacturing, and these remained on balance strongly pro-Labour; at the other extreme were those who lived in southern England, owned their own homes, were not union members, and worked for a private employer in a service industry, and these were about as likely to vote Conservative as Labour. There were few families that exactly represented either of these packages of variables, but the tendencies and correlations were very strong, and since manufacturing, employment in the North, union membership and council house tenancies were all becoming statistically rarer within the electorate as a whole, the social waves did indeed seem to be flowing the Conservative way. This was the culmination both of the long-term embourgeoisement of the working class detected since the early 1960s and of a direct response to council house sales, the decline of trades unions and Britain's deindustrialization in the 1980s. It could even be shown, indeed, that the Tories had done relatively badly in elections in the 1980s, since these measurable social and economic changes had improved the electoral battleground in their favour by a far bigger margin than their actual recovery of votes since 1974.

How, then, had the Conservatives, with such tides flowing, managed to score only 42 to 44 per cent of the national vote in the three elections that Thatcher won, a share that in previous generations would have produced only defeat or near-equality with Labour (as in both 1950 and 1964)? Most obviously, it was because politics in the 1980s was three-party in character, as it had not really been since 1929, but that answer tended to confuse cause and effect, for increased Liberal voting was itself a partial consequence of the failure of Conservatives to mobilize more support. The main underlying factor was that the rise in working-class support for Thatcher's Conservatives was offset by a loss of support among women and in the middle class, and by changes in the relative sizes of the classes themselves. Here, too, the pattern was more one of a division within class than of a shift that reflected a different form of class solidarity; middle-class voters who were (or were married to) managers in private industry or were self-employed were likely by 1987 to be as staunchly Conservative as ever, but the large number whose employment was in the public sector or in the liberal professions experienced a significant falling-off in Tory voting, with a shift of this 'salariat' first to the Liberals and then, after 1992, to Blair's Labour Party too. The reasons for this are not difficult to deduce: it was hard for public sector employees to remain for more than a decade supportive of a government which railed against the concept of public provision to which they had devoted their lives, and which frequently targeted the incomes and productivity of public sector employees as a means of keeping down government expenditure. It was equally difficult for such groups as lawyers and doctors (previously very solid Tory interest groups) to maintain their loyalty when even their traditionally self-governing havens of privilege were subjected to the Thatcherite new broom. To an extent, though, change in the size and membership of classes was as important as any changes within them; by 1990 the middle class (only a quarter of the electorate when Churchill returned to Downing Street in 1951) was for the first time a majority of the total electorate, but this meant that it now included a large section for whom educational opportunities had opened the door to improvement of income and occupational status; these people nevertheless imported into their new class and lifestyle attitudes learned at a working-class mother's knee and from a father's *Daily Mirror*.

This disappearance under Thatcher of the Conservatives' disproportionate support among women voters, recorded at every previous election since such evidence was collected, was on the face of it more paradoxical, for she was after all the first woman leader that any British party had put forward to appeal for women's votes. Since the older pattern reasserted itself and women once again became more Tory than men in 1992 and to an extent even in 1997, the explanation was almost certainly to do with Thatcher herself. Perhaps she was widely perceived as having particularly male, even machismo, characteristics – the 'best man among them', as she was sometimes described in the context of her own Cabinet. Perhaps her classically tough-minded articulation of the importance of competition, defence spending, battling enemies within and outside the state, and her insistence on self-reliance, were political characteristics that women voters generally distrusted and gave a lower priority to, than to caring and compassion. Perhaps there were simply more women voters who, as nurses, teachers, school cleaners and the like, were personally disadvantaged by the government's attempt to roll back the state which employed and paid them. The shift probably owed something to all of

Political postcard, c. 1989

these factors, but it was also a reminder that, in the stark polarization of political opinion that Thatcherism represented, Margaret Thatcher's own personality and style repelled some traditional Tory supporters even while attracting new ones.

One net effect of all these changes was a far more volatile electorate, more influenced by short-term and pragmatic considerations, with marginal seats now in rather different places than in the days of Macmillan – though the New Towns first captured by Conservatives in 1959, places like Basildon, could still be electoral weathercocks, as early declarations of Tory wins there in both 1987 and 1992 showed clearly enough. Another effect, much discussed and worried about by those who were concerned about the health of British democracy itself, was the increasing differentiation that voting trends introduced into the geography of British politics. In 1987, as in 1959, the Conservatives won a majority of a hundred in the Commons, but this time by winning four-fifths of the seats in southern England and the Midlands (where they had got three-fifths in 1959), and only a quarter of the seats in the rest of the United Kingdom (where they had half the MPs in 1959). In a decade that saw unusual levels of violence in British society (which investigators from such outside bodies as the Church of England attributed at least in part to the growing problems of

The Times, 13 May 1987.

poverty, to the widening gap between rich and poor, and to long-term urban unemployment) there was a dangerously narrowing geographical base beneath the government's representation in the Commons – though at the same time the Tories' class support was more broadly representative of the nation than ever before.

It was indeed a further sign of the unfixing of traditional political loyalties that the Church should have commissioned such a report in the first place, and then confronted the government head-on with calls for different policies when it was completed. 'The Conservative Party at prayer' of the Victorian era, still reliably supportive of Baldwin's anti-socialism in the 1920s though partly detaching itself from Macmillan's perceived gospel of materialism in the 1950s, was now quite clearly ranged against the Conservative Party. It was, though, characteristic of Thatcher that she responded to this turn of events not with any attempt to rebuild the party's bridges with a body that influenced many Tories' opinions, but with pointed requests to the bishops to stay off her turf, with the promotion of more conservative clerics when she had the chance, and with a sermon to the Church of Scotland in which she turned the parable of the Good Samaritan into a Victorian fable about self-help and thrift. Nobody could ever say that Thatcher shirked a fight, even in the most unpromising of circumstances, but neither could it be said that all her battles were either necessary or wise.

The confidence that underlay Margaret Thatcher's increasingly authoritarian tone when confronted by such independent entities within Britain's traditionally pluralist democracy was, however, hardly justified, for the foundations of her own authority lacked real solidity, being dependent on numerous factors outside her control. These can be listed as the narrow basis of her voter support, the contribution of the other parties to her victories, the timely procession of unpopular and easily demonized opponents, and – perhaps most crucially – her own inability to continue to operate with the shrewd mixture of strategic conviction and tactical pragmatism which had characterized her first term. These need to be examined in turn, for together they offer the explanation of how the Thatcher–Major governments were able for so long to defy the laws of political gravity, and to govern in defiance of an increasingly hostile 'middle' vote, which had exerted such a strong centrist pull on every other British government since the advent of democracy.

The narrowness of voter support was the most obvious problem to outsiders who were used to majoritarian electoral systems, but it was characteristic of the way in which British politics is conducted and reported that for four years out of every five it was the breadth of her parliamentary support rather than the narrowness of the voter-base on which it rested that attracted all the attention. And yet it was obvious that a party that could attract even in its moments of greatest triumph the support of only 42 to 44 per cent of the electorate was always vulnerable to the consolidation of the anti-Conservative vote. At by-elections this happened with great regularity, so that the Conservatives managed to hold only three of the twenty-three seats that they defended between 1985 and 1997 (with not even one being held in the eight contests after 1992). On the even lower turnouts in local government and European elections, the position was if anything worse (which is one reason why the government found itself at loggerheads with local government, overwhelmingly and permanently controlled by its opponents), and in opinion polls the Thatcher–Major governments were almost always behind Labour by very large margins. The Conservatives' survival in office was therefore basically due to their ability to mobilize the support of 42 to 44 per cent of the

Guardian, 11 April 1992.

electorate against a divided opposition once every four years, and it would come to an end as soon as either the Labour Party returned to its voting levels of 1945–70, or the Liberals and Labour together managed to use tactical voting to reduce the impotence of the majority of the electorate (both of which factors threatened in 1992 and then happened with a vengeance in 1997). The post-1981 rise of successive centre parties that split the anti-Tory vote without managing to win much for themselves therefore created years of false impressions of Tory security.

Thatcher was also able to hold back the swing of the electoral pendulum by exploiting the real weaknesses of the Labour alternative. Labour reacted to defeat in 1979 by taking a big leap away from the political centre, by adopting such left-wing policies as massive doses of nationalization, abolition of the House of Lords, and the unilateral abandonment of Britain's nuclear weapons. The lifelong nuclear disarmer and veteran left-winger Michael Foot became Leader and had, with his own defence views and his party's, little chance against the victor of the Falklands War in 1983 – quite apart from the rest of Labour's 'longest suicide note in history' manifesto and the extent to which Labour's actual campaign was outgunned in sophistication (and spending) by the Conservatives, and savagely denounced by most of the press. When, after 1983, Labour began to move in painful stages back to the political centre, they found that the Thatcherite 'ratchet' had anyway moved the political 'centre' still further right than it had been in 1979.

Neil Kinnock was the best Leader that Labour could realistically have chosen in 1983, since he was young, leftish in background but pragmatically right in current thinking, and prepared to fight the hard left at any personal cost. For Tory voters, however, he was irretrievably shop-soiled by his CND past (to which he was too emotionally committed ever to abandon it altogether) and by his tendency never to use one sentence where a couple of paragraphs would do. Kinnock could do little but bide his time in 1983–5, while Liverpool militants, 'loony-left' councils and striking miners dominated the political headlines, but he achieved a great deal in 1985–7 in dragging his party back to the centre, only to find in 1987 that the centre had once again been shifted rightwards by the government. Eventually, in 1992, Kinnock's problem was that he had moved so far in directions in which he had not originally wanted to go that he could not convincingly articulate anything at all except his determination to win.

Seen in this light, Labour's difficulties were clearly by no means all of their own making, but were also heavily influenced by the extent to which the political issues they opposed were always being moved in the wrong direction for them by the Conservatives in government. A party which, in 1984, could not decide whether to return telephones to a public sector monopoly (hardly a central point in the commanding heights of economic power) had to decide ten years later whether to fight – and if so how much – against the demolition of the jewels of Labour's 1945 crown: nationalized coal and the state-owned railways. This was an auction which Labour could not easily win – any more than the Conservatives could be more convincing than Labour as health reformers and advocates of fair shares all round in 1945 – so no wonder they found the adjustment difficult. Nevertheless, Labour under Kinnock did gradually lose its unelectable image as the party of hard-left militants, high taxers and unilateral disarmers, and had already by 1992 moved well to the right of where Harold Macmillan and Edward Heath had been as Conservative Prime Ministers. The Tory advantage from Labour unpopularity could be exploited for one last time in 1992, but sooner or later this windfall bonus would disappear. The ratchet could not work as a political weapon for ever, and its continued use risked eventually levering the Tories themselves off the edge of the politically acceptable spectrum of opinion in their efforts to stay clearly to Labour's right. A 'No turning back' group of Tory backbenchers had by then come into existence to press for the further pursuit of right-wing causes, but while 'no turning back' was actually a stance on which almost all Tories could agree, always pushing on was something quite different.

Conservatives were also united in their will to win against the miners' strike of 1984–5. The time was now ripe for the battle so carefully avoided in 1981–2, and it seems clear that the actual timing of a strike that began with the warm weather in 1984 also had something to do with the government. Once it did start, though, Arthur Scargill's posturing and his political mistakes (notably in refusing a ballot, so conceding to the government the democratic high ground) ensured public support of Thatcher and a complete victory after a year of hard pounding. By 1985, though, the supply of unpopular enemies was also likely to run out before much longer, not least because of the Thatcher government's single-minded determination to demonize and then defeat them. No foreign foe offered after 1982 a soft target as irresistible as General Galtieri of Argentina had been, while the utter destruction that came to the coal industry after 1984–5 ensured that no union leader would thereafter follow Arthur Scargill over the parapet. The trail of legislation needed to subdue the local government left was bloody and painful for the government as well as for its opponents, but a combination of abolishing actual councils, capping the expenditure of others, and introducing new codes of audit and of conduct had removed any likelihood of councils defying Whitehall after 1987, as the GLC and Liverpool had done in the early 1980s. Perhaps most seriously of all in this context, the gradual running-down of the Cold War after Mikhail Gorbachev took over the Soviet Union, while providing in the short term a rare international platform on which Thatcher herself could appear as a conciliator (and receive in 1987 an electorally valuable triumph on a walkabout in Moscow's Red Square of the sort Macmillan had enjoyed in 1959), deprived Conservatives of a key issue in domestic politics, exactly as it did for George Bush's Republicans in the United States. No longer could they pose as the only reliable defenders of the national interest against an anti-democratic Communist threat, a stance which had, ever since the late 1940s, helped to embarrass Labour and shore up the Tory vote. And no longer did 'unilateralism' have the relevance with the electorate which could be exploited in such Tory posters as that which in 1983 showed a British soldier with his hands raised in surrender, and the slogan 'Labour's defence policy'.

By the end of the 1980s Europe provided the only external or internal 'threat' that Thatcher could use, and Eurocommission President Jacques Delors did indeed come to occupy the role in British politics previously reserved for Leonid Brezhnev and Leopoldo Galtieri. But this was an issue which was as likely to split the Tories as Labour: it would in the end be the catalyst that wrecked Thatcher altogether and also played a major part in the downfall of her successor. Some enjoyed the poetic justice discernible in the fact that those who had lived by exploiting xenophobia should end by perishing on the same sword, but in Conservative history it may perhaps be better seen as evidence of the difficult balance that has to be struck between the triumph of Disraeli in 1878, when the exploitation of Russophobia brought great benefits, and the fate of Neville Chamberlain in 1940, when the *failure* to stand up for the national interest and be effectively rude to foreigners brought even swifter retribution than came to Thatcher in 1990.

Much, therefore, would come down to judgement, and in so presidential a regime as the Thatcher government was after the mid-1980s, this would depend mainly on the Leader. But here the government's problem deepened from within, for there is little doubt that Thatcher gradually succumbed to the same delusionary flaws that had doomed Heath in 1973–4 – if with her own very personal slant. She became increasingly convinced of her own rightness on all major political issues, less and less tolerant of different viewpoints, particularly as she really did become more experienced and more knowledgeable than almost everyone else around. Whereas in 1975 she had been a new Leader surrounded by men with longer and broader ministerial careers than her own, and was still in 1979 less well-qualified by experience than at least half of her own original Cabinet, by the time she fell in 1990 the steady processes of reshuffling, resignations, sackings and retirements meant that she was the *only* minister to have had eleven years continuously in the Cabinet. She was now surrounded by younger politicians who owed their appointments to her patronage, and it would have taken a much more modest – and less instinctively 'bossy' – politician than Thatcher ever was to avoid the steady boost to her self-esteem that these processes generated.

The native caution that had been an important part of her success in the first six years was on the wane after 1985, and the conviction that she alone knew what was best was on the rise, fuelled by flatterers and sycophants at her 'court', who fed her with the policies that she was thought likely to admire rather than giving dispassionate advice. The result of all this was the poll tax of 1989–90, a policy generated by some of the ablest minds in her government, in the sure knowledge that Thatcher herself had not forgotten the pledge to abolish domestic rates that she had been obliged to give (against her better judgement at the time) in 1974, and which she had not been able to persuade her Environment Secretary and Cabinet to redeem in the early 1980s. There were impeccably logical arguments in support of the poll tax, and its principles were perfectly consistent with 'late-Thatcherism' in its shifting of burdens from taxes to charges levied on consumers, but its adoption was none the less a massive political misjudgement, and exactly the sort of thing that the cautious Thatcher of 1981 would never have allowed her government to become committed to. In the government's internal discussions Thatcher was actually slow to endorse the poll tax, but once it was decided on and announced, the momentum became unstoppable. Thatcher's 'Damn the torpedoes' leadership style by that time ensured that she steered the government's 'flagship' policy personally, nailed her own flag to its mast, and went down with the ship when it sank.

There was also a broader problem generated by such a hands-on approach to the processes of government, which was that both the Prime Minister and her government (and Major's too after 1990) became increasingly reluctant to refuse to act on any problem brought to their notice. When savage dogs got out of control (as they had always done, at least as long as newspapers had been on the lookout for such stories during August), the government rushed into legislation which proved to be unenforceable and counter-productive, so hastily was it drawn up and pushed through both Houses. When there was criticism of educational standards in schools, the government imposed prescriptive rules for what must and must not be taught in all British schools, and then had to amend these provisions on an annual basis when they also proved to be ill thought-out and unworkable. When football supporters ran riot, the government announced that it would solve that problem too by allowing only the members of supporters' clubs to go to matches, though in this case sanity prevailed and saved football's financial viability. When the BBC proposed to stop broadcasting ball-by-ball commentary on test match cricket, it was sternly told to reverse policy, and the cricket authorities themselves were subsequently forbidden from selling the right to broadcast their matches to satellite companies (in direct contradiction of both the government's broadcasting policy and its belief in the market), though it was not clear that the government had the powers to do any such thing. In other areas, the overruling of the Home Secretary by the courts in the mid-1990s became so commonplace as scarcely even to merit mention on news bulletins.

The effect of this strange compulsion to rush into action on the slightest provocation was that a government that had promised to roll back the state and to introduce a moratorium on legislation became instead the most centralizing, regulatory and interfering that the country had ever had. All of this offended the various interest groups that were affected by each bold intervention, and rarely generated gratitude in return from those who had demanded reform but not got quite what they had asked for – legislation on gun control in the last days of the Major government being a fine example of this. More important politically, the process drastically reduced the powers and discretions of local government, health service managers and doctors, arts administrators, public industry managers and boards, vice chancellors and headteachers, and all the other multifarious intermediary bodies that had shared both the credit for success and the blame for failure when they had operated within a genuinely pluralist democracy. The Conservative government's 'nationalization of blame', as Simon Jenkins of *The Times* so neatly put it, ensured that to an ever-increasing extent all the focus of political criticism would fall on the government itself, and effectively on its Leader. By 1990 Thatcher was routinely answering twice weekly at Prime Minister's Questions a whole range of enquiries that had been a problem for people other than the government in 1979. While the government's luck held out and credit could plausibly be claimed for improved pass-rates in A-levels, or reductions in hospital queues, or better local authority housing services, then all was well and good, but when the government was failing in and after 1989, then all the chickens in the entire country would come fluttering around Number Ten's hen-house.

The final area of underlying weakness related entirely to the party rather than the government, for during the eighteen years of Thatcher–Major government the Conservative Party itself suffered a dreadful, unmitigated spiral of decline. At one level of explanation, this was but a further stage in the running-down of the membership, organization and financing of the party that had continued ever since the pinnacle reached in the early 1950s, and it was to be expected that an uninterrupted period of eighteen years in office would test the party severely, for on almost all previous occasions the party had waned when the Tories were in power (and when effort seemed unnecessary) but waxed when faced with Labour or the Liberals in power. All the same, the decline that set in after 1979 was more serious than that sanguine view would suggest, for the downward spiral reached in the 1990s a critical point at which the party apparatus could no longer properly fulfil even its basic functions, while the policies adopted to offset that decline brought other problems in their wake.

Membership was the most obvious yardstick of decline, for while in the mid-1970s there were still a million or more paid-up individuals who were party members, that figure collapsed after 1979; a survey in 1990 found that there were by then only about half a million (a large proportion of them over retiring age and fairly inactive), but estimates in 1997 put the figure at no more than 400,000 – and possibly even fewer than the 350,000 that Labour then claimed. This left an average of barely 500 members in each constituency, but since the members who did stay on were disproportionately concentrated in the safer seats, there were in practice marginal seats with far fewer members than that and safe Labour seats with virtually no Conservative organization at all. The consequences of that decline hit every aspect of the party's work. The inability even to fly the flag in local government contests in the northern cities led to the Liberals becoming the main challenger to Labour there, a pattern first set in Liverpool but soon followed elsewhere. By 1997 the Liberal Democrats rather than the Conservatives were also the main parliamentary challengers to Labour in places like Leeds and Sheffield. Fewer members meant less money raised, and this both affected the party's ability to employ professional staff nationally and locally, and forced an ever more desperate trawl for alternative sources of income – including recourse to some dubious overseas sources that would never have been tapped in the past. The organization had traditionally depended on paid professional agents to prepare for and coordinate campaigning by the member-amateurs, but the drop in the numbers of agents after 1979 meant less professional guidance at precisely the time when the shrinking membership most needed it.

By 1992 and 1997 it was clear that the local party machine was no longer capable (much as in 1945) of doing enough canvassing and 'knocking-up' on polling day to pull in even the reliable Tory vote, and the fact that in both elections the swings to Labour were higher in the marginals than in the country as a whole reflected that decline as well as Labour's corresponding advance. Finally, local decline reinforced the Tory retreat in local government, itself a direct effect of years of having the party in office and failing to elect councillors during long periods of mid-term unpopularity. The loss of control even of traditionally Tory authorities in the suburbs and the shires then in turn reinforced the government's damaging antagonism towards local government as such, and drove it to further centralization and regulation; it also ensured that in much of the political minutiae of local electoral politics (such as the placing of polling stations, the location of new building developments and the offering of community advice to boundary commissioners) only the voices of Labour and Liberal Democrats were officially heard. It was notable that, when parliamentary boundaries were redrawn before the 1997 election, the rock-bottom morale of local Tories prevented them from putting up much of a fight, and that the commissioners gave much weight (as they were legally bound to) to the advice of the local authorities, almost none of which now favoured the Conservatives. The 1997 redistribution of constituency boundaries was the first since 1832 not to produce a net Tory benefit.

Such a period of decline was unlikely also to be a time of reform, and this was certainly the case within the party. There had been during the Heath and early Thatcher period a considerable impetus for democratizing in some ways the structure itself, and some limited changes did take place. Heath as Party Leader attended the Conference (as none of his predecessors had ever done) rather than descending from the clouds at the end of the week only to address a mass rally. More of the Conference's time was spent on issues chosen by members, and it became possible to demand voting by ballot (as the Leader himself did in order to get the biggest possible show of support for European entry in 1971). The constituencies' views were formally collected and circulated before MPs voted for a new leader in 1975, and accounts were at last published in 1968. But these were limited concessions, and when a committee under Lord Chelmer was created in the late 1960s to consider a more participatory structure for the party as a whole, with more rights for members in return for their time, money and energies, even its cautious proposals were talked out by opponents of change (mainly by Tory MPs, reluctant to share their traditional monopoly of influence). This produced in the later 1970s quite a bit of noise from a 'Charter' group, which set out consciously to introduce party democracy, to 'set the Party free', but at the time succeeded more in antagonizing moderates than in widening support for reform.

Years of decline, then, set in after 1979, during which keeping the machinery going at all became the main preoccupation of constituency and National Union activists. But it was clear in the mid-1990s that, on such issues as the selection of women candidates on a fair and equal basis, rules mainly adopted in the 1940s would no longer do in the attempt to make Conservatism forward-looking. John Major was considering just such a package of reforms, which would probably have traded with the constituencies a partial voice in determining the election of the Leader, in return for some central say in the selection and re-selection of candidates, but the Major government came to its inglorious end before anything was actually done. On the form of 1868, 1911 and 1945, it would take a major defeat to create the impetus for structural reform of the party, and on 1 May 1997 the electorate duly obliged by giving the party its chance.

There were indirect effects of organizational decline too, in fundraising and in electioneering practice. To a large extent, the shortfall in locally raised money could be offset by increased national contributions from industry and from the rich (and there were certainly many of the newly rich who had every reason to wish for the continuation of Conservative government). So much money was needed because as the 1980s went on Labour steadily closed the financial gap that had previously separated it from the Conservatives and was in the 1990s able more or less to match the Conservatives' national campaigning budgets. The Conservatives resorted to the mortgaging of Central Office (though it was leased back straight away) to offset one financial crisis, and several local parties had to engage in similar sacrifices of capital to meet current account deficits. This was a policy that led to nowhere but disaster in the long term, and in 1997 the Conservatives were for the first time in the post-war era well behind Labour in terms of investment in electioneering technology, with results that showed to a positively embarrassing extent during the campaign.

The national party also had to respond to the campaigning deficit implied by local collapse – and to developments in the practices of campaigning in a media age, which might well have brought about such changes anyway – by placing a greater reliance on the outside advice of public relations specialists. Sir Tim Bell, one of Thatcher's favourite experts in this field, wielded influence during an election campaign comparable to that of the Party Chairman, though he held no party post at all, and in the last week of the 1987 campaign there was a semi-public battle between Central Office and the Prime Minister's staff over the way in which the campaign should be conducted – by no means the last such skirmish. There was also an increasingly dangerous reliance on the press support which such public relations experts were employed to achieve, and in particular on the owners of a small number of tabloid newspapers.

The Conservatives enjoyed during the period in which Margaret Thatcher was Prime Minister a greater preponderance of press support (in both titles and total daily circulation) than they had ever had before; in 1990 the Tory-supporting national newspapers sold over 9 million papers daily, compared with only 3.5 million for papers backing Labour, while in 1983 it had been estimated that three-quarters of the entire adult population regularly read a pro-Tory paper. The scale of that preponderance owed a good deal to the switch of the *Sun* from left to right when bought by Rupert Murdoch (who from 1987 owned well over half of the total pro-Tory circulation), but the convergence of interests between Murdoch's papers and the Thatcher government was far from accidental. Murdoch admired Thatcher personally. He had, like other press proprietors, a large vested interest in her campaign to destroy trades union influence (in which the transfer of his own papers to a union-busting new plant at Wapping was a key moment), and he recognized that a reader who bought the *Sun* was in any case likely to be the sort of 'new working class' person who liked Thatcher's populist style and her xenophobic politics.

The party's dependence on such support was nevertheless a source of vulnerability, as became clear after 1990, when Major failed to inspire in the press barons the same admiration that Thatcher had enjoyed, for by then they no longer needed the government's help to keep their own workers in order. For the most part, these were 'barons' only in the sense that major press owners had traditionally been described in that way, though at a lower level of political management of the media Thatcher was prepared to recommend knighthoods and other honours even for working editors and television interviewers, decisions that (whatever their actual purpose) seemed to smack of rewards for services rendered, as did the honours given to those who supported the party financially. In these various ways, then, the decline of the party as a campaigning, fundraising force, together with the demands of a changing media, contributed variously to the whiff of corruption that critics smelled in the air as the Thatcher period drew to a close, and to the 'sleaze' that was so widely associated with Toryism in the 1990s.

If all of this explains how Thatcher and Major successfully defied political gravity for so long, gravity does nevertheless always reassert itself in the end, and from the mid-1980s onwards the Thatcher regime was indeed on the way down, though it did not enter the free-fall phase of that decline until long after her own departure from office in 1990. In part this reflected the removal in stages of the various factors listed above which had held back the electoral pendulum. The Liberal Democrats discovered that by the steady concentration of their attention on building support at the grassroots and in rural and suburban local government they could become the second party to the Tories in these areas, and thus capitalize on tactical voting – and on mere anti-Toryism among moderate voters – to capture parliamentary seats in southern England in the 1990s. After 1987 Labour gradually lived down voters' memories of the 1979 winter of discontent and of its own abandonment of the political centre in the early 1980s, and was able under John Smith and (especially) Tony Blair to offer what the electors saw as a genuinely fresh approach. No new external enemies appeared on which the government could focus the electors' attention except in Europe, while the Tories' own party decline accelerated to such an extent that even such stockbroker shires of southern England as Surrey, and such archetypal middle-class suburbs as Croydon and Harrow, voted to terminate decades of Tory control. By May 1994 the Conservatives controlled only fifteen of the 198 local authorities in England and Wales, and held only 17 per cent of the council seats.

There was, however, a new weakness too, and in the end this was probably the one that was to prove fatally damaging: the narrowness of Thatcher's own base within the Conservative Party. For whereas in the first half of her premiership she had for the most part fought against political opponents whose departure strengthened her hand, she lost from 1986 onwards a number of senior ministers whose support she had enjoyed in the past and whose presence on the backbenches was to be a constant reminder of her increasing unwillingness to 'brook like the Turk no rival near the throne'. The first occasion was a trial of strength within the Cabinet in the winter of 1985–6 between Thatcher and Michael Heseltine, in which the point at issue (government policy on helicopter purchases for the armed forces) involved no great principle, but which escalated out of control into a battle of wills. Heseltine resigned dramatically in mid-Cabinet, in protest against Thatcher's refusal to allow him to raise there matters that she considered already settled at a lower level, and when the murky dealings, leaks and contrary briefings of the previous fortnight then came to light, Thatcher lost her Trade Secretary, Leon Brittan, as well. Heseltine was a dangerous man to antagonize, for his Conference oratory had made him over the previous decade a darling of the party faithful, and he now devoted himself to touring constituency events and cultivating backbenchers in an undeclared campaign to become Thatcher's successor.

Equally damaging, the fact that Heseltine himself attributed his resignation to her dictatorial methods provided the first line in a story that would get steadily longer. The loss of Norman Tebbit's support on 'wobbly Thursday' in 1987 was, if anything, even more careless. In the final week of the campaign, his advice as a very successful Party Chairman and highly experienced election campaigner was spurned in favour of alternative tactics suggested to the Prime Minister by her current favourite, Lord Young (who had never stood for election to anything in his life). The party wasted a sorely needed £2 million on unnecessary last-minute press advertisements, and when the Cabinet was reshuffled a week later Tebbit chose to leave the government. This was certainly understandable in view of injuries that he (and especially his wife) had suffered during an IRA bomb blast, but he surely could have been persuaded to stay on if his relations with Thatcher had been warmer at the time.

The loss of Cecil Parkinson (1983, as a result of a scandal), of John Biffen (1987, sacked) and Nicholas Ridley (1990, resigned after embarrassingly anti-German remarks were reported) deprived Thatcher of three of her keenest supporters, but the unnecessary departure of Nigel Lawson as Chancellor of the Exchequer in 1989 was symptomatic of pure hubris on her part. There were certainly policy disagreements over European issues, and over the details of financial policy, though these were hardly of deeper significance than those that Chancellors and Prime Ministers had surmounted in the past, and the issue once again developed from policy content to one of conflicting wills. Thatcher insisted on the right to take personal economic advice from Professor Alan Walters, who then made speeches and answered press queries in a way that was dismissive of the Treasury's declared policy (and suggested that the premier agreed with him rather than Lawson), so that financial markets were unsure as to just what the government's policy actually was. Eventually Lawson felt driven to resign, prompting an unforgiving Thatcher to attribute his departure to the fact that he had mismanaged the economy by over-stimulating demand and did not have the guts to take the necessary remedial measures. In the aftermath of Lawson's resignation, both Peter Walker and Norman Fowler also departed, in both cases quietly, but reducing yet further the number of those around Thatcher who could give independent advice on the basis of long experience in office. The cartoon from this time which showed twelve Thatchers lined up in a row, with the caption 'My Cabinet is completely behind me', captured neatly the sense of a political narrowing of the regime.

The final departure was, however, the least necessary of all. For all his monochrome appearance, Geoffrey Howe (until 1990 the only other survivor from her first Cabinet of 1979) had shared enthusiastically from 1975 onwards in Thatcher's personal project to transform Britain. He had patiently endured for years her dismissive treatment of him personally, both in conversation and in covert briefings of the press. By 1989 he had served for four years at the Exchequer and six years at the Foreign Office, where he had increasingly come into conflict with the Prime Minister over Europe. In the reshuffle of 1989 he had been kicked upstairs with the title of Deputy Prime Minister, so that the Foreign Office could be offered to the rising John Major, only for his new post to be undermined before he had even taken it up, through a press briefing that suggested that it was all title and no substance. Even this he loyally endured, until an off-the-cuff remark by Thatcher herself in November 1990 went back on a policy towards Europe hammered out with great difficulty in Cabinet, and he immediately resigned in protest. His resignation speech in the Commons in the following week recapitulated the essence of what first Heseltine and then Lawson had already said in similar circumstances about Thatcher's style of government, but went further than they had done by implying that the party should now change its Leader.

All of this occurred, quite accidentally, at exactly the time (at the start of a new parliamentary session) at which, under the 1975 rules, the Party Leader was open to annual challenge. On the next day Heseltine therefore announced that he would stand against Thatcher in order to restore the normalities of Cabinet government, to abandon the unpopular poll tax, and to provide leadership that would again be based on the whole breadth of the party.

Thatcher's position was especially vulnerable in November 1990 for a number of reasons. Over the years she had, like any long-serving leader, offended quite a lot of backbenchers by failing to promote them or by returning them to the backbenches fairly ruthlessly after undistinguished terms in office. Her government had also gradually alienated the more moderate Conservatives in the House (and indeed in the country too) by its almost Maoist insistence on continuous revolution in a radical-rightist direction. There were many who did not share Thatcher's personal economic creed but who had nevertheless backed her strongly in her first two terms, because they agreed on the need for strong leadership against the unions, unilateralists, the Labour left, the Argentinians and the Soviets.

There were in any case not many Conservatives of any stripe who were not enthused by her government's ability to bring within the orbit of practicality issues like privatization that had seemed utterly impossible to envisage under Macmillan and Heath. And, on the basis that omelettes cannot be made without breaking eggs, moderate Tories had accepted that even some conflict and social division had been a price worth paying. 'She gave us', as the very unThatcherite Kenneth Clarke later put it, 'the courage of our convictions.' 'Ours', please note, and not just 'hers'. But after 1987 such people tended to feel that things had gone far enough, that *unnecessary* damage to the social fabric was now being done, and that both the poll tax and continuing attacks on Europe put too great a strain on their continuing loyalty. The anti-poll tax riots in Trafalgar Square derived much of their popular support from the assumption that the government no longer represented the nation, and while Conservatives did not accept that view, some certainly did agree that the government ought to have healed the divisions in the nation that led to rioting rather than just confronting them on the streets. It was such reasoning which had already brought about a leadership contest in the autumn of 1989, in which the backbencher Sir Anthony Meyer fought a token contest against Thatcher and scored only thirty-three votes (though, since almost as many abstained, a sixth of all Tory MPs were already refusing to vote for their Leader to stay in office). It had been hoped that this would fire a warning shot across Thatcher's bows, but events in the meantime and the circumstances of Howe's departure seemed to prove otherwise.

The final, and perhaps in the end most crucial, factor in her fall was the depth to which the party had sunk in opinion polls, in local elections, and in the most recent by-election at Eastbourne just a fortnight before Howe resigned, when the Liberals had completely overrun a safe Tory seat. Despite her formidable record as an election-winner, many Tory MPs now saw Thatcher as an electoral liability and believed (as they had of Heath in 1975) that she – and the poll tax too, which she refused to ditch – would have to go if the party were to have a chance of winning next time. Heseltine was long committed against the poll tax and, unlike Meyer, fought a skilful and deadly serious campaign. Though the Cabinet remained unitedly behind Thatcher there was a detectable lack of enthusiasm in some of their endorsements of her candidacy. Thatcher herself left most of the campaigning to her parliamentary aides and chose to demonstrate her statesmanship by spending the final few days before the vote in Paris at an international conference. She had done the same thing during the 1987 general election and apparently impressed the voters, but Tory MPs were no doubt a more cynical electorate.

The outcome was almost as much of a shock as 1975's first ballot had been, for although Heseltine got only a very respectable 152 votes to Thatcher's 204, the seventeen abstentions meant that – even as an incumbent candidate with solid front-bench support – Thatcher had not been able quite to reach the threshold number required to win outright. Her immediate reaction, broadcast live on television from Paris, was that she would fight on and win in the following week, but within forty-eight hours wiser counsels prevailed. Some Cabinet ministers now felt absolved from the bonds of loyalty, since the ballot figures had for them shown that Thatcher could not reunite the party. Even those who shared her outlook advised that if she stood again she would get even fewer votes and that Heseltine would therefore win on the second ballot (the outcome that she was least likely to want). Reluctantly she agreed to withdraw, but not before playing a part in the choice of the minister selected to stop the Heseltine bandwagon: the Chancellor, John Major. The Foreign Secretary, Douglas Hurd, also chose to stand on a more distinctly moderate, traditionally one-nation platform.

Over the following weekend discreet campaigning by Thatcher and by most ministers, and the growing conviction that Heseltine would never be forgiven by the party's right wing for bringing Thatcher down, while Major could appeal to all sides, produced a strong surge in Major's direction. On 27 November 1990 Major won 185 votes – rather fewer than Thatcher had had a week earlier, and just under half the votes cast, since this time 131 went to Heseltine and fifty-six to Hurd. But MPs had clearly had enough of such things after two rounds of voting. Heseltine and Hurd could see that the party mood now wanted Major elected and they both withdrew, so that Major became Leader without the need for a further vote.

Major had been formally preferred only by the right-wing half of the parliamentary party, and as Thatcher's chosen heir, and this in itself made it difficult – in the end impossible – for him ever fully to emerge from her shadow. And those original supporters on the right would find their loyalties tested over the years ahead when he moved towards a centrist policy in order to hold the party together.

Reunification would anyway not prove an easy task, for Thatcher's supporters both in the Commons and in the constituencies would for years remain convinced that she had been unfairly struck down, and a survey of party members' attitudes conducted a year after her fall found that she was still their favourite Conservative politician. Major had to give Heseltine a big Cabinet post to reflect the breadth of his backing in the two recent ballots, but neatly chose to cancel out two of his problems against each other by sending his rival back to Environment to find a solution to the poll tax's unpopularity, which he had himself been exploiting against Thatcher. But no other former rebels returned. Major's own campaign manager, Norman Lamont, replaced him at the Exchequer, his friend Chris Patten went to Central Office as Party Chairman for the crucial run-up to the coming election, and for the most part other ministers remained in their existing posts.

Despite the continuing depth of feelings raised by November 1990, the party rallied remarkably well, almost as if the crisis had frightened it into a period of pulling together to save itself from electoral oblivion. Major, like Alec Douglas-Home in 1963–4, proved – as he now for the first time came within the ken of most party members – to be a likeable, decent man who had made few enemies. This was partly, of course, because it was never very clear what he actually stood for personally. But his willingness to appear to be all things to all men would only work in the short term; by 1996 the former Thatcher minister Lord Young was explaining that 'the trouble with John Major is that he doesn't believe in anything or look more than forty-eight hours ahead'. In the short term, though, this hardly mattered, for the right could see in him Thatcher's appointed heir, who would therefore carry on with her policies and programme, while the left could see that he was personally a more emollient figure than Thatcher and one who would seek consensus more readily than confrontation. The Cabinet basked in the restoration of something like normal Cabinet government after a decade of continuous high drama (much as Conservative ministers had felt when Bonar Law and Baldwin succeeded Lloyd George). Major offered, as Chris Patten has put it, 'continuity as well as a different face', though a less tactful version of the same view would be 'Thatcherism without Thatcher'. He proved efficient in the dispatch of business and skilled in the representation of the nation abroad – for example, returning from a European summit at Maastricht in December 1991 with enough concessions to enable him to steer the deal through the party, and so neutralize in the coming election year the most explosive current issue.

The passage of time did allow some of the passions of November 1990 to cool. On policy matters there was a ruinously expensive compromise package that buried the poll tax (but which, by piling up an eventual bill of some £20 billion, helped to wreck the control of public expenditure for years ahead and thus contributed signally to the Major government's fateful tax increases after 1992). The development of a more consumer-orientated approach to the public services was represented by a new 'Citizen's Charter' and its descendants then developed in areas like education, transport and health, and over time there was some slight easing of the economic problems that derived from the lengthy recession into which the country had fallen in 1988–9 after the 'Lawson boom' had over-heated the economy. Nevertheless, the economy stubbornly refused to recover in time to enable Major to campaign on a theme of prosperity achieved, as Thatcher had done in 1987 and to an extent even in 1983. Instead, the Conservatives were driven into an alternative stance as 1992 began, the year in which an election would have to be held. Instead of making implausible claims about economic success, the government would (as in February 1974) campaign on the theme that the country was in difficulties and could trust only to an experienced team to solve them. The Tory record would mainly be left to speak for itself, though the income tax cuts that continuing privatizations had funded could be highlighted in order to make a clear distinction from Labour's alleged 'tax and spend' instincts.

The campaign that the Conservatives began in the new year week of 1992 succeeded in moving the election year debate onto that favourable ground, and they were mainly able to hold it there until polling day in April. Assistance came from a poorly focused Labour campaign which sought to explain at length their policies on issues on which the public did not trust them anyway, and from the way in which Major's appearance as a new Prime Minister contrasted with that of Kinnock, who had by then been Labour Leader for nine years. Polls showed that, although most of his ministers were the same people, the public thought of Major as heading a different team from Thatcher's, and this largely neutralized the idea that it was 'time for a change' after thirteen years of Tory government. Finally, Major's brave personal campaigning, in the middle weeks of the campaign, when Labour seemed poised at least to deny the Conservatives a majority and possibly even to win one for itself, earned him much additional respect. Over the final weekend he was able to exploit the possibility of a hung parliament, with deals likely to be done between Liberals and Labour outside the electoral process, and to highlight what he saw as the threat to the constitution and the Union from Labour's devolution proposals. All of these things helped to turn the flow of the vote in the Conservative direction, but it seems overwhelmingly likely that the key issue remained taxation, with enough voters finally coming off the fence in the Tory direction simply to protect their pocket-books.

As in 1970, election night in 1992 was itself an exciting event, for the opinion polls were again comprehensively wrong in their predictions, while early results showed more correctly that Major had won for his party an unprecedented fourth term in office. Turnout, at 77.7 per cent, was unusually high (a level exceeded only twice in the ten elections since 1951). As both a cause and a result of this, the Conservatives polled in 1992 the largest popular vote that any party has ever had, for this was the only time that any party has exceeded 14 million votes. As in 1979 (to which the 1992 result bore a close overall resemblance) the Conservatives were about 7 per cent ahead of Labour, a margin smaller than in 1983 and 1987 but still a gap of well over 2 million votes. But this did not now translate as favourably as in 1979 into a parliamentary majority, for although Conservative and Labour each got almost exactly the same number of seats (336 to 271, compared with 339 to 269 in 1979), the increase in the number of MPs for other parties meant that whereas Thatcher's overall majority in 1979 had been forty-three, Major's in 1992 was only twenty-one. Over the next five years, as by-election defeats eroded and eventually removed this majority, and as maverick MPs discovered the leverage that they could exert when the government was routinely winning votes by margins in single figures (and indeed losing a few too), this element in the 1992 result would prove critical.

How then had it happened, for on all past form a government that won by 7 per cent of the vote would have expected an unassailable, by-election-proof majority. It was partly because the partisan divide of 1992 ensured that Tories piled up useless majorities in safe seats rather than winning key marginals (so that the overall relationship between votes and seats did not follow the traditional pattern); partly because the attenuated party organization could no longer win enough of the really tight contests where a thousand votes decided all; partly because tactical voting ensured that, in some areas at least, Liberals voted for Labour candidates and in others Labour voters supported the Liberals, a tacit collaboration rooted in the depth of hostility that both groups felt to the continuation of Tory government.

In the euphoria of victory, too little attention was paid to these factors – rather the converse in fact, for the winning of the 1992 election by any margin at all in such improbable circumstances bred among leading Conservatives a dangerous over-confidence, a 'We're in for ever' mood which would materially cloud judgements in the years to come.

It is too early to attempt a proper historical verdict on the Major government's term of office after 1992, but it seems likely that the historian of the future who seeks to explain the party's landslide defeat in 1997 will focus on three areas. Inside the party, there was poor leadership, self-indulgence by both ministers and backbenchers, and an almost suicidal disregard for the way in which the party was by now viewed by most neutral observers. From the outside, there was a further surge of electoral success from the Liberal Democrats and a near-transformation of Labour under Tony Blair. On the policy battlefield, the economy ceased to be an advantage, while Europe emerged, like the Corn Laws and tariff reform, as a wrecking issue on which members of the party at all levels put personal conviction before party, so that by 1997 it was the Conservatives that seemed weak, divided and preoccupied entirely with internal affairs, much like Labour in 1983.

The appeal that John Major had enjoyed when, in 1990–92, he offered Thatcherism without Thatcher soon faded after his election victory. Expectations of the role that a Conservative Leader should perform were still pitched at the high level generated by fifteen years of Thatcher, and measured by those standards the defiantly uncharismatic Major was simply too small a personality to wear her mantle. Her reluctance to fade quietly from the scene certainly did not help here, for interviews and press briefings hinted from time to time that Thatcher herself was less than enamoured of the consensual course that Major had to steer with such a small majority, while her keenest admirers still in the government never quite forgave Major for not actually being Thatcher. Heath had for years criticized Thatcher herself, but so lone a furrow did he plough, and so personally sour did his interventions become, that he could do her little real harm, while Thatcher – even when no more than a voice from the wings – was always able to upstage Major. It was notable that whereas Major was scrupulously careful to avoid criticizing Thatcher for these damaging interventions, as indeed he had to be for his own good, after his own withdrawal from the party leadership in 1997 he was quick to assure the party and his successor that he intended to behave better in retirement than either of his two predecessors. He would act as Arthur Balfour and Alec Douglas-Home had done under their successors, rather than follow the examples of Edward Heath and Margaret Thatcher.

Major was, though, a Leader who defied Machiavelli's advice to princes and sought his party's love rather than teaching it to fear him – as Thatcher had certainly done. But then so had others, though without making such a show of it: Enoch Powell remembered his conversations in Cabinet with the most undictatorial Harold Macmillan as being like negotiating with Henry VIII, since the axe was always within his reach, just beside the premier's chair. Released now from the burden of fear, and with little of the momentum in the Major government that charismatic leadership could in itself have generated, ministers and backbenchers alike began to flex their muscles in competitive briefings to the press, in self-indulgent speeches on issues of purely personal concern, and in contrary votes too – expressed in this parliament by a historically high cross section of Tory MPs.

Chris Patten later argued that 'Margaret [Thatcher] had driven the stagecoach at a furious pace. I always thought ... that when somebody tried to run the system more conventionally, which was driving along at a more sedate pace, pieces would start to come off.' As his majority slipped further away when by-elections were lost, Major's room for manoeuvre deteriorated further, and his reported complaints about 'the bastards' in his own Cabinet (who nevertheless remained unsacked) did nothing to add to his authority. The withdrawal of the whip from eight Eurosceptic MPs did not bring them into line, and the whip eventually had to be restored to them without either an apology or a promise of better behaviour, so vulnerable was the government now to ambush in the lobbies. Major's courageous decision to force a leadership contest in the spring of 1995, before his opponents were ready for the one that would probably have been forced on him in the autumn, flushed out his critics and rallied two-thirds of MPs behind his re-election campaign, against the candidature of John Redwood (a former close Thatcher associate who resigned from the Cabinet to stand against his Prime Minister).

This success bought Major time, and ensured that he would not be further challenged until the 1997 election was over, but it also deepened the wounds between party factions, for while Major had become Leader mainly on the votes of the right in 1990, he was re-elected mainly on the votes of centre and left in 1995. This was perhaps a more comfortable position for Major himself, one that accorded more with his own political instincts, but it reinforced the feeling on the right that he had betrayed their original expectations, and with Redwood out of office and behaving in 1995–7 both like Heseltine after leaving the Thatcher Cabinet and like

Joseph under Heath (in the sense that he founded a Conservative 2000 organization to promote his candidature as well as his views), the war was only scaled down to an armed truce. In effect, the Tory factions left it for the electorate to decide, though the scale of the defeat then administered to the party quickly changed Tory perspectives in ways that scarcely any faction had foreseen in advance.

Despite such visible troubles, the victory of 1992, seized as it was from the jaws of defeat by a not especially dynamic Leader, bred, as we have seen, a dangerous over-confidence, even complacency, among Conservatives during the fourth term. This in itself partly explained the self-indulgent political squabbling referred to above, but also showed itself in the various petty and real scandals that accumulated behind the *Guardian*'s investigative 'sleaze' campaign, and in the extremely unconvincing way in which both party and government reacted to that new threat. The problem was certainly exacerbated by the repudiation of the Major government by most of the press, quite early after the 1992 victory, a fruit both of editors' and proprietors' growing lack of respect for the premier and his record, and of the ineffective way in which the press was handled at exactly the time when it was being so assiduously courted by Labour. By 1997 there was scarcely a national newspaper that still backed the Conservatives actively in the election campaign, and the once-vital support of the *Sun* had turned to outright hostility. This in turn meant that the personal peccadilloes of Tory MPs (of which there were far too many in any case, another fruit of complacency) were emblazoned across the front pages, and that all the machinery of an investigative press – cash payments to informants, entrapments, long-lens photography – were turned on the Conservatives rather than on Labour.

The broad concept of 'sleaze' actually consisted of two quite different types of sin: the sexual adventures of Tory MPs, which clashed with their rhetoric about family values but very probably cost the party few votes, and the financial appetite of the greedy, which verged on corruption and was both a real political issue and extremely damaging. Some felt that this ethical decline followed naturally on from social change, and even in 1962 the Chairman of the National Union Executive had been arguing that 'nowadays too many MPs become [company] directors instead of too many directors becoming MPs' as before 1945. An older MP then remarked of 1983's intake that 'they may be a clever lot – everyone says they are – but they're not my idea of gentlemen', while in the 1990s one of Major's own staff thought that generation of Tory MPs to be 'ill-disciplined, greedy, self-indulgent, and with no sense of loyalty to the leadership of the party'.

After the 1997 election only 7 per cent of new Conservative MPs were Old Etonians whereas Etonians had still made up a quarter of new Tory MPs even in the meritocratic 'class of 1950', and there were now no Harrovians in the parliamentary party at all; almost a third of Tory MPs had not attended any public school. In place of the traditional social elite, the Conservative benches were filled by 1997 with men (only thirteen women out of 165) from less privileged backgrounds, typically with no experience of any career other than politics, and with little of the inherited wealth that had enabled earlier generations to rise above the temptations that come with parliamentary opportunities.

John Major's failure to distinguish publicly between the two different types of 'sleaze', his creditable determination to stand by colleagues until their faults had been proved – an honour code that some of his MP-colleagues exploited quite outrageously – and the lack of any rules to authorize the removal of peccant parliamentary candidates, combined to create the impression of a party no longer under any control at all. The result was that, as each scandal erupted, there was an attempt to limit the damage and then a second defeat when that proved to be impossible because of a hostile press. During the five years of the 1992 parliament there were three resignations from the government on policy, but no fewer than twelve resignations for personal misconduct, and almost every case was dragged out over a period of weeks; as the matchless verse of *Private Eye*'s E. J. Thribb put it on the eve of the 1997 campaign,

> So it's farewell then, Tory MPs.
> 'I shall not resign',
> That was your catch-phrase.
> But you usually did.

Attempts to show that the government was doing something to clean up its act, by the appointment of judicial investigations and of the Nolan enquiry into standards in public life, only confirmed the scale of the problem and ensured that time-bombs continued to tick away as the election approached, and indeed into the campaign itself. This was by any account a low point of modern Conservatism, both in the ethical standards that Tory MPs exhibited on their own behalf, and in the halting, even spineless, response of the leadership. Ian Gilmour has compared 1990s Conservatism with 'some crazed American religious cult ... intent

[Cartoon: "TOO MUCH VIOLENCE ON TELEVISION..."]

The Times, 11 December 1996.

on mass suicide. Unlike such cults, however, its leader was not intent on persuading his followers to commit suicide; he was merely unable to talk them out of it.'

Such disarray could not have come at a worse time, for the resignation of Neil Kinnock after his 1992 defeat had opened the way for a new leadership in the Labour Party which was in no way tarred by Labour's past, which appreciated more even than Kinnock had done that Labour must abandon old ideas if it was to win, and which committed itself unreservedly to the modern, campaigning technology which the Conservatives could not now match – and could not now afford to match, with a party overdraft that reached £19 million in 1993. By-elections after 1992 showed a far worse Tory performance than in the previous three terms in office; many produced gigantic swings to Labour and this time only one of the lost seats was regained in 1997. The gradual consolidation of Liberal Democratic strength in local government in the South was matched by the remorseless advance of Labour in the North and the Midlands. At precisely the moment that Conservatism was so weak and so divided, it faced real battles on two fronts for the first time since the 1920s, and a Labour Party more confident and more committed to winning than it had been since 1964.

Two policy failures allowed Labour to exploit the campaigning deficit which the Conservative government had allowed to emerge. First, on the economy, the several tax increases that the Major government introduced retrospectively invalidated its 1992 prospectus (and certainly removed from the pack the best card that Tories had been able to play against Labour), while sterling's humiliating exit from the European Exchange Rate Mechanism on 'Black Wednesday', 26 September 1992, completely ruined the government's reputation for basic economic competence, a reputation it was never able to regain even when the economy was booming for the 1997 election. It also destroyed Major's own reputation, for only six days earlier he had stated that withdrawal from the ERM would be a disaster for Britain, so that the man who had been a considerable party asset in April was by October thought to be doing a good job by only 16 per cent of the electorate. The *Sun*, ominously mocking the government and merging the issues of sleaze and competence, produced a headline on the morning following 'Black Wednesday' that read, 'NOW WE'VE ALL BEEN SCREWED BY THE CABINET'. The subsequent, but belated sacking of the Chancellor of the Exchequer, Norman Lamont, effectively a scapegoat for a collective policy failure, placed a dangerous critic on the backbenches and ensured that neither Major nor his new Chancellor Kenneth Clarke would be able to conduct subsequent policy without flanking fire from their own side. Lamont's astonishingly complacent resignation speech, talking of 'short-termism' and of a government that gave 'the impression of being in office but not in power' was an early taste of what was to come.

The paradox of the Conservative government being re-elected without economic success in 1992, but losing with a reasonable record in 1997, requires some explanation, though no doubt the humiliation of September 1992 cast a long shadow forward over later economic figures. Perhaps the long-term alibi that the economy was basically subject to market forces beyond any government's control prevented ministers from getting credit when things went well. Perhaps the very fact that the economy was stable in 1997 encouraged electors to take the risk of changing the government. Perhaps too many just did not believe that the economy *was* coming right, as polls tended to show. And perhaps the Tories themselves took too little time in 1997 to hammer home their economic success, because of their navel-gazing obsession with Europe.

The whole idea of a link, economically and politically, with the other countries of western Europe in a formal and permanent organization had divided Conservatives ever since the concept had first emerged in the late 1940s, when Churchill himself had called for 'a United States of Europe', and at least at some times had envisaged Britain as a full member of an organization with a single currency, postage stamps and all the other paraphernalia of supranationalism. But although there was Conservative opposition to Macmillan's first application, it was mainly associated with economic interest groups (particularly the farmers, who soon dropped their opposition when they saw benefits from EEC agricultural policy). It was characteristic of British debates in that period that they were always about a 'Common Market' rather than a Community (which is what its then members tended to call it). Even when Britain joined in 1972 and reaffirmed its decision in the 1975 referendum, the focus of the debate was economic, with supporters concentrating on the perceived benefits to the British economy, opponents on the dangers. When the long-term political objectives of the Treaty of Rome were debated at all by Tories, it was only in terms of distant aspirations that might never come about anyway, and which could be moulded to suit Britain's interests only if she were to be a participating member. The prevailing view was, indeed, that it was Britain's reluctance to join in the first place that had led to those political objectives being agreed on, and it was common ground that such a mistake must not be made a second time.

Even in Thatcher's early years as premier, the nature of the issue did not change, and clashes with Europe were mostly financial and economic rather than political. However, the Single European Act agreed at the Luxembourg Council in December 1985 more or less completed this phase of development, and the emphasis thereafter shifted in more political directions, as the admission of more member states necessitated a tightening-up of decision-making processes, the removal of national vetoes and greater powers for the European Court, the European Parliament and the Commission. For British Conservatives and others who were deeply sceptical about this trend of events, the key trumpet call was the speech that Margaret Thatcher made in Bruges in September 1988, rejecting that entire future model of European development. The creation soon afterwards of the Bruges Group to lobby for support for Thatcher's views marked the beginning of a new phase in British politics too, for there was a continuity of both personnel and organization from that time forwards on the Eurosceptic side, leading directly to those who demanded either a referendum on further integration or outright British withdrawal from the Community in 1997.

But the problem was that the economic arguments remained very similar to those which had persuaded most Conservatives to agree to join the EEC in the first place, even while the federalized, political shape of the future Community became ever less appealing politically. In her final two years as Prime Minister, Thatcher was therefore at constant loggerheads with the Treasury and her Chancellors and with the Foreign Office; the resignations of both Lawson and Howe derived substantially from their disagreements with the Prime Minister over Europe. Major's effective postponement of the issue between 1990 and the 1992 election only ensured that there was a greater explosion when it finally came. For, just like tariff reform (which had aimed at a sort of United States of the British Empire, via the same type of customs union as the EEC had at first been), 'Europe' in the 1990s involved almost every aspect of economic, social and foreign policy, and would sooner rather than later move on to encompass defence and the rest of domestic and industrial policy too. Again like tariff reform, it was an issue on which both sides felt passionately and were disinclined to compromise, believed indeed that compromise would be an illegitimate response to such a burning question. Britain must either enjoy the economic benefits of a more politically integrated Europe, or would lose economically in order to retain political independence. In these circumstances, both ministers and backbenchers behaved very badly indeed, and it is hard for a historian to argue with the verdict of the former whip Tristan Garel-Jones: 'This is a chapter in Conservative Party history that is an abomination ... I would never have imagined, in my wildest dreams, that I would see Conservative MPs behaving in that way ... It was without precedent.' Nor is it easy to disagree about the extreme discontent that other MPs and ordinary party members felt about the situation, as voiced by David Mellor when describing his 1997 defeat: 'the poor bloody infantry, of which I was one, were pretty fed up with the quality of the generalship that led us into the debacle'.

Because of the uncompromising views on both sides, Major had extreme difficulty in pushing his European policy through his Cabinet, and his European legislation through the Commons. Tactical arrangements and short-term convergences of interest with either the Liberal Democrats or the Ulster Unionists ensured that he did not often get defeated on votes of importance, but from the summer of 1992 there was always an air of panic about the lobbies and the whips' office each time Europe was to be debated. Twice Major responded to defeats in the lobbies, as Peel had done in 1843-5, by tabling votes of confidence which made his party critics swallow their pride and support him in order to avoid the fall of their government. As in the 1840s though, this was a tactic that produced diminishing returns and in the meantime reduced the mutual feelings of respect and loyalty on which collective party activity depends. Major had thus got himself locked into the position of having to up his own rhetorical ante of Euroscepticism in order to remain in touch with the party's right wing, while doing enough on actual policy to keep the party's pro-Europeans quiet. Both sides ignored Foreign Secretary Douglas Hurd's advice that the party must remember 1846 and 1903 and not make the same mistake again.

The tactical contortions thus required of Major did nothing to enhance the sense that he was a strong leader, while the increasingly Eurosceptic majority in the Cabinet and party were able to pull him further and further in the direction of their own position, which seemed far more straightforward than his tortuous compromises. Even this did not prevent the party from facing a direct electoral challenge from the Referendum Party (backed by, among other Conservatives, Lord McAlpine, a Thatcher acolyte who had been her Party Treasurer). In the 1997 election campaign this challenge cost the Conservatives many thousands of votes but nevertheless occupied too much of the party's attention (since it cost at most only one actual seat), as candidates indulged in a 'more sceptical than thou' leapfrog to hold the xenophobic vote. It was an utterly ungraceful process, and one that ensured that far too much of the reporting of the campaign reiterated stories of Tory divisions and ineffectiveness. Opinion polls showed that the public – whatever their own views on the subject – did not share the Conservatives' fascination with the minutiae of Europe's future. Within a few weeks after polling day, the party's desperate attempts during the campaign to second- and third-guess what might happen at the forthcoming Amsterdam Summit all seemed rather off-beam, when the summit came and went without much happening at all.

In these circumstances, it was hardly surprising that the party crashed to defeat in 1997, much as it had done in 1847 and 1906. Major allowed the 1992 parliament to run on until the end of the fifth year (the first time that this had happened since Douglas-Home had also had to await a late recovery in the party's fortunes in 1963–4), but the polls still failed to show a narrowing of the gap, until an election had to come in April–May 1997 anyway. In the early weeks of a long campaign Conservatives succeeded in unsettling even Labour's ultra-careful campaigning, and with memories of 1992's late recovery in everyone's mind the margin of defeat seemed likely to be less than the polls had been predicting for the previous two years. But the resurfacing of the European issue and renewed Tory divisions as polling day approached halted any party recovery in its tracks.

There was probably no chance in any case of the Conservatives winning in 1997, so devastating was the record since 1992, when added to the enormous forces of the 'time for a change' argument after eighteen years and the emergence of a bright, unthreatening and attractive alternative. Max Hastings, the editor of the *Evening Standard*, although he still intended to vote Conservative himself, remarked in a radio interview as the campaign began that the Major government did not deserve to win, and that if it had been an old dog it would have been put down long ago as an act of kindness. At about the same time the party's Director of Communications was reflecting privately that 'what we have to sort out is people's dislike of the Conservatives. We know we've a fight on our hands: it's so unfashionable now to even admit you vote Tory.' But when the campaign ended, as the BBC's Political Correspondent, Nicholas Jones, put it,

> shy and silent Tories stayed at home because they could not bring themselves to vote for a party which, in the public's mind, had become so discredited and so tainted. Voting Conservative in the 1997 election, even in the privacy of the polling booth, was not just unfashionable but, even for many of their traditional supporters, an act impossible to contemplate.

MORI's pollsters found plenty of statistical evidence of this – noting, for example, that while a quarter of Labour's supporters had encouraged others to join them, only a tenth of Conservatives did so, while only 3 per cent of the Tory voters admitted to having said anything to dissuade people from voting Labour. Even in 1992 the opinion polls had found it hard to identify Conservative voters who were prepared to admit their convictions to anyone but their nearest and dearest, and Conservative voters who actually displayed posters were by now an endangered species. In so far as the scale of the 1997 defeat was in part due to the refusal of Conservatives actually to come out and vote, in a contest that produced a lower turnout than 1992 even when Labour and Liberal supporters were brimming with enthusiasm, this turn of fashion may well have been the most fatal of handicaps.

And yet, in the end the margin of actual defeat *was* less than in the polls, for Labour led the Conservatives in the national vote by under 13 per cent (compared with the 20 per cent which the final polls had indicated). But even this was enough to produce what was generally seen as the worst Conservative deficit since the coming of democracy. As well as losing heavily to Labour all over England, and losing all that remained of their representation in Scotland, Wales and every large English city except London, Conservative candidates found that tactical voting and their long-term decline in local government produced many additional losses to the Liberals in southern England. The 165 Conservatives actually elected was the smallest number that had sat in any House of Commons since the 157 of 1906, and the casualties included a third of the outgoing Major Cabinet, though ironically both Eurosceptics and pro-Europeans were swept out by broadly comparable landslides of opinion. The fact that the party was divided on Europe seems to have been far more important than the political position actually taken up by any candidate.

Even before the last results were in, Major had resigned both the office of Prime Minister and the leadership of the party and retreated (as Baldwin might well have done) to watch a game of cricket. In the leadership contest that followed, every candidate spoke of the need to learn the lessons of defeat, to draw a line under recent events and to remake the Conservative Party on a new basis for the twenty-first century. The election as Leader of William Hague – who had barely been born when Harold Macmillan retired in 1963, had entered parliament after the middle of Thatcher's term as Prime Minister, had joined the Cabinet only a year before Major's election defeat, and had not even been mentioned in the national newscasts in a party campaign only just concluded – was fairly clear indication that the party's surviving MPs also saw the need to reinvent their party for a new century. The 1992 parliamentary party also had rather shallow roots in party history, for only seven of its MPs had been in the Commons before Heath became Prime Minister in 1970, and only thirty had arrived before Thatcher was elected Conservative Leader in 1975; the other 135 had no personal experience of any Conservative Leader except Thatcher and Major.

As Leader, Hague was within weeks demonstrating the open-mindedness that his election had foreshadowed, including some decisions that must have set his predecessors spinning in their graves. Countenance was given to a far more democratic structure in the party, with entrenched rights for ordinary members (and perhaps even the final say in the choice of the Leader), while other shibboleths summarily cast aside included the secrecy that had hitherto shrouded the Conservatives' financial backers and promises to end fundraising from foreign sources. This could all be seen (and was no doubt meant to be) as a very new way of doing things, a forward look which, like both MPs' behaviour in the 1992 parliament and the scale of the 1997 defeat, was without precedent in the party's history, and it was generally reported in those terms. But those who wrote in that way in the public prints tended to forget just how iconoclastic the Tories had also been in response to defeat in 1832, 1868, 1906 and 1945. Reinventing itself at periodic intervals – usually when under the impact of shattering defeats – has after all in itself been one of the Conservative Party's most hallowed traditions.

18

Ghosts and Portents

THE DEFEAT suffered by John Major's Conservative Party on 1 May 1997 was by any reckoning an especially heavy one, and made the more so by the extent to which it was both unexpected (despite so much evidence to the contrary) and, in some ways at least, self-inflicted. In drawing together the threads of this history of the party, it will be useful to place that 1997 defeat within the context of previous experience and to see how far the lessons of party history do indeed offer any guidance in its future task of restoration.

In many ways the Major government broke all records and precedents. Major himself scored the lowest satisfaction ratings since polling began in the 1930s. The whip had never previously been withdrawn from a number of Tory MPs. By-election swings to the Liberals at Christchurch in 1993 and to Labour at Dudley West in 1995 were each higher than ever recorded before for those parties. In 1996, for the first time since the First World War, the Liberals had more local councillors than the Conservatives. Three Conservative MPs defected to other parties, Alan Howarth's decision to join Labour being the first direct Conservative–Labour switch since Sir Oswald Mosley in 1924. The party was actually outspent by Labour in a national election campaign for the first time, during the 1994 European elections, and the Conservatives were unable to outspend Labour even at the constituency level in 1997. The party's membership probably also fell below Labour's for the first time. In the 1997 campaign the Conservatives were clearly at an organizational and technological disadvantage when compared with Labour, for the first time since at least 1945. Unprecedentedly, Labour was supported in 1997 by more national newspapers than the Conservatives, a lead of some 10 million copies in terms of combined circulations. Finally, and most remarkably, for the first time ever Labour won more middle-class and homeowners' votes than the Conservatives.

All of this may suggest that precedents cannot now count for much and that the 1997 Conservative defeat was different in kind from earlier setbacks, which would therefore offer no guidance at all for the future. In May 1997, reviews of the recent defeat and comparisons with 1906 and 1945 tended to conclude with just such a verdict, the irrelevance of all past experience. But that would surely be a facile view. After all, it was almost exactly the same electorate that smashed the Conservatives down in 1997 that had in 1992 given the party the largest popular vote ever, and it was to a large extent the same electors who in 1983 gave Labour an equally unprecedented thumping – after not three but dozens of its MPs had defected. All of this may suggest simply that with increasingly restless, rootless and volatile political behaviour on show at the end of the century on the part of press, politicians *and* public, our search for precedents should be, as it were, index-linked. Yesterday's 5 per cent swing is today's 15 per cent swing, and the difference in the numbers does not actually mean very much when prefiguring tomorrow.

In May 1997 the Conservatives elected fewer MPs than at any election since 1906. From that 1906 disaster, the party fought back to approximate equality with the Liberals fairly quickly, but was not able to go on and actually win power again until twelve years had passed and a world war had remade the political system. This widely made comparison was in itself rather bogus, for in 1906 Tory numbers included sixteen Irish (mainly Ulster) MPs, and without these the 1906 performance (141 MPs) would have been distinctly worse than 1997's 165. Losing so many actual seats in 1997 was in itself the consequence of a package of coincident difficulties – the collapse of Conservative voting in Scotland, Wales and the English cities; the necessity to fight on two electoral fronts in southern England (against both Liberals and Labour, and their tactical voting supporters); and the effect of a declining Tory organization reflected in the inability to win the marginals. None of these factors was unprecedented: Conservatives had also held no Welsh seats in 1906 and held only three as recently as 1966 when Labour last won a big majority; the collapse in the cities was visible during the previous period of Conservative unpopularity in 1974; the failure to do well in marginals was clear enough in 1992; and Scotland was very poor territory for the Conservatives for most of the nineteenth century and again between 1906 and 1914. What was unprecedented was for these factors all to strike at once and on so dramatic a scale that the traditional Disraelian claim that the Conservatives were the 'national' party became hard to justify. The charge that Thatcherism would turn the Conservatives into a narrow band of English South-Easterners, made even when the Lady was first running for the party leadership in 1975, seemed to have come true twenty-two years later. As a matter of fact, though, predictions of this kind had an even greater antiquity than 1975, for the Scottish Tory Walter Elliot was already making just such a prediction when the Conservatives lost so many northern seats in 1945, foreseeing in the party's future 'the rule of the Home Counties'.

If the criterion for evaluating performance is voting figures rather than seats and regional representation, then the 1997 position was if anything worse. The Conservatives' 1997 share of the national vote (30.7 per cent) was lower than any major party has achieved since 1945, but with the significant exception of Labour in 1983 and in 1987 (from which heavy defeats it took the Labour Party about as long to recover as it took the Edwardian Tories, but recover they did). The Conservatives themselves have never done so badly in terms of votes since modern electioneering began in 1832, though such comparisons do not mean very much once we go back into the nineteenth century world of uncontested constituencies and localized campaigns. Perhaps the best measurement of all is the *margin* by which the party lost, coming 12.5 per cent behind Labour in May 1997; this was worse than 1945, when Attlee led Churchill by 8.5 per cent, but not far off 1906, when the Liberals and Labour together outpolled Balfour's Unionists by 11.3 per cent. And yet, with the volatility of the modern electorate, and bearing in mind that 1997's low turnout was clearly caused – at least in part – by Conservatives staying at home, then a swing of 7 per cent, which is what the Conservatives would need in order to overtake Labour in the election due by 2002, would not be so very daunting a target after all. It is very much less than the swing that Labour itself achieved between 1992 and 1997 (a tidal wave which originated in a period in which most commentators were concluding that Labour would never win again) and not *much* more than the pro-Tory 5 per cent swings of 1970 and 1979.

If there were to be by 2001–2 a Conservative recovery that placed the party even near to such swing figures, then there would by then almost certainly have already been a recovery of party morale and of membership (with immediate effects on local organization, on campaigning activity and on funding). There has been a recovery of Conservative membership and organization every time Labour has been in office since 1924 – and arguably, when the 1870s and 1880s and 1910s are taken into account, every single time the Conservatives have been kicked out. An average swing of 5 per cent or more would produce gains in Wales and the English cities (all categories of seat where swings to Labour in 1997 were actually below the national average) as well as in the Home Counties and the London suburbs. In other words, something more like the 'normal' pattern of regional representation would follow the swing, much as it did in 1950–51 after the 1945 collapse, and in 1910 after the disaster of 1906. Scotland could very well prove a different matter, given the longer-term secular decline in Conservative voting north of the border and the Labour government's determination to satisfy Scottish aspirations towards self-government, though the actual advent of a Scottish parliament would in itself be likely to dislocate some of the trends that have been so damaging for the Scottish Tories over the past thirty years. It is after all a fairly clear rule of politics as well as physics that every action produces a reaction in due course – or, on Hannah Arendt's version of the same rule, 'the most radical revolutionary will become a conservative on the day after the revolution'.

The cold steel of the electoral statistics in the 1997 defeat do not then make entirely downbeat reading, and predictions of the Conservatives' inevitable withering into debility are no more justified by the facts after 1997 than they proved to be in 1832, 1880, 1906, 1945 or 1974. The sheer unexpectedness of heavy defeat in 1997 – unexpected because the party had in the previous three contests recovered so rapidly and so steeply in the final year of each parliament, and in 1992 as late as the final days of the campaign – contributed as much as anything to the morbidly gloomy tone of 1997's post mortems. So did the sense that it had all been unnecessary, both because the unhealed wounds of government between 1992 and 1997 had been self-inflicted anyway, and because the electorate seemed not to have voted against Conservative policies even while they were sweeping the Conservatives themselves out of power. In 1906 and in 1945 the electorate could be seen to be voting for a policy alternative as well as for different people, and the defeated Conservatives could therefore try to move their policy stance in a direction which would converge with the electorate's demands (though since, in 1945–51, the electorate's priorities had changed by the time the Tories made their come-back, that argument may be more apparent than real). What is clear is that in 1997 the Conservatives faced a new difficulty, for in seeing their main policy agenda once again endorsed by the electorate even while they themselves were being summarily dismissed, it is far from obvious what they should do as an opposition – European policy apart – to show that they have 'learned their lesson'.

The lesson that is easiest to point to is the consequence of disunity. In 1997, as in both 1906 and 1945, the Conservative Party that went down to defeat was riven by disunity and presented itself to the electorate while still in a state of disarray. In the BBC's exit poll on 1 May 1997 two-thirds of the actual voters rated Major a 'weak' leader, almost exactly the proportion that had voted against Conservative candidates. After defeat, unity was hard to restore in 1906 because the tariff issue that had divided Balfour's government continued to haunt the Balfour and Bonar Law Opposition right through to 1913–14, and this was certainly one reason why the recovery from 1906 was so slow and so patchy. Something similar can be said of the Conservatives' failure to gain much ground between 1847 and 1852, and between 1880 and 1885, whereas, despite their real problems as an Opposition, Churchill's Conservatives pulled together rather well after 1945 and presented a united, disciplined face to the electorate in 1950–51. Labour's experiences after 1979 provide an obvious recent example of the same point: recovery from defeat in 1979 and 1983 was seriously undermined by recriminations over the cause of those defeats and by continuing public disagreement about the party's future. How lasting a defeat 1997 turns out to be in Conservative history may well depend on how far the party can avoid the scenarios of 1846–52 and 1903–10, when policy divisions – much like the European issue has so far proved to be in the 1990s – made the party appear to floating voters as unfit for office for a longish period.

One factor in previous Conservative successes that seems on the face of it unlikely to apply is the contribution made by the other side. From the 1860s until the 1980s the Conservatives had been the regular recipients of transfusions of new blood from the left and centre: Liberal Imperialists, Liberal Unionists, Lloyd George Liberals and Constitutionalists, National Liberals, wartime Nationals, disaffected ex-socialists like Aidan Crawley in the 1950s and Reginald Prentice in the 1970s, and finally intellectuals who, like Max Beloff and Paul Johnson, found a leader to admire in Margaret Thatcher. In the 1990s, for the first time since the Peelite group crossed to the Liberals in the 1850s, there was a significant move the other way, with Conservative MPs defecting to Labour and the Liberals (mainly over Europe) and others making plain their readiness to go if party policies were to change further in a direction of which they disapproved. It must be the highest priority to end that haemorrhaging, since the defection of even one member of parliament gives an extremely damaging impression of a party that is already on the ropes, as Labour discovered in 1981. Moreover, since all the Tory defectors were from the left of the party and mainly from among its pro-Europeans, their departure makes it doubly difficult to win back those middle-of-the-road voters who were already lost after 1992. Chris Patten recently suggested that the Conservative Party had always had two wings, but that it had recently given the impression of trying to fly on one wing only, and that it could not expect to take off again unless both wings became fully functional. It is of course easier to say that this must be done than actually to do it, but the advent of proportional representation, which compels parties to select balanced tickets of candidates and policies in order to maximize the second- and third-preferences of the voters, would at least give the Conservatives a powerful shove in that direction.

The pragmatic reconstruction of a broad coalition of Conservatism would certainly not fall outside the party's historic mission, for, as Harold Macmillan somewhat romantically expressed it in 1957, 'I hear much about Left and Right. To the broad stream of our philosophy there are many tributaries. Indeed, we are always adding to this flow as the parties of the Left break up into a kind of delta of confusion. And so our great river flows on triumphantly to the sea.' It has sometimes been maintained, and never more forcefully than by Margaret Thatcher and her supporters in recent years, that when a coalition is that broad then it ends up believing in nothing and therefore doing nothing – the true current, so to speak, ceases to flow in any politically seaward direction at all. Such claims would hardly have worried most earlier generations of Tories, for whom a single over-arching current of ideas was neither necessary nor desirable. In his classic *The Case for Conservatism* (1947), Mrs Thatcher's Lord Chancellor, Quintin Hogg (as he then was), argued precisely this point; for Hogg, the Conservative Party's main historic role had lain in its scepticism rather than in its beliefs. When seventeenth- and eighteenth-century whigs reduced royal power and diluted exclusive Anglicanism, the Tories rallied to crown and Church; when nineteenth-century Liberals preached *laisser faire* individualism, the Conservatives defended the role of the state in ameliorating social conditions; and when twentieth-century state socialism threatened freedom and personal responsibility the Conservatives moved over to argue in defence of the individual and his rights. If all of this could be dismissed as a merely reactive approach, then so it should be, for in Hogg's view the proper Conservative function had always been a balancing one, sceptical about whatever nostrum the current party of change happened to be advocating. 'Conservatives do not believe that the political struggle is the most important thing in life' – and political ideology was even further from the centre of their being. For Hogg, fox-hunting was more likely to be central to a Tory's view of life than any actual political issue, a perspective with which Lord George Bentinck, Stanley Baldwin and Enoch Powell would all certainly have agreed. For, as Sir Peregrine Worsthorne once plaintively remarked, for a conservative the real news was never on the front pages of a newspaper – it was rather to be found on the social pages and in the small advertisements, where ships sailed every week (and did *not* sink), where vacancies awaited filling even in times of unemployment, and where the normal round of parties, marriages, weddings and funerals went along its uneventful way, in blithe disregard of the breathlessly topical questions that fascinate the leader-writers.

With such a view of life, traditional Conservatives could take an extremely relaxed view about political ideology as such, as even that systematic thinker Lord Salisbury came to do as he aged into a mellow Edwardian. And as Ian Gilmour has put it, 'although the inter-war Conservative Governments of Baldwin and Chamberlain made plenty of mistakes, they never became infected by ideology'. Sometimes, indeed, their refusal to present themselves and their party as coherently and tidily as political theorists would like the world always to be became positively a self-parody. As Stanley Baldwin rambled through the countryside with the young Frank Pakenham (then a Conservative), Pakenham asked his Leader which thinker had influenced him the most, and received the unexpected reply that it had been Sir Henry Maine. What then, asked Pakenham excitedly, had been Maine's great contribution to western political thought? Mr Baldwin, after rummaging into his memory for some time, carefully explained that Maine had been very well thought of when he had been up at Cambridge (which was by this time almost half a century earlier), for while Jean-Jacques Rousseau had argued that political relations in human societies had evolved from status to contract, Maine had conclusively proved that political society had actually evolved from contract to status. And then, after another excruciatingly long, pipe-smoker's pause, Baldwin added, with a winning smile, 'Or was it the other way round?' None of this fuzziness of thinking, lack of intellectual clarity, and unapologetic abstention from coherence – not to mention his indolent refusal even to read many of the policy papers prepared for him –

prevented Baldwin from being one of the Conservative Party's greatest leaders, and a tremendous electoral asset to boost.

In fact, there has almost been an inverse correlation between the Conservative Party leadership's intellectual clarity and its electoral record of success, not least because intellectual clarity invariably repels some potential supporters as much as it attracts others. The protectionists and Protestant bigots of 1847 and the tariff reformers of 1906 were both groups that knew very clearly what they wanted and were ready to argue their case with conviction and determination, but, after they captured the party, neither group was able to prevent its isolation into a permanent minority of the political nation. The more pragmatic Disraelians of the 1860s, the Salisburyans of the 1880s, the Baldwinites of the 1920s and the Butskellites of the 1950s were all ready to sacrifice some clarity to the belief that unity and diversity were more important – and each of them won long periods of Tory government. On the face of it, the Conservative Party's record of success under Margaret Thatcher would seem to undermine this correlation, for on the popular view the Lady was able to act only with and through the exclusively ideological 'one of us' brigade and yet hold power for eighteen years. But that would be to ignore two factors specific to the Thatcher regime and to the political world within which it operated. First, Thatcher herself, at least in her first decade as Party Leader, was far more pragmatically cautious in practice than either she or most of her critics were ever prepared to admit, and the disappearance of that caution later on was then matched by the erosion of her success at the polls. Second, her 'success' in winning parliamentary seats was really no success at all in terms of historic shares of the vote, since she never came near to capturing half or more of the total vote cast nationally – as Disraeli, Salisbury, Baldwin, Eden and Macmillan had all done for their party in the past. In 1951 Churchill had famously declared that a parliamentary majority of one would be enough; in 1997 the Conservatives discovered the hard way the dangers of their earlier pretence that a minority of about 42 per cent of the vote *had* been enough.

In this context of the necessary breadth of the Tory appeal, one factor entirely beyond the Conservatives' control but which has in the past contributed to the party's success is the extent of unity and coherence on the other side. Labour's divisions in the inter-war years, in the Bevanite splits of the 1950s and in the Bennite period of the 1980s, each contributed to the Conservative claim to be the better government on offer. Liberal divisions in the 1890s, in the 1920s and even in the 1980s (when, for example, a split centrist vote was necessary to enable William Hague to scrape into parliament at the 1989 Richmond by-election) were equally beneficial. Beyond this, the fact that the anti-Conservative vote was generally divided *between* Labour and the Liberals after 1918, at least until tactical anti-Tory voting came into its own in 1992 and 1997, was a significant contribution to Conservative success. It was that and that alone which allowed Margaret Thatcher to win three terms of office with a share of the vote that would have lost elections for most of the post-war years.

This factor may not be as accidental as has sometimes been alleged by those who, like Roy Jenkins, have bemoaned the division of the 'left-centre' since the First World War as a missed opportunity for all the progressives to work together, a mistake which handed power to the Conservatives. Many Liberal voters were always staunchly anti-socialist, and their decision to opt for Conservative rather than Labour candidates in 1924 and in 1951 owed a good deal to their own perception that Labour and the Liberals were opposites rather than near-relations. As recently as March 1974, the Liberal MPs who (almost) held the balance of power in the Commons were reluctant to join Heath in office, but recognized during negotiations that they had more policies in common with Heath's Conservatives than with Wilson's anti-European Labour Party. The long period of Conservative government since 1979, pursuing radical-right policies that many centrist voters found repugnant, together with the repositioning of the Liberals on the left rather than in the centre of British politics, has more recently realigned the triangular relationship between the three parties to the Conservatives' disadvantage. If the Conservatives were to achieve in 2001–2 a recovery that removed Labour's majority without creating a Conservative one, it is pretty clear that Liberal MPs would opt to maintain a Labour government, especially with the likelihood of proportional representation then coming their way – an eventuality which would in any case do terminal damage to the Conservatives' ability to exploit the split anti-Tory vote as so often in the past.

Such anticipation of the future are, however, no job for a historian, and all such psephological prediction is in any case reliant on a core assumption that voters would behave in a new electoral system much as they have done under the old one, which is in itself highly improbable. It is necessary, however, to note in passing the extent to which the Conservatives' own past success has depended on the fragility of the enemy forces and their lack of mutual coordination, and to point out that some at least of this is unlikely to recur in the near future. It may well be equally possible to note that the historic Conservative ability to pick up recruits from the left, both from voters and from professional politicians, has depended on the perception by those potential defectors that the party would be welcoming to people like themselves and sympathetic to their aspirations. In part this depended on creating openings for honest opportunism – Edward Stanley in 1834, Joseph Chamberlain in 1886, Winston Churchill in 1924, John Simon in 1931 and Reginald Prentice in 1977 were all heading towards ministerial office with the Tories when they made their decision to change parties – but often it depended on words as much as deeds. *The Tamworth Manifesto*, the Disraelian rhetoric that paved the way for middle-class vote-switchers in the 1870s, Baldwin's 'New Conservative' moderation that appealed so effectively to middle England (and indeed Scotland and Wales too) in the 1920s, and the Butlerian middle ground espoused by *The Industrial Charter* of 1947 were all effective moves to defuse the aspirant classes' natural suspicion that the possessing classes did not really have their interests at heart. It is hard to see how the Liberal–Labour alliance's hold on a high proportion of the middle vote in 1997 could be unfixed by a Conservative Opposition that offered merely more of the same to an electorate that has just thrown it out, and even less how it could make strategic sense for the Tories to move even further to the right in order to remain distinctive from 'New Labour'. This suggests a tactical situation not unlike the one that Derby and Disraeli failed to solve between 1855 and 1865, with the reactionary Lord Palmerston in charge of the allegedly progressive Liberal Party but pursuing a policy of which most Tories thoroughly approved. In their case the solution to the problem had to await Palmerston's death in 1865 – but then, when he became Prime Minister in 1855, Palmerston was already twice Tony Blair's age in 1997.

One clear lesson of the past that is more cheering for contemporary Conservatives is the party's quite remarkable facility for adaptation and, closely allied to this, its appetite for power, often indeed its readiness ruthlessly to subordinate all other considerations to that one objective. The Ultras who backed the distrusted Peel as the best way of responding to 1832; the gentlemen of England who accepted as Leader Benjamin Disraeli (even though one Tory MP as late as the 1870s was still calling him 'that hellish Jew'); the provincial party bosses who took up Lord Randolph Churchill's crusade for 'Tory Democracy' and then abandoned him, and the policy, to their fate without a backward glance when Salisbury seemed to offer the better chance actually to win and hold power; the

Edwardian aristocrats who opted for the Glaswegian ironmaster Bonar Law as their spokesman in the great battles over the Irish Union; the diehards who supported Baldwin ('that semi-socialist', as an ex-Party Chairman called him in 1926) as the best means of containing Labour in the 1920s; the knights of the shire who voted for the grammar-school boy Heath in 1965; and the misogynists who voted in the first woman to become a British party leader in 1975: all these were evidence of that fundamental subordination of all else to the drive for power. Sometimes this was in pursuit of a particular policy, more often it could be defensive, for in a party that has generally sought to resist rather than to introduce change, mere occupation of the Number Ten crease could indeed be an end in itself, if only because it keeps the other team out in the field where they can score no runs. For a Conservative, playing for a draw *is* in that sense playing to win. For as the 'delightfully Tory' West Country MP Robert Sanders told his Bridgwater supporters at his adoption meeting in 1903, 'our first object is to keep the Conservatives in, but, perhaps, as important an object is to keep the other side out'.

In office after 1992, Conservative MPs seemed to have lost this perspective as surely as they failed to behave with much sense of collective loyalty and common purpose, but if the principle were not to reassert itself in opposition then it would be the very first time in the party's history that it has not done so. As opponents can well testify, the Conservatives have been a formidable enemy when regrouped around that single-minded drive for power; the Salisburyan recovery of the party in 1884–6, Baldwin and Bonar Law's reclamation of the party from the clutches of Lloyd George, and the consumerist, tax-cutting electioneering of 1951, 1959, 1970 and 1979 are all cases in point – each example following a nadir in the party's fortunes when morale, unity and common purpose had been low. Like an experienced prize-fighter, the Conservative Party has never been more dangerous to opponents than when it was on the ropes, apparently dazed and looking as if it was about to be counted out.

Here much has depended on qualities of leadership, and in party history the men who have given their full attention to matters of party, at times over the competing claims of government and the national interest, have generally been those who both succeeded at the time and then left a positive legacy associated with their names – Disraeli, Salisbury, Bonar Law, Baldwin, Macmillan, Thatcher. In contrast, those who saw party as a taxi which would carry them to the door of Number Ten, but who then expected to have no further obligations when the electoral fare had once been paid, were likely not only to come a cropper in the process but also to leave a name behind them only as examples to good party men of how not to behave – Peel, Northcote, Balfour, both Austen and Neville Chamberlain, Churchill and Heath. Leading the Conservative Party has needed, after all, talents different from the requirements of ministerial office, and not all aspirants to leadership have either had those gifts or been prepared to work at developing them. Peel confessed privately in 1846 that he felt 'a want of many essential qualifications which are requisite in party leaders; among the rest, personal gratification in the game of politics and patience to listen to the sentiments of individuals whom it is equally imprudent to neglect and an intolerable bore to consult'. He might have been writing in advance a dramatist's character note on some of his successors, notably Northcote, Neville Chamberlain, and Edward Heath (except that Heath so pre-eminently lacked the gift to see himself as others saw him that he would not have recognized the description anyway).

Other leaders, and here Stanley Baldwin and Alec Douglas-Home come to mind, were attentive to the needs of party as such, but not good at providing the backbenchers with something partisan to cheer, especially when, in opposition, they found themselves wanting to support Labour governments whose policies they partly agreed with. Party leadership demanded, especially when in opposition, a readiness to be *seen* taking the front position and giving party a high priority in the allocation of personal time, not least by cheering up the parliamentary and National Union troops through morale-boosting rudeness to the enemy. That negative facility has on occasion done much in itself to restore the party's sense of being on the move, and was perhaps Churchill's only important contribution to the Conservative recovery after 1945; it was equally vital for Bonar Law in holding Unionists together between 1911 and 1914.

Leadership has, however, generally been about something more positive too, and that may be analysed under the twin headings of rhetoric about the party's identity and its policy-making tactics, though in practice neither has been likely to succeed without integration with the other. In a party that always respected hierarchy and order, and developed in any case from predominantly aristocratic, gentry and royalist roots, the Leader was invariably expected to articulate most of what the party stood for, even if in practice we can now see that this did not in the least add up to a dictatorial right of direction. As Bonar Law crudely summarized the position in 1922, 'Our system ... has hitherto gone on this principle: that the party elects a leader, and the leader chooses the policy, and if the party does not like it, they have to get another leader.' Taken literally, this was just what the Conservatives had *not* done in 1912–13, when Bonar Law allowed himself to be overruled by his party on a key issue but did not resign, and the same thing would happen to him in 1923 as Prime Minister. But as a statement of the public perception of the role it was exactly right, and even if his privately cynical maxim 'I am their leader – I must follow them' represented his real feelings on the subject, then this was far from evident from his public manner. The leadership principle, by which the Leader of the party set the tone, fixed the agenda and articulated the party's viewpoint, has created valuable illusions of unity where none actually existed, and has in any case facilitated the coherence of the party's electioneering. Reinforced since the 1950s by a broadcasting and tabloid media which sought in any case to concentrate on the clash of potential premiers, much came to depend on the 'strong lead' from the top. Churchill, Macmillan and Thatcher were obvious examples of those who could create the necessary sense of momentum from their personal input; Eden, Douglas-Home and Major the opposite cases of those whose failure derived in part from perceptions that they were simply not up to the extensive demands of the post in terms of visible personal authority. Nice, decent chaps make poor Leaders if the word *has* to be spelled with a capital L and then printed in bold type too. But then nobody who actually knew them was ever likely to consider Disraeli, Salisbury, Churchill, Macmillan or Thatcher to be nice, decent chaps.

As important as the style of the Leader's address to the party has been the ability to project its social identity, even if this has at times been an entirely bogus operation in itself. Disraeli was credited by his obituarists with initiating the party's appeal to the Conservative working man voter (to which privately he gave little weight); Salisbury was thought to exemplify the party's reassuring approach to the suburban middle class (of whom he and his circle were privately contemptuous); Macmillan was crucial in pulling in the votes of 'affluent' consumerist working-class voters (which consorted oddly with his preference for the company of grouse-shooting peers of the realm), and Thatcher (always a person of great wealth after her marriage) spoke out for 'Essex man' just up from the East End slums. The real trick in each case was to convey the openness of the party to the aspirant – those socially mobile groups whose political allegiance was becoming unfixed once they had begun to rise – without at the same time alienating the old conservatives who saw the Conservative Party as existing to protect their vested interests – but who rarely had anywhere else to go. The detection and adoption of a uniting philosophical trend was often of value here, giving respectability to a patently political manoeuvre, the best examples being Salisbury's espousal of the rights of property in the period in which socialist ideas arrived on the British scene, and Thatcher's discovery of the rights of taxpayers and public utility customers when socialism was on the way out. Baldwin's articulation of the *zeitgeist* of the 1920s was more subtle, combining an appeal to 'the real England', and its claimed inheritance of moderate good sense, with the determination to improve actual conditions, both of them ideas that struck uniting chords in the nostalgic era after the Great War. It is hard to see what philosophical mood of that type should be tapped for the twenty-first century, but then none of these earlier phenomena would have been foreseen either, even a couple of years before their time.

The final point that emerges from a study of the party's history and its leadership, then, is its ability to deliver the unexpected. Almost without exception, those men who had long been groomed for the party leadership were ineffective when once installed, perhaps precisely because their steady ascent made them unready to mould themselves and the party to the mood of the times when they arrived – Peel, Northcote, Balfour, Austen and Neville Chamberlain, Eden. Those whose chances of ever being Leader would have been discussed with incredulity even two or three years before it actually happened have done rather better – Disraeli, Bonar Law, Baldwin, Macmillan, Thatcher. Years as 'crown prince' (as Eden put it) are not necessarily the best preparation for being king. Of course – lest William Hague were to read too much into this apparent polarity – not all unexpected Party Leaders have done so well: Churchill was a disaster for the party, however well he did for the country, and neither Douglas-Home nor Major would be likely to be role models that any future Conservative Leader will wish to follow.

Forty years ago, during his tub-thumping, sea-bathing and bell-ringing time as Party Chairman, Lord Hailsham delivered, in another time of deep Conservative unpopularity, a public lecture to the Conservative Political Centre, in which he analysed the party's history:

> We have been abused by many opponents and our backs are broad. We were abused by the Roundheads, and we remained to see a popular Restoration. We were abused by the Whigs, and we lived to see them swallowed up by the Liberal Party. We were

abused by the Liberal Party, and we have survived to see them degenerate into a little, heterogeneous, mutual admiration society ... We are now abused by the Labour Party, and without being in the least impatient we realise that one day our successors will stand, crêpe-hatted and mournful, beside the open grave which, like all their predecessors, the Socialists will have dug for themselves.

Forty years on, with Labour replaced by 'New Labour' and socialism a word and a concept that has now been almost entirely removed from the British political debate, that sounds like a fairly shrewd prophecy, though 'triumphal' would be a better word than 'mournful' to describe the Thatcher Conservatives' appraisal of the actual process in the 1980s. This study of the party's history has been both more systematic and less romantic than Lord Hailsham could be in a single lecture, but it does nevertheless bear out his point. A party that has been so very successful in the past two centuries, in all manner of adverse circumstance, is unlikely just to die away in the aftermath of a single election defeat in the 1990s.

APPENDIX 1

Sources

The paragraphs below indicate the main sources that have been used in writing this history of the Conservative Party, including those from which quotations in the text have been taken. In addition to the specific references set out below, chapter by chapter, special acknowledgement must be made of sources that have informed the entire book but which may also provide readers with a different overall picture or more detail on particular issues than a single-volume work can do. Robert Blake, *The Conservative Party from Peel to Thatcher* (Methuen, London, 1985) is the best available single-volume history published to date, though Lord Butler of Saffron Walden, ed., *The Conservatives: A History from Their Origins to 1965* (Allen and Unwin, London, 1978) remains useful. For a general study of the earlier period, the best account is Bruce Coleman, *Conservatives and Conservatism in the Nineteenth Century* (Arnold, London, 1988), though on the development of ideas R. B. McDowell, *British Conservatism, 1832–1914* (Faber, London, 1959) remains valuable, as does Donald Southgate, *The Conservative Leadership, 1832–1932* (Macmillan, London, 1974), while Michael Pinto-Duschinsky, *British Political Finance, 1830–1980* (American Enterprise Institute, Washington, DC, 1981) is the sole useful source in its field. A thematic approach that offered insights into almost every aspect of the Conservative Party in the present century is Anthony Seldon and Stuart Ball, eds., *Conservative Century: The Conservative Party since 1900* (Oxford University Press, Oxford, 1994). A number of fresh perspectives appear in Martin Francis and Ina Zweiniger-Bargielowska, eds., *The Conservatives and British Society, 1880–1990* (University of Wales Press, Cardiff, 1996).

At a different level of specialization altogether from any other source is the six-volume Longman History of the Conservative Party (all published by Longman, London), which has been extensively used here, and grateful acknowledgement is made to Andrew Maclennan as the publisher, to Robert Blake as chairman of the Advisory Board and to Robert Stewart and Richard Shannon as authors of the first three volumes in that series, which consists of Robert Stewart, *The Foundation of the Conservative Party, 1830–1867* (1978); Richard Shannon, *The Age of Disraeli, 1867–1881* (1992); Richard Shannon, *The Age of Salisbury, 1881–1902* (1996); John Ramsden, *The Age of*

Balfour and Baldwin, 1902–1940 (1978); John Ramsden, *The Age of Churchill and Eden, 1940–1957* (1995); John Ramsden, *The Winds of Change: Macmillan to Heath, 1957–1975* (1996). These volumes, together with Seldon and Ball, *Conservative Century*, also provide substantial bibliographical guides to further reading.

For Chapter Two, 'Origins', there has been reliance on Stewart, *Foundation of the Conservative Party*. Other major inputs to the arguments advanced here were from Norman Gash, 'From the Origins to Sir Robert Peel', in Lord Butler, *The Conservatives*, Peter Jupp, *The Emergence of the Conservative Party, 1680–1830* (CPC, London, 1996), James J. Sack, *From Jacobite to Conservative: Reaction and Orthodoxy in Britain, c. 1760–1832* (Cambridge University Press, Cambridge, 1993), B. W. Hill, *British Parliamentary Parties, 1742–1832* (Allen and Unwin, London, 1985), Linda Colley, *Britons: Forging the Nation, 1707–1937* (Yale University Press, London, 1992), Robert Eccleshall, *English Conservatism since the Restoration* (Unwin Hyman, London, 1990), Roger Scruton, ed., *Conservative Texts: An Anthology* (Macmillan, London, 1981), and Frank O'Gorman, *The Emergence of the British Two-Party System, 1760–1832* (Arnold, London, 1982). More specific works on politics and politicians from 1812 were: W. R. Brock, *Lord Liverpool and Liberal Toryism* (Cass, London, 1941), Peter Dixon, *Canning* (Weidenfeld and Nicolson, London, 1976), W. D. Jones, *Prosperity Robinson: The Life of Viscount Goderich, 1782–1859* (Macmillan, London, 1967), Norman Gash, *Mr Secretary Peel* (Longman, London, 1961), Elizabeth Longford, *Wellington, Pillar of State* (Weidenfeld and Nicolson, London, 1972), J. E. Cookson, *Lord Liverpool's Administration, 1815–22* (Scottish Academic Press, Edinburgh, 1975), Boyd Hilton, *Cash, Corn and Commerce: The Economic Policies of the Tory Governments, 1815–30* (Clarendon Press, Oxford, 1977), John Cannon, *Parliamentary Reform, 1640–1832* (Cambridge University Press, Cambridge, 1972), Michael Brock, *The Great Reform Act* (Hutchinson, London, 1973), and Malcolm Thomis, *Politics and Society in Nottingham, 1785–1835* (Blackwell, Oxford, 1969).

For Chapter Three, 'Peel's Conservative Party', the main sources have been Stewart's *Foundation of the Conservative Party*, and his *The Politics of Protection: Lord Derby and the Protectionist Party, 1841–1852* (Cambridge University Press, Cambridge, 1971). A similar interpretation is offered, more from the viewpoint of issues than of party, by Travis L. Crosby in *Sir Robert Peel's Administration, 1841–46* (David and Charles, Newton Abbot, Devon, 1976) and in *English Farmers and the Politics of Protection, 1815–52* (Harvester, Hassocks, Sussex, 1977). The same issues and arguments as seen from the viewpoint of Peel can be traced in Norman Gash's section of Butler's *The Conservatives*, and in his biography of *Peel* (Longman, London, 1976). A different but equally sympathetic approach, in which Peel's fame rather than his actual policy is analysed, is Donald Read, *Peel and the Victorians* (Blackwell, Oxford, 1987). Other useful biographies include Robert Blake, *Disraeli* (Eyre and Spottiswoode, London, 1966), J. T. Ward, *Sir James Graham* (Macmillan, London, 1967), Richard Shannon, *Gladstone, 1809–1865* (Methuen, London, 1982), Colin Matthew, *Gladstone, 1809–1874* (Oxford University Press, Oxford, 1986), Muriel Chamberlain, *Lord Aberdeen: A Political Biography* (Longman, London, 1983) and Elizabeth Longford's *Wellington, Pillar of State*. Disraeli's early associates are analysed in Richard Faber, *Young England* (Faber, London, 1987). Quotations from Croker are to be found in Bernard Pool, ed., *The Croker Papers* (Batsford, London, 1967). John Vincent's analysis of Victorian voting is in his *Poll-Books: How Victorians Voted* (Cambridge University Press, Cambridge, 1967), and a good example of the national events as seen from the perspective of a very Tory county is in Richard W. Davis, *Political Change and Continuity, 1760–1885: A Buckinghamshire Study* (David and Charles, Newton Abbot, Devon, 1972). Peel's *Tamworth Manifesto* is reprinted in H. J. Hanham, ed., *The Victorian Constitution, Documents and Commentary* (Cambridge University Press, Cambridge, 1969).

For Chapter Four, 'Wilderness Years', there has been continued reliance on Robert Stewart's *Foundation of the Conservative Party* and his *Politics of Protection*. Valuable on the period after 1846 is J. B. Conacher, *The Peelites and the Party System, 1846–52* (David and Charles, Newton Abbot, Devon, 1972). Blake's *Disraeli* remains an essential source, as, despite its age, does W. D. Jones, *Lord Derby and Victorian Conservatism* (Oxford University Press, Oxford, 1956). Useful biographies of other Conservatives of this period have been few and far between, but there are two good edited diaries, John Vincent, *Disraeli, Derby and the Conservative Party: Journals and Diaries of Edward Henry, Lord Stanley, 1849–69* (Harvester, Hassocks, Sussex, 1978) and Nancy E. Johnson, *The Diary of Gathorne Hardy, later Lord Cranbrook, 1866–1892* (Oxford University Press, Oxford, 1981). Peter Ghosh, in 'Disraelian Conservatism, a financial approach' (*English Historical Review*, 1984), explored a neglected aspect of the party battle. Walter Bagehot's perceptive commentaries on the politics of his day were anthologized in Norman St John-Stevas, ed., *Bagehot's Historical Essays* (Dobson, London, 1965), while Cranborne's polemical commentary on Disraeli and his party can be followed in Paul Smith's edition of *Lord Salisbury on Politics: A Selection from the Quarterly Review 1860–1883* (Cambridge University Press, Cambridge, 1972). For the political crisis of 1866–7, reference has been made to R. B. Smith, *The Passing of the Second Reform Act* (Cambridge University Press, Cambridge, 1966) and to Maurice Cowling, *1867: Disraeli, Gladstone and Revolution* (Cambridge University Press, Cambridge, 1967). An essential background to any consideration of the political system in this period is H. J. Hanham, *Elections and Party Management: Politics in the Time of Gladstone and Disraeli* (2nd edn., Harvester, Hassocks, Sussex, 1978).

For Chapter Five, 'Disraeli's Indian Summer', Shannon's *The Age of Disraeli* and Blake's *Disraeli* have been heavily used, and continuing use has been made of Vincent's edition of the Derby diaries (for this period, *The Derby Diaries, 1869–1878*, Royal Historical Society, 1995), Johnson's *Diary of Gathorne Hardy*, Hanham's *Elections and Party Management*, and Smith's *Lord Salisbury on Politics*. For Disraeli's social policies, the essential source remains Paul Smith, *Disraelian Conservatism and Social Reform* (Routledge, London, 1967), while for the organizational side of things, much reference has been made to E. J. Feuchtwanger, *Disraeli, Democracy and the Tory Party* (Clarendon Press, Oxford, 1968), Cornelius O'Leary, *The Elimination of Corrupt Practices from British Elections, 1868–1911* (Clarendon Press, Oxford, 1962), and W. B. Gwyn, *Democracy and the Cost of Politics* (Athlone Press, London, 1962). Useful biographical material is to be found in Viscount Chilston's *W. H. Smith* (Routledge, London, 1965), Lady Gwendolyn Cecil's *Life of Robert, Marquis of Salisbury* (Hodder and Stoughton, London, 1931–2), and Robert Blake and Hugh Cecil's collection of essays on *Salisbury, the Man and His Policies* (Macmillan, London, 1987).

For Chapter Six, 'Salisbury and Unionism', there has been heavy reliance on Shannon's *Age of Disraeli* and his *Age of Salisbury*, and continuing use has been made of Blake's *Disraeli*, Lady Cecil's *Salisbury*, Blake and Cecil's *Salisbury*, Chilston's *Smith*, Vincent's *Derby Diaries* and Johnson's *Diary of Gathorne Hardy*. For specific events, Richard Shannon, *Gladstone and the Bulgarian Atrocities Agitation, 1876* (Nelson, London, 1963), Andrew Jones, *The Politics of Reform, 1884* (Cambridge University Press, Cambridge, 1972), and A. B. Cooke and John Vincent, *The Governing Passion: Cabinet Government and Party Politics in Britain, 1885–86* (Harvester, Hassocks, Sussex, 1974), are all essential sources. More generally on Salisbury's approach, reference is made to Peter Marsh, *The Discipline of Popular Government: Lord Salisbury's Domestic Statecraft 1881–1902* (Harvester, Hassocks, Sussex, 1978). Especially useful biographies include Roy Foster, *Lord Randolph Churchill* (Clarendon Press, Oxford, 1981), and Peter Marsh, *Joseph Chamberlain* (Yale University Press, London, 1994), but Northcote and Hartington still await modern biographers. Valuable primary sources are to be found in A. B. Cooke and A. P. W. Malcomson, eds., *The Ashbourne Papers, 1869–1912* (HMSO, Belfast, 1974), and Robin Harcourt-Williams, ed., *The Salisbury–Balfour Correspondence, 1869–92* (Hertfordshire Record Society, Hertford, 1988).

APPENDIX 1 505

For Chapter Seven, 'The Hotel Cecil', continuing acknowledgement is made to Shannon's *The Age of Salisbury*, Marsh's *Discipline of Popular Government*, Chilston's *Smith*, Lady Cecil's *Salisbury*, Blake and Cecil's *Salisbury*, Foster's *Randolph Churchill*, Cooke and Malcomson's *Ashbourne Papers*, Harcourt-Williams's *Salisbury–Balfour Correspondence*, and Marsh's *Joseph Chamberlain*. On the organizational side, Martin Pugh, *Toryism and the People, 1880–1935* (Blackwell, Oxford, 1985), M. Y. Ostrogorski, *Democracy and the Organisation of Political Parties*, vol. 1 (Macmillan, London, 1902), Viscount Chilston, *Chief Whip: The Political Life and Times of Aretas Akers-Douglas, 1st Viscount Chilston* (Routledge, London, 1961), Henry Pelling, *The Social Geography of British Elections, 1885–1910* (Macmillan, London, 1967), and James Cornford's 'The Transformation of Conservatism in Late Nineteenth Century Britain', in *Victorian Studies*, vol. 7 (1963), are all vital sources.

For Chapter Eight, 'Drifting', and Chapter Nine, 'Clambering Back', the main source has been John Ramsden's *Age of Balfour and Baldwin*. Continuing use has been made of Chilston, *Chief Whip*, Pelling, *Social Geography*, Marsh, *Joseph Chamberlain*, and Pugh, *Toryism and the People*. The Edwardian crisis of Conservatism is now best presented by Ewen Green, *The Crisis of Conservatism, 1880–1914* (Routledge, London, 1995), but use has also been made of Alan Sykes, *Tariff Reform in British Politics, 1903–1914* (Clarendon Press, Oxford, 1979), Richard Rempel, *Unionists Divided* (David and Charles, Newton Abbot, Devon, 1972), G. R. Searle, *The Quest for National Efficiency* (Blackwell, Oxford, 1971), Andrew Adonis, *Making Aristocracy Work: The Peerage and the Political System in Britain, 1884–1914* (Clarendon Press, Oxford, 1993), Rhodri Williams, *Defending the Empire* (Yale University Press, London, 1991), and Gregory Phillips, *The Diehards* (Harvard University Press, Cambridge, Mass., 1979). The Unionists' electioneering in the period is covered by A. K. Russell, *Liberal Landslide: The General Election of 1906* (David and Charles, Newton Abbot, Devon, 1973), and Neal Blewett, *The Peers, the Parties and the People: The General Elections of 1910* (Macmillan, London, 1972). Among the most useful biographical material is Blanche Dugdale, *Arthur James Balfour*, 2 vols. (Hutchinson, London, 1936), which should be supplemented by Ruddock Mackay, *Balfour, Intellectual Statesman* (Oxford University Press, Oxford, 1983), Julian Amery, *The Life of Joseph Chamberlain*, vols. 4–6 (Macmillan, London, 1951–69), David Dutton, *Austen Chamberlain, Gentleman in Politics* (Ross Anderson, Bolton, 1985), Robert Blake, *The Unknown Prime Minister: The Life and Times of Andrew Bonar Law* (Eyre and Spottiswoode, London, 1955), though advance sight of R. J. Q. Adams's forthcoming life of Bonar Law is also gratefully acknowledged, John Campbell, *F. E. Smith, First Earl of Birkenhead* (Cape, London, 1983), and Richard Cosgrave, 'Lord Halsbury', in J. A. Thompson and Arthur Mejia, eds.,

Edwardian Conservatism: Five Studies in Adaptation (Croom Helm, London, 1988). There is also now a wealth of primary material in print, much used in these and the following chapters: John Ramsden, ed., *Real Old Tory Politics: The Political Diaries of Sir Robert Sanders, Lord Bayford, 1910–35* (Historian's Press, London, 1984), John Vincent, ed., *The Crawford Papers: The Journals of David Lindsay, 10th Earl of Balcarres, 1892–1940* (Manchester University Press, Manchester, 1984), George Boyce, ed., *The Crisis of British Unionism: Lord Selborne's Domestic Political Papers, 1885–1922* (Historian's Press, London, 1987), and Philip Williamson, ed., *The Modernisation of Conservative Politics, the Diaries and Letters of William Bridgeman, 1904–35* (Historian's Press, London, 1988). For more specific material on the war and post-war years, much reference has been made to John Turner, *British Politics and the Great War* (Yale University Press, London, 1992), Martin Pugh, *Electoral Reform in War and Peace, 1906–18* (Routledge, London, 1978), Kenneth Morgan, *Consensus and Disunity: The Lloyd George Coalition Government, 1918–22* (Clarendon Press, Oxford, 1979), Michael Kinnear, *The Fall of Lloyd George* (Macmillan, London, 1973), Maurice Cowling, *The Impact of Labour, 1920–24* (Cambridge University Press, Cambridge, 1971), and Robert Rhodes James, ed., *Memoirs of a Conservative: J. C. C. Davidson's Letters and Papers, 1910–37* (Weidenfeld and Nicolson, London, 1969).

For Chapters Ten, 'Baldwin's Party', and Eleven, 'The Centre Holds', the most important source has again been Ramsden's *Age of Balfour and Baldwin*, together with *The Making of Conservative Policy: The Conservative Research Department since 1929* (Longman, London, 1980). The Sanders, Selborne, Crawford, Bridgeman and Davidson papers have again been used, as has Robert Self, ed., *The Austen Chamberlain Diary Letters, 1916–37* (Royal Historical Society, London, 1995), Keith Middlemas, ed., *Thomas Jones' Whitehall Diary, 1916–30*, 3 vols. (Oxford University Press, London, 1971), Thomas Jones, *A Diary with Letters, 1931–50* (Oxford University Press, London, 1954), and John Barnes and David Nicolson, eds., *The Leo Amery Diaries*, 2 vols. (Hutchinson, London, 1980 and 1988). The most useful biographical material has been Keith Middlemas and John Barnes, *Baldwin: A Biography* (Weidenfeld and Nicolson, London, 1969), H. Montgomery Hyde, *Baldwin, the Unexpected Prime Minister* (Hart-Davis, London, 1973), A. J. P. Taylor, *Beaverbrook* (Hamish Hamilton, London, 1972), David Dilks, *Neville Chamberlain, 1869–1929* (Cambridge University Press, Cambridge, 1984), Martin Gilbert, *Winston S. Churchill, 1922–39* (Heinemann, London, 1976; with associated documentary volumes, 1979), W. F. Deedes, *Dear Bill* (Macmillan, London, 1997), Randolph S. Churchill, *Lord Derby, 'King of Lancashire'* (Heinemann, London, 1959), J. A. Cross, *Sir Samuel Hoare* (Cape, London, 1977) and *Lord Swinton* (Clarendon Press, Oxford, 1982), David Dutton, *Simon: A Political Biography of Sir John Simon* (Aurum Press, London, 1992). On specific events within this period: Chris Cook, *The Age of Alignment: Electoral Politics in Britain 1922–29* (Macmillan, London, 1975), Stuart Ball, *Baldwin and the Conservative Party: The Crisis of 1929–31* (Yale University Press, London, 1988), Gillian Peele, 'St George's and the Empire Crusade', in Chris Cook and John Ramsden, eds., *By-Elections in British Politics* (2nd edn., UCL Press, London, 1997), Philip Williamson, *National Crisis and National Government: British Politics, the Economy and Empire, 1926–1932* (Cambridge University Press, Cambridge, 1992), Andrew Thorpe, *The British General Election of 1931* (Clarendon Press, Oxford, 1991), Tom Stannage, *Baldwin Thwarts the Opposition: The British General Election of 1935* (Croom Helm, London, 1980), Maurice Cowling, *The Impact of Hitler, British Politics and British Policy, 1933–1940* (Cambridge University Press, Cambridge, 1975), Nicholas Crowson, *Facing Fascism: The Conservative Party and the European Dictators, 1935–40* (Routledge, London, 1997), and Richard Cockett, *Twilight of Truth: Chamberlain, Appeasement and the Manipulation of the Press* (Weidenfeld and Nicolson, London, 1989).

For Chapters Twelve, 'War and Aftermath', and Thirteen, 'Post-War', the sources most used have been Ramsden's *Age of Churchill and Eden* and *Making of Conservative Policy*. The most valuable biographical sources for this period were: Martin Gilbert, *Winston S. Churchill*, vols. 6–8 (Heinemann, London, 1983–8), Robert Rhodes James, *Anthony Eden* (Weidenfeld and Nicolson, London, 1986), David Dutton, *Anthony Eden: A Life and Reputation* (Arnold, London, 1997), Randolph Churchill, *The Rise and Fall of Sir Anthony Eden* (MacGibbon and Key, London, 1959), Anthony Howard, *RAB: A Life of R. A. Butler* (Cape, London, 1986), Lord Butler of Saffron Walden, *The Art of the Possible: The Memoirs of Lord Butler* (Hamish Hamilton, London, 1971), Alistair Horne, *Macmillan, 1891–1956* (Macmillan, London, 1988), D. R. Thorpe, *Selwyn Lloyd* (Cape, London, 1989), Robert Shepherd, *Iain Macleod* (Hutchinson, London, 1994), Lord Birkenhead, *Walter Monckton* (Weidenfeld and Nicolson, London, 1969), Earl of Kilmuir, *Political Adventure: The Memoirs of the Earl of Kilmuir* (Weidenfeld and Nicolson, London, 1964), Robert Rhodes James, *Bob Boothby: A Portrait* (Headline, London, 1991), James Stuart, *Within the Fringe* (Bodley Head, London, 1967), John Turner, *Macmillan* (Longman, London, 1994), and the Earl of Woolton, *Memoirs of the Rt. Hon. Earl of Woolton* (Cassell, London, 1959). For editions of diaries and letters: Richard Cockett, ed., *My Dear Max: The Letters of Brendan Bracken to Lord Beaverbrook, 1925–58* (Historian's Press, London, 1990), John Colville, *The Fringes of Power: Downing Street Diaries, 1939–55* (Hodder and Stoughton, London, 1985), Anthony Eden, *Freedom and Order: Selected Speeches, 1939–46* (Faber, London, 1947), Nigel Nicolson, ed., *Diaries and Letters of Harold*

Nicolson, 3 vols. (Collins, London, 1966–8), Ben Pimlott, ed., *Hugh Dalton Diaries*, 2 vols. (Cape, London, 1986), Robert Rhodes James, ed., *Chips: The Diaries of Sir Henry Channon* (Weidenfeld and Nicolson, London, 1967). For studies of particular policies and issues: Samuel Brittan, *Steering the Economy* (Secker and Warburg, London, 1969), Kathleen Burk, *The First Privatisation: The Politicians, the City and the Denationalisation of Steel* (Historian's Press, London, 1988), Michael Cockerell, *Live from Number Ten: The Inside Story of Prime Ministers and Television* (Faber, London, 1988), William Crofts, *Coercion or Persuasion? Propaganda in Britain after 1945* (Routledge, London, 1989), Nigel Harris, *Competition and the Corporate Society: British Conservatives, the State and Industry, 1945–64* (Methuen, London, 1975), J. D. Hoffman, *The Conservative Party in Opposition, 1945–51* (MacGibbon and Kee, London, 1964), Kevin Jeffreys, *The Churchill Coalition and Wartime Politics, 1940–45* (Manchester University Press, Manchester, 1991), Harriet Jones and Michael Kandiah, eds., *The Myth of Consensus: New Views on British History, 1945–64* (Macmillan, London, 1996), Anthony Seldon, *Churchill's Indian Summer: The Conservative Government, 1951–55* (Hodder and Stoughton, London, 1981), Harold L. Smith, *Britain in the Second World War: A Social History* (Manchester University Press, Manchester, 1996), Justin Davis Smith, *The Attlee and Churchill Administrations and Industrial Unrest, 1945–55* (Pinter, London, 1990), Alan Thompson, *The Day Before Yesterday* (Panther, London, 1971), and Ina Zweiniger-Bargielowska, 'Rationing, Austerity and the Conservative Party Recovery after 1945', in the *Historical Journal*, vol. 37 (1994). The concept of 'social gardening' derives from John Turner, 'A Land Fit for Tories to Live in: The Political Ecology of the British Conservative Party, 1944–94', in *Contemporary European History*, vol. 4 (1995).

For Chapters Fourteen, 'Macmillan's Party', and Fifteen, 'Conservatives for a Change', most material is drawn from Ramsden, *The Winds of Change*, but much has also been derived from Ian Gilmour, *Whatever Happened to the Tories: The Conservative Party since 1945* (Fourth Estate, London, 1997), Seldon and Ball, *Conservative Century*, Butler, *Art of the Possible*, Howard's *RAB*, John Campbell, *Edward Heath* (Cape, London, 1993), W. F. Deedes, *Dear Bill*, Cockerell's *Live from Number Ten*, Philip Goodhart, *The 1922* (Macmillan, London, 1983), Lord Hailsham, *The Door Wherein I Went* (Collins, London, 1975), Alistair Horne, *Macmillan, 1957–86* (Macmillan, London, 1989), Vernon Bogdanor and Robert Skidelsky, eds., *The Age of Affluence, 1951–64* (Macmillan, London, 1970), Shepherd's *Iain Macleod*, Thompson's *Day Before Yesterday*, Thorpe's *Selwyn Lloyd*, and Turner's *Macmillan*. For specific events and issues: Jean Blondel, *Voters, Parties and Leaders* (Penguin, Harmondsworth, 1963), David Butler and Richard Rose, *The British General Election of 1959* (Macmillan, London, 1960), David Butler and Anthony King, *The British*

General Election of 1964 (Macmillan, London, 1965), David Butler and Michael Pinto-Duschinsky, *The British General Election of 1970* (Macmillan, London, 1971), David Butler and Denis Kavanagh, *The British General Election of February 1974* (Macmillan, London, 1974), Harold Evans, *Downing Street Diary, 1957–63* (Hodder and Stoughton, London, 1963), Tom Stacey and R. St Oswald, eds., *Here Comes the Tories* (Tom Stacey, London, 1970), Charles Hill, *Both Sides of the Hill* (Heinemann, London, 1964), Douglas Hurd, *An End to Promises: Sketch of a Government, 1970–74* (Collins, London, 1978), Uwe Kitzinger, *Diplomacy and Persuasion* (Thames and Hudson, London, 1973), Robert Rhodes James, *Ambitions and Strategies: British Politics 1964–70* (Weidenfeld and Nicolson, London, 1972), Reginald Maudling, *Memoirs* (Sidgwick and Jackson, London, 1978), Edward Pearce, *The Lost Leaders: The Best Prime Ministers We Never Had* (Little, Brown, London, 1997), Enoch Powell, *Reflections of a Statesman: The Writings and Speeches of Enoch Powell* (Bellew, London, 1991), Andrew Roth, *Heath and the Heathmen* (Routledge, London, 1972), Anthony Seldon and Stuart Ball, eds., *The Heath Government: A Reappraisal* (Longman, London, 1996), Robert Taylor, *The Trade Union Question in British Politics: Government and the Unions since 1945* (Blackwell, Oxford, 1993), Ian Trethowan, *Split Screen* (Hamish Hamilton, London, 1984), Peter Walker, *Staying Power* (Bloomsbury, London, 1991), Denis Walters, *Not Always with the Pack* (Constable, London, 1989), Phillip Whitehead, *The Writing on the Wall: Britain in the Seventies* (Michael Joseph, London, 1985), Lord Windlesham, *Communication and Political Power* (Cape, London, 1966).

For Chapters Sixteen and Seventeen, 'Thatcherism', further use has been made of Ramsden's *The Winds of Change*, Gilmour's *Whatever Happened to the Tories*, Seldon and Ball's *Conservative Century*, Cockerell's *Live from Number Ten*, and Whitehead's *Writing on the Wall*. Specific to these chapters were Kenneth Baker, *The Turbulent Years* (Faber, London, 1993), Malcolm Balen, *Kenneth Clarke* (Fourth Estate, London, 1994), David Butler and Denis Kavanagh, *The British General Election of 1979 . . . 1983 . . . 1987 . . . 1992* and *1997* (Macmillan, London, 1980, 1984, 1987, 1992, 1997), David Butler, Andrew Adonis and Tony Travers, *Failure in British Government: The Politics of the Poll Tax* (Oxford University Press, Oxford, 1994), Richard Cockett, *Thinking the Unthinkable: Think Tanks and the Economic Counter Revolution, 1931–83* (HarperCollins, London, 1994), Julian Critchley, *Heseltine* (Deutsch, London, 1987), Ian Gilmour, *Dancing with Dogma: Britain under Thatcherism* (Simon and Schuster, London, 1992), Morrison Halcrow, *Keith Joseph: A Single Mind* (Macmillan, London, 1989), Robert Harris, *Good and Faithful Servant* (Faber, London, 1990), Sarah Hogg and Jonathan Hill, *Too Close to Call: Power and Politics, John Major at Number Ten* (Little, Brown, London, 1995), Geoffrey Howe, *Conflict of Loyalty* (Macmillan, London, 1984), Simon Jenkins, *Account-*

able to None: The Tory Nationalization of Britain (Hamish Hamilton, London, 1995), Nicholas Jones, *Campaign 1997* (Inigo, London, 1997), Keith Joseph, *Reversing the Trend* (Barry Rose, Chichester, 1975), Denis Kavanagh, *Thatcherism and British Politics* (Oxford University Press, Oxford, 1987), Denis Kavanagh and Anthony Seldon, eds., *The Major Effect* (Macmillan, London, 1994), Nigel Lawson, *The View from Number Eleven* (Bantam, London, 1992), David Leigh and Ed Vulliamy, *Sleaze* (Fourth Estate, London, 1997), Cecil Parkinson, *Right at the Centre* (Weidenfeld and Nicolson, London, 1992), Jim Prior, *A Balance of Power* (Hamish Hamilton, London, 1986), Francis Pym, *The Politics of Consent* (Hamish Hamilton, London, 1994), John Ranelagh, *Thatcher's People* (HarperCollins, London, 1991), Anthony Seldon, *Major* (Weidenfeld and Nicolson, London, 1997), Norman Tebbit, *Upwardly Mobile* (Futura, London, 1989), William Whitelaw, *The Whitelaw Memoirs* (Aurum, London, 1989), Hugo Young, *One of Us: A Biography of Margaret Thatcher* (Macmillan, London, 1989). Some quotations were also drawn from *Bye-Bye Blues* (two-part documentary, Channel Four, November 1997).

APPENDIX 2

Officeholders in the Party since 1830

Leaders in the House of Lords

(Those asterisked recognized as 'Leader of the Party'. Before the Parliament Act of 1911, and to an extent even over the next decade, the Leaders in the Lords and the Commons were regarded as coequals unless one of them was Prime Minister or had been Prime Minister in the preceding Conservative government.)

1st Duke of Wellington: January 1828–July 1846 (* until 1834)
Lord Stanley [14th Earl of Derby, 1851]: July 1846–February 1868 (*)
3rd Earl of Malmesbury: February 1868–February 1869
1st Lord Cairns: February 1869–February 1870
6th Duke of Richmond: February 1870–August 1876
1st Earl of Beaconsfield: August 1876–April 1881 (*)
3rd Marquess of Salisbury: May 1881–July 1902 (* from 1885)
8th Duke of Devonshire: July 1902–October 1903
5th Marquess of Lansdowne: October 1903–December 1916
1st Earl Curzon: December 1916–April 1925
4th Marquess of Salisbury: April 1925–June 1931
1st Viscount Hailsham: June 1931–June 1935
7th Marquess of Londonderry: June–November 1935
3rd Earl of Halifax: November 1935–March 1938
7th Earl Stanhope: March 1938–May 1940
1st Viscount Caldecote: May–October 1940
3rd Earl of Halifax: October 1940–January 1941
1st Lord Lloyd: January–February 1941
1st Lord Moyne: February 1941–February 1942
Viscount Cranborne [5th Marquess of Salisbury, 1947]: February 1942–March 1957
14th Earl of Home: March 1957–July 1960
2nd Viscount Hailsham: July 1960–October 1963

6th Lord Carrington: October 1963–June 1970
2nd Earl Jellicoe: June 1970–June 1973
3rd Lord Windlesham: June 1973–October 1974
6th Lord Carrington: October 1974–May 1979
Lord Soames: May 1979–September 1981
Lady Young: September 1981–June 1983
1st Viscount Whitelaw: June 1983–January 1988
2nd Lord Belstead: January 1988–November 1990
Lord Waddington: November 1990–April 1992
Lord Wakeham: April 1992–July 1994
Viscount Cranborne: July 1994–

Leaders in the House of Commons

Sir Robert Peel: December 1834–July 1846 (*)
Lord George Bentinck: July 1846–December 1847
Marquess of Granby: February–March 1848
[no Leader appointed for 1848–9]
Benjamin Disraeli, Marquess of Granby and J. C. Herries: 1849–1852
Benjamin Disraeli: February 1852–August 1876 (* from 1868)
Sir Stafford Northcote: August 1876–June 1885
Sir Michael Hicks Beach: June 1885–August 1886
Lord Randolph Churchill: August–December 1886
W. H. Smith: December 1886–October 1891
Arthur James Balfour: October 1891–November 1911 (* from 1902)
Andrew Bonar Law: November 1911–March 1921 (* from 1916)
Austen Chamberlain: March 1921–October 1922
Andrew Bonar Law: October 1922–May 1923 (*)
Stanley Baldwin: May 1923–May 1937 (*)
Neville Chamberlain: May 1937–October 1940 (*)
[Sir] Winston Churchill: October 1940–April 1955 (*)
Sir Anthony Eden: April 1955–January 1957 (*)
Harold Macmillan: January 1957–October 1963 (*)
Sir Alec Douglas-Home: October 1963–July 1965 (*)
Edward Heath: August 1965–February 1975 (*)

Margaret Thatcher: February 1975–November 1990 (*)
John Major: November 1990–July 1997 (*)
William Hague: July 1997– (*)

Chief Whips, House of Lords since 1870

Lord Skelmersdale [1st Earl of Lothian, 1880]: 1870–85
9th Earl of Kintore: 1885–9
3rd Earl of Limerick: 1889–96
9th Earl Waldegrave: 1896–1911
9th Duke of Devonshire: 1911–16
3rd Lord Hylton: 1916–22
6th Earl of Clarendon: 1922–5
2nd Earl of Plymouth: 1925–9

5th Earl of Lucan: 1929–40
4th Lord Templemore: 1940–45
5th Earl Fortescue: 1945–58
2nd Earl St Aldwyn: 1958–77
2nd Lord Denham: 1977–91
3rd Lord Hesketh: 1991–93
2nd Viscount Ullswater: 1993–4
2nd Lord Strathclyde: 1994–

Chief Whips, House of Commons from 1835

Sir George Clerk: 1835–7
Sir Thomas Fremantle: 1837–44
Sir John Young: 1844–6
William Beresford: 1846–50
Forbes MacKenzie: 1850–53
Sir William Joliffe: 1853–9
Colonel T. E. Taylor: 1859–68
Gerard Noel: 1868–73
Colonel T. E. Taylor: 1873–4
Sir William Hart Dyke: 1874–80
Rowland Wynn: 1880–85
Aretas Akers-Douglas: 1885–95
Sir William Walrond: 1895–1902
Sir Alexander Acland-Hood: 1902–11
Lord Balcarres: 1911–12
Lord Edmund Talbot: 1912–21
Leslie Wilson: 1921–3

[Sir] Bolton Eyres-Monsell: 1923–31
David Margesson: 1931–41
James Stuart: 1941–8
Patrick Buchan-Hepburn: 1948–55
Edward Heath: 1955–9
Martin Redmayne: 1959–64
William Whitelaw: 1964–70
Francis Pym: 1970–73
Humphrey Atkins: 1973–9
Michael Jopling: 1979–83
John Wakeham: 1983–7
David Waddington: 1987–9
Timothy Renton: 1989–90
Richard Ryder: 1990–95
Alastair Goodlad: 1995–7
James Arbuthnot: 1997–

Chairmen of the Party Organization

[Sir] Arthur Steel-Maitland: 1911–16
Sir George Younger: 1916–23
Sir Stanley Jackson: 1923–6
J. C. C. Davidson, 1926–30
Neville Chamberlain: 1930–31
1st Lord Stonehaven: 1931–6
[Sir] Douglas Hacking: 1936–42
Thomas Dugdale: 1942–4
Ralph Assheton: 1944–6
Lord [1st Viscount] Woolton: 1946–55
Oliver [Lord] Poole: 1955–7
2nd Viscount Hailsham: 1957–9
R. A. Butler: 1959–61
Iain Macleod: 1961–3 (jointly with Lord Poole, 1963)
1st Viscount Blakenham: 1963–5
Edward du Cann: 1965–7
Anthony Barber: 1967–70
Peter Thomas: 1970–72
6th Lord Carrington: 1972–4
William Whitelaw: 1974–5
Lord Thorneycroft: 1975–81
Cecil Parkinson: 1981–3
John Selwyn Gummer: 1983–5
Norman Tebbit: 1985–7
Peter Brooke: 1987–9
Kenneth Baker: 1989–90
Chris Patten: 1990–92
Sir Norman Fowler: 1992–4
Jeremy Hanley: 1994–5
Brian Mawhinney: 1995–7
Lord Parkinson: 1997–

Party Treasurers (usually Joint Treasurers since 1948)

1st Earl Farquhar: 1911–23
1st Viscount Younger: 1923–9
Sir Samuel Hoare: 1929–31
1st Lord Ebbisham: 1931–3
1st Viscount Greenwood: 1933–8
1st Viscount Marchwood: 1938–47
Christopher Holland-Martin: 1947–60
6th Lord De L'Isle: 1948–52
Oliver Poole: 1952–5
Sir Henry Studholme: 1955–62
Robert Allan: 1960–65
Sir Arnold Silverstone [Lord Ashdown]: 1974–7
William Clark: 1974–5
Alastair [Lord] Macalpine: 1975–90
Lord Boardman: 1979–83
Sir Oulton Wade: 1982–90
Sir Charles [Lord] Johnston: 1984–8
Lord Laing: 1988–93
3rd Viscount Beaverbrook: 1990–92
Sir John Cope: 1991–2
Tim Smith: 1992–3

Richard Stanley: 1962–6
Lord Chelmer: 1965–77
Sir Tatton Brinton: 1964–74

Charles [Lord] Hambro: 1993–7
Sir Philip [Lord] Harris: 1993–7
Sir Graham Kirkham: 1997–
Michael Ashcroft: 1997–

Principal Party Organizers
Joseph Planta: 1831–2
Francis R. Bonham: 1832–46
Philip Rose: 1853–9
Markham Spofforth: 1859–70
[Sir] John Gorst, Principal Agent: 1870–77
W. B. Skene, Principal Agent: 1877–80
Sir John Gorst, Principal Agent: 1880–82
G. C. T. Bartley, Principal Agent: 1882–4
Captain Richard Middleton, Principal Agent: 1885–1903
Lionel Wells, Principal Agent: 1903–5
Alexander Haig, Principal Agent: 1905–6
Percival Hughes, Principal Agent: 1906–12
[Sir] John Boraston, Principal Agent: 1912–20 (jointly with William Jenkins, 1915–20)
[Sir] Malcolm Fraser, Principal Agent: 1920–23

Admiral Sir Reginald Hall, Principal Agent: 1923–4
[Sir] Herbert Blain, Principal Agent: 1924–7
[Sir] Leigh Maclachlan, Principal Agent: 1927–8
[Sir] Robert Topping, General Director: 1928–45
[Sir] Stephen Pierssené, General Director: 1945–57
[Sir] William Urton, General Director: 1957–66
[Sir] Richard Webster, Director of Organization: 1966–76
Michael Wolff, General Director: 1974–5
[Sir] Anthony Garner, Director of Organization: 1976–88
[Sir] John Lacy, Director of Organization and Campaigning: 1988–92
Paul Judge, Director-General, 1992–5
Tony Garrett, Director of Campaigning: 1992–
Martin Saunders, Director-General, 1995–7

Principal Publicity Officers

[Sir] Joseph Ball, 1927–30
Sir Patrick Gower, 1930–39
Edward O'Brien: 1945–6
Mark Chapman-Walker: 1946–55
Guy Schofield: 1955–7
Ronald Simms: 1957–61
George Hutchinson: 1961–4
Roger Pemberton: 1964–5
Tim Rathbone: 1966–8
Geoffrey Tucker: 1968–70
Russell Lewis: 1970–71
Donald Harker: 1971–5

Alec Todd: 1975–7
Tom Hooson: 1977–8
Gordon Reece: 1978–80
Sir Harry Boyne: 1980–82
Anthony Shrimsley: 1982–5
Harvey Thomas: 1985–6
Michael Dobbs: 1986–9
Brendan Bruce: 1989–91
Shaun Woodward: 1991–2
Tim Collins: 1992–4 and 1995
Hugh Colver: 1994–5
Charles Lewington: 1995–7
Francis Halewood: 1997–

Chairmen of the Conservative Research Department

Neville Chamberlain: 1930–40
Sir Kingsley Wood: 1940–43
Sir Joseph Ball, Acting Chairman, 1943–5

R. A. Butler: 1945–64
Sir Michael [Lord] Fraser: 1970–74
Sir Ian Gilmour: 1974–5
Angus Maude: 1974–9

(N.B. the post was left vacant between 1964 and 1970, and abolished in 1979, when its functions were assumed by the Chairman of the Party Organization.)

Directors of the Conservative Research Department

[Sir] Joseph Ball: 1930–39
David Clarke: 1945–51 (in 1948–50 jointly with Henry Hopkinson, and in 1948–51 jointly with Percy Cohen)
Michael Fraser: 1951–64 (in 1951–9 jointly with Percy Cohen)

Brendon Sewill: 1964–70
James Douglas: 1970–74
Chris Patten: 1970–79
Alan Howarth: 1979–82
Peter Cropper: 1982–4
Robin Harris: 1985–9
Andrew Lansley: 1989–95
Danny Finkelstein: 1995–

Chairmen of the 1922 Committee

[Sir] Gervase Rentoul: 1923–32
William Morrison: 1932–5
Sir Hugh O'Neill: 1935–9
Sir Annesley Somerville,
 Acting Chairman: 1939
William Spens: 1939–40
Sir Alexander Erskine Hill: 1940–44
John McEwen: 1944–5
Sir Arnold Gridley: 1945–51
Derek Walker-Smith: 1951–5
John Morrison: 1955–64
Sir William Anstruther-Gray:
 1964–6
Sir Arthur Vere Harvey: 1966–70
Sir Harry Legge-Bourke: 1970–72
Edward du Cann: 1972–84
Cranley Onslow, 1984–92
[Sir] Marcus Fox: 1992–7
Archie Hamilton: 1997–

APPENDIX 3

Conservative and Coalition Governments since 1834

(Non-Conservatives are underlined: Liberal Unionists between 1886 and 1912, Liberals between 1915 and 1922, National Labour and National Liberals between 1931 and 1935, Labour and non-party between 1940 and 1945.)

Year	Prime Minister	Foreign Secretary	Home Secretary	Chancellor of the Exchequer	Other Key Ministers
1834–5	Peel	Wellington	Goulburn	Peel	Lyndhurst [Ld Chan.]
1841–6	Peel	Aberdeen	Graham	Goulburn	Stanley [War], Gladstone [BoT]
1852	Derby	Malmesbury	Walpole	Disraeli	
1858–9	Derby	Malmesbury	Walpole/ Sotheron Escourt	Disraeli	Stanley [Colonies & India]
1866–8	Derby	Stanley	Walpole/ Gathorne Hardy	Disraeli	Carnarvon [Colonies], Cranborne [India
1868	Disraeli	Stanley	Gathorne Hardy	Hunt	Northcote [India], Cairns [Ld Chan.]
1874–80	Disraeli	Derby/ Salisbury	Cross	Northcote	Salisbury [India], Gathorne Hardy [War], Cairns [Ld Chan.]
1885–6	Salisbury	Salisbury	Cross	Hicks Beach	Churchill [India], Carnarvon [Ireland]
1886–92	Salisbury	Iddesleigh/ Salisbury	Matthews	Churchill/ Goschen	Smith/Balfour [HoC lead], Balfour [Ireland], Hamilton [Navy]

APPENDIX 3 519

Year	Prime Minister	Foreign Secretary	Home Secretary	Chancellor of the Exchequer	Other Key Ministers
1895–1902	Salisbury	Salisbury/ Lansdowne	Ridley/Ritchie	Hicks Beach	Chamberlain [Colonies], Balfour [HoC lead], Devonshire [Ld Pres.], Halsbury [Ld Chan.]
1902–5	Balfour	Lansdowne	Akers-Douglas	Ritchie/Austen Chamberlain	Chamberlain [Colonies], Devonshire [Ld Pres.], Halsbury [Ld Chan.], Wyndham [Ireland]
1915–16	Asquith	Grey/Cecil	Simon/Samuel	McKenna	Bonar Law [Colonies], Lloyd George [Munitions, War], Balfour [Navy]
1916–22	Lloyd George	Balfour/Curzon	Cave/Shortt	Bonar Law/ A. Chamberlain Horne	Birkenhead [Ld Chan.], Churchill [Munitions, War]
1922–3	Bonar Law	Curzon	Bridgeman	Baldwin	Salisbury [Ld Pres.]
1923–4	Baldwin	Curzon	Bridgeman	Neville Chamberlain	Salisbury [Ld Pres.]
1924–9	Baldwin	Austen Chamberlain	Joynson-Hicks	Churchill	Neville Chamberlain [Health], Birkenhead [India]
1931–5	MacDonald	Reading/Simon	Samuel/ Gilmour	Snowden/ Neville Chamberlain	Baldwin [Ld Pres.], Hoare [India]
1935–7	Baldwin	Hoare/Eden	Simon	Neville Chamberlain	Cunliffe-Lister [Air]
1937–40	Neville Chamberlain	Eden/Halifax	Hoare/ Anderson	Simon	Churchill [Navy], Wood [Health]

Year	Prime Minister	Foreign Secretary	Home Secretary	Chancellor of the Exchequer	Other Key Ministers
1940–45	Churchill	Halifax/Eden	Anderson/ Morrison	Wood/ Anderson	Attlee [Ld Pres.], Beaverbrook [Production], Bevin [Labour], Woolton [Reconst.]
1945	Churchill	Eden	Somervell	Anderson	
1951–5	Churchill	Eden	Maxwell Fyfe/ Lloyd George	Butler	Macmillan [Housing], Monckton [Labour]
1955–7	Eden	Macmillan/ Lloyd	Lloyd George	Butler/ Macmillan	Salisbury [Ld Pres.], Kilmuir [Ld Chan.]
1957–63	Macmillan	Lloyd/Home	Butler/Brooke	Thorneycroft/ Heathcoat Amory/Lloyd/ Maudling	Sandys [Defence], Macleod [Colonies], Kilmuir [Ld Chan.]
1963–4	Douglas-Home	Butler	Brooke	Maudling	Heath [BoT]
1970–74	Heath	Douglas-Home	Maudling/Carr	Macleod/ Barber	Carr [Labour], Whitelaw [N. Ireland]
1979–80	Thatcher	Carrington/ Pym/Howe/ Major/Hurd	Whitelaw/ Brittan/Hurd/ Waddington	Howe/Lawson/ Major	Prior [Employment], Tebbit [Employment], Baker [Education], Heseltine [Defence]
1990–97	Major	Hurd/Rifkind	Baker/Clarke/ Howard	Lamont/Clarke	Heseltine [Environment]

APPENDIX 4

Conferences of the National Union of Conservative and Unionist Associations

Year	Place	National Union President	Chairman
Nov. 1867	London		John Gorst
Dec. 1868	Birmingham	Earl of Dartmouth	Viscount Holmesdale
June 1869	Liverpool	Lord Skelmersdale	H. C. Raikes
April 1870	York	Earl of Feversham	H. C. Raikes
June 1871	Bristol	Earl of Feversham	H. C. Raikes
June 1872	London	Duke of Abercorn	H. C. Raikes
April 1873	Leeds	Earl of Wharncliffe	H. C. Raikes
July 1874	London	Lord Hampton	H. C. Raikes
June 1875	Brighton	Lord Colchester	Viscount Mahon
Oct. 1876	Manchester	Marquess of Abergavenny	Lord Claud Hamilton
June 1877	Portsmouth	Lord Winnerleigh	Lord Claud Hamilton
July 1878	Nottingham	Earl Cadogan	Lord Claud Hamilton
Oct. 1879	Birmingham	Earl Manvers	Earl Percy
July 1880	London	Marquess of Hertford	Earl Percy
Oct. 1881	Newcastle	Marquess of Salisbury	Earl Percy
Nov. 1882	Bristol	Duke of Northumberland	Earl Percy
Oct. 1883	Birmingham	Duke of Beaufort	Earl Percy
July 1884	Sheffield	Earl of Dartmouth	Lord Randolph Churchill/ Sir Michael Hicks Beach
Oct. 1885	Newport, Mon.	Duke of Norfolk	Lord Claud Hamilton
Oct. 1886	Bradford	Lord Tredegar	Ellis Ashmead Bartlett
Nov. 1887	Oxford	Earl of Londesborough	Ellis Ashmead Bartlett
Nov. 1888	Wolverhampton	Earl of Jenty	Ellis Ashmead Bartlett
Nov. 1889	Nottingham	Earl of Dartmouth	Sir A. K. Rollitt
Nov. 1890	Liverpool	Duke of Portland	F. Dixon-Hartland
Nov. 1891	Birmingham	Earl of Lathom	H. Byron-Reed
Dec. 1892	Sheffield	Lord Windsor	C. B. Stuart-Wortley
Nov. 1893	Cardiff	Earl of Scarborough	Sir S. Northcote

Year	Place	National Union President	Chairman
Nov. 1894	Newcastle	Earl of Dunraven	J. Rankin
Nov. 1895	Brighton	Marquess of Londonderry	Sir C. E. H. Vincent
Nov. 1896	Rochdale	Duke of Norfolk	Marquess of Granby
Nov. 1897	London	Earl of Derby	A. H. Smith-Barry
Nov. 1898	Bristol	Earl Cadogan	Sir B. Stone
Nov. 1899	Dewsbury	Duke of Beaufort	G. W. E. Loder
Dec. 1900	London	Marquess of Zetland	Lord Windsor
Nov. 1901	Wolverhampton	Lord Llangattock	Sir A. Hickman
Oct. 1902	Manchester	Earl of Dartmouth	Sir C. Cave
Oct. 1903	Sheffield	Earl of Derby	F. Lowe
Oct. 1904	Southampton	Duke of Norfolk	H. Gibson Bowles
Nov. 1905	Newcastle	Lord Montagu	Sir W. Plummer
July 1906	London	Duke of Northumberland	Henry Imbert-Terry
Nov. 1907	Birmingham	Duke of Northumberland	Duke of Rutland
Nov. 1908	Cardiff	Earl of Plymouth	Sir R. Hodge
Nov. 1909	Manchester	Earl Cawdor	Sir T. Wrightson
Nov. 1910	Nottingham	Earl of Derby	Henry Chaplin
Nov. 1911	Leeds	Duke of Portland	Lord Kenyon
Nov. 1912	London	Lord Faber	Sir William Crump
Nov. 1913	Norwich	Lord Farquhar	Archibald Salvidge
Dec. 1917	London	Sir A. Fellowes	Sir Harry Samuel
June 1920	Birmingham	Sir A. Fellowes	J. C. Williams
Nov. 1921	Liverpool	Austen Chamberlain	Sir Arthur Benn
Dec. 1922	London	Earl of Derby	Sir Alexander Leith
Oct. 1923	Plymouth	Lord Mildmay	Sir Herbert Nield
Oct. 1924	Newcastle	Duke of Northumberland	Earl of Selborne
Oct. 1925	Brighton	G. Loder	Sir Percy Woodhouse
Oct. 1926	Scarborough	George Lane-Fox	Dame Caroline Bridgeman
Oct. 1927	Cardiff	Viscount Tredegar	Sir Robert Sanders
Sept. 1928	Great Yarmouth	Lord Queenborough	John Gretton
Nov. 1929	London	Lord Faringdon	Gwylim Rowlands
July 1930	London	Neville Chamberlain	Lady Iveagh
Oct. 1932	Blackpool	Lord Stanley	Earl Howe
Oct. 1933	Birmingham	Earl of Plymouth	Sir Geoffrey Ellis
Oct. 1934	Bristol	Lord Bayford	Miss R. Evans
Oct. 1935	Bournemouth	G. Herbert	Sir W. Cope
Oct. 1936	Margate	Lord Ebbisham	Sir L. Brassey

APPENDIX 4

Year	Place	National Union President	Chairman
Oct. 1937	Scarborough	Lord Bingley	Miss C. Fyfe
May 1943	London	Marquess of Salisbury	R. Catterall
March 1945	London	Lord Courthorpe	R. A. Butler
Oct. 1946	Blackpool	Oliver Stanley	Richard Proby
Oct. 1947	Brighton	Harold Macmillan	Mrs Hornyold-Strickland
Oct. 1948	Llandudno	G. Summers	Sir Herbert Williams
Oct. 1949	London	Viscount Swinton	D. Graham
Oct. 1950	Blackpool	Sir David Maxwell Fyfe	Anthony Nutting
Oct. 1952	Scarborough	Sir Thomas Dugdale	Charles Waterhouse
Oct. 1953	Margate	Marquess of Salisbury	Mrs J. Warde
Oct. 1954	Blackpool	Sir Anthony Eden	Sir G. Llewelyn
Oct. 1955	Bournemouth	Mrs L. Sayers	Mrs Evelyn Emmet
Oct. 1956	Llandudno	R. A. Butler	Sir Eric Edwards
Oct. 1957	Brighton	Earl of Woolton	Mrs W. Elliot
Oct. 1958	Blackpool	Sir Richard Proby	Sir Stanley Bell
Oct. 1960	Scarborough	Henry Brooke	Edward Brown
Oct. 1961	Brighton	Viscount Hailsham	Sir Douglas Glover
Oct. 1962	Llandudno	Sir G. Llewelyn	Sir John Howard
Oct. 1963	Blackpool	Earl of Home	Mrs T. Shepherd
Oct. 1965	Brighton	Viscountess Davidson	Sir Max Bemrose
Oct. 1966	Blackpool	Selwyn Lloyd	Sir Dan Mason
Oct. 1967	Brighton	Lord Chelmer	Mrs A. Doughty
Oct. 1968	Blackpool	Reginald Maudling	Sir Theo Constantine
Oct. 1969	Brighton	Lady Brooke	Derek Crossman
Oct. 1970	Blackpool	[Iain Macleod]	Sir Edwin Leather
Oct. 1971	Blackpool	William Whitelaw	Miss Unity Lister
Oct. 1972	Brighton	Dame M. Shepherd	William Harris
Oct. 1973	Blackpool	Anthony Barber	Mrs R. Smith
Oct. 1975	Blackpool	Peter Thomas	Sir Alastair Graesser
Oct. 1976	Brighton	Lord Hewlett	Miss Shelagh Roberts
Oct. 1977	Blackpool	Lord Carrington	David Sells
Oct. 1978	Brighton	Dame A. Doughty	Sir Herbert Redfearn
Oct. 1979	Blackpool	Francis Pym	D. Davenport-Handley
Oct. 1980	Brighton	Sir Theo Constantine	Dame A. Springman
Oct. 1981	Blackpool	Edward du Cann	Fred Hardman
Oct. 1982	Brighton	Sir John Taylor	Donald Walters
Oct. 1983	Blackpool	Sir Geoffrey Howe	Peter Lane
Oct. 1984	Brighton	Sir Alastair Graesser	Dame P. Hunter
Oct. 1985	Blackpool	Sir Humphrey Atkins	Sir Basil Feldman
Oct. 1986	Bournemouth	Sir Charles Johnston	Patrick Lawrence

Year	Place	National Union President	Chairman
Oct. 1987	Blackpool	George Younger	Dame J. Seccombe
Oct. 1988	Brighton	Dame Shelagh Roberts	Sir I. McLeod
Oct. 1989	Blackpool	Viscount Whitelaw	Sir S. Odell
Oct. 1990	Bournemouth	Sir D. Davenport-Handley	Dame M. Fry
Oct. 1991	Blackpool	John Wakeham	Sir J. Barnard
Oct. 1992	Brighton	Sir D. Walters	J. Mason
Oct. 1993	Blackpool	Dame W. Mitchell	Sir Basil Feldman
Oct. 1994	Bournemouth	William Stuttaford	Sir Basil Feldman
Oct. 1995	Blackpool	David Kelly	Sir Basil Feldman
Oct. 1996	Bournemouth	Dame H. Byford	Robin Hodgson
Oct. 1997	Blackpool	John Taylor	Robin Hodgson

(N.B. No Party Conference was held in 1914–16 or in 1918–19 because of the First World War, in 1938–42 or in 1944 because of the Second World War, and in 1931, 1951, 1959, 1964 and 1974 because of autumn general elections.)

APPENDIX 5

Glossary of Organizations and Principal Personalities

Akers-Douglas, Aretas, 1st Viscount Chilston (1851–1926): Conservative MP from 1880 and Chief Whip 1885–1895, then Cabinet posts 1895–1905; active party organizer and chairman of the 1911 Unionist Organization Committee.

Advisory Committee on Policy: created in 1949 after earlier experiments, to bring together representatives of MPs, peers and National Union and chaired by the Party Leader or a senior colleague; confidentially discussed party policy proposals prior to publication and so provided Central Office and the leadership with a valuable sounding-board of representative party opinion.

Baldwin, Stanley, 1st Earl Baldwin of Bewdley (1867–1947): late developer who became MP after a business career only when forty-one and a minister only when fifty; sudden rise to prominence after helping to overthrow the Lloyd George coalition, 1922, and became Party Leader, 1923–37, three times Prime Minister; a fiercely moral man, determined on centrist and reformist ideas; one of the best ever political communicators; a spokesman for rural England, he also found leading the Conservative Party 'like driving pigs to market'.

Balfour, Arthur James, 1st Earl of Balfour (1848–1930): nephew of Salisbury, and politically active from entry to the Commons in 1874 until his death; Irish Secretary, 1887–91, and Conservative Commons Leader, 1891–1902, before becoming Prime Minister, 1902–5; overthrown as Conservative Leader after the constitutional crisis of 1911, but served under three later Leaders, and as Foreign Secretary made the 'Balfour Declaration' on a future state of Israel; his dilettante air of 'philosophic detachment' encouraged such views as Lloyd George's, that Balfour's impact on history would be 'no more than the whiff of scent on a lady's pocket handkerchief'.

Beaconsfield, *see* **Disraeli**

Birkenhead, *see* **Smith**

Bow Group: founded by a group of university friends in 1950, including Peter Emery and Dennis Walters, both later Conservative MPs, in order to provide a forum for younger thinking Conservatives; initially named after its first meeting place at the Bow and Bromley Conservative Club; effectively re-launched in 1957, when it began the magazine *Crossbow*, and thereafter provided an avenue towards a parliamentary career for many future ministers, notably ex-Group chairmen like Geoffrey Howe; often thought of as being on the left of the party but combined concern for social policy and human rights with a belief in sound finance.

Butler, R. A., 'Rab', Lord Butler of Saffron Walden (1902–82): Conservative MP from 1929 and Baldwinite minister in the 1930s, implementing Appeasement at the Foreign Office, 1938–41; wartime success as Minister of Education and the key figure in the post-war policy review; Chancellor of the Exchequer, 1951–5, but twice failed to become Party Leader in 1957 and 1963, when the right were critical and the left not unitedly supportive; a good party man often accused of spinelessness by those who confused loyalty with cowardice.

Cairns, 1st Earl (1819–1885): Ulsterman and lawyer, Belfast MP from 1852; law officer under Derby and twice Lord Chancellor under Disraeli.

Canning George (1770–1827): lawyer and political writer as a young man, MP from 1794, opponent of the French Revolution and supporter of Pitt; Foreign Secretary, 1807–9 and 1822–7; regularly appointed to other offices and equally regularly resigned on points of principle and the incompatibility of personalities; Prime Minister, 1827, under whom the Tory Party split, but revered by some later Tories like Disraeli.

Carlton Club: since the 1830s the senior Conservative gentlemen's club in the West End of London, its membership limited to Conservatives and until recently containing almost all Conservative MPs as members; located in Pall Mall and after wartime bombing in St James's, premises in which several notable party meetings have been held, including the one that overthrew Lloyd George on 19 October 1922.

Centre for Policy Studies: founded in 1974 by Sir Keith Joseph and Margaret Thatcher to propagate politically the economic ideas associated with the free market; initially headed by Alfred Sherman, associated with Joseph's 1974 speeches, which marked a decisive step towards bringing 'monetarism' into the British debate, and supported Thatcher in her early years as Conservative Leader but thereafter became less politically committed.

APPENDIX 5   527

Central Office: the headquarters of the Conservative Party Organization since 1870, run initially by the Principal Agent under the aegis of the Chief Whip, but since 1911 under the authority of the Party Chairman; housed since 1958 at 32 Smith Square.

Chamberlain, Sir Austen (1863–1937): elder son of Joseph Chamberlain and his intended political heir; Chancellor of the Exchequer, 1903–5, and tariff reform leader in opposition from 1906; failed to win the party leadership in 1911, but 'emerged' unopposed when Bonar Law retired in 1921; strong coalitionist who resigned when party abandoned coalition in 1922, but returned to Foreign Office under Baldwin, 1924–9; an austere and uncharming man, obsessed with honour and the need to live down his father's reputation as a wrecker, Churchill observed that he had always 'played the game' and therefore always lost.

Chamberlain, Joseph (1836–1914): Unitarian and radical Liberal, reforming Mayor of Birmingham; discontented member of Gladstone's 1880 government and the author of the 1884 'Unauthorized Programme'; became a Liberal Unionist in opposition to Home Rule, 1886; supported Salisbury's Conservatives from 1886 and then joined the Unionist government as Colonial Secretary, 1895–1903; resigned over tariff reform in 1903 and was poised to capture the party when incapacitated by a stroke in 1906; one of the most dynamic and individual figures of British political history.

Chamberlain, Neville (1869–1940): younger son of Joseph Chamberlain; Mayor of Birmingham and entered the Commons only in 1918; in the Cabinet from 1922 and Chancellor of the Exchequer in 1923 and 1931–7, but his favourite post was as Minister of Health, 1924–9; Baldwin's heir-apparent by 1930 and so Prime Minister, 1937–40; credibility wrecked by the failure both of Appeasement and of the first year of war, and overthrown after Tory rebellion; true political professional, a sensitive man and keen angler, but one accused of viewing all political issues 'through the wrong end of a municipal drainpipe'.

Churchill, Lord Randolph (1849–94): younger son of 6th Duke of Marlborough; rose to prominence through the 'Fourth Party' then challenged Northcote and Salisbury for control of the party, 1884–5; involved in intricate negotiations over Ireland, 1885–6, but then played 'the Orange card' enthusiastically, leading Ulster's fight against Home Rule; a restless and inordinately ambitious political adventurer, he never recovered from his resignation from Salisbury's Cabinet in

1886; later remembered as a supporter of 'Tory Democracy', an idea he could not define and probably never meant anyway.

Churchill, Sir Winston (1874–1965): son of Lord Randolph Churchill; war hero after escape from Boer captivity and always then seen as (his own words) 'a war man'; defected to the Liberals, 1904, and held major posts under Asquith and Lloyd George, but then 're-ratted' to the Conservatives on grounds of anti-socialism in 1924; Chancellor of the Exchequer under Baldwin, 1924–9, but then left front bench over India and was regular critic of 1930s Conservative Leaders; Prime Minister in war crisis of 1940–45 and again in 1951–5, but an inactive Conservative Leader, 1940–55; died as the world's most revered national hero after a chequered earlier career. Lloyd George thought his ambition to be such that 'he would make a drum out of the skin of his mother in order to sound his own praises'.

Confederacy: undercover organization created by the extreme tariff reformers of the Edwardian period to propagate their ideas and to harass free traders.

Conservative Action for Electoral Reform: pressure group set up after the party's defeats in 1974 to press for constitutional reform, including a Bill of Rights; favoured the introduction of the Additional Member System for British elections; withered after the party's return to power in 1979.

Conservative Political Centre: a body created after the Second World War to foster political discussion among party members through meetings and publications, and hence in part following on the work of the inter-war Conservative Education Department, for which its first director, Cuthbert Alport, had worked; main activities included 'two-way contact programme' of party debates in the constituencies, publication of pamphlets, and major annual lectures.

Conservative Research Department: policy unit founded in 1929–30 and given its initial shape by Neville Chamberlain (chairman, 1930–40); under the chairmanship of R. A. Butler (1945–64) it became the foundation of all the party's official policy work and was responsible for drafting all policy statements and manifestos, servicing shadow ministers and parliamentary committees, assisting Central Office with publicity work; merged into Central Office in 1979.

Cooper, Duff, 1st Viscount Norwich (1890–1954): moderate Conservative MP and Baldwin supporter, helping to save Baldwin's leadership at 1931 by-election; ministerial office from 1931 but resigned over

Munich, 1938; restored to office by Churchill, and subsequently Ambassador to France.

Cranborne, *see* **Salisbury**

Cunliffe-Lister, Sir Philip, 1st Earl of Swinton (1884–1972): meteoric rise in government during the Lloyd George coalition, then Cabinet under Bonar Law and Baldwin; responsible as Air Minister for rearmament plans in mid-1930s, then left politics for security work; returned to ministerial office under Churchill and gave his home Swinton Castle as a post-war party college.

Curzon, George Nathaniel, 1st Marquess Curzon of Kedleston (1859–1925): Conservative MP from 1886; junior office under Salisbury and Viceroy of India, 1898–1905; took pragmatic line in 1911 Parliament Act crisis, but was a leading Unionist by 1914; War Cabinet 1916, and then Foreign Secretary, 1919–23; beaten by Baldwin in leadership contest of May 1923, but served loyally under a successor he despised; so keenly aristocratic that the 17th Earl of Derby said 'he makes one feel so terribly plebeian'.

Davidson, J. C. C., 1st Viscount Davidson (1889–1970): political secretary and then Conservative MP; junior office under Baldwin and then an active Party Chairman, 1926–30, but sacrificed by Baldwin to appease his critics; close family friend of the Baldwins; his wife Mimi succeeded him as MP for Hemel Hempstead and went on to a considerable career in her own right, both in parliament and in the National Union.

Derby, 14th Earl of, Edward Stanley (1799–1869): known as Lord Stanley until 1851; Whig MP and minister until 1834, then crossed in the 'Derby Dilly' to support Peel's first government and serve in his second; broke with Peel over the Corn Laws, 1845, and then Leader of the Conservative Party, 1845–68; Prime Minister in 1852, 1858–9 and 1866–8.

Devonshire, 8th Duke of (1833–1908): styled Marquess of Hartington, 1858–91; a Whig of conservative views, sitting in the Commons from 1857 to 1891 and leading the Liberals after Gladstone first retired in 1875; Liberal minister 1870–74 and 1880–85, then became Liberal Unionist Leader over Home Rule in 1886; supported Salisbury's Unionist governments and joined the 1895 Cabinet as Lord President; resigned in defence of free trade, 1903; a keen sportsman, responsive landlord and generous benefactor, but a politician of limited imagination; widely known as 'Harty-Tarty'.

Diehard: a particularly determined party man whose true blue instincts would not come out in the political wash, especially in the Edwardian period.

Disraeli, Benjamin, first Earl of Beaconsfield (1804–81): son of Isaac D'Israeli, Jewish writer; colourful early career during which he sought election under several party labels, then rose to fame as critic of Peel; Conservative Leader in the Commons from 1849 and Party Leader from 1868; Prime Minister 1868 and 1874–80; successful novelist; Lord Randolph Churchill summarized his career as 'failure, failure, failure, moderate success, renewed failure, sudden and absolute triumph'.

'Ditchers': the Conservatives who wanted to 'die in the last ditch' in resisting the 1911 Parliament Act (as opposed to 'Hedgers' who reluctantly agreed to compromise).

Douglas-Home, Sir Alec, 14th Earl of Home (1903–95): styled Lord Dunglass until 1951, and was Earl of Home, 1951–63; Chamberlain's PPS when Prime Minister but career then interrupted by polio; seen as diplomatic specialist, and Foreign Secretary, 1960–63 and 1970–74; Conservative Leader and Prime Minister after disputed succession crisis of 1963; facilitated system of election for future Leaders, and then resigned, 1965, but was then loyal backer of his successors; life peer as Lord Home of the Hirsel, 1974.

Eden, Sir Anthony, 1st Earl of Avon (1897–1977): war service in the Great War, and liberal Conservative MP from 1923; foreign affairs specialist from becoming PPS to the Foreign Secretary in 1926, and himself Foreign Secretary, 1935–8, 1940–45 and 1951–5; Churchill's designated successor from 1942 but kept overlong in the waiting room, and unsuccessful Prime Minister even before being wrecked by the Suez crisis in 1956; Conservative Leader, 1955–7.

Fourth Party: ginger group of four Conservative MPs, John Gorst, Drummond Wolff, Lord Randolph Churchill and (for a time) A. J. Balfour, created to harass the Commons leadership of Sir Stafford Northcote and largely succeeding in doing so, 1881–4.

Gathorne Hardy, Gathorne, 1st Earl of Cranbrook (1814–1906): active Anglican politician from election as MP in 1856; ministerial office under Disraeli from 1868, and a leading Commons Conservative under Disraeli and Salisbury.

Goderich, Frederick Robinson, 1st Viscount and later 1st Earl of Ripon (1782–1859): MP from 1806 and liberalizing minister under Liverpool and Canning; an ineffective Prime Minister 1827–8; minister in Whig government, 1830–34, but served as Conservative under Peel, 1841–6, and was later a Peelite.

Gorst, Sir John (1835–1916): Conservative MP from 1866 and party organizer, creator of Central Office; junior ministerial office under Disraeli and Salisbury, but increasingly discontented over the failure to advance 'Tory Democracy'; left the party in defence of free trade after 1903.

Hailsham, Quintin Hogg, 2nd Viscount (1907–): son of 1st Lord Hailsham, Lord Chancellor under Baldwin; Conservative MP from 1938 and a leading member of the wartime Tory Reform Group; author of the 1947 *The Case for Conservatism*; office under Eden and Macmillan, and a successful, ebullient Party Chairman, 1957–9; disclaimed his peerage but failed to win the party leadership in 1963, and continued to serve under Douglas-Home and Heath, becoming Lord Chancellor (as life peer Lord Hailsham), 1970–74 and 1979–87.

Halifax, 1st Earl of, Edward Wood, Lord Irwin (1881–1959): moderate Conservative MP and supporter of Baldwin, Cabinet office from 1922; Viceroy and advocate of a progressive Indian policy, then Foreign Secretary and an architect of Appeasement, 1938–40; stood back to allow Churchill the premiership in 1940 and was sent as Ambassador to the USA, 1941–6.

Hartington, *see* **Devonshire**

Heath, Sir Edward (1916–): entered Commons in the 'class of 1950' and then rose quickly, becoming Chief Whip in 1955; conducted EEC negotiations, 1962, and became Conservative Leader (1965–75), partly chosen to offset Wilson's meritocratic appeal but showing few presentational gifts; a Prime Minister after 1970 beset by an avalanche of problems and not seemingly in control; first Conservative to be elected Leader and first to be overthrown in a ballot.

'Hedgers', *see* **Ditchers**

Hicks Beach, Sir Michael, 1st Earl St Aldwyn (1837–1916): Conservative MP from 1864, and minister under Disraeli; Chancellor of the Exchequer, 1885–6 and 1895–1902; keen free trader after 1903; known as 'Black Michael' in deference to his appearance and alleged similarities to a character in *The Prisoner of Zenda*.

Howe, Sir Geoffrey, Lord Howe of Aberavon (1926–): an early chairman of the Bow Group and a law officer under Heath, before distancing himself from Heath in 1974 over economic policy; stood in the second ballot for the leadership in 1975 but subsequently served as Thatcher's shadow Chancellor and Chancellor, 1975–83; Foreign Secretary, 1983–9, and then Deputy Prime Minister, but clashed repeatedly with Thatcher over Europe and finally quit in 1990, his resignation speech provoking the end of her leadership.

Industrial Charter, The: Party policy review document emanating from the Industrial Policy Committee set up under Butler's chairmanship in 1946; report accepted by the 1947 Party Conference and formed the basis of much of the party's post-war domestic policy.

Joseph, Sir Keith, Lord Joseph (1918–95): a rare Jewish MP on the Conservative benches when first elected in 1956; in Cabinet first under Macmillan in 1962, and subsequently served under Heath and Thatcher until retiring in 1986; publicly disagreed about policy issues with Heath in 1974 and founded the Centre for Policy Studies to promote his free market views, thus becoming a key formative influence on 'Thatcherism'; a more effective thinker than he ever was a minister, he intended standing for the leadership of 1974–5, but subsequently withdrew and supported Thatcher.

Joynson-Hicks, Sir William, 1st Viscount Brentford (1865–1932): Conservative and Anglican politician, MP from 1908; early specialist on road traffic law and military use of air power; Cabinet from 1923 and Home Secretary, 1924–9, during which he made well-publicized gaffes and offended liberal opinion with a moral campaign to clean up London's nightlife; an early politician of the religious right; generally known as 'Jix'.

Junior Imperial League: the party's youth wing in the first four decades of the twentieth century, known as 'Imps'; had its own even younger wing, the Young Britons; in decline in the 1930s and the Fraser report of 1939 recommended drastic reforms which led in 1945 to its evolution into the Young Conservatives.

Kilmuir, *see* **Maxwell Fyfe**

Lansdowne, 5th Marquess of (1845–1927): a Liberal Unionist from 1886, and was successively Governor General of Canada and Viceroy of India; served under Salisbury, becoming Foreign Secretary, 1900–05; led the Unionists in the Lords from 1903 and hence had to negotiate the Parliament Act crisis of 1911 when the Unionist peers split three ways; member of the Asquith War Cabinet, 1915–16, but left the party over the continuation of the Great War, 1916–17.

Law, Andrew Bonar (1858–1923): from Canadian Ulster stock and a son of the manse, brought up in Glasgow, where he became a successful businessman; tariff reformer and MP from 1900, rising to become the compromise choice for Party Leader in 1911; key supporter of the Lloyd George government, 1916–21, but also overthrew Lloyd George, 1922; Prime Minister, 1922–3, before ill-health forced retirement; a taciturn and sometimes gloomy man who thought as well as acted in the framework of party; Asquith thought him 'the unknown Prime Minister'.

Lawson, Nigel, Lord Lawson (1932–): Conservative financial journalist and then MP from 1974; supporter of Thatcher in early battles within her Cabinet and Chancellor of the Exchequer, 1983–9, before resigning in a disagreement over policy advisers.

Liberal Unionists: section of the Gladstonian Liberal Party which rejected Irish Home Rule in 1886, containing both radicals led by Joseph Chamberlain and Whigs under Hartington; supported Salisbury in office 1886–92 and joined his government, 1895; remained a separate party with its own local and national structures, and with considerable strength in Scotland and in the West Midlands, until formally merged with the Conservatives in 1912.

Liverpool, 2nd Earl of (1770–1827): son of 1st Earl who was a politician in the 1760s and 1770s and minister under Pitt; MP from 1790, Foreign Secretary, 1801–3, and then occupied Home, War and Colonies departments before being Prime Minister, 1812–27; a man of strong convictions but limited inspirational gifts.

Lloyd, Selwyn (1904–78): MP from 1945 after earlier being a Liberal; Foreign Secretary 1957–60 and then Chancellor of the Exchequer before being sacked in 1962; compiled 'Selwyn Lloyd Report' into the Party Organization, 1963, and then returned in Douglas-Home Cabinet, but was dropped by Heath in opposition; Speaker of the Commons, 1971–6.

Long, Walter, 1st Viscount Long of Wraxall (1854–1921): Conservative MP from 1880, presenting himself as representative of Conservative squires; junior office under Salisbury and Cabinet from 1895; choleric critic of Balfour as Party Leader but failed to become his successor in succession crisis of 1911; then thorn in the flesh of Bonar Law, and of Lloyd George as coalition premier.

Macleod, Iain (1913–70): Conservative Research Department, 1945–50, then Conservative MP; quick rise to Minister of Health and then Labour, and courageous decolonizing Colonies Minister, 1959–61; Party Chairman in a time of Tory unpopularity 1961–3, and then refused office under Douglas-Home; his subsequent recovery of his position culminated in just a few weeks as Chancellor of the Exchequer in 1970 before his early death; a most effective party communicator and a tireless campaigner for moderate Conservative causes.

Macmillan, Harold, 1st Earl of Stockton (1894–1986): Great War service, then maverick inter-war MP; first junior ministerial post only in 1940, but rose quickly in Churchill's wartime coalition and post-war Opposition; critical success as Minister of Housing, 1951–4, then after quick moves through three posts became Party Leader and Prime Minister, 1957–63; credited with the party recovery after Suez and the 1959 victory, but less successful after 1960; consistent advocate of a left-wing Conservatism and later critic of Margaret Thatcher's policies.

Major John (1943–): undistinguished early career before election to the Commons in 1979; whip's office and then meteoric rise through Treasury and Foreign Office, 1987–90; uniting choice as Party Leader and Prime Minister in 1990 after bruising Thatcher–Heseltine contest; credited with 1992 victory, but never recovered credibility after 'Black Wednesday'; led party to largest ever defeat in 1997 and resigned as Leader.

Maudling, Reginald (1917–79): post-war Conservative Research Department, including work on *The Industrial Charter*, then Conservative MP from 1950; office under Churchill, Eden and Macmillan, Chancellor of the Exchequer, 1962–4; failed to win leadership in 1963 or in the election of 1965, but Deputy Leader under both Douglas-Home and Heath; Home Secretary, 1970–72, but then resigned over a financial scandal.

Maxwell Fyfe, Sir David, 1st Earl of Kilmuir (1900–1967): Conservative MP and lawyer, worked on prosecution of Nazi war criminals at Nuremberg 1946; compiler of 'Maxwell Fyfe Report', 1948; Cabinet office under Churchill, Eden and Macmillan, a highly conservative Home Secretary and Lord Chancellor, especially on moral issues; unceremoniously sacked in 1962's 'night of the long knives', shortly after he had told John Mackintosh that loyalty was the Conservatives' secret weapon.

Middle Way, The: book by Harold Macmillan, 1938, which advocated a centrist policy, government intervention and adoption of Keynesian economic ideas, later seen as prophetic of much post-war Conservative thinking.

Milner, Sir Alfred, 1st Viscount (1854–1925): initially a journalist and one of the founders of the Liberal Unionist Association; colonial administration in Egypt and then High Commissioner in South

Africa, 1897–1905, involving responsibility for the Boer War; after 1905 a 'diehard' Unionist and leader of the Lords' resistance to the 1911 Parliament Act, but member of War Cabinet under Lloyd George.

Monday Club: a right-wing pressure group within the Conservative Party founded in 1961 to fight against decolonization and taking its name from the day of Macmillan's 'winds of change' speech in Cape Town; attracted significant support in constituency associations and made life uncomfortable for Conservative MPs on the left, especially when it also took up the cause of immigration; waned during the 1970s as the party leadership became more attuned to its views.

National Liberals: name sometimes given to Lloyd George's Liberal supporters who allied with Conservatives 1916–22, but more usually associated with the 'Simonites' who followed Sir John Simon into permanent alliance with the Conservatives after 1931; retained entirely separate organization until 1947, when the Woolton–Teviot pact created a single party, though 'Conservative and National Liberal' remained a label under which candidates campaigned for election until the 1960s.

National Union: federative organization which has since 1867 brought together the voluntary side of the Conservative Party; slow to get going, but by the 1870s a significant factor and involved in the battles between Churchill, Northcote and Salisbury in the 1880s; its small secretarial team housed in Central Office but technically subject to the National Union rather than to the Party Chairman; organizes the annual 'Party Conference' and several other regional and more specialized consultative activities; supervises local association rulebooks and arbitrates in disputes.

Northcote, Sir Stafford, 1st Earl of Iddesleigh (1818–87): Gladstone's private secretary and framer of civil service recruitment proposals, then Conservative MP from 1855; Chancellor of the Exchequer, 1874–80, and Party Leader in the Commons, 1877–85, but attacked by the 'Fourth Party' and outwitted by Salisbury; removed to the Lords, 1885.

One Nation Group: backbench discussion and dining group formed by new Conservative MPs in the intake of 1950, taking its name from Disraeli's phrase (also the title of its first publication); early members included Carr, Macleod, Powell and Heath; its impact fluctuated as some members left to become ministers but it remained significant into the 1970s.

Peel, Sir Robert (1788–1850): son of Sir Robert Peel, calico manufacturer,

1st baronet, MP, and factory law reformer; MP for various constituencies, then Tamworth from 1830; Home Secretary under Liverpool and Wellington, 1822–7 and 1828–30; Prime Minister, 1834–5 and 1841–6; Conservative Leader, 1834–6, splitting party over the Corn Laws, 1846; subsequently the inspirer of the Peelite group and after his death widely revered as a wise statesman, and as the man who had by keeping down food prices avoided a major social explosion in Victorian Britain.

'Peelites': the Conservative MPs who backed Peel in the Corn Law crisis, and who remained supportive after his fall in 1846; a talented group that included Gladstone and many other front-benchers, most of whom gradually shifted to the Liberal Party into which the group merged in 1859.

Pitt, William 'the Younger' (1759–1806): 2nd son of 1st Earl of Chatham; George III's choice as Prime Minister when only twenty-three, and served 1783–1801 and 1804–6; moderate financial reformer in the 1780s but then mobilizer and inspirer of British resistance to French Revolution and Napoleon; looked back to by later Tories as the party's founder, though always called himself a Whig.

Post-War Problems Central Committee: hybrid body set up by the National Union in 1941, but including members of both Houses as well as the voluntary side of the party; aimed to fill the vacuum in party policy research created by the Second World War but failed to attract the support of the Party Leader, Churchill.

Powell, Enoch (1912–98): post-war Conservative Research Department and MP from 1950; early member and secretary of One Nation Group but also member of Suez Group; resigned from Treasury with Thorneycroft, 1958, but was Minister of Health under Macmillan; refused to serve under Douglas-Home, 1963, but rejoined Heath's shadow cabinet before being sacked over Birmingham speech on race, 1968; subsequently widened his disagreement to include opposition to EEC and left party in 1974, having a later parliamentary career as an Ulster Unionist; father within British politics of much economic thinking later linked with 'Thatcherism'.

Primrose League: a voluntary supporters' club for Conservative principles, named after Disraeli's allegedly favourite flower when launched in the 1880s; attracted a huge following and did much to socialize especially working-class and women members into support for the party; far less effective after women joined ordinary party organizations after 1918.

Reveille: ginger group dedicated to fighting the battle for tariffs in the party in the Edwardian period.

Robinson, *see* **Goderich**

Salisbury, 3rd Marquess of (1830–1903): styled Viscount Cranborne until 1868; caustic right-wing critic of Disraeli and Derby in the *Quarterly Review* and resigned from Cabinet over 1867 Reform Act; rejoined Cabinet in 1874, becoming one of Britain's greatest Foreign Secretaries, 1877–80, 1885–6, 1887–92 and 1895–1900; Conservative Leader, 1885–1902, and three times Prime Minister; a determined pessimist who failed entirely to understand the political trends of his time.

Simonites, *see* **National Liberals**

Smith, Sir F. E., 1st Earl of Birkenhead (1872–1930): from humble roots but rose through Oxford and the bar to become an MP in 1906, galvanizing a weak Unionist opposition with the wit and force of his early speeches; helped to mobilize Ulster resistance to Home Rule, and earned the reputation of an extreme right-winger, but in coalition office from 1915 was more pragmatic; Lord Chancellor and a strong coalitionist, 1919–22; refused to serve under Bonar Law, 1922, but returned to office under Baldwin in 1924; an advertisement for the opportunities available to a man with wit and ambition.

Stanley, *see* **Derby**

Steel-Maitland, Sir Arthur (1876–1935): disciple of Milner and Birmingham MP from 1910; first Party Chairman and determined reformer of the organization, 1911–17; junior office in wartime but a disappointed man by the time he conspired against the coalition in 1920–22; Minister of Labour under Baldwin, 1924–9, but generally a career that did not deliver on its early promise; an able and energetic man but also widely distrusted.

Swinton, *see* **Cunliffe-Lister**

Swinton College: at Masham near Ripon, opened as the 'Conservative College of the North' in 1948, and then became Swinton Conservative College until 1984.

Tariff Reform League: body set up by Joseph Chamberlain in 1903 to propagandize through meetings, posters, leaflets and foreign visits, and generally to promote the cause of tariffs in the public debate; one of the first such pressure groups in Britain, but less effective after Chamberlain's stroke in 1906.

Thatcher, Margaret, Baroness Thatcher (1925–): Conservative MP from

1959 with uneventful early ministerial career; both lucky and courageous in seizing the leadership in 1975 and then holding it for fifteen years, as Prime Minister 1979–90; the 'iron lady' of the last phase of the Cold War, warrior-queen of the Falklands War, and destroyer of the Cabinet wets; gradually fell out with too many natural allies and overthrown as an electoral liability, 1990; critic of her successor as betrayer of her legacy; supported Hague for Leader, 1997.

Thorneycroft, Peter, Lord Thorneycroft (1909–94): Conservative MP from 1938 and Cabinet under Churchill; Chancellor of the Exchequer, 1957, resigning in 1958, but returned later to Macmillan's government; retired on losing seat in 1966, but Party Chairman under Thatcher, 1975–81.

Tory Reform Group: during the Second World War, an informal body of enthusiastic younger MPs on the party's left wing, led by Quintin Hogg, Hugh Molson and Viscount Hinchingbroke, who lobbied for the party to accept the Beveridge Report and other wartime reforms, mainly unsuccessfully.

Ulster Unionists: evolved from within the broader ranks of Irish Unionists as support for the Irish Union shrank into Protestant areas only in the 1870s and 1880s; in full alliance with British Conservatives from 1880s until the 1970s, its MPs took the Conservative whip until 1972 and its Ulster Unionist Council was affiliated to the National Union until 1975, though never subject to the same rules as British constituency parties; the governing party in the devolved Northern Ireland parliament, 1920–72.

Unionist Business Committee: informal backbench group which sought in 1915–16 to press the Liberal and then Coalition government into a more active prosecution of the Great War; played a part, along with the even more active Unionist War Committee in bringing down Asquith in 1916, but less effective after Unionists allied with Lloyd George in office.

Unionist Social Reform Committee: a backbench group chaired by F. E. Smith, which sought in 1911–14 to rebut the charge that Conservatives had no social policies; had support from Central Office but never officially backed by the party's leaders; some of its thinking resurfaced in Conservative social policy in the 1920s and several of its members were by then ministers.

Wellington, 1st Duke of, Arthur Wellesley (1769–1852); younger son of 1st Earl of Mornington and brother of 1st Marquess Wellesley, Foreign Secretary, 1809–12; Anglo-Irish professional soldier, rising to Field

Marshal Duke after victories in India and in the Napoleonic Wars; in Cabinet under Liverpool, 1818–27, Prime Minister, 1828–30, and served in both of Peel's governments; the father of the 'the show must go on' school of Conservatism.

Woolton, Frederick Marquis, 1st Earl of (1883–1964): early career in large-scale retailing led to his involvement in government preparations for war in the 1930s, and to inclusion in Churchill's war coalition as Minister of Food and then of Reconstruction; joined the Conservative Party after defeat in 1945 and then became its inspirational Party Chairman, 1946–55; ill-health prevented him from playing a major governmental role after 1951.

'YMCA': nickname given in the 1924–9 parliament to a group of earnest, left-wing Conservative MPs, notably Harold Macmillan, Gerald Loder, Noel Skelton and Robert Boothby, whose collective book *Industry and the State* urged greater commitment to government intervention in the economy and in social policy.

Young Conservatives: the party's youth wing since 1945, and hence successor to the Junior Imperial League; a partially social organization sometimes derided as a marriage market, initially limited to members under thirty but extending the age limit when membership fell away in the 1960s and afterwards.

Young England: small group of MPs led by Disraeli and Lord John Manners which harassed Peel from the back benches in the 1841–6 parliament; its members romanticized a vanishing, rural and feudal Englishness, contrasted sharply with Peel's more commercial approach to policy and the party.

Younger, Sir George (1851–1929): brewer and local political activist in Scotland; MP from 1906; whip and from 1917 Party Chairman, negotiator of the 'coupon' deal of 1918 and one of the Conservative Party's rescuers from the Lloyd George coalition, 1922; subsequently Party Treasurer.

APPENDIX 6

The Conservative Party's Electoral Performance

Seats won by Conservatives in the parts of the United Kingdom since 1832

Year	England	Wales	Scotland	Ireland
1832	123/471	13/29	10/53	33/105
1835	205/471	17/29	15/53	38/105
1837	239/471	18/29	20/53	32/105
1841	284/471	19/29	22/53	43/105
1847*	247/469	19/29	19/53	42/105
1852*	251/467	18/29	20/53	42/105
1857	201/467	15/29	15/53	50/105
1859	220/467	15/29	15/53	57/105
1865	225/471	11/29	12/53	50/105
1868	223/463	8/30	8/60	40/105
1874	288/459	11/30	20/60	33/103
1880	203/459	2/30	7/60	26/103
1885	219/461	3/34	10/72	18/103
1886**	329/461	7/34	29/72	19/103
1892	268/461	3/34	22/72	23/103
1895	348/461	9/34	33/72	21/103
1900	337/461	6/34	38/72	21/103
1906	137/461	0/34	12/72	18/103
Jan. 1910	239/461	2/34	11/72	21/103
Dec. 1910	238/461	3/34	11/72	19/103
1918	321/492	4/36	31/73	23/101
1922	312/492	6/36	15/73	11/13
1923	227/492	4/36	16/73	10/13
1924	352/492	9/36	38/73	13/13
1929	226/492	1/36	22/73	11/13

Year	England	Wales	Scotland	Ireland
1931	402/492	6/36	50/73	11/13
1935***	355/492	10/36	45/73	11/13
1945	168/517	4/36	29/73	9/13
1950	253/506	4/36	31/71	10/12
1951	271/506	6/36	35/71	9/12
1955	293/511	6/36	36/71	10/12
1959	315/511	7/36	31/71	12/12
1964	262/511	6/36	24/71	12/12
1966	219/511	3/26	20/71	11/12
1970	294/511	7/36	23/71	8/12
Feb. 1974	269/515	8/37	21/71	0/12
Oct. 1974	253/515	8/37	16/71	0/12
1979	306/515	11/37	22/71	0/12
1983	362/523	14/38	21/72	0/17
1987	358/523	8/38	10/72	0/17
1992	319/523	6/38	11/72	0/17
1997	165/535	0/40	0/72	0/18

* includes Peelites
** includes Liberal Unionists in 1886 and all subsequent elections
***includes National Liberals in 1935 and all subsequent elections

Candidates and Votes since 1880

Year	Conservative Candidates	Cons. Mus Elected Unopposed	Total Number of Cons. Votes	Cons. % Share of Total Votes Cast
1880	458	58	881,566	44.8
1885	601	10	1,935,216	44.1
1886*	567	120	1,423,765	51.5
1892	600	39	2,056,737	47.3

Year	Conservative Candidates	Cons. Mus Elected Unopposed	Total Number of Cons. Votes	Cons. % Share of Total Votes Cast
1895	587	131	1,780,753	49.2
1900	579	163	1,797,444	51.1
1906	574	13	2,451,454	44.1
Jan. 1910	600	19	3,127,887	47.5
Dec. 1910	550	72	2,420,566	47.9
1918	382	41	4,144,192	38.4
1922	482	42	5,502,298	38.5
1923	536	35	5,514,541	38.0
1924	546	16	8,039,598	48.0
1929	590	4	8,656,225	38.1
1931	517	49	10,398,650	57.6
1935**	573	26	11,415,843	51.8
1945	555	1	9,972,010	39.6
1950	619	2	12,492,404	43.5
1951	617	4	13,718,199	48.0
1955	624	0	13,310,891	49.7
1959	625	0	13,750,875	49.3
1964	630	0	12,002,642	43.4
1966	629	0	11,418,455	41.9
1970	628	0	13,145,123	46.4
Feb. 1974	623	0	11,868,906	37.9
Oct. 1974	623	0	10,464,817	35.8
1979	622	0	13,697,690	43.9
1983	633	0	13,012,315	42.4
1987	633	0	13,763,066	43.4
1992	645	0	14,092,891	42.3
1997	649	0	9,600,943	30.7

* includes Liberal Unionists in 1886 and all subsequent elections
**includes National Liberals in 1935 and all subsequent elections

INDEX

Abrams, Mark 367
Abyssinia 107, 114, 116, 294
Aberdeen, Earl of 64, 77, 85, 90
Acland-Hood, Sir Alexander 180, 212, 213
Act of Union (1801) 36
Adam Smith Institute 425
Adams, R.J.Q. 11
Addison, Christopher 232
Admiralty 124, 170
advertising 356, 366–7
Advisory Committee on Policy 342, 348, 376, 390, 392, 408, 425, 525
Afghanistan 133
agriculture 33, 35, 51; Conservative voters 64; corn duty 194, 200–1; Disraeli's loan proposal 80, 84; and EEC 373, 480; Great Depression 134, 137, 175; Liberal policies 177; mechanization 87; Peel and 55; protectionism in 61, 64, 70; smallholdings 153; versus industry 70, 73; wage boards 219; *see also* Corn Laws
Aims of Industry 336
Aitken, Max 214
Akers-Douglas, Aretas 149, 167, 173, 179, 212, 525
Alabama 114
Allotments Act 171
Amery, Julian 332
Amery, Leo 212, 285, 287, 302, 312
Amory, Viscount, *see* Heathcoat Amory, D.
Anderson, Sir John 302
Anglican Church, *see* Church of England
Anglican Church of Ireland 36, 68, 91; Irish Church Act 102–4
Angry Silence, The (film) 376
Anne, Queen 18–19
Annual Register, the 42
Anti-Corn Law League 64, 69, 70
Anti-Jacobin Review, the 47
Anti-Maynooth Committee 69
Anti-Waste League 241
Appeasement 294, 295–7, 302–3, 325–6, 329
Arendt, Hannah 489
Argyll, Duke of 139

army: artillery 223; Bureau of Current Affairs 305; conscription 192, 224–5, 363–4, 382; officers' links with Unionism 218; reform 91, 104, 111, 184–5, 191
'Army of a Dream, The' (Kipling) 192
Arnold, Matthew 94
Arthur James Balfour (Dugdale) 9
Artisans' Dwelling Act (1875) 126–7, 164
Ashbourne, Lord 151
Ashley, Lord 52, 63–4, 66, 67, 113
Asquith, Herbert: Bonar Law on 217; and conscription 225; and Irish Home Rule 217–19, 226–7; and Lloyd George 239; ousted 231, 238; as Prime Minister 207, 519; wartime coalition of 230–1
Assheton, Ralph 310
Association of Conservative Clubs (ACC) 172–3
Association of Independent Peers 228
Atkins, Humphrey 417
Attlee, Clement: and BBC 346; in Churchill's coalition 302; government 322; leadership qualities 253; nationalization 346
Auden, W.H. 303

Bagehot, Walter 8, 85–6, 89, 99
Baldwin, Stanley 499, 525; and abdication crisis 290; anti-Baldwin right 268, 272–3, 276, 278–9; attitude to Labour 237, 256, 267, 272; background of 257; at Board of Trade 241; on Bonar Law 248; Burkeian influence 28; Cabinet of 265; Cabinet posts 250; Carlton Club speech 250; cartoons 252, 254–5, 266, 275; as champion of caring conservatism 271–2; and Churchill 252, 253, 276, 285, 298, 299; and coalitionism 244, 245, 270; on concessions to miners 437; on Conservatism 22; and Davidson 273; election defeats 262, 270; Englishness of 258, 260; as ex-Leader 423; foreign affairs 294, 295; and Great War 293; and ideology 492; image of 381; and India 268, 276, 277–8, 285, 287; and industrial relations 265, 267–8; as

Baldwin, Stanley – *cont.*
    leadership contender 249–50; legacy of 251;
    literature on 11; and MacDonald 283; as
    media performer 254–6, 267; and
    membership 259; national appeal 265, 270,
    284, 293; in National Government 281, 283,
    287, 291; New Conservatism of 5, 495; on
    1924 election 271; in opposition 260, 262,
    272, 276, 280, 383, 497; as Party Leader 250,
    270, 496, 497; as party man 5; personality of
    256, 258; as pipe-smoker 254–5; political
    motivation of 257–60; political style of
    251–3, 256; press and 273–5, 279; as Prime
    Minister 246, 250, 262, 265–8, 283, 287, 519;
    reputation of 305, 326–7; speeches of 253–4,
    256, 258; support crumbles 279; and tariffs
    262, 276–7, 281, 282; on Zinoviev letter 264
Baldwin and the Conservative Party (Ball) 11
Balfour, Arthur James 525; at Admiralty 230;
    aristocratic strain in 189; as backbencher
    249; on Baldwin 252, 253; biography 9; and
    Boer War 184; Cabinet of 198, 202–3;
    cartoons 165, 169, 204; and Central Office
    206; and Chamberlain 163, 178, 197, 201–2,
    206; Churchill on 183; as coalitionist 4,
    243; and constitutional crisis (1911) 4;
    defence policy 223; as ex-Leader 423, 474;
    foreign policy 191; Fourth Party member
    138; and Home Rule Bill 177; as Irish
    Secretary 167–70; as Leader of Commons
    168, 179, 180, 188, 194; and leadership
    contest 250; and Lords 206–7; loses seat
    205; nicknames 168; in opposition 206–7;
    and party organization 199, 212–13, 214; on
    Peel 50, 72; personality of 198–9; as Prime
    Minister 197–8, 200, 202–3, 519; on
    Randolph Churchill's resignation 167; re-
    elected 205–6; relation with MPs 67;
    resignation 204, 211–12, 214; in Salisbury
    Cabinet 164–5, 167–8, 179, 187; and
    Salisbury succession 188–9, 197; and tariff
    reform 200–1, 203, 206, 210, 490; Unionist
    leader 163; on Unionist merger 178;
    'Valentine compact' 206; on Wellington
    44; on Westminster model 4
Balfour, Gerald 181, 187, 198
Balkans 131
Ball, Stuart 11
Ballot Act (1872) 112
Banbury 48, 61
Bank Charter Act (1844) 64
Barber, Anthony 390, 393, 439
Barchester Towers (Trollope) 3
Bath clique 94, 95
BBC 254, 305, 312, 346, 460, 490
Beaconsfield, Earl of, *see* Disraeli, Benjamin

Beaverbrook, Lord 318; anti-Labour fantasies
    312; cartoons 263, 275; in Churchill's
    coalition 302; Macmillan on 342; personal
    vituperation of 304; as press lord 273–4, 279
Bell, Sir Tim 464
Beloff, Max 490
Bennett, Alan 326
Bentinck, Lord George Cavendish 492;
    attacks Peel 75, 78; biography 82; death 82;
    and Disraeli 81–3; as Leader of Commons
    74–5, 81–2; resignation 82
Beresford, Admiral Lord Charles 223
Beresford, William 68, 69, 74, 78, 88
Berlin, Congress of (1878) 132, 133
Bevan, Aneurin 344, 348
Beveridge, William 291
Beveridge Report (1942) 309–10
Bevin, Ernest 238
Beyond the Fringe 369
Biffen, John 436, 467
Bill of Rights 429, 430
Birkenhead, Earl of, *see* Smith, F.E.
Birmingham 163, 176, 339, 446
Blackwood's Magazine 27, 51
Blair, Tony 452, 466, 474, 495
Blake, Robert 9, 10–11, 124, 424
Blakenham, Lord 391
Blunt, W.S. 144
Boer War (1899–1902) 150, 183–6, 190–1,
    193, 194, 222
Bolingbroke, Viscount 23
Bonham, F.R. 60, 61, 78
Booth, Charles 192
Boothby, Robert 261, 272, 302
Bow Group 342, 526
Bowles, John 26
Boy Scouts 192, 224
Boyle, Edward 372, 403, 404
Boyson, Dr Rhodes 16
Bracken, Brendan 302, 318, 321
Bradlaugh, Charles 140
brewers 111–12, 229
Bridgeman, William 215, 221, 226, 229
Bright, John 91
Bristol 51
British Commonwealth 278, 362, 365, 373
British Empire 133; Africa 170, 372; Boer War
    and 190–1, 194; decolonization 357, 372;
    Disraeli on 116–17; imperial preference
    scheme 200, 275, 276, 283; independence
    movements 331; India 200, 241, 277–9;
    Ireland and 228; trading arrangements
    193–4; transition to Commonwealth 278;
    see also imperialism
British Housewives' League 347
British Movietone News 255

INDEX   545

British Political Parties (McKenzie) 10
British Telecom 447
British Union of Fascists 290
British United Industrialists 336
Brittan, Leon 440, 466
Brittan, Samuel 4
broadcasting 498; Central Office department 336; competition in 345, 346; political balance 411; radio 254, 312; television 356, 359, 365, 367, 369, 381, 460
Brodrick, St John 198
Brooke, Henry 261, 306, 369
Brooks's Club 32, 163
Bruges Group 480
Buchan, John 261
Buchan-Hepburn, Patrick 318
Buchanan report 371, 374
Buckinghamshire 62, 103
Buckinghamshire Herald, the 64
Buckle, G.E. 9, 51
Budget Protest League 208
budgets: Chamberlain's 288; Disraeli's (1852) 84–5; Gladstone's 87; Heathcoat Amory's (1959) 366; Howe's (1981–2) 439, 446; Lloyd George's 'people's budget' (1909) 207–10; Peel's (1842) 66; Ritchie's (1903) 201; Wood's (1941) 304
Bulgaria 131
Burghley House 114
Burke, Edmond 14, 16, 23–9, 33, 48
Bush, George 458
Butler, R.A. 52, 351, 526; as acting Prime Minister 329; as Appeaser 329; Baldwin's influence on 251; at Board of Education 301–2; Butskellism 343; and caring conservatism 272; cartoon 307; chairs PWPCC 306; as Chancellor 329, 343, 352; and Churchill's centrism 3; on Douglas-Home 380; on 'dries' 442; Education Act (1944) 306, 357; and EEC 373; failing powers 369; and *Industrial Charter* 321, 322, 324, 495; as leadership contender 329–30; and Lib-Con pact 319; on Macmillan 361, 370; in Macmillan's Cabinet 372; and Macmillan succession 376–7, 378–80; on Peel 51, 379–80; on Pitt 31; policy work of 306, 308, 311, 318, 321, 322, 342, 345; on postwar Conservatism 335; retirement 383; and Suez 333, 334; on Thatcher 432
by-elections 74, 179; (1845) 69; (1848–9) 80; (1872–3) 115; (1874–80) 131, 135; (1886–92) 172; (1895–1900) 185; (1900–5) 197; (1903–4) 203–4; (1907–8) 207; (1911–14) 220, 237; (1921–2) 241, 243; (1923) 249; (1927–9) 270; (1930) 274; (1931 St George's) 279–80; (1933–4) 290;

(1935–9) 291; (1942–5) 311; (1946–50) 351; (1958, Rochdale) 365; (1960) 367; (1962, Orpington) 382; (1973) 411; (1978 North Ilford) 426–7; (1985–97) 455; (1989, Richmond) 494; (1990, Eastbourne) 469; (1992–7) 475, 478, 486
Byron, Lord 32–3

Cairns, 1st Earl 102, 103, 134, 526
Callaghan, James 427–8, 429, 435
Campaign Guide/Notes 152
Campbell-Bannerman, Sir Henry 207
Canada 67, 193
Canning, George 526; Burkeian influence 27; death 38, 53; defends electoral system 27; at Foreign Office 34; influences Liverpool 35; as Prime Minister 37; as 'Tory' 32; unpopularity 37–8; on victory over revolutionaries 35
Canningites 38–9, 40, 42, 53, 57
capitalism: defence of 345–6; industrialists 109–10, 173, 336–7; share-ownership 447; unacceptable face of 408
Cardwell, Edward 77
Carlisle, Mark 439
Carlton Club 76, 88, 172, 526; founded 47; Liberal Unionists and 162–3, 215; as party headquarters 60; Peelite resignations 85; 1922 meeting at 244–5, 250
Carlton Club, The (Petrie) 9
Carnarvon, Lord: in Bath clique 95; and Churchill 150, 164; as Colonial Secretary 122; in Derby ministry 93; as Lord Lieutenant of Ireland 151; resignation 132, 155; as Salisbury's acolyte 117, 122
Caroline, Queen 33
Carr, Robert 251, 340, 423
Carrington, Lord 390, 417, 436
Carson, Sir Edward 214, 229, 231
Case for Conservatism, The (Hogg) 342, 491
Castlereagh, Lord 34
Catholic League 40
Catholicism 17–18, 36–8, 40–1, 103
Cato Street conspiracy 33
Cecil, Lady Gwendolyn 9, 146
Cecil, Lord Hugh 187, 203, 215
Cecil, Lord Robert 187, 203
Central Agricultural Protection Society (CAPS) 74
Central Office 47, 119, 171, 173, 527; and Baldwin's unpopularity 279; expansion of 213; inadequacies of 213; mortgaging of 464; National Union and 143, 206; Party Chairman and 213; premises 336; publications 152, 173, 178; Salisbury and 174; Thatcher and 464; under Woolton 336

Central Policy Review Staff 393
Centre for Policy Studies 414, 425, 526
Chamberlain, Sir Austen 206, 527; as backbencher 249; background of 257; on Baldwin 252; and Balfour 203; biography of 9; and Bonar Law government 248; as Chancellor 202; as coalitionist 242–3, 244; Eden and 328; as ex-Leader 423; at Foreign Office 265; as leadership contender 214, 215; on Lib-Lab pact 197, 209; Party and 3; as Party Leader 242–4; rejoins Conservative ranks 262; resignation 244; as social reformer 265
Chamberlain, Joseph 176, 527; ally of Randolph Churchill 161, 166–7; and Balfour 163, 178, 197, 201–3, 206; cartoon 154; as Colonial Secretary 179, 183–4, 187, 193, 197, 201; combativeness 186; Conservative attitude to 178, 205; crosses floor 109, 156, 159, 495; on election losses 174; and Home Rule Bill 177; ill-health 206; imperialism of 179, 201; as mayor of Birmingham 126, 127; and press 184; radicalism 139, 163, 189; re-election 205; refuses Premiership 160; reputation of 242; resignation 202; and Salisbury succession 188; and social legislation 171, 178, 194, 207, 228; and South Africa 184, 186; and tariff reform 182, 193–4, 197–8, 202–3, 206; and trades unions 196; as Unionist 163–4, 169, 171, 176, 186; 'Valentine compact' 206; Winston Churchill on 183
Chamberlain, Neville 527; Appeasement 294, 295–7, 326, 459; attitude to Labour 298; background 257; and Baldwin 251, 253, 257; biography 326; in Bonar Law Cabinet 249; as Chancellor 260, 283, 288; character-assassination of 302; and Churchill 268, 299, 326; at CRD 280, 288; death 299, 301; as Deputy Prime Minister 299; as ex-Leader 423; fall of 292, 298–9; foreign policy 294–7; heads National Government 291; as leader in waiting 273; as Minister for Health 260; as Party Chairman 273; as Party Leader 300; and policy formation 260–1; as pragmatist 52; as Prime Minister 291, 519; reputation of 302–5, 326–7; as social reformer 261, 265, 288, 305; and tariff reform 283; in wartime 297–9
Chandos, Viscount 45–6
Charles I 16
Charles II 16, 17, 39
Charles Street gang 47
'Charter' group 463
Chartism 49, 65, 87, 89
Chelmer, Lord 463

Cheshire 233
Christchurch 63
Church of England: and Catholic emancipation 36; Conservative voters in 63; Disraeli and 115, 125, 132; growth of 51; in Lords 43; on social violence 453–4; and state 31; Tories and 16, 17, 20, 21–2, 23, 31, 454
Churchill, Lord Randolph 124, 402, 527; biography of 9, 144; cartoons 154, 157; as Chancellor 164–6; Dartford programme 166; death 166; and Disraeli 101, 140; failing health 166, 167; and Irish question 150–1, 155–6; leader of Fourth Party 138; as Leader of House 164; mental instability 166; and National Union 142–3; and Northcote 138, 140, 150; opportunism of 144; paternalism of 349; personal political agenda of 166; premiership campaign 166; resignation 166–7; and Salisbury 138–9, 143, 161, 166; as Secretary for India 150–1; as social reformer 166, 219, 228; and Tory Democracy 138, 144–5, 163, 495; and Toryism 14; and Whigs 139, 155, 156
Churchill, Randolph 332
Churchill, Sir Winston 12, 528; in abdication debate 290; absence from Commons 317, 328; at Admiralty 223, 230; as anti-socialist 264, 300, 318; anti-working class 299; and Appeasement 294, 325–6; and Baldwin 252, 253, 276, 279, 285, 298, 299; and BBC 346; and Beveridge Report 309; biography of father 9, 144; on Britain's international role 373; Cabinets 301–2, 320; campaigning (1945) 312–15; caretaker government 311; cartoons 286, 300; centrism of 3, 317, 318–20; as Chancellor 265; Conservative Party under 310–11; defection to Liberals 3, 9, 203, 205, 231; de-selection attempt 290; distrusted 285, 295; and Eden 328, 331; election defeat (1945) 315–16; and Europe 480; failing health 329; fixation with war 293; foreign policy 316, 331; on Gandhi 279; and General Strike 267; and housing 349; imperialism of 117; and India 285–6, 327; 'iron curtain' speech 316; on Joseph Chamberlain 183; Liberal alliance proposals 318–20, 351; loses seat 207; national credentials of 300, 313, 314; nationalism of 4; and Neville Chamberlain 268, 295, 296, 299; in Opposition 317–18, 320, 327–8, 490; partisanship of 5; as Party Leader 293–4, 301, 313, 315–17, 325, 327–9, 497, 498, 499; on party name 7, 317; patronage of 301, 318, 360; and policy-making 307–8, 320, 324, 343; post-war team of 302; as Prime Minister 298–300, 320, 351, 520;

rejoins Conservatives 262, 495; resigns from front bench 279; returns to office 297–8; rising reputation of 297; and Royalist ancestor 17; self-justification 325; speeches 254; as statesman 316, 327; succeeds Chamberlain 299; and Suez 331–2; and tariff reform 277; Toryism of 301; and trades unions 376; and Ulster 227, 236; Unionist antagonism towards 231; *War Memoirs* 299, 325, 331; wartime coalition of 3, 5, 300, 302, 308, 311; and Woolton 335
cinema 255
cities 31, 46, 63, 148, 487, 489
Citizen's Charter 472
civil service 91, 111
Clarke, Edward 105
Clarke, Kenneth 469, 479
class: changes in 451–2; electoral alignments 353–4, 356–8, 454; and party identity 498; *see also* middle class; working class
clubs 30–1, 32, 47–8, 61, 110, 172–3
Coal Board 437
Cobden, Richard 64, 70, 87
Cobdenites 74
Cold War 331, 363, 428, 458
Coleridge, Samuel Taylor 27
Colville, Jock 313
Committee of Imperial Defence 223
Communists 240, 263–4, 289, 376, 410, 411, 458
Confederacy 528
Conference 317, 521–4; first (1867) 106; second (1868) 119; sixth (1872) 116; (1883/84) 142; (1887) 174; (1894) 178; (1911, Leeds) 212, 214, 215; (1917) 221; (1923) 262; (1928) 259; (1934) 287; (1946) 320; (1947) 323, 343; (1950) 348; (1956) 333; (1963) 376–8; (1981) 442; (1982) 445; (1989) 449; under Baldwin 253; democratization of 463; manipulation of 430; tariff reform motions 202
Congested Districts Act (1890) 170
Congress Party (India) 277
Coningsby (Disraeli) 65, 69
Conservatism 14, 15, 49; aristocratic image of 356, 380, 497; caring 272; Churchill's 301; consumerism 346–7, 351; Disraelian 56, 117, 301; free markets 347; freedom rhetoric of 310, 344, 347–8, 351, 360, 364; and ideology 491–2; intellectual dimension 27, 342, 493; Leader's rhetoric on 497–8; loyalty in 2, 51, 365, 379, 417, 423, 441; and modernization 374–6; 394, 395; 1990s 477; outdatedness 369, 380, 385; paternalism in 164, 293, 349; Peelite 52, 55–6, 63; post-war 335; pragmatism of 491, 493; and 'sleaze' 465, 476–7; unity 2, 60, 490, 493;

Victorian values 54–5; working class 357
Conservative Action for Electoral Reform 429, 528
Conservative Board of Finance 336
Conservative Club 172
Conservative Local Government Conference 389
Conservative Party: adoption of name 48–9, 56, 81; decline 461–6; defections from 3, 57, 486, 490–1; defections to 490, 495; democratization 463, 484; dominance 7–8, 148, 180, 353, 367; formation of 13–16; histories of 9–11; identity of, *see* Conservatism; lack of constitution 14; longevity of 8, 45, 50; make-up of 29; as natural party of Government 8; patriotism of 4; recovery 246; relationship with monarchy 29; reunited 262; roots of 14–16, 22; split 51, 62, 77, 80, 309; survival of 50–2, 57; and Tories 13–18, 28–30; *see also* Toryism; Unionist Party
Conservative Party from Peel to Churchill, The (Blake) 11
Conservative Philosophy Group 425
Conservative Political Centre (CPC) 342, 434, 499, 528
Conservative Research Department 324, 528; Chairmen 516; Chamberlain and 261, 280, 288; Directors 516; Heath and 390; and housing policy 348; merged with Central Office 425; publications 342; re-created (1946) 321, 341–2; reduced influence of 306, 425; set up 261
Conservative 2000 476
Conspiracy and Protection of Property Act 127
constituencies: associations 47–8, 121, 149, 172, 259; boundary changes 233, 234, 235–6, 237, 339, 351, 463; candidates and 60, 61, 120, 213, 463–4; candidates' rules 339–40; and leadership elections 463–4; marginal 355, 453, 473, 487; party organization in 47–8, 60–1, 172, 338–9; single-member 148; size of 86–7; redistribution 145–9; uncontested 61, 89, 174, 186; university 234; urban 46, 63
constitution 32, 115–16, 429
Constitutional Club 172
Constitutional Year Book, the 152
Contarini Fleming (Disraeli) 9
Cooper, Alfred Duff 272, 284, 294, 295, 302, 528
Corn Laws 50, 67, 69; abandonment of 80; changes in 35, 66; defence organizations 74; party splits over 77, 79; passed 33; repealed 1, 3, 69–76, 79, 84

Corn Laws and Social England, The (Fay) 69
Corrupt Practices Act (1883) 143
Corry, Monty 105, 108, 136
Council on Prices and Incomes 375
Cranborne, Lord, *see* Salisbury, Marquess of
Cranbrook, Lord, *see* Gathorne, Hardy
Crawford, Lord 225
Crawley, Aidan 490
Crimean War (1854–5) 90, 131
Crimes Bill 168
Crisis of Conservatism, 1880–1914, The (Green) 11
Critchley, Julian 441
Croker, John Wilson 27, 34, 66; on Canning 37; on Conservative party 48, 49; on Peel 62, 73; on political parties 32, 60; on Tory peers 43; and Wellington 44, 46
Crosland, Anthony 393
Cross, Richard 150, 164, 179, 187; at Home Office 122, 124; social reforms 125, 126–8, 137
Cruickshank, Harry 361
Crystal Palace rallies 106, 115, 116–17
Culture and Anarchy (Arnold) 94
Cumberland, Duke of 59
Cunliffe-Lister, Sir Philip 529
Curzon, Lord 149, 212, 529; on Baldwin 252; on Balfour 198–9; deserts coalition 244, 245; in India 200; as Leader in Lords 228; as leadership contender 249, 250; on MacDonald 264; personality of 249; wartime standing of 229–30
Cyprus 132, 331
Czechoslovakia 295, 297

Daily Express, the 240, 273–4, 279, 303, 304, 312, 342, 360
Daily Mail, the 184, 193, 222, 240, 263–4, 273–4, 279, 303, 304, 369
Daily Mirror, the 303, 304, 452
Daily Telegraph, the 207, 274, 332, 394, 401, 421
Darwin, Charles 191
Davidson, J.C.C. 245, 255, 273, 390, 529
Davidson, Lady 358
Davies, Clement 320
Davies, John 399–400
Deedes, William 251, 341, 371
defence policy: Heath's 387; inter-war 295; Labour policy 456; nuclear weapons 363, 428; post-war 330; Pre-Great War 223–4; Salisbury's 170; unilateralism 456, 458
Delors, Jacques 459
democracy 147, 234, 258, 284; party 463, 484; *see also* Tory Democracy
Democracy and the Organisation of Political Parties (Ostrogorski) 172

De Quincey, Thomas 27
Derby, 14th Earl (Edward Stanley) 529; architect of Conservative recovery 76; constituency of 55, 58; and Corn Laws 70, 72–3; death 110; defection to Conservatives 57–8, 495; 'Derby Dilly' 57; Disraeli and 17, 83, 86, 95, 99; opposes Peel 72–3, 74; as Party Leader 1, 73, 75, 86, 89; in Peel's Cabinet 64; as Prime Minister 1, 84, 90–1, 93–4, 518; protectionist leader 77–80, 83; refuses office 73–4, 90; resignation 1, 57, 85, 99; Second Reform Bill of 93, 94–5, 97–8; visits provinces 108; as Whig minister 42
Derby, Edward Stanley, 15th Earl 91, 94, 110; on Churchill 166; and Disraeli 117; at Foreign Office 122, 130; as Liberal 137; on liquor 111; refuses leadership 114; as reluctant Conservative 103, 130–1; resignation 132; on social programme 113
Derby, Edward Stanley, 16th Earl 202, 210, 215, 216, 244
Devonshire, 8th Duke of (Marquess of Hartington) 529; cartoon 159; Liberal Unionist leader 160, 162, 163, 201; refuses Premiership 160, 167; and Salisbury Cabinet 178; and tariff reform 203; Whip in Lords 163; Whig Leader 128, 139, 155
Dicey, A.V. 158
Diehard 530
Dilke, Sir Charles 183
Disestablishment Bill (1869) 104
Disraeli, Benjamin (Earl of Beaconsfield) 91, 495, 530; appetite for power 83; architect of Conservative recovery 76, 101; on Ballot Act 112; and Bath clique 94; and Bentinck 81–3; biographies 9, 10, 51; and Burke 26, 27–8; Cabinets 102, 122–4; in Carlton Club 47; cartoons 96, 118, 123, 141; as Chancellor 84, 94; and Church of England 115, 125, 132; Conservatism of 56, 117; death 130, 138, 140; as democrat 140; and Derby 84, 86, 91, 95; distrusted 78, 102; economic policy 135; election campaigning 136–7; and electoral reform 234; elevation to Lords 128, 131, 138; emergence of 81; exoticism of 166; failing health of 128, 133, 138; foreign policy 114, 116, 128, 130, 131–2, 459; and Gladstone 85, 102, 105, 113, 114, 116; imperialism 107, 116–17; inheritance of 5; and Irish matters 103–4, 110, 125; as landowner 82–3; as Leader of Commons 82, 84, 94; Liberal support for 95; on Liverpool 33; myth of 140; as national statesman 101; and Northcote 140; as novelist 9, 65, 69, 111; obituary 99; on 'one

nation' 98; in opposition 89, 104–5, 110–12, 114; and Palmerston 83, 116; on party 2, 3; as Party Leader 99–100, 110–11, 114, 117, 138, 215, 495; on party name 48; at party rallies 107, 108, 115; and Peel 3, 38, 53, 64, 67, 69, 74, 75, 78; on Pitt 31; popularity of 115; as Prime Minister 99–100, 101–2, 122, 125, 130–3, 518; and protectionism 80, 174; resignation 104; revolt against 114; and Salisbury 104, 122, 140, 146; and Second Reform Act 92, 94–7, 99; as social reformer 113, 125–8, 140, 219; on Stanley 17; success of 85–6; and Whigs 139; and working class vote 498; and Young England 65

Disraeli (Blake) 10, 124

Ditchers 530

domestic policy, *see* social policy

Don Pacifico crisis 107

Douglas-Home, Sir Alec (Lord Home) 530; cartoons 379, 381; committees led by 419, 430; as ex-Leader 423, 474; at Foreign Office 369; government of 374; and Heath 388, 394, 419; leadership contender 245, 330, 418; in Macmillan's Cabinet 372; and Macmillan succession 376, 378–9; at Munich 295; in opposition 383, 497; as Party Leader 497, 498; popularity of 380, 471; as Prime Minister 380, 520; resignation 383

Dublin 177

Du Cann, Edward 121, 390, 408, 419, 420, 424

Dugdale, Blanche 9

Dyer, General 278

Eccles, David 321, 324

Ecclesiastical Causes Act 54

economic policy: competition 347; ERM 479; free enterprise 345, 346, 399; free trade 35, 70, 87, 201–3; incomes policy 397–8, 435, 437, 438; Keynesian 277, 304, 343, 358, 360, 361, 366, 407, 432, 434; Major's 479; monetarism 365, 414, 421, 432; public expenditure 183, 240–1, 280, 288, 352, 364, 365–6, 437, 438, 443, 472; rightwards shift in 433–4; split over 399; wage and price controls 409–10

Economic Policy Group 397

Economist, The 85, 99, 158, 315, 343

economy: Boer War and 185, 194; decline in 193; under Douglas-Home 382; financial crisis (1931) 280–1;
in Great Depression (1875–8) 134–5; inflation 361, 364, 365–6, 396–8, 407, 409, 414, 438–9; under Labour 427; under Macmillan 364–6, 375; mixed 322, 345, 346; oil exports 439; post-war austerity 326, 338, 346–7; recession 277, 382, 439, 472; upturn in 289; *see also* economic policy

Eden, Sir Anthony 499, 530; attacks on 332–3; Cabinet of 198; and caring conservatism 272; and Churchill 316, 328, 331; as Deputy Leader 328–9; as ex-Leader 423; foreign policy 330–1; as Foreign Secretary 331; and *The Industrial Charter* 323; and nationalization 345; as Party Leader 498; paternalism of 293; and post-war policy 308; as Prime Minister 332–3, 520; resignations 294, 295, 329, 330, 334; return to office 297; serves under Churchill 302; and Suez 331, 333–4

Edinburgh 49, 108

Edinburgh Review, the 27

education: 'Balfour' Act 194–5; 'Butler' Act 306; Disraeli's reforms 127; extended provision 171, 374; free milk 288; Gladstone's reforms 91, 111; reform bill withdrawn 182; Robbins report 371; Thatcher and 460; university reforms 111, 115

Education Act: (1870) 127; (1902) 194–5; (1944) 306, 357

Edward VII, King 210

Edward VIII, King 290

Eisenhower, Dwight D. 362

elections: campaigning 54, 234–5, 259, 312, 338, 355, 436, 464; canvassing 120, 144, 259, 462; class alignments 353–4, 356–7; electioneering 173; electoral volatility 357; geographical voting trends 453–4; *see also* by-elections; general elections; local government: elections

electoral system: birth of 233; electoral management 147; first-past-the-post 6–7; mass electorate 234; postal votes 339, 351; proportional representation 320, 429–30, 491, 494; reform 36, 38, 41–6, 92, 97–8, 112, 130, 143, 145–9, 232–7; registration 60–1, 78, 88–9, 102, 120, 147, 220; secret ballot 112; tactical voting 473, 487, 494

Egypt 331–4

Elizabeth I, Queen 23

Elizabeth II, Queen 379

Elliot, Walter 488

Emerson, Ralph Waldo 8

Employer and Workmen Act 127

English Civil War 16, 17

English Constitution, The (Bagehot) 8

Ensor, Robert 156

Europe 180, 479–80; Churchill and 480; Disraeli on 114; EEC 274, 332, 402, 408, 480–1; Eurosceptic MPs 475; Heath and 372, 387, 392, 402; Macmillan and 362–3,

Europe – *cont.*
372–4; Major and 471, 474, 481–2, 484; Thatcher and 443, 444, 458, 480–1
European Exchange Rate Mechanism (ERM) 479
European Free Trade Area 363, 372
European Parliament elections 429, 455
Evening Standard, the 49, 120, 121, 420, 483
Exclusion Crisis (1679–81) 17

Factory Acts 52, 99, 124
factory reform 66, 67–8, 69, 124, 288
Fair Deal at Work (1968) 396
Falkland, Viscount 16, 17
Falklands War 108, 332, 421, 444–6
Falmouth, Lord 41
Faraday, Michael 27
Fashoda affair 183, 184
Fay, C.R. 69
Feiling, Sir Keith 9, 13
Fielding, Henry 20
Filmer, Robert 23
Finer, Professor Samuel 367
Fisher, Nigel 2
Fitzgerald, Vesey 40
Foot, Michael 304, 448, 456
foreign policy: Balfour's 191; Churchill's 331; Disraeli's 130–3; Gladstone and 113–14; Macmillan's 362–3; pre-war 294–5; right-wing split in 332; Salisbury's 170, 180, 183–4, 191; social imperialism 107; Thatcher;s 443–5
Fortnightly Review 109
Forty Years On (Bennett) 326
Fourth Party 138, 140, 142, 530
Fourth Party, The (Gorst) 144
Fowler, Norman 467
Fox, Charles James 30, 109, 163
France: EEC veto 373–4; entente (1904) 191, 192, 204; Fashoda affair 183; Revolution 14, 24, 29, 31, 32; and Suez 333, 334; wars against 29, 30, 32, 33
Franchise Bill (1884) 147, 232, 235
Franco, General Francisco 294
Franco-Prussian war 114
Fraser, Michael 322, 373
Fraser's Magazine 27
Free Food League 202
Freedom Association 425
Fremantle, Sir Thomas 59–60, 88
Frere, John Hookham 56
Friedman, Milton 432
Future of Socialism, The (Crosland) 393

Gaitskell, Hugh 333, 343
Gandhi, Mahatma 277, 278, 279
Garel-Jones, Tristan 481
Garvin, J.L. 188
Gascoigne, General 45
Gash, Norman 10, 24, 38
Gathorne, Hardy (Lord Cranbrook) 93, 103, 110, 124, 149, 164, 531
Gaumont British News 258
general elections 540–2; (1807) 32; (1830) 41–2; (1831) 43, 46; (1832) 46, 47, 58; (1835) 53, 56, 57, 61; (1837) 61–2; (1841) 62, 64; (1847) 62, 78–9; (1852) 84; (1857) 89; (1859) 89; (1865) 89; (1868) 101, 104, 106, 108–10; (1874) 101, 113, 119, 121–2; (1880) 130, 133, 134, 135–7; (1885) 130, 152–3, 156; (1886) 130, 158–60; (1892) 172, 174–6; (1895) 179–80, 185; (1900) 180, 185, 186, 190; (1906) 205, 487, 488; (1910) 208, 209, 210, 489; (1918) 233, 236, 239–40; (1922) 245–6, 248; (1923) 253, 262, 271; (1924) 260, 263, 264, 271; (1929) 264, 269, 270, 271, 278; (1931) 281–2; (1935) 284–5, 287, 291; (1945) 292, 311–12, 315, 488; (1950) 319, 351, 489; (1951) 319, 327, 351; (1955) 352, 354; (1959) 358, 367, 432, 436; (1964) 370, 380, 382–3, 391; (1966) 385, 391, 394; (1970) 400–1, 405, 436; (1974) 405, 411–13, 414, 415, 417, 431; (1979) 428, 430–1, 436, 473; (1983) 446, 448; (1987) 449, 453; (1992) 457, 462, 472–3; (1997) 462, 464, 482–4, 486–90
General Strike (1926) 5, 257, 265, 266–8, 437
George I, King 19, 21
George II, King 19, 21
George III, King 20, 23, 28–9
George IV, King 29, 33, 36, 37, 38, 41, 99
George V, King 210, 218
Germany 132; anti-Germanism 222–3; Appeasement 294, 295, 302–3; deteriorating relations 192; industrial rivalry 193; navy 183, 222; Nazi 294; rapprochement 191; rise of 114; threat of 193, 207; unification (1871) 170; World War I 222
Gilbert, W.S. 5, 124
Gillray, James 30
Gilmour, Ian 3, 417, 435, 439, 477, 492
Gladstone, William 68; at Board of Trade 70; Bulgarian campaign 128, 131; and Carlton Club 76, 85; cartoon 154; censure motion 150; as Chancellor 66; and Corn Laws 70; death 162; defection to Liberalism 57; and Disraeli 85, 102, 105, 113, 114; dissolution of parliament (1874) 119; election campaigning 136; foreign policy 113–14; imperial policy 116; Ireland policy 101, 102–4, 115, 117, 121, 133, 142, 156–9, 162, 172, 174–7; intellect of 86; legislative

INDEX

programme 102–5, 111–12, 121, 145–7; Liberal leader in Commons 92; loss of office 93; Midlothian campaigns 128, 135, 253; Northcote and 125; and Peel 52, 58–9, 66; in Peel's Cabinet 64; as Peelite 77; as Prime Minister 108, 116, 137, 176–8; radicalism 87, 139; reappearance of 130, 131–2; resignation 117, 150; retirement 128, 162; rise of 91; royal prerogative used by 104–5; and Second Reform Bill 92, 93; unpopularity of 115
Glasgow 115, 186
Globe, the 120
Gloucester 47
Goderich, 1st Viscount (Frederick Robinson, Lord Ripon) 530; as Chancellor 34–5; in Peel's Cabinet 57, 64; as Prime Minister 38; in Whig ministry 42
Gorbachev, Mikhail 458
Gordon, General 133, 150
Gorst, Harold 144
Gorst, Sir John 530; as borough organizer 105; member of Fourth Party 138; on party leadership 142; as Principal Agent 119–20, 137, 138, 149; replaced 136, 145
Goschen, G.J. 167
Gould, Joseph 120
Government of India Act (1935) 251, 285
Government of Ireland Act (1920) 227
Government of National Unity 3
Graham, Sir James 57, 58; economic policy 70; on party unity 60; as Peelite 77; resigns from Carlton Club 76
Granby, Marquess of 82
Great Contemporaries (Churchill) 183
Greater London Council 448, 458
Green, Ewen 11
Greville, Charles 58
Grenvillites 32
Grey, Earl 38, 41–3
Guardian, the 476
Guilty Men 302–3, 326

Hague, William 388, 484, 494, 499
Hailsham, Lord (Quintin Hogg) 531; and Bill of Rights 429, 430; CPC lecture 499–500; and leadership contests 330, 378, 383; Oxford by-election 294; as Party Chairman 121, 366, 390; as principled liberal 403; writings 303, 342, 491–2
Halifax, 1st Earl 299, 301, 531
Halsbury, Lord 195, 196
Halsbury Club 212
Hamilton, Lord George 109, 119, 127, 170, 223
Hanover, House of 19–20
Hansard Society 429

Harrison, Frederick 113
Hartington, Marquess of, *see* Devonshire
Hastings, Max 483
Hastings, Warren 25
Hayek, Friedrich von 310, 432
Hazlitt, William 27
Healey, Denis 428
health provision 291, 308, 344
Heath, Sir Edward 531; as administrator 386, 393–4; anti-political manner of 389; attends Conference 463; background of 341, 384, 386–7, 388; begins political career 294, 387; at Board of Trade 380–1; cartoons 386, 412, 415, 422; consumer measures of 374, 381; defence policy 387; duels with Wilson 4, 385; economic policy 396–400, 406, 409, 414; and Europe 372, 387, 392, 402; as ex-Leader 423, 474; at Foreign Office 372; founder of One Nation Group 340; front bench team of 390, 414, 417–18; and immigration 405–6; leadership contests 383, 388, 418–22; and Macmillan 359, 372, 387; and miners' strikes 407, 410–11; as Minister of Labour 376; mutinous rumblings against 3, 418–19; national unity approach of 3, 403, 414–16, 418, 429, 494; and Northern Ireland 403; in opposition 385–99, 414; as Party Leader 385, 388, 390, 417–19, 496, 497; patronage of 390; and policy review 390–3; policy U-turns 402–3, 406–9, 442; political career 387–8; political ideas 387; as Prime Minister 399, 401, 520; relation with MPs 67, 388–9, 400, 406, 408–9, 418, 420; and RPM 374, 381, 388; speeches 389; and Thatcher 423, 474; and working-class vote 357
Heathcote Amory, Derick (Viscount Amory) 324, 365, 366, 369, 395
Herries, J.C. 82, 84
Heseltine, Michael 436, 440, 466–7, 468–71
Hicks-Beach, Sir Michael 531; as Chancellor 194; in Disraeli Cabinet 124; at Irish Office 164, 167, 168; as party organizer 148; retirement 197
Hill, R.L. 9
Hints for Candidates 121
History of the Great Rebellion, The (Clarendon) 42
History of the Tory Party, The (Feiling) 9, 13
History of the Tory Party (Woods) 9
Hitler, Adolf 289, 294–7
H.M.S. Pinafore (Gilbert) 124
Hoare, Sir Samuel 223, 249, 285, 301
Hobbes, Thomas 23
Hodgkinson (Liberal MP) 96–7
Hogg, Quintin, *see* Hailsham, Lord

Home, Lord, see Douglas-Home, Sir Alec
Home Rule Party 181, 137
Hooker, Bishop Richard 23
House of Commons: Chief Whips 513; confrontational style of 215–16; Conservative domination of 8; family factions in 32; independent MPs 32, 60; management of business 32; Party Leaders 512–13; social background of MPs 477
House of Lords: attempt to restore powers of 268; Balfour and 4; Chief Whips 513; commercial men in 173; confrontational style of 216; Conservative strength in 8, 43–4, 51, 78; constitutional crisis over 4, 207, 208–9; Disraeli's defence of 115; and Gladstone and 104, 137, 176–8; and Home Rule Bill 176–7, 208; Labour absence from 249; and monarchy 32; Party Leaders 511–12; power of veto of 142, 209, 211; Prime Ministers in 249; reconstruction of 209, 241; and Reform Bill 43; Salisbury Doctrine 142; threat of extinction 105; and trades union litigation 196; Unionists in 176, 177, 205, 206–7; vote down 'people's budget' 208
housing: boom 289, 348–9, 351; 382; council house sales 393, 446–7, 451; finance 402; home-ownership 289, 349; housing estates 349, 353; Macmillan and 349, 350; New Towns 357, 358; slum clearance 288; working-class 126–7; 164
Housing of the Working Classes Act (1890) 164
Howarth, Alan 486
Howe, Sir Geoffrey 531; as Chancellor 436, 437, 439; as leadership contender 422; as monetarist 434; resignation 468, 469, 481; as shadow chancellor 425
Howell, David 394, 436
Hughenden Manor 82
Hughes, Percival 212
Hunt, Ward 102
Hurd, Douglas 51, 389, 407, 470, 482
Huskisson, William 34–5, 39
Hyde, Edward 16, 17
Hyde Park riots 94

I'm All Right, Jack (film) 376
Iddesleigh, Earl of, see Northcote, Sir S.
immigration 193, 357, 364, 403–6, 426
Imperial Airways 321–2
Imperial Economic Conference (1932) 282
imperialism 4, 130, 132; Boer War and 190–1; Chamberlain's 183, 201; Disraeli's 116–17; Ireland and 158; patriotic 108; Salisbury's 170; social 107; and World War I 229–30

Importance of Being Earnest, The (Wilde) 162
India 91, 116, 131; Amritsar massacre 277; Baldwin and 268, 276, 277–9; Curzon in 200; debates on 131, 287; Irwin in 278; legislation 285; self-government 228, 241, 278
Indian Empire Society 285
Industrial Charter, The 321–4, 342–6, 360, 365, 375, 433, 495, 532
Industrial Policy Committee 320–1, 323, 343, 345, 361
industrial relations 351; Baldwin and 265; under Churchill 343; collaborative approach 375, 395, 409–10; failure to act 195; legislation 127, 265, 268, 376, 395–6, 406–7, 433; Thatcher and 395, 3,96, 433, 437; trade union immunities challenged 195–6
Industrial Relations Act (1971) 396, 402, 406–7, 409, 433
industry: coal 265, 345, 407, 410, 458; deindustrialization 442, 451; expansion 87; free-market view of 399–400, 407; industrial policy 320–2, 345; Industrial Revolution 35; iron and steel 346, 393, 439; manpower shortages 364; manufacturing decline 193, 439; modernization 374; party donations from 336–7; Peel and 63, 64–6; privatizations 393, 447, 457. 469; public sector 315, 321–2, 345–6, 351, 447, 452; recession in 65; three-day week in 410; unrest in 238; versus agriculture 70, 73; Whig links with 51
Industry Act (1972) 408
Ingham, Bernard 440–1
Institute of Economic Affairs 399
International Monetary Fund 427, 432
interventionism 310, 322, 347, 360, 407–8, 409, 434
Invasion of 1910, The (Le Queux) 222
Iolanthe (Gilbert) 5
Ireland 51, 130; Balfour and 169–70; Buckingham Palace conference 218, 221; Catholic emancipation 36, 40; constituencies 145; devolution 151, 200; Disraeli and 125; Easter Rising (1916) 227; election campaigning on 136–7; election results 84, 108, 121, 137, 153, 540–1; electoral reform 102; emergency measures 168–9; famine 70–2; Gladstone's Bills 101, 102–4, 115, 117, 121, 142; Home Rule 139, 151, 152, 154–9, 161, 162, 172, 176–8, 180, 181, 205, 209, 216–19, 226–7; land purchase 169, 181, 200; partition 218, 227; Peel and 67–9; Pitt and 36; rent strike 168; Salisbury and 104, 151–2, 158, 161, 168;

Union 36, 136, 152, 168, 170, 172, 209; university 115, 117, 169, 181; Wyndham and 200; *see also* Northern Ireland; Ulster
Irish and Land Purchase Act (1891) 169, 181
Irish Church, *see* Anglican Church of Ireland
Irish Church Act (1869)
Irish Coercion Acts 125, 152
Irish Free State 236
Irish Home Rule Bill: (1893) 155, 156–9, 177, 180, 186; (1914) 226–7
Irish Land Act: (1870) 104; (1881) 140, 142
Irish Nationalist Party 168, 181, 218, 227
Irish Party 121, 128, 134, 137, 139, 150, 153, 176
Irish Republican Army (IRA) 467
Irish Unionists 214, 218, 228, 241
Irwin, Lord (Edward Wood) 249, 278

Jacobitism 19, 21
Jamaica 131
James II, King 17–18
Japan 191, 294, 308
Jay, Douglas 348
Jenkins, Roy 494
Jenkins, Simon 461
Jews 82, 91, 193
jingoism 4, 132, 180, 184
Johnson, Paul 490
Johnson, Dr Samuel 22
Jolliffe, Sir William 88
Jones, Nicholas 483
Jones, Tom 283
Joseph, Sir Keith 532; on Conservative guilt 326; eugenics speech 420; Heath and 414; as Industry Secretary 436; in Macmillan's Cabinet 372; as monetarist 396, 399, 421, 434; policy work of 425; and public spending 366; *Reversing the Trend* 433; and Thatcher 414
Joynson-Hicks, Sir William 223, 249, 532
Junior Imperial League 532

Kennedy, John F. 369, 372
Kenya 331, 404
Khrushchev, Nikita 362
Kilmuir, Lord, *see* Maxwell Fyfe
Kinnock, Neil 457, 472, 478
Kipling, Rudyard 192–3, 222, 280
Kitchener, Lord 200
Korean War 366

Labouchere, Henry 109
Labour Party: advance of 478; anti-Labour coalitionism 238–40, 243, 247, 270; Blair's 452, 466, 474; class alignment 235, 353, 357–8; and Communism 263–4; confidence debate lost 428; constituencies 259, 353–4; defections 487; and devolution 431; in disarray 287, 456–7; divisions 448, 490, 493; and EEC 373; economic policy 280; election campaigning 351, 352, 472; election results 205, 351; fear of 237, 240, 265, 268, 270, 352; foundation 13, 182, 190, 195; funding 464; and General Strike 268; governments 235, 262, 270, 272, 315, 427; housing policy 348; leftwards shift 456; Lib-Lab pacts 190, 195, 196–7, 209, 220–1, 237, 248, 427–8; major party status 235, 246, 264; moderation of 272; and National Government 280–1; and nationalization 345; New Labour 500; and NHS 344; and planning 310, 343, 347; and privatization 457; refusal to serve under Chamberlain 298; sectarianism of 5; and tariff reform 277; trades union affiliations 196; unpopularity 400; and wartime coalitions 237, 302, 311, 313; and World War II 295, 307, 309
Lamont, Norman 471, 479
Lancashire 108–10, 122, 137, 172, 176, 179, 202, 205, 209, 210, 215, 216
Lansdowne, Marquess of 532; appeals for negotiated peace 228; Balfour on 198; as Foreign Secretary 187, 198; as Leader in Lords 163, 208, 216, 228; resignation 139; and tariff reform 216; as War Secretary 187
Law, Andrew Bonar 205, 532; achievements of 247–8; and Asquith 217–19; background of 214, 215, 257; biography of 9, 11; Cabinet of 249; as Chancellor 232; as Colonial Secretary 230; confrontational style of 215–16, 385; death 247, 249; elected 186; on fusion with Liberals 241–2; and Irish Home Rule 217–18, 225–7; leadership contender 214–15; leads Commons walk-out 226; and Lloyd George 214, 215, 231–2; and Loyalists 117; negativism of 248; as Party Leader 215, 496, 497–8; as Prime Minister 245, 248–9, 519; retirement 242, 249–50; return of 245; and social reform 219; and tariff reform 216–17, 262, 490; at Treasury 229; and World War I 226, 230–2
Laws of Ecclesiastical Polity (Hooker) 23
Lawson, Nigel 436, 440, 467, 468, 472, 481, 533
League of Empire Loyalists 332
Lechy, W.E. 17
Lecky, W.H. 158
Leeds 88, 172, 462
Left Book Club 302
Left Were Never Right, The (Hogg) 303
Le Queux, William 222

Lewisham by-election (1903) 203
Liberal Democrats 446, 462, 463, 466, 474, 478, 481, 484
Liberal Party: anti-socialism 494; and Boer War 185; by-election gains 270, 335, 382, 469; Churchill and 317; coalitions 3, 4, 210, 230–1, 240–5; decline of 7, 122, 179, 262, 264, 270, 281, 291, 247–8, 315, 319, 351; defections from 130, 235, 262; defections to 57; defence policy 223–4; Disraeli and 95; divisions 77, 93, 186, 232, 239–40, 245, 248, 282, 493–4; electoral pacts 239–40, 280; and electoral system 7; foreign policy 114; foundation 13, 80, 91; fusion with Conservatives contemplated 241–2; under Gladstone 92, 101, 108, 111–12, 135; governments 85, 101, 104, 115, 137, 149–50, 176–8, 205, 208–9, 211; House of Lords and 206–7; and Labour Party 190, 196–7; leave National Government 283; leave wartime coalition 311; Lib-Con alliance 318–20, 413; Lib-Lab pacts 190, 196–7, 209, 220–1, 237, 248, 427–8, 494; in local government 462, 486; minor party status 264; moderates resign 139; Newcastle Programme 176; and nonconformists 195; party organization 136; press 120; radicalism 87, 91, 95, 139, 145, 153, 163; revival 7, 174, 195, 204, 262, 271, 382, 413, 451–2; Scottish 108; and social reform 171, 177, 205, 206; and tariff reform 277; Whigs in 91, 139; and World War I 225–6; see also Liberal Democrats; National Liberals
Liberal Unionists 57, 77, 533; Cabinet Posts 178–9; conservatism of 163; cooperation with Conservatives 162–4, 171; Council 202; and education reforms 195; election results 160, 174–6, 179; electoral alliance 158–9; and Home Rule Bill 177; merger with Conservatives 176, 178, 181, 215; party funds 173; and tariff reform 202
Licensing Act (1872) 111
Life of Benjamin Disraeli (Monypenny and Buckle) 9, 51
Life of Robert, Marquess of Salisbury (Cecil) 9
Lincoln, Lord 74, 77
Liverpool 46, 135, 172, 440, 458, 462
Liverpool, 2nd Earl 32, 55, 449, 533; and Cabinet government 33; Canning's influence on 35; and Catholic emancipation 36–7; and electoral reform 36; and George IV 29, 33; government of 15, 33–7, 58; Grenvillites join 32; ministers of 34–5; parliamentary defeats 33–4; party divisions under 35, 37; policy modernized 49; suffers stroke 37

Lloyd, Geoffrey 261
Lloyd, Selwyn 369, 371, 533
Lloyd George, David: attacks Tory peers 208; and Bonar Law 214, 215, 231–2; censure debate 238; as Chancellor 207; coalitions 3, 5, 240–3, 246; on Communism 264; election broadcast 254; loss of office 248; 'people's budget' (1909) 207–11; as Prime Minister 231, 238, 519; resignation 244; scents Liberal revival 268; and Unionists 232, 238–9; War Cabinet 230, 232
Lloyd-Greame, Philip 249
local government: Conservative Conference 389; county councils 171, 172; elections 120, 220, 351, 411, 455, 462, 469; Irish 169, 181; Liberals in 462, 478, 486; London 182; modernization 374; pacts 207; reform 268, 391, 402; Thatcher and 447–8, 458, 461, 463; Tory retreat in 462–3, 466, 486
Locke, John 23
Lockhart, J.G. 27
London: boundary changes 148; City 158, 346; clubs 172; election results 109, 122, 137, 160, 176, 179, 354; local government 171, 172, 179, 182, 220, 374; rioting in 171; suburbs 489
London County Council 171, 172, 179, 207
London Passenger Transport Board 288
Londonderry, Lord 59
Long, Walter 533; biography 9; and Chamberlain 188, 205; election defeat 174; heads Budget Protest League 208; as leadership contender 214, 215; in Lords 242; on wartime party truce 230
Looking Ahead (policy document) 260
Lord Randolph Churchill (Churchill) 9, 144
Low, David 304; cartoons 252, 269, 319
Lyttelton, Oliver 321, 345

McAlpine, Lord 482
Macaulay, Thomas 22, 53
MacDonald, J. Ramsay: and Baldwin 283; as 'British Kerensky' 235; election broadcast 254; expelled from Labour Party 281; heads National Government 280, 283; ill-health 287; National Labour Party of 281–2; as Prime Minister 262, 270, 279, 280, 519; recognises Soviet Russia 263–4
McKenzie, Robert 6, 10
Macleod, Iain 533; Baldwin's influence on 251; biography of Chamberlain 326; as Colonial Secretary 372; death 390, 399; founder of One Nation Group 340; in Macmillan's Cabinet 372; as Minister of Health 344; on 1966 manifesto 394; as principled liberal 403, 404; refuses to serve under Home 380, 388; rejoins front bench

INDEX

383; in Research Department 261, 341; as shadow chancellor 397–8; and Toryism 14
Macmillan, Harold 190, 534; ambition of 330; as backbencher 284, 330, 361; background of 359; Baldwin's influence on 251; on Beaverbrook 342; on broad coalition 491; and Butler 51, 361, 377; Cabinet of 368, 369–70, 371–2; caring conservatism of 272; cartoons 350, 362, 363, 368, 371, 377; censure debate 370; and Churchill 302, 318, 360; critic of Chamberlain 294; defence policy 363; economic policy 364–6, 375, 439; and EEC 373–4; as ex-Leader 423; foreign policy 362–3, 372–3; as front bencher 317; Heath and 387; as Housing Minister 349, 350; immigration controls 403; and *The Industrial Charter* 321, 324; and industrial relations 375–6; intellectualism 342, 360; as international statesman 362; as interventionist 345, 360; as leadership contender 329; materialist appeal of 358; *The Middle Way* 317, 360–1; as Minister of Housing 330; modernization policy 374–6; on nature of Party 16; on negative campaigning 352; 'night of the long knives' 371–2; as Party Leader 498; as paternalist 293, 361; personality of 359, 368, 372; political theories of 360–1; as Prime Minister 334–5, 358–9, 361–2, 367, 371, 475, 520; retirement 370–1, 374, 376–7; on Stanleys 203; succession 330, 376–9; and Suez 334, 362; and television 359; unpopularity 368–70; on Woolton 336; and working class vote 498
Maidstone Advertiser, the 66
Maine, Sir Henry 158, 492
Major, John 52, 534; background of 388; Baldwin's influence on 251; Cabinet 'bastards' 475; confidence votes 481–2; and Disraelian Conservatism 117; economic policy 479; election victory 472–3; and Europe 471, 474, 481–2; at Foreign Office 468; government of 474, 486; gun control legislation 461; leadership contests 419, 470, 475; as Party Leader 498; party reform proposals 464; and Peel 51; personality of 471; and press 465; as Prime Minister 471, 475, 486, 490, 520; resignation 484; and 'sleaze' 477
Malaya 331
Mallock, W.H. 158
Manchester 88, 108, 109, 115, 205, 215, 282
Manifesto: (1880) 136; (1924) 260; (1928–9) 261; (1935) 288; (1939–40) 291; (1945) 309; (1950) 343; (1966) 391, 394; (1970) 399; (1983) 447

Manners, Lord John 65, 84, 150
Marconi scandal 216
Marlborough, Duke of 17, 136
Marples, Ernest 348–9
Mary, Queen 18, 19
Mass Observation surveys 313
Maude, Angus 400, 421, 424, 425, 430, 434
Maudling, Reginald 340, 534; as Chancellor 380, 382, 396; and Heath 390; as Home Secretary 402; and *The Industrial Charter* 323–4; as leadership contender 383, 385; in Macmillan's Cabinet 372; in Research Department 261, 341
Maxse, Leo 188
Maxwell Fyfe, Sir David (Lord Kilmuir) 51, 306, 365, 417, 441, 534
Maxwell Fyfe Report (1949) 339, 341
Maynooth Bill 68–9
Mediterranean Agreements 170
Melbourne, Lord 42
Mellor, David 481
Methodism 31, 63
Metropolitan Conservative Association 99, 119
Metropolitan London and Westminster Association 106
Meyer, Sir Anthony 441, 469
middle class 106, 153, 354, 498; growth in 148–9; home-ownership 289; Labour support 353, 452, 486; Liberal defectors 112, 122, 125, 149, 451–2; suburban 109, 149; 'villa Toryism' 148
Middle Class Alliance 425
Middle Way, The (Macmillan) 317, 360–1, 534
Middlesex 109, 122
Middleton, Captain 47, 109, 167, 172, 173; as Principal Agent 145, 149, 179, 186; retirement 179
Mill, John Stuart 26, 109
Miller, John 48
Mills, Lord 349
Milner, Sir Alfred 200, 209, 215, 229–30, 534
Mines Regulation Act (1887) 171
monarchy 17–19, 51, 115
Monday Club 332, 376, 403, 405, 535
Monypenny, W.R. 9, 51
MORI 483
Morley, John 109
Morning Journal, the 41
Morning Post, the 120, 199, 201, 204, 273–4, 278
Morrison, Herbert 302, 349
Mosley, Sir Oswald 275, 290, 486
Munich Conference 295, 297
Murdoch, Rupert 465

Mussolini, Benito 275, 294
myths: Disraelian 117, 129, 140; of inter-war Britain 302–4, 326–7; of loyalty 441; of Tory imperialism 333

Napier, Sir Robert 107, 108
Napoleonic Wars 15, 29, 30, 32, 33
Nasser, Colonel 333
National Debt 33
National Economic Development Council (NEDC) 375, 376
National Front 426
National Government (1931) 5, 270, 276, 280–91, 293; under Baldwin 287, 291; under Chamberlain 291; emergency Cabinet 281; under MacDonald 280–1, 283; post-election 282; of World War II 300
National Health Service 321, 344, 351
National Incomes Commission (NIC) 375, 376
National Labour Party 281–2, 284
National Liberals (Simonites) 57, 280, 282–4, 315, 318, 535
National Review, the 188, 199, 211, 214, 273
National Service League 192–3, 224
National Union 172, 535; accepts party re-organization 213; attitude to coalition government 243; Balfour and 168, 212; Central Council 142, 287, 339, 426; Chamberlain's address 163; Churchill and 142–3, 166, 167; conferences, *see* Conference; Executive 3, 206, 286, 476; Gorst at 119–20; as 'handmaid to party' 149; headquarters 143; link with Central Office broken 206; Organization Committee 142; proposed launch 105–6; restructured 145; seized by tariff reformers 206; Thatcher and 423
National Union Gleanings 173
National Union of Mineworkers 448; 'Red Friday' 265; strikes 267, 407, 410–12, 458; under Thatcher's incomes policy 437
Naval Defence Act (1889) 170
Navigation Acts 80
Navy League 193, 223
Neave, Airey 420
Nevill, Lord 105
New Social Alliance 112
Newcastle, Duke of 41
1922 Committee 287, 317, 332, 408, 418, 419, 424; Chairmen 517
'No turning back' group 457–8
Nolan enquiry 477
North, Lord 28
Northcote, Sir Stafford (1st Earl of Iddesleigh) 110, 535; attacked by Fourth Party 138; Cabinet Posts 93, 124; as consensual centrist 139; elevation to Lords 150; as Foreign Secretary 164, 167; as Leader of House 128, 134, 138, 139–40, 142; pragmatism of 52; socialism of 113; tax increase 135; weakness of 139, 150
Northern Ireland 402–3; *see also* Ulster
Northumberland, Duke of 124
Norway 298
Nott, John 436
Nottingham 31, 47

Oastler, Richard 49, 52, 69, 113
Observer, the 273
O'Connell, Daniel 40, 83
O'Gorman, Frank 29
old age pensions 192, 194, 207, 288, 291
One Nation Group 340, 535
Opposition 490; under Baldwin 260, 262, 272, 276; under Churchill 317–18, 320, 490; confrontational style of 215–16; under Derby 87; emergence of concept 29, 31–2; leadership elections during 385; role of 44–5; under Peel 50–3, 56; quiescent 87, 89–90, 91, 139; under Thatcher 427
Organization for the Maintenance of Supplies 266
Orpington by-election 382
Orwell, George 258
Ostrogorski, M.I. 144, 172

Paine, Tom 23, 26
Pakenham, Frank 261, 492
Palmer, Roundell 77
Palmerston, Lord 42, 53, 91; death 77, 92; Disraeli and 83, 116; gunboat diplomacy 107; limited opposition to 87, 89–90, 91; as reactionary 87, 495; refuses to serve under Derby 90
Parkington, Sir John 84, 113
Parkinson, Cecil 440, 467
Parliament Act (1911) 142, 209, 211, 212, 217, 226, 241
parliamentary reform, *see* electoral system: reform
Parnell, Charles Stewart 152; and Churchill 151; death 169; and Gladstone 150, 155; Irish Party of 139, 153, 160, 169; *Times* attack on 168
party funding: accounts 463; Board of Finance 336; cash for peerages 173; declining 436, 461, 464, 478; donations 259, 336–7, 462, 464; election budget 88, 106, 173, 486; Hague and 484–5; industrial donors 336–7, 339; membership subscriptions 259, 338; organizational 143–4; Party Treasurer 213, 514–15; quota system 339–40; sale of whip's letter 60

INDEX 557

Party Leader 73, 142, 324, 496–9; in Commons 512–13; contests 385, 419, 463–4, 468, 475, 484; in Lords 512–13
Party Organization 101; agents 109, 120, 144–5, 172, 212, 339, 425, 462; Balfour and 199, 212–13; Bonham and 78; Chairmen 213, 390, 514; decline 136, 179–80, 205, 206, 461–4, 486, 487; funding of 143–4; Gorst and 119–21; farming out of 88; improvements 105, 119, 121, 152, 172, 212, 220, 351, 436, 488; local 87–8, 105, 305, 338–40, 462; membership 259, 337–8, 354, 355–6, 462, 486, 488; Organization Committee 142, 212, 213; Peel and 59, 60–1; post-war 312; pre-war 291; Principal Party Organizers 515; Principal Publicity Officers 516; professionalism of 173, 273; reformed 212–14; Salisbury and 149; tripartite management 213; in wartime 305, 311; under Woolton 335–41; youth 291
Patriotic Association 133
patriotism 4, 29, 31, 116; anti-Germanism 223; as campaigning ploy 235; Disraeli and 133, 235; patriotic imperialism 107–8; Unionist 229; working-class 98, 235
Patten, Christopher 251, 425, 427, 471, 475, 491
Peace and Plenty (film) 302
Peacock, Thomas Love 27
Pearce, Edward 389
Peel, General Jonathan 91, 95
Peel, Sir Robert 535; administrative abilities 52, 63; Burkeian influence 27–8; Butler on 51, 379–80; by-election defeat 40; on Canningites 39; and capitalists 109; cartoon 71; and Catholic emancipation 40, 52; as Chancellor 66; collapse of government 60, 76, 77; confidence votes 481; as 'Conservative' 56; and Conservative recovery 47; and Corn Laws 1, 69–75; death 80; and death of Canning 38; defence of electoral system 27; Disraeli and 3, 64; economic policy 64–7; governments 50, 53–4, 57, 64, 518; growth in Conservative support under 62; at Home Office 34, 52; 'Hundred Days' of 53–4; and industrial economy 63, 64–6; and Ireland 67–9; as Leader of Commons 39, 52; literature on 10; middle way advocated by 55–6; mistrusted 53; on mood of country 34; in opposition 50–3, 56, 59; parliamentary defeats 67, 76; and parliamentary party 67, 68, 74–6; as Party Leader 13, 15, 50, 52–3, 59, 497; and party organization 59, 60–1; as Prime Minister 53, 62–3, 67; and Reform Bill 45, 53, 54, 92; resignation 1, 37, 73; and split party 51, 62, 77, 79; statue of 81; *Tamworth Manifesto* 49, 54–6, 73, 267, 321, 495; unpopularity of 67–9; and Wellington 43, 53, 59; and Whig defectors 58
Peelites 52, 57, 62, 536; attack Disraeli 85; in Liberal Party 91; and Peel's legacy 80; split from protectionists 77, 83; support Whigs 77, 79, 80, 85, 160
Percival, Spencer 32
Perth, declaration of 430
Peterloo massacre 33
Petrie, Sir Charles 9
Peyton, John 422
philosophy, *see* Conservatism
Picture Post 303
Pitt, William, the Younger 55, 449, 536; biographies 26; Cabinet government under 29; and Catholics 36; and electoral reform 36; legacy of 33, 116, 117; Pittites 15; political alliances 15, 28, 29–30; reputation of 31
Pitt clubs 30, 48
Place, Francis 109
Planta, Joseph 47
policy 260–1, 356, 489–90; Central Policy Review Staff 393; CRD's role in 261, 288, 291, 341–2; Heath and 390–2, 397–8; in *The Industrial Charter* 320–4, 342–5; Leader's role in 324, 497–8; Policy Secretariat 260; postwar 342; Thatcher and 426–7; wartime 305–10
Politics in the Age of Peel (Gash) 10
poll books 62, 63, 98
Poole, Lord 366
Poor Law 99; Royal Commission on 192
Pope, Alexander 22, 54
Popish Plot (1679) 17
Portland, Duke of 32
Post-War Problems Central Committee (PWPCC) 305–6, 309, 324, 536
Pound, Ezra 12
Powell, Enoch 492, 536; cartoons 404, 406; in CRD 261; desertion of party 3, 405; as Health Minister 366; on Heath 389, 402; and immigration 404–5; as leadership contender 383; on Macmillan 475; and means testing 344; as monetarist 365, 396–7, 399, 421; and public spending 366; refuses to serve under Home 380, 388; rejoins front bench 383; in Research Department 341; resignation 365, 390; sacking 405; in Suez Group 332; and Toryism 14; as Ulster Unionist 405
Prentice, Reginald 490, 495

press 356; anti-Baldwin right and 273–6, 279; anti-Conservatism 303–4, 476, 486; Conservative 110, 120, 240, 273, 312, 332, 369, 464–5; Major and 465; press agency purchased 120; press bureau 213; scale of influence of 273–4; Thatcher and 440–1, 465; Unionist 212, 213, 243
Pretyman, E.G. 242
Priestley, J.B. 304
Primrose Day 152
Primrose League 11, 140, 143–4, 170, 172, 178, 536
Prior, Jim: cartoons 438, 440; on Heath 418; as leadership contender 422; as Northern Ireland Secretary 440; in shadow cabinet 433, 434; on Thatcher 427; and trades union legislation 436–7; as 'wet' 439–40
Private Eye 369, 394, 477
Profumo affair 370, 374, 381
protectionism 51; abandoned 87; agricultural 61, 64, 66, 135; Balfour and 203; by-election victories 80; defeat of 80; Disraeli and 80, 174; Robinson on 35; *see also* tariffs
protectionists 61, 62, 70; as 'Conservatives' 81; split with Peelites 77–8, 80
Protestantism 62, 63, 69, 103, 109, 152
Public Health Act 127
Public Sector Research Unit 394
Pugh, Martin 11
Punch cartoons 71, 96, 118, 123, 141, 175, 211, 220, 266, 307
Putting Britain Right Ahead (1965) 391, 394, 395, 435
Pym, Francis 421, 436
Pym, Wollaston 120

Quarterly Review, the 27, 32, 48, 56, 104, 117

radicals/radicalism 5, 35; abatement of 87, 109; Conservative alliances with 49, 52; Disraeli and 83; Liberal 87, 91, 95, 139, 145, 153, 163; Tory 163; Tory repression of 15, 29–30, 31
Rag Trade, The 376
Raikes, H.C. 105
rallies 49, 106, 108, 115, 253
Reaction and Reconstruction in English Politics in the 1830s and 1840s (Gash) 10
Reagan, Ronald 445
Redistribution Act (1885) 148–9
Redwood, John 475
Reeves, John 24, 26
Referendum Party 482
Reflections on the Revolution in France (Burke) 26
Reform Act (1832) 15, 42–6, 51, 54, 60, 86, 91;

Second (1867) 5, 14, 62, 85, 93, 95–9, 102, 105, 174, 180, 235
Reform Club 47
Reith, John 254
Representation of the People Act (1918) 232, 233–4, 264
Resale Price Maintenance (RPM) 374, 381, 382, 388
Research Department, *see* Conservative Research Department
Reveille 537
Reversing the Trend (Joseph) 433
Rhodesia 404
Richard II (Shakespeare) 21
Richmond, Duke of 41, 42, 121, 150
Riddle of the Sands, The (Childers) 222
Ridley, Nicholas 393, 408, 467
Right Approach, The (1976) 434, 435
Right Approach to the Economy, The (1977) 434
Right Road for Britain, The (1949) 343, 435
Rights of Man, The (Paine) 26
Ripon, Lord, *see* Robinson, J.F.
Rippon, Geoffrey 423
Ritchie, C.T. 198, 201
Road to Serfdom, The (Hayek) 310
Robert, J.M. 16
Roberts, Lord 185, 192
Robinson, J.F., *see* Goderich
Rochdale by-election (1958) 365
Rockingham Whigs 38
Rolls-Royce 407
Romanticism 24, 27
Rome, Treaty of 480
Roosevelt, Franklin 295
Rosebery, Lord 178, 180
Rothermere, Lord 273–5, 279; cartoons 263, 275
Rousseau, Jean-Jacques 23
Rowntree, Seebohm 192
Royal Commission on Poor Laws 192
Royal Navy 170, 207, 223
Royal Society of St George 258
Royalists 16–17
Russell, Lord John 45, 77, 79, 92, 93
Russell, W.H. 90
Russia 131–2, 331; diplomatic relations broken 268; Labour and 263–4; Macmillan in 362; Revolution 235, 237, 243; Thatcher in 458

Saatchi & Saatchi 436
Sack, James 15–16
Sadler, Michael 49
Safeguarding of Industry Act 241
St John-Stevas, Norman 439

INDEX

Salford 109
Salisbury, Lady 144, 173
Salisbury, Robert Cecil, 3rd Marquess (Lord Cranborne) 492, 499, 537; and agricultural relief 134; alliance with Whigs 30; attacks on party 110, 117; and Balfour 168; biography 9; Cabinets 150, 164–5, 167, 178–9, 187–8; Cabinet posts 93, 122, 198; cartoons 146, 154, 175; on Conservative dominance 180; defence of Protestantism 152; and Disraeli 104, 122, 140, 146; on election defeat (1880) 137; and electoral reform 147–8, 234; foreign policy 131, 170, 180, 183–4; as Foreign Secretary 132, 133, 164, 167, 179; and Gladstone 145, 147; and Hartington 160, 167; and Home Rule Bill 177; 'Hotel Cecil' regime of 188–9, 198, 215; and Ireland 104, 151–2, 158, 161, 168; as Leader in Lords 138, 140, 142, 146–7, 178; and Liberal Unionists 164; and London County Council 171; and middle-class 160, 498; new management team 149; opposes Reform Bill 97; as Party Leader 130, 139, 155; and party organization 173–4, 180; paternalism of 164; on Peel 50; pessimism of 25; as Prime Minister 117, 147, 150–1, 160–1, 162, 164, 167, 187–9, 194, 518–19; on radicalism 5; and Randolph Churchill 138–9, 143, 156, 166–7; resignations 95, 155–6, 176; retirement 190, 197; social reforms 164, 171, 187; succession 188; and tariffs 174; and trade unions 196; visits provinces 108; and Whigs 139
Salisbury, Lord (4th Marquess) 244, 250, 259
Salisbury, 5th Marquess (Viscount Cranborne): and appeasement 294; at Foreign Office 329; Salisbury doctrine 142
Salisbury Review, the 425
Sandars, Jack 199, 212
Sanders, Robert 215, 496
Sandon, Viscount 113, 122–3
Sandys, Duncan 318, 363, 404
Scargill, Arthur 458
Scotland: declining support 403, 431, 487, 489; devolution 427, 430–1, 489; Disraeli and 108; election results 42, 43, 108, 121, 137, 153, 160, 176, 179, 186, 205, 354, 431, 432, 540–1; electoral reform 97, 102; Liberals in 159, 186; Unionists in 186
Scott, Sir Walter 27, 65
Scottish Church 152
Scottish National Party 430–1
Second Tory Party, The (Feiling) 9, 13
Seeley, J.R. 158
Selborne, Lord 226

Selsdon Group 425
Selsdon Park conference (1970) 398, 399
Shaftesbury, Earl of, *see* Ashley, Lord
Shakespeare, William 21
Shannon, Richard 126, 148
Sheffield 135, 282, 462
Shop Hours Act (1892) 171
Shrewsbury, Earl of 89
Sidmouth, Lord 34
Signpost (booklets) 306
Simon, Sir John 277, 278, 495
Simon Commission 278
Simonites, see National Liberals
Single European Act 480
Sinn Fein 227, 236
Skene, W.B. 136
Smith, Adam 35
Smith, Sir F.E. (1st Earl of Birkenhead) 537; on Baldwin 252; chairs Social Reform Committee 219; as coalitionist 243; and General Strike 267; joins front bench 205; as Lord Chancellor 243; out of office 249
Smith, John 466
Smith, W.H.: agent of 120; on Churchill's resignation 167; death 168; election 109; as Leader of Commons 167; in Salisbury Cabinet 122, 164; satirized by Gilbert 124
Smithers, Waldron 246
Soames, Christopher 420, 424, 425, 439
Social Democratic Party (SDP) 446, 448
social policy: Baldwin and 261, 265; Balfour and 192; Beveridge Report 309–10; Chamberlain and 171, 178, 194; Church and 453–4; Disraeli and 112–13, 115, 117, 125–8, 129, 137; Liberal 177; of National Government 288; postwar 344–5; Randolph Churchill and 166; Salisbury and 164, 171, 182, 192; 'social gardening' 349, 446; state interventionism 228, 345; Unionist Social Reform Committee 219
socialism 207, 272, 500; anti-socialism 263–4, 268, 274, 300, 318, 494; anti-socialist coalitionism 238–40, 243, 247, 270; Butler and 322; 'pink' 345; revolutionary 237–8, 240
South Africa 183, 184, 200, 201
South African War, *see* Boer War
Southey, Robert 27
Soviet Union, *see* Russia
Spanish Civil War 294
Speaker's Conference (1916) 232
Spectator, the 156, 198, 199, 201, 203, 400, 420
Spofforth and Rose 88, 105
Stalin, Joseph 295
Stanley, Lord, *see* Derby, Earl of
Stanley, Oliver 302, 318, 329, 345

Steel-Maitland, Sir Arthur 121, 213, 219, 537
Stewart, Robert 43, 93
Stuart, House of 17
Stuart, James 312
Suez Canal Company 116, 131, 333
Suez crisis (1954) 329, 333–5, 352, 357, 362, 387, 445
Suez Group 332, 333
Sun, the 441, 465, 476, 479
Sunday Express, the 369
Sunday Mirror, the 384
Swinton College 537
Sybil (Disraeli) 65

Taff Vale judgement 196, 207, 443
Tamworth 55
Tamworth Manifesto, The 49, 54–6, 73, 267, 321, 495
Tariff Commission 202
tariffs 268, 271, 274, 481, 490; abolition of 66; and agricultural depression 134–5; Baldwin and 262, 276–7, 279, 281; Bonar Law and 216; Chamberlain and 182, 193–4, 197–8; Disraeli and 134–5; and fair trade 174, 193; in 1931 election 280, 282; Peel and 66; Salisbury and 174; on statute book 283; Unionists and 200–2, 205, 206, 210–11, 241
Tariff Reform League 202, 260, 537
taxation: capital 392–3; cuts 365–6, 437, 450, 472; and defence programme 224; direct 205; on food 201, 276; income tax 33, 66, 80, 85, 119, 135, 194, 240, 352, 366, 472–3, 479; poll tax 459–60, 468, 469, 471, 472; rating tax 182; redistrubutive 207; reform 392–3, 402; VAT 438; wartime 229
Taylor, A.J.P. 12
Taylor, Colonel Edward 88, 105
Taylor, Teddy 431
Tebbit, Norman 440, 442, 467
Territorial Army 223
Test and Corporation Acts 20, 38, 39
That Was the Week That Was 369, 381
Thatcher Margaret 499, 537; background 388; bilateralist approach 426, 432, 436; on broad coalition 491; Cabinets 436, 441, 453, 459, 466–7; cartoons 401, 422, 424, 429, 438, 440, 444, 450, 454; and Church 454–5; and devolution 431–2; and Disraelian Conservatism 117; economic policy 433–5; and Essex man 498; and Europe 443, 444, 458, 480–1; as ex-Leader 474; fall of 468–71; foreign policy 443–5; in Heath government 402, 420; jingoism of 4; leadership contests 419, 420–3, 469–70; legislative interventions 460–1; male characteristics of 452; and miners' strike 410, 458; and monetarism 414, 421; narrow base of 456, 466, 488, 493; in opposition 427, 432; and parliamentary party 468–9; as Party Leader 215, 423–4, 425–7, 496, 498; personal initiatives of 426–7; policy role 426–7; political ethics of 441; and poll tax 459–60, 469; populist agenda of 442, 443; pragmatism of 493; presidential regime of 453, 459; and press 440–1, 465; as Prime Minister 436, 449, 520; and public relations 435–6, 464; and public spending 366; rightwing policies of 435; shadow cabinet 424, 425–6, 432, 435; and Thorneycroft 365; toughness of 117, 401–2, 428; and trades unions 395, 396, 433, 437, 442–3; and 'wets' 439–41
Thomas, Peter 390
Theodore, Emperor of Abyssinia 107
This is the Road 343
Thomas, Jim 318
Thorneycroft, Peter 375, 383, 538; as Chancellor 364; as Party Chairman 365, 424–5, 436
Thoughts on the English Government (Reeves) 24
Time and Tide 332
Times, The 90, 99, 103, 120, 167, 168, 264, 273–4, 312, 364
Tocqueville, Alexis de 12
Tom Jones (Fielding) 20
Tories and the People, The (Pugh) 11
Tories/Toryism: as ancestors of Conservatives 13–15; under Canning 38; and Church 16, 17, 20, 21–2; in decline 28; divisions in 35, 37–8; dominance of 19, 21, 32; and electoral reform 43–7, 54; emergence of 17; High Tories, see Ultras; identity of 36; 'Liberal' 34, 49, 66; under Liverpool 34, 35; in Lords 43, 51; loss of office 19–20, 50; and monarchy 17–19, 21–2, 28–9; MPs 20; name change 48, 56; party identity 45; party organization 47; popularity of 29–30; principles of 20–2, 29–32, 34, 36, 38, 48; and radicalism 15, 29–30, 31; return to political world 21; Royalist roots 16–17; survival of 50; use of term 16, 21, 28, 32; and Whigs 29–30, 37, 38, 41
Tory Democracy/Democrats 137, 142; Derby's 93; Disraeli and 100, 113, 129, 140; negative impact of Liberal Unionists on 163; Randolph Churchill and 138, 144–5, 495
Tory MP (Left Book Club publication) 302
Tory Reform Group 309, 538
Toryism and the People (Hill) 9
Trades Disputes Act (1927) 265
trades unions: decline in 443, 451; and

General Strike 267–8; Heath and 391, 395–6, 407, 409–10; immunities attacked 195–6; *Industrial Charter* on 321, 343, 345; and Labour Party 196; membership 353, 443; Thatcher and 395, 396, 433, 437, 442–3, 447; Trades Union Congress (TUC) 267; 'winter of discontent' 428; workers' soviets resolution 238; *see also* industrial relations
Traffic in Towns (report) 374
Trethowan, Ian 397
Trollope, Anthony 3
Truck Act 171
True Blue Club 31
'Trust the People' exhibition (1947) 326
Turkey 131–2
Turner, John 349
Twain, Mark 2

Uganda 406
Ulster 225; army in 218; Churchill on 155–6, 227; election funding 340; election results 153, 354; electoral reform in 145; MPs 236; partition 227, 236, 239; resistance to Home Rule 177, 217, 226; *see also* Northern Ireland
Ulster Unionists 354, 402–3, 414, 481, 538
Ultras 37, 38–41, 42, 45, 49, 55, 59, 495
unemployment 438; assistance 288; and election results 289; inter-war 268, 270, 277, 304–5; low 382; post-war 343; rising 407, 438; and tariff reform 262; Tebbit on 442; under Thatcher 438, 442, 446
Unionist Business Committee 228, 538
Unionist Organization Committee 212, 213
Unionist Party/Unionism 4, 129, 131, 156; alliance 163–4, 168, 171–2, 176–7, 181; Balfour government 199; cartoon 220; Chamberlain and 183; clubs 172; coalitions 210, 230–2, 240–3; commercial and financial men in 173; defeat of 236; disintegration of 200, 204; election results 186, 205, 209, 211–12; as government in crisis 190–7; and Home Rule Bill 177; and Liberals 238–42; merger 176, 178, 181, 215; obstructionism by 181–2; in opposition 206–7, 208–9, 223; Queen's Speech discussions 176; Scottish 431; support Boer War 184, 185; and tariff reform 200–2, 205, 206, 210–11, 241; and Ulster 227; unconstitutional acts of 217–18; and worker's rights 195, 200; in World War I 225, 226–32; *see also* Liberal Unionists; Ulster Unionists
Unionist Social Reform League 219, 260, 538
Unionist War Committee 228

United Empire Party 279
United States 114; Anglo-American relations 362, 372–3, 445; and end of Cold War 458; and Suez 333–4
Unknown Prime Minister, The (Blake) 9
Upper Clyde Shipbuilders 408

Vassall spy scandal 370
Vicky 362; cartoons 350, 363
Victoria, Queen 59, 83, 140–1; conservatism of 6, 93; death 190; Diamond Jubilee 180, 184; and Disraeli 99–100, 102, 115, 116, 128; as Empress of India 116, 133; widowhood 115
Vincent, John 63, 217

Wales: Assembly 429; counties 46; declining support 403, 487, 489; devolution 431; election results 108, 137, 153, 176, 179, 186, 205, 354, 432, 540–1; electoral reform 97, 102; Liberal Unionists in 159, 160; nonconformists 186, 195
Walker, Peter 393, 399, 423, 436, 440, 467
Wall, Patrick 4
Wall Street Crash 270
Walpole, Spencer 84
Walrond, Sir William 180
Walters, Professor Alan 467
War Memoirs (Churchill) 299, 325, 331
Watney, James 111
Webb, Beatrice 186
Welbeck Abbey rally 253
Welch, Colin 394
Wellington, Duke of (Arthur Wellesley) 84, 538; Cabinet 39; on Canning 37; and Catholic emancipation 36, 40; as 'conservative' 48; contribution to Conservatism 44; fights duel 40; and George IV 29; government of 39–41; on Liverpool 34; and Lords 43–4, 51; 'loses' general election 42; parliamentary defeats 39–40, 42; and Peel 45, 53, 59, 64; as pragmatist 39; and Reform Act 43–4, 46; reliance on Whig votes 41; reputation of 53; resignation 37
Wesley, John and Charles 31
Westminster 109
Westminster, Statute of (1931) 278
Westminster Gazette, the: cartoon 204
Whigs 17; alliances 30, 37, 38, 80, 85, 93, 155, 156, 163; Burke and 26; and Corn Law repeal 75; defectors 57–8, 62, 139; as differentiated from Tories 22; dismissed from office 53–4; Disraeli and 83; dominance of 19–20; and electoral reform 50; governments 41, 42, 53, 77, 79, 83–4;

Whigs – *cont.*
    industrial links 51; Liberal 91, 139, 163;
    Peelite cooperation 77, 79, 80, 85; and
    radicalism 31, 139; split 83; support for
    Tories 41, 42
Whips 32, 136: Chief Whip 59, 88, 149,
    179–80, 206, 212, 213, 318, 513; effectiveness
    of 233; Heath as 387; and National Union
    143; under Peel 59–60; Salisbury's team
    149; withdrawal of whip 486
White Lion Club 31
White's club 32
Whitelaw, William: as deputy leader 423, 425,
    426; and economic policy 434; in Heath's
    Cabinet 403; as Home Secretary 436; as
    leadership contender 418, 422–3; as Party
    Chairman 390, 417; as shadow home
    secretary 426; as 'wet' 440
Wilde, Oscar 162
Wilkes, John 109
William III, King 18, 19
William IV, King 41, 42, 53–4, 61
Wilson, Harold: background of 388; and
    Douglas-Home 380, 381; and Heath 4; as
    pipe-smoker 254; as Prime Minister 414; on
    'Selsdon Man' 398; and trades unions 395
Winn, Rowland 149
Wolff, Sir Henry Drummond 138, 143
Wolff, Michael 417, 424
Wolmer, Lord 159
women: candidates 463; Conservative voters
    234; and Primrose League 143; suffrage 232,
    234, 268; Thatcher loses support of 452
Wood, Edward, *see* Irwin, Lord
Wood, Sir Kingsley 304
Woods, Maurice 9
Woolton, Frederick Marquis 319, 351, 539; on
    council estates 349; as Minister of
    Reconstruction 302; as Party Chairman 47,
    318, 336–9, 355, 390; political career 335–6
Wordsworth, William 26, 27
working class: agitation 94, 113; clubs 172–3;
    Conservative voters 98–9, 113, 122, 125–7,
    182, 221, 271, 354, 356–7, 451, 498; dual 451;
    'embourgeoisement' of 358, 451; franchise
    92, 95, 98, 147, 235; home-ownership 349;
    housing 126–7, 164, 349; Labour Party
    support 195, 337, 353, 357–8; legislation 171,
    182, 192; organizations 105–6; patriotism
    95, 235; quiescent 87; and unemployment
    assistance 288; Unionists and 195, 200; and
    Whigs 51–2
Working Men's Compensation Act (1897) 182
World War I 191, 226, 293; coalition 230–2;
    conscription 225, 231; effect on Labour
    Party 237; end of 232, 238; Irish Union and
    227; outbreak of 218, 220–1; post-war
    reconstruction 240; Unionist backing for
    war effort 226, 228–30, 232
World War II 290, 292–3, 297, 325; new
    perspectives created by 304–5;
    reconstruction planning 305–9
Worsthorne, Sir Peregrine 492
Wyndham, George 184, 198, 200

Yeomanry 223
YMCA 539
Yorkshire 176
Young, Lord 467, 471
Young Conservatives 291, 338, 436, 539
Young England 65, 67, 69, 108, 143, 539
Younger, Sir George 242, 246, 273, 539
Your MP ('Gracchus') 303

Zinoviev letter 263–4, 269
Zululand 133